☑ Facts On File, Inc.

11 Penn Plaza
New York, NY 10001-2006
(212) 967-8800
Fax 212-967-9196

Dear Librarian,

   Here is your **FREE COPY** of the new *Editorials On File* book, *Great Events, Great Debates: A Quarter Century of Editorial Opinion.* It's our gift to you for agreeing to a trial subscription to *Editorials On File*.

   Great Events, Great Debates is but a sample of the unique current and historical record that *Editorials On File* provides to students, researchers, debaters and most importantly to librarians.

   No other library reference source surveys the entire spectrum of key newspaper editorial opinion across the U.S. and Canada to put events and issues in context.

   When one of our telephone representatives contacts you in the near future, please say, "Yes, our library is going to subscribe to Editorials On File." You won't be sorry. You'll be bringing a resource into your library that will used again and again.

Sincerely,

Steve Orlofsky

Steve Orlofsky,
Director, Subscription Services

The Information Publisher Since 1941

Great Events, Great Debates

A Quarter Century of Editorial Opinion

Great Events, Great Debates

A Quarter Century of Editorial Opinion

An Editorials On File Book

Editor: Oliver Trager

Facts On File, Inc.

AN INFOBASE HOLDINGS COMPANY

Great Events, Great Debates: A Quarter Century of Editorial Opinion

Published by Facts On File, Inc. An Infobase Holdings Company

© Copyright 1996 by Facts On File, Inc.

Library of Congress Cataloging-in-Publication Data

Great Events, Great Debates / editor, Oliver Trager
p. cm. — (An editorials on file book)
Includes index.

ISBN 0-8160-3550-8
I. Trager, Oliver. II. Series

96-083125
CIP
AP

Printed in the United States of America
987654321
This book is printed on acid-free paper

Contents

Preface

In today's information age, the force of editorial opinion is more vital than ever. The growth of new forums for debate, from talk radio to cable television to "chat rooms" on the Internet, offers us access to exchanges of opinion ranging from the polite to the combative to the raucous. But for all their power, words exchanged electronically all too often fade unrecorded and unremembered.

America has seen no forum of expression more vigorous — or more enduring — than the newspaper editorial. And it remains true that newspaper editorials are the only permanent, printed record of our national debate. Nothing else illuminates the facts, crystallizes the sides of an issue or captures the rich diversity of our people and politics as editorials do.

Editorials On File, published every two weeks since 1970, has chronicled the events and debates that shaped the nation, as they were played out on American newspapers' editorial pages. Drawing from that publication's rich archive, *Great Events, Great Debates* offers an overview of the most hotly contested issues of the last quarter century. This collection of journalistic debate on a host of controversies, tragedies and triumphs gives the reader a unique insight into how America has viewed itself and the world.

Combing our files in preparation of this volume was a daunting task, if for no other reason than because debate on almost any "hot topic" in recent history was a prism on American life that was worth including. We have often let one major development stand for a host of smaller ones so that we could cover the widest possible range of topics: from domestic crises like the Oklahoma City bombing to foreign ones like the Vietnam War; from social-issue debates like abortion to political struggles like the Iran–contra scandal. Whether the events themselves will ultimately be seen as historical watermarks or historical footnotes, to read these pages is to revisit the events that shaped our recent history.

Editorials On File — still going strong in its 26th year — has reprinted more than 100,000 editorials on some 6,500 topics and issues in the news. Like its parent publication, *Great Events, Great Debates* is an invaluable research tool for students, scholars, researchers, teachers and historians. And like our biweekly compendium, this book provides — for the writer, the student, the debater — an unmatched anthology of forceful expository writing, offering hundreds of examples of how facts and words can be marshaled subtly in the service of persuasion.

December 1995

Oliver Trager

CAMBODIAN CRISIS: INVASION AND AFTERMATH

The Vietnam War became the Indochina War after President Nixon told the nation April 30 he was ordering U.S. troops into Cambodia. Even before the speech, however, the Saigon government announced that American advisers, artillery and air support had been operating with South Vietnamese troops 24 miles into the Parrot's Beak section of Cambodia.

The widening conflict caused an outpouring of dissent, both at home and abroad. Congressional criticism was considerable, especially in the Senate where there was a growing concern over the Constitutional question about the authority to wage war. But the most explosive dissent was triggered on the college campuses. The worst, a confrontation between National Guardsmen and students at Kent State University in Ohio, resulted in the deaths of four students May 4.

The massiveness and vehemence of the dissent ultimately forced President Nixon into a more conciliatory stance. In a televised news conference May 8, the President promised that all U.S. ground forces would be out of Cambodia by June 30.

The Washington Post
Times Herald
Washington, D.C., April 30, 1970

From the very beginning of our effort in Vietnam we have rested our case on the sanctity of frontiers; North Vietnam had *invaded* South Vietnam, we argued, so it was aggression pure and simple. From this flowed our right to come to Saigon's aid, and bomb the North and all the rest. When North Vietnamese troops began in recent weeks to menace the new government in Cambodia, the refrain was the same; the White House wasted no time calling it "a foreign invasion" and never mind that the presence of large numbers of North Vietnamese troops in Cambodia had been a fact of life which we had accepted, without doing anything about it, for several years.

So now, because we don't like the turn of events in Cambodia, we have lent ourselves, with combat support and moral backing, to a *South Vietnamese* invasion of that country, without the slightest evidence that this support has been requested by Pnom Penh.

This is a stupefying development, which makes you wonder where in the world this Nixon crowd was when we were working our way insidiously into the Vietnam War? Does nobody in this administration remember how that scenario went: first, try it with the South Vietnamese Army (ARVN), with American advisers and American equipment and American encouragement, and then if it doesn't do it, throw in air support, and then, if that doesn't work, American combat troops. Call it temporary, of course, something quick and surgical to buy time until our allies can pull themselves together and go it alone. If this administration can't remember how it went before, it ought to consider the possibility that a lot of people do— that we have been conned, once, by experts and that there are a lot of people, as the reaction in the Senate yesterday plainly suggests, who are in no mood to be conned again.

It may be, of course, that there is something to this that we haven't been told in the communique from the Saigon government, announcing the ARVN drive into Cambodia, and also the American collaboration in it, with military advisers, helicopters and air support. The President will have an opportunity to explain tonight in his television address just what there is about this adventure which distinguishes it from the follies of the past. For it is difficult, on the basis of what Saigon has said, and what the Pentagon has confirmed, to find any quarrel with Senator Mansfield's assessment: "Cambodia is a whole new ball game. If we become involved directly or indirectly, it becomes a general Indochina war."

Since we obviously *have* become involved, not only indirectly but directly, it certainly gives every appearance of being a step toward a "general Indochina war." And the hard questions come immediately to mind. Why, and why now, of all times, when we are supposed to be paring commitments and scaling down involvements and concentrating on Vietnamizing Vietnam? The obvious argument is that this will remove a great thorn in our Vietnam effort and thereby hasten our exit from the scene— or at least prevent it from being delayed. That is what we were told about the bombing of North Vietnam, and it is no more believable in this instance. For one thing, we would need far better evidence than anybody has offered in advance of this decision that the South Vietnamese can clear out the Cambodian sanctuary; still less is there any evidence that they can keep it cleared out. Even if they could, what is to stop the North Vietnamese, in the meantime, from turning around and giving their full attention to the subjugation of Cambodia? And where does this end, if not in an ever-increasing effort to make good on Mr. Ronald Ziegler's ambiguous implication that we suddenly have an obligation to keep Cambodia neutral and out of Communist control?

Frankly it did not occur to us, when the President first announced his new, "low profile" approach to foreign policy that its first real application would come in the form of active American collaboration in a South Vietnamese invasion of Cambodia. But we are, perhaps, getting ahead of things; we await the President's explanation tonight of what is new, let alone even remotely promising, about this policy.

THE COMMERCIAL APPEAL
Memphis, Tenn., April 30, 1970

PRESIDENT NIXON and his defense chiefs have taken a big gamble in Cambodia. The decision to provide advisers and tactical and logistics support to South Vietnamese troops raiding Communist bases across the Cambodian border is risky.

The question is: Will this help or hinder the President's program to withdraw American troops from South Vietnam?

Mr. Nixon plans to tell the nation tonight why he felt this move necessary. And the people of this country, from villages to Congress, certainly are looking for an explanation.

The country knows it was a tough decision reached in a deteriorating situation.

The Defense Department defends the limited support of Cambodian border raiding this way: "These bases and depots have posed an increasing threat to the security of free world forces in South Vietnam as a result of increased enemy activities."

A department spokesman called the action "a necessary and effective measure to save American and other free world lives and to strengthen the Vietnamization program."

The South Vietnamese say their troops have been ordered to withdraw from Cambodia as soon as their mission is completed.

We sincerely hope the action serves its announced purpose—and quickly. As might be expected, there already is loud criticism in congressional circles. And millions of Americans undoubtedly received the news with mixed feelings.

President Nixon's past policy statements make it explicit that he does not want the United States to become trapped in another trouble spot such as Cambodia. He himself has stressed the lessons learned from Vietnam.

ADMITTEDLY, there is a vast difference between the massive military aid recently requested by the new Cambodian government and the defense of South Vietnam from outside attack.

A buildup of North Vietnamese and Viet Cong troops within 35 miles of the South Vietnam capital of Saigon and almost within sight of the sprawling Mekong Delta poses a hard dilemma for American decision makers. For instance, it is in the Mekong area where so much emphasis has been put on Vietnamization and American withdrawal. Until South Vietnam's army is able to defend itself internally and externally, the United States withdrawal planned by Mr. Nixon will be impeded.

So let us hope that this new development is limited to minimal American support, kept in South Vietnamese control, and that it serve to speed, rather than interrupt continued American withdrawal from South Vietnam.

ST. LOUIS POST-DISPATCH
St. Louis, Mo., April 30, 1970

If Congress has a proper regard for the welfare of the American people it will repudiate President Nixon's shocking escalation of his Vietnam war and limit the spending of United States funds in Cambodia. It is all too clear now that Mr. Nixon lacks either the will or the ability to extricate the country from the Asian morass, and this places a heavy responsibility on Congress.

Sad to relate, there was more than a little deception in the Administration's new Cambodian commitment. Only last Monday Secretary of State Rogers told the Senate Foreign Relations Committee the Administration had not reached a decision on Cambodian aid; which may have been the literal truth but not all of it. Mr. Nixon was on notice that a large majority of the Foreign Relations Committee was opposed to extending military assistance.

So it was necessary to act in s e c r e t. Mr. Nixon himself kept out of sight, though he now plans to offer an explanation this evening — after the decision has been taken. The Pentagon hatched its plans with its Saigon clients but did not inform Congress or the people. Senator Eagleton of Missouri tried to find out yesterday morning what was going on but got a run-around at the Pentagon (until finally somebody read him a press release). If this is not contempt of Congress, what is?

After the South Vietnamese launched an assault into Cambodia that had been in preparation for at least several days, the Pentagon announced the United States would furnish advisers, tactical air strikes, medical evacuation and some logistics assistance. A United States command spokesman said in Saigon American ground troops were not and would not be involved.

We would like to believe American ground troops will not become involved, but the facts suggest otherwise. The whole history of Vietnam has been one tragic misstep after another, each one leading deeper into the mire. We are not persuaded the South Vietnamese are capable of fighting a war on their own.

Since the Cambodian army is tiny and practically worthless, the question is not one of helping the Cambodian forces. They are being bypassed. The South Vietnamese are moving into Cambodia to fight the North Vietnamese and the Viet Cong guerrillas and, with American help, the end will be the devastation of Cambodia.

Tragically, all this may be totally unnecessary. North Vietnamese and Viet Cong troops have been in parts of Cambodia for years; it was Cambodia's military impotence that forced the deposed Prince Norodom Sihanouk to allow the interlopers to remain — despite the centuries-old racial hatred between Cambodians and Vietnamese.

These troops could have enlarged their hold at any time, but they did not. There is no indication North Vietnam wants to conquer Cambodia. It is quite likely Hanoi wants to control only the small portion it has controlled in the past, and that the North Vietnamese would have settled for the same status they enjoyed under Sihanouk, which was a status the U.S. lived with for a long time. But the U.S.-backed South Vietnamese invasion of Cambodia upset this likely possibility.

What Mr. Nixon has now done is to bring all of Indochina into the war. The Administration did everything possible to prevent the public from finding out about the secret war in Laos, but much of it was revealed through the diligence of Senator Symington. The Cambodian decision was taken secretly. If Congress, which controls the purse, cannot stop this process, where will it end?

The Pentagon's excuse for moving into Cambodia is that the action was "a necessary and effective measure to save American and other free world lives and to strengthen the Vietnamization program." This is nothing but empty press agentry. If it were accepted it would provide the rationale for moving anywhere — into Thailand, Burma, China — and endlessly wasting lives and treasure while the American dream dissolved into a nightmare.

Yet in all this gloom there may be a fragile ray of hope. Congress can, if it will, apply a brake. Now that Mr. Nixon's war has become an Indochina war, Congress can insist that the Administration s e e k a negotiated settlement covering all of Indochina.

SUN-TIMES
Chicago, Ill., April 30, 1970

The U.S. Senate should act at once to adopt a resolution specifically forbidding any U.S. military involvement in Cambodia.

This should be done to remove any basis the administration (or the Defense Department) might believe exists for extending U.S. military involvement in Southeast Asia without the express consent of the Congress.

The grim shadow of Vietnam hangs over the action in Cambodia yesterday. U.S. military combat support was given to South Vietnam's army for an invasion of Cambodia. The support takes the form of U.S. "advisers," tactical air and artillery support and other forms of military aid—as was the case in the beginning in Vietnam.

On Monday Sec. of State William P. Rogers told the Senate Foreign Relations Committee that North Vietnamese troops in Cambodia threatened the Vietnamization program.

This is nonsense. North Vietnam has had troops in Cambodia for at least five years. During the past year the Vietnamization program, according to Defense and State Department spokesmen, has been increasingly successful.

> The Vietnam toll — as of April 18
> United States — 49,334 dead
> South Vietnam—105,800
> Why more?

Sec. Rogers also said it was not necessary to get the consent of Congress to give military aid to Cambodia. He said the deciding point for such approval was the "amount (of aid) given."

The use of U.S. troops in a combat role in Cambodia goes beyond any arbitrary "deciding" point set by Rogers. The issue is no longer whether the United States should give arms aid to Cambodia. It is clearly whether the United States should expand its military combat role in Southeast Asia.

To do so would run counter to the overwhelming sentiment of the American people, who want to get out of Vietnam. It is the duty of the Senate to recognize that sentiment as well as the economic dangers and further divisions among Americans that would inevitably result if the Vietnam war is widened to include Cambodia.

The Senate must act quickly before it is too late.

THE LOUISVILLE TIMES
Louisville, Ky., April 30, 1970

If the American government's goal in Indochina is to shore up or establish, by military means if necessary, governments compatible with our own, then President Nixon's decision to involve the United States directly in the war in Cambodia was, we suppose, inevitable.

Presumably a case can be made militarily for a widening of the war —we will be protecting our flank in Vietnam, we will be denying the enemy (if we are successful) territory from which to attack us.

But we have heard all that before. We have heard it over and over as an explanation as we took one step and then another deeper into the Vietnamese quagmire. And all that ever resulted was a constantly bigger commitment, with longer casualty lists.

To us, the President's decision is doubly dangerous. It means the acceptance of unknowable risks militarily. Will the Red Chinese or Russians intervene? Will the Cambodians, whose support by the South Vietnamese we are now supporting, collapse before there is anything to support?

But beyond what happens on the battlefields, the decision implies great risks at home. How will the people react when they realize that the policy of withdrawal, on which so many had such high hopes, has been contradicted in deed if not in word?

For no matter what the rationalizations, this means a widening of the war. The Pentagon speaks of the move as "a necessary and effective measure to save American and other free-world lives and to strengthen the Vietnamization program." So we will save American lives not by withdrawing men more swiftly from the fighting front but by expanding the fighting front.

If our goal is a military victory in Indochina, this may well make military sense. But for all those who had hoped—and who had been led to believe—that our goal was disengagement, it is irrational and disillusioning, as well as dangerous.

KENT STATE KILLINGS

The worst outbreak of violence following President Nixon's decision to send American forces into Cambodia occurred at Kent State University in Ohio. Four students, two of them women, were killed at Kent State May 4 when 100 National Guardsmen fired their M-1 rifles into a group of antiwar demonstrators. Eleven other students were wounded. None of the four victims was described as radical. One was second in his ROTC class. According to friends, the two girls were going their separate ways to class when they were killed. After the shooting, Ohio Adjutant Gen. Sylvester Del Corso said the troops who had run out of tear gas fired in reaction to sniper fire. The next day Corso declared, "there is no evidence" of sniper fire.

The New York Times

New York, N.Y., May 6, 1970

The four students, including two women, killed by M-1 bullets fired by Ohio National Guardsmen, did not die on their campus because they were known to be committing acts of violence or engaging in illegal dissent. They were victims of panic, ineptness or worse on the part of National Guard officers and soldiers with loaded weapons—almost as if Kent, Ohio, were Parrot's Beak, Cambodia.

Many students at Kent State University had indeed been demonstrating with inexcusable violence against expansion of the Vietnam war. The National Guard had been called in after an Army R.O.T.C. building had been burned down. Rocks and vile names were thrown at Guardsmen; Guardsmen laid down a tear-gas barrage against the provocative students. But shooting the students down? According to a New York Times reporter standing ten feet away from one of the students who was killed, there was no audible or visible gunfire until the National Guardsmen set to. And the Ohio National Guard itself said yesterday it was unable to find evidence of sniper fire.

The State of Ohio has an obligation thoroughly to investigate this tragedy and tell the American people how and why these four students were killed—and if there is criminal responsibility. The statements by National Guard officials reveal at the very least a gross lack of control of the men under their command. Do individual Guardsmen have an option to fire without orders? Are Guardsmen allowed to fire point-blank into crowds without warning or warning shots? Did these Guardsmen and their commanders fail to carry out guidelines issued by the Pentagon on civil disturbances and riot control?

The deplorably unfeeling statement by the President of the United States—through an intermediary—certainly does not provide either any answer or any comfort—nor does it show any compassion or even understanding. Mr. Nixon says that the needless deaths "should remind us all once again that when dissent turns to violence it invites tragedy," which of course is true but turns this tragedy upside down by placing the blame on the victims instead of the killers. The way this dreadful incident has been handled could hardly have been better calculated to drive the mass of moderate students—the great majority—over to the side of the alienated. It is nothing short of a disaster for the United States, and it is doubly tragic that the President does not seem to realize that this is so.

AKRON BEACON JOURNAL
Akron, Ohio, May 8, 1970

Does President Nixon have any understanding of the intensity and the honesty of the college students who are opposed to the war in Vietnam?

Until Wednesday, all evidence would indicate that the answer is "No."

Maybe the national reaction to the Kent State University tragedy finally wakened him. At least, he had the decency and the courtesy to receive six students from Kent and to listen to their reports of how they saw four of their fellow students shot down by the Ohio National Guard.

It was reassuring to hear these students say that the President listened attentively and that he promised to get a full report on "where the errors were made."

But, until the very moment on Wednesday when the Kent Staters went to the White House, evidence had mounted that our President had shut himself off from any exposure to or understanding of the attitudes of the younger generation.

After extending the war into Cambodia, he went to the Pentagon last Friday and, in impromptu remarks, cast a slur on all college students with his references to "these bums . . . blowing up the campuses."

This surely contributed to the violent reaction over the weekend on many campuses, including Kent State's.

As Thomas Wicker says in a column in the Beacon Journal today, the President was "obtuse and heartless" when he said of the Kent State killings only that "when dissent turns to violence it invites tragedy."

This showed a disregard for the possibility that some of the students were deeply sincere in their protest, that some or all of the victims might have been totally uninvolved and that the forces of "law and order" could have accomplished their purpose in a less inept and disastrous manner.

Rarely has a President encountered such open disaffection within administration ranks as was shown Wednesday in two separate instances:

1— A young assistant in the Department of Education, Anthony J. Moffett Jr., assigned to involve young persons in government, angrily quit in protest against the "irresponsible statements" of the President concerning student protest.

2— More significant, because of the stature of the protester, was the letter from the Secretary of the Interior Walter J. Hickel, to President Nixon.

"A continued attack on the young," the Cabinet member told the President, "not on their attitudes as much as their motives, can serve little purpose other than to further cement those attitudes to a solidity impossible to penetrate with reason."

Mr. Hickel, as the father of eight, is undoubtedly in closer touch with the attitudes and aspirations of the younger generation than is Mr. Nixon.

In what may be his swan song as a member of the administration, the Interior Secretary was so bold as to suggest to the President that "you consider meeting, on an individual and conversational basis, with members of your cabinet."

Surely, the President has spent too much time lately listening only to his favorite Cabinet crony, the hard-nosed John Mitchell.

But when public opinion does finally seep through the barriers, Dick Nixon has a way of reacting.

Maybe that's why he adjusted his schedule on Wednesday to meet the six from Kent State.

On Thursday, eight university presidents gained an audience with him. They reported that he pledged that hostile comments by administration officials about college students would cease.

Tonight, the President will meet the press—and the public—on nationwide television. Will there be a "new Nixon" insofar as his attitudes toward the students are concerned?

THE BLADE

Toledo, Ohio, May 6, 1970

AS The Blade's staff writer, Tom Gearhart, reported from the grieving campus of Kent State University, what actually happened at each stage of the escalating violence there that ended with four students shot to death is still in question. It may, in fact, be some time before all is known about this tragedy, if indeed it ever can be—what triggered the actual firing by National Guard troops, whether they reacted simply to panic, and so forth.

Even so, it goes without saying that sympathy is manifest for those who paid such a terrible price at a fatal spot and a fatal moment during a violent demonstration. That it was even necessary to ring a campus of an American university—and Kent State was but one such—with helmeted troops, armed with gas and bullets and bayonets, is profound testimony to the bitterness eating at the fabric of our national life. It was a shocking and appalling commentary on the divisive tensions breeding across the land today, fueled by the deep feeling of disenchantment of a younger generation which believes that its peaceful dissent goes unheard and fed in part by an Administration in Washington that has shown all of the sensitiveness of a dinosaur to the longings and frustration of great segments of our people, particularly the young.

That having been said, one cannot deny the basic truth in one part of President Nixon's comment on the deadly clash at Kent State:

This should remind us all once and again that when dissent turns to violence, it invites tragedy.

The violence that has marred campus life and torn some universities asunder in recent years is thoroughly deplorable. There is a state of mind building among young dissidents that seems to have led them to embrace the notion that they can carry their dissent to any lengths without fear of any meaningful punishment. Thus, early campus demonstrations against the Vietnam war of the Johnson era have given way to increasingly destructive tactics. Dormitories, libraries, laboratories have been burned to the ground. University offices have been bombed, seized, and ransacked. Institutions and private establishments near campuses have been savagely sacked. The public has been terrorized, faculties cowed, activity disrupted, and other students assaulted—all this ostensibly in the name of peace.

Frankly, we believe that this nation is reaching the point where it will have to support the use of whatever force is necessary to protect our campuses and colleges from destruction and preserve the right of the vast majority of students to pursue an education. When students go on rampages—as they did at Kent—smash store windows, trample on the rights of others, burn down an ROTC building, harass police and the militia, their conduct amounts to little more than guerrilla warfare. And in that type of warfare, as in all others, people do get hurt; some may even die.

It happened at Kent to the sorrow and dismay of all who believe there must be no surrender to anarchy. It may very well happen again on other campuses or in other confrontations unless those who would replace idealism with nihilism, maturity with mayhem, recognize that violence only breeds more violence.

the San Juan Star

San Juan, P. R., May 6, 1970

The tragedy at Kent State University in Ohio is appalling evidence of the dangers that accompany the confrontations that are taking place on campuses across the nation, in Puerto Rico and around the world.

Young National Guardsmen, supplied with live ammunition in a gross error of judgment by somebody, face young students threatening them with thrown rocks and chunks of concrete. The guardsmen panic and students, some of them only bystanders, are mowed down.

Who is to blame?

Student activists who had burned the university's ROTC building to the ground as part of raucous demonstrations against President Nixon's decision to send U.S. troops into Southeast Asia?

National Guardsmen who, under orders to "take cover and return any fire," are incited to shoot before they are shot at?

It is a senseless situation and there is little use in trying to uncover a thread of logic in it. But the most senseless part of it all is to confront students with loaded and bayoneted rifles (and then man those rifles with people undoubtedly inexperienced in coping with such a predicament) — unless one wants to happen what happened at Kent University Monday.

The Cincinnati Post

TIMES ⚓ STAR

Cincinnati, Ohio, May 5, 1970

The slaying of the four students during demonstrations at Kent State University yesterday is a tragedy for all of us—for families and friends of the dead youths for the National Guardsmen who participated in the event, and for Ohio officials and citizens alike.

In the words of UPI reporter Robert Corbett, an eyewitness, "It was inconceivable to me that the troops could fire such a barrage at the demonstrators."

THE STATE ADJUTANT General, S. T. Del Corso, stated that a sniper opened fire against the Guardsmen from a nearby rooftop. That is disputed by eyewitnesses. But either way, how could Guardsmen have opened fire against unarmed students, including co-eds, at pointblank range?

Was an order given? Were the Guardsmen trigger-happy? Did they cut loose out of fear in the tense situation, or out of anger at the barrage of student-thrown rocks? We can think of no understandable reason why the troops levelled their M-1 rifles on the students, leaving nearly a score dead or wounded.

The students at Kent who burned down the ROTC building over the week end, tossed missiles at the Guardsmen and taunted them with obscenities are not blameless in this tragedy, either. The atmosphere of violence was created by them. The deadly fusillade from National Guard rifles was not inevitable. But the lesson of history is that violence often begets violence, whether by design or accident.

As we ask students to fix reasonable, nonviolent limits for their protest, so we ask those in authority to use the force at their disposal with restraint.

DIDN'T THE GOVERNOR realize that to dispatch a contingent of Guardsmen—many of them relatively inexperienced, yet armed with the weapons of war—was to send both too much and too little to the Kent campus? From all appearances, the troop commanders had too much firepower and not enough brainpower.

And the president of Kent—did he do all he could to stay in communication with the students, to persuade them to quiet down and disperse—or did the administration in effect abdicate its role to the Guard?

Nothing would be more fitting, in memory of the slain students at Kent State University, than a profound expression of remorse on all sides, and a pledge to end the name-calling, the rock-throwing, the tear-gassing, the arson and the gunfire that threatens to rip to shreds our lives—and our future.

Record American

Boston, Mass., May 8, 1970

The news from Kent State University in Ohio last Monday came as a stunning shock, immediately followed by a feeling of alarm. So the campus disorders had finally come to this—four students shot to death during a confrontation with National Guardsmen!

Nothing, of course, can diminish the tragedy of four young lives so needlessly lost. On the other hand, responsible second thought suggests how much can be done to prevent a recurrence of similar tragedies. The shootings at Kent, hopefully, could be the first and last of their kind.

We are not unduly hopeful. The most unusual fact about the occurrence is that something of the sort had not happened before. Young guardsmen, pelted by rocks in an all too familiar scene of anarchy, apparently panicked. They could do so again elsewhere in the angry chain reaction of new student demonstrations already under way.

What is needed immediately—and no doubt is being provided—is a fresh crash course in mob control for guardsmen everywhere.

Also required immediately—and already under way by the Justice Department—is a series of the most thorough probes of all agencies with jurisdiction. Guardsmen found guilty of breaking discipline at Kent must be punished. And so must the student radicals whose irresponsible leadership led to the tragedy.

What is needed most of all is a sober reassessment by student extremists of what they have been doing to their colleges and their country. At Kent they have experienced the inevitable result of what many thought was a kind of fun and games exercise. It is a bitter lesson, but not half so bitter as what would have happened to them elsewhere in the world.

Hopefully—and the word is stressed—what happened at Kent may also have instructed others in positions of authority. Some college officials may have learned, at last, that permissiveness and compromise can literally be fatal. And perhaps President Nixon may come to realize that all campus demonstrators are not necessarily "bums."

There are many lessons to be learned from the tragedy at the Kent State campus—by many people. If a sincere effort to learn them is made by all concerned, the needless deaths of four young Americans will not have been in vain.

Chicago Daily Defender

Chicago, Ill., May 11, 1970

The practice of stationing National Guardsmen on campuses to curb legitimate student demonstrations has proved to be a tragic error. There is no defense for the shooting to death of the four students at Kent State University who had committed no acts of violence and were not engaged in illegal dissent.

The Ohio National Guardsmen who fired the M-1 bullets that took the lives of those harmless students did so on an impulse well rooted in the conviction that they were doing the right thing in the light of the unpopularity of student demonstrations among public officials, both state and federal.

The bullets that penetrated the bodies of t h o s e young people will not stop anti-war protests. If anything, the martyrdom of the helpless four will serve as a holy cause for more massive and angry demonstrations against the Asian war.

President Nixon's enlargement of the theatre of the Vietnamese war by going into Cambodia is responsible for the intensification of the anti-war hysteria which is gripping the colleges.

Prolongation of the conflict may bring us closer to a global confrontation than any miscalculation this nation has made since the Korean war. The young men who bear the brunt of any armed conflict wish to vent their opposition now before it is too late.

But they are not only complaining against senseless wars. They want a greater voice in campus affairs, a decent society in which all men have an equal opportunity to advance according to their abilities.

We are going through a period of agony which will be augmented by greater and more painful and costly commitments to the present flaming struggle. There will be more mass protests, more angry demonstrations in which Americans of all political persuasions and ethnic identity will join hands. For the steps that the Nixon Administration is taking are poor harbingers of peace.

The Evening Bulletin

Philadelphia, Pa., May 6, 1970

The tragedy of four killed and eight wounded at Kent State University in Ohio casts a chilling shadow across the campuses of the country, indeed the country itself.

It may be, as President Nixon asserts, that "when dissent turns to violence, it invites tragedy." But this tragedy could have been and should have been avoided.

The State of Ohio has begun an investigation into the shooting by National Guard troops. It should be pressed with utmost vigor and objectivity to find, if possible, who was responsible and bring them to justice.

There is no condoning the burning of the university's ROTC building and the wholesale smashing of windows in Kent's business district which brought in the Guard in the first place. And the troops undoubtedly were provoked by rock-throwing students.

But mowing down unarmed students is unthinkable. Even if a sniper's shot did provoke the fire—and numerous witnesses, including two seasoned reporters, neither heard nor saw any sign of one—firing into a crowd denotes panic and a perversion of the purpose of troop presence.

The soldiers' conduct raises some old questions. The Kerner Commission report said that National Guard "use of the rifle in riot control operations is generally inappropriate. It is a lethal weapon with ammunition designed to kill at great distance."

It recommended immediate research to develop new weapons in riot control. That was in 1968. Similarly, it raised serious questions about the use of the bayonet, much in evidence at Kent, on such occasions.

These questions and others, such as whether the Ohio Guard's 18 hours' riot training is sufficient, are apart from the fundamental issues of why students are demonstrating in the first place.

Humane control of demonstrations is essential pending resolution of those issues. This means more careful attention to command control of troops, to the experience and training of the troops employed, and to the kind of crowd-control devices used.

THE 🏔 SUN

Baltimore, Md.
May 6, 1970

The dreadful events at Kent State University must be fully investigated if a shocked nation is to learn just what fatal mixture of provocation, panic and immaturity brought about the tragic shooting to death of four students by National Guardsmen. It will be an even greater tragedy if intolerable campus violence and unforgivably violent reaction are driven to a higher pitch.

What has happened in Ohio makes terribly clear the urgency and the force of the appeal 34 college and university presidents have addressed to President Nixon. In extraordinary language reflecting their sense of the menace now overhanging the whole of higher education in America, these presidents—the chief administrators of the Johns Hopkins, Princeton, Dartmouth, Notre Dame, Fordham, Amherst, Bryn Mawr, Vassar, Tuskegee, Columbia and Radcliffe among them—have said to Mr. Nixon:

"We implore you to consider the incalculable dangers of an unprecedented alienation of America's youth and to take immediate action to demonstrate unequivocably your determination to end the war quickly."

Could any expression by responsible and representative academic spokesmen of their deep anxiety be stronger? Of course, herd-like, destructive student riotousness must be kept under control. But it is not enough simply to protect buildings and punish those who resort to stones and fire. Nor can the trouble be met by denunciation as when Mr. Nixon last week in an unguarded moment—or so, for the sake of presidential dignity, we hope it was—spoke of college "bums," or when Vice President Agnew talks about a "smug elite." The 34 college and university presidents are far closer to the reality and to the nature of the danger when they say that "among a major part of our students and faculty members the desire for a prompt end of military involvement in Southeast Asia is extremely intense."

What is needed is not more anger and rhetoric—there has been too much already—or more "confrontations" — though admittedly they cannot be entirely avoided. Rather the pressing need is for a better understanding of the causes of this new surge of bitter discontent on the campuses, which cannot be wholly ascribed to mischief-making "activist" minorities, and for responses to it more carefully measured in language and in action.

The Sun 🦅 Reporter

San Francisco, Calif.
May 9, 1970

The death of four students at Kent State University is a sad, sickening and unforgivable event. We fear that the fate of these fallen young heroes is a harbinger of the violence and repression which the Nixon administration intends to use in the suppression of the people's mounting efforts to end the war in Indochina. Although the loss of any young life causes tremendous grief, we mourn ever more for the soul of the nation which is bing destroyed in the quagmire of Indochina, by national leaders insensitive to the crescendo of non-violent protest which has existed for the past six years against the U.S. war in Southeast Asia. John Mitchell, Spiro Agnew and Richard Milhous Nixon can no longer use the slogan of "law and order" to camouflage the true nature of their misdeeds--in Indochina and at home. The same mentality that could brush off the deaths at My Lai as one of the unfortunate vicissitudes of war now disposes of the shooting and killing of four unarmed students in Ohio by describing it as the inevitable result of "resorting to violence as a means of dissent."

No one would have believed six years ago that a generation of American youth escaping reality via panty-raids, goldfish swallowing contests and crowding phone booths, could have produced such martyrs as Schwerner, Chaney and Goodman, the fallen heroes of the SNCC Summer in Philadelphia, Miss., 1964; nor could one have imagined that the youth contingent of the U.S. peace forces would produce a breed hardy enough to suffer police rioting in Chicago, 1968--and now, in their determination through people's power to force our insensitive and nonresponsive Establishment to end violence and racism at home and in Indochina, young people unafraid to face the firepower of the Establishment.

The one bright spot in the troubled present is the determination of our children cleanse this nation of racism, poverty and war. In this dark hour this willingness of young Americans to pay the greatest price--if required, life itself--in the struggle for peace is America's one great redemption.

Des Moines Tribune

Des Moines, Iowa, May 6, 1970

When policemen faced the Irish riots of 1863 in New York City, they were armed with two weapons — a wooden stick and a gun. When ghetto riots rocked U.S. cities more than 100 years later, police were armed with the same two weapons. And when the Ohio National Guard faced a student mob on the Kent State University campus, they used guns to kill four students and injure 11.

The 1968 Kerner Commission report pointed to the unchanging police weaponry to show the importance of developing alternatives to the use of deadly force. The Kent deaths might have been avoided if this advice had been taken.

The commission urged immediate research to develop a new type of ammunition for use in civil disorders which would strike with deterrent, but not lethal, force. British units in Hong Kong, when faced with violent rioting, fired a wooden peg from their guns with great effectiveness but with little danger of killing or maiming rioters.

New methods of delivering chemical deterrents have been developed, the commission reported. They allow tear gas or nausea-producing gas to be used more discriminately. At the Kent disorder, old-style tear gas cannisters were used with little effect.

The commission suggested using distinctive marking dyes or odors on rioters or filming them both to deter and to positively identify persons committing illegal acts.

Researchers told the commission that sticky tapes, adhesive blobs and liquid foam could be used to immobilize or block rioters. They reported that intensely bright lights and loud, distressing sounds might be capable of disabling rioters.

A nation with the technological ability to go to the moon should be able to devise effective methods of controlling rioters without gunning them down like milling livestock.

Amsterdam News

New York, N.Y., May 9, 1970

The tragic deaths of the four Kent State College students brings a feeling of shock and revulsion to us as it does to millions of Americans, especially so to the outraged students who are demonstrating and striking on campuses across the country.

We cannot but note, however, that this national shock was lamentably lacking two years ago when three youths were slain at South Carolina State College, shot down by state troopers.

Those black youths were demonstrating, too. But not against some undeclared war miles and miles away from home. They were demonstrating for their rights as free men in a free society in their own country, their own state, their own town.

It made no difference. They were shot down. Twenty-seven others were wounded. They were all black.

The fact that there were then no national outcries for an independent commission of inquiry into their deaths as is the demand now being made in the Kent State tragedy, is almost as tragic as the fatal shootings themselves.

Olympic Massacre:

ARABS KILL 11 ISRAELI ATHLETES; MOURNING HALTS GAME FOR ONE DAY

Palestinian commandos slipped into the Olympic village in Munich, West Germany during the early hours of Sept. 5, killing two members of the Israeli Olympic team and seizing nine others as hostages. All nine were murdered by the terrorists nearly 24 hours later when German police sharpshooters attempted to ambush the Arabs at a military airport outside of Munich. Five of the commandos were killed and three captured during the gun battle, which also took the life of a German policeman.

Negotiations between the Arabs and German authorities had continued throughout the day on the patio of the Israeli dormitory. The Arabs had demanded the release of 200 commandos imprisoned in Israel. German offers to pay an unlimited ransom or to substitute German officials for the Israeli hostages were rejected by the terrorists. The stalemate was broken about 9 p.m. when an ostensible bargain was reached to transport the Arabs with their hostages by helicopter to the airport where they would be provided with a jet to take them to Cairo. Apparently unaware of the precise number of terrorists, the police sprung their ambush at the airport before all the Arabs were out of the helicopters.

Responsibility for the attack on the athletes was claimed by an Arab guerrilla organization called Black September in a statement issued in Cairo. In a warning to the Palestinian guerrilla groups that they would be held accountable for the raid, the Israeli government charged that the Arab nations and particularly Egypt had to accept some responsibility for the attack since they had encouraged and financed the terrorists. Israeli Premier Golda Meir expressed her personal appreciation Sept. 6 to the West German government for its decision to "take action for the liberation of the Israeli hostages and to employ force to this end."

While most Arab governments remained officially silent on the attack, many newspapers and radio stations in the Arab world expressed admiration for the commando operation. The governments of Jordan and Lebanon, however, expressed concern and sorrow over the deaths.

Israeli jets carried out a damaging attack Sept. 8 against 10 Arab guerrilla bases and naval installations deep inside Lebanon and Syria. Lt. Gen. David Elazar, Israel's chief of staff, said Sept. 10 that the raids were not only in retaliation for the Munich murders, but also for the increasing attacks on Israel's borders from the two countries. When a resolution calling for Israel to "cease immediately all military operations" but failing to condemn the Munich raid came to a vote in the U.N. Security Council Sept. 10, the U.S. vetoed it on the ground that it was one-sided.

Even as the West German negotiators were bargaining with the Arabs, athletic competition continued Sept. 5 in 11 of the 22 sports on the day's program. It was not until 4 p.m. that International Olympic Committee President Avery Brundage ordered the games suspended. More than 80,000 persons filled the Olympic Stadium Sept. 6 for a 1$\frac{1}{2}$-hour memorial service for the slain Israelis. The resumption of the games later that afternoon was the subject of considerable controversy among the athletes, officials, spectators and journalists attending the games. Many, including the Israelis, had said the remaining events on the program should have been cancelled or postponed for a longer period of mourning.

The Evening Bulletin

Philadelphia, Pa., September 6, 1972

The deadly assault on Israeli athletes at the Munich Olympics by Palestinian terrorists—a bloody and maniacal intrusion on that peaceful scene devoted to international understanding—**is a** blow not against Israel alone but against civilized communion among all nations and peoples.

Innocents have been murdered. The sacred laws of hospitality have been breached. The ideal of the Olympic contest, already strained by the jarring political disputes of our age, has now been indelibly stained by a horrible act of political criminality. We mourn the victims, but we had better weep for our society as well.

Israel besieged, a nation of citizen-soldiers, has conditioned itself to withstand and fight back against such terrorism. Aerial hijackings, abduction, blackmail, and assassination have been the order of the day. Only a few months ago the world shuddered at the Tel Aviv airport massacre in which Japanese fanatics employed by Arab guerillas indiscriminately slaughtered passengers.

But surely, now that a murderous vendetta dares reach into the peaceful international Olympics assembly for its **victims,** governments cannot permit themselves the luxury of mere expressions of outrage.

There must be action, and not the kind of action that is a frightened retreat into walled security.

It has been said by some that West Germany, which tried so hard to make this Olympics contest a model of friendliness, did not maintain tight enough security at the Olympic Village. That may be so, but the degree of security that would suffice to wall out such fanatical terrorists as these might well also completely stultify the spirit of such a gathering as the Olympics.

Sealing off people is not so much the answer as sealing off terrorists of all kinds, not only the murderous Palestinian variety.

They should be denied sanctuary anywhere. No matter what the cause in whose name they violate considerations of humanity, they should find every decent man's hand against them.

Any government that tolerates or encourages terrorist groups should be the object of international sanctions.

If the civilized world does not recognize that organized murderous violence is a spreading plague—that the urban guerilla and the aerial hijacker and the political kidnaper threatens every social order — there will be little point in the superpowers guarding civilization against the larger atomic terrors.

Killer fanatics such as those that were loose in Munich's Olympic Village can, if they go unchecked, atomize our very society.

Arkansas Democrat

Little Rock, Ark., September 7, 1972

With the Germans' investment in the Olympic games and their opportunity for profit, both to their image and their pocketbooks, it is surprising that they were so lax in security for the 6,000 athletes. People saw the Arab gunmen leaping the fence and making their way to the dormitory housing the Israelis, but they thought it was simply some fun-loving athletes out past curfew. Relatives and reporters were meticulously kept out of the compound but not athletes who cheat on the rules or fanatics with submachine guns.

Then, once the hostages had been seized, it is even more amazing that the Germans bungled the rescue attempt. The Germans have a great capacity for organization and thoroughness, not to mention military operations. We predict that Chancellor Willy Brandt, one of the handful of real statesmen on the world scene today, will be seriously damaged by this tragedy. After all, he flew to Munich and took personal command of the situation, and the Munich police chief said that the orders for sharpshooters to start firing (in the dark) at the Arabs came from the "top level." Really, the surprise is not so much that the attack was made but that it ended so dreadfully.

Arab fanatics have carried out dozens of cowardly and senseless attacks against Jews in all parts of the world. In fact, network commentators have said there were reports several days ago that Arab terrorists would use the Olympics for some kind of extortion plot against Israel. And why not?

The Olympics already had caved in once to blackmail. A group of blacks, including some of the star athletes and some Americans, had threatened to leave if Rhodesia were not expelled because of its anti-black government. The walkout, the Olympic officials feared, might spoil the games, so Rhodesia's team (although integrated and previously certified) was sent packing.

The games must go on no matter if 17 human beings have been killed and the original purpose of the games — noncommercial and nonpolitical tests of skill and strength among amateur athletes of all countries of the world — had long since disappeared in the glitter of Olympic village. We in Arkansas are familiar with the game-must-go-on philosophy, the Razorbacks having been one of the few football teams that insisted on playing its regularly-scheduled game the day after President John F. Kennedy was assassinated.

Should the Olympic games have been canceled? We think so. Brandt's sorrowful first reaction, "The joyous games are over," probably was the correct one. Maybe it wouldn't have accomplished anything except to tell the Jews, more meaningfully than with lip service, that the decent people of the world, as represented by the apostles of fair play gathered in Munich, share their grief at the unfairness that once again has been heaped upon them.

Assassination, skyjacking, fragging, blackmail, bombing, massacre, terrorism, kidnaping, mugging, torture . . . These are horrible things that we no longer seem to regard as horrible. At least not to the extent that we are willing to discontinue business as usual, to make some sacrifice even so slight as giving up our entertainment, or getting to the airport 20 minutes early. Until we reduce our tolerance for horrors like the one in Munich, they are likely to increase.

New York Post

New York, N.Y., September 7, 1972

After the Munich madness the whole world—with a few obvious exceptions—mourned the slain young Israeli athletes who (as their Chief of Mission put it) "died in the bloom of their lives." But the question of how to turn the grief into action remains.

It would have been better to cancel the Olympic Games right after the memorial service. For the killing of the Israeli hostages took the heart out of the rest of the games and make them a meaningless mummery.

The international term for stern penalties on sovereign states is "sanctions." The time for sanctions is here. What Israel will do will depend largely on what the rest of the world does. If the UN could get over its current case of paralysis, or if the 17-nation aviation meeting in Washington were to act decisively to stop hijacking, it would be a signal to the Arab states harboring the guerrillas that the world will no longer tolerate terrorism, and a signal to Israel that it does not stand alone. In that case direct Israeli reprisals would lose much of their urgency.

But if the civilized world community doesn't act, the Israeli people who mourn their dead will pressure their government irresistibly to act. One action being demanded is to apply the death penalty to terrorists judged guilty by Israeli courts. Another is through commando raids on terrorist bases in Lebanon and Syria, to hit at "the cells and branches of terrorist organizations," as the official Israeli statement puts it.

The Israeli officials won't do this with any eagerness or relish. They know that it will endanger the delicate current moves toward direct peace talks with Egypt. There is also the risk of dissipating the large fund of world good-will which is today heavily on Israel's side. But in the absence of world action by other nations, no Israeli government which failed to take action of its own could hope to survive.

The problem is one of the sanctuaries which a few Arab states—Lebanon, Syria, Egypt—have provided for the terrorists. This is where their bases are, their offices, their information centers. This is where they hold press conferences and publish their newspapers. Whatever the ruling groups of these three Arab states may feel about the gruesome deed of the terrorists at Munich, they carry a direct responsibility for it by furnishing the sanctuaries. They can divest themselves of the responsibility only by stripping the terrorists of their sanctuaries.

*   *   *

If they refuse, then they will have no moral basis for protesting against sanctions that the rest of the world may decide to impose. Even the Soviet Union, which has tried to establish a power base in the Arab states, must take an official stand against terrorism from whatever source it comes, including its allies.

But the lead must come from the U. S., West Germany, France, Great Britian and Japan, who have the strength to impose economic sanctions on governments willing to offer sanctuaries to terrorists. They cannot absolve themselves from this task, even by deep-felt words of shock and grief.

The Oregonian

Portland, Ore., September 8, 1972

The reaction of some elements in Arab nations, official and unofficial, to the death-dealing assault on the Olympics by Arab terrorists is despicable. In blaming West German police for the tragedy and implying that the terrorists were martyred, they encourage repetition of such outrageous acts.

The principal offenders are Egypt and Libya. The Egyptian government, to its great discredit, said through a spokesman that "the West German government is fully responsible for the consequences of the incident." A Cairo newspaper had previously said that the guerrillas had acted "courageously and cautiously, killed the Israelis and fell martyrs." A Libyan government-controlled newspaper called the Bonn government "criminally responsible for the murder of both the Israelis and the Palestinian guerrillas," and the Libyan government offered to charter a plane to fly the bodies of the five dead guerrillas to Libya for a martyrs' burial.

Such incredible responses to the ghastly crime of the guerrillas unquestionably reflect the sympathies for the Palestinian cause in the Arab world. But they fly in the face of world revulsion.

King Hussein of Jordan, who recognizes the barbarism of the guerrillas, was alone among his sometime allies in reacting in humane fashion, denouncing the Palestinians' "shameful crime." Lebanon's government expressed itself as "sorry" it had happened. Other Arab governments withheld their opinions.

Circumstances call for drastic action against those nations giving sympathy, support, sanctuary or any aid and comfort to such murderers as sparked the fray in Munich. Both the U. S. House of Representatives and Senate overwhelmingly called for such action by resolutions. So has U. S. Secretary of State William P. Rogers at the direction of President Nixon.

But it is all too possible that such calls to action will be lost in the complications of international politics.

The West German government of Chancellor Willy Brandt, whose territory was violated by the guerrillas, could be the first to take retaliatory action against Egypt. Cairo has been promoting a rapprochement with Bonn. Egypt recognized West Germany in June after a seven-year hiatus in relations between the two countries. Egyptian Foreign Minister Murad Ghaleb is scheduled to visit Bonn late this month.

West Germany would be justified in reconsidering its relations with Egypt in light of the Cairo government's wholly unacceptable response to the guerrillas' slaughter. Other countries, including the United States, should do the same. Egypt and those who follow its lead must be shown that civilized nations will not tolerate those who openly or covertly sponsor or condone acts of international banditry.

NIXON'S VISIT TO CHINA: 'WEEK THAT CHANGED THE WORLD'

President Nixon's heralded journey to the People's Republic of China became history in late February. The President, who had startled the world last July with his announcement of a China summit [See Vol. 2, pp. 908-940], had to travel half way around the world to shake hands with the Chinese Communists. Nixon left Washington Feb. 17, accompanied by Mrs. Nixon, Secretary of State William Rogers, National Security Adviser Henry Kissinger and a party of about 300 persons.

After stopovers in Honolulu and Guam, the party arrived Feb. 21 in Peking, where they were welcomed at the airport by Premier Chou En-lai himself. Within hours of his arrival, Nixon was granted a surprise hour-long audience with Chairman Mao Tse-tung. It was his only meeting with the 78-year-old Communist leader during the week-long visit. Although the substance of the Mao-Nixon talk was kept secret, it was described afterwards as "frank and serious." But Nixon's most important contacts in China were with Chou. The two leaders spent at least 14 hours together in formal policy discussions and considerably more time at banquets, receptions, concerts and walking tours. They were said to have gotten along well together; the atmosphere was described as relaxed and communicative. But even though there was extensive coverage of the Nixon's sight-seeing excursions in China, including visits to the Great Wall and the Forbidden City, journalists complained that there was a lack of "hard news." So it was left to the President himself to describe the meaning of his visit and in Shanghai, on the eve of his departure, Nixon called it "the week that changed the world."

The day before he left China, President Nixon issued a communique jointly with Premier Chou En-lai indicating that their talks had resulted in agreement on the need for increased Sino-American contacts and for eventual withdrawal of U.S. troops from Taiwan. The Feb. 27 communique called on all countries to "conduct their relations on the principles of respect for the sovereignty and territorial integrity of all states, nonaggression against other states, noninterference in the internal affairs of other states, equality and mutual benefit, and peaceful coexistence."

The most important part of the communique dealt with Taiwan. The Chinese declared that the status of Taiwan was "the crucial question obstructing the normalization of relations" between Washington and Peking. They said that the Chinese government firmly opposed the creation of "one China, one Taiwan," "one China, two governments," "two Chinas" or an "independent Taiwan." The Americans acknowledged that "all Chinese on either side of the Taiwan Strait maintain there is but one China and that Taiwan is a part of China" and that they did not challenge that position. According to the communique, the U.S. reaffirmed its "interest in a peaceful settlement of the Taiwan question by the Chinese themselves." "With this prospect in mind," the statement went on, the U.S. "affirms the ultimate objective of the withdrawal of all U.S. forces and military installations from Taiwan. In the meantime, it will progressively reduce its forces and military installations on Taiwan as the tension in the area diminishes."

The Pittsburgh Press

Pittsburgh, Pa., February 28, 1972

If President Nixon's visit to Communist China is judged only in light of the 1,800-word communique issued near the end, the United States did not come off too well.

As Mr. Nixon and adviser Dr. Henry A. Kissinger themselves acknowledged, the document contained no concessions by Chairman Mao Tse-tung and Premier Chou En-lai.

On the other hand, there was notable "give" by the United States as Mr. Nixon moved closer to Peking's view that the future of Taiwan is an "internal" Chinese matter that must be settled without outside 'interference,' meaning by the U. S.

It was a considerable concession by Mr. Nixon to sign a communique with Chinese Communists pledging "the ultimate . . . withdrawal of all U. S. forces and military installations from Taiwan."

Although Mr. Nixon said it would be done only "as the tension in the area diminishes" —meaning when there are no signs of a Communist invasion—it still comes as a hard blow to the Nationalist government on Taiwan.

★ ★ ★

The 9,000 American servicemen on Taiwan cannot stay forever.

Most of them are there to support our Vietnam operations, which are winding down.

But the way to withdraw troops from an ally's soil is after careful negotiations with the ally, not through a joint announcement with his sworn enemy.

The communique talked of America's "close ties" to South Korea and "close bonds" with Japan. But the Nixon-Kissinger team could not get a friendly word in the communique for Taiwan, to which this country has a defense commitment.

It would not be surprising, therefore, if the Taiwan regime, feeling abandoned by Washington, thinks of making the best deal it can with Peking.

The same can be said about countries like Thailand and the Philippines, which may question the value of their American ties and look to accommodation with Red China.

Of course, in 18 hours of secret talks with Mao and Chou, Mr. Nixon may have received assurances of China's cooperation in keeping peace and stability in Asia and the Pacific. Let's hope so.

That would go a long way toward balancing the one-sidedness of the communique.

Despite his inability to show concrete gains today, Mr. Nixon's visit may in time prove to have had great value.

As he put it, building "a bridge across 16,000 miles and 22 years of hostility that have divided us" can be more important than the details of a communique.

★ ★ ★

Nevertheless, the v i s i t has reinforced doubts about the value of summit diplomacy.

Mr. Nixon was up until 5 a.m. Saturday overseeing the wording of the joint statement. That is not a safe way to do business.

In such meetings, the head of a democracy —especially one running for re-election—is at a disadvantage.

His public and his career demand a success, while the totalitarians he is dealing with are unworried by public opinion, which they manipulate, and by elections, which are uncontested.

Let's hope Mr. Nixon will keep such pitfalls and his Peking experience in mind when he moves up to the real big leagues: Moscow in May.

The Courier-Journal

Louisville, Ky., February 29, 1972

THE BLADE

Toledo, Ohio, February 29, 1972

DIPLOMATS, China scholars, and other far-from-casual observers no doubt will be poring for some time to come over the words and phrases of the communique summing up the talks between President Nixon and Premier Chou En-lai. And those analytical exercises will be neither futile nor inappropriate, for the presidential visit to Red China was a momentous enough event and the concluding statement was certainly carefully enough drafted to warrant the closest attention to nuance and profundity by experts concerned with underlying meanings.

But it may well be that the greatest significance of the joint document lies less in its specifics than in its format. Considerably more length is given to expressions of the separate views of the two sides than to declaring what they agree on. This was emphasized not only in broad, introductory-type statements by each but in divergent comments on certain issues such as Indochina and Taiwan. And in more than one instance the two sides underscored that they were affirming or reaffirming positions—words obviously chosen to make it plain that they were not saying anything that should come as a surprise to anybody.

The essential point of all this is that the Nixon-Chou communique took a distinctively opposite tack from most formal declarations on diplomatic summitry. Instead of the usual paper of platitudes contrived to mask points of difference, there was a studied attempt to lay out in the open the fact that major disagreements between the United States and Communist China remain virtually unchanged at this point. Indeed, it is particularly notable that the overall tone and substance of the joint statement were much more low-keyed and calculatedly cool than some of the courteous rhetoric exchanged at the formal banquets and during the presidential sightseeing jaunts of the preceding week. And even some of the points on which the leaders said they agreed "in principle" carried strong hints that they would probably have sharply different interpretations for the generalities.

This deliberate effort to focus on the persistence of large disagreements constitutes, paradoxically, the most encouraging aspect of the entire occasion. It is a reminder that the purpose and the hope of the new move toward "normalization of relations" between Washington and Peking were not to raise the rosy-hued prospect of an instant end to old animosities but to begin dealing with them on a realistic basis.

The resistance to the temptation inherent in most summitry to hide fundamental divisions under a glossy surface of diplomatic verbiage is a good sign that, in truth, an important step has been made toward approaching the problems on the basis of facts rather than the fantasies of nearly a quarter-century past.

THERE IS AN old Chinese saying: "Loud noise on staircase, but nobody comes down stairs." This bit of ancient cynicism is recalled by President Nixon's descriptions of his visit to the People's Republic of China. When first announced, it was "a great breakthrough." At its conclusion it became "the week that changed the world."

The President's habit of overselling his case makes the episode difficult to judge fairly. It gives credibility to such comments as that of George Ball, who was Undersecretary of State in two Democratic administrations: "The journey was television overkill, as it has been diplomatic overkill."

It would have been better to stick more closely to the cool, guarded, sometimes vague language of the joint communique issued by the American and Chinese negotiators. But the President in his exuberance has declared that the communique itself is unimportant compared to the actions that will follow. What actions? It will take much more time to winnow out the wheat of actual accomplishment from the chaff of propaganda, publicity and politics.

This newspaper supported Mr. Nixon's decision to make the journey to China. It welcomed so dramatic a change of direction on the part of a man who had done as much as any other American to fix our country on a course of blind antagonism to everything that stemmed from the governments in Peking and in Moscow. We have applauded his courage in being willing to open a door long bolted shut. We have noted that a man with such a reputation as a hard-line anti-Communist would be better able to persuade the American public to take a look with him at the realities between the Iron and the Bamboo Curtains than any of the opposition leaders he has accused in the past of being "soft on communism."

The trip has had its exciting and sometimes entertaining points, and certainly it has had its educational values for a great many Americans. The unblinking eye of the television camera has stared into the entire scene, from the initial cool reception at the airport to the exchange of convivial toasts at later banquets, from the snowy grandeur of the Great Wall to the classic beauty of the Ming Tombs. Burton Holmes never produced such a travelogue.

As to actual results, experts disagree, and the jury will long be out. Reports from Shanghai indicate that some foreign observers think the sophisticated and sagacious Chou En-lai got everything he wanted and gave nothing of consequence in return.

There are some indications of at least limited progress, however. There apparently will be an exchange of persons, and talks on increased trade. It appears that the issue of Taiwan, though it remains "the crucial question obstructing the normalization of relations between China and the United States," will not be allowed to create a violent rupture.

It must be noted that Chiang Kai-shek, who has carried the cause of Taiwan on his shoulders for two decades, is now 84 years old. Peking reaffirms its sacred claim to the island he occupies. The mainland leaders may be willing to exert Oriental patience, however, and wait for Chiang's inevitable departure. It has long been suspected that his son and heir would find it easier to make an accommodation with Peking. Meanwhile, the United States agrees to "progressively reduce its forces and military installations on Taiwan as the tension in the area diminishes." The final phrase is conveniently vague as to time, but the agreement is another overdue step in our disengagement from a myth—Chiang's claim to all of China—that Mr. Nixon did so much in the beginning to make American policy.

But "the week that changed the world"? The description would perhaps be justified if the United States and China had been on the verge of a nuclear war against each other, and it had been averted by the Nixon visit. After such hyperbole, what can the President say when he concludes his visit three months from now to the Soviet Union, which is indeed a potential nuclear foe?

There is a danger that the whole episode will deepen a familiar delusion, the Wilson-Chamberlain Syndrome, it might be called: that all the world's troubles could be settled if a few powerful men would sit down at a table and discuss them together. After all, such rival figures as Richard Nixon and Chou En-lai shared a Chinese dinner and managed to "change the world," and in only a week. What if they'd had a month, and Russia's Leonid Brezhnev had been present, too?

As Nixon and Chou En-lai said goodby

Such oversimplification of the facts of life is a peculiar peril to Americans. We are always subject to the twin lures of isolationism, the impulse to shut our doors and pull down our curtains and ignore the rest of the troublesome world, and of idealism, the notion that since everyone wants peace, all it takes is straight talk. Always present is the seductive hope that we could stop spending our money and sacrificing our young men abroad if the leaders of foreign powers would talk things over sensibly with our top policymakers. It was in much this mood that John Kennedy, soon after his inauguration, undertook to exert the power of sweet reason on Premier Khrushchev in Vienna. The rebuff he received was followed not long after by the missile crisis in Cuba.

This is the inherent danger of summitry, including the concessions a participant may make in advance to ensure that the coming talks don't collapse and take with them both his dreams and his political aspirations. It is increased when the chief American participant suggests after the summit that historic goals have been accomplished, though they cannot be immediately disclosed. The dialogue in Peking was surely of some value. It would be folly to assume, however, that one week of conversations in the gaps between banquets and sightseeing trips could level the mountainous differences of philosophy that lie between us and China. The President would serve his cause better if he would curb his overweening enthusiasm in days to come when he reports on his trip to the American people.

TWIN CITY SENTINEL

Winston-Salem, N.C., February 29, 1972

PRESIDENT NIXON must have every reason to be pleased with the effect of his China trip on the American public.

For more than a week he dominated the front-pages and television screens of the nation. At all times he appeared the self-assured leader — dignified, courteous, good-humored. And Mrs. Nixon, moving with equal poise through the classrooms and clinics, created her own favorable image. Not even a fearsome ballet depicting the unmasking and flaying of a capitalist oppressor could upset the aplomb of the presidential couple.

The President, however, could not have been overly pleased with the results of the visit in the field of foreign policy.

As the joint statement reveals, Mr. Nixon had to concede the offshore island of Taiwan to the Chinese Communists. They are free to take it by persuasion or intrigue any time they can, and the United States will not interfere. That eventually dooms the nationalist government of President Chiang Kai-shek, which has survived on the island for 22 years. It also warns the Japanese, who ruled the island from 1895 to 1945, that they are to keep hands off.

The joint statement is therefore a shocker for Chiang and his government. That shock was inevitable, of course. sooner or later.

But the whole effect of the Nixon visit on Japan, from the failure to consult Japan's pro-American government in the first place to the final statement, is a much more serious matter. Japan is the most powerful nation in Asia, the third industrial power of the world and the most valuable U.S. ally in the Far East. The United States cannot afford to alienate the Japanese for a mess of Peking duck.

India, another big factor in the Asia power balance, was also irritated by the Nixon visit from its origins to the end. The gratuitous reference to Kashmir in the joint statement was enough to ruffle the feathers of Prime Minister Indira Gandhi and send American prestige still lower in India.

No doubt we shall learn more about the visit in the days ahead. But the joint statement provides reason to believe that it did the United States no more good than other foreign excursions by previous American presidents.

The Washington Post

Washington, D.C., February 28, 1972

"A trip to China is like going to the moon"— President Nixon, in his Man of the Year interview with Time Magazine.

"Where an event is a great event it does not need a lot of rhetoric. Where you need a lot of rhetoric, a lot of jazz, a lot of flamboyance, is when you don't have much to sell." — Mr. Nixon, in the same interview.

We cite these thoughts of President Nixon not in any effort to denigrate his trip to China or what he may have accomplished there, but because we think there is much truth in them which has some relevance to what has—and hasn't—happened this past week in Peking. To begin with, it was undeniably a "great event." We can be sure that things will never be the same again between the United States and the Peoples Republic of China, or between both countries and Russia, or between us and Japan, and the rest of Asia—and certainly between us and Chiang Kai-shek. An opening exists where there has not been one for 22 years; a beginning has been made; the potential is vast and for this much the President is entitled to great credit for it was a bold stroke, skillfully brought off by painstaking and clandestine preparations tracing back to the beginning of Mr. Nixon's term.

In this sense, it was something like going to the moon. It was a daring and dramatic voyage, long in the making, which produced an authentic First. But it was also like a moonshot in other ways: by his own choice, the President made it a TV spectacular; yet, apart from the spine-tingling touchdown at Peking Airport of the Spirit of '76, the first, fateful, Presidential footfall on Chinese soil, the opening banquet and the other touristic highlights, it was not, in its essence a visual event. What millions of Americans were witnessing was merely the outward, symbolic expression of decisions taken secretly by both countries months ago, and of profound and amorphous geopolitical shiftings which can only be dimly perceived or understood, let alone transmitted through a television tube. In their substantive preoccupations, the President and his aides became shadowy figures, bounding off unseen on diplomatic probes. And so the voids were filled, as television must fill them, with pageantry and Peking cityscapes and badminton matches and, in large measure, banalaties. We saw some splendid sights and learned some history and shared the sense of barriers breaking down. We also learned, among other things, that Bob Haldeman is a tireless taker of home movies and, from Barbara Walters, that "the people all say (all 800 million of them) that their life is better now than it was in the days of the landlords." But there was no way to see what really was happening in those 20 critical hours of conversations behind closed doors; you cannot simulate a diplomatic docking, as it were, between President Nixon and Chairman Mao. So as the week wore on, and the bloom wore off, the necessity for so much secrecy became a burning issue and in the absence of substance what we were getting was in fact a large dose of rhetoric, flamboyance and jazz. There will be more of the same, one would imagine, with the President's re-entry and splashdown tonight, which will presumably come in the form of a nationally-televised presidential report.

And then what? The astronauts bring back rocks for expert analysis, but these have not yet unlocked the secrets of the universe and the public interest in moonshots is, by all indications, on the wane. The President has brought back a communique, which will similarly be worked over by the experts, and the pickings, we would judge, will likewise be relatively slim. It will be argued by some that Mr. Nixon has performed too sweeping a kowtow, that in his eagerness to produce something of substance he has bartered away our commitment to Nationalist China—with his promise of total military withdrawal from Taiwan and his concession that "there is but one China and that Taiwan is a part of China"— for rather modest gains; cultural and scientific exchanges; sporadic, high-level diplomatic contacts; and increased trade. Others will doubtless question his literal acceptance of the Bandung principles of peaceful co-existence which the Chinese themselves inspired in 1955 and which this country has refused to embrace until now. There is a danger, in short, of a disillusionment on the part of some which could be as damaging, in its way, as the euphoria which the President has done so much to inspire.

There are two things to be said, it seems to us, about giving way at this point either to a morning-after depression or to visions of that generation of peace that Mr. Nixon would have us accept as the inevitable consequence of his journey to Peking. First, we would simply repeat the warning expressed on this page a few days ago by Chalmers Roberts: don't jump to conclusions; Spirits, whether of Geneva or Camp David or Hollybush—or Peking—can prove evanescent; there are too many uncertainties. If history tells us anything about summit meetings it is that you cannot measure their impact quickly, or reliably; we have Yalta, Geneva, the Nassau meeting between President Kennedy and Prime Minister MacMillan, and perhaps most tellingly, the Kennedy-Khrushchev meeting in Vienna to testify to that. Just as we could not tell until the Cuban missile crisis a year later how badly Mr. Khrushchev had misread Mr. Kennedy, so we cannot begin to know now how well, or badly, the Chinese may have read Mr. Nixon, or what the Russians will read into the Peking summit, or what the impact will be on other leaders in other lands.

The second thing we would say on first reading is that Mr. Nixon, in his concessions to the Chinese, has probably paid a heavy, but not unreasonable price for the excesses of American foreign policy in the post-war years; that this was a payment made higher by the fact that it was long overdue; that it will be painful for many Americans in the short run; but that it may well be richly profitable in the long run, if for no other reason than because we may now come to perceive more clearly an Asian order of priorities and power realities, which will enable us to approach our role in the world in general, and the problem of our disengagement from Vietnam in particular, in more realistic terms. It will not be easy for the President to square the downgrading of this country's obligation to Chiang Kai-shek with an overly-rigid, excessively protective attitude toward President Thieu, or to reconcile an open-ended struggle in Vietnam for the larger purpose of containing China, with the "peaceful co-existence" now subscribed to by the Chinese.

But neither will it be easy for him to make the most of what he has achieved in Peking if he continues to overstate — or misstate — the forseeable gains. "This was the week we changed the world," he declared in Shanghai, as his visit ended, and nobody would deny him that. Whether, as he went on to say, "generations in the years ahead will look back and thank us for this meeting," is something nobody can know. It is enough, for now, to acknowledge a great event, which speaks for itself, and speaks well for the President. To embellish it with rhetoric and flamboyance and jazz, as Mr. Nixon has himself suggested, is to encourage the suspicion that he doesn't have all that much to sell.

THE MILWAUKEE JOURNAL

Milwaukee, Wis., February 28, 1972

Generally, the communique issued by the United States and China following a week of talks justifies President Nixon's early warning that not much could be expected from the first direct contact between the two nations in more than two decades.

What was startling was the president's agreement that Taiwan is part of China and that this country will withdraw all military forces from that island "as tension in the area diminishes." That, of course, could take years. But the Chinese have won a major concession — and, if the communique is the sum total of agreement, they yielded nothing in return.

Once more, the former Nationalist China on Taiwan has been dealt a serious blow. This one comes on the heels of its dismissal from the United Nations and mainland China's assumption of the China seat, with American backing. It may be all but fatal.

Taiwan is part of China, of course. But the United States has been father and perpetuator of the myth that it is China. This complete turnabout without advance warning will undoubtedly outrage the pro-Taiwan forces in this country. It will jar such allies as Japan, which the United States has been urging to undertake closer relationships with the Nationalist government.

As is normal in communiques, this one pledges both nations to a course of peace and denies the right of any country to interfere with the internal affairs of others. In this connection, China continues to stand firmly behind North Vietnam and North Korea. Hopes that some steps might be taken toward solution of the problems these countries pose were not realized in the communique.

Still, there was an overall gain from the Nixon visit. The way has been paved for improved relations, starting with cultural and other exchanges and efforts to establish trade. The door to China has been opened. Americans almost overnight have been taken through that door via television and have seen glimpses of a society that has been closed to them since 1949.

China is once again in the family of nations. That is important to the world. And while the Nixon visit may not have the dramatic results that the president proclaimed as he was about to leave China — he called it a dawning of a new age — it does ease tensions in one more huge area of the world.

And now, on to Moscow and the Kremlin, from which Russia's leaders have been watching the China meetings with misgivings and apprehension.

THE NASHVILLE TENNESSEAN

Nashville, Tenn., February 29, 1972

PRESIDENT NIXON has returned home from Communist China after joining with Peking leaders in issuing a lengthy summary of the week-long visit.

Parts of the statement gave the U.S. view on certain matters. Parts of it gave the Chinese view. Still other parts reflected the view of both nations when these coincided.

There was agreement on generalities such as the need to broaden understanding between the two peoples, to work for peace and to oppose aggression and the interference by one nation into the affairs of other nations.

On more sensitive subjects such as Vietnam, Korea, Japan and some others, the two nations set out their divergent attitudes in firm but moderate terms. There was little change by either side in previously held views on any of these subjects.

* * *

Perhaps the most important parts of the summary dealt with the question of Taiwan and the future U.S. policy toward that island province of China and its current leader, Gen. Chiang Kai-shek.

The U.S. part of the summary on this topic in effect recognized Red China's claim to Taiwan and repudiated this nation's long-standing policy of supporting Chiang's right of rule.

"The United States," the statement said, "acknowledges that all Chinese on either side of the Taiwan Strait maintain there is but one China and that Taiwan is a part of China. The United States position does not challenge that. It

reaffirms its interest in a peaceful settlement of the Taiwan question by the Chinese themselves.

"With this prospect in mind, it affirms the ultimate objective of the withdrawal of all U.S. forces and military installation from Taiwan. In the meantime, it will progressively reduce its forces and military installations on Taiwan as the tension in the area diminishes."

The Chinese Communists have considered the Taiwan question to be the biggest obstacle in the way of peaceful relations between China and the U.S. The Reds have been adamant in their insistence that Taiwan belongs to them, and it seems likely they would consider any negotiation with the U.S. a success to their side if they could get recognition of their claim.

Thus, it is likely to be claimed that the President was bested in his negotiations with Premier Chou En-lai and Chairman Mao, and that in yielding on the Taiwan question he made a major concession without getting anything comparable in return. At least one conservative spokesman Mr. William Rusher, the magazine publisher, used the word "betrayed" in reacting to the U.S. position.

Mr. Nixon's present stand on Taiwan at least seems to be a reversal of the view he held when he was General Eisenhower's vice president and when he was campaigning for the presidency against the late John F. Kennedy in 1960. In television debates with Mr. Kennedy, Mr. Nixon repeatedly asserted that not only Taiwan, but

the off-shore islands of Quemoy and Matsu as well, belonged to the Nationalist government of General Chiang and should not be abandoned to the Communists either through force of arms or diplomacy.

Mr. Nixon contended then that the Communist Chinese leaders— the same ones with whom the President negotiated last week— could not be trusted, and that a concession to them would be an invitation to war.

In upholding the Eisenhower policy of defending the Formosa Straits, and criticizing Mr. Kennedy for recommending that the nation not risk war to defend the off-shore islands, Mr. Nixon said in one of the debates:

"Why did the President (Eisenhower) feel this (abandoning Quemoy and Matsu) was wrong? Because again, this showed a lack of understanding of dictators, a lack of understanding particularly of Communists because every time you make such a concession it does not lead to peace. It only encourages them to blackmail you. It encourages them to begin a war . . . we are dealing with the most ruthless, fanatical leaders that the world has ever seen."

Well, every person, perhaps, should be forgiven for changing his mind once in awhile—although some of Mr. Nixon's right-wing supporters will never forgive him for changing his mind about Taiwan. But the President's change of mind on Taiwan is bound to be suspect because of the surreptitious manner in which he went about it.

It was apparent when the U.S. supported Red China's admittance to the United Nations last fall that changes were coming about in Asian policy. Although the U.S. opposed kicking the Nationalist Chinese out of the U.N., it could be read in the tea leaves at the time that Chiang Kai-shek's days as a free-loader on American hospitality were coming to an end and that something more closely approaching a realistic Asian policy was coming into being.

But if the President did not try to hide this shift of policy from the American people, he did not go out of his way to make it clear that Chiang was being dumped until after he had spent seven days conferring with Chou and Mao.

* * *

This makes it appear the President's change of mind about Taiwan resulted from the persuasions of the leaders in Peking, and left him open to charges that he had been euchered by Chou and Mao.

At any rate, everybody now should understand that it is only a matter of time before nationalist China goes the way of Mao.

About the most that can be said of Mr. Nixon's new idea about China is that he expects now that whatever happens will be peaceful.

When it is all considered it may be concluded that the trip to China is far less impressive than Mr. Nixon makes it all appear. But despite the political motives behind it, it represents a step in the direction of progress.

STATE ANTI-ABORTION LAWS VOIDED BY SUPREME COURT IN 7-2 DECISION

The U.S. Supreme Court ruled 7-2 Jan. 22 that a state may not prevent a woman from aborting her pregnancy during the first six months of the gestation period, thereby invalidating laws prohibiting abortion in Texas and Georgia and, by implication, overturning restrictive abortion laws in 44 other states. Justice Harry A. Blackmun, writing the majority opinion, denied the contention that the unborn fetus was a "person" entitled to due process under the 14th Amendment. To the contrary, Blackmun said that "the 14th Amendment's concept of personal liberty and restrictions upon state action" guaranteed a right of privacy that included "a woman's decision whether or not to terminate her pregnancy." By interfering with that decision, the justice wrote, the state could harm the pregnant woman medically or psychologically, or could "force upon the woman a distressful life and future" and bring "a child into a family already unable, psychologically and otherwise, to care for it."

The majority opinion denied that a woman's rights with regard to abortion were absolute, since "a state may properly assert important interests in safeguarding health, in maintaining medical standards and in protecting potential life." After the first three months of pregnancy, during which time "mortality in abortion is less than mortality in normal childbirth," the state may intervene to protect the health of the woman, by licensing and procedural rules, Blackmun said. In the last 10 weeks of pregnancy, Blackmun wrote, when the fetus "presumably has the capability of meaningful life outside the mother's womb," the state "may go so far as to proscribe abortion during that period except when it is necessary to preserve the life or health of the mother." The court barred state residency laws and procedural obstacles to abortions.

Justice William H. Rehnquist supported Justice Byron R. White's dissent. White argued that the court's ruling meant that "the people and the legislatures of the 50 states are constitutionally disentitled to weigh the relative importance of the continued existence and development of the fetus on the one hand against a spectrum of possible impacts on the mother," which White characterized as "convenience, family planning, economics, dislike of children, the embarrassment of illegitimacy, etc." White said the court was "interpreting a constitutional barrier to state efforts to protect human life" while "investing mothers and doctors with the constititonally protected right to exterminate it."

Justice Blackmun said the state has an interest in the unborn child. The court would not define when life begins, but said that the state may interfere in the "right of privacy" in the last three months of pregnancy when the child is developed enough to live outside the mother.

That's clear, also.

But there is more. And it is not at all clear that at this point the majority of the supposedly strict constructionist court confined itself to the constitutional issues.

Justice Blackmun divided the normal nine-month pregnancy into "trimesters."

* * *

In the first three months, he said, the Constitution doesn't permit any state ban on doctor-approved abortions.

The second three months are a gray area in which the state may express its interest in the pregnant woman's welfare by requiring a doctor to perform abortions, requiring that the procedure be done in licensed facilities and providing for emergency after-care.

In the final three months the state can go so far as to forbid abortion except to preserve the life or health of the expectant mother.

This extensive qualification of "the right of privacy" moved Justice Rehnquist to say in his dissenting opinion that the ruling "partakes more of judicial legislation than it does of . . . the Fourteenth Amendment."

While we have advocated liberalization of abortion laws, we share Justice Rehnquist's concern that the court is drawing up detailed legislation rather than ruling on constitutional points.

* * *

Moreover, the Burger Court is going right down the road of the Warren Court in falling back on the judge's personal feelings and sociological considerations to do what it says it is doing in the name of the Constitution.

Said Justice Blackmun:

"Maternity, or additional offspring, may force upon the woman a distressful life and future, psychological harm may be imminent . . . There is also the distress for all concerned, associated with the unwanted child . . . The additional difficulties and continuing stigma of unwed motherhood may be involved."

All this may be true, but what, we ask, do these things have to do with the Fourteenth Amendment and the right of privacy? Are these federal constitutional considerations?

If they are properly the business of governmental concern and action, surely they are the business of legislators, not of would-be legislators and sociologists on the nation's highest court.

* * *

Nebraska and Iowa legislators, like those of most states, have the task of devising laws that fit the decision. In Nebraska, Sen. DeCamp says he will introduce a bill which may be more restrictive, as regards the middle months of pregnancy, than the Supreme Court guidelines appear to permit.

Whether DeCamp's colleagues support him is another matter, but we see no reason why the state should not push its views into what is admittedly a gray area of the decision as far as its legislators believe is practicable.

Omaha World-Herald

Omaha, Neb., January 28, 1973

In striking down Texas and Georgia laws, the Supreme Court Monday knocked out the abortion statutes of at least 45 states, including those of Nebraska and Iowa.

The majority opinion written by Justice Blackmun based the decision on the woman's right of privacy. It said in part.

"The Constitution does not explicitly mention any right of privacy. In a line of decisions, however, going back perhaps as far as Union Pacific R. Co. vs. Botsford (141 U.S. 250, 251—1891) the court has recognized that a right of personal privacy or a guarantee of certain areas or zones of privacy does exist under the Constitution . . .

"This right of privacy, whether it is founded on the Fourteenth Amendment's concept of personal liberty and restrictions upon state action, as we feel it is, or, as the District Court determined, in the Ninth Amendment's reservation of rights . . . is broad enough to encompass a woman's decision whether or not to terminate her pregnancy."

* * *

That's clear enough: Most state abortion laws violate the right of privacy and are therefore unconstitutional, says the Supreme Court.

The Evening Star
The News

Washington, D.C., January 27, 1973

The Supreme Court's long-awaited ruling on abortion is a landmark decision for two reasons. It recognizes a woman's right of privacy and freedom of choice in the first months of pregnancy. And it cuts through the controversy raging over the abortion issue by nullifying the laws in 31 states where abortion up till now has been a crime. In most other states the abortion laws will have to be modified.

At first glance it looks like a liberal decision by a conservative court. However, Justice Harry A. Blackmun, who wrote the 7-2 majority opinion, made it clear that the ruling was based, not on emotional grounds, but on the constitutional rights of the individual. He said the right of privacy under the Constitution is "broad enough to encompass a woman's decision whether or not to terminate pregnancy."

It is noteworthy that, in addition to Justice Blackmun, himself, two of the four justices appointed by President Nixon sided with the majority. But Mr. Nixon less than a year ago came out strongly against liberalizing abortion and defended what he termed "the right to life of literally hundreds of thousands of unborn children."

The court's ruling sets out guidelines for states with antiabortion laws. It says that in the first three months of pregnancy the decision whether or not to have an abortion rests with the woman and her doctor and the states have no right to interfere. In the first trimester the risk of death through abortion is considered slight. Beyond the three-month period, the court says, a state "may regulate the abortion procedure." This means, for instance, that a state may stipulate that abortions take place in hospitals and not in clinics, as New York State has already done. For the last three months of pregnancy, the period when the fetus is considered capable of surviving on its own, a state may declare abortion illegal except when deemed necessary to preserve the life or health of the mother.

It is on this last recommendation that the court's ruling appears most open to criticism. In accepting the theory that the fetus is viable only in the last three months of pregnancy it is entering the domain of medical and biological research. If the medical findings on the viability of the fetus change, presumably the court would have to revise its guidelines. The court rejected the theological argument that the fetus should at all times be considered a person. It ruled that the word "person" as used in the 14th Amendment does not apply to the unborn.

Undeniably there are positive aspects to the court's decision. It will give the unmarried woman who does not want a child an opportunity to solve her problem in private and to restore herself. To end a pregnancy in the hope of preventing a broken life could be a lesser of two evils. The ruling will relieve the burden of the very poor who have more children than they are equipped to raise or care for. In this respect it will be an additional aid in family planning. The provision of safe, inexpensive abortion clinics will eliminate the lucrative and obnoxious clandestine abortion industry, and protect women from the dangers and indignities of illicit operations often carried out in highly questionable conditions.

However, there is an evident risk of a proliferation of abortions under liberalized abortion laws. In New York City the figures are running at the rate of one abortion for one birth, although that ratio is undoubtedly distorted by the number of women from out of state going to New York clinics for abortions.

At best abortion is only a palliative. It is not a solution for the social problem of unwanted pregnancies, a problem aggravated by the growth of permissiveness. There are other, more constructive ways in which the problem should be tackled. In the case of the very poor, where birth occurs year after year, the need is for better education and counseling of both parents on birth control and family responsibilities. In the case of a single woman, the alternatives should be compassionately explained to her, particularly the possibilities of adoption. With the ever wider use of contraceptives and the growing practice of abortion, adoption agencies already have reported that the number of couples waiting to take babies exceeds the children available. It is heartwarming to learn that some couples are prepared to adopt, not only children of a different skin color, but even physically handicapped or mentally retarded children.

The pregnant woman should never be made to feel that abortion is an easy or a cheap way out of her problem, nor be rushed into a snap decision under emotional stress which she might afterwards regret.

Ultimately the answer for the indiscipline of permissiveness and sexual license must be found in a return to the moral and spiritual standards of the Bible and in a higher sense of life. The Biblical promise is: "Blessed are they that do his commandments, that they may have right to the tree of life . . ." (Rev. 22:14). The answer must be found by the individual in the privacy of his own thinking, through his own search for the meaning of such sayings as the Beatitude: "Blessed are the pure in heart: for they shall see God." (Matt. 5:8) No material palliative through surgical intervention can ever take the place of the discipline and self-control that come from an understanding of man's relationship to his divine source, and from love and respect for the good, pure and noble in one's self and in one's neighbor.

THE CHRISTIAN SCIENCE MONITOR

Boston, Mass., January 29, 1973

No victory for women's rights since enactment of the 19th Amendment has been greater than the one achieved Monday in the Supreme Court. The historic decree on abortion at last extended the protections of the Constitution broadly to an area of the law in which women are most singularly and severely affected.

As expected, it is being criticized on one hand as too sweeping and permissive, and on the other as not going far enough. Some liberationists will argue that a woman's absolute right to an abortion at any period of pregnancy should have been affirmed. But it seems to us that the court struck a judicious balance, weighing law and morality as best it could.

The justices held that a state may not forbid an abortion — provided the woman's doctor approves — in the first six months of pregnancy. But the states' regulatory powers are by no means swept away. They may, for the middle three months of pregnancy, impose requirements to protect the health of the mother in operations. And in the final three months, they may prohibit abortions, except to save the "life or health" of the mother, though the manner of deciding that may not be made excessively rigorous. Hence, the states still are empowered to set standards under which abortions may be administered.

But the new power given to women is solidly fixed in a single sentence of the ruling: The right of privacy under the 14th Amendment "is broad enough to encompass a woman's decision whether or not to terminate her pregnancy." This is a decision that women should have the right to make, within the bounds of safe medical practice, and six months should be more than sufficient for deciding in most cases. The court, though, has properly circumscribed that right in the advanced stages of pregnancy, in which the unborn child could live outside its mother's womb. So enough leeway is given, it seems, to prevent unsafe and wholesale abortions, and the sanctity of life, both adult and unborn, is recognized.

This latter question is the hard moral hurdle which many Americans won't be able to scale as readily as the court has. But it is now established in law at what point the unborn begin to share the rights of persons, and states no longer may forbid abortions except to save the life of a mother. That is indeed a long step in the law, altering the practices of most states.

And the remarkable aspect is that only two justices dissented from this difficult decision, and only one of President Nixon's conservative appointees to the court. Those judicial observers who have foreseen a retreat from activism by this newly rearranged court — a hesitancy to stretch the application of the 14th Amendment — find their prophecies confounded. The court continues to be unpredictable, and in this delicate case, we think it was right.

The Courier-Journal

Louisville, Ky., January 24, 1973

SINCE MORAL QUESTIONS are involved in any discussion of abortion, the controversy over whether it should be freely permitted is likely to continue, despite the Supreme Court's latest ruling. But at least the court's bold and unequivocal decision has settled the main legal arguments: the state has no right to prohibit or restrict an abortion in the earliest months of pregnancy, and it may impose regulations in the interests of the woman's health during the middle period. Only during the last trimester, when the fetus would be capable of an independent life outside the woman's body, may the state intervene to forbid the operation.

This ruling is understandably a deep disappointment to those who were counting on the highest court of the land to vindicate their belief that the unborn fetus, from the moment of conception, has rights equal to those of any living person. Yet, although they have failed in their struggle to engrave their personal conviction in the law, their efforts have not been entirely in vain. The attention they have focused on the moral aspects of the abortion issue will surely help put the issues into sharper perspective for the many thousands of women who every year face the prospect of an unplanned pregnancy and who are now free to decide what, if anything, they will do.

This insistence on freedom of choice has been the whole thrust of the pro-abortion lobby. It is possible, as a result of the Supreme Court ruling, that in the future there may be pressures, either social or bureaucratic, for insisting on abortions in certain circumstances — for instance, pregnant women on welfare, or women who already have more than a certain number of children. This is a potential development we should all be on guard against, for the state has no more right to demand abortions than it has to refuse them.

No problem for the rich

That attitudes have been changing was demonstrated by a Gallup Poll last summer showing that 64 per cent of Americans accepted the idea that the decision was one for the individual woman and her doctor, compared with only 15 per cent four years earlier. Many people doubtless had become aware in the interim that however generally discouraging the laws were intended to be, their effect was in fact blatantly discriminatory. A pregnant woman with money and easy access to good medical facilities has never had any difficulty in getting a safe abortion. But for the great majority, the only alternatives up to now have been the back-street abortionist or the unwanted child. Even some of the so-called "liberalized" abortion laws, such as the Georgia statute that the Supreme Court struck down, penalized those women who lived in remote areas, far from accredited hospitals, and those lacking the fees to pay the number of doctors who had to approve the operation.

It was also unfair and impractical that access to abortion was determined by state boundaries. What gave New York City the unsavory reputation of an abortion mill was not its own broadly liberalized law, but the lack of such freedom in most other Eastern states. But the chances of federal legislation resolving these anomalies were never rated high; congressmen generally preferred to duck the issue by claiming that it was really up to the states to decide. Even President Nixon, who made his own personal aversion to abortion perfectly clear when he intervened in the New York state legislature's debate a year ago, stressed that such laws lay "outside federal jurisdiction."

It was because Mr. Nixon had expressed himself so forcibly on this question that the Supreme Court's opinion came as such a surprise. Three of the four Nixon appointees to the court were among the seven-member majority, thus partially dispelling the notion that the thinking of all Nixon-appointed judges would inevitably reflect his sometimes odd views of what true conservatism, starting with individual liberty, is all about. Now that the court has asserted the right of independent judgment on the legal and constitutional issues involved in abortion, the controversy over its moral validity can return to its rightful place in the consciences of the American people.

THE RICHMOND NEWS LEADER

Richmond, Va., January 24, 1973

It was inevitable that the Supreme Court decision voiding the majority of State laws on abortion should arouse a storm of reaction. The issue is so charged with emotional and religious controversy that the response would have been as great regardless of how the court ruled.

In deciding that the state has no right to interfere with a woman's decision to have or not to have a baby during her first six months of pregnancy, the court followed an impeccable line of reasoning: The Fourteenth Amendment guarantees a right to privacy to all Americans, including women. During the first six months of pregnancy, a fetus cannot survive independent of its mother's body; therefore, a fetus does not constitute a "person" covered by constitutional guarantees.

The court's logic continued: During the first trimester, especially, pregnancy is a medical matter, and thus any decisions made about that pregnancy rightfully rest with the woman and her doctor. The efforts of the state to infringe on a doctor's practice of his profession, through the requirement for boards of approval, or for certification by other physicians, cannot be permitted under the Constitution. During the second trimester of pregnancy, the state can interfere only to the point of regulating medical circumstances under which abortions are performed, to guarantee a woman the best possible medical services. In the last trimester, when life theoretically could be sustained independently of the woman, the state has more compelling interests in the well-being of both mother and child.

Given the perceptible trends toward more libertarian interpretations of the rights of privacy in recent years, the court hardly could have ruled any other way on the abortion issue and maintained any consistency. Granted, abortion is the worst possible means of birth control. In an ideal society, there would be no unwanted pregnancies. Owing to the efforts of family planning programs, there are fewer unwanted pregnancies today than ever before, but there still are too many, especially among teen-agers who lack even fundamental knowledge of how conception occurs.

Millions of Americans do not believe in abortion at any stage of pregnancy. That is their right. Millions of other Americans do believe that women have the right to govern their own bodies to the extent of having a legal, safe abortion if they choose. Abortion proponents recognize the special agonies that can result from rape, incest, or deformed fetuses. Aside from these special instances, they also know that no birth control method is guaranteed to be 100 per cent effective, and unwanted pregnancies also can ruin lives and marriages when the state exercises absolute control over the circumstances under which abortions can be permitted. As in any other instance where the state attempts to regulate morals, stringent anti-abortion laws merely drive abortionists underground, where quacks and amateurs can maim and kill desperate women.

The issue offers no middle ground for opinion. Some men, still clinging to outdated chauvinistic views of women's role in society, feel that men alone should have the ultimate decision on abortion laws. Yet men never experience unwanted pregnancies. This may permit them to consider the issue dispassionately, but it also leads them to cruel conclusions. Catholic Church leaders may call the high court's opinion an "unspeakable tragedy," but the Catholic injunction against abortion is of rather recent origin in a religion two thousand years old. While Catholic spokesmen's horror at the decision can be understood, a majority of the high court properly recognized that no religion has a constitutional license to force its beliefs upon others.

The court's ruling does not compel any woman to have an abortion against her will. Neither does it prevent any woman from having an abortion under optimal medical conditions when she chooses. That decision now is hers alone to make. As long as a fetus, under the most conservative medical interpretation, cannot sustain its own life system, the continuation of a pregnancy is a medical concern. The high court was right in taking the state out of the doctor's consulting room.

The Globe and Mail
Toronto, Ont., January 27, 1973

In a historic and surprisingly definite 7-to-2 decision, the United States Supreme Court this week overturned all state laws that prohibit or restrict in any way a woman's right to obtain an abortion during her first three months of pregnancy.

The court also established a new and detailed set of national guidelines which will require abortion laws in 46 states to be broadly liberalized.

In brief, the Supreme Court has ruled that, in the first three months of pregnancy, the decision to have an abortion lies entirely with the woman and her doctor. The state has no right to intervene in any way. For the next six months, a state may regulate the abortion procedure in ways that are "reasonably related to the preservation and protection of maternal health". This could involve licencing and regulating of the doctors and facilities available. Only in the last 10 weeks of pregnancy—when the fetus is judged to be viable or capable of surviving independently if born—may the state forbid abortions except where they may be necessary to preserve the life or health of the mother.

The sweeping Supreme Court ruling is certain to create waves well beyond the United States. By its very geographic position, if not by a system of osmosis, Canada has always been conditioned to a greater or lesser degree by U.S. cultural and social values. Our cautious moves toward qualified abortion reform in 1969 might not have been possible or at least so readily acceptable had there not been more relaxed laws in areas outside our borders. If the Supreme Court ruling provokes strong challenges in the United States, then the abortion controversy in Canada, after being relatively quiet for the past few months, may rage again here, too.

Catholic Church leaders in the United States have predictably denounced the ruling. Already there has been talk of lobbying for a legislative amendment to throw out the court's decision. In the recent U.S. elections, two states rejected abortion reform in a referendum. President Richard Nixon last May took the unusual step of intervening in the New York State fight to overturn abortion reform by sending a personal letter to Terence Cardinal Cooke, telling the cardinal—for publication—of his admiration and support for the anti-abortion forces. In a nation caught up in a hard-hat reaction to what is seen as excessive liberalism, there will be much heat generated before the issue is finally resolved.

Of more immediate concern to Canadians is the fact that the new U.S. law will be available to Canadians, too. No longer will it be necessary for Canadian women to live within easy distance of the New York border to take advantage of easier abortion opportunities. Now women living anywhere within reach of Maine, Vermont, Michigan, Minnesota, Washington or any other U.S. border state can cut the red tape of Canada's abortion procedures by a quick trip south.

The U.S. decision will force us to re-examine the functioning of our own abortion laws. Despite the good intentions of 1969, many women still cannot get the abortions they seek. Hospital abortion review committees in some areas cannot handle the volume of applications, in other areas they put too severe an interpretation on the law's requirements. In many cases, delays are frequent, dangerous and costly. Certain hospitals and doctors are not only reluctant but refuse to participate in abortions.

This is not to argue for abortion on demand, or to suggest that abortion should take the place of responsible methods of family planning. There is certainly still a place for reasonable restrictions and reasonable safeguards. But the law must be made workable. Abortion procedures need to be speeded, simplified and carried out impartially and there should be better assurances that one person's moral or professional convictions will not be used in such a manner as to cause needless delays in an area where time is of the essence, or to enforce feelings of shame in the applicant, or to effectively deny to anyone the provisions of the present law. Without those provisions, the clamor for change to match the U.S. court's decision will mount.

Chicago, Ill., January 25, 1973

THE SUPREME Court's 7-to-2 decision striking down state antiabortion laws, at least as they apply during the first 12 weeks of pregnancy, is being hailed and attacked with equal fervor. The attacks, tho, seem to be more deeply rooted in conviction than the praise, and are likely to outlast it.

We are pulled two ways by this ruling, being able to see both benefits and dangers in it, but our net reaction is one of uneasiness. The court seems to have answered an immensely difficult problem just too readily, as tho it weren't aware of the difficulty. As an exercise in balanced legal logic, its ruling is excellent; the trouble is that it deals with matters deeper than logic, feelings on a fundamental level where legal reasoning cannot reach.

In favor of this finding, it is clearly not right that the feelings of some people should have the force of law over others, merely because these feelings are very strongly held. That is particularly true when such laws can and do bring about personal tragedies—unwanted and uncared-for children, families whose parents cannot support them, young girls who find themselves pregnant before they can understand what's happened or cope with it.

The decision makes a kind of de facto distinction between the embryonic and the fetal stage of growth—which is as reasonable as any such distinction could be—and upholds legal protections for the unborn in the later stages of pregnancy. And of course it doesn't require anyone to have an abortion; it just makes that choice available, and less dangerous to the mother.

And yet what we are talking about is the granting of an unappealable right of decision over life or death—and that question can never be wholly divorced from the feeling that life is sacred and the law should reflect its sacredness. We may never be quite comfortable with a doctrine that ranks a question of life or death as a purely private and personal decision.

We do not claim the wisdom to settle this question. There is only one viewpoint that seems to us wholly wrong: The idea that it's an easy question to settle.

THE BLADE
Toledo, Ohio, January 28, 1973

JUSTICE Harry A. Blackmun has written a landmark opinion — supported, 7 to 2, by his colleagues — that goes far toward ending the long legal controversy over abortion with strong statements in behalf of women's and physicians' rights. The ruling, based on women's constitutional right of privacy, avoids the vague areas surrounding questions of when life begins such as abortion foes have raised.

In practical terms, the court struck down anti-abortion laws in Georgia and Texas which forbade abortion for any reason other than to save a woman's life. Because Ohio and 29 other states have similar laws, the decision will have a sweeping impact and must be deemed a victory for those who have long held with the view Justice Blackmun has formally articulated.

At the same time, the court decision restrains those who would permit abortion — at any time and for any reason — on demand. Justice Blackmun rejected the idea that a pregnant woman has "an absolute constitutional right to an abortion on her demand." He took the middle ground holding that, while abortions are permissible, they become less permissible as pregnancy advances: In the first three months only a woman's physician, not the state, should have the right to permit or deny an abortion. In the next three months, the state may regulate abortion procedures in the interest of the mother's health. In the final three months, the state may regulate or even prohibit abortions if it chooses.

Justice Blackmun, a Nixon appointee bringing with him the identity of a "strict constructionist" hewing to conservative interpretation of the Constitution, based his opinion on the 14th Amendment. It says that the state shall not "deprive any person of life, liberty, or property without due process of law; nor deny any person within its jurisdiction the equal protection of the laws."

Rejecting the thesis that a fetus is a "person" within constitutional terms —hence entitled to protection by the state—he said that in the Constitution "use of the word is such that it has application only postnatally."

Foes of this view accuse the court of "trying to impose its own philosophical understanding of a biological principle on a total society." We would repeat, as the court has now answered, that the foes of abortion have had no clear right to bind all citizens under one rational interpretation of religious denial.

Until now, the principal person concerned — the woman — has been virtually ignored. This decision, granting the dignity of an ethical judgment and the privacy of individual conscience, restores to women their equal protection as a matter of right.

Although the issue is at the moment fraught with legal intensity and ethical emotion, it may as a practical matter have become academic a relative few years hence. Continuing scientific research and progress in development of various means of conception control very likely will bring the day — and probably sooner rather than later — when abortion will be the rare and last resort as the means of dealing with unwanted pregnancy.

VIETNAM CEASE-FIRE ACCORD SIGNED BY FOUR PARTIES IN PARIS CEREMONY

President Nixon appeared on nationwide television Jan. 23 to announce that Dr. Henry Kissinger and North Vietnamese negotiator Le Duc Tho had initialed in Paris that day the "Agreement on Ending the War and Restoring Peace in Vietnam." The initialing followed a Jan. 15 halt in all U.S. offensive operations against North Vietnam. Representatives of the U.S., South Vietnam, North Vietnam and the Viet Cong formally signed the accord in the French capital Jan. 27. These were the principal provisions of the accord as revealed by Dr. Kissinger at a Jan. 24 news conference:

■A ceasefire throughout North and South Vietnam effective Jan. 28 local time.

■Complete withdrawal of all U.S. troops and military advisers and dismantling of American bases in South Vietnam within 60 days of the signing of the agreement.

■The return of all U.S. and other prisoners of war and civilians throughout Indochina and the release of captured North Vietnamese and Viet Cong troops within 60 days.

■North Vietnamese troops were to remain in South Vietnam but they could not be replaced. Additional arms could be introduced into South Vietnam, but only to replace existing weapons.

■Foreign troops were to be withdrawn from Cambodia and Laos, with no deadline set. Troop and supply movements through the two countries were banned.

■The demilitarized zone separating the two Vietnams was to remain a provisional dividing line, with the eventual unification of the country to be settled "through peaceful means."

■The formation of a 1,160 man International Commission of Control and Supervision to supervise the release of prisoners, troop withdrawals, elections, and other aspects of the agreement. Canada, Hungary, Indonesia and Poland were to contribute personnel for the commission which was to be based throughout South Vietnam and at border crossings.

■The U.S. agreed to contribute to the postwar reconstruction of Indochina.

■An international political conference on Indochina would be called within 30 days to "acknowledge the signed agreements." Its participants would include China and the Soviet Union.

■The South Vietnamese government of President Thieu would remain in office pending elections. The U.S. and North Vietnam were to respect "the South Vietnamese people's right to self-determination." A Council of National Reconciliation and Concord would supervise the South Vietnamese elections. Its members would represent the Saigon government, the Communists and neutralists.

Kissinger said the Nixon Administration had "substantially achieved" the negotiating goals it had established for "an honorable agreement." Kissinger said the breakdown of the peace talks in December and the subsequent massive bombing of North Vietnam had been ordered "to make clear that the U.S. could not stand for an indefinite delay in the negotiations." He indicated that the U.S. had achieved a number of changes in the original October accord, especially those relating to Laos and Cambodia, and the size of the truce supervision team.

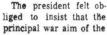

The Toronto Star

Toronto, Ont., January 24, 1973

It's evidently impossible for a president of the United States to come clean about Viet Nam; there is too much shame and failure in the American record there to be even hinted at. Thus President Nixon kept proclaiming the achievement of "peace with honor" last night, when all he can really promise is that the Americans are going to pull out of that wretched war in fairly good order, with their prisoners returned, instead of fleeing in abject humiliation.

"Exit with face saved" would have been a more accurate phrase than peace with honor; for, whatever the terms of the Paris agreement may say, it's obvious that there is no guarantee of peace between North and South Viet Nam. Hanoi maintains its goal of unifying all Viet Nam under Communist rule, while the government of South Viet Nam and a considerable number of its people mean to resist that dubious blessing.

The president felt obliged to insist that the principal war aim of the

RICHARD NIXON

United States had been achieved; he told the South Vietnamese that their right to determine their own future has been won. That's uncertain, to put it mildly, since they have so far been incapable of defeating the Communists with the full participation of the United States on their side.

It would have been enough good news for Nixon to say what he can say credibly, that the United States is getting out. Not that the basic purpose of the American intervention—to keep South Viet Nam from being taken over by the Communists—was dishonorable. But the way the Americans fought the war has been calamitous for both Viet Nam and the United States.

The United States waged war with incredible stupidity and callousness. Counting social as well as material and human destruction, it probably harmed its ally South Viet Nam more than its enemy North Viet Nam. The land was transformed from one of hamlets and villages to one of shantytown cities living off the American war machine. Bombing and clearance orders—in South Viet Nam —created millions of refugees and caused hundreds of thousands of civilian casualties. In terms of military efficiency, the profligate American operation was comparable to shooting mosquitoes with a machine-gun. The Viet Cong and the North Vietnamese troops were equally callous, but couldn't match the American power to destroy and disrupt.

Let us hope that peace is indeed near for the tortured people of Viet Nam. But the prospects are highly doubtful, and depend heavily on the willingness of the Soviet Union and China on one side, and the United States on the other, to restrain their respective allies. For now, it is sufficient to know that the most blunderingly destructive element of all—the American presence—is to be removed.

The San Diego Union

San Diego, Calif., January 24, 1973

At last, at long last, the war in Vietnam is over for the United States of America.

It is a great moment for President Nixon as well as for the nation. For four years the President has had the courage to adhere to his convictions that the peace in Vietnam should be just and honorable. He rejected often the fierce pressures for a quick and easy out. He held on, as he said last night, for the "right kind of peace."

Because the President has had the courage of his convictions we may rest assured that the cease-fire agreement he reached will guarantee the unequivocal safety of our troops, the return of all prisoners of war and an accounting of all those missing in action. These are our first priorities.

By the same token the Administration's insistence that every sentence in the treaty must be exactly right offers hope to the South Vietnamese people that their chances for freedom are as good as the U.S. can arrange under the circumstances.

Now the first order of business for the people of the United States is to give the Administration the support that it will need to bring the men and prisoners home, assimilate them into our everyday life smoothly and to adjust to an economy that does not contemplate the support to American forces in Vietnam.

The second domestic order of business is to heal whatever wounds the war in Vietnam has inflicted on us. We can begin, we believe, by asking ourselves whether there really is any point in torturing ourselves about our role in that war. After all, we must remember that four American Presidents of both major political parties have seen the value of an enclave of freedom in Southeast Asia.

The history is plain. Communist North Vietnam coveted the entire nation and deliberately set out in 1946 to win it by force. South Vietnam, guided by the flickering candle of freedom, fought desperately for more than a quarter of a century for its right to self determination.

The first American combat troops were committed to Vietnam in 1963, and that was when the United States also made its biggest mistake of the war. We sent our men into battle without a full commitment to assure a military victory and without the national will to win the war. This is not the stuff of which victories are made, and we pray that the lesson is not lost on coming generations of Americans.

Despite its faint heart, the United States has done relatively well. While we did not win the war, we did not lose it either. South Vietnam has a fighting chance to stand on its own feet. Its government is stable and accepted by the people, South Vietnamese troops have been tested in battle and have withstood the heat of the crucible.

The South will, of course, have to continue to defend itself. North Vietnam probably will have more than 100,000 well armed and supplied troops in the South after the United States leaves, and its desire to control the entire peninsula is unchanged.

We probably will continue to supply the arms that South Vietnam will need in the continuing battle against the Communists. Additionally we could be a force for freedom through our assistance in the reconstruction of all of Indochina.

Realistically, we must acknowledge that the document that the United States signs in Paris undoubtedly will be far less than ideal. Like Korea, Vietnam was a war whose strategies, and even its tactics, were often guided by political circumstance rather than by military necessity.

The phrase "No more Vietnams" will resound around our country today. We must endorse those words most sincerely, hoping that they mean to every American, "when you go to war, fight to win."

AKRON BEACON JOURNAL
Akron, Ohio, January 24, 1973

John Lane of Canton, whose daughter, Army nurse Sharon Lane, was killed in the Vietnam war, said it all: "Thank God it's over."

The war in Vietnam, the longest nightmare in America's history, will stop in silence with a cease-fire at 7 p. m. Saturday, Akron time, the President said.

And in the next 60 days all Americans will be pulled out of there and all the American prisoners throughout Indochina released and started on their way home.

It's strange:

At the end of World War II in Europe there was a great leap in spirits, and at its end in Asia an even greater one. Crowds collected to rejoice; there was dancing in the streets.

At the end of the Korean thing, there was at least a massive surge of relief.

But with this one, there is a sort of numbness

Maybe it will take a day or so for the news to sink in. The words are flat; they spill off the sides of the tired mind.

" ... The agreement on ending the war and restoring peace in Vietnam was initialed . . . The agreement will be formally signed by the parties participating in the Paris Conference on Vietnam on Jan. 27, 1973 . . . The cease-fire will take effect on 2400 Greenwich Mean Time, Jan. 27, 1973. The United States and the Democratic Republic of Vietnam express the hope that this agreement will insure stable peace in Vietnam and contribute to the preservation of lasting peace in Indochina and Southeast Asia."

The listener struggles for the meaning. Not hope of peace. Not progress toward peace. Not peace at hand. Peace. Silence. An end of killing. No war. Saturday.

The mind reaches for memory of what is was like with no war. The image is unreal.

It has been 18 years since the first American soldiers were sent there; for many there is no memory of a time before that — the war has been a lifetime condition.

It's 45,933 American deaths in action ago, and more than 10,000 others dead of "non-hostile causes;" the ungraspable and uncertain statistic of 1,084,000 Vietnamese military deaths ago; nobody knows how many civilian deaths; perhaps six million refugees.

The mind grapples hard to feel what the prisoners and the families of prisoner and missing-in-actions must feel: The surge of relief, the iron effort to control it, after all the blows of past disappointment; for some, bracing for the hurt of finding out now, after years of hoping and fearing and unknowing, "My man is dead."

May God grant them a swift deliverance from all fears, and the rest of us reverence for all who have sacrificed and been sacrificed in a cruel conflict that has seemed to have no end.

The Montreal Star

Montreal, Que., January 24, 1973

THE joy is profound, the sense of relief, for the Vietnamese, for the world, is immeasurable. Both sides obviously have yielded to make possible a ceasefire. As of 7 p.m. on Saturday the killing and the destruction will be over while international supervisory teams attempt to ensure the peace until a formal, sturdy treaty follows in time. One hopes it is, indeed, in the words of President Nixon last night, "the right kind of peace."

Meanwhile, is there a victor? Obviously not. Certainly the United States, the most awesome force in the world's history, cannot claim satisfaction. "All we did," Arthur Schlesinger has written, "was show how 500,000 troops and vast technology couldn't cope with a few thousand guerrillas in black pyjamas." The reckoning in statistics is pitiful: 55,000 young Americans dead, a dollar cost of more than $400 billion.

The Vietnamese? U.S. planes dropped on a tiny territory three and a half times the tonnage of bombs let loose on all of Germany and Japan during the Second World War; in North Vietnam cities were almost wiped out, with unknown numbers of casualties. In the South itself, with the lines fluid, 400,000 civilians were killed in all forms of fighting and 900,000 wounded between 1965 and 1972; as many as eight million dispersed from their villages.

The list goes on, adding to the grief, and the injuries within the structure of American society alone are searing. Many patriotic Americans now regard their country with apprehension and distrust; the alienation is not confined to the younger generation alone. If the U.S. military power could not kill off the opposition in Vietnam, one might conclude gloomily that it succeeded in killing part of the American dream.

Ultimately Thieu will go, and reunification probably will take place, with the South possibly under the same ideology as the North, for that is where the dedication lies; to sense the dedication one needs only to look at the tenacity with which the Viet Cong and North Vietnamese fought. But this portend should not be the preoccupation now. The Vietnamese have to heal themselves first, and we — not only the U.S., as Mr. Nixon suggested last night, but the whole of the West — must help. More than a quarter of a century of warfare has shaken a people in a fashion unparalleled in modern history.

The answer to the big question Washington should be asking—was U.S. involvement worth while?— is clear. In an immediate sense, the human sacrifice and the material waste are deplorable. In longer terms, however, the lesson will have been learned if President Nixon's pledge in his second inaugural address is maintained: That no longer will the United States feel impelled arbitrarily to function as the world's policeman, that other nations will be allowed self-determination without interference. Partly this is because the U.S. itself feels that old notions about "containing" communism no longer are valid. At least the simplistic view of the good guy versus the bad can now be altered with a degree of sophistication.

The Globe and Mail

Toronto, Ont., January 24, 1973

So much blood, so much suffering, so much destruction—to what end? The world's greatest power is now coming to terms with one of the world's littlest, and the American war in Vietnam is ending. For the United States, there is neither victory nor defeat. For North and South Vietnam, there is no settlement of the essential issue on which the war was fought. The Vietnamese struggle of unification is again largely where it was in 1954, when the period of French colonial rule came to its close.

Now the Vietnamese people will be left to settle their own affairs. We may hope and pray that they can do so peacefully, but there is no assurance against further bloodshed to come. What the United States has achieved, then, is to delay for a dozen years or so the final resolution of the problem of Vietnam.

The tragic involvement of U.S. power in Southeast Asia began in a world political climate that seems almost incomprehensible now. U.S. policy was driven by its view of a global life-or-death struggle against a Communist world conspiracy. For the then Secretary of State, John Foster Dulles, it was a crusade—the struggle for God against the devil.

He therefore made the United States the protector of South Vietnam while deploring the Geneva agreements that let the North go Communist.

Like all diplomatic settlements that do not reflect political reality, the Geneva agreements crumbled away. Their terms were violated on both sides, and the international commission (Canada, Poland and India) that was supposed to oversee the peace became an exercise in futility.

In its own appointed role, the United States progressed from financial and political support of South Vietnam, to the provision of logistical services and weapons, and ultimately to the deployment of more than half a million troops on a hopeless, cruel battlefield. At every stage, the only U.S. answer for an immediate problem seemed to be the application of still greater force. The Vietnam war made "escalation" a familiar term in military and diplomatic jargon.

But the issue would not yield to American firepower. On the contrary, the power fractured and corroded the society whose leaders tried to use it so overwhelmingly. The cost to the United States of the Vietnam war is far more than $125-billion in war expenditure. Nearly 55,000 young men died and 300,000 were wounded.

The war destroyed a U.S. President, whose death made a footnote to the final peace negotiations in Paris, and in so doing it gravely weakened the confidence of U.S. citizens in their government and leadership. "Credibility gap" is another term spawned by the ruinous Vietnam involvement.

The war frayed the basic loyalty of the young Americans whose age made them liable to be drafted for service in Vietnam. It turned youth against its parent generation, and created the "silent majority" and the "hard hats" as symbols of reaction. It wrecked discipline in a once-proud army and soiled its honor with such incidents as the My Lai massacre. The fear and despair of service in Vietnam turned thousands of young men into hard drug addicts; their addiction and their knowledge of arms are now significant factors in U.S. crime rates.

The experience of this war, its blunders and its savagery, have altogether damaged the confidence of the United States in itself, and debased the American ideal throughout the world. For whatever the United States set out to do in Southeast Asia, it ended up bickering over peace terms designed to protect a corrupt dictatorship in South Vietnam. And whatever the objectives were, the world has mainly seen the most powerful weapons of mass killing and destruction being used against a poor people in a tormented land.

The cost of the Vietnam war has been exorbitant even if its lessons are taken to have led President Richard Nixon into his new international policy of détente and conciliation. That it has helped produce this result, however, is at least some compensation. And now that the agony is ending, perhaps the bitterness will begin to subside—within the United States as well as in its relations with the world.

"The time has passed," Mr. Nixon said in his second inaugural address, "when America will make every other nation's conflict our own, or make every other nation's future our responsibility, or presume to tell the people of other nations how to manage their own affairs."

The statement makes a hopeful guide to the future of U.S. world relations, for all that it is an admission of astounding self-righteous arrogance in the past.

The Boston Globe

Boston, Mass., January 25, 1973

After 18 years of military involvement and four years of painful negotiations and false hopes, Americans greeted news of a standing cease fire in Vietnam, not with a cheer, but a sigh. We are glad to be out and we must thank President Nixon and his advisor Henry Kissinger for their perseverence in getting us out.

Triumph can have no part in our grateful relief at the ending of a conflict in which, most Americans now agree, we should never have taken part; a conflict that has destroyed a nation we hoped to protect; that has taken the lives, the health and the liberty of hundreds of thousands; that has tarnished the American image, bringing division and disaffection at home and abroad; and that has seen the world's mightiest powers facing each other over the wounded body of Southeast Asia.

Whether the present agreement meets the conditions of "peace with honor" is immaterial. More important, as President Nixon pointed out, is the cooperation of all parties in working together to "see to it that this is a peace that lasts and also a peace that heals."

Both sides have made concessions in the long haul of negotiations. We gave in on the sovereignty of the Thieu government and on the withdrawal of 145,000 North Vietnamese troops from the south. But the North Vietnamese gave in on an imposed coalition government in favor of a tripartite Council, on the release of political prisoners, and on prohibitions against infiltration or replacement of troops in the south. In addition the agreement allows the United States to retain forces offshore and in Thailand and to provide unlimited economic assistance and replacement weapons to South Vietnam.

It is too soon to tell how these concessions will affect the stability of the truce. But four years ago and, in fact, up to last October 8, the North Vietnamese would not even discuss an agreement until the Thieu government had been disbanded and replaced. The final agreement is clearer and stronger than either the draft of last fall or the Geneva Accords of 1954. And, where details are not spelled out, a system of checks is offered.

In an extraordinary and convincing one hour and forty-five minutes televised press conference, Dr. Kissinger left it up to each American to reach a verdict on the pre-Christmas bombing (and on the mining of Haiphon Harbor in May), saying only that "we carried out what we considered necessary to make it clear that the United States could not stand for an indefinite delay in the negotiations." A deadlock in December, he pointed out, was broken when the North Vietnamese came back to the negotiating table on January 3rd and the major breakthrough came six days later.

Pragmatism is a key to the approach on many of the terms. Assigning status to North Vietnam under the agreement, Dr. Kissinger said, was "a point of greatest bitterness and we believed it was better not to deal with it legalistically." Thus, in calling for a peaceful resolution of differences, the agreement avoids the issue of whether North Vietnam is a foreign entity or one of a divided country. If this paves the way for self-determination in Vietnam, it does offer hope of a lasting peace.

And clearly there is an expectation that the provision for replacing destroyed or damaged military equipment on a one-to-one basis, will be an incentive to North Vietnam and its allies not to engage in an arms race. If it works, this provision may also serve to decrease the chance of a bloodbath once outside forces leave. We pray it does.

That our part in the bloodshed and holocaust is over is a certain blessing. The war has had an untold impact on the spirit and confidence of this country, sapping the economy, depriving Americans of a chance to live and work for more valuable ends, turning young people against those in authority and dimming their faith in the nation and in their own futures.

At last our prisoners of war and those who have been missing in action will come home. For many the return to a country that has changed in their absence will not be easy. They and their families will need our help. And we must help each other to heal the wounds and divisions caused by our part in Vietnam. Today's truce must become tomorrow's peace and it must be made to last and to heal so the world can move forward.

DAYTON DAILY NEWS

Dayton, Ohio, January 26, 1973

The fine print of the Vietnam cease-fire agreement and protocols is pretty much what leaked out in advance. It offers the prospect of a reduced level of violence but little hope that the long struggle for control of Southeast Asia will end any time soon.

The combat role of the United States is obviously finished, though the possibility remains that this nation might reintroduce air power in the event of flagrant violations of the accord by North Vietnam or of air attacks on South Vietnam by the high-performance M I G -21s of North Vietnam.

Otherwise, the problems that caused the conflict remain. North Vietnam wishes to extend its sovereignty over South Vietnam and probably over Laos, Cambodia and even Thailand. The current regimes and the bulk of the populations of these countries want to remain independent.

In such circumstances, the chances of eliminating armed conflict are extremely low. The new accord likely will follow the example of the Geneva agreements of 1954 and 1962, both of which were violated almost immediately. The 1954 accord got the French out of old Indo-China but was never observed otherwise, either in North or South Vietnam. In fairness, to the South Vietnamese government, it at least had not signed.

The 1962 agreement was traduced immediately by North Vietnam, which promptly announced its intention of maintaining an insurgency in Laos and Thailand in direct violation of the terms of the arrangement. Far from pulling out of Laos, as it had agreed, Hanoi immediately began a build-up along the Ho Chi Minh trails.

Something of the kind is highly likely again, probably after a quiet interval to insure the U.S. exit. Then North a n d South Vietnam will slug it out, with the survival of Laos and Cambodia as independent entities perhaps awaiting the outcome.

South Vietnam is considerably stronger now than it was a few years ago and has a reasonable chance of making it. Time will tell. Whether the level of conflict r e m a i n s low or re-escalates depends largely upon whether Russia, China and the United States reduce the flow of arms or keep pouring in sophisticated weaponry.

There is a possibility that North Vietnam might relent and take advantage of U.S. offers of economic assistance, but that chance is slight. Hanoi has been extremely open about its ambitions with respect to South Vietnam. Barring a miracle, the North Vietnamese will continue to mount an armed aggression to effect that goal.

The proper American role is clear. While working to limit weapons to both sides, and strictly abiding by any agreement on military assistance that binds the other side in verifiable ways, we are obligated to supply whatever arms the South Vietnamese require for a reasonable chance to defend themselves. To do less would be to default upon a solemn commitment and an obligation written in years of shared sacrifice.

NIXON FIRES COX, THEN CONCEDES ON TAPES

President Nixon agreed Oct. 23 to submit tapes containing White House conversations about the Watergate case to Federal District Court Judge John J. Sirica. For three months, Nixon had insisted that the tapes remain in the White House under his absolute control. The President abruptly reversed himself in the midst of a mounting government crisis, laced with the threat of an impeachment effort, that resulted from his abrupt discharge Oct. 20 of special Watergate prosecutor Archibald Cox and return of the federal Watergate prosecution to Justice Department jurisdiction.

Cox had rejected a White House compromise plan to end the tapes dispute by furnishing investigators with a "summary" of the taped presidential conversations that would be verified by Sen. John Stennis (D, Miss.). Nixon's compromise plan was his response to an order Oct. 12 by the U.S. Circuit Court of Appeals for the District of Columbia that he turn over the tapes to Sirica. [See pp. 1328–1333] The President directed Attorney General Elliot L. Richardson to discharge Cox. Richardson refused and resigned Oct. 20. Deputy Attorney General William D. Ruckelshaus was then asked to fire Cox, and after refusing was in turn fired the same day. Solicitor General Robert H. Bork, who became acting attorney general after Ruckelshaus' discharge, dismissed Cox.

The crisis began Oct. 19 when Nixon announced his "compromise" plan. He said it had been drawn up by Richardson and agreed to by Senate Watergate committee Chairman Sam J. Ervin (D, N.C.) and Vice Chairman Howard H. Baker Jr. (R, Tenn.). Cox had rejected his compromise plan, Nixon said, but he had decided to take "decisive actions" anyway in order to avert a "constitutional crisis" and "lay the groundwork upon which we can assure unity of purpose at home and end the temptation abroad to test our resolve." He had decided, therefore, Nixon said, not to seek Supreme Court review of the appeals court decision Oct. 12 ordering him to surrender the tapes to the U.S. district court supervising the Watergate probe. It was not in the national interest, the President contended, "to leave this matter unresolved for the period that might be required for a review by the highest court." "Though," he continued, "I have not wished to intrude upon the independence of the special prosecutor, I have felt it necessary to direct him, as an employe of the executive branch, to make no further attempts by judicial process to obtain tapes, notes or memoranda of presidential conversations."

Cox rejected Nixon's "compromise" tapes plan later Oct. 19 and said he would take his objections to it before the court. In his judgment, Cox said, "the President is refusing to comply with the court decrees." Cox said the proposed summary would lack "the evidentiary value of the tapes themselves" and "no steps are being taken to turn over the important notes, memoranda and other documents that the court orders require."

The announcement that Cox had been fired came on Saturday evening Oct. 20. White House Press Secretary Ronald L. Ziegler said Richardson had resigned rather than discharge Cox. Ruckelshaus was then asked to carry out the President's order to discharge Cox. When he refused, according to Ziegler, Ruckelshaus was fired. Cox's dismissal was finally carried out by Solicitor General Bork, who was appointed acting attorney general.

The President also announced through Ziegler that he had abolished the special Watergate prosecutor's office as of 8 p.m. and transferred its duties back to the Justice Department where they would "be carried out with thoroughness and vigor." Ziegler said Cox had been discharged because he had "pressed for a confrontation at a time of serious world crisis."

FBI agents were sent later that evening to seal off the special prosecutor's offices. The next day, they were replaced by U.S. marshals. Nixon aide Alexander Haig conceded Oct. 23 he was "guilty" of ordering the FBI to seal off the offices. He said he acted to preserve the files after hearing reports that staffers were leaving with "huge bundles under their arms." Acting Attorney General Bork announced Oct. 22 that he had placed Henry E. Petersen in direct charge of the Watergate case "and all related matters previously being directed by the special prosecutor." Petersen would use the evidence and staff already assembled, as well as other department personnel, Bork said, "to see that these cases are pressed to a conclusion and that justice is done."

A flood of protest erupted over the abrupt ouster of Cox and resultant departures of Richardson and Ruckelshaus Oct. 20. Telegrams and letters of protest began arriving at the White House and at the Capitol. By Oct. 23, Western Union in Washington had been "inundated" with messages, according to a company official—more than 150,000 telegrams, "the heaviest concentrated volume on record." Even conservative members of Congress reported the preponderant tone of the messages was "negative" advocating impeachment.

American Bar Association (ABA) President Chesterfield Smith warned Oct. 22 that Nixon was attempting to "abort the established processes of justice." He urged the courts and Congress to take "appropriate action" to "repel" the "attacks" by the President. Delegates to the 10th biennial convention of the American Federation of Labor and Congress of Industrial Organizations (AFL-CIO), meeting in Bal Harbour, Fla. Oct. 18–23, passed a resolution by acclamation Oct. 22 calling on President Nixon to resign and the House to impeach him "forthwith" if he did not.

The threat of impeachment began to take shape in Congress Oct. 23. Eight impeachment resolutions, co-sponsored by a total of 31 Democrats, were offered in the House, where impeachment charges could be brought by majority vote. House Democratic leaders agreed unanimously Oct. 23 to have the Judiciary Committee begin an inquiry into possible impeachment. House Republican leaders, facing the Democratic move, endorsed the inquiry. The President's decision to yield the tapes to the court did not deter the move toward an opening of the impeachment process. House Judiciary Committee chairman Peter W. Rodino Jr. (D, N.J.) said Oct. 24, after conferring with 19 other Democrats on the panel, that its impeachment investigation would "proceed full steam ahead."

The President's reversal of position and consent to turn over the tapes to the court was revealed in a dramatic and brief announcement before Judge Sirica Oct. 23. At that time, the administration had been expected to present the response of the President to the court's decision insisting upon surrender of the tapes.

Sirica asked the President's attorneys if they were prepared to file "the response of the President" to his Aug. 29 order as modified by the appeals court. Charles Alan Wright, chief of the President's Watergate legal defense team, stepped forward and said "the President of the United States would comply in all respects" with Sirica's order as modified by the higher court. The announcement was totally unexpected. Wright explained that the President still maintained that his previous posture was correct and the "summary" would satisfy the court's needs, but the problem was that even if the court agreed with him "there would have been those who would have said the President is defying the law." "This President does not defy the law," Wright declared, "and he has authorized me to say he will comply in full with the orders of the court."

At a news conference later Oct. 23 with Nixon's chief of staff Alexander M. Haig, Wright said "we all miscalculated" the reaction to the President's recent course.

THE SPRINGFIELD UNION
Springfield, Mass., October 22, 1973

In the light of the sensational weekend developments in Washington, crucial days lie ahead for the stability of the federal government — and its image before the nation and the world.

Part of the dismal picture is the prospect of impeachment moves when Congress convenes tomorrow.

It is questionable whether President Nixon would ultimately be removed from office. If the House completes the impeachment, or indictment, stage, the Senate might not convict him.

Nevertheless, Nixon's firing of Archibald Cox and William Ruckelshaus, and his forcing of Elliot Richardson's resignation, for their insistence on doing their job, has fueled powerful support for impeachment, at least.

As Williams College Prof. James M. Burns has said, the course to be taken by Congress will depend in some degree on whether the court holds Nixon in contempt for his actions.

But the shocking display of willfulness by the President in turning his back on the judicial system, disposing of officials highly dedicated to its support, will also be a factor.

In this, Nixon has strengthened the belief of many Americans (perhaps most by now) that he is hiding an involvement of his own in all phases of the Watergate affair.

At one time, he declared he would abide by a "definitive" decision of the Supreme Court on the matter of turning over his Watergate tapes. Now he appears unwilling to risk any decision by that court.

Also, he turned down U.S. District Court Judge Sirica's ruling that the tapes should be examined privately by the judge himself, with Cox and presidential representatives.

The purpose of that would be to determine what parts of the tapes were pertinent to the Watergate prosecution, and what parts should be withheld for national security or other urgent reasons.

In his hard-handed preoccupation with "executive privilege," President Nixon has shaken the nation's confidence in him — and the world's, at a point when diplomacy could be vital to a peace in the Mideast.

This is a momentous time in American history. The wisdom of Congress will have to make up for the lack of it in the White House.

Detroit Free Press
Detroit, Mich., October 16, 1973

AS THE NATION struggles to define the limits of presidential power, it needs all the guideposts it can get. Surely one of the best guides yet offered is to be found in the opinion by the U.S. Circuit Court of Appeals on the President's attempt to withhold his Watergate tapes.

Those tapes, the court concluded in upholding Judge John Sirica's order, should be turned over to the courts to shed whatever light they can on possible criminal actions by members of the President's staff.

The appeals court's 5-2 decision was even more forceful and direct than Judge Sirica's carefully balanced original decision, which forbade the President to withhold the tapes. To the majority on the Court of Appeals, the positions taken by the President's lawyers "are invitations to refashion the Constitution, and we reject them."

Far from posing a threat to "the continued existence of the presidency as a functioning institution," as the President's lawyers argued it would be, Judge Sirica's decision was found to be based on sound doctrine. "The Constitution makes no mention of special presidential immunities," the court said. "Indeed, the executive branch is afforded none."

In ringing terms, the court reiterated the fundamental principle that no man, not even the President, is above the law. "Incumbency," said the court, "does not relieve the President of the routine legal obligations that confine all citizens."

If there is a single buttress that has been strengthening the country as it has faced the Agnew and Watergate scandals, it has been the renewed demonstration that the laws do indeed apply to those in high places. Sometimes the processes seem to work with painful slowness, but in the end they have worked to force the vice president out of office and to punish many of the President's closest associates.

The complaint can be and is being made that former Vice President Agnew escaped with too light a punishment, and the point has some force to it. It can also be argued that the President has too often gotten by with arrogant assertions that the law does not restrict his actions — in impoundment of appropriated funds, in the illegal Cambodian bombing, in his refusal thus far to turn over the tapes.

Slowly, though, the nation's institutions —the courts, the federal prosecutors, the Justice Department—are calling the executive branch to account. The President is subject to the law. The lawful society can deal with its own evils.

All of us must hope that the President recognizes that he must obey the decisions of the courts, if ratified by the Supreme Court, and turn over the tapes of White House conversations where they are relevant. If he should fail to get the message, he will find an aroused electorate ready to demand that he be made to comply.

The rule of law is being restored, and the public official who tries to ignore its claim does so at his own peril. This includes especially the President of the United States.

The Miami Herald
Miami, Fla., October 21, 1973

AT first glance the arrangement between the Senate's Watergate cochairmen and President Nixon to audit The White House Tapes seemed ideally tailored to avert a constitutional crisis.

Sens. Sam Ervin and Howard Baker agreed that Mr. Nixon could provide a written summary of the tapes, which supposedly include all Oval Office discussions of Watergate and everything else, and that Sen. John Stennis of Mississippi would privately hear the tapes to confirm or deny the President's interpretation. Also, U.S. District Judge John Sirica would get the statement but not the tapes.

This was the course in part we and others advocated several months ago when it developed that the White House walls had ears and that what they recorded was the only way of determining who really said what.

All of this came unhinged when President Nixon last night dismissed Special Prosecutor Archibald Cox, who protested the compromise solution most eloquently a few hours before. His firing was followed by the resignation of Attorney General Elliot Richardson and his deputy, William Ruckelshaus. The fat now is deep, deep in the fire.

When Mr. Cox, Solicitor General in the Kennedy and Johnson administrations, was appointed by Attorney General-designate Richardson May 18 to head the federal investigation he said he had "not the slightest doubt I will be independent."

Subsequently Mr. Nixon gave him a presidential blessing, and at the Richardson confirmation hearing on May 21 Mr. Cox promised the Senate Judiciary Committee he would follow the "trail of federal crime wherever that trail may lead." This was enough for the senators.

Evidently it proved too much for President Nixon. When Mr. Cox objected to the Ervin-Baker-Nixon deal the President said that "though I have not wished to intrude upon the independence of the special prosecutor, I have felt it necessary to direct him as an employe of the executive branch, to make no further attempts by judicial process to obtain tapes, notes or memoranda of presidential conversations."

So, after all, in Mr. Nixon's eyes the special prosecutor pledged so much independence and latitude was really a lackey of the White House and, without appeal to the Supreme Court, Judge Sirica's order and the order of the Court of Appeals will be defied.

This was all to neatly tricky, too dissimulating, too patently political.

If it avoided a confrontation over expecutive privilege it retreated from principle and hangs a big question mark, not unlike the truth about a political assassination, over the head of Watergate and President Nixon.

It has never been determined conclusively whether a President may disobey a court, but it is increasingly clear that he may not abuse public opinion and expect to avoid constitutional consequences. Mr. Nixon has only succeeded in digging himself in deeper, and we deplore his judgment as prejudicial to open and honest government.

THE KNICKERBOCKER NEWS
··· UNION-STAR ···
Albany, N.Y., October 22, 1973

The man who said he would obey a "definitive order" of the Supreme Court has taken steps designed to prevent the court from having an opportunity to issue such an order.

The man who would have had us believe that Archibald Cox, the special Watergate prosecutor would have a free hand in that Watergate inquiry sought to tie his hands and failing that, had him fired.

The man who appointed the forthright and able Elliot Richardson as attorney general of the United States has forced Mr. Richardson to resign by asking him to go back on his word. That same man also fired William B. Ruckelshaus, the deputy attorney general for likewise refusing to fire Mr. Cox.

And then, in a gesture that can only be considered insulting to the special prosecutor, he had FBI agents swoop down on that special prosecutor's office, seal it off, and deny the prosecutor's staff the right of admittance, even to do so much as pick up personal papers.

All this was done by President Richard M. Nixon as he desperately and slyly sought to inflict his will on the courts, the Congress and the nation.

Earlier that same day there had been confusion over whether the President would make available to the Senate Watergate committee and the special prosecutor a "summary" or a "transcript" of the controversial Watergate tapes. The confusion was resolved, but there is evidence that for a time the White House had been engaged in "double-speak," a language it speaks very well and too frequently.

What is apparent today is that the President had sought to avoid having to obey a court order to produce the Watergate tapes by offering to provide a transcript of sorts. It is apparent that he did not want the issue of the tapes to reach the Supreme Court. An appeal to the Supreme Court from rulings of lower courts that he produce the tapes for private inspection of Judge John Sirica was not to the President's liking.

And when Mr. Cox refused to accept the transcript as a substitute for the tapes themselves and documents associated with them, Mr. Nixon chose to turn ruthless. In an arrogant display of power, he ordered heads to fall.

So he inflicts further turmoil on a nation that is weary of turmoil. He adds to the number of all those who have fallen victim to his administration. (And, looking back, Metroland has reason to remember that the late Dr. James Allen, who had been state commissioner of education before taking a post in that Nixon administration, was one of the first of the victims.)

Above all, by seeking to avoid the rule of law, he has challenged the entire American concept of equal justice. This nation has reason to be alarmed.

THE ☼ SUN
Baltimore, Md., October 21, 1973

With reckless, almost irrational disregard for the national interest, President Nixon has embarked on a course that leaves the Congress little choice but to consider impeachment proceedings. Mr. Nixon's dismissal of Archibald Cox, the special Watergate prosecutor, constitutes a brazen obstruction of justice without parallel in history. Attorney General Elliot Richardson, by his resignation, and Deputy Attorney General William Ruckelshaus, by inviting his own dismissal, have courageously shown how far the President has lost touch with truth and principle. Their departure robs the faltering administration of two of the finest men who have served it. How far the unraveling will go on is a numbing speculation, but it is not too early to foresee that even the supposedly assured confirmation of Vice President-designate Gerald Ford may be stymied by these developments. Nor does there appear to be much chance the country will be spared the appalling trauma of an impeachment action—perhaps an impeachment at a moment when we lack a Vice President and thus the man next in line of succession is a Speaker who is a member of the opposition party. This is the stuff of political novels, but it is hardly what the people of this country should suffer at a time of international tension and unmet needs at home.

Mr. Nixon has brought upon the country the constitutional crisis he has long and piously protested against. He seems to be a man in panic, flailing out in a self-destructive way over an issue that hardly seems worth the candle. For if the President is to be believed, the evidence in the Watergate tapes he refused to give the courts or Mr. Cox is inconclusive as to his personal guilt in the Watergate break-in or the coverup that followed. Moreover, it was Mr. Nixon who assured the country only a few months ago that he would abide by a "definitive" decision of the Supreme Court ordering him to release Watergate documentation. Now when that moment of justice was fast approaching, he has used all the power at his disposal to block the issue from getting to the Supreme Court. Thus, his arrangement with Senators Ervin and Baker of the Senate Watergate committee to have Senator Stennis vet tapes denied the government's own prosecutors. Thus, his dismissal of Mr. Cox after that distinguished lawyer let it be known he would ask the courts to hold the President in contempt or force him to "clarify" the Stennis arrangement. The situation is so unprecedented it is risky to speculate on what the courts might do. For if Mr. Nixon is willing to fire his own law officers, he may in his present mood be ready to defy the courts directly.

It had been bad enough to have a President under suspicion of having condoned illegal breaking and entering, of having discussed hush money and other impediments to justice, of having fostered an attitude of "dirty tricks" subversive to the electoral process. But now we have a President using his office to stop the nation from ever finding out the truth of these allegations. The public has every right to be dismayed.

This newspaper has repeatedly stated its longing for a compromise on the release of information that the President believes is confidential but the courts and the Senate committee consider pertinent to Watergate and related transgressions. There still remains a chance the Stennis arrangement can be modified to meet the public need. But the chance is slim and appears quickly to be slipping from sight. Mr. Nixon has shown once again that he believes this is a government of men rather than laws so far as he personally is concerned. This is an attitude that challenges the separation of powers, threatens our most basic institutions and promises to cripple the political life of our country.

The Washington Post

Washington, D.C., October 21, 1973

In particular, the Special Prosecutor shall have full authority . . . for . . . determining whether or not to contest the assertion of "Executive privilege" or any other testimonial privilege . . . The Attorney General will not countermand or interfere with the Special Prosecutor's decisions or actions . . . The Special Prosecutor will not be removed from his duties except for extraordinary improprieties on his part."

Those are the crucial provisions from the original order setting up the office of Special Prosecutor Archibald Cox—an order which also gave him full authority to investigate and prosecute offenses arising out of just about any aspect of the Watergate case, in its broadest sense, including specifically "allegations involving the President, members of the White House staff, or presidential appointees . . ." And these are also a part of the guidelines for Mr. Cox which were presented in advance to the Senate Judiciary Committee in its hearings on the appointment of Elliot Richardson as Attorney General. They formed the basis, in other words, of a solemn compact between the Nixon administration and the Senate, which was a condition for Mr. Richardson's confirmation for reasons which are all too familiar to all of us.

It was President Nixon's brutal violation of this compact which directly brought about the crisis in government which is now upon us, with the resignations of Attorney General Richardson and his his deputy, William Ruckelshaus.

It is impossible at this stage to measure the full consequences of what has happened, or to predict how events will now unfold. What is important for now is to be very clear in our minds about the defaults and abuses of presidential power that brought us to this critical juncture.

Two successive "investigations" of Watergate by the President had been demonstrably incomplete if not criminally negligent. John W. Dean III, who allegedly conducted the first, pleaded guilty Friday to actual obstruction of justice; the second investigation was supposedly conducted by John Ehrlichman, who has conceded that he thought of it as no more than an "inquiry." Throughout, it appears from testimony before the Senate Watergate committee, there was a singular lack of cooperation with Justice Department investigators; access to White House officials and materials was systematically impeded. The President himself had conceded that there may have been a cover-up, while denying participation in it—or even knowledge of it—until early this year.

It was this stark and demoralizing record which caused the Senate Judiciary Committee to demand strict commitments from Mr. Richardson and from Mr. Cox that the latter would be given a totally free hand. And it is against this background that one must examine the extraordinary statement by President Nixon on Friday night recounting his failed effort to seek a compromise with Mr. Cox over the latter's demand for tapes of presidential conversations, memoranda, notes and other material which he deemed to be essential to his work. The U.S. Court of Appeals has held that this material should be turned over to Judge John Sirica of the federal district court here for a determination as to which parts, if any, should be presented to the grand jury as a part of Mr. Cox's evidence. In his statement, the President said he had decided against further appeal to the Supreme Court, but that he wouldn't abide by the appeals court ruling that he must submit the material in the absence of an out-of-court agreement with the special prosecutor. Instead, he described in great detail his efforts to work out a settlement with Mr. Cox—and then

announced that it had failed. Accordingly, the President said, he had "felt it necessary to direct (Mr. Cox), *as an employee of the executive branch,* to make no further attempts by judicial process to obtain tapes, notes or memoranda of presidential conversations."

In other words, faced with three choices, the President failed to adopt any of the three. Instead, he, in effect, shredded the compact with the Senate which was a condition precedent to Mr. Richardson's confirmation for his job and to Mr. Cox's acceptance of his—a compact which plainly precluded interference in the special prosecutor's work and specifically authorized the special prosecutor to make any effort he saw fit to obtain precisely the material that the President finally sought, in defiance of the court, to place beyond his reach.

The proposed bargain, as described by the President's statement, was that he would prepare a summary of the relevant portions of the requested tapes and would have Sen. John Stennis authenticate it by listening to the tapes and comparing them with the summary. Along the way, the President elicited some kind of agreement—the extent and nature of that agreement is not yet clear—from Sen. Sam Ervin and Sen. Howard Baker of the Watergate committee to this arrangement. He also cited large questions of national interest as his reason for wanting to dispose of this matter now, without taking it to the Supreme Court.

In return for the summaries he was willing to provide, Mr. Nixon wanted Mr. Cox to agree that "there would be no further attempt by the special prosecutor to subpoena still more tapes or other presidential papers of a similar nature." After Mr. Cox turned the deal down, Mr. Nixon went ahead and announced that he was going to pursue the route suggested in his aborted bargain anyway and that the summaries, after having been duly authenticated by Senator Stennis, would then be made available to Judge Sirica and to the Senate Watergate committee.

What, in sum, did Mr. Nixon do? Having lost two rounds in court, he attempted to seize immediate control of the prosecution of a series of criminal cases in which he is at least potentially a defendant. He further sought to substitute his own judgment and enforcement power for that of the federal courts, whose jurisdiction he acknowledged by sending his lawyers to plead his case there in the first place. In recent days people have been heard to observe that Vice President Agnew got a very lenient deal in his tangle with federal prosecutors. But consider by comparison the arrangement Mr. Nixon contrived for himself: In matters in which he and many of his most important associates are under examination for possible misconduct in office, he proposes to define what the prosecutor may or may not do and what the grand jury may or may not hear and, in many important senses, to preside as judge, as well.

Mr. Nixon, in other words, has served notice to the world that, in one crucial aspect touching on his own conduct, the Watergate investigation had gone as far as he intends to permit it to go. For his part, Mr. Cox served notice that he would carry out his responsibilities for as long as he would be permitted to do so. He responded, in other words, as a man of honor and integrity, as did the two senior officials of the Justice Department. Honor has been a rarity in the long, dismal history of the Nixon administration's performance in this affair. To recall this history is to raise the most profound questions about Mr. Nixon's own honor—as well as his competence to conduct the affairs of government.

THE ATLANTA CONSTITUTION
Atlanta, Ga.
October 22, 1973

No man is above the law. That includes the President of the United States.

The U.S. House of Representatives should move promptly to begin impeachment proceedings against Richard M. Nixon, the 37th President of the United States.

We do not say such a thing lightly. This is a grave time in American history. The impeachment of a President is a frightening concept. It has occurred only once since the nation was founded. Yet President Nixon, with the near incredible arrogance of his action in firing Archibald Cox, has left the Congress and the American people little choice.

Cox, the special prosecutor for the Watergate investigation, was named to the sensitive position by U.S. Attorney General Elliot L. Richardson with the apparent approval of President Nixon. Cox, a distinguished attorney, was approved also by the U.S. Senate after a careful public hearing aimed at establishing that Cox would conduct an independent thorough investigation of the Watergate scandal.

Cox was fired by President Nixon because he persisted in doing just that, insisting that White House tapes of conversations and White House papers bearing directly on the criminal activities of Watergate were important to the investigation.

Attorney General Richardson, a man of courage and integrity, resigned his office rather than fire Cox. Richardson noted that in appointing the special prosecutor he had promised that such a prosecutor would be independent and "aware that his ultimate accountability is to the American people." That is still true, and this is also the measure of President Nixon's accountability. Deputy Attorney General William Ruckelshaus succeeded Richardson; he was fired by the President when he too refused to fire Cox.

President Nixon has made the beginnings of impeachment proceedings a near certainty. It is a measure of what has happened when a conservative South Georgia Congressman, W.S. "Bill" Stuckey of Eastman, can say as he did in the immediate aftermath: "The country and the House of Representatives will demand impeachment proceedings in order to get the facts out in the open." We agree with that. We think most Americans do,

In addition, President Nixon is now in open defiance of a direct federal court order to release the White House tapes.

Nixon's abrupt action has done another thing. It has scuttled any chance that Congress will act swiftly to approve Congressman Gerald Ford as the new Vice President. Not now. Not until the question of impeachment is settled.

The President of the United States is, in Richardson's phrase, ultimately accountable to the American people. President Nixon is no exception. The Watergate investigation will —and should—go on. President Nixon will not block it by firing one special prosecutor, nor can he long maintain a position of being above and beyond the law.

AGNEW QUITS AS PART OF PLEA BARGAIN

After strenuously denying any improper or illegal behavior for more than two months, Spiro T. Agnew resigned the vice presidency and pleaded no contest (nolo contendere) to one count of evading income tax on $29,500 during 1967 in a dramatic courtroom hearing in Baltimore Oct. 10. [See pp. 1208–1218] In return for Agnew's resignation and no-contest plea, the Justice Department agreed to drop all other pending charges and request leniency on the tax evasion charge. (Agnew had faced federal indictment for violation of bribery, conspiracy and tax laws.) After Agnew entered his plea, U.S. District Court Judge Walter E. Hoffman asked Agnew if he understood that waiving indictment and pleading no contest was "the full equivalent of a plea of guilty." Agnew concurred and Hoffman sentenced him to a fine of $10,000 and three year's unsupervised probation. Hoffman said that without the recommendation for leniency by Attorney General Elliot L. Richardson, he would have been inclined to follow his usual procedure in tax evasion cases of imposing a fine and prison sentence of two to five months.

In a statement read to the court, Richardson said no agreement could have been reached without a provision that he appeal for leniency. Richardson emphasized that a central element of the agreement was that the department be allowed to present the details of its other evidence against Agnew while agreeing to waive prosecution based on it.

Richardson said that for the people to "fairly judge the outcome" of the Agnew case, he would offer an "exposition of evidence" which "establishes a pattern of substantial cash payments to the defendant during the period when he served as governor of Maryland in return for engineering contracts with the State of Maryland."

According to the "exposition of evidence," Agnew—shortly after becoming governor in 1967 —established a system of taking payments from engineering firms. I. H. Hammerman 2d, a Baltimore investment banker, acted as "collector" from companies designated by Jerome B. Wolff, then chairman of the Maryland State Roads Commission. The three agreed—on Agnew's order—that the payments would be divided 50% for Agnew and 25% each for Hammerman and Wolff.

The evidence also detailed the relationship between Agnew and the presidents of two engineering firms who made direct cash payments. One, Lester Matz of Matz, Childs and Associates, continued making "corrupt payments" to Agnew after he became vice president.

As required by law, Agnew's formal instrument of resignation was a statement transmitted to Secretary of State Henry A. Kissinger. Agnew also formally notified President Nixon by letter, saying "the accusations against me cannot be resolved without a long, divisive and debilitating struggle in the Congress and in the courts." Agnew had concluded that it was "in the best interest of the nation" that he relinquish the office. In his reply, Nixon praised Agnew's "strong patriotism" and "all that you have contributed to the nation by your years of service as vice president."

Agnew's action touched off an immediate search by President Nixon for a successor. [See pp. 1294–1303] House Speaker Carl Albert (D, Okla.) became next in line for the presidency until the office of vice president was filled, for the first time, under the provisions of the 25th Amendment to the Constitution, ratified in 1967.

During the two weeks preceding the surprise hearing in Baltimore, there were the following major developments in the Agnew affair:

In a Los Angeles speech Sept. 29, Agnew declared to a cheering audience of Republican women, "I will not resign if indicted." He went on to bitterly denounce the Justice Department and, without specifically naming him, Assistant Attorney General Henry Petersen for leaking malicious information to the media. The Vice President claimed that "individuals in the upper professional echelons" of the department who had been "severely stung by their ineptness" in the Watergate case were "trying to recoup their reputation at my expense." "I'm a big trophy," Agnew declared.

President Nixon told a news conference Oct. 3 that Agnew's refusal to resign was "altogether proper," but took issue with Agnew's criticism of Petersen's handling of the investigation. Nixon said the charges against Agnew were "serious and not frivolous."

In an unusual action, Judge Hoffman Oct. 3 authorized Agnew's attorneys to investigate— with full powers of subpoena—the alleged news leaks by Justice Department officials. Under Hoffman's order, the lawyers could privately question under oath and take sworn depositions from any persons they deemed "appropriate and necessary." Some lawyers were quoted Oct. 4 as believing that Hoffman's order was unprecedented in that a person under criminal investigation but not yet under indictment was granted such broad authority to question prosecutors and others involved. The order was also seen as a potential source of further constitutional issues in the Agnew case if reporters questioned by his attorneys refused to reveal their sources.

In another action Oct. 3, Judge Hoffman summoned the grand jurors and delivered a special charge cautioning them to "disregard totally any comments you might have seen or heard from any source, save and except what you have heard or seen in your grand jury room while in official session." Hoffman called the press "integral and necessary," but added that "unfortunately, in the present-day grab for priority in getting news items, the news media frequently overlook the rights of others, especially where criminal matters are involved."

Democrat and Chronicle

Rochester, N.Y., October 11, 1973

It's better this way.

Tragic and shocking event though it is, the resignation of Spiro T. Agnew from the Vice Presidency puts an end to an ugly mess that was placing heavy strains on the nation.

And there would have been worse to come. In Agnew's own words, there could have been no resolution of the conflict "without a long, divisive and deliberating struggle."

Attorney General Elliot Richardson has said that the resignation should be perceived as a "just and honorable" decision. So it was, and so it will probably be received. Americans are not a vindictive people.

But it can also be seen now as an inevitable decision for Agnew, the tide was unstemmable. His reputation was gone and public esteem low. And it's now been confirmed that he had been involved in the past in wrong-doing.

Even a man who was never a quitter could not take that kind of knowledge into battle with him and have much real chance of coming out on top.

Agnew's plea of no contest to a charge of federal income tax evasion was, in the judge's opinion, tantamount to an admission of guilt.

Agnew has denied that the unreported payments received from contractors while he was Maryland governor affected his official actions, and has said further: "My acceptance of contributions was part of a long-established pattern of political fund raising in the state."

Agnew apparently did nothing more than others had done before him. But that didn't make the practice right even in those days. And what may have been considered normal behavior then is no longer acceptable in the wake of Watergate and heightened public demands for greater political morality.

If anything good can come out of this unhappy affair, it may be a much greater sensitivity, among politicians and public alike, to the need for integrity in the conduct of the public's affairs. The nation is tired of graft and dirty tricks.

And it is of course crucially important that the man who is chosen to follow Agnew be above all suspicions. America needs nothing so much as a shiny new knight. One man that the President will certainly want to consider is former Secretary of State William P. Rogers. The next Vice President must be first and foremost a person of unstained reputation.

The Sun Reporter

San Francisco, Calif., October 13, 1973

While the full terms of the negotiated deal achieved between the U. S. Department of Justice and former Vice President Spiro Agnew are not fully known, we find the punishment of resignation as fine for income tax evasion, with the promise of no further prosecution, another example which violates the concept that we are a nation of laws and not men.

Spiro Agnew began as a ward dealing politician who used his opportunities for political advancement to one heartbeat away from the most powerful politicial position in the world. Along the way, he violated the nation's laws and used his high political position to ride herd on some of the nation's most honored principles: freedom of the press, the right to peacefully assemble, and, above, all, the concept of law and order without justice. He ignored the first dictum of politics: that Caesar's wife must be above reproach.

We have insisted that no individual in America is guilty until the verdict has been rendered in the court of law by a jury of his peers. Moreover, we do not believe that the president or the Vice President are men who are placed above the law. We cannot agree that Agnew's resignation from the Vice Presidency and his plea of nolo contendere, with the $10,000 fine and three years probation, equates itself on the scale of justice with penalties that have been levied against others who without fame or position, dare to cheat Uncle Sam and the Internal Revenue Service. If men in high places pay so little as a result of crimes against the state, how can we justify long prison terms for lesser mortals not provided with a position of trust from which to steal and rob the people?

The Charlotte Observer

Charlotte, N.C., October 12, 1973

The disgrace and fall of Spiro T. Agnew as vice president of the United States delivers yet another profound shock to the American political system. The second-ranking officer of the land, a man put forward by his President and his party as a righteous advocate of law, order and decency, is revealed to be personally corrupt. He is forced to plead no contest to a charge of income tax evasion in order to escape a certain prison term for even shabbier crimes.

It is enough to disillusion American voters, who have been disillusioned only too often in recent elections. The John Kennedy "Camelot" turns out to have been a land of mere mortals and grave compromises. The Lyndon Johnson campaign for peace was actually a declaration of war. The Richard Nixon pledge to "bring us together" has torn us apart and left us with a snarl of moral and legal issues known simply as "Watergate."

The hypocrisy of the country's overblown politics, in which appearance means more than substance, has caught up with us. It is an hypocrisy made worse by 20th century communications and advertising methods, in which symbols and images mean more than reality and dimension. The people are regarded as children who must be protected from the truth and spared the hard facts necessary to make intelligent decisions.

Hypocrisy's Toll

Even before the Agnew case reached crisis proportions, the hypocrisy was beginning to take its toll. Men of conscience in American political life, aroused by Watergate and its disgusting picture of what politics has become, announced they were washing their hands of it. Sen. Harold Hughes of Iowa has announced his retirement. Sen. William Saxbe of Ohio has announced his. Sen. Marlowe Cook of Kentucky is said to be on the brink of an announcement. In their private conversations, local and state political figures are expressing the same disgust.

Yet, so ingrained is the habit, the sham continues even in the wake of Agnew's exposure and resignation. Asked for their reactions, senators, congressmen, national and state political leaders dissemble before the cameras. They express sorrow for the fallen vice president's personal tragedy rather than outrage over his betrayal of the people's trust.

And at the White House, where Agnew's capitulation is a supreme embarrassment, President Nixon lights the stage for another distracting round of the politics of appearance. Limousines come and go in the night, bearing key advisors and political figures the President is said to be consulting. Congressmen and senators are asked to submit names of possible successors; governors are polled over the telephone.

More Theatrics

But the President has known since before July that his vice president was under serious investigation and since late summer that the investigation was building toward a crisis. He was kept abreast of the findings and participated in decisions regarding the plea bargaining, knowing full well what that would mean. Obviously, he has been deliberating over his choice of a new vice president for weeks; today's theatrics are simply a distraction aimed at lifting the sagging confidence of the American people.

The people have had too many distractions. If the President has a firm choice (and by now he probably has) he should bring him on for public examination, without the effort to pre-condition the people's response. It is reminiscent of President Johnson's coy indecision over whether to make Hubert Humphrey his running mate during the 1964 Democratic Convention.

The Choice In '68

The nation got into this situation because Mr. Nixon played to appearances in choosing Agnew as his running mate in 1968 and stubbornly stayed with him in 1972, when prudence suggested making another choice. He did not look for a man of stature and substance. He chose a man who would project the desired image: a suburbanite to appeal to the growing suburban constituency, a man reputed to be tough on dissenters and street demonstrators, a man knowledgeable in local (but not national) affairs, a man of ethnic appeal.

Elevated overnight to national prominence, Mr. Agnew gratefully carried out whatever dubious tasks the President found for him, though some of them demeaned him and his high public office.

In choosing his successor, Mr. Nixon will do the nation added disservice if his choice again is dictated by appearance rather than honesty and national need. The next vice president must be a man capable of governing in a nation and world rushing toward profound change. He must not be another of the President's political guided missiles.

Among the men said to be foremost in the President's favor are several who, at cursory glance, seem to be less than the national trust requires. Would John Connally restore confidence by dealing directly and candidly with the American people and the nation's problems? Would Gov. Nelson Rockefeller, whose political views are said to be undergoing basic change? Would Ronald Reagan?

No Caretaker

There are many political figures of conscience and honor available to the President, experienced men capable of standing up to the challenges of the nation and the world. They need not be instantly recognizable to the electorate; they must be able to prove themselves under the glare of the congressional scrutiny that is ahead. We hope the President will look to such a person.

The Congress will play a major role in the outcome. The Senate and the House each must approve the President's nominee by majority vote. There is talk among Democrats of demanding a caretaker who will not seek the presidency in 1976. That talk should be disregarded. When the Congress wrote the succession amendment in 1965, it pledged that partisan considerations would not bear on the confirmation decision. That pledge should be honored today. The nation needs a man capable of leading. The President and the Congress must work to nominate and confirm him.

ARABS LIFT ANTI-U.S. OIL EMBARGO; PRODUCTION INCREASED BY SAUDIS

Seven of nine Arab petroleum-producing countries agreed at a meeting in Vienna March 18 to lift the oil embargo they had imposed against the U.S. in October 1973. One of the seven nations, Algeria, said it was removing the ban provisionally until June 1. The Arab producers were to meet again on that date in Cairo to review their decision. The embargo was to remain in effect against the Netherlands and Denmark. The delegates placed Italy and West Germany on the list of "friendly nations," assuring them of larger supplies.

The Arab action, taken at a meeting of the Organization of Petroleum Exporting Countries (OPEC), was approved by Algeria, Saudi Arabia, Kuwait, Qatar, Bahrain, Egypt and Abu Dhabi. Libya and Syria refused to join the majority. Iraq boycotted the talks. The meeting, which had begun March 16, confirmed the Arab decision which had been approved in principle at a conference in Tripoli, Libya March 13. The Vienna delegates had agreed at the March 17 meeting that oil prices would not be rolled back, despite protests and appeals from consumer nations. A communique said the oil ministers would convene a new meeting if any of the countries asked for one before July "with a view to revising the posted prices" for oil. The posted price for the next three months was to remain at $11.65 a barrel for Arabian light crude oil, in effect since Jan. 1. Saudi Arabia was the only country which pressed for a lower price for oil. Other countries, led by Indonesia, Algeria, Nigeria and Iran, sought an increase above the $11.65 posted price.

With the announcement of the agreement to end the oil embargo, Saudi Arabia pledged March 18 an immediate production increase of a million barrels a day for the U.S. market. A formal statement on the Arab decision did not mention the restoration of production cutbacks. The communique explained that a shift in American policy away from Israel had prompted the producers to terminate the embargo.

Syrian resistance to abandon the "oil weapon" because of its belief that the U.S. had not done enough to insure Israeli withdrawal had delayed until March 18 the formal announcement of the end of the embargo, despite the majority decision taken at the Tripoli meeting March 13.

Washington officials reacted cautiously to news that most Arab states were lifting the oil embargo. In his opening statement before a meeting of the National Association of Broadcasters March 19, however, President Nixon announced four basic energy policy decisions made as a result of the lifting of the embargo. He flatly ruled out the need for compulsory gasoline rationing and rescinded an order banning Sunday sales of gasoline, effective March 24. Nixon said he had directed the Federal Energy Office to increase fuel allocations to industry and agriculture. He also pledged to increase gasoline allocations to the states "with the purpose of diminishing ... and eventually eliminating" lengthy lines at gasoline stations. Nixon urged motorists to continue their voluntary fuel conservation efforts, such as car pooling, and to maintain reduced driving speeds because, despite the embargo's end, "we still have an anticipated shortage of perhaps 5%–8% in the U.S."

Saudi Arabia had resumed shipment of oil to the United States, it was reported March 25.

The Miami Herald

Miami, Fla., March 14, 1974

WE KNOW Sen. Henry Jackson would love to have the Democratic nomination for the presidency in 1976 and that he is using the energy crunch as a stump for political potshotting at the Republican administration. One of his sharp shots came yesterday when Sen. Jackson questioned the state of detente between Washington and Moscow when Soviet broadcasts in Arabic to the Middle East were urging opposition to Secretary Kissinger's peacemaking efforts and continuation of the oil embargo against the United States.

In the cool atmosphere of the State Department, the senator might be accused of an oversimplification and single-minded pursuit of an inflammatory issue, which is one classic definition of demagoguery. But out here where the voters are, the senator will raise doubts about Russia's talk of conciliation and long-range goals of trade and lasting friendship.

Being leery about the progress of President Nixon's new-found friendship with Russia is not strictly a partisan matter. Pennsylvania Republican Sen. Richard Schweiker has been wondering about the legality and wisdom of making low-interest loans to develop oil and gas fields in the Soviet Union. The President had said that such extension of credit was in the best interests of the United States because of Russian promises to deliver some of the new energy to American consumers.

The General Accounting Office has now agreed with Sen. Schweiker on the question of legality. Credit for the $7.6 billion project has been cut off and the administration will now have to make a case of national interest for pushing the loan through the Export-Import Bank. You can bet Sen. Schweiker will find much support for his view that Mr. Nixon's Operation Independence could be helped a great deal by offering American industry those low-interest loans for search for more energy.

It would certainly have more political sex appeal than lending that immense amount of money to the Russians who are siding with the most radical of the Arab leaders.

San Francisco Chronicle

San Francisco, Calif., March 19, 1974

TO THE AUTOCRATIC and aristocratic King Faisal, above all other Arab oil potentates, is owed, no doubt, the unconditional lifting of the embargo on crude oil shipments to the United States which the oil producers announced in Vienna yesterday.

Faisal's Saudi Arabia is the world's largest oil-exporting country, at 8.3 million barrels a day. It is an absolute monarchy, ruled by the law of the Koran, of which the grand theme and refrain are "Allah is merciful." King Faisal has found it politic and possible to be merciful too. And so, despite the economic and political bloodthirstiness of Libya's Colonel Khadafy, who with Syria held out against relaxing the embargo, our gasoline stringency in this country will be eased. The oil weapon has been thrown aside.

IT IS A WEAPON, which, it must be conceded, served the Arabs well. By tripling their prices while pumping less oil, they have gotten richer. They also have heard screams of blackmail from the victim countries. But their weapon did re-establish self respect and a sense of global power in the Arab leaders as they saw some of their customers split up ignobly among themselves, kick little Israel and little Holland around, and generally salivate.

It must be said with considerable pride that the United States did not engage in this demeaning servility, possibly because even with the embargo the pressure of shortages here was not, as it proved, all that great.

IT IS HARD TO SAY whether the resumption of Arab oil shipments to this country will not again be interrupted. Algeria, for one, says it will reconsider the matter in June, but the Persian Gulf states were unconditional and their decision may signify more than a temporary letup. Their easing of the embargo may well mean that the Arab states are willing, even anxious, to have peace in the Middle East on a stable basis along lines that they — President Sadat most notably — are trusting Dr. Kissinger, not Moscow, to work out.

The Virginian-Pilot

Norfolk, Va., March 20, 1974

In the weeks before the qualified lifting of the five-month-long embargo on sales of Arab oil to the United States, some Americans began behaving as though bountiful quantities of petroleum were again in prospect.

That wasn't smart.

For six weeks hence the Arabs are to review their decision ending the boycott, in light of Washington's progress, or lack of it, in Middle East peacemaking. Their appraisal will coincide roughly with the arrival on these shores of the first post-embargo shipments of Persian Gulf crude—eight weeks being the tanker-sailing time from Saudi Arabia, Abu Dhabi, Bahrain, Qatar, and Kuwait.

Meanwhile, an earlier review of the Arabs' oil policy should not be ruled out; the oil sheikhs may well be made unhappy by any number of things—Secretary of State Kissinger's diplomacy, or world oil prices, or whatever. Furthermore, it is not yet clear when, or if, Arab production will return to pre-embargo levels.

Yet U.S. gasoline consumption during the first week in March leaped one million barrels a day over the previous week, to 6.4 million barrels. (Gasoline consumption last March was 6.5 million barrels a day and in the peak month of last August was 7.2 million.) This means that gasoline usage was down but 5 per cent from what it would have been had there been no embargo, instead of the 20 per cent recorded the previous week.

Standard Oil Company of California warns that even if the flow of Arab crude reaches pre-embargo strength, it will not mean an abundance of petroleum for Americans. There is insufficient refinery capacity to cope with the rapid growth in demand that was normal before the fourth Arab-Israeli war and was threatening to bring on an energy shortage with no help from the Arabs.

The oil cutoff inspired many Americans to rethink personal, organizational, and national energy-usage habits. It would be unfortunate were the conditional turnabout by the oil-rich Arab states to halt the self-examination that the embargo necessitated.

Within weeks after the embargo households and corporations adopted stratagems that produced astonishing fuel savings. Torrents of suggestions—some good, some half-baked, some exotic—for conserving fossil-fuel resources and harnessing wind and sun power poured forth for public and private consideration.

We learned that slower highway speeds save not only gasoline but lives and limbs, that small cars offer distinct advantages in an era of rising gasoline prices, that crystal sky scrapers are energy gluttons, that the neglect of urban mass transit systems and railroads had left us without strong alternatives to private automobiles and trucks in an emergency. We learned that we can have all the oil and coal we want if we are willing to pay the price—in money and in environmental deterioration.

Many comfortable Americans seem to have relearned what earlier Americans learned automatically—that thrift is a virtue in itself; that the rich and powerful, no less than the poor and powerless, should not be profligate; and that thoughtless waste is wicked. We had thought there was no end to cheap energy. We have been disabused of that assumption. We should continue to conduct ourselves as though the Arabs had not relented.

DESERET NEWS

Salt Lake City, Utah, March 19, 1974

Despite the relaxation of the Arab oil embargo, there's still no room for Americans to become complacent.

Even though Saudi Arabia alone has promised the U.S. all the oil it needs, the embargo can be reimposed at any time. If that point wasn't clear before, it certainly was emphasized by the Arabs' decision to meet again June 1 and reassess the situation.

Unless the Arab petroleum exporters increase their output, the U.S. will still be competing in the world market for short supplies.

Yet, with the Arabs now receiving more income from lower production, there is less incentive for them to increase oil production.

Despite the inconveniences of the past and the challenges of the future, in the long run the Arabs may have done the U.S. a favor by turning off the oil spigot.

If the embargo didn't make it clear that the energy crisis is not the figment of some publicist's imagination, what can? For years the U.S. has been consuming more and more energy than it produces, and for years there have been warnings that the day of reckoning could not long

be postponed. Only since the embargo have those warnings seemed to make much impact.

By putting a strain on U.S. oil supplies, the Arabs exposed some shortcomings in the machinery for allocating America's resources. Data on petroleum consumption, as well as on supply systems, was found to be scattered and inadequate. Acting tardily and on short notice, Congress gave the Federal Energy Office instructions that were at times vague and contradictory. Moreover, as has been documented by a recent report from the Federal Trade Commission, the FEO tried to impose too many regulations with a staff that was inexperienced besides being spread too thin. Next time the U.S. ought to be better prepared to deal with oil blackmail — if there really must be a next time.

In contrast to such weaknesses, the embargo also exposed some American strengths. There was no truckling to the Arabs on Washington's part, as was the case with some western nations heavily dependent on oil imports. The U.S. was not pressured into forcing Israel into submission to the Arabs. Indeed, Ameri-

cans were not even incited into castigating Israel as a scapegoat. If anything, America's performance during the embargo demonstrated the U.S.'s desire to be fair and to maintain good relations with both the Arabs and Israelis.

Moreover, the embargo helped draw attention to America's vast coal deposits as a potential source of oil and gasoline, as well as giving impetus to the development of the West's oil shale deposits.

Likewise, because of some tendencies that the embargo brought to a head, the style of life in America may never again be the same. By driving more slowly to save gas, Americans have saved many lives on the highways. Mass transit has been given a solid boost, and a concerted effort has been mounted to make the U.S. self-sufficient in fuel.

Americans are glad the embargo has been lifted, of course, and wouldn't want to repeat the experience. But if ever there has been a practical demonstration of the uses of adversity, it has been this episode — and the U.S. can generally take pride in its performance during the embargo.

THE DALLAS TIMES HERALD

Dallas, Tex., March 20, 1974

LIFTING OF the oil embargo by the Arab nations gives no cause to dance in the streets or rush to the nearest service station for a fill-up.

It will be weeks, possibly up to 10, before even the semblance of normal consumer service. But, more importantly, it is a tenuous arrangement that could topple again.

In no sense does it affect the long-range energy program that confronts the United States. Self-sufficiency is the ultimate goal, but it is nowhere in sight at the moment.

Shortage of gasoline refining capacity in both the United States and Europe still is an immediate problem, but lifting of the embargo almost assures that gasoline rationing will not be needed and that fuel supplies will be greatly improved come the summer tourist season.

Tankers have been in dry dock for several weeks, undergoing barnacle cleaning and maintenance. They must be put back to sea and rushed to Arab ports—and all of that takes time.

Federal Energy Office officials indicate that cautious reduction of existing stocks, something that would have been considered unwise during the embargo, could give immediate relief. Stocks will be replenished with the flow of new oil from the Middle East.

The lifting of the embargo is contingent upon the United States taking further action in persuading Israel to negotiate a withdrawal from the Syrian front. And when oil and politics mix, there develops a slippery situation that could collapse again if the Arabs feel that the United States is weakening in its efforts to build acceptable peace in the Middle East.

On June 1, the Arab nations will come back again in a Cairo meeting to assess the picture. If they are unhappy, the spigots could be turned off again.

Unquestionably, the American consumer will still see fuel conservation measures and high prices. The reasons? Gasoline demand, at the high prices now in effect; actual crude oil import levels; the availability of imported gasoline as the embargo lifts still further in Europe and policy decisions on the use of gasoline inventories and a late summer shift of refinery production towards other fuels.

DAYTON DAILY NEWS

Dayton, Ohio, March 19, 1974

The decision of the Arab states to release the United States temporarily from their oil embargo will require considerably more policy poise by the Nixon administration than did the imposition of the embargo.

Wanting not to further rile an electorate already disenchanted with him, President Nixon made few long-range plans for surviving an oil siege when the embargo went into effect. He asked of the nation only the minimum, nuisance efforts that would let the United States improvise its way through the recent winter. Had not the embargo been lifted now, or soon, the United States would have been in for gasoline rationing and for serious inconveniences in its general energy arrangements.

The President must be relieved that the Arabs, who put him on it, have taken him off the hook. Relieved — and deeply fearful of what decision the Arabs will make when they decide on June 1 whether or not to revive the embargo. They have given Mr. Nixon until then to arrange a troop disengagement between Israel and Syria. What that means is that they have told the President to muscle Israel into making a deal that is more advantageous to Syria than Syria would be able to make on its own.

There is, alas, little reason to think Mr. Nixon will balk at doing that.

The President's reaction to the oil embargo from the beginning has been to minimize the domestic political problems it would cause for him. He was tardy and inept in offering to share America's energy resources with embargoed allies that were harder hit. He pushed, as solutions, a lifting of environmental controls and the fast development of new coal and oil supplies, rather than conservation and the more time-consuming development of new kinds of energy.

The United States has not kept itself in a posture that would allow it comfortably to stand by the basic interests of its ally Israel. The Arabs acted brutishly when they imposed the embargo. But by lifting it with a plausible threat that they will re-impose the embargo if they don't get their way, the Arabs are now playing Mr. Nixon in a masterly manner. The question is whether the President will let them.

The Oregonian

Portland, Ore., March 20, 1974

Lifting of the Arab oil embargo will substantially ease the gasoline shortage in the United States this spring and summer, but it could have damaging psychological impact on the gas-thirsty American public.

Despite all the lip service given to self-reliance, energy independence and goals to make the nation selfsufficient in oil resources, the fact remains that Americans didn't function very well during the Arab embargo and that the embargo itself was a highly successful tool in influencing foreign policy.

Americans, indeed, were in pain during December, January and February, and the long lines at service stations only enhanced our dependency on Arabian crude. It was during the height of the gasoline crunch that the government, through the Federal Energy Office, yielded to pressure and began borrowing against inventories — a dangerous ploy had the Arabs decided against lifting the embargo.

Federal energy chief William E. Simon told The Oregonian just last week that the decision to tap our existing oil reserves to ease gasoline shortages was spurred by public and political pressures because the gasoline shortage was painful.

Simon said he felt the government could take the risk of drawing down inventories because the lifting of the embargo was imminent. So, under pressure, the government opted to remain dependent on Arab oil, eliminating the more popular alternative of making do without it.

Yet the blackmail threat implied by initiation of the embargo last September — a threat which inspired energy-independence rhetoric from many U.S. politicians — is still very much alive today as reflected by Arab intentions to review the world climate June 1 in Cairo.

So nothing has really changed on the international oil front. The Arabs still hold the trumps, and we have shown in this first test that we are, indeed, dependent on imported oil resources and susceptible to international blackmail. Those who wanted the United States to turn down Arab oil once the embargo was lifted in a show of self-reliance should consider public response to the energy crisis a serious weakness inherent in a nation that has achieved such a high standard of living, much of it greased by petroleum products. They thought the Arabs were doing us a favor with their embargo. They were proved wrong.

In the short-run, the transfusion of Arab crude into the United States in the next 60 to 90 days will permit our refineries to expand from 82 per cent of capacity to perhaps 95 per cent, thus replenishing the inventories from which we borrowed to ease the February and March crunch and assuring ourselves a rather normal tourist season this summer.

Of course, we will be paying more for oil products than ever before and we will be just as vulnerable to future Arab blackmail as we were last September. Given a choice, we opted for comfort and convenience at the expense of self-sufficiency.

The TENNESSEAN
Nashville, Tenn., March 20, 1974

WHILE THE decision by most oil producing countries to lift the embargo against the United States was greeted with a sigh of relief, it has failed to elicit much real joy on Wall Street or in Washington.

For several good reasons both government and private interests view the action with cautious optimism, but realize that the public must wait to see how much real effect the decision will have on supplies and prices.

* * *

In the first place, the Arabs were anything but united. Two countries, Libya and Syria, violently opposed any change in the previous policy of using oil as a weapon against the U.S. Libya, which used to export about 10% of Mideast oil to the U.S. went so far as to term the vote by other Arab states as treachery. Syria, which exports no oil to the U.S. was almost as critical of the decision.

Striking such poses has become routine for these two states and it is obvious that the U.S. can get along quite well without either nation helping relieve its oil needs. But it is also obvious that such divisive influences can spell genuine trouble for the U.S. in coming months. The oil ministers will meet in Cairo in June to review the lifting of the boycott. This will give Libya and Syria time and opportunity to reverse the decision.

Egypt and Saudi Arabia may be the principal leaders of the Arabs in this situation, but it has not been forgotten that it was the Libyans, under dictator Moammar Khadafy, who first convinced the Arab states that oil would be a potent weapon to use against the industrial nations of the West.

Publicly the Arabs are saying that the embargo lift is a reward for the U.S. for having helped negotiate an end to Israeli occupation of the Suez and in hopes that Secretary of State Henry Kissinger can be as successful in securing the withdrawal of Israeli troops from the Syrian front. If that is true then a failure to resolve the Syrian question would give Arab states cause to reintroduce the embargo.

But there is considerable question why the embargo strategy was used in the first place. Although its view obviously serves its own self interests, the Israeli argument nevertheless makes sense. Tel Aviv and some U.S. observers insist that the Yom Kippur war and U.S. support of Israel only provided the Arabs with an excuse to boycott Western nations. The Arabs, it is believed, realize that vast oil reserves will be worth far more in the future, so the embargo enabled them to drive up prices while at the same time preserve finite resources.

* * *

What ever the real motivation of the Arab states, it is apparent that they have found a way to combine their strengths through the oil weapon to accomplish what they wish. Thus the oil weapon will continue to be a threat to the U.S. and every other nation. Whether employed to drive up prices, justify seizure of private company holdings, conserve oil or force U.S. foreign policy changes, the effect on the U.S. will be the same.

The question then is not whether the flow of oil from the Mideast will help America's current energy supply problem, but rather: How long can anyone count on Arab oil?

THE INDIANAPOLIS STAR
Indianapolis, Ind., March 20, 1974

The lifting of the embargo on shipments to the United States by the Arab oil-producing nations is welcome, but it does not mean that oil supply problems are behind us.

There have been rumors in recent weeks, affirmed the other day in a statement to Associated Press by an unnamed oil company executive, that tankers carrying crude oil that could have come to U.S. ports have been diverted to other nations. It's only logical that this may indeed have occurred.

Two reasons intertwine—price controls and the Federally mandated allocations system. Companies importing crude oil into the U.S. may be required by Federal allocators to resell it to other companies rather than using it in their own refineries. Even more absurdly, they may be required to resell it at a loss under the price controls.

In those circumstances the natural thing for companies to do is to restrict their imports—to avoid bringing in oil on which they cannot reap profits and may even have to take losses.

Lifting of the embargo should mean restoration of normal availability of oil for import. But significantly increased quantities of crude oil will not be imported unless the importers can earn profits on that crude. Their ability to do so is problematical as long as the government is deciding where oil shall go and what prices shall be, whether for crude oil or final consumer products.

If controls are removed the prices of gasoline, diesel fuel and heating oil may rise higher. But they will rise only until supply and demand come into balance, and if the government stops interfering supply will rise and prices will become more competitive.

The neighborhood service station operator does not want to limit purchases of gasoline, but on the contrary he wants to sell as much as he can. And in order to do that he wants to sell at prices that will attract customers to his pumps rather than the other fellow's.

Motives of the big oil companies are the same. If government will get out of the way, and let the companies go after maximum profits, the fuel supply problems will be solved in minimum time.

The Birmingham News
Birmingham, Ala., March 23, 1974

Keeping a lot of heavy qualifications in mind, the lifting of the Arab oil embargo against the United States is good news.

It won't mean an automatic end to the fuel shortage, however. It won't mean that prices will drop or that lines at service stations will be eliminated.

The help that the lifting of the embargo brings is just too small in terms of total U.S. energy consumption. Furthermore, the capriciousness of the Arab oil suppliers is the same as ever. At any time, the Arab oil cartel could decide that U. S. Mideast policy doesn't suit them and slap the embargo on again.

All of this means that the need for energy conservation is still as great as ever Americans can't afford to view the lifting of the embargo as a signal to drop restraints on energy consumption. Not that they would, anyway, with prices expected to remain high.

And the post-embargo situation demands, as ever, that the U.S. make every effort to become self-sufficient in energy in the shortest time possible. Mideast sources, even when plentiful, are not reliable. The United States cannot afford to be permanently in a position to be blackmailed whenever the whim strikes Arab oil producers

It is unlikely that the changes in the economy brought about by the energy shortage will reverse themselves. Trends to smaller cars, smaller engines and less driving are probably here to stay. People have been made aware of the high cost of wasted energy, whether in the home or in industry. That awareness can be expected to develop more fully in the years ahead.

The energy shortage was inevitable and has been predicted for several years. In a sense, the Arabs have done the U.S. a favor by raising prices to outrageous levels and slapping on the embargo. Those actions made this country painfully aware that it cannot go on allowing consumption of energy to increase at the expense of national security and to the detriment of the national economy.

The Arab oil manipulations have helped raise the issue of energy to the top of the national list of priorities, where it should have been for years.

Now the nation must begin looking to the energy needs not only of the present but of the distant future and begin crash programs to develop new sources of energy, sources which will not be dependent on the relatively limited supply of natural fossil fuels with which the earth is endowed by nature.

The Des Moines Register
Des Moines, Iowa, March 24, 1974

"Inappropriate" was U.S. Secretary of State Henry Kissinger's word for the Arab oil embargo against the United States. That is a good word for the Arab oil weapon generally. The weapon is blunt, often hit the wrong people and distributed hurts in strange ways, mostly through price.

It hurt most of all the underdeveloped countries against which the Arabs had no grievance. It hurt Israel very little. It bludgeoned most Western European governments and Japan into being somewhat more pro-Arab than they had been anway, but the effect was minor.

If it affected United States policy at all (Secretary Kissinger said it didn't), the oil weapon merely made the United States somewhat more diligent in its chosen role as peace mediator.

In two other countries, the effects were paradoxical. The Netherlands and South Africa were both subjected to total embargo on Arab oil, like the United States. The embargo did not work in either country.

The Netherlands suffered hardly at all after the first few days of confusion. It got the oil it needed for internal use and for its great export refineries from non-Arab sources.

South Africa, instead of collapsing, boomed. South Africa is only marginally dependent on imported oil (local coal is its big energy source) and it was able to get what oil it needed. But the financial effects of the world energy crisis drove up the price of gold as dramatically as it drove up the price of oil. South Africa's gold mines made money, and old, outworn mines reopened to cash in on the high prices.

Arabs of the oil countries didn't know what to do with all the money they made with the high new oil prices, and bought a lot of gold. From South Africa, mainly.

RICHARD NIXON RESIGNS PRESIDENCY

Richard Milhous Nixon, 61, resigned as President of the United States Aug. 8, and Vice President Gerald Rudolph Ford, 61, was sworn in as his successor. It was the first time in the history of the nation that the president has resigned.

The resignation was announced Aug. 8, three days after Nixon's disclosures on Monday, Aug. 5 that he had ordered the Federal Bureau of Investigation to halt its probe into the break-in at the Democratic Party's national headquarters in the Watergate building in Washington D.C. Transcripts of three tapes released on Aug. 5 proved that in his conversations with H.R. Haldeman Nixon had known and interfered with the FBI's investigation as early as June 23, 1972, six days after the break-in. Furthermore, Nixon stated, he had kept this part of the record secret from investigating bodies, his own counsel and the public.

The admission Aug. 5 destroyed what remained of Nixon's support in Congress, fading since the House Judiciary Committee had drawn, with substantial bipartisan backing, three articles of impeachment to be considered on the House floor. [See pp. 864–876] Within 48 hours of his statement of complicity, which he stated did not in his opinion justify "the extreme step of impeachment," the 10 committee members who had voted against impeachment reversed themselves, on the basis of the new evidence, and announced they would vote for impeachment. This, in effect, made the committee vote for impeachment unanimous.

The development was accompanied by serious defections in the Republican Congressional leadership and acknowledgment from all sides that the vote for impeachment in the House was a foregone conclusion and conviction by the Senate certain.

This assessment was delivered to the President by the senior Republican leaders of the Congress. Shortly afterwards, Nixon made his final decision to resign. He announced his decision the evening of Aug. 8, to a television audience estimated at 110–130 million persons. In his 16-minute address, Nixon conceded he had made "some" wrong judgments. He said he was resigning because he no longer had "a strong enough political base in Congress" to carry out his duties of office. He also reviewed what he hoped would be his legacy of accomplishment in office.

Some of the events of Nixon's last week in office:

■ July 30—The third of the articles on impeachment is approved by the House Judiciary Committee.

■ July 31—Patrick J. Buchanan, special consultant to the President, says that the President had "not ruled out" the plan to bypass the House debate on impeachment and move quickly to the Senate for the impeachment trial. Later that day, the White House drops the plan after Congressional opposition.

■ Aug. 2—Rep. Paul Findley (R, Ill.) proposes that the House consider censure of the President, rather than impeachment. Findley himself abandons the idea in favor of impeachment after the Aug. 5 statement.

■ Aug. 4—Sen. William Proxmire (D, Wisc.) calls on Nixon to transfer presidential powers to Vice President Ford until the impeachment proceedings are completed. Proxmire cites the 25th Amendment's clause on presidential incapacity.

■ Aug. 5—Sen. Robert P. Griffin (Mich.), assistant Senate Republican leader, calls for Nixon's resignation: "I think we've arrived at a point where both the national interest and his own interest would best be served by resigning." Sens. Edward W. Brooke (R, Mass.), James L. Buckley (Cons-R, N.Y.) and Richard S. Schweiker (R. Pa.) also call for the President's resignation. [See pp. 311–321]

■ Aug. 5—Nixon issues his statement on blocking investigation of Watergate break-in.

■ Aug. 6—Nixon tells the Cabinet he will not resign.

■ Aug. 8—Nixon announces his resignation.

Although there was general agreement that Congress did not have the power to grant immunity from prosecution, Sen. Brooke and Rep. John H. Buchanan Jr. (R, Ala.) introduced companion resolutions Aug. 8 expressing the "sense of Congress" that Nixon should not be prosecuted after he left office. Such a measure would not be binding on the prosecution or the courts. Brooke said the next day, however, that he would not press for passage of the resolution because of the lack of contrition or confession in Nixon's televised announcement.

Speculation was widespread both before and after Nixon's resignation as to what legal action, if any, might be taken against him as a private citizen. A key element in the issue was the fact that Nixon had been named as an unindicted co-conspirator in the cover-up case. The grand jury had reportedly wanted to indict Nixon but had been dissuaded by Watergate special prosecutor Leon Jaworski. In a statement released after the resignation announcement Aug. 8, Jaworski said that bargaining regarding possible immunity from prosecution had not played a part in Nixon's decision to leave office. "There has been no agreement or understanding of any sort between the President and his representatives and the special prosecutor relating in any way to the President's resignation," the statement said. Jaworski said his office "was not asked for any such agreement or understanding and offered none."

THE CHRISTIAN SCIENCE MONITOR
Boston, Mass., August 12, 1974

Though Richard Nixon left office under a cloud, his career had been in many respects an exemplary American success story. The storekeeper's son did become president, and along the way he amassed a record of achievement that history will have to weigh against the wrongs that brought his downfall.

Long ago, as a congressional proponent of the Marshall Plan, he hinted at the international statesmanship that culminated in his second-term breakthroughs toward providing the conditions for world peace.

With Henry Kissinger's help, Mr. Nixon risked alienating many of his long-time cold-war supporters by opening America's door to the Communist world. In one year, 1972, his visits to China and Russia led the way to a new era of the nations living together. By 1974 a Moscow summit could seem almost the normal thing.

Then came the triumph of Mr. Nixon's emissary, Dr. Kissinger, in bringing an end to the 1973 Middle East war and laying the groundwork for the difficult continuing negotiations for peace.

These strides forward followed Mr. Nixon's fulfillment of his pledge to end America's military involvement in Vietnam, albeit with deeply controversial methods and timetable.

As the Watergate momentum increased, erosion threatened Mr. Nixon's foreign policy successes. Yet their basic easing of world tensions remains a legacy to the succeeding administration, which must act decisively to prevent further slippage and to move ahead toward lastingly peaceful relations with all. It is to the credit of President Ford that he immediately assured world leaders of his intentions to continue on this path.

Presiding over the visit of the first men to the moon and the return of the last POW from Vietnam, Mr. Nixon led his country during a time that deserves to be remembered for much in addition to the first presidential impeachment proceedings in a century.

Ten years earlier no one would have predicted that Richard Nixon would be in the White House. He had been defeated not only for the presidency but for the governorship of California. The charges of unfair campaign practices lingered over him from his first congressional and senatorial races, as did the Checkers speech about the Nixon fund, and his controversial role in the Hiss case. As Vice-President, he had coped with what he called one of his "six crises," the illness of President Eisenhower. But now he was labeled a "loser."

Yet Mr. Nixon talked and traveled and labored and won his way back to the leadership of his party and of his country. Though his presidential domestic record was weak in comparison with his foreign policy, he did take highly debated steps that could have lasting impact.

For example, Mr. Nixon began to turn away from the Johnsonian "war on poverty" sort of federal program, and toward the revenue-sharing approach — with all the strengths and pitfalls of increasing state and local options in the use of federal aid. He left his influence on the Supreme Court through the appointment of four justices tending toward conservatism and away from the social activism of the Warren court. He ended the draft. If he finally failed to stop inflation, he made a start on a national energy policy.

Less publicized was Mr. Nixon's firm support of more and more federal funding for the arts and humanities, and there is no telling how much this investment may affect the future quality of life in America.

No one can be certain of what history will choose to emphasize among the events of the Nixon years. But it does not condone any of Mr. Nixon's wrongdoing to recall his positive contributions.

THE INDIANAPOLIS NEWS
Indianapolis, Ind., August 9, 1974

It is little comfort to a nation in anguish to lament "what might have been." Richard Nixon, acclaimed in 1972 as the most popular president in this nation's history, is giving up his office to Gerald Ford, the man he chose as vice-president.

Set in the political morality of our time, Watergate, a political burglary, seems a petty crime to exact such a high price. Explained quickly and openly, coupled with a humble request for public forgiveness, Watergate could now have been a dim memory. In his determination to protect his friends and advisers, however, the President became embroiled in a complex and prolonged defense which ended in tragedy.

All of which points up a landmark for the future and especially for Gerald Ford: A president can not be "brought down" by communications media or by opposition politicians, but he can be destroyed — and was — by unprincipled advisers.

History will tell us more about Richard Nixon's presidency, but a few facts stand out above the din. First, he achieved what his mentor, President Eisenhower, wanted to achieve but could not; he opened the iron and bamboo curtains of Russia and China and set in motion machinery which may help create world peace.

He helped to settle the conflicts in Vietnam and the Middle East. It is a tribute to his wisdom and to the ability of his appointees that he led the nation to a high point in international esteem and respect.

Beyond international affairs, Richard Nixon brought into his government a host of brilliant and competent persons. Many of his most recent appointments were men of outstanding ability. His Supreme Court appointments, for the most part, emphasized legal expertise and not political ideology.

While he failed to turn around a free-spending legislative branch, he made valiant — and unappreciated — efforts on many occasions. He made some impact with his "new federalism" and with revenue-sharing to reverse the flow of funds and authority from Washington to local communities.

There are other achievements, not the least of which is the model he, his wife and daughters set as a devoted and close-knit family. They imparted a genuineness of affection and respect which all of us could emulate.

Richard Nixon, finally, may have become the victim of a new level of political morality. His mistakes would have been blinked at and forgiven in another time; they would be "normal" among political leaders in any other nation in the world.

Here, in these times, no. The people are saying they expect more — more of their president than of themselves. In their sorrow for what might have been, they must be calling for a higher level of integrity than their leaders have ever had before. If they are and if they are ready to support what they seem to be saying, it is a hopeful sign for the future of this republic.

THE EMPORIA GAZETTE
Emporia, Kans., August 9, 1974

Thank God it is over.

THE INDIANAPOLIS STAR
Indianapolis, Ind., August 4, 1974

Americans should be acutely conscious that they may be witnessing "the eating of the guts" of their country in the headlong stampede to impeach President Nixon.

Field Marshal Viscount Montgomery coined the phrase to describe the epochal battle of el-Alamein in World War II. It was, he said, "the eating of the guts" of Hitler's famed Afrika Corps which later enabled him to chase the Germans some 1,200 miles across the North African desert and ultimately — with American help — out of Africa.

But "the eating of the guts" is a political as well as a military stratagem. History — including that of Imperial Rome — shows that whole nations have collapsed, or gone down to calamitous defeat in war, because they had been so consumed internally as to become impotent.

Recent history's most glaring example, the fall of France in 1940, resulted directly from the internal weakness contrived by such disloyal yet influential figures as Pierre Laval, a Socialist-inclined demagogue — ultimately shot as a traitor— who twice rose to be premier. Furthered by self-serving politicians and other misguided Frenchmen, unaware they were in fact butchering their country, the machinations of Laval and his accomplices proved to be the incisive instrument for delivering once-great France defeated and helpless to Hitler's invading Nazis.

Stunned, the French people were utterly unable to comprehend what had happened. They could not grasp that "the eating of the guts" of their country had been going on right under their noses, that the France they thought so strong had in fact been reduced to a shell.

Has "the eating of the guts" of America been going on right under the noses of the American people? Is it now reaching a climax in the impeachment proceedings against President Nixon?

Consider that America's latter-day Lavals and their fellow travelers have long been entrenched at almost every significant point of leverage in the nation — government; legal, educational and ecclesiastical establishments; foundations; organized labor; segments of the business community; and news media.

Consider that under prodding of these seldom visible wielders of power — comparatively few in number, but immensely influential — America has taken giant strides away from the open, free-enterprise society that made her great and toward an authoritarian, bureaucratically controlled society of the type that has made other great nations small.

Consider some of their stratagems for laming America, for turning her institutions upside down, for spreading dissatisfaction and discord among her people — contortion of the Constitution, emasculation of the criminal justice system, encouragement of lawlessness in the name of freedom of expression, maneuvering the nation into war as a prelude to screaming bloody murder at those inheriting the carnage, deliberate creation of an octopus-like welfare state, taxation contrived to penalize success, inflationary debauchment of the people's money, and the subjugation of America's separate sovereign states to an ever-growing Federal bureaucracy.

Consider that these insidious schemes were proceeding apace, virtually unchecked until Mr. Nixon, a seeming castaway, arose to be President. His sin has been not Watergate — a stupid political shenanigan blown up and rigged to involve him in scandal and disgrace — but that he has tried to set America's feet back on the road that in the past has led her to peace and prosperity.

Will the American people watch while Mr. Nixon's implacable enemies push on with their avowed purpose to elbow him out of their way by impeachment? If so, they had better be aware they may be witnessing right now "the eating of the guts" of their country.

The Des Moines Register
Des Moines, Iowa, August 10, 1974

Former President Nixon was not bitter or recriminatory in his farewell address. He was not forthright, either, or the least bit apologetic for the agony he inflicted on this nation during the course of what he referred to—only once—as "the Watergate matter."

The address was historic, for no other U.S. president ever resigned the office. But the absence of candor and remorse bars it from greatness.

The national TV appearance was moving, because the hurt of another human being is always moving. Richard Nixon's pain at being the first U.S. president ever forced from office for misconduct was plain beneath his veneer of manful calm.

Mr. Nixon took justifiable pride in his achievements in foreign relations and in his goals for domestic progress. His listeners would agree on these matters.

But rather than face, with the nation, the reality of the events which had brought him to such a moment, Nixon indulged in euphemisms which tended to cloud, in the best public relations fashion, what had happened and why.

He did not acknowledge that there had been a conspiracy to obstruct justice after the Watergate break-in, that he knew about it, and that he lied about that knowledge for months — until the Supreme Court forced him to yield the taped evidence that he knew. He only said, "Some of my judgments were wrong."

He did not acknowledge that one-time supporters on the House Judiciary Committee were persuaded by the evidence to say they would vote for his impeachment. He only said he didn't have a "strong enough political base in the Congress" to continue his effort to complete his term.

It is true that the former president's words had to be guarded on the Watergate crimes, for he may face trial on criminal charges arising from the actions which led to his resignation.

But that would not prevent a frank admission of why he had to resign. Mr. Nixon, in his final words, revealed the same obliviousness to moral questions and the same obsession with "PR" that dismayed so many when the first White House transcripts were released. He seemed to be inviting doubt among his supporters that he really had committed the crimes with which he was charged. He even seemed in doubt himself that he had done anything wrong.

CHICAGO DAILY NEWS
Chicago, Ill., August 10, 1974

Shakespeare had a phrase for it — "hoist by his own petard" — referring to a man destroyed by his own explosive device. Richard Nixon lighted the fuse of his own destruction when he installed the automatic tape machine to record conversations in the Oval Office and other strategic locations in the White House.

The tapes were his undoing. The day their existence became known the fuse began sputtering toward the explosion that came this week. The tapes, meant to provide a historical record of a great and successful Presidency, provided instead the clinching evidence of lawless conspiracy, of a mean, amoral spirit that invaded and finally engulfed the White House, until the only remedy was a thorough cleansing.

Without the record of the tapes, the nature and extent of the Watergate scandal would have remained a matter of conjecture, of suspicion without proof. The long battle to conceal, withhold and in some instances erase the tapes — all in the name of national security or executive privilege — nearly succeeded. But a stubborn judge, some persistent reporters, a stubborn prosecutor (taking over after the first one was fired) and a Supreme Court heavy with Nixon appointees finally broke through the barriers. And the tale of the tapes toppled the President.

Why would a President "bug" himself and everyone he talked with? Recording messages of state, or ensuring the accuracy of oral instructions and decisions — in such cases a tape record becomes understandable. But every spoken word?

Surely Richard Nixon, the astute politician, the consummate statesman with the prodigious memory for detail, would not forget that his every word was being recorded. Yet the words that finally emerged were so self-incriminating that it is hard to believe he remained aware of his own sanctioned eavesdropping.

There may be no logical, reasonable answer to the puzzle of the tapes. One can only speculate that an overpowering ego created the system — in a desire, perhaps, to preserve a private record from which to cull in later years the "definitive" memoir of a President at work. The idea first advanced — that this was to be a public record for historians of the future — can hardly be given credence in the light of the tawdry conversations actually recorded.

But a historic record was certainly made. The ego-massaging tape machine dutifully tucked away all the evidence of corruption, of deception, of a mortally flawed Presidency. And in due course it spewed that evidence forth, and in so doing turned upon its master and destroyed him. Not even Dr. Frankenstein did a more thorough job.

THE ROANOKE TIMES
Roanoke, Va., August 11, 1974

A longer-range view would almost certainly see today and the past several weeks as times that lifted the spirit. A Congress which had been in full retreat for 30 years has reasserted itself. A President who marred his achievement and potential by a gross abuse of power has resigned. The performance of the judiciary has been nothing less than magnificent.

U.S. District Judge John J. Sirica, probably the most important person in shaking loose the scandals and the wrongdoers, is an example of how a seemingly average judge can rise to greatness on the occasion. District Judges Gerhard Gesell and George L. Hart, Jr., are beginning to share judicial responsibilities arising out of the Watergate

scandals and they, too, seem to be honest and learned men.

The United States Supreme Court rendered the vital decision that a President is not above law and that President Nixon had to surrender the Watergate tapes for a criminal trial. The eight unanimous judges included three appointees of Mr. Nixon and proved that they put devotion to law above politics.

Certainly something must be said for special Watergate prosecutor Leon Jaworski. Doubtful eyes were cast upon him when he came on the scene because he replaced Archibald Cox, the original prosecutor whose popularity increased when he was fired by President Nixon. But Mr. Jaworski has done his

duty and may have some more stern duties to perform.

Our previous praise of James D. St. Clair needs extension. In addition to his previous difficulty defending a weak case Mr. St. Clair also had, as was learned last Monday, a client that misled him: Almost the worst thing that can happen to a lawyer in action. Among those who understand the value of adversary proceedings, Mr. St. Clair's reputation has not suffered one whit.

All in all, the previously distorted parts of government are falling back into the place originally intended for them. We invite a reading on this page today of the heart of Federalist Paper No. 51, explaining the separation of powers. It was

written by either a Virginian, James Madison, or New Yorker Alexander Hamilton.

If men were angels, no government would be necessary, No. 51 reads. That is a good closing point for a review of an exciting month. The members of the House Judiciary Committee which recommended impeachment (at a time when it was politically dangerous so to do), did not look like angels. But they looked like good, honest and sincere men—more like the typical Congressman than the cynics would have us believe. When good honest men—in the executive, legislative and judiciary branches—are properly disposed as intended by a good Constitution, surely we are all better off.

THE MILWAUKEE JOURNAL
Milwaukee, Wis., August 9, 1974

There is no joy in the fall of Richard Nixon. He came to the presidency declaring great goals and seeking an honored place in posterity, but the quest ended wretchedly. He will be chiefly remembered as the first president driven from office in disgrace.

For the man, his family, his friends — it is deep human tragedy. And for millions who will no longer call him president it is a melancholy moment. The cold immensity of what has occurred is numbing.

In his somber televised farewell, Nixon was the model of dignity under severe stress, expressing malice toward none, saying he had put the national interest first, urging unity in his wake. The words were touching. Yet the omissions were almost eerie. Aside from vaguely conceding some wrong judgments, there was no recognition of what produced the roar for resignation, no admission of serious misconduct or broken faith. He even lightly implied that "vindication" might have been possible if supporters in Congress had not buckled.

Clearly, resignation is not the ideal way to get rid of a chief executive who has violated his oath, stained his office and cannot bring himself to say so. Impeachment and trial would not have left these loose ends.

Even so, only a partisan zealot can contend that Nixon was hounded from the White House without warrant. His wrongdoing — so often confirmed, directly or circumstantially, by those amazing tapes — placed his incumbency beyond tolerance in a land of law. Clearly visible in Congress

and across the country was a verdict of cumulative unworthiness, a judgment rooted in voluminous proof and ultimately shared by dogged defenders who had given Nixon the benefit of so many doubts.

Some will say that other presidents have abused their authority, that Nixon's tenure climaxed a steady aggrandizement of the presidency, a trend of swelling arrogance and declining accountability. However true, none of this excuses Nixonian excesses, or lessens the need to make his tumble from the top a vivid warning that no successor will be allowed to wipe his shoes on the Constitution. Impeachment and conviction would have scorched the message onto the White House lawn — but the lesson is not lost. And to deny Nixon blanket immunity against the reach of criminal justice in private life would make the point doubly distinct.

As the most durable politician of the post World War II era, Nixon leaves a swirl of memories, a mix of historic feats and tawdry failures. At one point considered washed up, he had, until now, outfought or outlasted all rivals, from John Kennedy to Nelson Rockefeller. Yet he remains largely an enigma, a complex, contradictory man who very few claim to really know.

What was the fatal flaw? Perhaps it was the craving for power, the thirst to prove worth through domination. Perhaps it was the temperament that restricted his reach for openness and diversity, that caused him to snuggle into an Oval Office cocoon, surrounded by narrow counselors and stern

gatekeepers. Perhaps it was the bent of mind that saw life as perpetual war and cast critics as enemies to be destroyed.

In any case, Nixon did not capture the presidency without warning. Foes harped on his reputation as a humorless, ruthless opportunist, lacking deep moral conviction. Yet the worst was discounted, or at least obscured, by his lengthy preparation for lofty office, his impressive grasp of foreign affairs, his plays to prevailing sentiment, his mastery of TV as a campaign weapon.

And his first term was touched with promise. Despite many ominous shortcomings in domestic affairs, he did bring the troops back from Vietnam, draw Red China into the family of nations, lessen tension with Russia. But by the time of his smashing re-election against a feeble foe, clouds of scandals were growing. The second term, envisioned as a crowning achievement, became a nightmare. As the Watergate coverup unraveled and other outrageous activity surfaced, public confidence crumbled.

His pledge that there would be "no whitewash at the White House" proved ludicrous. His initial pleas of aloof purity were eclipsed by tape transcripts that made America cringe. His indignant declaration, "I am no crook," was answered by a grand jury naming him an unindicted co-conspirator. His confident assertion, "I do not expect to be impeached," withered when he finally admitted to living a colossal lie for two years.

Looking back, it's hard to be-

lieve that it all happened — the hammer blows of stubborn Judge Sirica, the piercing accusations of John Dean, the Senate Watergate Committee's astonishing discovery of secret tapes, the firestorm after Archibald Cox was crudely axed as special prosecutor, the parade of top aides bound for prison, the toppling of an errant Agnew, the Supreme Court rebuff of presidential imperialism, the memorable impeachment debates.

Could it have ended differently? Possibly. If Nixon had come clean soon after the Watergate burglary, he would have damaged his re-election bid, but he probably could have won and pressed ahead without mortal wounds. And who is to say what he might have accomplished — from welfare reform to nuclear disarmament?

Yet, it seems plain now that Nixon and his inner circle were afflicted with disastrous fear of the democratic process. It was something to manipulate or subvert, but not trust. Indeed, this Machiavellian mentality, reinforced by the angry challenges of the Vietnam years, spawned the family of obscenities called Watergate — the bugging and burgling, the twisting of government agencies to political ends, the enemy lists and dirty tricks. And, when the pivotal moment came, it was this mentality that made purifying candor impossible.

So it was that Richard Nixon, the extraordinary scrambler who yearned for lasting glory, sealed his doom in layers of falsehood. Now, he may seek personal peace. Sadly, it will be peace with dishonor.

Indochina War:

INDOCHINA'S 30-YEAR WAR ENDS; SAIGON GOVERNMENT SURRENDERS

The 30-year war in South Vietnam came to an end April 30 [April 29 U.S. time] as the government surrendered to the Communists, and Viet Cong and North Vietnamese troops entered Saigon. Hours before the fall of the capital, the U.S. completed an emergency airlift from the city ordered by President Ford, bringing out all Americans remaining in Vietnam, as well as thousands of South Vietnamese, who feared their lives would be endangered by a Communist take-over.

The Communists' accelerated offensive around Saigon in the previous seven days had quickened the collapse of the government's forces. In their final military victory before entering the capital, the Communists earlier April 30 had captured Bien Hoa air base 15 miles northeast of the city and seized Vung Tau, the port city southeast of Saigon from which only hours earlier thousands of refugees had left in boats.

Saigon's unconditional surrender was announced by President Duong Van Minh, who had assumed the office April 28 as one of the Communists' conditions for ending the war; the other demand was the total departure of the Americans. (Minh replaced Tran Van Huong, who had become president upon the resignation of Nguyen Van Thieu April 21.)

Addressing the Viet Cong's Provisional Revolutionary Government (PRG) in his surrender announcement, Minh called on his forces and the Communists' "to cease hostilities" and offered to meet with the PRG representatives to discuss the "orderly transfer of power so as to avoid any unnecessary bloodshed of the population." Upon the entry of the Communist troops into Saigon later April 30, Minh broadcast another appeal to South Vietnamese troops throughout the nation to surrender their arms. Minh was directed to deliver the plea by North Vietnamese troops, who later took him to an undisclosed destination.

With Saigon on the verge of falling to the Communists, President Ford April 29 [April 28 U.S. time] ordered the airlifting of Americans and South Vietnamese from the capital. A sealift operation to rescue fleeing Vietnamese also was undertaken. In a 19-hour operation extending through part of April 30, a fleet of 81 helicopters at Saigon's Tan Son Nhut airport evacuated 4,475 South Vietnamese and 395 Americans, bringing them to U.S. warships waiting offshore, while 1,120 South Vietnamese and 978 Americans were helicoptered from the roof of the U.S. embassy to the ships.

The evacuation was completed when the last 11 of the 800 Marines on guard were flown by helicopter from the embassy roof. U.S. Ambassador Graham Martin was one of the last civilians flown out in the final regular lift of 19 helicopters.

The U.S. embassy April 29 was the scene of pandemonium as thousands of other Vietnamese sought to join the helicopter lift to escape the approaching Communist troops. Many tried to push through the gate, while others attempting to scale the compound walls were dislodged by U.S. Marines and civilians striking out with pistols and rifle butts. At the airport, Vietnamese guards fired in the air and in the direction of the evacuation buses, shouting, "We want to go too."

Soon after the U.S. embassy was abandoned April 30, thousands of Vietnamese invaded the building and looted everything in sight.

The Washington Post
Washington, D.C., April 30, 1975

THE LAST STAGE of an era-long American involvement in Vietnam was distinctive, not only because it brought a particular agony to an end but also because during that brief stage the United States acted with notable responsibility and care. All Americans, save the few inadvertently lost, were removed safely and in a way which deterred any larger accident and which provided time and an atmosphere in which tens of thousands of Vietnamese who chose to leave could do so. The effort made to assist those Vietnamese was an admirable demonstration of loyalty to a group of human beings otherwise bereft of hope. It may not have nullified so many other excesses committed during long years of war, but it had this virtue: it was the right thing to do. The United States also, in the last days, made what seems to us an entirely genuine and selfless attempt to facilitate a political solution that would spare the Vietnamese further suffering. That the outcome of this attempt remains in doubt is no reflection on the motives of those who made it.

Americans, in other words, can include a positive judgment of their government's final acts in Vietnam in their larger judgment of the war as a whole. And they should. For if much of the actual conduct of Vietnam policy over the years was wrong and misguided— even tragic— it cannot be denied that some part of the purpose of that policy was right and defensible. Specifically, it was right to hope that the people of South Vietnam would be able to decide on their own form of government and social order. The American public is entitled, indeed obligated, to explore how good impulses came to be transmuted into bad policy, but we cannot afford to cast out all remembrance of that earlier impulse. For the fundamental "lesson" of Vietnam surely is not that we as a people are intrinsically bad, but rather that we are capable of error—and on a gigantic scale. That is the spirit in which the postmortems on Vietnam ought now to go forward. Not just the absence of recrimination, but also the presence of insight and honesty is required to bind up the nation's wounds.

Dr. Kissinger was wise, in his news conference last evening, not to make stark predictions one way or the other about how the foreign policy of the United States would henceforth unfold. That is not just because there are so many obvious uncertainties. It is also because foreign policy proceeds a great deal more from the character and outlook of a people than from the specific manipulations of public men. Vietnam—by which we mean the whole play through the years—has made Americans extremely sensitive to limitations on American power, but it has provided so far no clear guide to or consensus on how that power should be used. The large sprawling domestic debate on foreign policy that has gone on in recent years will not end now. It will intensify. Fortunately, the United States still has the great power, measured in conventional military and economic terms, to afford the luxury of a debate. For the moment, it is perhaps enough to say the country will fare better if it regards what has finally happened in Vietnam as bearing, for Americans, the potential for deliverance as well as disaster. Such a perception is the best foundation on which the future can be built.

The Virginian-Pilot

Norfolk, Va., April 30, 1975

South Vietnamese President Duong Van Minh—the neutralist "Big Minh" to whom Saigon turned when there was no course but to ask the Communists for peace terms—solved for the United States its final dilemma in two decades of involvement in the Vietnam War. He ordered from the country the last of the American diplomatic and military personnel. Lately the United States strategy had been to support General Minh—and Presidents Tran Van Huong and Nguyen Van Thieu just before him—as best it could while indicating to Hanoi, whose troops ringed the South Vietnamese capital, that it was ready to depart.

For an accommodating official to expel us was always a way of getting out of that quagmire, as President Kennedy once noted. But when the jest came to reality, three harried Administrations and close to 50,000 American war deaths later, all humor had been drained from it. Yesterday's evacuation was, despite Washington's careful planning and direction, confused and violent. Two U.S. Marines in an evacuee protection force were killed. Resentful South Vietnamese soldiers fired on buses carrying Americans—and, contributing enormously to the disorder, frantic South Vietnamese squeezed among them—to the air base.

Ugliness stemming from South Vietnamese anger at the Americans' departure had been a fearful prospect from the time, early last month, it became apparent that North Vietnam and the Viet Cong were going to win the long war that this country quit, as their foe's combat ally, with President Nixon's "peace with honor" acceptance of the Paris Accords in early 1973. Saigon's mood was reflected in the denunciation of Washington that Mr. Thieu delivered on resigning the presidency last week. But by then the American corps had trickled from about 6,000 down to a couple of thousand. When a great swarm of U.S. helicopters went to work yesterday, shuttling between the Saigon airport and five aircraft carriers off the coast, the passenger list was no more than 600.

Whatever else may be said about President Ford's handling of the Vietnam wind-down, during which he urged Congress to pour more money into Saigon's broken defenses while knowing it should not and in any event would not, he avoided for the last Americans on the scene a catastrophe. He opened the way for the escape of about 60,000 intimidated South Vietnamese. He gave Saigon what little diplomatic credit he had left in petitioning for a cease-fire and peace settlement.

Now the Communists are in control of that unhappy capital. Any further military activity by them would be cruel and unnecessary. Among the South Vietnamese there is neither ability nor will to make a last stand. The victors will cheapen their accomplishment and complicate their responsibility for order and their task of administration if they refuse now to show restraint.

The Cleveland Press

Cleveland, Ohio, April 30, 1975

Even though two decades of U.S. efforts in Indochina were a costly failure, Americans have nothing to be ashamed of about their final days in South Vietnam.

President Ford, Secretary of State Kissinger, embassy officials in Saigon and above all the oft-criticized U.S. military succeeded in salvaging what could be salvaged from a lost and dying cause.

In the difficult and dangerous circumstances of South Vietnam's military collapse, they evacuated almost without a hitch 55,000 Vietnamese judged to be in peril because they worked with Americans for years.

They also removed 6500 Americans at a gradual rate that neither touched off uncontrollable panic in Saigon nor reprisals by angry Vietnamese against departing U.S. citizens.

And all the while, through secret diplomatic maneuvers, they tried to arrange a peaceful turnover of Saigon to the Communists, one that would avoid senseless bloodshed in a country that has bled too much.

Of course the best-conducted withdrawal does not change defeat into victory. But leaving Vietnam in a decent way makes it easier for Americans to come to terms with the setback and cope with the future.

Ford struck the right note, we thought, when he announced the end of the emergency evacuation of Americans by helicopter and said:

"This action closes a chapter in the American experience. I ask all Americans to close ranks, to avoid recriminations about the past, to look ahead to the many goals we share and to work together on the great tasks that remain to be accomplished."

Kissinger also appeared to have drawn the right conclusion when he said "one lesson we must learn" from Vietnam "must be to be very careful in the commitments we make, but scrupulously honor those we do make."

South Vietnam's failure to withstand the Communist offensive without U.S. combat support is painful, disappointing, diplomatically embarrassing and probably will lead to probes against U.S. friends in other places.

But it should not be exaggerated nor cause black despair. It does not vitally affect our national interests. It is not the end of the world nor of America's role in the world.

As Ford implied, much remains to be done: working for stability on the international plane; working for economic recovery, energy independence and fair play for the disadvantaged domestically.

With honest explanation of problems to the public and with closer cooperation between Congress and the White House, there probably is nothing on America's agenda that cannot be solved, despite Vietnam.

THE SACRAMENTO BEE

Sacramento, Calif., April 30, 1975

The successful evacuation of virtually all Americans and thousands of Vietnamese with close American connections from Saigon is an occasion for both a sigh of relief and a feeling of sadness.

There's a relief that the operation was completed with few casualties and with relatively little panic among the citizens of the besieged South Vietnamese capital. But it is sad that South Vietnam was left without even the moral support of a token American diplomatic presence as it tried to negotiate an end to the fighting with the victorious Viet Cong.

The Viet Cong today entered the once beautiful but now battered capital city after President Duong Van Minh announced an unconditional surrender of South Vietnam.

So a milestone has been reached. The United States' involvement in Vietnam has, at long last, ended. Still, there is no disguising the immediate humiliation for this country. An enterprise this nation undertook in good faith went sour before its eyes, foundered, and now we have the denouement — the surrender of South Vietnam.

Probably no issue, except perhaps slavery, has torn up this country politically and emotionally in quite the same traumatic way as the war in Vietnam. Over the long years of American involvement several million U.S. servicemen and women were funneled through the Vietnam war. Some 50,000 American service personnel did not return. Several hundred thousand more were wounded, many of them permanently disabled.

Now the shooting is over and the Americans are totally disengaged from the South Vietnamese government but some monumental problems remain.

The refugees from South Vietnam must be cared for. These are this country's friends, in a place and over a time span when profession of such friendship for America was far from universal. Americans must not respond by dumping the new immigrants into tented ghettos, called relocation centers, by grudging them anything beyond the merest subsistence.

Now we will see whether Americans are actually as concerned with the Vietnamese welfare as for years they have been saying they were.

St. Louis Globe-Democrat

St. Louis, Mo., April 30, 1975

The evacuation of Americans from South Vietnam has been completed, marking an ignominious end to the United States role in all of Indochina. The evacuation itself was an efficient and impressive operation carried out by naval and Marine forces, but the event it symbolized was a saddening — even sickening — spectacle that became necessary because of United States blunders weeks, months and years ago.

Contrary to the drivel advanced by some, the South Vietnamese did not turn on the Americans as they left. The only "unseemly" action was the pathetic situation of thousands of Vietnamese asking to be whisked away from the Communist brutality and tyranny to come, some of them even begging Americans to take their children on the flights.

Obviously, the Americans had to be evacuated when they were. Because Congress had procrastinated since Jan. 28 on supplemental military aid — actually, just a restoration of the original Administration request covering minimum needs — the South Vietnamese first had to retreat from their military lines (which turned into a rout), and then had to try to preserve what remained without American assistance in arms, fuel and supplies. The situation became hopeless because Congress kept saying it would be hopeless.

By never lifting a finger to help the South Vietnamese, and on the contrary by undercutting them while North Vietnam was receiving massive new aid from the Soviets and Chinese, Congress guaranteed the final tail-between-the-legs evacuation. It is true that Congress was responding to public sentiment, but such a grave issue should hinge on probity rather than plebiscite.

In retrospect, the evacuation was the result of the U.S. decision years ago to fight for a tie rather than a victory in Vietnam. Once that policy failed dismally, as it was destined to do, the U.S. decided that South Vietnam should fight alone — thus the Paris agreement. For two years that effort succeeded, but then Congress changed the rules: Saigon was to fight with only one hand, even as Hanoi was being equipped with a powerful new club.

As Prince Sihanouk said of Cambodia some years ago, the country would be overrun by Communists because China was near and had perseverance, and the United States was far away and lacked perseverance. It's really that simple. The Communists are not on the verge of victory because their cause is just, but merely because the Soviets and Chinese had perseverance in supplying Hanoi, while the U.S. lacked perseverance in supplying Saigon.

North Vietnam and South Vietnam were almost incidental characters in the drama, and would have held each other at bay indefinitely without outside support. When the Communist superpowers aided Hanoi, the U.S. responded with aid to Saigon. But the U.S. tired of the effort, even financially, and the penultimate moment, the evacuation of the last Americans, resulted. Now only the ultimate, consummate act remains to be performed.

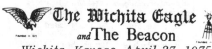

The Wichita Eagle and The Beacon

Wichita, Kansas, April 27, 1975

It's ironic that we seem to have lost a war — a war we pulled out of more than two years ago, a war we possibly never should have been in — so close to our nation's 200th birthday.

We can now engage in self-recrimination, argue over which politicians, still active and retired, to blame for the way it all turned out and let ourselves become even more divided than we were when we were actively participating in the war in Vietnam and elsewhere in Southeast Asia.

Or we can ponder the lessons we have learned, consider what our forefathers were trying to accomplish when they founded our nation in 1776, and make up our minds to try to do better in the next 200 years, the next 100 years, the next 10 years.

We can understand why South Vietnam's President Thieu was so bitter as he resigned from office with enemy forces so close to his capital city, Saigon. He felt he had been let down by our failure to deliver additional aid he thought he had been promised and possibly was — by American leaders who had no right to make such a promise

He cried out that we had "led the South Vietnamese people to death." But it wasn't our war we had been fighting when our military forces were engaged in Southeast Asia. We thought it was for South Vietnam that some 59,000 American lives were sacrificed.

We were given to understand, when we pulled out, leaving vast amounts of materiel and numerous advisers behind, that South Vietnam was prepared to go it alone.

Or, suppose that we had stayed in, blasting Hanoi off the map with hydrogen bombs — and possibly setting off a really worldwide conflict — what would we have accomplished?

Would we really have proved that the Vietnamese people were entitled to peaceful self-government — for which they had fought French colonialists for some years earlier?

Would we then have been prepared to pour additional billions into the rebuilding of a war blackened land? The rehabilitation of vanquished enemies is an American tradition, too, you know.

The outcome in Vietnam is indeed a tragedy. The war which helped turn part of a generation of Americans into drug users was also a war involving human beings and the toll in both human lives and human relationships was enormous.

Americans have always tended to want to help other people less fortunate. Through various programs, we have given away food, American know-how and educational opportunities. American religious bodies have done vast amounts of good work abroad.

We have dedicated at least two wars to the purpose of trying to stop communism. Perhaps our efforts should better have been aimed at trying to spread democracy. In neither Korea nor Vietnam have we really achieved much for democracy.

Our forefathers who rebelled against tyranny two centuries ago might have been as disheartened by the tyranny we have helped foster in South Korea, for example, as many more modern Americans for many reasons by the outcome of events in Vietnam.

When things seem to be completely in a mess, it's always wise to get out the blueprints to see what the original goals were and where things went wrong.

We can't change history, but we think our original American ideals were good ones. Perhaps we should study them as they spelled out in our Constitution and its Amendments. To understand why we did what we did back in 1776, perhaps we should study the Declaration of Independence, too.

You might find something significant, also, in George Washington's Farewell Address. He warned us about foreign entanglements.

"Observe good faith and justice toward all nations," he counseled. But a couple of paragraphs later he warned: ". . . a passionate attachment of one nation to another produces a variety of evils. Sympathy for the favorite nation, facilitating the illusion of an imaginary common interest, in cases where no real common interest exists, and infusing into one the enmities of the other, betrays the former into quarrels and wars of the latter, without adequate inducement or justification. . . . Against the insidious wiles of foreign influence, (I conjure you to believe me, fellow citizens,) the jealousy of a free people ought to be constantly awake. . . ."

The Des Moines Register

Des Moines, Iowa, April 30, 1975

The war in Vietnam, like the war in Cambodia, has ended with a victory for the Communist-led revolutionary forces and a defeat for the upholders of the old ruling classes. That includes the United States, which for 25 years — since the first aid to France in support of that country's effort to maintain its Indochina colony — has been upholding the old regimes.

The incredible thing, still, is the stubborn failure of United States leaders to see what was going on, to see the hopelessness of their cause and to get out. A quarter of a century!

The American public and press must share the blame for this disaster of American foreign policy. With rare and honorable exceptions, Americans went along, bemused by the concept of American leadership of a "free world" struggle against Communism.

A succession of American presidents, secretaries of state, defense secretaries and generals told the people over and over that America was winning. They distorted the evidence; they told outright lies. The facts were that the side America was supporting was losing.

Each American president since Eisenhower has had the opportunity to move toward a political compromise in Vietnam. Each one lacked the courage to take a step which he feared might look like an American "defeat" or, as President Ford and Secretary Kissinger have been putting it, like a failure to make good on a commitment.

In the end, this policy led to a much worse defeat and a much worse discrediting of America's international be-

havior than early withdrawal would have meant.

The fear of Communist takeovers, of a phony "domino" theory of collapsing "democracies", has been dominant in U.S. policy — even after the moves toward detente with the big Communist countries.

The misguided quarter century is now behind America, as President Ford said recently, although not in those words. Instead of losing face or encouraging Communism or losing confidence of the rest of the world, the United States probably will gain in these respects from finally ending its military role in Asia.

The nation would have gained respect sooner if the government had acted on its own — 10, 15 or more years ago. Instead, action to end the Indochina connection came only after the arousal of public opinion which drove one president out of public life, and led to the near-impeachment of another on charges of abuse of constitutional power. Even the ending was a foot-dragging business with Ford, Kissinger and Ambassador Graham Martin holding the line in Saigon.

But public opinion finally did prevail; the machinery of democracy did work, though slowly. The country will be stronger, wiser and more effective in world affairs, we believe, as a result of ending this misadventure. The illusions of imperialism, of world leadership in terms of military power, of executive primacy in foreign affairs — those illusions, we hope and believe, are vanishing.

THE ATLANTA CONSTITUTION

Atlanta, Ga., April 30, 1975

The poet Robert Frost was there, his white hair blowing in the cold winter breeze of that January in Washington. The youngest American President in decades, lean and committed and intense, spoke of the world and of freedom and said that this nation would "bear any burden" in the defense of freedom and in support of our friends. Most Americans had never heard of Vietnam.

That was 15 years ago, and the bearing of that "any burden" in Vietnam came in the end to seem tragic even to the very Americans who applauded President John F. Kennedy when he first made that pledge.

It is over now. Two American Marines died in an artillery attack on the base at Tan Son Nhut Monday, the first Americans to die in combat in fully 16 months. Their deaths are sad, tragic. But no more sad and no more tragic than the deaths of more than 50,000 Americans during our long torturous involvement in Vietnam. There may yet be other American deaths or injuries this week, but not for long, not for long. President Ford has ordered the immediate evacuation of all Americans from Vietnam after a request from South Vietnam's new president, Duong Van Minh. The last Americans(except perhaps for newsmen) will probably be out of Vietnam today.

North Vietnamese military forces surround Saigon in massive numbers. President Minh's new government hopes, at best, only to manage a negotiated peace on North Vietnamese terms. The North Vietnamese may yet act to claim a complete military victory, and there is little indication that their troops would meet with significant opposition.

So, then, it is over.

Americans are so exhausted emotionally by the bitter controversies of Vietnam that the ending of them only dimly tears at the heart. Our hearts have already been torn through the years of spilling of American blood and treasure in what proved to be a massive national failure.

We did not succeed, as we had hoped, in preserving South Vietnam as an independent government. We did not stop the North Vietnamese Communists from overrunning South Vietnam. We learned, as did the French 21 years before us, that it is not possible perhaps in the long run for a Western nation to determine the kind of government and society that can survive and exist in Vietnam.

And yet, and this should be said, there is a nobility and a glory in some sides even of failure. No one should try to glorify the torturous warfare of Vietnam. Yet many young Americans fought and died in Vietnam in the deeply held conviction that the South Vietnamese deserved a chance to live their own way, without being taken over by the totalitarian Communist regime of North Vietnam. The effort to create that chance can, even now, be viewed as something worthy and idealistic. Whatever the mistakes in judgment in American policy in Vietnam, there is no God-given principle asserting that the absolutely dictatorial regime of North Vietnam always had the right to rule all Vietnamese.

In retrospect, all Americans can probably regret the mistakes and the suffering of Vietnam. But it is not unimportant too to remember why many Americans believed the effort a worthy cause.

THE DALLAS TIMES HERALD

Dallas, Texas, April 30, 1975

THE UNITED STATES has withdrawn finally from the miseries and frustrations of Vietnam.

It is finished.

The American involvement is ended and those we sought to save are left behind in pitiable climax to 30 years of fratricidal war.

The years of Vietnam finished as they started a dozen years ago—in supplication to the thousands who swarmed the embassy evacuating the last Americans in rocket-glare eeriness of the night.

"Please help me! Please help me!"

It was the same cry that took us there first with advisor groups and then with a half million men to help them gain the free life. The Americans left 55,000 dead, 165,-000 wounded and billions upon billions of dollars in their cause.

And when President Ford during the night ordered the emergency helicopter evacuation of the remaining few hundred Americans, the men, women and children of South Vietnam were still clinging to the United States for last-minute escape from the oncoming Communists.

One of the last of the American correspondents, Chad Huntley of UPI, stood with U.S. Marines and embassy officials behind compound walls and told of their last hour.

"The wealthy bribed, the poor pleaded and others stood with bowed heads hoping the Americans would show mercy and take them out. The Marines listened to the Viernamese pleas with harried but sad looks . . . .

"Red flares and smoke of grenades thrown to mark landing areas for the helicopters made the night look like something out of a horror movie.

"Please help me! Please help me! The cries will echo for years."

The tactics, the failures, the humiliations, the decisions of a Vietnam war that finally brought public demand for American withdrawal, will be argued through countless chapters of history.

It will be known as the first American defeat. A defeat that ironically came from doing what we know best — trying to help others salvage the treasures of freedom.

It was a strange and unfamiliar war for Americans who had dominated other conventional conflicts through desire, resourcefulness and superior equipment. The stealth of jungle tactics was new and decimating to our forces.

We refrained, through four Presidents, from walking the edge of another World War through use of nuclear and power tactics that could long ago have ended it in "victory."

It was the way we chose. We felt we could leave well-trained and equipped South Vietnamese to their own ends.

In suddenness born of internal conflict and lack of leadership, it all collapsed. Now, God be with the South Vietnamese who reached so desperately for their freedoms.

For the United States, the restoration process ahead must assure others that American commitments to free peoples will not again crumble.

MAO TSE-TUNG DIES; HAD LED COMMUNIST CHINA SINCE 1949

Mao Tse-tung, the preeminent leader of the People's Republic of China since its creation in 1949 and a founder of the Chinese Communist Party, died Sept. 9 in Peking at the age of 82. The announcement of Mao's death came over Radio Peking at 4 p.m. Peking time, 16 hours after he died at 12:10 a.m. The message said Mao died "because of the worsening of his illness and despite all treatment, although meticulous medical care was given him in every way after he fell ill." It also included an appeal to the people to "continue to carry out Chairman Mao's revolutionary line and policies in foreign affairs resolutely."

The announcement was made by Hsinhua, the official Chinese news agency, on behalf of the party's central committee, the central committee's military commission, the state council of the People's Republic and the standing committee of the National People's Congress. The message also urged the country to "deepen the criticism" of former Deputy Premier Teng Hsiao-ping, who had fallen from power in the political struggle that followed Premier Chou En-lai's death in January. [See pp. 482–485] The broadcast asked the Chinese to "uphold the unity and unification of the party and closely rally round the party central committee." The message did not name any possible successor to Mao.

The cause of Mao's death remained unclear, although the *Washington Post* reported Sept. 10 that Chinese officials had told one foreign visitor that Mao had suffered a stroke recently. In addition, the *New York Times* Sept. 10 quoted a Viennese doctor as saying he had been told that Mao had suffered from Parkinson's disease. Mao's last public appearance had been May 1, 1971 when he viewed a fireworks display in Peking.

Outpourings of popular grief were reported throughout China Sept. 9. The "Internationale," the socialist anthem, was played throughout Peking as 2,000 persons gathered in Tien An Men Square. Some wept openly; many wore black armbands or white mourning flowers. Front pages of Sept. 10 newspapers displayed full-page photographs of Mao bordered in black. Reports from the countryside outside Peking cited immediate work stoppages and funeral processions after the announcement. Within minutes of the broadcast, which was replayed throughout the night of Sept. 9, peasants had put on black armbands. Officials immediately scheduled eight days of memorial ceremonies, beginning Sept. 11 and ending Sept. 18. For the last day of mourning a televised memorial rally was scheduled for Tien An Men Square. Until that date, Mao's body would lie in state in the Great Hall of the People, and flags would fly at half-staff.

Mao Tse-tung was one of the 12 founders of the Chinese Communist Party in Shanghai in July 1921. The Communists were at first allied with Chiang Kai-Shek's Nationalists, but Chiang broke with the Communists in April 1927. The two groups fought a civil war during the 1930s, joined in an uneasy united front agreement when the Japanese invaded China, and resumed their civil war in 1946. The Communists eventually won, and Mao proclaimed the creation of the People's Republic of China on Oct. 1, 1949. He was named chairman of the committees of the party, government, and army.

SAN JOSE NEWS
San Jose, Calif., September 10, 1976

Chinese Communist party Chairman Mao Tse-tung was devoted to perpetual revolution. Not surprisingly, his death threatens to unleash new turmoil as leftists and moderates struggle for control of the world's most populous nation.

The ingredients for upheaval are at hand.

In a matter of months the two giants of Chinese communism, first Premier Chou En-lai and now Chairman Mao, have fallen. Those who had been viewed as Mao's most likely successors — including Chou and the late Minister of Defense Lin Piao who died in a plane crash in 1971 after an abortive coup — are gone.

The party leadership that remains is dominated by old men of much lesser stature. It is as if Mao resisted orderly succession.

In addition, China is strained by a fierce ideological struggle between those who would resist "revisionism" and those who favor a more moderate and pragmatic policy. Ironically, Mao and Chou were viewed by many China watchers as embodiments of the contrasting philosophies.

To compound uncertainty, China is struggling to recover from the scars of a devastating earthquake that may have claimed as many as a million lives while seriously crippling its mining and steel industries.

Loss of the nation's two most prominent leaders, a philosophical struggle that saw Maoists unleash a severe political attack against Deputy Premier Teng Hsiao-ping early this year, and a natural catastrophe — these are sufficient to test the stability of any government.

The announcement that foreign dignitaries will not be invited to China for Mao's memorial services indicates the outside world will be given little mind as the struggle of succession unfolds.

The ranking party leader for the moment is Premier Hua Kuo-feng. China watchers aren't even sure of Hua's age. Little is known of his early background. It was a surprise to Western observers in January when he was catapulted from sixth-ranked deputy premier and public security minister to the post of acting premier, succeeding Chou En-lai. The favorite for the post had been the now discredited Teng.

The American who may have spent the most time with Hua since his rise to prominence is former President Richard Nixon. Hua hosted the Nixons at a banquet during their Feb. 21-29 visit.

Hua is a protege of Mao and the anti-revisionists, who look with disfavor on a softening of the revolutionary fervor, but — as Mao was — he is committed to U.S.-Chinese rapprochement. In fact, at the banquet for the Nixons, he praised the former President's "farsightedness" in improving relations between the two countries. He also castigated the Soviet Union for pursuing a policy of "rabid expansionsim."

Something else was notable about that toast: Hua's acknowledgement that "a revolutionary mass debate in such circles as education, science and technology" is under way inside China as part of "a deeping of the Great Proletarian Cultural Revolution."

As long as that "debate" and the struggle of succession continue to be focused inward, the rest of the world will experience little impact from the passing of Chou and Mao. But all of us must hold our breaths for fear that an uneasy leadership could turn outward for an enemy or cause to consolidate its hold on the Chinese people.

THE SAGINAW NEWS
Saginaw, Mich., September 10, 1976

The mystique of Mao Tse-tung's god-like grip on more than 800 million mainland Chinese will not vanish with the aged revolutionary's death at 82.

World leaders with the skill and the power to attract mass following for well over a quarter of a century become legends in their time — subjects for historians to study endlessly.

Mao was all of that. Tough at times. Shrewd at others. Benign always in the eyes of his people. From the time this farmer's son led peasant troops into Peking to start Communist reform in 1949, he inspired not merely obedience but awe and reverence as well. And for most of the intervening years when he was building the new China from ashes of proletariate revolution, he held most of the world in the same grip of fascination, sometimes even

fear.

In death which comes after years of infirmities, Mao leaves one indelible reminder. There were premiers, prime ministers and pretenders during the Mao rule. There was only one chairman of the Chinese Communist party. Even with his miscalculations he survived.

Yet death is final — if it doesn't answer all questions. And in Mao's passing new questions arise with another indelible reminder. The earlier death of Chou En-lai and now that of Mao signals the end of the old guard.

What now and who now rises to take their places? These are uppermost questions in the minds of government heads, foreign diplomats and China watchers everywhere. If Mao was an enigma to some, he was an anath-

ema to others. The "others" are not sad. They hope for a severe change back to 10 years ago.

The result may be slow in coming. It may be swifter than we think. Mao may have left some direction. It may not be followed. Political unrest has been accented of late in China with Mao's declining months. But even to the end, the old revolutionary — who raised China from the ash heap to world power status — insisted he liked "class struggle."

Possibly a new struggle somewhat on that order is about to begin. The role of recently appointed Premier Hua Kuo-feng, a Mao protege, will be watched.

But however the passing of power turns out, it will have its special meaning to all governments. Not the least of them is

our own. The new era of more open relationships between the U.S. and the once closed Communist China society has been vital to improved world stability.

It was Mao who parted the bamboo curtain, Chou En-lai who played host and greeter. And it has been that which enabled the People's Republic to play off the U.S. against Russia in recent years. Clever, perhaps, but enough to keep the Soviet Union temperate at important moments in world politics.

Thus the importance of the new politics of Red China. If it pursues nothing worse than the recent course of guarded openness, if for no other reason than in the cause of "parallel interests with caution," as Henry Kissinger opines, Washington will consider it good fortune.

Chicago Tribune
Chicago, Ill., September 10, 1976

"Now that the country has become Red, who will be its guardian? Our mission, unfinished, may take a thousand years. The struggle tires us . . ."

Mao Tse-tung wrote these words last year in a poem directed to his old comrade, Prime Minister Chou En-lai, who preceded Mao in death by eight months. A quarter of a century after his soldiers had triumphed, after he had unified China as it never had been unified before, and even in the late evening of his life, Mao was still thinking of struggle.

In his long life he was many things—military leader, guiding figure of one of the bloodiest revolutions in history, organizer, poet, philosopher, and god—but most of all, he was a revolutionary. From his boyhood, when he rebelled against his father, through the years of fighting and intriguing to take over China, and into his dotage, Mao was the opponent of authority. After completing his revolution, he did not weep as Alexander the Great did because there were no more worlds to conquer; instead he proclaimed that the revolution was not complete. It would go on forever.

Thus, in the 1960s he inflamed the Red Guards and plunged China into a "Cultural Revolution" which almost turned the country upside down. Yet it eventually ended, falling far short of the thousand year struggle he preferred.

His antagonism toward any authority except his own may even have extended to his choice of a successor. More than one was chosen—and then rejected. First there was Liu Shao-chi, who was head of state for eight years but who was found wanting during the Cultural Revolution. Next Lin Piao was anointed, only to die in a mysterious plane crash after being accused of trying to assassinate Mao. More recently, Teng Hsiao-ping was brought back from limbo—and then returned to it. So, at his death Thursday, Mao remained without a clear successor, and there was wide speculation about who would take his place.

Probably, the best answer is that no one will take his place, or can. As Robert Payne, the author and student of China, once wrote: Mao "alone possessed the charismatic power to induce the entire population to follow him blind-

ly. No doubt another dictatorship will be formed, but it will lack the authority which is vested in his person and in his name, for he was the sole ruler, the single emperor, and there is no one who can replace him."

That is very likely true, in the sense that no one in the Soviet Union ever replaced Lenin. He had successors but not replacements. For one thing, dictatorships are not easily bequeathable. Stalin was not the early favorite to succeed Lenin, and Khrushchev was scarcely mentioned in the first speculation after Stalin died.

If it is fruitless to speculate about Mao's successor, it is easier, for the short range, at least, to predict what his death may mean in foreign affairs, what it may mean to the United States and the world. It is generally thought, for example, that China's differences with the Soviet Union are so deep and painful that no conciliatory steps can be expected soon. China is wary about Soviet expansionism and fears encirclement. This is important, because the continued split of those countries improves the U.S. position. The world would be far more dangerous for us if they were allies.

China's domestic course is harder to predict—yet in large measure it will determine Mao's place in history. History can be fickle in judging a man's stature. If a moderate internal policy is pursued, the world's most populous country may at last settle down and consolidate the economic, agricultural, and industrial gains made since the Communists took power. If that happens, history will probably remember Mao as a unifier and a conqueror of starvation and corruption; the millions who were trampled to death in his march to power will slip from memory.

If more radical elements from the so-called Shanghai group come to the fore, China will probably continue to have internal upheavals and the ultimate outcome will be uncertain. History may then remember Mao as the bloody revolutionary rather than as the constructive leader. And with *that* Mao will be remembered a quotation which seems to sum up his belief in the desirability of eternal struggle: "There is turmoil in the heavens; the situation is excellent."

THE DAILY OKLAHOMAN
Oklahoma City, Okla., September 10, 1976

DEATH has come to Mao Tsetung at 82. The oldest of the world's absolute dictators, Mao represented a sort of benevolent emperor to many outside China, and a demi-god to those hundreds of millions who had known no other leadership for the past quarter of a century. His brand of communism has been called Maoism. It is a way of life unlike anything in modern human history. Whether it can survive its founder and teacher is a question that only time will tell.

To some Western intellectuals in search of one living Communist philosopher who could be held in reverence, Mao was the epitome of idealism in action. To his victims—and they were many—he was the embodiment of Satan. To millions of Chinese, he was the father figure who had welded the far-flung Chinese people into a single nation-empire for the first time in ages—perhaps ever.

The Little Red Book, "Quotations from Chairman Mao," and its more complete counterpart, "The Thoughts of Mao," were used as missals and for meditation by millions who had learned to read by reading excerpts of his writings and speeches. There were liberal sprinklings of moralist teachings, economic homilies preaching thrift and productivity, and advice on how to help one's fellow man. There were also many citations from his writings about the necessity for constant warfare against the evils of capitalism, private property, and personal ambition. There is no question of the effect these books have had on millions of Chinese. They have become subservient to a degree unthinkable in most nations, but most have willingly done the leader's bidding after learning their lessons well.

The price of establishing communism in China after the military victory of 1949 did not become immediately apparent to the outside world. But between 1955 and 1965, international civil rights study groups published a series of summaries of the Peking regime's own figures, and the result was horrifying. By the Mao government's own reckoning, it had been necessary to eliminate—by their deaths—some 15 million Chinese. The victims of this "purification of the people" were described as "notorious landlords and religionists, exploiters of the people," etc. But with their deaths, there were no opposition groups left to espouse Christian, Buddhist, or Confucian ideas of duty, deity, or personal responsibility. Only Mao's thoughts remained—it was assumed.

While Mainland China established an economy like that of Egypt under the Pharoahs, the "other China" on Taiwan built modern cities, shipyards, factories, nuclear power plants, turnpikes and a wholly different society. Taipeh warned the rest of the world that Mao's regime was a threat, and dreamed of the day it would end. But gradually, Mao and Chou En-Lai won seats at international councils, and broke down the strong opposition to recognition of Peking's legitimacy. Taiwan's frustration has grown as Maoism survived the death of Chou and other upheavals. Its grip today is supposed to be tight.

There are indications of increased decay of that hold, however. Bank robberies and other crimes are increasing. Some of the outer provinces are reported almost self-governing under warlords like in the "old China" of 50 years ago.

Mao is dead. Maoism lives. But it runs counter to the natural aspirations of mankind. Will it survive?

The Topeka Daily Capital
Topeka, Kans., September 12, 1976

The death Thursday of Chinese Communist Party Chairman Mao Tse-tung marked the end of one era and the beginning of another for the world's most populous nation.

Mao, who for decades has been an ideological enemy of America and the West, must nonetheless be recognized as one of history's most dynamic leaders; a man who raised millions of people from the chaos of feudalism to the order and prosperity of industrialized society.

It is ironic to consider, in that vein, that Mao, as one of the foremost leaders of the international "revolution of the proletariat" accomplished little more or less than to westernize China in the image of the social order he sought to overthrow. And that Mao, who was through his life dedicated to the advance of communism, opened China to the world finally through Richard Nixon, who for most of his life was dedicated to opposing communism.

It is possible, therefore, to view Mao as a national leader of vision, no matter what one may think of his politics.

Mao's death leaves a great vacuum in China's upper echelons, and the rush of wind to fill that vacuum may well prove violent and convulsive for that nation. Unfortunately China is still such a mystery to most of the West that we have no way of knowing just what might occur in the weeks and months ahead. Our recently improved relations with China may remain unchanged with the chairman's death. They may vanish, and they may improve further still.

The storm has already begun, apparently. The day before Mao died, sources reported political rifts had become so serious in China that the government was taking unusual steps to mollify the masses. And immediately after Mao's death, the party's central committee issued an appeal for unity, obviously anticipating further political power plays.

The world's eyes and ears will be attentive to the situation in China for some time to come, but just as with the massive earthquake that ripped China's land apart, the Chinese may remain secretive about the effects of Mao's death, the political consequences of which will prove surely as massive a convulsion for China's society as was the earthquake for China's soil.

ALBUQUERQUE JOURNAL
Albuquerque, N.M., September 10, 1976

Mao Tse-Tung — for good, for evil and for widely devious combinations of the two — was perhaps the most dynamic and accomplished leader of human society to rise in the 20th century, a century that stands alone for its elevation of giants among men.

Only in historic perspective can the quality and the wisdom of Mao's leadership be evaluated objectively. None of his contemporaries can say today that there was a better course then the one he chose in achieving the unity and the collective greatness of a quarter of the world's population.

But while history tediously unfolds the perspective, the long impending passing of Mao Tse-tung precipitates immediate crises, challenges and — springing from those crises and challenges — opportunities for men and nations to fill the vacuums and bridge the voids that will result from the termination of his leadership.

Within China itself, the struggle for power among Mao's own lieutenants could generate world-wide repercussions. Mao's lifetime work could be nullified, or it could prove to be the foundation for China's ascent to world leadership.

And the outcome of that struggle poses momentous decisions, the nature and the expediency for which are not predictable, for every other nation, including the United States.

For this reason alone, Mao's passing must be viewed as a crisis in itself — one imposing on the United States an urgent need for dynamic leadership — a leadership characterized by perception, wisdom and the judgment to know when and how to act.

THE DALLAS TIMES HERALD
Dallas, Tex., September 10, 1976

MAO TSE-TUNG, a peasant's son who became a poet, a political philosopher, a military strategist and the architect and founder of Chinese communism, always denied that he was his country's indispensable man.

"How can the death of a single person be such a tremendous loss?" he used to ask. "There is no such thing. Man always must die . . . We must be prepared at all times to leave our work posts, and we must be ready with successors at all times."

Few men knew death as intimately as he. He assumed leadership of his party in a time of death, while the Communist army was in retreat before Generalissimo Chiang Kai-shek in 1936. When the 8,000 miles from China's east coast to Shensi province were crossed and the "Long March" was over, 100,000 of Mao's 120,000 soldiers were dead.

He knew death during World War II, and during the civil war against his old rival Chiang which ended with Communist victory in 1949. And Mao slaughtered millions to consolidate his rule over the country and the party.

Now he is dead, too. And China will decide how tremendous its loss is. The "work post" that Mao left is huge. Who will be the successor to a man who, even his foes must admit, was one of the giants of his century?

For the Communist leaders of China have been united only in their reverence and fear of him. By periodic purges and nationwide cataclysms such as the Cultural Revolution of 1966-69, he kept potential rivals off balance, simultaneously holding the Soviet Union at bay along the 5,000-mile border between the jealous Communist giants, finally opening the Chinese door to his old enemies, Richard Nixon and the Americans.

Now, just as China seems to have outlived its outlaw image in the community of nations, the man who made it an outlaw — and a world power — is gone.

"You must not always think that you alone will do," he used to say, "and that everything done by others is no good, as if without you in the world, the earth would not turn and there would be no party."

But years of intrigue and tumult might pass before his true successor emerges. And no one can say how China is about to change, nor what new role it will play tomorrow in our dangerous world.

THE INDIANAPOLIS NEWS
Indianapolis, Ind., September 10, 1976

For a generation Mao Tse-tung presided as the Chinese people's unchallenged leader, their father figure, and at times it seemed their god.

His presence pervaded Chinese society through giant posters and heroic statues. His little red book of earthy sayings became its bible. His maxims were the standard to which every aspect of Chinese life had to conform on penalty of death or other stern sanctions.

Now, at age 82, Chairman Mao is gone. The small "g" god of China has gone the way, as the Bible puts it, "of all flesh."

A society which has lost such a pervasive personage is bound to go through a period of instability, self-doubt, and re-appraisal. A struggle for power is the immediate prosepect, followed by changes in the institutional structures and methods of governing, as Chinese society gradually frees itself from its Maoist straitjacket.

Chairman Mao asserted his personal leadership by the device of "continuing revolution." It exacted over the years a fearful price in human lives, and it inhibited the genius and productive capacity of the Chinese people. But it kept him in power.

There is no likely successor to Mao in this sense. There is presently no leader on the Chinese scene with a mass following sufficiently strong to keep the Communist party bureaucracy in a constant state of upheaval. The long-term outlook is for bureaucrats and technocrats to assert themselves, with emphasis on production rather than revolution.

The potential dangers of the transition period, however, are real and immediate. The West must be prepared for the possibility of diversionary actions by China's new leaders. It is a time for U.S. vigilance in the western Pacific and a strong reaffirmation of commitments to Taiwan and South Korea, lest the new Chinese leaders be tempted into military adventures to consolidate their position at home.

Another challenge to American diplomacy is the possible inclination of the Chinese Communist party, without Mao, to revert to its ties with the Soviet Union, giving the Communist bloc a monolithic stance once again.

Without Mao, China could develop along more normal, humane lines. But, unhindered by Maoist maxim and myth, it could also become a formidable military power.

St. Petersburg Times

St. Petersburg, Fla., September 10, 1976

In death as in life, Mao Tse-tung is not an easy man for Westerners to measure. He was at once a conceited dictator and a visionary leader, a better than average poet and a politician whose concepts were totally alien to Western values, especially as they relate to individual initiative and freedom.

HE WAS THE son of a peasant who accomplished a feat many thought impossible. He organized one fourth of the world's population into an entity with which the world's most powerful nations have been unable to deal effectively. They can't even understand it.

In China, Mao is nothing less than a god. In all the world, he must be recognized as one of the Twentieth Century's most effective leaders of men and women.

Mao built a Communist society upon a framework laid down by Marx and Lenin. Yet his version was distinctive. It has allowed to exist factions with different opinions on how to attain China's goals, factions that sometimes seem almost like political parties.

Like so many strong leaders, Mao was unable to leave a successor so China now faces the most difficult of all political problems, the transfer of political power. The unanswered question is how China's leadership, without the unifying force of a living god, will manage a contradictory system that on the one hand provides for dissent but on the other is rigidly totalitarian.

AFTER THE long march to the Yenan Valley that ended in 1935, Mao's home was a cave. Whatever the future holds for China, that country can be expected always to carry the imprint of the man who slept in that cave on a crude bed made of planks stretched across two sawhorses.

WINSTON-SALEM JOURNAL

Winston-Salem, N.C., September 10, 1976

In recent years, predictions of Mao Tse-Tung's impending demise became more regular than the Chairman's purges of political foes. The predictions regularly flopped, of course — so often that rumors about Mao's failing health were a sure sign of his real robustness. Ironically, Mao died this week at the age of 82 during one of those periods when his physical condition was not the subject of speculation.

No matter: Speculation enough on other subjects will now ensue, for the death of Mao is a watershed event of vast consequence for the People's Republic of China. Grief — genuine grief — will flow from the souls of the Chinese people in a display of mourning beyond Western comprehension. A god, the only god of the Chinese, has died, and the foundations of the PRC will be shaken.

For Mao was the PRC, and vice versa: from the Long March in the 1930s to the defeat of the Nationalist Chinese in the 1940s to the Great Leap Forward in the 1950s to the Cultural Revolution in the 1960s to the rapprochement with the United States in the 1970s. Through all that, Mao wielded god-like power, killing and creating, building and destroying, winning and losing and winning. He dragged a country steeped in backwardness and barbarity into the 20th Century. He made a nation of the world's largest population grouping. He guided China to military and technological viability. And he gave his people a material well-being they had never known before. He revolutionized China, and when he feared the pace of change was too fast or the quality of change too Western, he revolutionized the revolution by purge and mass purification.

But Mao's accomplishments came at an awful price. He took a spirited people and subordinated them entirely to his will. Those who would not be broken were executed. Those who erred were purged. In the end, Mao presided over a nation of semi-robots who had never known true freedom before him, and certainly will never know it after him. That part of the Chinese character that was nourished in Nationalist China in creating a quasi-democracy was stamped out in the PRC to create an absolute Communist tyranny.

And now the Mao men mourn. Their sadness at this moment, however, will give way to even deeper grief. For Mao, both as god and tyrant, was unique in the Chinese system, and hence irreplaceable. A power struggle within the PRC's hierarchy is inevitable — a power struggle far more vicious than any to date.

Just last January, the Chinese system was severely strained as a result of the death of Premier Chou En-lai. Chou was widely supposed to be Mao's chosen successor. His death ended that possibility, and led to a desperate fight between Chou's own supposed successor, Teng Hsiao-ping, and the ultimate victor, now-Premier Hua Kuo-feng. Hua in turn is seemingly first in line today for Mao's powers.

But Mao committed himself to no one publicly before his death this week, so chances for an orderly succession are remote. Hua will fight and perhaps win, but the Chinese hierarchy and the Chinese people will necessarily be ravaged in the process. The precise dimensions of the wounds to come are subject to speculation, but this is not: In life, Mao's essence was revolution; in death, revolution is his legacy.

THE BLADE

Toledo, Ohio, September 11, 1976

"There are no straight roads in the world; we must be prepared to follow a road which twists and turns . . ."
—Chairman Mao Tse-tung

WHATEVER the effects of the death of Mao Tse-tung on the leadership of China, they probably will not become visible to western eyes for some time to come. But they could be vitally important to the United States because China, under Chairman Mao, has been a balance wheel between the two superpowers, this country and the Soviet Union. Which way that wheel tips in the future could have a profound effect on global relationships as they now exist.

There is no question that many of Mr. Mao's twists and turns were of his own making. But what is unmistakably clear is the tremendous impact the chairman has had on his nation and on the outside world as well. Few men in history, in fact, have left a stronger imprint on their own countries as has Chairman Mao, who died at 82 after having led the Chinese Communist party for 50 years and China itself for more than 25.

It is impossible, for instance, to think of modern China without equating it with Mao Tse-tung and remembering his party's famous Long March of 1934-35, his abortive Great Leap Forward of the late 1950s, and his controversial Cultural Revolution of the mid-1960s. His great accomplishment was that he literally single-handedly dragged China into the 20th century in the less than three decades that the People's Republic has been in existence.

One does not transform a nation of 800 million people in that length of time, of course, by cajoling or pussyfooting. His revolution left a bloody trail of victims, and Mr. Mao was regarded as a master manipulator of power. He is quoted, in fact, as having remarked that "political power grows out of the barrel of a gun." In the process, however, he lifted China far beyond anything it had known previously in material terms and he became almost deified by the masses of that country.

Beyond China's borders, the enigmatic Chairman Mao's influence was most fundamentally felt in his ideological break with the Soviet Union in the early 1950s. In one stroke, he ended the monolithic character of world communism and injected a new dimension into the relationship between the United States and the USSR.

The precarious global balance thus created leaned dramatically in America's favor following the 1972 visit of former President Nixon to Peking and the formulation of the so-called Shanghai Communique, which spelled out a new understanding. Although Sino-American relations have cooled somewhat since then, the Chinese anti-Soviet stance has remained firm. How the new leadership in Peking deals with that situation will be a matter of considerable interest and no little apprehension to the United States and other western nations.

CARTER WINS PRESIDENTIAL ELECTION; DEMOCRATS RETAIN LEAD IN CONGRESS

Democrat James Earl Carter Jr. plucked the presidency from the Republican incumbent Gerald Rudolph Ford Nov. 2 in one of the closest presidential elections of the century. Sen. Walter F. Mondale (Minn.) was elected vice president on the Carter ticket. Ford's running mate was Sen. Robert J. Dole (Kan.).

Carter, 52, of Plains, Ga. was the first man from the Deep South to be elected president since the Civil War. Ford became the first president to lose since Herbert Hoover was beaten by Franklin D. Roosevelt in 1932 during the Great Depression. It was the eighth time in the nation's 200 years that an incumbent was defeated. Carter's inauguration as the nation's 39th President was set for Jan. 20, 1977.

Carter won 23 states and the District of Columbia with 297 electoral votes—27 more than the required majority of 270. Ford won 27 states with 241 electoral votes. The margin in popular votes was greater. Carter got 40,287,283, or 51%; Ford 38,557,855, or 48% (unofficial totals). The voter turnout of 80 million was the largest in U.S. history. Preliminary estimates put participation at 53.3% of those eligible, down from 1972's 55.4% figure. In 1960, a record 62.8% of the electorate voted.

Carter's victory was based on a sweep of the South and the Border states. He added a tier of industrial states in the Northeast—New York, Pennsylvania, Massachusetts, Delaware and Rhode Island—Texas and the liberal Middle West states of Wisconsin and Minnesota. In the West he won only Hawaii. But that state's four electoral votes, along with Mississippi's seven, were among the last to fall to Carter and gave him the almost bare majority of 272 after an agonizing hold for hours just short of victory. Ohio was added to the Carter column later in the day, pushing his electoral vote total to the final 297. In state after state, the margin between the candidates was wafer thin. In Ohio, the edge was 1%, as it was in Mississippi, California, Pennsylvania, Iowa and New Jersey. In Maine and Oregon, the difference was less than 1%.

Voters Nov. 2 elected a House with virtually the same party lineup as in the preceding House, once again granting the Democrats a 2–1 majority. The results represented a consolidation of Democratic strength and a reversal of the political tendency reflected in the congressional elections of 1960 and 1966. In those years, Republicans had recouped losses sustained in the previous election.

The Democrats maintained their 3–2 edge in the Senate. There were changes in party control for 14 of the 33 seats that were filled Nov. 2, but gains balanced losses so that the partisan lineup for the Senate of the 95th Congress matched that for the 94th. (New York's Sen. James Buckley, who was defeated in his bid for reelection, had been counted as a Republican in the Senate lineup although he had been elected as a Conservative.)

Los Angeles Times

Los Angeles, Calif., November 4, 1976

In choosing Jimmy Carter as their 39th President, the people have said many things. The clearest of them, we believe, is that they prefer the unknown of a Carter administration to the continuation of President Ford's policies.

The people said they wanted change, and stronger leadership to effect that change.

We are going through hard times, and Carter's call for a reordering of economic and social priorities was more credible than Ford's insistence that his present policies would, over the long run, put the country back on its feet and distribute its bounty more equitably.

We are going through cynical times, and Carter's call for national reconciliation and for greater integrity in Washington was more credible than Ford's insistence that he already had led the nation out of the despair of Watergate and that the institutions of government were no longer suspect.

Most voters could not agree with Ford's complacent vision of the country, and thought they saw in Carter a hope for more realistic and aggressive leadership.

There may have been other factors in Carter's victory. His choice of a running mate may have been decisive in such a close election. Walter F. Mondale obviously was the more acceptable of the potential inheritors of the Presidency, in sharp contrast to the inadequate Robert Dole.

But the country's desire for change probably was the main determinant. No one attributes qualities of greatness to Ford, but most Americans knew what they could or could not expect of this sincere and likable man.

Yet the triumph went, instead, to the candidate the voters didn't know as well, and with whom they seem to have felt a deepening sense of unease as time ran out before the election. His winning margin was much narrower than was forecast in the early polls.

But despite a vigorously fought campaign, the country appears to have come out of the election without rancorous division. Ford's generous concession set the tone for what should be an amicable and orderly transfer of power. "You have my complete and wholehearted support," he told the winner. ". . . I believe we must now put the divisions of the campaign behind us and unite the country once again in the common pursuit of peace and prosperity." And Carter paid tribute to Ford for what he is, "A good, a decent man."

The candidates' disagreements during the campaign were many and vigorous, but none is likely to harm the prospect for consensus in this country or the integrity of our commitments to other nations.

Finally, it must be said that Carter's achievement was a remarkable one, and a measure of his energy and tenacity. Two years ago, he was an almost anonymous former governor of Georgia. But he was willing to work harder and longer than all the other potential Democratic nominees, many of them with national followings. He overcame the bias against Southern politicians. He spoke to the people's frustrations over the remoteness and seeming indifference of government, and to their hope that their voices could and would be heard. And with that message, and with a genius for political organization, he was able to claim the leadership of his party, and now of the nation.

The more difficult challenges lie ahead. It is now up to Carter to apply the same energy, tenacity and persuasiveness to the Presidency that he did to the struggle to win it, and to fulfill the many promises he has made to his fellow citizens.

THE SAGINAW NEWS
Saginaw, Mich., November 3, 1976

Jimmy Carter's long night climb to presidential election as the soon-to-be 39th chief executive of the United States will put a famous smile in the White House and undoubtedly usher in a new approach to national problems such as unemployment, inflation, crime, tax and social reform.

We trust that in the 80 days ahead before Mr. Carter takes the oath of highest office, he will recapture the vigor drained from him in a long and arduous campaign that has led him from the plains to the pinnacle. He may need that. And he has earned it.

No man, within our memory, seeking the presidency ever put as much of himself into it than Mr. Carter. Actually his victory culminates an effort begun four years ago. It was launched in quiet talks with close friends and in a great deal of soul searching. It escalated into a hard decision — and finally into a nonstop meet-the-people campaign of close to two years in duration.

Thus Mr. Carter's victory is no accident. It was meticulously drafted, implemented and fought for by a man who showed indefatigable campaign energy and bulldog determination blended with a pleasing sort of self-confidence.

More the quality of his victory that he defeated a man holding the presidency and one of Gerald R. Ford's stature.

Carter's victory as of today's early unofficial tabulation is not large. This was the hard, close election that was predicted. What was not predicted was the national enthusiasm for it. But Mr. Carter's victory, if no overwhelming mandate, is sufficient — both in the popular vote and electoral columns.

And like all presidential elections, it will be inspected and dissected for weeks to determine why and how a virtually unknown outsider from Georgia, a former governor and a peanut farmer from Plains, beat all of the odds to beat an incumbent president. And why an incumbent president could not have fared better.

There are hundreds of answers for that. Just quickly, three occur. Carter made the most of his arguments that the country needed a fresh start in the White House. He capitalized on a soggy domestic economy. And he appealed to sufficient numbers of independent voters to pull him through. Simply, he put all of that together with a solid coalition of labor and minority support.

And now to the future. Mr. Carter has made many promises to the people. They are mapped out in an imposing array of changes he intends to institute over the next four years.

His interests range from achieving greater federal tax equity, a balanced federal budget and getting people back to work to national health care, reforming the federal bureaucracy and the Pentagon budget — and granting greater protection to the consumer and the environment.

This is hardly a modest blueprint. It evokes skepticism in many places. Yet he impresses us as a man of action and ideas, this first southerner in a century to win the presidency. And as a Democrat, he will have a Democratic Congress to work with. That will ease his path some. But to achieve he will need the vigor, good health, wisdom and basic decency so evident in his campaign.

We congratulate James Earl Carter — or Jimmy as he prefers it — and offer him our prayers for success in the great burden of the presidency he will shortly assume. In defeat, we salute a gracious and good loser — Gerald Ford — who did so much in so short a time to restore public faith in the dignity of the office he will soon vacate for his successor.

We are certain a nation shares with us these sentiments.

CHARLESTON EVENING POST
Charleston, S.C., November 4, 1976

With a Democrat in the White House and Congress still strongly Democratic, the political power in Washington again is in the hands of a single party. Responsibility will be clearcut, and there should be no question about whom to praise or blame for the good and bad things that may be happening after the inauguration of Jimmy Carter.

Hoping for the best, we also believe in balancing the contending forces of politics lest the country be pushed into undesirable extremes of any variety.

Picking up the pieces after defeat of Gerald Ford will be a hard assignment for the Republican Party. The closeness of the election does not, in our judgment, signal the death of the party, as some people have feared.

It cannot be denied, nevertheless, that recapture of the South as a Democratic province has provided a strong base of power. Whether the South will stay solid is a question we cannot answer.

Manipulation of a bloc vote, including both whites and blacks, requires great skill.

As the leader of the party, Jimmy Carter has demonstrated professional dexterity.

It would be hard to believe, however, that smooth sailing will continue indefinitely. Difficult decisions lie ahead. Not all of them will be pleasing to everybody.

The closeness of the presidential election confirms that our people are deeply divided on many political issues. Had Gerald Ford been a more appealing candidate, the outcome might have been different. When Jimmy Carter takes the helm, he no longer can play the part of popular candidate, promising all things to everybody.

As loyal Americans, all of us will want to rally around our leaders. We have a right to demand that they behave like leaders of the Republic, not vote-chasers in a campaign.

The Ottawa Citizen
Ottawa, Ont., November 3, 1976

So it is going to be President Jimmy Carter for the next four years, and probably eight, and that means that the American people have a new, untried but promising leader.

The president-elect has promised to unify the nation and he has a good chance now that Vietnam and even Watergate belong to the history books. President Ford owed his being in the White House to the Watergate scandal, and his pardoning of former president Richard Nixon cost him much support. As Carter prepares to take over, all this is left behind. A new era begins, with the Democrats in control of the White House, the House of Representatives and the Senate.

It is far from clear what kind of president Carter will make. Americans themselves have their doubts and that is a prime factor in why Carter, who once led in the polls by 33 per cent, barely won what had become a very tight race.

Carter stood for motherhood issues — open government, tax reforms, more jobs, help to the cities, control of inflation, the fight against pollution, war against waste, and so on. How these issues will be tackled remains very much to be seen.

Nor is it known who the main pillars of a Carter administration will be. What is clear is that there is no going back.

Under the Ford administration, Americans had overcome much of the Watergate shock as well as the economic recession. Ford had taken the nation well on the road to recovery in both the political and economic fields. Carter pledged to do better and, given his party's control of Congress, should be able to do so.

For a president who was appointed to the post, and that too by Nixon, Ford had done remarkably well — especially since he is from the minority Republican party. But in the end his own mistakes, perhaps more so than Carter's attacks, convinced the voters that Carter was the more promising leader.

The election was much too close for Carter to feel that he has a clear mandate from the people. But the issues he raised drew a responsive chord.

The U.S. today is at peace. More Americans are working than ever before. The inflation rate has been halved to 6 per cent. But all of this is not good enough.

The world today is still an insecure and unjust place. Eight per cent of Americans are out of work. Inflation is putting more and more people in the ghettos of poverty.

Carter now has his chance.

Canadians, with such close ties to the United States, can only watch and hope that the new U.S. leader is able to perform as effectively as he says he will.

The Evening Gazette

Worcester, Mass.,
November 3, 1976

Jimmy Carter's victory yesterday capped one of the most extraordinary political chapters in the American history book. Against all the rules, flouting all the conventional ideas about presidential campaigns, this man from the hamlet of Plains, Georgia, has captured the mightiest office in the world.

Just why a majority of the voters decided on Carter will be debated for months. But it was perhaps a combination of positive, if confused, feelings about C a r t e r, and a reluctance to see Gerald Ford in the White House for another four years. Although Ford made an amazing comeback in the last weeks of the campaign, the memories of Watergate, the feeling that it was time for a change, and doubts about the ability of Ford to provide forceful leadership combined to tip the scales against him.

Just what kind of president Carter will be cannot be answered, as is always the case when a new candidate makes it to the White House. But Carter is a particularly difficult man to fathom. Although he has made himself clear on some issues, he has seemed to straddle others, some of them very important. Some who voted for him think of him as essentially conservative. That was the impression he gave during his primary campaign. But others voted for him because of the more liberal stands he espoused in the last weeks of the campaign. At this point, it is impossible to say whether he plans to plunge into big spending programs financed by a looser money policy or whether he intends to make good on balancing the budget, as he has promised a number of times. Our feeling is that Carter is essentially a pragmatist, and that he will not be tied down to traditional party policies.

The loss of this election, just when it seemed that he might win it at the last moment, was a cruel disappointment for President Ford. Yet, ironically, Ford may be the most popular defeated candidate in our history, liked by just about everybody. Although the American people decided narrowly that they did not want to give him and his party another four years in the White House, there is a deep feeling of gratitude for the calm and steady way he handled things after the Watergate fiasco. His place in history is assured, along with his place in the hearts of the people.

So another presidential election goes down in the history books. In turning out in far larger numbers t h a n expected, the American people confounded their critics again. Down deep they may be angry, c o n f u s e d, suspicious and dubious about politics. But they are not apathetic. They do care more than anyone can measure about the United States of America.

The Evening Bulletin

Philadelphia, Pa., November 3, 1976

The people can take a lot of satisfaction out of the way things went in yesterday's presidential election.

For one thing, the turnout was far better than had been expected. Just as important, the fact that the popular vote has been so close between Gerald R. Ford and James Earl (Jimmy) Carter, Jr., shows that the millions who did vote did a lot of soul searching, and cast their ballots carefully and critically. And this is all to the good.

The people can take satisfaction from the fact that in the year of our nation's Bicentennial we have chosen as our next President the first person from the Deep South since Civil War's Reconstruction Period. This should, we hope, wipe out the last traces of the bitterness remaining from that struggle of more than a century ago.

It was good to hear Mr. Carter, in a pre-Dawn talk to his supporters, pledge to help bring all of the people of the nation together. It was reassuring to hear him pledge to tap the greatness that is in the American people to make America itself greater.

The uncertainty during the morning hours was probably irksome to many, but we should remember that since we last voted for president, we have seen two presidents and three vice presidents. Our top law enforcement agencies, the military and some giant corporations as well as the Congress have been tainted with scandal.

President Ford was certainly hurt, in the final days of the campaign, by the fact that few of the economic indicators supported his claim that we had "turned the corner" on what has been a severe economic decline.

In addition, Mr. Ford's failure to call upon the people to make real sacrifices, as part his pledge to cut back on government spending, left many wondering whether he really possessed the necessary leadership qualities.

What the people were seeking yesterday, then, was the leader they thought could do the better job of making our government work, and they made their choice without any seeming bitterness or partisan rancor. One reason for this is that many voters apparently were still making up their minds as they actually entered the polling places.

The uncertainty that went on the morning continued for so long, while disappointing to many eager for all of the final details, shows that the American people are making their post-Watergate judgments very, very carefully.

And the likelihood is that the next president will be watched even more critically in twe years just ahead. This is as it should be as we move into our next century of our national history.

St. Louis Review

St. Louis, Mo., November 5, 1976

A lackluster campaign was climaxed by an interesting and even exciting election as the American people voted strongly for the Democratic Party and selected as their new president Jimmy Carter.

The pundits and pollsters, who were about as right and about as wrong in this election as they usually are, will argue whether Jimmy Carter won the election and brought a strongly Democratic Congress along with him or whether the Democratic Party won the election and swept Carter into office in the process. In any event, Mr. Carter will be our new president, and he brings to the office a stamp indisputably his own.

His campaign was based strongly upon moral commitment. Mr. Carter reflects much of the populist political philosophy that believes that government exists to assist the individual directly. Mr. Carter believes, he says, that unemployment is demeaning to the human person and is morally wrong, and so he promises to combat unemployment, even at some risk of inflation. Mr. Carter believes that every family should have access to decent housing, and so he promises to work to provide that housing, even at some risk to the free economic market.

We hope that this moral concern of Mr. Carter will extend to even other areas. Mr. Carter has said that he believes abortion to be wrong, that government should not fund abortions and that government should do everything possible to minimize abortions. We would rather see him go further and translate this moral concern into action to prevent abortions in the same strong manner in which he promises to prevent unemployment and housing inadequacy.

We are also concerned by Mr. Carter's revival of cold war rhetoric in the campaign. We hope that his bellicosity was intended for the consumption of potential voters and that his presidency will reflect a courageous search for peace rather than a destructive and fearful preparation for war.

Every American—including American Catholics who apparently were cool in their support of Mr. Carter—will pray for his success and that of the country which he leads.

We will all also remember the very real contributions to American history of Gerald Ford. For most of us, the degradation of American government represented by Watergate is past history. Yet it was only two short years ago that we were a nation shamed by the resignation of a vice-president, the indictment of high government officials and even the resignation of a president. In a competent, quiet way, Mr. Ford reflected the essential decency of most Americans and restored very quickly a respect for government and a pride in America, reflected in the outburst of patriotism celebrating the nation's Bicentennial. Unelected, "a Ford, not a Lincoln" by his own admission, and defeated in his attempt to be an elected president, Mr. Ford's place in history is nevertheless a crucial one. He served his country exceedingly well and America is better because of him.

—*Father Edward J. O'Donnell*

DESERET NEWS
Salt Lake City, Utah, November 3, 1976

Jimmy Carter has done for Southerners what John F. Kennedy did for Roman Catholics.

That is, by his efforts the former Georgia governor has opened up presidential politics to 50 million Southerners whom custom and prejudice have long excluded from the White House.

For the first time in this century, a man from the Deep South has won this nation's highest office, ousting a sitting President in the process.

In one of the closest and most tense presidential races of modern times, Mr. Carter demonstrated that even a one-term governor with determination and a hard-working staff can seize control of a national party from better-known politicians and win the right to occupy the White House for the next four years.

If there is a lesson in this experience for other candidates, it's that there is no substitute for starting as early as the day after election and not letting up if the natural head start of one's competitors is to be overcome.

At the same time, Mr. Carter has brought at least a temporary end to divided government, with Congress in control of one party and the White House in the hands of the other — a condition that has existed for 14 of the past 24 years.

But in the understandable euphoria over his victory, President-elect Carter needs to keep certain points firmly in mind:

First, despite a high rate of unemployment and the lull in the economic recovery, there clearly is really not much dissatisfaction among Americans. Not when an election is as close as Tuesday night's cliff-hanger was.

Second, with a mandate as narrow and as subject to erosion as his is, the Carter administration should go extremely slow in instituting anything that can be interpreted as sharp changes in the direction of government programs. America is still best governed the same way elections are normally won: By appealing to the broad segment of the public in the middle of the political spectrum, rather than to the extremes.

Third, despite his appearance in three televised debates and even though his staff issued dozens of position papers, many Americans still perceive Jimmy Carter as a man without a detailed blueprint for his administration. That image helps explain the large segment of supposedly undecided voters so late in the campaign.

To some extent this continuing lack of specifics represents an attempt to please as many voters as possible, no matter how diverse they are. To an extent this situation also reflects Carter's conviction from the outset that 1976 wasn't an "issue" year; rather, it was a time when Americans were looking for someone from outside Washington to help restore faith in government. But faith can feed on promises of integrity and preachments of love only so long. And Mr. Carter has lost some of the look of an outsider by aligning himself with such old Democratic politicians as Chicago Mayor Richard Daley. The real Jimmy Carter has got to start standing up now. The Oval Office is no place for anyone without real convictions.

Fourth, if Mr. Carter is to make good on his promises to balance the budget, formulate an energy policy, and reduce an overgrown federal bureaucracy, he will have to work through a Democratic Congress that is responsible for creating some of the very problems he proposes to attack. Americans could soon discover that divided government is not necessarily an aberration to be avoided at all costs, and that unless Congress is changed, little else will change either.

Fifth, more than a little humility is in order from a man who saw a lead of 30% in the polls dwindle to almost the vanishing point in only two months. Some erosion set in as Mr. Carter pretended so many things were wrong with America it became increasingly hard to believe him. Still more erosion set in as he came to look more liberal in a nation where, according to the latest poll, 51% of the public rates itself conservative, 12% middle of the road, and only 37% liberal. With even a slightly better economy, the outcome Tuesday could have been quite different.

With his victory, Jimmy Carter has shown himself to be one of this century's most remarkable political figures. As little as a year ago few Americans had ever heard of him. His victory in the presidential sweepstakes is a triumph of personality, perseverance, and intelligence. For all our sakes, let's hope he wears as well during the next four years as he has during the past 12 months.

The Washington Star
and Daily News
Washington, D.C., November 4, 1976

Even on ordinary inauguration days, no ritual so well expresses the nature of our political system as the peaceful replacement of one President by another. Vast power shifts quietly from one party to another; the only shots are fired by ceremonial guns.

That moment, solemn enough at ordinary times, will be exceptionally so when Gov. Jimmy Carter takes his oath as 39th President next January, having defeated President Ford by a whisker. Not only will a sitting President involuntarily give up his office for the first time since 1933; his successor will be the first man of the Old South to win the presidency on his own since before the Civil War. In this transition, then, both sadness and pride will be mingled.

For many of us, it will be sad to bid farewell to President Ford. He has served us well. He came to the White House at a grim time when nerves were frayed and spirits cast down by war and scandal. He will leave it enhanced by a generous presence. And he will leave it knowing that his good work is not unappreciated. In an election that came so close to a draw, he has been in no sense repudiated.

For many of us also — to consider the other historic aspect of the occasion — Mr. Carter's inaugural will symbolize something quite important: It will at last ring down a curtain on the racial and regional divisions that lingered so long from the Civil War. Only the reconciliation of blacks and white southerners made Mr. Carter's candidacy workable. His success is built, as he must know best of all, on the labors of a generation to purge racism from American politics.

Of course, the new administration will not rest on theatrical or symbolic functions, however satisfying, and Mr. Carter will immediately confront some problems so obvious as to need little elaboration here.

He campaigned on a theme of national renewal, with high moralistic voltage. He offered the voters a flattering proposition: that recent national disappointments, generating a sour mistrust of once trusted institutions, resulted from the failure of the government to trust or consult the "goodness" and high-mindedness of the people. We hope that Mr. Carter has not fostered another national illusion. Perhaps he can start a vital flow of confidence between the people and the presidency. In this naughty world, it will not be easy.

The inward nature of Mr. Carter's program and personality is also a puzzle, even after a long campaign. In its early stages his campaign featured a fashionable anti-political iconoclasm, and in its late stages programmatic commitments (tax reform, economic growth, openness in the conduct of foreign policy) that will demand skilled mobilization of the very political machinery he at first attacked. Starting as a highly untraditional kind of presidential campaign, Mr. Carter's became at the last quite orthodox, full of familiar appeals and promises to the natural Democratic constituency which, having elected him, will demand that these chips be cashed. Whether this is a built-in contradiction, bound to trouble him, or a minor adjustment, will depend perhaps on his understanding and use of the office. The anti-Washington tone was muted toward the end, but Governor Carter cannot have forgotten that the issue of the "imperial presidency" is merely dormant and could be reawakened.

Finally Mr. Carter is, and may remain for some time, a paradoxical personal presence. It has not been easy to determine how the piety and the pragmatism fit together, the deacon and the nuclear engineer. The voters obviously wanted a change this year — wanted it badly enough to unseat a President of considerable appeal — but they appear to have wondered to the very end whether Mr. Carter was the change they wanted.

No doubt, a President-elect who came from obscurity to the doorstep of the White House in the space of a calendar year is not politically unequipped to deal with these challenges and doubts. He will be, in many ways, the most untried and untested of Presidents for some years. If there is mystery about him, it is obvious that there is capacity also. He will begin, next January, with all our good wishes.

CAPITAL PUNISHMENT RESUMES IN U.S. AFTER DECADE AS GILMORE EXECUTED

Convicted murderer Gary Mark Gilmore, 36, Jan. 17 was shot to death by a firing squad at the Utah State Prison at Point of the Mountain. Gilmore was the first person to suffer the death penalty in the United States since 1967. [See 1976, pp. 1493–1497]

Gilmore had been convicted of the July 20, 1976 slaying of a Provo, Utah motel clerk, Bennie Bushnell, 26, and had admitted killing Max Jensen, 24, a law student working as a service station attendant in nearby Orem, the previous night. Gilmore had been sentenced to death for the Bushnell murder. He had demanded that the state carry out the sentence and had disparaged those individuals and groups who had attempted to block his execution. He had emphasized his wish to die by twice attempting suicide in 1976. Gilmore's actions, and the struggle to keep him alive, had been heavily publicized by the news media.

Opponents of the death penalty made several futile efforts to delay the execution. The Supreme Court Jan. 11 rejected one such request from Douglas A. Wallace, a Vancouver, Wash. lawyer, on the ground that he lacked standing, or the legal right to bring a court action. Attorneys representing two convicted Utah killers Jan. 14 unsuccessfully sought orders to stay the Gilmore execution from U.S. District Court Judge Aldon J. Anderson and Utah District Court Judge Dean E. Condor. Utah Gov. Scott Matheson Jan. 14 also denied a request for an executive stay, citing a stay order granted by his predecessor in 1976. (The state parole board had refused to commute Gilmore's death sentence after the temporary stay had been granted.) A petition from the convicts on Utah's Death Row was presented Jan. 16 to Supreme Court Justice Byron R. White, who rejected it. Although White said he spoke for the majority, the same petition was brought before Justice Harry A. Blackmun the same day. Blackmun also rejected it.

THE ROANOKE TIMES
Roanoke, Va., January 26, 1977

On the eve of a legislative vote on capital punishment the General Assembly has received an impressive, eloquent appeal against capital punishment signed by bishops and ministers representing a broad range of churches and denominations. The document should be treated with great respect; it is a reminder of the source of life and the circumspection that should accompany any governmental taking of it.

The legislators need not feel overawed, however. A degree in divinity or a place in a pulpit does not preclude other ways of reaching a conclusion on the question: How to punish the violation of a commandment of all established religions: Thou Shall Not Kill.

We hold to the premise that respect for life diminishes when the penalty is diminished for the wanton taking of life. When the penalty for the taking of life is no more than the penalty for a particularly outrageous theft or series of lesser crimes, society has lost its nerve. It has lost the capacity to provide a scale of punishments equal to the offenses.

There is admittedly a practical frustration in applying the rule. The American Civil Liberties Union (ACLU) and other opponents of capital punishments will interfere even in cases where they are not invited to participate. They will stage such a cat-and-mouse spectacle of delay as to inflict a punishment more "cruel and unusual" than the swift one imposed by the courts as directed by the legislature.

Also the opponents of the law (with the aid of the media) will cause the public to think of Gary Gilmore when the public ought to see the two college boys killed by Gary Gilmore, one of them killed while he lay helpless and unthreatening on the floor. Soon attention will be centered on some apparently clean-cut Texan when what should be remembered is a 10-year-old girl first raped, then killed, then thrown into a river

The distractions are great: the possibilities of deterrent are lost during the distraction. The practical reasons for giving up on the death sentence are more visible than the reasons for not having one. Nonetheless the principle is sound that the greatest crime should have the greatest punishment. Legislators who believe that principle need not be deterred from voting for capital punishment in those cases clearly deserving it. If they hold to the principle, the sense of the people generally may yet prevail.

DESERET NEWS
Salt Lake City, Utah, January 18, 1977

It isn't an easy task for a state to be the first in nearly 10 years to execute a condemned criminal. Not even when the criminal has vigorously fought for the right to die for his murders.

For most Utahns, along with sorrow for the loss of human life — any life — there is a profound sense of relief that the tension and the glare of worldwide publicity are about over, now that Gary Gilmore is dead.

It has been a long ordeal, for Gilmore most of all, but also for every person sensitive to problems of justice, of law, and of human suffering. The anguish of indecision and uncertainty lasted to the very end, due to the ill-considered midnight stay of execution by Judge Willis Ritter after all other courts, both lower and higher, had made their firm decisions. America's long, sad history of legal executions has seen many last-hour reprieves, but the 10th Circuit Court's overturn of Ritter's stay may be the first last-hour — indeed, last-minute — death order on record.

No one can be happy or satisfied with the record of this bizarre case. But sober reflection will show it is hard to fault any Utah official, agency, or court. Governor Rampton acted properly in granting the first stay; to do otherwise would have been an unseemly rush to death. The Board of Pardons acted conscientiously and with dignity. So did the various Utah courts. The Attorney General's office properly and effectively fulfilled its role in seeking Gilmore's execution. Warden Sam Smith did his job as well as a man could do under these difficult, tension-packed circumstances.

As this page has previously noted, putting a human being to death is a grisly business and should be carried out only under the most stringent legal safeguards.

As the Gilmore case has so dramatically exemplified, the first order of business must be to write into Utah law a provision for mandatory court review of all death sentences. That would help safeguard the rights of the defendant in capital cases, while still satisfying the demands of justice. Had Utah had such a provision, much of the circus aspects of this case would have been avoided.

Mandatory review would assure that no Utah prisoner in the future will be legally executed on the basis of one set of testimony heard by one group of men and women. Surely human life, even that of an accused killer, is worth more than that. But, on the other side of the coin, the courts should speed up the review process as much as legally and morally possible.

Utah's execution this week has, in effect, reopened the door to the legal taking of human life. The state now has an obligation to do what it can to make that taking of life as carefully considered, as orderly, and as humane as possible.

The Salt Lake Tribune

Salt Lake City, Utah, January 18, 1977

Capital punishment, by its grim and final nature, inspires extraordinary efforts to stay its imposition. So there is no way the condemned or those opposed to the death penalty can be prevented from pushing last minute, longshot appeals in the courts and otherwise. Nor should there be.

Because of unique aspects of the Gary Mark Gilmore case, down-to-the-wire legal maneuvers sometimes bordered on the theatrical. They tested many a layman's patience with the judicial system. And all of them failed.

Unlike Gilmore, few persons sentenced to death seek to hasten their departures. His eagerness to die was a critical element that set this bizarre case apart.

Public attention was further generated by the fact that Gilmore figured to be, and indeed was, the first person executed in the United States in almost a decade. Now that he has been shot by a Utah firing squad and capital punishment, for better or worse, is again in force, other executions will lack the novelty of the first one.

These factors and Gilmore's flair for the sensational, gave impetus to last-ditch efforts to block his execution. And a previously unnoticed flaw in Utah's death penalty statute produced a ready vehicle.

Focus of the final legal jousting was the fact that Utah law does not provide for automatic review of all death sentences.

Lawyers opposing the Gilmore execution, but not Gilmore himself, maintained that lack of review would cause the appellate courts to declare the Utah death law unconstitutional. It was noted that the United States Supreme Court's latest decisions seemed to hold that automatic review was necessary if state capital punishment laws were to pass muster.

The United States Supreme Court may or may not have agreed with this position. It did not get the opportunity because Gilmore refused to raise the question and the court would not hear it from others.

Never mind. Utah law should provide for mandatory review in capital cases as a matter of simple justice and orderly procedure.

A bill to provide this additional safeguard is before the Legislature. Its passage will remove one cause for attacking future death sentences.

Automatic review would go far to assure society that in taking a killer's life it had acted well within society's laws. It could have prevented some of the highly publicized legal sparring that marked the Gilmore case and in future death penalty dramas as well.

Mandatory review would not mean an end to 11th hour appeals which, despite their sometimes exasperating aspects, constitute a final chance to prevent a possibly tragic miscarriage of justice.

THE DAILY HERALD

Biloxi, Miss., January 18, 1977

Gary Mark Gilmore has brought capital punishment back into American society after an absence of nearly ten years. Our society needs it.

His death yesterday by firing squad gives concrete meaning to the Supreme Court's finding that the death penalty does not constitute cruel and unusual punishment.

There's another execution scheduled in Texas where Jerry Lane Jurek, a convicted child-killer, is to die in the electric chair, barring intervention by the government or the Supreme Court.

For a decade, arguments about the death penalty have swirled about in the courts, in the press, in magazines and in legislatures. In that interim of remission, the deterrent effect of the ultimate sentence has been effectively reduced, not only in the minds of those who would break the laws covered by the death penalty, but also in the minds of those citizens with no intentions of breaking those, or any other, laws.

Gilmore's death has changed that. If Texas does execute Jurek, with news and television cameras recording the deed, there is every possibility that visions of capital punishment may appear on television screens in millions of American homes. Remembering the impact upon America from watching the first war televised in bits and pieces nightly, it is impossible to assess the changes that might be stimulated from the televising of a rash of executions.

Capital punishment has had an inconsistent history in America. The movement to abolish it peaked in the years before World War I when, in a 10-year period, nine states and Puerto Rico outlawed the death penalty for most crimes. After that, a number of states abolished the death penalty only to reinstate it later. After 1917, no state succeeded in abolishing capital punishment for 40 years.

There are no accurate statistics on the total number of Americans who have been executed because of the lack of an accurate accounting in the years prior to 1930. But testimony before a Congressional subcommittee in 1972 contains an estimate that the total has been "something on the order of 7,000 executions in this century under state and federal law."

Abolitionists will argue that the rising crime statistics refute any contention that the death penalty has been effective as a deterrent. Others will reply that each execution has effectively deterred any repetition by the criminals so dispatched.

Opinion polls show that the public favors the death penalty, but by a vacillating margin over recent years. Those poll results can be expected to swing to disfavor should the televising of executions become anywhere near as common as the Vietnam war reports once were.

Until that happens, if it does, the death penalty has returned.

It is necessary if this country is to be a nation of laws that include a system of of justice wherein a variety of punishments are meted out, increasing in severity as the crimes increase in heinousness. There must be a maximum punishment for the most heinous of crimes.

THE DALLAS TIMES HERALD

Dallas, Tex., January 18, 1977

GARY MARK GILMORE is dead at last. His body is still. He is gone.

He kept saying that he wanted to go, and he will not be missed by many for long. He is dead because the deeds that he did were so terrible that society said he had to go, and he apparently agreed. At least he did not want to stay where he was.

Society thought long and hard before it did to Gilmore what Gilmore did to others, but for some the decision was easy and right. "An eye for an eye" has been in the human mind for a long time, and its simple fairness is hard to refute.

But many even among those who wanted Gilmore's death — and the death of hundreds more on the nation's death rows — were not motivated by revenge. The deed must be done, legislatures and juries and judges have said, to protect society itself, to save that fragile thing we call civilization from those who would carry us back to the animal past. To deter others who are tempted to go Gilmore's way. The death penalty may not be a perfect antidote to crime, their reasoning goes, but this is an imperfect world, and at least we will not have to be afraid of this *one* criminal anymore.

Others say that to do to Gilmore what Gilmore did to others is to pull all of us down to his level; that for society to take Gilmore's life is to make Gilmores of us all. It is this doubt which kept alive for months a man who said he wished to die. No defense lawyer wanted to believe that he could have saved a man's life and did not. No judge wanted to say the final, irrevocable yes. No state was eager to be the first in a decade to officially and deliberately snuff out a human life.

During the long months of hesitation, Gilmore became something more than a man, more than a murderer. He became a cause, the vehicle for renewal of an old, old debate: What is justice? To whom should the state show mercy?

The debate will begin anew, again and again, as each of the hundreds sitting in cages on our death rows moves along his own Last Mile. We shall have new flurries of legal briefs and arguments, more news accounts of last meals and last words, perhaps even television film of the death throes. Although others will go out with less fanfare and senationalism than Gilmore, who had the fortune or misfortune to be first, none of it will be nice to see.

But the Supreme Court has said that to kill a criminal is not cruel or unusual if the killing is done without bias. And by so ruling, the Court has refused to force us to be merciful.

If we wish to be merciful, we can, of course. We could order our legislatures to allow no more firing squads, no more electric chairs, no more gas chambers, no more hangmen's ropes. We could even amend the Constitution.

But for now, the people of Utah and Texas and other states say, "An eye for an eye." And we shall see whether any good comes of that exchange.

ARGUS-LEADER
Sioux Falls, S.D., January 18, 1977

It is a matter of note that the first execution to take place in the United States in almost 10 years occurred because the condemned man conducted a lengthy fight to have the sentence carried out.

A last-minute effort by opponents of capital punishment to have Gary Gilmore's sentence stayed was unsuccessful when a federal appeals court lifted the stay order of another federal judge.

The last previous execution in this country occurred in Colorado's gas chamber.

Gilmore's execution likely will mean that other executions in other states will follow.

There are situations in which the imposition of the death penalty is appropriate. The crimes of hijacking, kidnaping and murder of the kind committed by Gilmore are justifiable reasons for exacting the death penalty.

Gilmore was sentenced for killing Bennie Bushnell, 26, a Provo, Utah motel clerk last July. He also admitted killing Max David Jensen, 24, the night before. Mr. Jensen was a service station attendant. Both murders were during robberies and each victim left a young widow and child.

Executing Gilmore won't bring back the two young men he murdered, but it may deter some other hood in Utah from killing a victim during a robbery. The state of Utah will also be spared the problem and expense of looking after Gilmore for what would have been the rest of his life.

The arguments, pro and con, about capital punishment in this country during the last 10 years have served a good purpose. State and federal laws have been changed to protect the accused, and to attempt to get a more even application of the extreme penalty.

This country faces a real problem in combating crime. The application of the death penalty in a number of states may make wouldbe murderers think twice before they take somebody else's life. An effort by local governments to prosecute more criminal cases, whether or not they're capital offenses, to the end that punishment is virtually certain, would do much to counter the crime problems confronting this country.

The Birmingham News
Birmingham, Ala., January 18, 1977

After 10 years in which there were no executions in America, the nation still is divided over the issue even though the suspension has been broken by a firing squad in Utah.

Gary Mark Gilmore, who died yesterday, was a curious candidate for the death penalty. He freely admitted he was a killer and wanted death rather than a life sentence.

But what Gilmore wanted or didn't want is not the yardstick by which the nation should measure the pros and cons of capital punishment. The principles are of a general nature; they must be determined on the basis of what is just for society and most effective in protecting the innocent from hardened criminals such as Gilmore.

A number of arguments can be made against the death penalty. Other arguments can be made in favor of the death penalty. Many earnest people these days find themselves morally torn over the question, and now, with the execution of Gilmore, that question has been made very real.

It is argued that capital punishment is not a deterrent to the heinous crimes it is meant to punish. Possibly other would-be murderers will not be deterred by the death of Gilmore. Certainly Gilmore was deterred neither by death nor life in prison, and he killed in cold blood.

The fact is, no punishment has proven effective as a deterrent against heinous crimes. If the death penalty must be abolished because it does not deter, then imprisonment must also be abolished, because it doesn't deter, either. But, of course, that would be absurd.

What is certain now is that Gilmore will never harm another soul. If his execution does not cause even one other person to relent from murder in cold blood, we all may rest assured that Gilmore has claimed his last victim. To some individual who might otherwise have been killed by Gilmore, that is a blessing of the highest order.

Even a life sentence does not effectively isolate a hardened killer from potential victims. Prison officers and other inmates come in contact with the killer every day. The only weapon the killer needs is a sharpened screw driver or any honed piece of metal if he wants to kill someone else in that micro-society behind bars. Killings in prisons are not rare.

The argument can be made that society places a lower value on human life if it kills someone in the name of justice. But to whom would society be communicating this value system except to those whose respect for life already deters them from violence? It is a nuance which is lost upon the killers and would-be killers in society. If such a value system prevailed in the law, the only persons to be executed would be the victims of crime.

The best argument, perhaps, against capital punishment is that there is always the potential for error—that an innocent person might be forced to die. No one can guarantee that any particular judgment of the criminal justice system is accurate and fair. It is not unusual for the system to malfunction because it, as any other human activity, is subject to human error.

But behind this argument is the tendency to want to err in favor of the accused rather than in favor of potential victims. It is not impossible for innocent persons to be convicted, but it is rare that a guilty verdict is maintained after the usual appeals and after all legal safeguards have been observed. However, it is not unusual for innocent persons to be killed every day behind grocery counters, on the streets and so on.

The death penalty is not so valuable for the last victim of crime as it is for the next potential victim of crime. There is no lack of certainty that Gilmore was guilty, and he will never kill again.

In executing Gilmore, the state of Utah has acted with justice and resolve. If criminal justice were carried out with equal resolve in every jurisdiction, the public safety would be immeasurably enhanced.

Richmond Times-Dispatch
Richmond, Va., January 18, 1977

How many people, we wonder, can readily identify Max David Jensen or Bennie Bushnell? Not many, we suspect. How many can readily identify Gary Mark Gilmore? Nearly everyone, for his name has been on the front pages of the nation's newspapers for the past two days and had been there several times before.

Max David Jensen, who died violently last year at the age of 24, was a young law student with a wife and infant daughter. He worked at an automobile service station to make ends meet. Bennie Bushnell also died violently last year, the very day after Max David Jensen's death, at the age of 25. Bennie Bushnell worked at a service station too, supporting a wife and child and trying to make enough money to return to college.

Cause of both deaths? Gary Mark Gilmore, who robbed and mercilessly shot both men last summer. Yesterday he was executed by a Utah firing squad. He was 36.

Gary Gilmore's victims were decent and law-abiding citizens who posed no threat to society, but he had been a menace since he was 14, robbing, mugging, raping and shooting his way through life. He displayed his sociopathic tendencies even in prison, where he once permanently paralyzed an inmate by hitting him with a hammer. His callous attitude toward life he expressed in a letter he wrote to a girl friend soon after killing the two men last year:

"If I feel like murder, it doesn't necessarily matter who gets murdered. Murder is just a thing of itself, a rage, and rage is not reason, so what does it matter who? It vents a rage."

Opponents of capital punishment treated the man who expressed these views as a martyr and fought hard to save him from execution. Their efforts made him a celebrity whose life will be remembered in a book and a movie.

After his execution yesterday, a spokesman for the American Civil Liberties Union, which led the fight against it, tearfully accused Utah of being barbaric. But might it not have been more barbaric to allow the man to live and endanger the lives of even more human beings? Considering his willingness to kill anyone simply to vent a rage, no one within his reach, in prison or on the streets, would have been safe.

If ever a man deserved to die at the hands of the state, Gary Mark Gilmore did. We are sorry that his life was such a bloody tragedy, but we shall shed our tears for Max David Jensen and Bennie Bushnell.

The State

Columbia, S.C., January 19, 1977

THE American news media are taking their lumps from some critics for the coverage given to the legal maneuvers involving convicted murderer Gary Mark Gilmore — and for the coverage of his execution by firing squad.

The thrust of the criticism is that the news media have whipped up the morbid interests of too many Americans, that too much attention was focused on Gilmore.

Perhaps the criticism is justified in some specifics, but as a matter of news the Gilmore case was more than just a run-of-the-mill one in that he was the first person to be executed in all of the United States since 1967. And with that fact rode all of the controversy over capital punishment, and the rising concern for victims of crime.

There were other elements in the Gilmore story which set it apart — his own wish to die and the efforts of lawyers to keep him alive; his own suicide attempts, and that of his girl friend. And finally, the commercial overtones that involved one of his attorneys.

If Americans seize on the Gilmore stories to whet a morbid thirst, we are persuaded they would have found what they were seeking in other news stories or events even if Gilmore had not existed.

It is possible the news media may have told many Americans more than they really wanted to know about Gary Gilmore. But the telling of his story could no more be avoided by the news media than Gilmore could have escaped his own destiny before the firing squad Monday morning.

The Seattle Times

Seattle, Wash., January 18, 1977

GARY Gilmore and the State of Utah both got what they wanted yesterday — America's first legal execution in 10 years.

Befitting the circus nature of the event, the only witnesses to Gilmore's execution, other than his uncle and prison officials, were a Hollywood literary agent and two lawyers involved in arranging book and movie rights to the story of Gilmore's ignoble life and death.

Given the bizarre nature of that modern tale of crime and punishment, those rights no doubt will be among the most profitable "literary" investments of the decade.

The noxious ballyhoo of the "Gilmore legend" has yet to reach its peak.

Grotesqueries aside, Gilmore's execution is a historic event that opens a new chapter in the long and tortuous debate over capital punishment in the United States and each of the 50 states.

One category of participants in the debate opposes capital punishment, on principle, in any and all circumstances.

But for a larger number of people, the question boils down to whether or not the death penalty is an effective deterrent to murder and other heinous crimes such as kidnaping and treason.

There are well-qualified criminologists on both sides of that question.

The United States Supreme Court opened the door to Gilmore's execution and that of others on "death rows" elsewhere around the country with a finding last summer that capital punishment does not constitute "cruel and unusual punishment" as forbidden by the Constitution.

The high court held further, however, that state capital-punishment laws are acceptable only when they provide adequate restraints against arbitrary or capricious imposition.

In November, 1975, Washington State voters, by a better than 2-to-1 margin, approved an initiative providing mandatory capital punishment for murder in especially aggravated situations.

Since the compulsory feature of the initiative does not meet the ground rules subsequently set forth by the Supreme Court, this state's legislators are left with the responsibility to modify the law both to meet the federal requirements and the overwhelmingly voiced sentiments of voters in this state.

The lawmakers now in session in Olympia ought to act without delay.

Meanwhile, it can be said that the fates chose well in determining which convicted killer should be the one to open a new era in the history of capital punishment.

Relatives of the two young men whom Gilmore senselessly gunned down while commiting robberies will testify to that.

Fort Worth Star-Telegram

Fort Worth, Tex., January 19, 1977

Gary Mark Gilmore is dead.

There was little rejoicing at his passing that we can detect.

The news that a rifle squad had, after exercise of every avenue of judicial appeal, finally taken his life came with shocking impact.

Though we have editorially supported resumption of the death penalty as a deterrent to crime, we join all who are sorrowed by the seemingly unnecessary death of another human.

Gilmore's execution came only after every possibility of delay or reversal was at last denied through due process.

Here was a man who had capriciously killed two persons, and who admitted if he hadn't been caught, he would have killed others.

Yet emotions run high on the subject of capital punishment. The Supreme Court by a 5-4 vote in 1972 declared the death penalty unconstitutional as it was at that time imposed. But the justices found it necessary to write nine separate opinions.

The emotions cloud the issue.

That Gilmore was guilty of murder was never in doubt. His crime was so heinous as to deserve the maximum penalty legally permissible. Few would argue that point.

The significance of Gilmore's execution, then, is not that he was wrongly punished, but that he was the first to legally die for a crime in almost 10 years, and that his execution might lead to a resumption of capital punishment.

We join all who regret that this human chose to misuse his life and, in so doing, sacrificed it. We join all those, also, who mourn his victims. We find satisfaction only in that he had no further opportunity to kill.

On capital punishment, the Star-Telegram noted editorially Jan. 19, 1972:

"The swift and certain execution of the law — punishment by a means bearing a just proportion to the enormity of the crime — is the best deterrent known."

That reasoning, regrettably, still stands.

The Topeka Daily Capital

Topeka, Kans., January 20, 1977

The long ordeal of the Gary Mark Gilmore case is over.

Gilmore, who committed a cruel murder in a motel robbery and who wanted to die for it, was executed Monday by a Utah firing squad.

For the first time in nearly 10 years, a state executed a criminal.

Though courts approve capital punishment in certain cases, many Americans oppose it. They argue it is wrong to kill under any circumstances and that executions by the state involve all citizens in killing. That argument is wrong.

Many other Americans favor the death penalty, arguing that it is needed to prevent the worst of crimes. It can save lives, they maintain.

Gilmore's case was unusual. He wanted to die; others fought to keep him alive. His mother's efforts for him were understandable.

However, the American Civil Liberties Union and other liberals took up the cause. Determined to stop capital punishment at all costs, they ignored what Gilmore wanted, being more interested in protecting others on death row. Their appeals delayed the case unnecessarily.

It is appalling to think there may be similar long wrangles about every murderer on death row. There may be valid issues in some of these cases; if there are, courts should decide on them.

But since the Supreme Court has declared the death penalty constitutional under certain circumstances, the struggle over it should be transferred to state legislatures.

Let those favoring capital punishment seek laws that comply with Supreme Court rulings. Kansas' lawmakers should pass such a statute.

Groups opposing it should fight in legislatures. not in courts. Let's have no more Gary Gilmore cases.

Bakke Admitted To School; Affirmative Action Policy OKd

A split ruling by the U.S. Supreme Court June 28 granted Allan P. Bakke admission to a University of California medical school, upholding the 38-year-old white engineer's contention that he had been a victim of "reverse discrimination." The case, *University of California Regents v. Bakke*, challenged the medical school's special admissions policy, whereby 16 of 100 places were set aside for minority students. Bakke, twice rejected by the school, had charged in state court that his civil rights had been violated under both the 14th Amendment (guaranteeing equal protection of the laws to all citizens) and the Civil Rights Act of 1964 (prohibiting discrimination based on "race. color or national origin" in any federally funded institution or program.) [See 1977, pp. 1214–1233]

A California superior court had ruled in Bakke's favor on both grounds, while the state Supreme Court supported Bakke's right to be admitted solely on the basis of the 14th Amendment.

In the U.S. Supreme Court's decision, two differently comprised majorities ruled (5–4) 1) that the special admissions program that set racial quotas at the Davis school was illegal and 2) that universities could consider race as on of several factors in choosing among applicants for admission. Justice Lewis F. Powell Jr. cast the pivotal vote in each decision.

Four justices—John Paul Stevens, Potter Stewart, William Rehnquist and Chief Justice Warren Burger—contended that the Davis program violated Title VI of the Civil Rights Act (see above) and that the broad question of "whether race can ever be used in an admissions decision" was not an issue in the Bakke case. In an opinion by Justice Stevens, discussion of the subject (the constitutionality of affirmative action programs) was "inappropriate" since the "settled practice" of the high court was to "avoid the decision of a constitutional issue if a case can be fairly decided on statutory ground [Title VI]."

A second group of four justices—William Brennan, Byron White, Thurgood Marshall and Harry Blackmun—held that the special Davis admissions plan was constitutional under the 14th Amendment. The civil rights statute (by implication a restatement of the 14th Amendment), Brennan wrote, did not "bar the preferential treatment of racial minorities as a means of remedying past societal discrimination to the extent that such action is consistent" with the 14th Amendment. Brennan and his group maintained that Davis's program was acceptable according to those terms and voted to deny Bakke admission to the school.

Justice Powell agreed with the Stevens group that the Davis plan was illegal and that Bakke should be admitted, but he did so on the basis of the 14th Amendment rather than on the more narrow ground of Title VI. Powell held that Davis "preferential program" contained a "fatal flaw" in its denial of equal protection of the law to white applicants.

In the second part of the high court's ruling, Justice Powell joined Justices Brennan, White, Marshall and Blackmun in finding that college admission policies could use race or ethnic background as one of several factors in considering an applicant. The decision to allow race to be taken into consideration reversed a lower court ruling prohibiting the university from establishing race-conscious programs in the future.

Powell stated that the attainment of a diverse student body was a "constitutionally permissible goal for an institution of higher learnings." This goal was improper, he indicated, if it was attained through a system of quotas based on race or ethnicity. An applicant's origin, he said, was "but a single though important element."

Universities could attain "beneficial educational pluralism," Powell said, by considering, in addition to race, an applicant's "exceptional personal talents, unique work or service experience, maturity" or "history of overcoming disadvantage." Powell urged schools to adopt programs that treated "each applicant as an individual in the admissions process."

Powell cited Harvard as a school that employed a special-admissions plan to expand "the concept of diversity" to include students from all types of racial and economic backgrounds.

Harvard's admission program was described by the school as unstructured and subjective. In a brief submitted by Harvard on the Bakke case, the university said that only about 150 persons in each incoming undergraduate class were admitted on the basis of academic preeminence. The admission's committee gave some weight to an applicant's race. in addition to such nonacademic criteria as geographic origin, socioeconomic class and extracurricular interests.

The Supreme Court rejected the University of California's claim that the high court had, in the past, handed down broad rulings in support of the preferential treatment of minorities. Justice Powell warned that in such areas as school desegregation, employment discrimination and sex discrimination, the court had "never approved a classification that aids persons perceived as members of relatively victimized groups at the expense of other innocent individuals in the absence of judicial, legislative or administrative findings of constitutional or statutory violations."

Justice Thurgood Marshall, the only black justice, agreed with the court's ruling "only insofar as it permits a university to consider the race of an applicant in making admissions decisions." He did not find the Davis minority program in violation of the Constitution. In his dissent, he wrote that "it must be remembered that during most of the past 200 years, the Constitution as interpreted by this court did not prohibit the most ingenious and pervasive forms of discrimination against the Negro. Now. when a state acts to remedy the effects of that legacy of discrimination, I cannot believe that this same Constitution stands as a barrier."

The Carter Administration praised the Supreme Court decision. Attorney General Griffin Bell said the ruling was a "great gain for affirmative action. It's the first time the Supreme Court ever upheld affirmative action and it did in as strong a way as possible."

Joseph Califano, secretary of the Department of Health. Education and Welfare, said the ruling "strongly supports this nation's continuing effort to live up to its historic promise—to bring minorities and other disadvantaged groups into the mainstream of American society through admissions policies that recognize the importance of diverse, integrated educational institutions."

Rocky Mountain News
Denver, Colo., June 30, 1978

BY A 5-4 DECISION in the now famous Bakke case, the Supreme Court has handed down a ruling on the touchy issue of racial preference that can be supported by fair-minded Americans.

The court upheld the principle of affirmative action — giving minorities a break to redress past discrimination.

Many civil rights leaders and educators were fearful a victory for Allan Bakke would be the death knell for university efforts across the country to help qualified minority students gain entry into the professions. Bakke won — he will start medical school this fall — but affirmative action was preserved.

Bakke, a 38-year-old white engineer, was twice denied admission to the University of California Medical School at Davis even though he did better on entrance examinations than minority applicants who were admitted.

Bakke argued and the unversity conceded he had been rejected solely because of his race. At the same time the court ordered him admitted, it struck down the practice at Davis of reserving 16 of 100 places in entering classes for minority students, declaring that such a scheme violates the Constitution and federal civil rights law.

On that point we side with Justice William J. Brennan Jr. and the three other court dissenters that the Davis program was reasonable in light of its objective of assisting minorities, long handicapped by past discrimination, to gain entry to medical school.

Instead, the majority suggested that colleges emulate Harvard's method of dealing with the issue. The school fixes no quotas for minority students but does consider race as one factor in selecting among qualified applicants.

The court seems to be recommending that schools be subtle like Harvard and not crude like Davis in discriminating in favor of minorities. It will be interesting to see how schools manage to give meaningful consideration to race without opening themselves to the charge of establishing a quota system.

AS NOTED by Justice Thurgood Marshall, during most of the past 200 years, "the Constitution as interpreted by this court did not prohibit the most ingenious and pervasive forms of discrimination against the Negro. Now, when a state acts to remedy the effects of that legacy of discrimination, I cannot believe that this same Constitution stands as a barrier."

To be sure, many Americans are tired of endless governmental and educational tilting toward one group or another to make up for injustice. But can we do any less until America is truly color blind with equal opportunity for all?

THE BLADE
Toledo, Ohio, July 2, 1978

THE Supreme Court's multifaceted ruling in the Bakke case was decisive in two respects but did not resolve the fundamental issue underlying the surface dispute. That is hardly surprising in a situation in which the nine-member court produced majorities on both sides of the case and enough individual viewpoints to fill 154 pages with six separate opinions.

Decided by one five-justice majority is that the engineer whose name has become a sort of household word symbolizing the reverse-discrimination controversy in this country is entitled to admission to the University of California's medical school at Davis. Decided by an almost entirely different group of five justices is that schools may nevertheless consider racial and ethnic factors in choosing their students.

Left unanswered by that judicial division is the most crucial question involved: To what extent, or in what manner, can race and nationality be considered without getting into the trouble the Davis medical college did? And the ambiguity of the Supreme Court's handling of the matter was emphasized by the fact that two opinions used essentially the same argument to arrive at opposite conclusions on the Davis medical school's policy of reserving 16 places for members of certain minorities.

Justice Powell, the swing man on both court factions, said the "semantic distinction" between calling this a goal and calling it a quota was beside the point; he held that the Davis approach is not permissible. But the four justices who dissented from that part of his opinion said that "for purposes of constitutional adjudication there is no difference" between setting a predetermined number of openings for minorities and using minority status as a positive factor in evaluating applicants, which Justice Powell suggested would be permissible.

The constitutional argument must be left to the court, but from a practical standpoint the dissenting justices are closer to the mark. For the real problem in affirmative-action programs — which are necessary to help overcome the consequences of centuries of discrimination against blacks in this country — is how there can be any assurance of effectiveness in working toward the goals unless there are quotas. It is hard to avoid the presumption that even the so-called "diversity" approaches which Justice Powell favored have quotas — albeit unspecified ones — lurking in the background.

The question may be one not of semantics but of candor. Apparently the essential mistake the Davis school made was that it came right out and said it was designating 16 of 100 openings in each entering class for members of minorities.

By ruling, in effect, that this is wrong but that affirmative action is allowable, Justice Powell has laid the groundwork for a great deal more litigation on what constitutes an acceptable "diversity" approach. And although he meant to offer some guidance, his reference to Harvard University as an "illuminating example" was unfortunately not very helpful. For it sets up an institution in unique circumstances as the model for schools with situations that are not really comparable.

Harvard's medical school and perhaps a handful of other similarly prestigious ones can with minimum effort attract such a range of top-quality applicants — blacks and other minority-group members included — that these institutions may indeed find it unnecessary to set any fixed numerical goals in order to achieve the desired "educational diversity." But other schools — notably ones like Davis and the Medical College of Ohio which are new and still establishing their reputations — do not enjoy the luxury of being able to select from such riches of applicant talent. Yet they know that the Government is most unlikely to accept that fact as a reason for their having what it considers too few blacks or other minorities among their student bodies.

Thus the setting and filling of quotas becomes the only feasible route to the affirmative-action objective for most schools. As one law school dean commented, with an obvious touch of cynicism, after the Supreme Court ruling: "I'll be very interested in hearing how you take race into consideration without setting up some kind of quota." The answer may well be years in coming from the court — if indeed it ever does.

The Hartford Courant
Hartford, Conn., June 29, 1978

The U.S. Supreme Court decision in the Allan Bakke case is limited in scope and reasonable in conclusion.

The University of California medical school admissions policy for minorities was clearly affirmative action at its worst, well deserving of the popular label, "reverse discrimination." The arbitrary nature of the 16-person quota of minority students to be admitted was found unconstitutional by the court's majority; the principle of affirmative action is still intact.

In his oral argument before the court, Mr. Bakke's attorney stressed that he was more interested in winning his client a place in medical school than resolving the ideological issues that made the case so important. In a broad sense, the five-judge majority accepted his strategy.

The ruling is clearly a narrow one, aimed at the particular defects of the California plan. The court's order to admit Mr. Bakke to the medical school in Davis does not do damage to minority rights, but it does stand as a warning that the rights of white men cannot be artificially distorted to serve another purpose.

The irony of the high court's reliance on the Civil Rights Act of 1964 to overturn a program of benefit to minorities should not be lost on those administrators who must now re-evaluate other such programs. Title VI of the act says that "no person in the United States shall, on the ground of race, color or national origin, be excluded from participation in, be denied the benefits of, or be subjected to discrimination under any program or activity receiving federal financial assistance."

The "person" Congress had in mind in 1964 was clearly not the blond, blue-eyed, professionally successful Allan Bakke. But can the wisdom of the civil rights act be denied him? We should not need a decision of the Supreme Court to tell us that the answer is no.

In the shorthand sometimes relied on to evaluate a high court decision, Justice Lewis F. Powell Jr. can be labeled the swing man — the deciding vote on an issue that has divided the court evenly. While he was clearly sympathetic with the justices who supported the California program, Mr. Powell voted with the other side, unconvinced that the objectives of the medical school program could not be achieved in a better way.

That message from Mr. Powell, and in a less direct way, from the other majority justices, should be the guiding principle to come from the Bakke case. The medical school in Davis developed its plan with the expressed desire to assist candidates handicapped by economic or racial barriers. In truth, the program represented a rather unappetizing decision to fill 16 of the 100 available slots each year with blacks, Puerto Ricans and several other approved minorities.

That the noble experiment to help the deprived was not open to whites was made embarrassingly clear last year when a Russian-born Jew, economically deprived and a victim of religious discrimination, was refused consideration under the special criteria. She was admitted to UC-Davis under a federal court order.

The message from the Supreme Court in the Bakke case is a call for colleges to be as intellectually honest and creative in their affirmative action programs as they are in their classrooms. The effort to encourage, recruit and train victims of society must entail more than selecting black or brown or yellow or red faces to provide an esthetically pleasing mix.

If there had been no affirmative action program at the University of California medical school, Mr. Bakke would probably still have been turned down, as he was at a number of other institutions. He won his case not because his academic credentials were better than some of the minority students, not because he was white, but because the weak and arbitrary nature of the school's affirmative action program did not provide compelling justification for excluding him.

THE CAMP DAVID SUMMIT:
Thirteen-Day Meeting Produces Israeli-Egyptian Accords

The Middle East summit talks at Camp David, Md. ended Sept. 17 with an agreement between Israel and Egypt on a "comprehensive framework for peace" and on the future of the controversial West Bank and Gaza Strip. The U.S.-sponsored meeting produced two separate documents, signed at a White House ceremony by Israeli Premier Menahem Begin and Egyptian President Anwar Sadat. President Carter, who had been conducting the meetings since Sept. 6, signed the accords as a witness. Carter made the contents of the documents public Sept. 18 in an address to a joint session of Congress.

Under the Egyptian-Israeli accord, both nations were to conclude a peace treaty within three months. Israel would withdraw from the entire Sinai Peninsula and turn it back to Egypt. The area would be demilitarized. The Israeli pullout would occur in phases, with the first one taking place within three to nine months after the signing of the peace treaty. Normal diplomatic relations between Israel and Egypt would then be established. The final Israeli withdrawal would be carried out within two to three years after the peace pact was signed.

Among the major points of the agreement dealing with the West Bank and Gaza Strip:

- Israel, Egypt, Jordan and elected Palestinian representatives would negotiate the key question of sovereignty of the Israeli-occupied territory after a five-year transition period. Israel and Jordan would conclude a peacy treaty at the end of that time.
- Israel would keep troops in specified areas of the West Bank during the five-year period.
- Israel would dismantle its military government and permit the Palestinians to elect representatives and to decide on a form of local government.
- New Israeli settlements on the West Bank would be frozen during the peace negotiations.
- Palestinian police would join Egyptian and Israeli and possibly Jordanian security forces in maintaining public order.

Carter cautioned that the "magnitude of the obstacles that still remain" could not be overlooked. Among those issues cited by the President and not specifically mentioned in the document on the proposed Egyptian-Israeli treaty was the question of the removal of Israeli settlements in the Sinai, which required the approval of the Israeli Knesset (parliament). [See pp. 1159–1167] Also, the accords made no mention of Arab demands for control of East Jerusalem, which Israel had annexed in 1967.

An almost immediate dispute arose over the question of Israeli settlements on the West Bank, when Begin contended in an interview Sept. 20 that Jewish settlements would be halted only for the maximum three-month period during which the bilateral treaty with Egypt was being negotiated. U.S. officials insisted that Begin had promised to bar new settlements throughout the period of negotiations concerning the disposition of the West Bank.

The Chattanooga Times
Chattanooga, Tenn., September 22, 1978

The primary beneficiaries of the Camp David Summit meeting between Egyptian President Anwar Sadat and Israeli Prime Minister Menachem Begin are the two leaders' countries, especially if the agreed-upon "framework for peace" is implemented along the lines outlined at Sunday's press conference. But there can be no doubt that President Carter, the host and mediator for the leaders, has emerged from the meeting with a greatly enhanced reputation for leadership. It belies the pre-summit carping by "Carter baiters" and exposes the speculation that he will be a one-term president for what it is: premature exaggeration.

All of this is not to say that Mr. Carter is home free, despite the open affection showered upon him by Messrs. Begin and Sadat, and the tumultuous reception he received in his speech to Congress Monday night. Moreover, several weeks of crucial negotiations remain, which mean at least part of the Sadat-Begin deal could fall through.

But Mr. Carter has already profited in tnagible measure, as the brief item on a CBS News poll published below makes clear. Not only has his popularity rating taken off, he is also retrieving the loyalty of the Jewish community in this country which, while traditionally Democratic, has been upset in its belief that Mr. Carter has been too hard on Israel and too easy on Egypt in the past.

There is more to the benefits Mr. Carter has derived from the summit, however. Even though it has dampened criticism of the president within his own party, and rebuffed those who have insisted at length that Mr. Carter was somehow "in over his head" in the presidency, the Middle East is not everyone's idea of the number one problem today.

In this country, that "honor" obviously belongs to the state of the economy. If Mr. Carter can achieve a success in his anti-inflation effort that is at least relatively as far - reaching as the agreement at Camp David, he will have established himself as a leader to be reckoned with — not only by his political opponents but by historians.

This point is bolstered by the fact that the president has not just been scoring heavily in foreign diplomacy. He won, for instance, most of what he sought in his Civil Service reform legislation. And after months of painstaking negotiations with Congress, the administration may soon achieve a substantial success in an energy program. In an effort to reduce drastically the government's deficit, the administration is already working on a leaner budget for next year.

All of this is coming about at a time when the public continues to expect much from the president (more, perhaps, than any man can deliver) while openly voicing cynicism and pessimism about what government can do.

Much of what happens now in the Middle East depends on negotiations between the principals and on the amount of cooperation by the other Arab states. The United States, of course, will continue to help out by doing what it can, perhaps in mediation. The prospects for success are bright, however, because of President Carter's invaluable leadership and concern.

The Hartford Courant

Hartford, Conn., September 19, 1978

The Mideast summit concluded at Camp David now brings the world true hope for peace in that embattled area. With that heightened expectation also comes a frightening potential for disappointment — and tragedy.

The paper and ink of Camp David hold great promise; it must now be translated by the flesh-and-blood political forces in the United States, Israel, Egypt and Jordan.

Already, in the face of opposition from the most conservative elements within his political alliance, Israeli Prime Minister Menachem Begin has cautioned against from the most positive interpretation that could be placed on the summit agreement, in an interview with Israeli journalists.

Egyptian President Anwar Sadat, as he was preparing to sign the historic documents, saw his second foreign minister resign since he began the stunning rapprochment that has carried Egypt and Israel to this new place in their histories.

From the isolation of Camp David, with the comforting encouragement of President Carter, both Mr. Sadat and Mr. Begin must now venture forth and defend themselves to constituencies far more difficult to please than an American president.

Clearly, Mr. Begin has the more difficult chore. If the signed agreements at Camp David can be believed, the Israeli prime minister has taken an admirable step forward from the intransigence he had exhibited in years past. He has apparently curbed his enthusiasm for controlling all the lands for which he can find an appropriate Biblical reference. He is apparently willing to risk a political fight from the right-wing, religious settlers he has encouraged to populate Arab lands, as a divine mandate.

What is not yet clear is how far Mr. Begin can go, or is willing to go, to risk his fragile political alliance. Can he survive an agreement that would place Sinai settlers under an Egyptian flag? Can he survive an agreement that concedes even a modest amount of sovereignty in East Jerusalem?

Mr. Sadat, on the other hand, is blessed with a nation given to puppy-dog loyalty to national leaders. The Egyptian president must grapple with hostile Arab neighbors, and a Palestinian people who have long suspected that others acting in their name are usually acting first for themselves.

Mr. Sadat has thrown off the last pretext of uneasiness about representing the Palestinians; he is negotiating for their political rights, whether they like it or not. It is a gamble worth taking, at least in these initial stages. Except for the radical fringe, the Palestinians are weary of war and uncertainty.

Mr. Sadat has taken a major step toward peace and his apparent willingness to resolve the less difficult problem of Israeli settlements in the Sinai, whether or not immediate progress is made in the more difficult areas of the West Bank and Gaza, coupled with the issue of Palestinian sovereignty.

For real peace to be assured in the Middle East, the Palestinians must now assume an important role in the ongoing negotiations. With Jordan now written into the negotiations as an important partner, the Palestinians are in danger of being thrust aside, as Jordan's King Hussein and Mr. Begin settle political and security questions in the Palestinian-populated West Bank area.

Palestinian nationalism was somewhat lulled to sleep under the original Jordanian annexation, and brought back to life during the years of Israeli-Arab warfare. Now, both sides must concede an important amount of autonomy to the Palestinian people, whose trust has been violated consistently for 30 years.

With the triumphant, yet cautious, Congressional appearance of Monday night now over, all sides return home to defend themselves and prepare for true peace. Even with the sketchy and imperfect information now available, it is clear that Mr. Sadat and Mr. Begin are prepared to put some trust in a piece of paper — a peace treaty — guaranteeing only as much as a signature on paper can guarantee. But if peace is to become reality in the Middle East, such trust must be engendered.

THE ANN ARBOR NEWS

Ann Arbor, Mich., September 20, 1978

IT HAS BEEN a long time since Americans could feel genuinely proud of something accomplished by their President. It is an experience unknown to the generation now in its 20s, whose personal memories of public affairs are dominated by the Vietnam war and Watergate. It is no wonder that skepticism and disbelief are mixed with relief in the reactions to President Carter's reports on the Camp David agreements.

Carter could have made much more of his personal achievement, as more than a mediator but less than an imposer of solutions, during his Sunday appearance with Prime Minister Begin and President Sadat, or during his Monday address to Congress. He didn't, and more than modesty must be involved. Carter effectively made the point that whatever his role was in getting the Camp David agreements written and signed, success or failure in getting them carried out rests largely beyond the control of any government outside the Middle East.

* * *

OPTIMISM seems justified, because of a single pragmatic consideration:

If Egypt, with its population of about 38 million, signs a formal peace treaty with Israel's approximately 3.5 million citizens, it is difficult to imagine Jordan (about 3 million), Syria (about 7.7 million), Saudi Arabia (not quite 10 million), Lebanon (about Jordan's size, but in constant danger of civil war), or Iraq (11.5 million) refusing indefinitely to settle with Israel.

There will undeniably remain a possibility of a new Egyptian/Israeli war, in which some or all the other Arab countries might join, until a peace treaty between Cairo and Israel is actually signed. A failure by Israeli leaders to live up to the spirit of the Camp David agreements, by pushing new settlements in occupied territory as vigorously as Begin and Foreign Minister Moshe Dayan have often encouraged, could bring another such disaster. The best hope that this won't be allowed to happen rests in the large demonstrations that have been taking place in Israel during recent weeks, organized around the slogan, "Compromise is not a dirty word."

Efforts to create settlements in occupied regions, such as the Sinai Peninsula, have not brought Israel security; many Israelis realize this, and Begin has now acknowledged it.

Sadat has acknowledged that Israel cannot be expected to give up all military occupied lands unless an experiment with self-government shows that most Palestinians in those lands do not wish to be politically dominated by the Palestine Liberation Organization terrorists. Good evidence of how the PLO leaders expect that experiment to turn out is provided by their quick denouncement of the Camp David agreements.

Evidence that it will be an honest experiment in self-government is provided by Begin's emphasis on "real autonomy," plus his acceptance of Carter's reference to the "legitimate rights" of Palestinians — a phrase that Begin has until now considered intolerable.

* * *

IN HIS ADDRESS to Congress on Monday, Carter made a point of describing the United States as a "full partner in the search for peace." He emphasized that a key reason for this major effort in the Middle East is to discourage further efforts by the USSR to dominate certain Arab governments. These are not empty phrases.

Carter has, on one hand, placed the United States far ahead of the USSR as a facilitator of the real interests of nations in one of the world's most perennially troubled regions. But he is being careful not to present this as a U.S. victory over the USSR. He is making clear that the USSR, while no help in the Camp David agreements, is recognized as the other necessary "full partner" if there are to be any genuine assurances of peace anywhere. Gestures of that nature, at moments of personal triumph, can turn politicians into statesmen. Carter is moving in that direction.

THE DAILY HERALD

Biloxi, Miss., September 19, 1978

Those who watched the dramatic conclusion of the Camp lDavid summit meeting Sunday night on television might be tempted to be swept away into a feeling of triumph, a feeling that peace has, at last, come to the volatile Mideast.

Peace has not come, not yet. Tremendous strides remain to be taken and complex problems remain to be solved. The next three months will be crucial in determining if those solutions can be reached. Camp David's accords strongly indicate that they can.

The accords were surprising. The talks had been cloaked in secrecy and that tight blackout of information may have been a key ingredient to the success of the conference.

Egyptian President Anwar Sadat and Israeli Prime Minister Menachem Begin unanimously and unstintingly applauded the efforts of President Jimmy Carter in arranging and conducting the meeting.

At significant risk, the president assumed the role of being the moving force that produced the two historic documents, "A Framework for Peace in the Middle East" and a "Framework for the Conclusion of a Peace Treaty Between Egypt and Israel."

That the heads of both of these nations have come together onto this much common ground, and have spoken enthusiastically of signing a peace treaty in less than three months, is certain to generate additional momentum to this peace initiative.

That momentum will be needed as the Camp David participants set about convincing others, whose support and cooperation are vital to peace, to join with them.

The world must also hope that the spirit of Camp David will be contagious and that the other parties will be willing to negotiate with the degree of sincerity and flexibility exemplified by Sadat and Begin.

Egypt's Arab neighbors, especially Jordan, Syria and Lebanon, represent a particularly difficult challenge to Sadat. Israel's Knesset, the parliament, will be as challenging for Begin.

Sadat and Begin are buttressed by the message from Camp David that peace is achievable. The troublesome issues that were evaded at the summit, the Camp David accords say, may also succumb to the reasoned efforts of men of good will.

When the summit opened, there was a consensus that it would be successful if it only achieved an agreement between Sadat and Begin to continue negotiating.

The summit has done so much more than that. It has constructed a foundation upon which these two former enemy nations, their neighbors and the world may realize the dream of a Mideast peace.

The Des Moines Register

Des Moines, Iowa, September 19, 1978

For all its ambiguities and shortcomings, the Middle East peace breakthrough announced at the White House Sunday night was an extraordinary diplomatic and historic achievement.

Since Israel was born 30 years ago, its most intractable foe has been Egypt. Egypt is the Arab world's largest state and usually its most influential — the heartland of pan-Arab nationalism, the heart of whose creed has been a strident anti-Zionism. Egypt has fought four wars with Israel.

Less than a year ago, Egyptian President Anwar Sadat was saying that face-to-face negotiations between top Egyptian and Israeli leaders would not come in his lifetime.

Today, after 12 days of the most intense, face-to-face negotiations, top Egyptian and Israeli leaders have solemnly agreed to replace nation-destroying with nation-building.

But they did more than replace 30 years of war and bitterness with a commitment to build a new era of realism and detente; they also agreed on a reasonable framework to achieve that goal. That achievement is not only new, but revolutionary.

President Carter described the agreement as a "framework for peace," and so it is. Like any framework, or blueprint, the document contains a lot of open spaces for questions, ambiguities, possibilities, risks and hopes. Yet it is these open spaces that will furnish new opportunities to shape the future of the Middle East.

The 1.1 million Palestinian Arabs in the West Bank and Gaza

were promised "full autonomy." Will they be content with this language, or will they insist on forming a state that will pose a danger to Israel's security?

Will Jordan's King Hussein be both willing and able to play a "security role" in a five-year transition period leading to Palestinian autonomy?

Will Saudi Arabia — the Arab world's richest nation and the one with the most conservative, pro-Western stance — give this agreement the support it needs?

Will Israel and Egypt be able to settle the nagging, volatile issue of Jewish settlements in the Sinai and the West Bank?

Will Sadat be able to convince his brother Arabs that he has not betrayed them and the cause of Arab unity?

Some diehards like Syria and Libya can be expected to make this charge, even though the accord gives Jordan a specific role in the five-year transition to Palestinian autonomy.

Tough decisions and sacrifices will be needed to give flesh and meaning to the framework.

When Sadat flew to Jerusalem in November, the world anticipated that further progress would be swift and solid. Instead, it was followed by a nine-month-long stalemate. So the events of the weekend must be regarded with equal measures of hope and caution. The two sides have fashioned a blueprint, not an edifice.

But in an area where battle maps and casualty lists have been the rule for 30 years, a blueprint for peace is a precious and, indeed, unique commodity.

The Knickerbocker News

Albany, N.Y., September 20, 1978

While President Carter deserves the highest praise for his courage, perseverance and skill in arranging the risky Camp David summit meetings that brought Egypt's President Sadat and Israel's Prime Minister Begin to an agreement on "a framework for peace" in the Middle East, it would be unrealistic to be much more than guardedly optimistic at this point over the final outcome.

It is fair to say that the results of the summit exceeded expectations, for the fact that Sadat and Begin were able to agree on any major points during their 13 days at Camp David is, in itself, remarkable. The odds were against any substantive agreement and indeed, the principals themselves have disclosed that the summit came close to foundering several times.

An examination of the Camp David agreements indicates that what has been forged is not a settlement but a basis for negotiations for a peace treaty. What is significant is that the preliminary agreements offer a much better chance for a final settlement than ever has been possible up to this point.

For example, under the agreement, Egypt would regain sovereignty over the Sinai and Israeli troops would be withdrawn to specified defensive positions. However the future of Israeli positions on the West Bank and Gaza strip are left somewhat fuzzy. Moreover, the fate of the highly controversial Israeli settlements on the West Bank and the Sinai has been left for the Israeli Knesset (Parliament) to decide, although President Sadat in-

sists that dissolution of the settlements is a precondition to any peace treaty.

Another possible major problem could be the failure to agree on any clear-cut plan for the permanent location of the 1.5 million Palestinian refugees, other than a vague promise to give the refugees the opportunity for self-determination. Without a more definite plan, there can be no peace in the Middle East. The militant Palestine Liberation Organization (PLO) will see to that.

So while, as President Carter said in his eloquent address to Congress — without doubt the high point of his presidency to date — "no one should underestimate the historic importance of what has been achieved," neither should the difficulty of what lies ahead be underestimated, either.

For one thing, President Sadat at the moment stands alone among the Arab leaders in moving toward a settlement with Israel and in fact is being bitterly criticized in the Arab world for what is being called a "sellout." And Jordan's King Hussein, whose agreement on any plan for solution of the Palestinian refugee problem is essential, so far has been non-committal.

But no one ever said the path toward peace in the Middle East would be easy.

Now, however, thanks to the prodigious efforts of President Carter, President Sadat and Prime Minister Begin at Camp David, chances for peace are brighter than they have been at any time since Israel became a nation.

Press Herald

Portland, Me., September 20, 1978

Americans should not have much difficulty in providing the support President Carter asked for the accomplishments of the Camp David summit.

But Americans must also regard the epilogue of the meeting just as they did the prologue—very cautiously. Without detracting one iota from the achievement of the summit, it must be remembered that what has been produced is not a peace agreement. It is precisely what it has been labeled—a framework for peace.

President Carter obviously is elated with the result. But even in his elation, the president solemnly reminded us that a tremendous amount of work will be necessary to build what he called a comprehensive peace on that framework.

That framework already is under attack by some sources in the Middle East. Americans may well display a greater unanimity of support for it than will be evident in any of the countries directly involved.

President Carter said the world may stand near "one of the bright moments in human history."

It may be just as close to one of the great disappointments of human history.

While enthusiastically applauding the result of the Camp David summit, we just as fervently hope time will not reduce it to just another false promise of peace.

The Washington Star

Washington, D.C., September 19, 1978

If it was the major hope of the Camp David summit to revive President Sadat's historic peace initiative, now almost a year old and fading, that hope has been triumphantly realized. The results, said President Carter Sunday evening, went "beyond our expectations."

The modest hope was that the peace process could be kept moving, that the parties would at least decide how to decide. And so they have. And if we are not mistaken, there is a large bonus — how large, time will tell.

Under President Carter's mediation, President Sadat and Prime Minister Begin broke from their stalemate. With his November 1977 journey to Jerusalem Mr. Sadat had proclaimed a break with pan-Arabist hostility toward Israel. Even so, he insisted that Israel, in turn, must accept him as something like the plenipotentiary spokesman of other Arab states, accepting from him commitments that only they could keep. This was a gallant but unrealistic expectation and it needed substantial modification. At Camp David Mr. Sadat in the end modified it.

Thus the worry word "comprehensive" — as in "comprehensive settlement" — nowhere appears in the two documents he co-signed with Mr. Begin. There is a "framework" for the negotiation of a peace treaty between Egypt and Israel. Hope is expressed that the plan will become a model for other bilateral settlements; but there is no assurance that it will and no threat that if the model is scorned the recalcitrance of Israel's other neighbors will undermine bilateral peacemaking.

This was Mr. Sadat's most striking concession. What does Mr. Sadat receive in return? Much more, we believe, than is suggested by any portrayal of the Camp David agreements as one-sided.

Egypt will get an Israeli withdrawal from all the Sinai — including, we must suppose and hope, the Knesset's assent to the abolition of Israeli settlements there. Mr. Sadat, for his part, clung to the earlier demand for larger Israeli concessions on the future of the West Bank, Gaza, and "the legitimate rights of the Palestinian people." But his dogged devotion to those demands and to his claim to act as peacemaker in a larger sense did not go unrewarded in the proceedings at Camp David.

Therein lies the major *quid pro quo*.

For even under the pressure of President Sadat's historic *demarche* of last year, Mr. Begin's policies as to the West Bank, Gaza and the Palestinian future remained all along a study in diplomatic ambiguity. Not even Mr. Begin's 26-point plan for the West Bank looked as far or as explicitly as the Camp David agreement into the future. And that offer was clouded by reservations. Mr. Begin appeared at times to deny the applicability of UN Resolution 242 to the West Bank, which he preferred to call Judea and Samaria. And only on the eve of the Camp David meeting did Mr. Begin respond at all flexibly to President Sadat's insistence that some sort of independent Palestinian rule there must lie at the end of the road.

The "framework" for a peace settlement, even without the word "comprehensive," thus modifies Israeli reservations quite remarkably. It speaks clearly of a "transfer of authority" and "full autonomy to the inhabitants" of the West Bank; and it establishes for the first time Israel's recognition of "the legitimate rights of the Palestinian people and their just requirements," at least as the basis of negotiation. Finally, it cites Resolution 242 "in all its parts" as the "agreed basis" for a settlement.

It is difficult to imagine that a negotiation governed by Resolution 242 and looking to "full autonomy" for the West Bank and Gaza Arabs could end in Israeli control. For all practical purposes, then, Mr. Begin's government has renounced the cloudy title it asserted in those areas.

These two agreements, the one on a peace treaty between Egypt and Israel and the other establishing principles for negotiating an end to the Israeli occupation of the 1967 conquests, may have been obtainable many months ago. At times, in fact, the positions of the two sides seemed as close as the frayed ends of a broken rope only waiting to be spliced. What was needed was a splicer. That, it now appears, has been President Carter's role at Camp David and he deserves great credit for having done his work so well.

Should this happy beginning live up to its promise, the president's mediation will be of great historical significance. A genuine peace between Egypt and Israel after three decades of conflict would render most other hostilities in the Middle East manageable. The optimistic, among whom we number ourselves, will be searching their modern history for a parallel. One that occurs to us is the Anglo-French entente which, in the closing years of the 19th century, ended a century of war and colonial rivalry. And the comparison, we might add, is distinctly flattering to the work at Camp David.

Chicago Tribune

Chicago, Ill., September 19, 1978

There is nothing to gain by trying to determine whether it was Egypt or Israel that "won" the 13-day encounter at Camp David. As Plato and other perceptive writers have noted, victories can be short-lived—even military victories; and in diplomacy, the greatest victory is an agreement in which neither side can claim a victory.

The real victor at Camp David was President Carter, who called the meeting, acted as mediator [the American compromise proposal went through 23 drafts before both sides found it acceptable], and deserves the credit for whatever was achieved. As he says, there is still a lot of work to be done. Hopes for peace have been raised many times in the past, only to be dashed once again. But at least the momentum toward a settlement has been restored, and that is probably the most that could be expected from Camp David.

The major losers are the rejectionist Arabs who fear that peace would leave them without a cause—and their Soviet backers. They have consistently opposed bilateral talks between Egypt and Israel and insisted that the whole assortment of Middle East problems be dealt with at once, which of course would make any agreement almost impossible.

It was to draw support away from these militants that the Camp David talks went beyond the outlines of a settlement between Egypt and Israel over the Sinai. A second and potentially more important agreement created a "framework" for peace on the West Bank and in the Gaza Strip.

The framework calls for an end to the Israeli military government, full autonomy for Palestinians, and an embargo on new Israeli settlements. It evidently stops short of the independence which even moderate Palestinians want; but the question of an independent Palestinian state is a thorny one even for Arabs. The conservative governments of Jordan and Saudi Arabia, whose support is essential if negotiations are going to move ahead, are no more eager than Israel to have a zealous and probably left-wing Palestinian state as their neighbor.

The Sinai agreement is along the lines that have seemed promising for some time: the return of sovereignty to Egypt, the withdrawal of Israeli forces within two or three years, the resumption of diplomatic relations, and the prohibition of military airfields in the area.

The agreement does not call for American help in the form of manpower. But the series of supplementary "letters" between the United States and Egypt, to be made public on Tuesday, presumably involve other types of commitments — perhaps financial aid; and to Israel there is an apparent commitment to replace its military airfields in the Sinai with new, American-built airfields in the Israeli Negev, a 10 minute flight to the east.

But the important thing is that Mr. Carter has restored American leadership in the move toward peace and thus to restore American prestige worldwide. If further talks are to succeed, they will need continued encouragement from the United States as well as the support of moderate Arabs. And if this calls for financial help from the U. S., it could well be one of the best investments available to us today.

IRANIAN CRISIS:

Iranian Students Seize U.S. Embassy in Teheran, Hold Hostages

About 500 Iranian students Nov. 4 seized the U.S. Embassy in Teheran along with about 90 hostages, including 60-65 Americans. They vowed not to release their captives until ousted Shah Mohammed Riza Pahlevi, under medical treatment in New York, was returned by the U.S. to stand trial in Iran.'[See p. 567, 191, 114, 16]

The U.S. rejected the demands and sent two mediators to Iran to seek the release of the hostages. The mediators were denied entry and the Palestine Liberation Organization intervened with Iranian authorities in an effort to free the Americans. As a direct result of the crisis, Premier Mehdi Bazargan and his government resigned Nov. 6, giving Ayatollah Ruholla Khomeini, de facto ruler of Iran, and his Revolutionary Council complete control of the country.

When the U.S. Embassy was stormed, Revolutionary Guards at the embassy gates made no move to intervene. The students, who called themselves "Followers of the Imam's [Khomeini's] Line," read a statement by Khomeini in which he said Iran "must clean up its situation vis-a-vis the United States. This action is a kind of recognition of the situation." The Iranian Foreign Ministry said the embassy takeover was "a natural reaction to the U.S. government's indifference to the hurt feelings of the Iranian people about the presence of the deposed shah, who is in the United States under the pretext of illness. If the U.S. authorities respected the feelings of the Iranian people . . . , they should not have allowed the shah into the country and should have returned his property."

U.S. State Department officials Nov. 9 said Iran had assured the U.S. Embassy in Teheran three times that it would receive adequate protection, despite the presence of the shah in the U.S. When the embassy was stormed by the students Nov. 4, U.S. Marine guards there held them off for about two hours behind a steel door, while others in the embassy repeatedly called the Iranian government for help, according to the State Department. The government promised to send security forces, only two blocks away, but help never came, the department said. An anti-American rally had been held near the U.S. Embassy Nov. 2, two days before its takeover, and Iran provided security then as it had promised.

A spokesman for the students Nov. 5 disclosed that Iranian members of the U.S. Embassy staff had been released and that those remaining in the building were Americans, Pakistanis, South Koreans and Bangladeshis. Two more Americans were seized at their hotel in Teheran Nov. 7 and taken to the U.S. Embassy. U.S. Charge d'Affaires L. Bruce Laingen was detained by the Iranians at their Foreign Ministry building in Teheran. The Iranians said they could not guarantee his security if he left. (Laingen had been named U.S. ambassador to Iran in October but had yet to assume the post.)

The Iranian government Nov. 5 announced that it was canceling its military treaties with the U.S. and the Soviet Union. The pacts theoretically gave both powers the right to intervene militarily in Iran. In other protest actions Nov. 5, student demonstrators seized the two empty U.S. consulates in Tabriz and Shiraz, which had been closed earlier in the year, and occupied the British Embassy in Teheran for five hours. The embassy was seized after Khomeini accused Britain of providing asylum to former Premier Shahpur Bakhtiar, who was, in fact, living in France.

In response to an appeal from the U.S., United Nations Secretary General Kurt Waldheim Nov. 6 said he would use his authority to obtain the release of the hostages. The U.S. also appealed to others for help, including Syria, Pakistan and Pope John Paul II.

The Ottawa Citizen
Ottawa, Ont., November 6, 1979

Is there method in Ayatollah Khomeini's madness? From all indications there seems to be more madness than method in the Iranian leader's conduct. From the frying pan of the deposed Shah's tyrannical dictatorship, the Iranian people seem to have fallen into the fire of this misguided, intolerant despot.

With his tacit encouragement, hordes of Iranian students have invaded the U.S. embassy in Tehran and taken dozens of Americans hostages. Their demand is that the Shah of Iran, now under treatment in the U.S. for cancer, be returned to Iran for trial and his assets in Iran be turned over to the Iranian government.

Both demands have some validity. The Shah of Iran did amass a huge fortune during his long rule and the Iranian people are entitled to the return of what the Shah, in effect, looted from them. Because the Shah had ruled ruthlessly — his opponents were imprisoned, tortured and even killed — there is merit even in the demand that the Shah be tried for his deeds.

But the merits of the demand do not justify the method through which the goal is being pursued. The Iranian students who attacked the U.S. embassy violated international law and they did so with the backing of their spiritual dictator.

Now they are saying that they won't release American hostages unless the Shah is returned to Iran. It is a foregone conclusion that the Americans won't return a sick man to Iran — under the relentless pressure of hysterical goons. To do so would be to demean America and also to encourage terrorists and blackmailers to indulge in an orgy of kidnappings and hostage-taking for all kinds of demands.

What are the Iranians going to do? Keep the hostages in confinement indefinitely? Threaten harm to them? If they did hurt the innocent diplomats, that would be a horrible crime. The world will not forgive them. The Iranians will simply become international pariahs.

As it is, their relations with many of their neighbors are severely strained. Within Iran itself, there is confusion that borders on anarchy.

Khomeini has often threatened to "crush" all those who do not see eye to eye with him. The hundreds of Iranians who have been executed are proof that the man is deadly serious. But his real victims are the Iranian people who had struggled for freedom and democracy, but who now find their country being dragged back to a medieval dictatorship under a ruler who seems as intolerant as the one he replaced.

The Washington Post
Times Herald

Washington, D.C., November 6, 1979

THE ADMINISTRATION obviously should not act in a way likely to endanger the lives of the Americans being held hostage at the U.S. embassy in Tehran. But to say that is not to counsel pussycat acquiescence in the reckless way the Iranian authorities-cum-mob are behaving. It is fraudulent to suggest that the poor officials are helpless to control the mob's passions. They are not. On many other occasions they have shown they can keep control, and they must be held accountable for discharging the basic duty of safeguarding foreigners. That the invaders of the embassy are followers of Ayatollah Khomeini, who has personally endorsed their deed, pinpoints the responsibility. This is no mob on the loose. It is a force under tight control.

The invaders' demand that the United States send back the shah, who is in a New York hospital undergoing cancer treatment, is, in equal parts, contemptible and frivolous. No extradition treaty exists under which Iran could gain his return, and even this administration—which declined to admit the ousted shah until cancer made him eligible for "humanitarian" entry—rejects the suggestion that the terms of his sojourn are negotiable with a mob. And speaking of mobs, the U.S. government surely can find ways to return some of those visiting and protesting Iranians in this country, if they have violated the terms of their stay.

The ayatollah's people say they find in the hospitality offered the shah reason to break off relations with the United States, which is, among other things, Iran's chief arms supplier and the chief educator of its students abroad. That is Iran's privilege. It has to be said, however, that the invasion of the embassy fully demonstrates the futility of the administration's trying to keep lines open to the Khomeini regime. A power struggle is going on between fundamentalists led by Ayatollah Khomeini and pragmatists led by the nominal prime minister, Mehdi Bazargan. The fundamentalists seem to have seized on the shah-in-America issue (no pressure was put on Mexico in the shah's months there) to paint the pragmatists as softliners. When politics comes down to a competition in anti-Americanism, there is little room for an official American role. Specifically, we do not see how the American embassy in Tehran, or the Iranian mission in Washington, can stay open in these conditions.

Precisely because suspicion of the United States is so widespread, however, the administration cannot let itself be drawn into any sort of crude campaign against the ayatollah. He has alienated the unfanatical segment of Iranians, including the hard-core left, and the non-Persian ethnic minorities, and he has provoked virtually every one of Iran's neighbors. But it should be left to Iran's citizens, or neighbors, to deal with him as they will. Any other course promises only to hand the ayatollah, or a successor, the unifying platform of anti-Americanism. It is frustrating to wait for events to sort things out in Iran—especially because things will almost surely get worse before they get better—but events are moving.

The Boston Globe

Boston, Mass., November 6, 1979

Sooner or later Iran will have to decide the terms under which it chooses to live with the rest of the world. That decision cannot possibly be made in the context of seizing the embassies of foreign countries or the holding of hostages to achieve some act of merely symbolic value, like the return of a deposed shah deeply ill with cancer.

Meanwhile, the State Department has done what it practically can by saying that the next move must be made by the Iranians; only they can decide how to treat hostages or whether to back off from their unwise and, in the long run, self-destructive threat to the American embassy and its staff in Tehran. And the Carter Administration has acted humanely in refusing to consider returning the shah to Iran for trial and certain death.

Many Americans may feel that the United States ought to react with a show of strength, as the Israelis did when terrorists captured one of their airliners and flew it to Uganda. Why can't we, as they did, send a detachment of troops to whisk the potential victims from under the noses of their captors?

There are practical considerations, first of all. At Entebbe, the hostages were held at an isolated airport, which the Israelis had helped to build. The American embassy is deep in the heart of a city populated with hundreds of thousands of profoundly agitated and xenophobic Iranians. Many of them are armed. The military prospects of an American raid succeeding are overwhelmingly bleak.

Further, and more important in the long run, many Iranians are deeply commited to the creation of an Islamic state, which many of them believe is naturally antagonistic to foreign creeds. Ayatollah Khomeini has encouraged their belief that Americans are enemies. Any attempt to deal with the situation physically would merely reinforce that mistaken belief.

It is very much in the American interest to seek the best possible relations with Iran. The obvious reason is oil, of course, but there is also the larger issue of general stability in the Mideast, stability that seems increasingly fragile. Threats to that stability are a matter of concern for the entire world, as well as the United States, and we owe it to all countries to do what we can to contribute to sane developments in the region. That contribution will sometimes come in the form of restraint in the face of insults, even of heavy provocation like the threat to the life of American citizens.

There is reason to hope for improvement within the Iranian community itself. Thousands of Iranian leaders in government, industry and the univerities have taken part in the modernization of Iran's economy and the increase in its standard of living. They understand the value of reliable relationships with the rest of the world for the sake of their own economic development. How can they possibly view the temporary seizing of the American and British embassies as being in the best interests of Iran? What are they saying to Ayatollah Khomeini? What are they saying to each other? How long will they accept the mood of madness still gripping Iran?

Events are moving swiftly in Iran and there is great danger that, at any minute, some group of Iranians will lose internal control, with lethal consequences for hostages or other Iranians. The violence now so close to the surface is almost certain to be self-destructive, and that is sad for all Iranians.

But American interests will be best served if we can avoid overreacting. We must try to be firm with the Iranian government and perhaps look for new ways of conveying messages to the Iranian leaders that will ease this or some future crisis. The current actions in Tehran undercut but cannot obliterate Iran's need for reasonable relations with the world around it.

St. Louis Globe-Democrat

St. Louis, Mo.,
December 18, 1979

Who's on first in Iran?

Trying to deal with a terrorist government is bad enough. But when those who supposedly speak for that government are constantly contradicted by the "students" who are holding 50 Americans prisoners, the situation becomes almost impossible.

Sunday morning President Carter had some grounds for optimism when Iran's Foreign Minister Sadegh Ghotbzadeh said he hoped some of the hostages could be released by Christmas and that the spy trials might be avoided by establishment of an international commission which would judge U.S. actions in Iran rather than try the captives.

But the militants at the U.S. Embassy, who say they take orders only from Ayatollah Ruhollah Khomeini, almost immediately contradicted Ghotbzadeh, saying that all of the hostages would be tried and none of them would be home by Christmas.

The Revolutionary Council meanwhile issued a statement contending that the shah's departure from the U.S. for Panama was a "victory" for the Iranian revolution. Previously, militants at the embassy had warned they "would take it out on the hostages" if the shah left the U.S. for any country other than Iran.

This same council also rejected the decision over the weekend by the International Court of Justice of The Hague, claiming it was "one-sided." The world court ruled that the hostages should be released because their seizure was a violation of international law.

There is some evidence that treatment of the hostages is improving. Their captors are allowing them to make more regular phone calls home. They reportedly will be permitted to attend religious services on Christmas and Ghotbzadeh promised — for what it's worth — that a team of representatives from other countries would visit the hostages soon to certify they are being treated humanely.

All of which doesn't change the fact that the government of Iran is still using terrorism in an attempt to force the U.S. to capitulate to its insane demands and is behaving in a barbaric way toward American diplomats and military personnel that it should be protecting under international law.

Unless, Iran now frees the hostages President Carter should move at once to obtain economic sanctions against that country through the United Nations. If this fails, Mr. Carter should take whatever actions are necessary, including a naval blockade and military action, to gain the release of the captives.

Americans have been tremendously patient with the mad behavior of Iranian leaders but they aren't going to allow demagogues running that country to hold the hostages indefinitely and to endlessly heap abuse on the United States. Mr. Carter absolutely should not permit the Iranian government to conduct a "show trial" of the hostages or harm them in any way.

The honor and the credibility of the United States has taken a tremendous beating in this whole disgusting affair. At some point this disgraceful episode has to be brought to an end. If Iranian leaders choose to believe they can hold our diplomats and military personnel prisoner indefinitely and herd them around like animals, then they and their country should be made to pay a very high price for this insult to the American people.

THE CHRISTIAN SCIENCE MONITOR

Boston, Mass., November 6, 1979

The United States confronts an extremely difficult situation in Iran. If it acts with insufficient firmness to secure release of the Americans being held hostage by Muslim students in the US Embassy in Tehran, it will be faulted for weakness in the face of outrageous provocation. If it acts too toughly, too soon, it may prevent the more responsible elements on the Iranian scene from defusing the crisis and endanger the lives of its citizens. The prudent course is to say as little as possible publicly and to work vigorously behind the scenes to resolve the problem. It can do so from the standpoint that the Iranian Government has the responsibility, under international law, to protect a foreign embassy and respect its inviolability.

We would like to think that it is misguided Persian nationalism rather than the religion of Islam which motivates the students who have seized the embassy (and, as we write, the British Embassy) and are angrily demanding the return of the deposed Shah. Surely it is not a tenet of Shia Islam that it is justifiable to make innocent people pay for someone else's wrongdoings.

In any case, the US cannot submit to such blackmail. In political terms, the Carter administration would have preferred not to let the Shah enter the United States, at least at this time. The diplomatic difficulties of doing so were foreseen. But it would have offended the moral sensibilities of all Americans to refuse the Shah sanctuary for the humanitarian purpose of medical treatment. Furthermore, no one of humane and democratic persuasion could countenance turning over the former Iranian leader to a dubious system of justice and to political forces with such an uncontrolled desire for vengeance. That is not the way of the West and on this point there can be no compromise, even though many Westerners would be the first to concede the Shah's sweeping misdeeds that undercut his positive achievements.

It is sad, but perhaps significant, that such a crisis should have arisen at the very time that Washington seeks to improve its relations with Iran. Only recently US adviser Zbigniew Brzezinski met with Prime Minister Mehdi Bazargan in Algiers, to spell out among other things the US position on the Shah. It could be precisely because of this effort to repair US-Iranian ties that hard-line religious fundamentalists and the Ayatollah Khomeini supported the student siege on the US Embassy. Behind this violent act some observers see an intensifying power struggle at the top between the religious fundamentalists, who seek the establishment of a theocratic republic run by the Muslim clergy, and the pragmatists, who favor a secular government but one sensitive to Islamic feelings.

The United States thus finds itself snared in Iran's ongoing revolutionary struggle, which far from bringing instant democracy to that unhappy land has brought in its wake regional revolt, popular unrest, institutional confusion, heavy-handed justice, and bitter political and clerical infighting. It clearly will take time for the struggle to play itself out and the West, fundamentally sympathetic to the aspirations of most Iranians for a democratically based society, can only watch with patience and forebearance.

But this does not mean the United States must not stand up for its interests. The Bazargan government and Ayatollah Khomeini must be given every reasonable opportunity to resolve the embassy crisis. They did so once before, it will be recalled, when pro-Khomeini forces drove revolutionaries from the US compound. But, even while exercising diplomatic restraint, the US must accompany such restraint with firmness. It goes without saying that, if quiet persuasion does not succeed, President Carter will have to consider other measures, such as enlisting international diplomatic help, to free the Americans from unlawful detention.

The Sun

Vancouver, B.C., November 7, 1979

Ayatollah Ruhollah Khomeini's religious fanaticism is thrusting Iran back into the Dark Ages. In doing so, it is affronting the civilized world and besmirching the name of Islam.

Symptomatic of the global wave of revulsion against the ayatollah's excesses was yesterday's unanimous vote in the House of Commons to protest to the Iranian government the "latest acts of criminal aggression" in Tehran.

The ayatollah and his followers, particularly the student gangs who invaded the United States and British embassies in Tehran and attacked American consulates in Tabriz and Shiraz, have transgressed the norms of decency in international relations.

There is an appalling depravity about a national leader who calls on the faithful to kill and tear apart the sick and ousted Shah, compounded by the gangsters who, with their leader's blessing, seize and humiliate hostages, attempting to use the threat to the lives of their prisoners to force the extradition of Mohammad Reza Pahlavi, to give the ayatollah the pleasure of having the shah mocked, probably tortured, and certainly executed in Tehran.

President Jimmy Carter of course has rejected out of hand the demands for the shah's extradition. His agonizing problem is how to safeguard the lives of Americans at the mercy of the Iranian mobs.

But the challenge is to the West as a whole, not only to the U.S. After the American and British embassies, it could be the turn tomorrow of Canada or any other non-Islamic nation.

The resignation yesterday of the ineffectual government headed by Mehdi Bazargan gives all power to the mullah-dominated Revolutionary Council. That development probably presages more outbursts of fanaticism.

Anger over Ayatollah Khomeini's behavior has led to some talk in Washington and Western European capitals of military intervention. Such action, in existing circumstances, is totally out of the question.

For the most pressing problem, the safety of the hostages and other foreigners in Iran, the best hope is probably through diplomacy by United Nations Secretary-General Kurt Waldheim. The UN, possibly including an emergency meeting of the Security Council, should be used as a forum to denounce the Iranian rulers.

If the zealots in Tehran persist with their violation of acceptable standards of international conduct, Western governments will undoubtedly consider economic and diplomatic sanctions.

Ultimately the task of restoring sanity to their government lies with the Iranian people. Before that is effected, a period of chaos and bloodshed seems inevitable.

The Courier-Journal

Louisville, Ky., November 7, 1979

SELDOM has patience been more difficult — or more necessary — than in dealing with the madness gripping Iran. Even with American hostages at the mercy of fanatic students unleashed by the Ayatollah Khomeini's anti-U.S. propaganda, a low-key response is our proper course.

That doesn't set easily with a nation prideful of such maxims as "Damn the torpedoes," "Speak softly but carry a big stick," and the more contemporary "Can do." Great countries once endured only so much trouble from lesser ones before retaliating with a vengeance. But even great nations now face constraints unknown to our forebears. As we learned painfully in North Korea's seizure of the Pueblo and our abortive commando raid on a North Vietnamese prison camp, sometimes the only recourse is diplomacy.

There are limits, in short, to what can be accomplished by force. We can gnash our teeth and listen to macho types like John Connally irresponsibly cry "appeasement" following the Carter administration's careful reaction to the events in Tehran. We can fantasize images of U.S. Marines mowing down hysterical waves of Iranian students or kidnaping the Ayatollah. But armed reaction to Sunday's takeover of the U.S. embassy would be hollow heroics — a probable death sentence for the hostages and our military force, too.

It has been clear since the Iranian revolution began that the security of all Americans there, including embassy personnel, was exceedingly fragile. But a continued diplomatic presence, to serve as our ears in an important nation undergoing tremendous upheaval, is imperative if it's possible at all. Now, our best hope is to give the agitated captors of our personnel no excuse to turn more savage, but instead to hope that their frenzy will fade.

This does not mean that the Carter administration should cave in to the Ayatollah's demand to hand over the Shah. The fanatic who is trying to guide Iran into the 7th century may not recognize the ancient rules of asylum, safe conduct and diplomatic immunity, or even the concept of compassion for the stricken. But we must. That puts us into the dilemma any nation faces when its countrymen are the pawns of terrorists. And no civilized nation has yet found a totally satisfactory answer to that problem.

If the present crisis passes without tragedy, the Carter administration still will have to maintain a steady course. Obviously, we will have to make bitter protests. But we should resist taking reprisals — military or otherwise — if our citizens are freed. And we must try as long as possible to maintain a presence inside Iran to keep abreast of the whirling events there. Iran is still an important factor in world politics and economics, and one day soon it is bound to come to its senses.

So our only present course, however frustrating, is to sit tight. This is no time for cheap-shot politics or White House heroics aimed at proving leadership. It is not pleasant to watch a once-emerging people revert to barbarism. It's horrifying when some of our own citizens are caught up in the terror, and when we are impotent to find a dramatic solution. But the better part of wisdom in world affairs is knowing when to keep cool.

Los Angeles Times

Los Angeles, Calif., November 6, 1979

There appears to be virtually nothing that the United States can do about the assaults against its citizens and diplomatic property in Iran except to wait and hope that in time the occupiers of the U.S. Embassy and consulates will grow tired of their sport and bring it to an end. A situation has arisen in which the United States is without leverage, and with few if any choices. Its only right move is to wait things out. If it makes the wrong move, the lives of scores of Americans could be forfeited.

The students who invaded the U.S. diplomatic missions, and the regime that has endorsed their actions, demand that the deposed Shah Mohammed Reza Pahlavi be turned over to Iran. That is not going to happen. So the stage has been set for further anti-American measures. The threat has been made to break relations entirely. The threat has been made to halt Iranian oil sales to the U.S.

market. And always, the threat remains to the Americans still in Iran.

For some weeks the Ayatollah Ruhollah Khomaini has been increasing his fulminations against America, most lately adding plots of "underground treason" to the list of alleged crimes committed or conspired in by Washington. These rantings were all the sanction needed for the latest anti-American explosion. The shah's presence in the United States for medical treatment provided the occasion. With Iran's politics in confusion and the economy in disarray, a distraction of the kind now provided is not only welcome to its leaders but needed. And it is a risk-free operation. Iran is holding the hostages, it is holding the oil card, it has little to fear from any reactive U.S. response. It is an uncomfortable if not humiliating experience for this country, but it is not one that should have been unanticipated.

The Miami Herald

Miami, Fla., November 7, 1979

AS THIS nation seethes in outrage, its government has had to mask its ultimate intentions while negotiating — with dwindling power and options — for the release of 60 American hostages, held under threat of death in our own embassy in Tehran.

Once those Americans are safe, there is one course of action and one point on which the U.S. Government can agree with the portable mob that masquerades as the "government" of Iran: All ties between the United States and Iran must be terminated.

The final vestige of civilized contact disappeared Tuesday with the resignation of Prime Minister Mehdi Bazargan and his cabinet, powerless anyway in face of Ayatollah Khomeini's Islamic Revolutionary Council. This left President Carter and his Administration with nobody to negotiate with except a maddened clique of Islamic clergy that draws its power from the frenzy of murderous slogans.

It is the inability of Khomeini and his blood-cult brothers to govern Iran that resulted in the descent into hysteria. Only by distracting Iranians by setting up devils can Khomeini cloak the chaos of his uncivilized rule. "Death to the shah," and demands for his delivery into Iranian hands by the "Satan" United States are the polarizing elements in a coalition of hate.

But the United States will not hand over the dying shah to a Khomeini who, we must remember, is mortal, too. Whatever sensible and civilized thought exists in Iran cannot be heard now, but now is not forever.

With the disappearance of American personnel and technicians from Iran, a stoppage of military parts and in fact all commerce, and the loss of a market for oil that must be sold somewhere if Iran's situation is not to deteriorate internally even more, Khomeini cannot over the long or even medium term be expected to survive.

But the United States will survive, and without paying blackmail, and will have its honor reestablished at a cost cheap by compare. This nation's oil consumption depends on only 2.5 per cent from Iran. Other oil-producing nations can increase their supply to us — or we can make do with less oil, and make a start on finally facing up to an individual, and a national, policy of energy conservation.

To help us we will have the resolve to not be humiliated at the hands of wild, terrorist sects disguised as a government. We will have moral reason not to trade in the comfort and convenience of a full tank for national dishonor.

And, it is time.

THE SACRAMENTO BEE

Sacramento, Calif., November 7, 1979

The appalling truth about the American hostages in Tehran is that their fate hangs upon the whims of a fanatical religious leader whose regime is becoming an outlaw among nations. The Ayatollah Ruhollah Khomeini, having assumed direct personal control after the resignation of Prime Minister Mehdi Bazargan, has embarked on a reckless and dangerous course which demonstrates, more than anything else, that Iran is governed by mob rule. The dilemma thus presented to Washington is how to deal with a madman who holds traditional diplomacy in contempt and whose revolution, facing an economic debacle, must be fed by ever more fevered hatred of the West in general and of America in particular.

It would be shameful to capitulate to Khomeini's demand to hand over the exiled shah. Neither should this nation be cowed by the ayatollah's threatened cutoff of oil; even if the supplies from Iran were of major importance to the United States — and they are not — such a course would open the door to every imaginable kind of blackmail from elsewhere.

In dealing with the irrationality now in command in Iran, the administration must proceed coolly and patiently. At this writing, the hostages have not been harmed. Unless that circumstance changes, it would be folly to talk, as some in Congress are, about sending in military force to get them out; long before any such effort might succeed, their throats would be cut. Even for the government to discuss that option publicly might endanger their lives. The irony should escape no one, of course, that the Iranian embassy in Washington, fearful of reprisals by American demonstrators, has demanded protection of the kind Iran flagrantly failed to give the U.S. embassy in Tehran.

But while there are limits to Washington's options in the immediate situation, this nation must make it clear to Khomeini that it will react in the sternest possible way, including possible military retaliation, if the hostages are harmed. Meanwhile, in attempting to effect their safe release, Washington is not without leverage. The ayatollah's chaotic regime faces grave difficulties; the resigned Bazargan found the economy almost impossible to administer with the Moslem imams in de facto control. As a result, there's wide internal unrest over the revolution's failure to deliver on its promises, particularly in the cities.

The United States and other governments, including other nations in the Persian Gulf, can apply economic pressures and, in the extreme, sever diplomatic relations, isolating Khomeini. Iran's Arab neighbors, fearful that the ayatollah intends to export his brand of Islamic revolution, have a clear stake in helping to assure that the present crisis doesn't become the trigger to destabilize the entire oil-producing region.

Admittedly, those temporizing measures may not succeed with the fanatic and unpredictable ayatollah. Yet, considering that any impetuous rescue mission at this moment would almost certainly result in the deaths of the hostages at the hands of the terrorist mob, wisdom calls for using that kind of restraint until it is clear tougher sanctions are unavoidable. Time is on Washington's side, time to let Khomeini, for all his fervid Islamic visions, contemplate the prospect of an economic isolation which might very well hasten the ultimate breakdown of his faltering regime. In the end, it must be assumed that even madmen retain some sense of self-preservation.

Soviet Forces Invade Afghanistan After Coup; Deposed Leader Executed

Hafizullah Amin, president of Afghanistan, was ousted Dec. 27 in a coup backed and reportedly engineered by the Soviet Union. His overthrow had been preceded and was followed by the airlifting of thousands of Soviet troops across the border into Afghanistan. By Dec. 29, the invading Soviet force numbered more than 30,000 men, according to U.S. estimates. Moscow said its troops had been invited in by the Afghan government to help it combat "provocation of external enemies."

An Afghan broadcast from Kabul said Amin was executed after a revolutionary court sentenced him to death for "crimes against the state." He was replaced by former Deputy Premier Babrak Karmal, who was installed with a new government on his return from exile in Eastern Europe. In a proclamation issued on his assumption of power, President Karmal declared in a broadcast Dec. 27 that the Afghan people had been liberated from "the bloody apparatus of Hafizullah Amin and his henchmen, the agents of United States imperialism."

The Soviet Union Dec. 30 publicly acknowledged for the first time that it had intervened in Afghanistan. The Communist Party newspaper Pravda said that Moscow had sent a "limited" military contingent to Afghanistan in the face of "imperialist interference" in Afghan affairs that was "taking forms and acquiring a scale that placed the very existence of the republic in danger." The Soviet troops would withdraw when they were no longer needed, Pravda said. Soviet forces were said to have fought a two-hour battle Dec. 31 in the center of Kabul with dissident Afghan army troops opposed to the Soviet military presence. Other Afghan army units were said to be resisting the Soviet soldiers in the eastern and southern parts of the country.

President Carter told Soviet President Leonid Brezhnev Dec. 28 that the Soviet action in Afghanistan, if not "corrected, could have serious consequences to United States-Soviet relations." Carter's warning was contained in a message sent to the Soviet leader on the Washington-Moscow hot line installed for emergency communications. Carter disclosed the sending of the message Dec. 29 and elaborated on it in a television interview Dec. 31. The President denounced the reply he had received from Brezhnev, asserting that the Soviet leader was "not telling the facts accurately." Carter said Brezhnev's explanation that the Soviet Union had been invited to send troops into Afghanistan "was obviously false, because the person he claimed invited him in, President Amin, was murdered or assassinated after the Soviets pulled their coup." Carter added that it was "imperative that within the next few days that [world] leaders make it clear to the Soviets that they cannot take such actions as to violate world peace without severe political consequences."

THE SUN
Baltimore, Md., December 28, 1979

The world cannot accept a Brezhnev doctrine for Afghanistan.

That rationale for the Soviet invasion of Czechoslovakia in 1968 held that the socialist community (Moscow) has a right to invade a socialist state threatened by non-communism within. No free government accepted the doctrine, but none tried to stop the tanks. Czechoslovakia was tacitly recognized as a Soviet satellite.

Afghanistan is not.

In Africa, Moscow has restricted its military role to supply and instruction, with Cubans to do the fighting where needed. In Afghanistan, a neighboring state long coveted by Russian imperialism, Soviet troops are intervening as never before in the Third World. Russian soldiers are being sent to Afghanistan to kill Afghanis and be killed by them.

Afghanistan's Communist revolution of April, 1978, antagonized a whole people. The regime in Kabul would long since have disintegrated without Soviet aid and personnel. Rebellion has spread throughout the country, not limited to tribal, religious or political factions. Though the Russians have built good roads into Afghanistan, they probably could not have moved their troops and material into Kabul on them. Only the airways are secure.

The coup reported yesterday was the second that was stage-managed within the hated Communist regime in hopes of making it more acceptable. Two chosen puppets have been discarded and denounced, and the third installed, possibly by Soviet troops sent for the purpose. Babrek Karmal, the reported new strong man, was considered too Muscovite until now, and had been banished as ambassador to Czechoslovakia. His broadcast promises of liberation from tyranny can have no credibility with Afghanis.

The desperate Soviet escalation is doomed to defeat. Soviet tanks and planes can destroy any town or military concentration in the country, but Russian infantry cannot hold the frigid valleys of the Hindu Kush, where earlier British imperialism had to retreat.

Washington should make every effort to have this intervention condemned in the United Nations and other world councils. Moscow has applauded the maneuvers of the tyrants of Iran to create the semblance of war between the United States and Islam, with which the United States has no quarrel. Next door in Afghanistan, Moscow is truly doing what Washington is falsely accused of doing in Iran.

In trying to consolidate a failed imperialist grab of a non-aligned but friendly Third World country, the Kremlin has thrown its customary caution to the howling winds of the Hindu Kush. This effort seems intended to destabilize all of Central and Western Asia outside Moscow's grasp. It risks backlash at home, where public opinion survives underground, and contamination of Soviet Muslims by the Islamic revival.

The United States alone cannot stop the grab, and should not try. But Washington has a secret ally, and that is the folly of what Moscow is doing.

The Kansas City Times
Kansas City, Mo., December 28, 1979

If the United States is confused about what to do with the Islamic revolution, the Soviet Union is not. If any wild-eyed Muslims have the idea they can overthrow a Soviet-supported ruler, then they can expect to have their mufti stomped on.

Although the Ayatollah Khomeini apparently has missed this basic lesson in Mideast life, his brothers in Afghanistan have not. Islamic rebels there who at one time controlled as much as 60 percent of the Afghan countryside are experiencing the Soviets' idea of a negotiated settlement — keep quiet and we won't shoot you. Thus did they bring instant peace to Hungary.

The more than 5,000 Soviet combat troops sent to back up Afghan strongman Hafizullah Amin are a clear indication of how Moscow strategists plan to deal with Islam's much-heralded revival. There won't be a lot of pondering the Muslim mind or heroic attempts to mend age-old differences. There will be a lot of tanks and AK-47s.

The Soviets, far more than the industrialized West, have reason to fear an Islamic revolution. Three militant Islamic states sit on their southern border, Afganistan, Iran and Pakistan. More importantly, a respectable percentage of the Soviet population is Muslim — subdued Muslim to be sure, but still Muslim. To allow a Khomeini to establish a successful Islamic nation and export Muslim identity to the Soviet Union would be suicide to Moscow's mind.

That such Islamic states as Iran, Iraq, Libya and Syria still insist the United States is their "No. 1" enemy is a perversion of political logic not equaled since the Aztecs welcomed Cortez as their pale-faced savior.

THE WALL STREET JOURNAL.
New York, N.Y., December 28, 1979

Soviet troops were reported fighting in the streets of Kabul yesterday as Afghanistan underwent its latest coup. The troops had arrived in a massive airlift over the past few days. This marks a pivotal change in world affairs. For years the Soviets have used Cubans and other surrogate troops to do the dirty work beyond their immediate sphere of influence in Eastern Europe. Here the Russians are committing their own sons to fight Afghan rebels.

The question is why, and the first response that comes to mind is, why not? Events of the last few years certainly must suggest to the Soviets that there is very little risk of serious opposition from the U.S. to Soviet aggression, overt or covert, in most parts of the globe. In this case, for example, an American spokesman accuses the Soviets of "blatant military intervention," but the response does not extend beyond the State Department press room.

However, a broader answer is needed. The Russians will pay some price, in lives and expense, in trying to subdue Afghan anti-Marxists, and

they risk alienating even those few Afghans who supported the puppet Marxist government. They are obviously making some calculations, not the least of which is that this is an inexpensive way of demonstrating their military capability and the will to use it. With 150 planes, including AN 22 transports capable of delivering 175 fully equipped troops each, they showed that they could put 5,000 troops and supporting heavy weapons into the Kabul area in two days. The lesson for the rest of Asia and the Middle East is that what can be done there can be done elsewhere:

There can be little doubt that the message has been heard. Islamabad, the capital of Pakistan, is only a short hop from Kabul; the Pakistanis would have noticed how quickly the Russians projected direct and forceful power. China and India are only a little further away. Afghanistan has a long flanking border with troubled Iran. You can be sure that the Saudis, already uneasy about Soviet destabilizing influences conducted through South Yemen, and quite possibly, through elements of the PLO, noticed as well. And the message could hardly

have been lost on Israel, or even, say, Iraq, of how military balances in the Middle East could suddenly shift if a similar Soviet airlift should deliver Soviet troops and armor to Syria.

The Russians are, in short, telling the Middle East and the rest of the world that they are not loath to send their own troops into any situation where a political opportunity presents itself. And while their direct interventions have so far been confined to places where great care had first been taken to install a friendly regime, that too carries a message. Any would-be power-grabber who is willing to call himself a Marxist and conduct his overthrow in the name of Communist liberation can count on the kind of backing that really means something, even if he has a very small power base and nothing to offer the people. His chances for success, as opposed to having his head chopped off, suddenly look much better. Hence, there is suddenly greater incentive for Marxist revolution. Such an event in, say, Saudi Arabia, would have dire consequences for the West.

The Soviets are obviously banking

on the United States, Europe and Japan watching the performance from a safe distance, hoping that something will go wrong—that the Russians will get themselves into "their own Vietnam." Even today the curious myth persists that Vietnam was a spontaneous uprising, rather than a calculated war supported by massive Soviet logistical support and in the end settled not by guerrillas but by armor striking across borders. Is the U.S. prepared to supply the outside support that would turn Afghanistan into a Soviet Vietnam? Does it presently have the ability for such covert support even if it had the will?

The broadest lesson of the Afghan airlift is that we cannot bank on the old idea that the Soviets are supercautious in committing their military power. When the occasion is right, when what they call the correlation of forces is in their favor, they are quite capable of bold and direct moves. The caution we have observed over the last three decades was the result of American military power, which is now failing to match Soviet advances and gradually being withdrawn from much of the world.

The Dallas Morning News
Dallas, Texas, December 29, 1979

CHALK UP another triumph for the Carter administration's foreign policy of kindness, geniality, love and restraint. Afghanistan goes the way of Iran and Nicaragua, only more so, as it converts to the status of Soviet satellite.

What are we going to do about it? You guessed it. Raise our voices in righteous shock is what we are going to do.

"We certainly protest," says Defense Secretary Brown, "and we think international condemnation is in order." As of course it is, given the Soviets' blatant and unabashed intrusion of at least 10,000 troops into neighboring Afghanistan and their engineering of a coup in which President Amin was replaced with a Soviet puppet, Babrak Karmal.

Is it clearly understood what is happening? The Soviets are in the process of achieving a century-old Russian objective — the subjugation of Afghanistan, which, as the British so well recognized in bygone days, is the pathway to India.

Worse, Afghanistan borders Iran and makes, accordingly, a splendid base for further subversion of that unhappy country.

We say that the Sovietization of Afghanistan is in process, and for a very good reason. With the militant Moslem tribesmen of that country, the predecessor Marxist government had nothing but trouble; indeed it

was almost certainly the government's failure to quell the tribal revolt that brought Soviet troops directly into play. The Soviets will have to crush the tribesmen before they take total charge of the country. But who can suppose that their modern weapons and ruthlessness must not, in the end, prevail?

For the Afghanistan disaster — it is just that — the Carter administration is largely to blame. Sedulously, Carter has courted the Soviets' good will, going so far as to negotiate with them a one-sided arms limitation agreement in the expectation of coaxing from them a nicer standard of behavior. Nowhere, not even on America's doorstep, Cuba, has Carter challenged or defied the Soviets. They have been allowed to run about the world making trouble. The CIA, which used deftly to handle problems like Afghanistan, did nothing there — at least nothing visible to the naked eye.

So a fine kettle of fish simmers and stinks in the Middle East. The White House wrings its hands over the United Nations' failure to get the hostages out of Iran. Afghanistan falls to the Soviets. Slowly, slowly, Soviet pincers encircle the region, with all its vast oil wealth. What next? Saudi Arabia, where armed revolt has broken out once already? Surely the key question of 1980 is not whether Jimmy Carter can survive; it is whether the nation can survive Jimmy Carter.

The Seattle Times
Seattle, Wash., December 31, 1979

THE Russians are moving boldly to convert Afghanistan, by brute force of arms, from the status of a Marxist state oriented toward Moscow to that of a total satellite like Outer Mongolia, on the opposite flank of China.

Thousands of Soviet soldiers, some from as far away as the Moscow military region, have been airlifted into remote and mountainous Afghanistan with two immediate objectives, the first of which already has been achieved.

That was to install in power, by means of a bloody coup, a puppet, Babrak Karmal. His complete willingness to serve Moscow contrasts with the somewhat independent leanings of his slain predecessor, President Hafizullah Amin.

The second objective — which will not be so easy — is, of course, to crush the Islamic rebels who control much of the Afghan countryside and who say they "will not be deceived by the change in pawns" in the capital, Kabul.

Afghanistan has little in the way of oil or other important economic resources. But it is a strategic prize for the Russians for at least two reasons.

Under Moscow's control, it contributes to the encirclement of China by Soviet or pro-Soviet

forces. And it is one of a layer of Moslem states that stand between the Soviet Union and the free world's oil-supply sea routes.

The naked power play in Afghanistan, the largest Soviet troop movement outside Eastern Europe since World War II, establishes the Kremlin's willingness to use its own forces — in addition to proxy troops like the Cubans in Africa — to expand its satellite empire.

This point was nailed down by the similarity of official Soviet statements justifying the military move into Afghanistan and that into Czechoslovakia 11 years ago. In both cases, Moscow spoke of a need to "defend revolutionary gains."

For the free world, the implications of this newest chapter in Russian imperialiasm are enormous. Defense Secretary Harold Brown says "international condemnation is in order."

But even though the armed opposition to the Russian designs in Afghanistan is the Islamic fundamentalist movement in that country, there have been no outcries from other Moslem capitals and no mob take-overs of Russian embassies by "Islamic revolutionaries."

St. Louis Globe-Democrat

St. Louis, Mo., December 28, 1979

What is happening in the Middle East and Africa bears a strong resemblance to the events that preceded World War II in the late 1930s.

In the late 1930s Adolf Hitler became convinced his Third Reich war machine was superior to any in the world and could do as it pleased. As isolationists in Britain and the United States stood by and did nothing, Hitler unleashed his Panzer divisions to conquer Denmark, Norway, Czechoslovakia, France, East Poland and other Balkan states while the Russians gobbled up West Poland, Finland and the Baltic countries.

Then in June of 1941 Hitler sent three million troops against the Soviet Union as he envisioned a final conquest of the continent.

Today the Russians, apparently certain their military power can't be challenged by the United States, have airlifted thousands of armed troops and equipment into Afghanistan to install a new puppet Communist regime in Kabul and crush a full-scale rebellion by anti-Communist Moslem guerrillas in the mountainous northeastern province of Badakhshan.

One of the first actions reportedly taken by the encroaching Russians was to install Babrek Karmel, a leader of the Parcham faction of the Afghanistan Communist Party, as the new head of state.

The State Department says the Soviets have carried out a 150-plane airlift of as many as 4,000 combat soldiers and their equipment in a two-day period, bringing the number of Russian troops in that country to 5,500 men. These are in addition to 3,500 Soviet military advisers who have been there for the last year. The Russians also are said to have mobilized five divisions—50,000 men—on the Soviet side of the Afghan border.

It is reported that the planned offensive against the Moslem rebels in Badakhshan would be mounted by 5,000 Afghan Communist and 800 Russian combat troops backed by 300 Soviet-supplied tanks.

This is the third time in recent years the Russians have openly intervened militarily to crush anti-Communist forces in the Middle East and Africa. They transported more than 12,000 Cubans to Angola to defeat pro-western forces in that country. They sent massive aid to Ethiopia's Communist rulers to crush the Somali forces in the Ogaden region. Now they appear to be converting Afghanistan from a buffer state into another tightly-controlled satellite.

In the previous instances the U.S. protested weakly. This time a State Department spokesman accused the Russians of "blatant military interference" in Afghanistan but the Russians again paid no attention.

But look what happens when the U.S. contemplates possible military action against Iran for the seizure of 50 American hostages. The Russians growl that they would go to Iran's aid in the event of a U.S. attack. So the nation once regarded as the strongest in the world meekly accepts the imprisonment and harassment of our diplomats and military personnel, as well as daily insults from the fanatic Ayatollah Ruhollah Khomeini.

Should the Russians now put Afghanistan in their orbit, Iran and Pakistan could soon be in danger of a Soviet takeover. The Russians apparently have decided they can ignore the muted protests of the Carter administration and velvet-gloved doves in Congress. This is a highly dangerous situation. Like Neville Chamberlain, the U.S. appeasers believe they can stop the Communist advances with words. But the Soviets simply aren't listening.

The Cincinnati Post

TIMES ✦ STAR

Cincinnati, Ohio, December 28, 1979

At long last the Carter administration has publicly denounced the Soviet Union's "blatant military interference" in strategically placed Afghanistan. That is a good start but not enough.

Through coups in April 1978 and just this week that put pro-Moscow communists in power in Kabul, the Kremlin has been struggling to turn the fiercely independent, deeply religious Afghan people into docile subjects.

Unfortunately for Moscow's ambitions, its puppets in Kabul are seen as godless and foreign-dominated. Islamic tribesmen are in revolt all over the country and would overrun the capital in weeks if it were not for the Russians.

Moscow has 3500 "advisers" on the scene running the war against the rebels.

It is this threat to regional stability that jarred Washington out of polite silence. A major Soviet military presence in Afghanistan endangers neighboring Iran and Pakistan. It gives Russia a chance to move through Pakistan to the Indian Ocean, a goal since czarist days.

Given Russia's proximity and America's distance, Afghanistan is no place for the United States to get involved militarily. But that should not rule out covert gun-running to the rebels and other moves.

Moscow's power grab should be taken to the United Nations as a breach of the peace. Radio broadcasting to Moslem nations should brand the Kremlin for what it is — an enemy of Islam.

The Soviet Union is badly trying to change the balance of power in Southwest Asia. Washington can, at little risk, enormously raise the cost of Moscow's effort, if it has the will to do so.

The Evening Bulletin

Philadelphia, Pa., December 28, 1979

The fast moving events in Afghanistan, where for the first time the Soviet Union airlifted thousands of its fully equipped combat troops into a non-Eastern European satellite, may well surpass the crisis in Iran in terms of lasting importance to the U.S. and to our allies.

For what happens in Afghanistan, which borders on Iran — what influence the Russians gain there — will have a continuing economic as well as military impact on the entire Persian Gulf area, a region that holds nearly two-thirds of the world's proven reserves of oil. The Persian Gulf not only washes Iran. It also touches on Saudi Arabia, Iraq, Kuwait, the United Arab Emirates and other oil producing states. And fully 16 percent of the oil we use comes from there.

Just after World War II, before we had to depend upon others for oil to run our cars and heat our homes, we didn't worry about the Persian Gulf. It was England's problem, and for years it kept thousands of British troops occupied. But by the time the British pulled out we couldn't do without Persian Gulf oil. And with the British gone we had to look around for a proxy policeman to keep the Russians from flowing into the power vacuum and threatening our oil supply.

It was then, back in the 50s, that we turned to the shah of Iran and poured money and military hardware into his country. With the shah banished, a victim of his own as well as our excesses, we're once more fearful that Russia will keep us away from the oil supply.

The rules of the game have changed, though. Military power isn't enough. There is a Muslim tide and Third World aspirations that must be considered. It most likely would be fatal for any ruler to allow himself to be designated as anyone's proxy. So if we are to be a force in the Persian Gulf-Indian Ocean area it will have to be with the consent of the Saudis and others there. It will cost us a lot of money, probably worsen our inflation. But until we discipline ourselves to use less foreign oil, we have little choice.

Our continuing testing in Iran has brought us closer together and erased many of the self-doubts and guilt feelings left over from Vietnam. This is all to the good, for we may need a great deal of national unity in the months just ahead.

DAILY ☒ NEWS

New York, N.Y., December 29, 1979

President Carter has good reason to be alarmed over the Soviet Union's naked use of military force to set up a trusty stooge government in Afghanistan.

With a slavishly obedient regime in Kabul, Moscow will be able to expand its base of operations in Afghanistan and extend its penetration into an area vital to the free world. The bold move also was calculated to impress Middle East friends of the U.S. with the USSR's military might—and its willingness to use it.

But if he hopes to thwart Russia's ambitions, the President is going to have to do more than voice a strong protest and consult with allies. For openers, he should get cracking on acquisition of air and naval bases in the region. The nations of the Middle East aren't going to believe in American power unless they can see and feel its presence.

Let's act quickly and decisively, even at the risk of offending the Third World. We can't retreat from an area vital to our national interest simply out of fear that we will be denounced as "American imperialists." We are a great power and we should act like one.

Lincoln Journal

Lincoln, Neb., December 28, 1979

Soviet military muscle is being flexed again, and it is not a reassuring sight. Moscow's "aid" to Afghanistan in putting down a Moslem rebellion seems to have amounted virtually to an invasion, perhaps the largest Soviet troop movement outside of Eastern Europe since World War II.

The upshot, as best it can be determined from a distance, is that Moscow's erstwhile buddy in Kabul was executed in a coup and has been replaced by a stooge even more willing to do the Kremlin's bidding. The conclusion has to be: the Soviets will take any steps necessary to end the 20-month-long civil war and crush the Moslem insurrection which seeks to erase any traces of atheistic Marxism from the government.

This development occurred despite U.S. warnings to Moscow to tread lightly in Afghanistan. One American official called the heavy-handed military operation "the grossest form of international behavior." Obviously it is not likely to make things easier for the United States in a part of the world where it already has trouble enough.

Still, there may be some sources of comfort in the generally depressing situation. America's civilized course in trying to solve its own problems in Iran stands in sharp contrast to the crude Soviet response in next-door Afghanistan. That should not be lost on neighbors of the two countries, or on the world community in general.

Further, it is important to realize this *was* a response. The Soviet Union was not taking an initiative as part of some global plan of subjugation, but rather was reacting to a situation even more dangerous to it than the Iran crisis is to the United States.

Iran, on the U.S.S.R.'s southern border, is now a fundamentalist Moslem state. Had Afghanistan's rebels prevailed, that nation could have ended up another. The prospect of two such neighbors frightened Moscow.

And with cause. Already there are reports of unrest among the Soviet Union's Moslem population. Though little heard of in the West, these ethnic and religious minorities are sizable segments of the Soviet people — and, indeed, in another quarter century may no longer be a minority.

Quelling a second Moslem uprising on its doorstep may make sense from the Kremlin's point of view, but there is no guarantee that in the long run it will keep the Islamic areas of the U.S.S.R. immune to insurrection.

If Western societies have underestimated the power of religion, the atheistic Soviet Union certainly has. Islamic stirrings in several lands suggest we may be entering a period of — archaic as the term sounds — religious wars. If these fires of fervor spread, the Kremlin's chief problem will be dousing flames at home, not on its border.

THE INDIANAPOLIS STAR

Indianapolis, Ind., December 29, 1979

History repeats itself — sometimes with extraordinary exactness.

In the armed aggression against Afghanistan by the Soviet Union history has produced almost a mirror image of the Soviet march into Hungary in 1956.

At that fateful time, it will be recalled, the eyes of the world were riveted on the so-called Suez crisis — an abortive struggle involving Britain, France, Israel and Egypt, with the shadowy form of the Soviet Union in the background. The United States government was shaken. It administered a tongue-lashing to Britain and France — unwisely committed to the struggle — and a stalemate resulted.

But while this event commanded center stage, the Soviets cannily jumped at the chance to solve a problem of their own. The Hungarian people just then had risen against their Soviet-installed communist government, which had been maneuvered into power in direct contradiction of the Yalta and Potsdam agreements at the close of World War II.

What did the USSR do? While the rest of the world was looking the other way — at Suez — it sent massive detachments of the Red Army into Hungary. It smashed the Hungarian people's revolt. It reinstalled its puppet regime in Hungary — where it has been in power ever since.

Then the rest of the world awoke. Led by the U.S., it let out a wail. It protested. It wrung its collective hands. But it *did* nothing.

And isn't that the almost exact same scenario seen today in the Afghanistan coup?

For weeks the world has been engrossed in the Iran crisis, the hostages, the Ayatollah Khomeini, the gang of "students" holding the U.S. embassy in Tehran. And meanwhile the Russians have been having a problem. They've been wrestling with a Moslem uprising in Afghanistan directed at the tyrannical Moscow-backed communist government in Kabul.

But the Soviets have found a way to solve their problem. How? While the rest of the world gazed at Iran, they seized on the chance to send massive detachments of the Red Army into Afghanistan, where its dirty work could be done almost unnoticed.

Reports indicate the Soviets have smashed — or at least forestalled — the Afghan people's revolt. They even appear to have gone one better than in Hungary. Not only have they reinstalled their puppet regime in Kabul, they have set in power a man — oh, yes, a Moslem Afghan — yet more amenable to their purposes than his predecessor.

So what will the world do? Will it yell, wring its hands, protest, run to the United Nations for "help"? Or will it *do* something?

We shall see. But the smart money will be on nothing, nix, zilch — until the now clearly impending avalanche finally breaks loose.

DAYTON DAILY NEWS

Dayton, Ohio, December 28, 1979

If the world had its consciousness raised by the American misadventure in Vietnam, you can't tell it from the reaction to the Soviet Union's military intervention in Afghanistan. For the Soviet Union's power play, there are only a few tsk-tsks.

But the general indifference does not diminish the rawness of the Soviet move. The Kremlin threw in thousands of Russian troops to order to assure itself a pro-Soviet government there.

The latest coup, won in part with Russian troops, obviously advanced the Soviet aims, though whether it secured them remains to be seen. In any event, the involvement of Russsian troops raised the stakes dangerously in the hardening Soviet-American contest in the Middle East and southern Asia. In effect, Moscow has announced that it now believes the prizes, oil and position, so great that it will not settle for attempting to influence and manipulate political events to its favor. At least sometimes, it is willing to compel events to its advantage.

The Russians have been trying to force Afghanistan into their orbit as firmly as they have forced their East European satellites, in the course eliminating some of the neutral counterweight in the region that both superpowers allowed in the past as a way to keep their rivalry there from becoming total.

Make no mistake. This is a grave change in the rules by which the superpowers have played in the Middle East and southern Asia. The Soviet Union is now taking up the line from *Butch Cassidy and the Sundance Kid:* "Rules? In a knife fight?"

Whether it really must become a knife fight probably will depend upon how things go for the Soviet Union in Afghanistan — whether it can maintain its toady regime against the seething, Khomeini-like Islamic upheaval without undue cost, whether the world accepts the Soviet grab with the double standard by which it often measures the acts of Washington and Moscow.

The Carter adminstration is trying almost desperately to overturn the habits of that double standard in order to force world recognition of the gravity of the Soviet move. There should be some allies for American concerns. India, Pakistan and China must fear the advance of the Soviet military into the heart of their region. Iran, next door, should fear for its revolution, much the same sort the Russians are suppressing in Afghanistan. The Mideast oil states must fear the influence that Soviet power in Afghanistan could have on Iranian oil policy, even if the Russians never step into the Iranian fields just across the border.

It is impossible to guess all the consequences now, but the politics of the region will be badly shaken for years to come. Whether it succeeds or fails, the Soviet move on Afghanistan is one of the most reckless disturbances in years in what has passed for world order.

IRANIAN CRISIS:
U.S. Hostage Rescue Mission Fails; Iran Displays Commandos' Bodies

The U.S. April 24 launched an airborne attempt to free the American hostages in Teheran, but the mission was called off after one of the helicopters involved in the operation developed engine trouble in a staging area in the Iranian desert. Eight Americans were killed and several injured in the collision of two planes during the withdrawal of the U.S. force. An official report on the ill-fated U.S. mission was first made public April 25 by Defense Secretary Harold Brown. A more detailed account was provided by President Carter April 27.

According to Carter's report: six U.S. C-130 Hercules transport planes and eight RH-53 helicopters "entered Iranian airspace" April 24. The transport planes had taken off from Egypt and the helicopters left the aircraft carrier *Nimitz* in the Arabian Sea.

During the flight to the rendezvous point in Dasht-i-Kavir, two of the eight helicopters developed operating problems. One returned to the *Nimitz* and the second landed in the desert, where its crew was picked up by another helicopter and flown on to the landing site.

One of the six helicopters that arrived at Dasht-i-Kavir "developed a serious hydraulic problem and was unable to continue with the mission." Since the plan called for a minimum of six helicopters to carry out the rescue, "it was determined not to proceed as planned." At this point, Carter said he had decided, on the recommendation of the force commander and his military advisers, to cancel the operation.

During the pullout, one helicopter collided with a C-130, which was about to take off, resulting in the death of eight men and injury of five others. All surviving members of the party then boarded the five C-130s and left; the remaining five helicopters were left behind as were the eight dead.

Altogether, the U.S. force remained on the ground for about three hours.

During the operation, the U.S. force at the landing site stopped a passing Iranian bus on a nearby road. All its 44 occupants were detained and later released unharmed just before the Americans departed.

Iran announced April 26 that it had moved the hostages from the U.S. Embassy and scattered them among other Iranian cities to prevent further rescue attempts. Iranian authorities April 27 displayed the bodies of the Americans killed during the ill-fated rescue attempt. The ruling Revolutionary Council announced April 28 that it would not turn the bodies over directly to the U.S. but would transfer them to representatives of Pope John Paul II and the Red Cross for repatriation to their families.

THE INDIANAPOLIS NEWS
Indianapolis, Ind., April 25, 1980

President Carter's gamble in mounting a rescue of the American hostages in Iran has ended in a tragic loss of eight Americans who volunteered for this military effort.

If the rescue had been successful, the President would have been hailed around the world as a hero. At home, his prestige would have been immeasurably enhanced and no one would have dared speak a critical word.

Now that he has failed, his critics have additional evidence of his incompetence to handle what must be appraised as one of the most difficult foreign policy decisions in the nation's history.

Dismayed by another failure in the international arena, Americans will be pondering and discussing the obvious questions: Was the timing of this rescue forced upon the President by developments known only to him? Why was the rescue launched at the very moment when most of the American allies appeared to be joining a collaborative attempt to press Iran into surrender of the hostages? Was it wise to divert — and perhaps destroy — the growing support of an international economic assault upon Iran? Was this commando-type raid dictated by political pressures at home? Why was an obviously dangerous military technique chosen at the moment when a less dangerous naval blockade was achieving international support? Was it wise, in the light of finally achieving such international cooperation, to shock the allies with what appears to them to be a rash solo act?

Answers to these questions will not be easy to sort out in the aftermath of a military effort now diminished by "equipment failure." What had in the course of .74 days become a humiliating national experience has now assumed traumatic dimensions. The President has, as he put it, lived through the "longest night of his presidency."

While they may condemn him for poor judgment, Americans share his agonies and will surely stand with him in his — and their — search for an effective response to an international outlaw.

THE PLAIN DEALER

Cleveland, Ohio, April 26, 1980

"It was worse than a mistake, it was a blunder."

This famous crack by the 18th-century French diplomat Talleyrand best describes the United States' fiasco in Iran. President Carter has accepted the blame. He deserves it. The Russians describe it as "laughable, ridiculous, wild." Allies so far have been more subtle, but they have left little doubt about their concern.

In short, the United States is a laughingstock.

Without opposition, the supposed greatest power in the world attempted a risky operation and simply ran into itself and was forced to withdraw. The picture of the president of the United States having to explain this mess to the public was bad enough. Then the secretary of defense and the chairman of the Joint Chiefs of Staff added more embarrassing details.

But even if the rescue operation of the hostages in Tehran had been successful, was the risk worth it? The Russians have massed troops on the Iranian border. Iran, in retaliation to the United States and its allies, could seal off the Persian Gulf and prevent passage of oil from Saudi Arabia and other nations. Such retaliation and potential military escalation must be weighed against the genuine concern for the American hostages.

This fiasco serves to damage our working relationship with our allies who have just publicly acted to support us. Our enemies and allies have been given good reason to question Carter's repeated statements that the United States is the strongest power in the world.

Strangely, the presidential political candidates have been very restrained in their comments. Even Sen. Howard H. Baker, a Republican who withdrew from the presidential sweepstakes, was not critical of the Democratic president after Baker was briefed about the situation. Perhaps President Carter had checked all this with the Russians in advance. Perhaps the Joint Chiefs had a great many volunteers who thought they knew how to pull off a secret military operation at night. Perhaps some people in high places don't know what they are doing and don't know what they are talking about. Something clearly is haywire.

Americans have been mystified, embarrassed and disgusted and saddened by the death of eight of their countrymen.

The Atlanta Journal
AND
THE ATLANTA CONSTITUTION

Atlanta, Ga., April 26, 1980

It isn't over. It may scarcely even have begun. That the United States should now abandon its attempt to free the hostages in Tehran, even after the humiliating failure of its first attempt, seems unthinkable.

The risk to the hostages? It may be less great now than many people had feared. At every turn the militants in our embassy have threatened to kill the hostages if Americans attempted anything of this kind. We did, and they didn't — and now, if there is any lucidity of thought left in that demented land, they have to realize that they have lost something in the way of a psychological edge that can never be regained.

And they may have to reassess their possibly superficial impressions about the lack of American will. The eight men who lost their lives in the aborted rescue mission were as courageous and determined as any who charged up the hill at Gettysburg or fought their way onto the beaches of Normandy — and there will be others, equally brave, ready to take up where these men left off.

So it isn't over. And it may be that no one would be happier to see it over — and successfully concluded — than the Iranian Revolutionary Council itself. No one knows better than the council members how much the Soviet Union stands to gain from a prolongation of the hostage crisis — and how, inevitably, if it continues, Iran itself will be brought under Soviet domination.

If they're not actually Soviet agents armed and equipped by Moscow, the embassy militants know that as well. And now they know something else too: that they may have to die for whatever gains they hope to achieve.

Chicago Tribune

Chicago, Ill., April 26, 1980

We believe, and the nation must believe, that President Carter made the right decision in sending the rescue team to Iran. It is wrong to criticize him now for making the decision. It is wrong to criticize him for failing to consult in advance with Congress or with the allies. It is outrageous to suggest that he acted for domestic political reasons. There are but three proper emotions for Americans in the tragic aftermath of the mission's failure: gratitude to the brave volunteers who undertook it; grief for the eight who died in it; and intense disappointment over the bad luck that aborted it.

It cannot be said that the White House acted in ignorance or in folly despite the widely voiced and apparently compelling arguments against a military rescue effort. People with access to far more information than is available to the rest of us determined that the chances of success were sufficient to risk the dangers—such dangers as the enormous physical problems involved in mounting such an operation over great distances and in the heart of a major city, the shock to allies who had just begun to join in sanctions against Iran; and the political embarrassment that would attend a failure. Defense Secretary Harold Brown said the operation had been rehearsed repeatedly and successfully. It was the unforeseen and apparently unforeseeable breakdowns of three helicopters, plus the tragedy of the ground collision, that turned it into a debacle. The timing, too, was justified. The continued strains on the hostages and Iran's deteriorating domestic political situation argued strongly for a rescue attempt. Moreover, according to Secretary Brown, summertime heat and diminishing hours of darkness would have ruled it out for many more months had it not been undertaken when it was. The fact that the allies had begun to move on sanctions was not sufficiently relevant to delay. For one thing, allied movement was so sluggish as to be nearly useless. For another, the very fact that the administration seemed to be turning away from military action helped to insure secrecy and surprise.

Secrecy obviously was of paramount importance, and critics in Congress are wrong in attacking President Carter for failing to consult with them under the terms of the War Powers Act. One congressman went so far as to call him "stupid." But what the President ordered was a rescue mission, not a war. He would have been genuinely stupid to jeopardize the mission by informing even a single member of our leak-happy Congress, and stupider still to broadcast it around the world by telling our allies.

We can hope that the failure will not lead to reprisals against the hostages. Iranian officials are counseling restraint, and the embassy kidnappers' mood is one of smug delight rather than homicidal rage—a factor that the planners must have considered in contemplating failure.

So although Americans will feel frustration and rage over the gloating that will come from Tehran, there is no call for shame or embarrassment. Brave men did their courageous best to rescue their countrymen, and only the most undeserved bad luck prevented them from doing it.

They, and the President, deserve only praise for what they did. As Sen. Howard Baker so succinctly put it: "I'm glad we tried it; I'm sorry we failed."

The Seattle Times

Seattle, Wash., April 25, 1980

TODAY is a day of mourning for America. Also a day of concern and rage.

There is mourning for the eight lives lost in last night's abortive rescue operation in Iran.

There is concern for the future of the 53 Tehran hostages, whose status at first report, at least, remains unchanged.

There is rage at incompetence in high places, beginning in the Oval Office.

In a nation that is officially at peace, members of the armed forces are still sacrificing their lives in distant, God-forsaken areas of the globe. In a world where a major regional power is run by outlaws who seize diplomats as hostages, it is not surprising that such sacrifices become necessary.

America's heart goes out to the families of the brave men who died last night and to the families of the hostages, who have endured nearly nearly half a year of agonized waiting and now must face even greater uncertainties.

President Carter shoulders full responsibility for the desert fiasco. He could scarcely have done otherwise. To him would have accrued the cheers and the political benefits had the operation been successful.

Obviously there is a high element of luck in a venture of that kind. Any number of things could have gone wrong. Mr. Carter cannot be blamed personally for the helicopter functions that did go wrong. He had to trust the judgment of his military advisers. —

But the issue of competence in the Oval Office goes far beyond the "nuts and bolts" of a military operation.

Huge questions remain about the wisdom of attempting the raid at a time when — at long last — all of America's major allies were beginning to act in concert to apply real pressure on Iran.

The allies, albeit with considerable misgivings, were moving to get in step with Uncle Sam, partly because they feared the possibility of exactly what happened last night — a bold, unilateral American strike posing risks for all the industrial democracies.

Now there are fresh threats from Tehran to "set the Persian Gulf aflame." U.S. prestige is at its lowest ebb since the Bay of Pigs. And all plans, all hopes, are in disarray.

CUBA:

Carter Orders Halt to Refugee Flow; Haitians Demand Asylum

Cuban refugees began reaching the shores of Key West in late April, after Premier Fidel Castro terminated a two-day airlift of refugees to Costa Rica. Private boats, bought or chartered by Cuban-Americans, headed for the port of Mariel to pick up relatives or other Cubans who had been allowed to leave the country. The refugee flood reached serious proportions by mid-May, prompting President Carter May 14 to reverse himself on his initial pledge to welcome the Cubans with "open arms." Carter ordered the U.S. Coast Guard to prevent boats from leaving Florida, and he called for measures to screen incoming Cubans in Miami. By May 15, a total of 46,000 Cubans had landed in Key West, and there were reports that criminals and mental patients were among them. Most were flown to U.S. military bases to await processing. Aside from the problem of handling such a large flood of refugees, there was fear that the influx of Cubans would give rise to anti-Hispanic sentiment in Florida, whose Cuban population was already quite large.

The refugee exodus stirred up anti-U.S. sentiment in Cuba. The U.S. May 4 closed its interests section in the Swiss Embassy in Havana and ordered all personnel to leave May 15. Cubans waiting to enter the interests section had been attacked by pro-Castro mobs.

Meanwhile, Haitians who had reached Miami by boat told a federal court judge May 7 that they should be classified as political refugees like the Cubans. The U.S. listed Haitians as economic refugees, which did not entitle them to asylum. About 26,000 Haitians had fled poverty and repression in their country to reach Miami, where they were considered illegal aliens and ineligible to work. Carter was criticized by labor, human rights and black groups for the different treatment of the Haitians. They charged the Administration with racial prejudice, noting that most of the Cubans were white, while the Haitians were black.

The Seattle Times

Seattle, Wash., May 9, 1980

THEY come in waves, sometimes thousands in a single day. There are Communist spies among them. And criminals and prostitutes. Nearly all are destitute.

Yet the United States has not barred the gates to this newest of the world's repeated floods of political refugees.

Cuba's "Freedom Flotilla" poses a wide array of problems for the U.S., including the urgently necessary one of screening out the spies and other undesirables. This country is being called upon to assimilate the new waves of refugees even while a similar task remains far from complete in regard to the transplanted Vietnamese and Cambodians.

Yet President Carter was reacting in line with the best of this country's traditions — and with majority American sentiment — when he pledged to accept thousands more Cuban refugees and declared that they are welcomed with "open arms and an open heart."

The earlier generation of Cuban refugees, who fled to these shores when Fidel Castro was first consolidating his power, has proven to be a national asset — a successful ethnic community not unlike the European ethnic communities that took root in the U.S. in the last century.

We have no doubt that the ultimate verdict on the newcomers will be the same.

For the short range, though, there is obvious validity in a federal official's observation that "Castro is jiggling us. He is playing games with us, is trying to embarrass us."

The U.S. is helping the Cuban Communist dictator ease his problems of overcrowding, political dissent and economic stagnation.

But the larger reality is an admission of failure on the part of the Castro revolution. In the last analysis, the U.S. — for all of its tactical blundering during more than two decades of indecision as to how to "handle" Castro — has a reason for pride.

THE MILWAUKEE JOURNAL

Milwaukee, Wisc., May 1, 1980

In attempting to cope with the flood of refugees from Fidel Castro's authoritarian Cuba, the US government should not forget this country's tradition of providing a haven for the disinherited and politically repressed.

Granted, Castro is cynically testing America's hospitality by urging hundreds of thousands of dissatisfied Cubans to move to the US. But the US government, which criticized Malaysia and Thailand for being reluctant to accommodate the boat people from Vietnam, will appear callous and hypocritical if it slams its "golden door" on Cuban refugees.

Confronted with a similar Cuban exodus in 1965, President Lyndon Johnson stood at the base of the Statue of Liberty and enunciated a policy that permitted 265,000 Cubans to systematically enter the US over an eight year period. As a group they have proved to be responsible and self-sufficient.

So far, the Carter administration's policy is confusing. Some officials have been threatening to fine boat owners who illegally transport refugees to the US; others seem mainly concerned with filtering out the criminals (Castro reportedly is emptying his prisons). Commendably, President Carter has at least decided to provide Navy escort for the boatlift.

There's no denying that the influx of Cubans, particularly if it comes too fast, can create problems in a country already worried about unemployment and perplexed over a growing population of illegal aliens. Therefore, it would be reasonable to try to stretch out the admission of Cubans over a period of time. It is also sensible to screen the refugees, seeking to distinguish between, say, a political dissident and a common criminal. And it is proper to call upon other countries to share the refugee burden.

The thing to avoid, however, is any suggestion that the US has forgotten its historic invitation to the "huddled masses yearning to breathe free."

The News and Courier
Charleston, S.C., May 8, 1980

President Carter's pledge that the United States will accept with "an open heart and open arms" tens of thousands of Cuban refugees typifies the humanitarian spirit that freedom-loving people in other lands long have associated with America. The president's promise of sanctuary, made as small boats continued to land refugees in Florida, puts in sharp contrast the ways of life in the U.S. and in Castro's Cuba. The exodus has made the differences stand out for the world — and especially for Latin Americans — to see.

Accepting thousands and thousands of Cubans fleeing a repressive regime is not without complications, however. Reaction to the stream of refugees has put U.S. immigration policies in disarray. Aliens without proper papers are welcomed, while the masters of the boats which brought them are fined. Laws bent or broken for reasons of compassion inevitably will invite charges of unfairness. How does a government justify taking in illegal aliens escaping oppression in one country, while turning away those fleeing another?

Beyond that are the strains imposed in receiving and absorbing the Cubans now joining the 800,000 who have come to this country since Castro came to power 20 years ago. Millions in federal funds are going to help Florida cope with the influx. The economic impact will, of course, spread, extending to employment and welfare fields where populations are concentrated. Job competition will create animosities, if experience is any guide.

There is, additionally, a screening problem. Immigration officials say there is evidence Fidel Castro is unloading his jails, pushing criminals into the immigrant stream to the U.S. The scope of that problem can only be guessed at.

Welcoming refugees with open heart and open arms presents difficulties even in a nation as large as the United States, because most go not to the open spaces, but to overcrowded metropolitan areas.

The Cleveland Press
Cleveland, Ohio, May 1, 1980

The challenge flung down to the United States by Fidel Castro in the matter of the Cuban boat refugees demands a bold response.

Here is a chance to strike a telling psychological and propaganda blow against Cuba's Communist dictatorship. Here is an opportunity to wipe away some of the humiliation this country suffered in the hostage-rescue debacle in Iran.

In our fancy, we hear President Carter proclaiming, as President Johnson did during a similar opportunity in 1965, an "open door" policy for Cuban refugees.

We picture him going beyond Johnson's limited airlift and chartering a fleet of Caribbean cruise ships, each capable of carrying hundreds of passengers, and every other large ship he can, and sending them to Havana harbor in full view of the world.

We imagine the Voice of America saturating Cuban airwaves unto the remotest parts of the island with the news that transportation to freedom awaited everyone who could make his way to the coast.

Fanciful, of course. But the fact is that the Castro regime stands very close to being fatally discredited, for today's refugees, unlike the earlier great wave in the 1960s, are Cubans who have grown up under communism.

Sadly, this sincere champion of human rights around the world has so far mustered only a feeble, legalistic response to the greatest human rights challenge of his administration — one taking place right on the nation's doorstep.

U.S. authorities are seizing boats and fining their captains for bringing refugees to Miami. It is a field day for hucksters in human lives who are charging exorbitant boat rental fees. Caught in storms in tiny, unseaworthy craft, an unknown number of refugees have drowned.

We implore the president to rise to this challenge.

The London Free Press
London, Ont., May 7, 1980

The Communist dictatorship put together by Fidel Castro is still capable of bringing out hundreds of thousands of Cubans for a May Day propaganda rally in Havana. But the thousands of other Cubans fleeing the island in small boats at grave risk to their lives attest to the political oppression and economic inefficiency of this self-styled "paradise of socialism" in the Caribbean.

Judging from the number of requests for exit visas, diplomats in Havana estimate from 200,000 to 400,000 Cubans would like to quit the island. Most prefer to go to the United States, of course, but as the 10,000 would-be emigrants who jammed into the Peruvian embassy grounds last month indicated, many thousands of Cubans would be pleased to settle in almost any other impoverished Latin American country just to get out from under Castro's yoke.

To be sure, conditions in Cuba today are in many respects much improved over the injustices which existed under the previous Batista dictatorship. Unlike most other Latin American countries, few children in Cuba now go barefoot and almost all have an opportunity to attend school. In many Latin American countries, half the population goes hungry, but in Cuba, almost everyone has an adequate, if bland, diet as well as access to minimal health-care services.

So what's wrong with Cuba? The main problem seems to be that initial gains in social justice have given way to continuing economic stagnation and political oppression.

For 1976, the Castro regime admitted that production fell 2.2 per cent or $200 million below the planned target level. Corresponding figures have not been released for any year since — a good indication that no improvement in productivity has occurred.

Economic conditions would be much worse without support from the Soviet Union. U.S. experts estimate that out of a total gross national product for Cuba of about $10 billion a year, no less than $3 billion depends on Soviet subsidies. That's an expensive drain for the Kremlin, which already has serious economic difficulties to contend with at home.

Indeed, the economic problems of Cuba and the Soviet Union have an important common cause; namely, the collectivization of agriculture. Nowhere has this system of farming proven efficient in promoting long-term gains in food production. Not in the Soviet Union, not in Tanzania, and certainly not in Cuba.

Land reformers in Latin America and elsewhere would do better to look not to Cuba but to rural North America of the last century. There can be no doubt that in comparison with communal farming and large landed estates, a system of privately owned family farms is far more conducive to promoting social justice, economic growth and political freedom. The end results might not be utopia, but that's a delusion pursued by political fanatics like Castro at great expense in suffering for thousands of his countrymen.

THE SAGINAW NEWS
Saginaw, Mich., May 11, 1980

The flood of Cuban refugees braving death to reach America's shores says something about Fidel Castro's Cuba. It says more about America. And Americans should listen.

While paranoid ayatollahs and two-bit dictators are kicking our country around, the people they rule are still voting their own feelings. On the issue of America, their ballots are emphatically marked yes.

It's yes, also, that the refugees are coming while our nation is in an economic slump — although many of them gladly take menial jobs and seek only opportunities for advancement, not guarantees of it. It's true they create temporary settlement problems and that Castro is trying to foist criminals off on the U.S.

Even that is indicative of the spite of a dictator sharply rebuked by his own people in their eagerness to escape, to taste freedom, to make a new life in the one land where that more than anywhere else remains possible.

It's sad that so much of the world shares this yearning, one above and beyond political mouthings. But in our own malaise, it must be encouraging that Liberty's torch remains visible and bright beyond our shores. We cannot extinguish it without darkening the reflection it casts on us and our nation.

1980 ELECTION:

Ronald Reagan Wins Election in Massive Sweep of States

Ronald Reagan was elected the 40th President of the United States Nov. 4 in a sweep of electoral votes that took most election analysts completely by surprise. The Republican challenger reaped 489 electoral votes to only 49 for President Jimmy Carter. The vote count, although less lopsided, nevertheless indicated a resounding defeat for the incumbent—51% for Reagan and 41% for Carter. Independent candidate John Anderson won 7% of the vote, which made him eligible for Federal campaign reimbursements.

Carter won in only six states, plus the District of Columbia: Rhode Island, West Virginia, Maryland, Georgia, Minnesota and Hawaii. He became the first elected president since Herbert Hoover in 1932 to be defeated while in office. His concession speech at 9:50 p.m. (EST) was the earliest since 1904. He congratulated his opponent for "a fine victory" and pledged to work with Reagan for "a very fine transition period." Speaking to supporters in Washington, he said, "I promised you four years ago that I would never lie to you, so I can't stand here tonight and say it doesn't hurt."

The major factor in Reagan's victory, according to analysts, was dissatisfaction with Carter. Traditional Democratic voters, including blue-collar workers, Southerners, Roman Catholics and Jews, flocked to Reagan in substantial numbers. The economy and Carter's effectiveness as a leader were the main worries of the voters. The 52.3% turnout was the lowest since 1948, however.

THE DENVER POST
Denver, Colo., November 15, 1980

AFTER 12 YEARS of non-stop campaigning, Ronald Reagan has finally made it to the top. American voters Tuesday gave him a landslide victory whose dimensions were startling; having decided it was time for a change, they ordered it emphatically.

Even so, Reagan has not been granted *carte blanche* to lead the nation down mysterious and uncharted paths. We've had enough of that. America's instructions at the polls to the man who on Jan. 20 will become our 40th president were simple: Get the U.S. economy functioning again; restore America to a position of leadership in the world *by peaceful means*; guarantee our safety on a troubled globe. It's quite an order.

We know precious little of Reagan's specific plans for accomplishing all of this; the campaign dealt mainly with personalities while issues largely were ignored. It might be said that millions of Americans voted *against* Carter than *for* Reagan.

Nonetheless, Reagan has his share of credentials. His years as governor of California taught him the arts of leadership in a two-party milieu. He knows how to delegate authority to able subordinates and has mastered the art of compromise as an administrative tactic. These are assets of incalculable value, missing in Carter.

Moreover, George Bush will be a capable No. 2 man in the Reagan administration, fully qualified to take charge in any emergency.

For Jimmy Carter, Tuesday was a full-scale disaster. He came to Washington four years ago as an admitted amateur in two-party politics, elected without ever having created a true constituency. To this day, he remains something of an outsider. The shallowness of his popular support handicapped his presidency and doomed his re-election bid.

Jimmy Carter remains a thoroughly decent man — as evidenced by his offer to assist Reagan in any way possible during what surely will be a difficult transition period. He had more than his share of failures, but they were failures of execution, not of conception. And there *were* more than a few triumphs. On the home front, he did much to equalize the opportunities formerly available only to some Americans; his advocacy of human rights raised man's spirits round the world.

Even if Carter had compiled a far better record of accomplishment, it might not have been enough to stave off Tuesday's defeat. The temper of the people has changed dramatically in the United States; millions of Americans have been edging toward more conservative positions. Nor is this trend likely to be reversed quickly. Unless the Democrats can regroup and sharpen their blurred image, they may not capture many presidential elections between now and the end of the century.

It was the demonstrated belief of the American people that a Reagan-led Republican administration stands a better chance of taming the lurching beast that is our body politic than did the Democrats under Carter. But they'll assess the results carefully four years hence.

Our congratulations to Ronald Reagan and George Bush as they make ready to head our government; they fought well and won. Our condolences to Jimmy Carter and Walter Mondale who tried as best they could — and failed.

The Des Moines Register
Des Moines, Iowa, November 6, 1980

The American people announced emphatically Tuesday their conviction that one inept term does not deserve another. Jimmy Carter's scant 41 percent of the popular vote amounts to a massive vote of "no confidence" in his administration.

Ronald Reagan's showing falls short of a thumping endorsement of his policies. He will come into office knowing that he has the support of a majority of Americans, which is healthy. It is healthy, too, that his support is broad-based — nationwide, not regional. But it is a slim majority of 51 percent — clear notice that substantial numbers of Americans are leery of Reagan.

In an election in which many voters had their doubts about Carter and Reagan, John Anderson served as a useful outlet. Millions utilized the chance to declare a plague on both major-party houses. In Iowa, Anderson won a respectable 9 percent of the vote; he took 7 percent nationwide.

Reagan made the economy the centerpiece of his campaign. The Carter administration's record on inflation was a major factor in its defeat. It is a tribute to Reagan as a campaigner that he was able to score heavily on the inflation issue without offering a credible anti-inflation program of his own.

It's a tribute to Reagan, too, that he persuaded Americans to overlook his inexperience in national and international affairs after the nation has just paid the price of inexperience in the White House. The president-elect did that partly on the basis of his record as governor of California, partly on personal qualities. He comes across as a trustworthy and genuinely nice human being.

Americans have shown by their rejection of Carter that they want results, not pieties or appearances. Reagan will be judged ultimately by his ability to tame inflation, keep the peace and take the pragmatic steps necessary to cope with the other problems that worry Americans.

The president-elect is masterful at capsuling his beliefs in one-liners. Government cannot be run by slogan. The sight of Jimmy Carter figuratively crumpled on the sidewalk after being tossed from the White House by dissatisfied voters is one for Republicans to ponder.

Nevada State Journal

Reno, Nev., November 5, 1980

The overwhelming electoral-vote victory for Republican Ronald Reagan is a rejection of President Jimmy Carter's policies. There can be no doubt of that.

But it is also a victory for conservative principles. The Reagan triumph, coupled with the defeat of such important liberal senators as George McGovern and Birch Bayh, gives clear evidence of the growing power of the conservative philosophy in this nation.

As for Jimmy Carter, he was dismissed because he failed in both major areas of presidential responsibility: world affairs and domestic governance.

During Carter's four years in office, international relationships grew steadily more unstable and threatening. If there were some achievements, such as the Camp David peace between Israel and Egypt, there were many more setbacks. The growing power of the OPEC oil cartel went unchecked; Russian combat troops went through maneuvers unmolested in Cuba; Russia became more aggressive and finally invaded Afghanistan, ignoring American power; and, perhaps most damaging of all to Carter, a vehemently unfriendly government took over in Iran, and more than 50 American hostages remained imprisoned by militant students for one solid year while Carter and America stood by helplessly.

Concerns about defense grew, and no fourth-year Carter commitment to U.S. military power could make voters forget three years devoted to the lessening of that power. These international problems planted the seeds for Carter's defeat.

But even more important was the faltering economy. Inflation soared from 4.8 percent to 12 percent and higher during the Carter years. And during a Carter-induced recession, employment also grew without achieving any appreciable reduction of inflation.

Millions are out of jobs. And even the employed feel the daily sting of rising bills for food and other essentials. Droves of potential home buyers find inflation-puffed interest rates preventing them from fulfilling the American dream of owning their own residence. Here is where many blue collar votes were lost, as were the votes of many other traditional members of the Roosevelt Democratic coalition. The economy, even more than international problems, rang the death knell for the Carter presidency.

But there is more to this election than a Carter loss. It is also true that Ronald Reagan won this election, and won it convincingly. Despite the candidacy of John Anderson, Reagan gathered in a majority of the popular vote and goes into office not as a minority president, but as a true selection of a majority of the voters.

Also, Reagan goes to Washington carrying the solid credentials of a true conservative. He modified his stands somewhat as the campaign progressed, but generally he held to his conservative beliefs on the economy, defense, and many other matters. He is the first true conservative to sit in the White House for many years. And he sits there because the American people want a new way of doing things.

A majority of American voters now appear ready to try the policies they rejected in the Goldwater-Johnson election of 1964. They want to see a balanced budget; they want to see less government in their lives; they want to see — not war — but the military strength through which they believe war can be prevented. Most important of all, they want to see if the conservative approach can defeat the twin evils of inflation and recession.

Reagan cannot accomplish anything alone. He will have to work with Congress and the Washington establishment; he will have to do so not merely passably well, but extremely well. However, his record in California shows that he *can* work well with political adversaries, in a way that Carter apparently could not. His record also shows that he appoints good, capable, knowledgeable men to key government posts; the nation has every reason to believe this tendency will serve the United States well in the coming four years.

President Carter, in his graceful and conciliatory concession speech, pledged full cooperation with Reagan in the coming weeks. This is an American tradition, although one honored as much in its absence as in its fulfillment. However, Carter, despite all his difficulties, remains basically an honest man, and his graciousness must be taken at face value. Certainly the new president, and the nation, will need this type of cooperation to deal successfully with important matters during the transition period — especially the handling of the hostage negotiations, whose outcome and tenor could well set the tone for American-Mideast relationships for years to come.

As for President Reagan, we would urge him to reject the more extreme and unpleasant philosphies of some of his far right supporters. But at the same time we would urge him in no way to desert his longtime principles, but to inject into government as much of his conservative beliefs as possible.

There is always much talk of the middle road being the best road in American politics and government. To a large extent, this is true. But at the same time a real change is needed — a change from the traditional liberalism which has guided this nation since the days of the New Deal, but which now has grown threadbare and tired. New paths must be followed now — that is part of the message from the American people.

It is along these paths that Ronald Reagan is prepared to lead us. And as he does so, the entire nation must wish him Godspeed.

St. Louis Globe-Democrat

St. Louis, Mo., November 5, 1980

Ronald Reagan's sweeping triumph over President Jimmy Carter was by a truly astonishing margin, beyond the wildest imagination of some observers who had predicted a close race.

From the moment of the first returns it was apparent that Governor Reagan was on his way to a stunning success. By 9 o'clock St. Louis time President Carter had conceded defeat. And Jimmy Carter can forever be proud of the gracious manner in which he manfully congratulated the winner, promising Governor Reagan the best transition cooperation possible.

Ronald Reagan's landslide victory adds up to a popular demand for a sharp change in direction at the top level of federal government.

Kingpin liberal Democratic senators went down to defeat along with Mr. Carter, giving President-elect Reagan the kind of supporting cast needed to improve matters in Washington.

Gone from the Senate will be liberal stalwarts like George McGovern of South Dakota, Birch Bayh of Indiana, Frank Church of Idaho and John Culver of Iowa.

Analysts may be busy from now until Inauguration Day offering reasons why the voters preferred Reagan by such huge margins across the country. The simplest explanation is that the American people historically exercise sound judgment in periods of crisis. They saw fit to place their trust in Governor Reagan.

Voters all over America, from President Carter's Deep South to the Far West, expressed their confidence in Ronald Reagan. Missouri and Illinois appeared to be in the Reagan column.

The winner's popular margin over Mr. Carter appeared substantial enough to eliminate John B. Anderson as a factor in causing the president's defeat.

In choosing Ronald Reagan as their next president the voters expressed their displeasure for Mr. Carter's disappointing record at home and abroad. Undeniably the American people showed most concern for the economic failures that have brought double-digit inflation, sky-high interest rates and massive unemployment. They also demonstrated they want the U.S. restored as the Number One nation in the world in defense capability.

Roanoke Times & World-News

Roanoke, Va., November 5, 1980

The traditional realist might say that hard times, foreign and domestic, did in Jimmy Carter. But there is more than that in the victory of former California Governor Ronald Reagan for the presidency of the United States. He was the beneficiary of a conservative trend away from regulation by the federal government, away from excessive government spending and inflation, away from weakness in the world.

In a recognizable, although unprovable, sense, the Republican candidate's victory also represented a wish for traditional values which, until about 1960, dominated the country's thinking and moral behavior.

Governor Reagan deserves congratulations and, for today, at least, no provisos indicating ifs, ands & buts. But beginning tomorrow, certainly no later than a week, he must approach the job of the presidency as he did the governorship of California. He must find strong, young and able advisers, and to them he must be prepared to delegate. He and they must begin the process of establishing a sound relationship with the Congress.

Governor Reagan is not fitted, by age or by temperament, to be the strong president in the style of either of the Roosevelts, or of Harry Truman, Jack Kennedy or Richard Nixon in his best days. He will succeed by setting the style, tone and general directions, leaving the execution to able lieutenants.

In several respects he must be prepared to take the advice of, and compromise with, Congress. During the campaign, he did not face up to the truth about Social Security, although he came closer to it than did Jimmy Carter. His support of the Kemp-Roth tax cuts will bring him warnings from able and conservative economists who are just as desirous as he is of increasing productivity and reducing government spending.

In the field of foreign policy, he will wish to move the country from the policies founded on the revisionist theory that the United States is to be blamed for the Cold War. That theory held that if the United States would become less militarily strong and less provocative, the Russians would behave, the probabilities for world peace would improve. That theory collapsed with the Soviet invasion of Afghanistan, to the astonishment of President Carter whose policies were based on that theory, whether or not he realized it.

In an important way, the campaign improved Governor Reagan's stature. His doctrinaire opponents tried hard to depict him as a bomb-throwing war monger and a "racist" and "sexist," to boot. He kept his cool and came across as an amiable American with good instincts. He has a respect for the American past which amounts to reverence. They are good attitudes, good qualities. If Ronald Reagan can bring to his side the brains and energy to help reach his goals, the restoration of the United States might begin in the next four years.

THE DAILY HERALD

Biloxi, Miss., November 6, 1980

The Republicans' smashing victory in Tuesday's election must be interpreted as a mandate from the American people for a change in the conduct of the government in Washington and the course of the nation.

The conservative sweep not only carried former California Gov. Ronald Reagan and running mate George Bush into the White House, the unpredicted landslide also helped the GOP to capture control of the U. S. Senate for the first time in 26 years. In the process, several leading, targeted Democratic liberals tasted defeat.

Although the House remains nominally under control of the Democrats, it would appear the voters' message will register strongly in the lower chamber as well.

The historic change, which pre-election pollsters missed by a mile, offers a rare opportunity for the GOP to show in meeting the nation's needs it can outperform the Democrats — whose policies have largely prevailed since Franklin Delano Roosevelt initiated the New Deal and the growth of bureaucracy in the 1930s.

What are those needs as expressed by the vast "silent majority" of disenchanted voters, Republican, Democrat and Independent alike, who said they wanted no more of Jimmy Carter's administration?

Analysts may disagree on the ranking of the factors, but we would have to place the pocketbook issue of the economy at the top of the list. Unchecked inflation, high interest rates and a declining standard of living have hit everyone, regardless of their income or philosophical bent.

The hostage situation is an emotional factor, symptomatic of a deep uneasiness that America is failing in world leadership, in military superiority and in commanding respect of the community of nations. Certainly, it was perceived as President Carter's unsolved problem, indeed by many as of his own creation.

Broad segments of American society also have been distressed by what they perceive as a steady drift into Big Brother government, excessive federal red tape and burdensome fiscal irresponsibility, mandating a diversion of an ever higher proportion of their personal income into federal taxes.

And, for many, a trend toward permissive conduct which flaunts strongly held moral standards is viewed as a threat to the God-fearing foundations of the nation — a deep-seated feeling which some liberals obviously misjudged.

While the responsibility for these and other irritations cannot be blamed solely on the Carter administration, which indeed struggled to overcome some trends, the failure of the president and the Democratic majority to take effective action created a groundswell of dissatisfaction.

The challenges which will face the Reagan administration are monumental, but the opportunities to implement change are greatly enhanced by the GOP's new-found clout.

The nation stands today at an historic crossroads, ready to march to the tune of a different drummer. Let's pray we have found the right leader.

The News American

Baltimore, Md., November 5, 1980

Yesterday the American people dismissed the Democratic president they had embraced four years ago, and elected in his stead a Republican of vastly different political and personal stripe. They made their decision not by the tens of thousands, or the hundreds of thousands, but by the millions, and left public-opinion wizards reeling in their wake. They projected their sentiments at other targets inside the polling booths, tossing out even mildly liberal senators and congressmen in favor of younger and more conservative substitutes.

It is not easy, even now, to reckon with the prospect of a President Reagan. He still seems like candidate Reagan — and still, to many, movie star Reagan. But he will enter the White House with a mandate not matched since Lyndon Johnson's in 1964: His popular vote is solid, his electoral vote astonishing, his philosophies seemingly at the dead center of a new American political mainstream. Even so, that remarkable vote is driven by a deep disappointment about the administration of Jimmy Carter in particular and the dominance of the Democratic Party in Washington in general. That emotional element makes the Reagan triumph more brittle than it may seem, as much an act of rejection as an act of desire.

Throwing the rascals out has always been the electorate's version of a cheap thrill, and liberals have savored it no less passionately than conservatives may be doing today. But the work that follows is seldom so satisfying or so simple. President-elect Reagan's victory is impressive — the fruit of hard work and good judgment about the national mood — but as his predecessor has just learned, a campaign is peanuts compared to what follows.

It may be patronizing to say that nothing so became President Carter as his leaving, but when he stood there in the hotel ballroom in Washington last night, accepting his defeat with a brave smile, it came back to us — his victory four years ago, and the sense of renewal and confidence that surrounded it, as the door to Watergate and Vietnam closed behind.

What then faced him, and all of us, were more rooted and intractable problems — of energy, inflation, international turmoil — that have not gone away. The president's fault? In part, certainly, and voters seemed to think so, whatever merit in the blame. But Mr. Reagan now faces the same problems — yet another outsider with ambitious ideas — and we don't know that he is any better equipped to address them, except that he begins with a clean slate, which is by definition a promising one.

Ronald Reagan begins, too, as the symbol of a sea change in American politics, one that has left good people like Birch Bayh, Frank Church, John Brademas, George McGovern, Al Ullman, John Culver, Elizabeth Holtzman, Gaylord Nelson and Warren Magnuson far behind, and the United States Senate firmly in Republican hands — and under conservative committee chairmen — for the first time in a quarter-century.

The shift — it has been a drift, really, only too dimly perceived by many of us — will be telling on the congressional reapportionment of the national population two years from now, a redrawing of the political map that will carry to the end of the century. In Washington, it will mean that members of the Democratic establishment will go into hibernation, and Republicans will emerge from their exile since the Nixon-Ford years to take their places in a zillion niches of influence. In Baltimore, it may well mean a more slender and more skeptical federal presence, less attuned to the rebuilding and rejuvenation that the Carter administration has sponsored in the last four years, but conceivably willing to learn.

And speaking of which, all of us who supported Jimmy Carter, whether institutionally or personally, ought to have the same frame of mind in approaching Ronald Reagan. We have a new president, or will have shortly. There is no profit in grumbling. He has a big job ahead of him, and, as we hope he will tell the American people right off, so do we all.

The Afro American

Baltimore, Md., November 5, 1980

Outgoing President Jimmy Carter was right: President-elect Ronald Reagan's landslide victory hurt.

Also on target was the NAACP official who declared that black Americans are concerned yet hopeful.

The size of Reagan's win and the sharpness of the swing to the right was stunning.

More than a little disturbing was the success the rightwing and one-issue groups scored in replacing liberal-moderate U.S. senators and House members with conservatives. They delivered control of the Senate to the Republicans and weakened Democratic control in the House.

Thus the stage has been set for conservatism Reagan to have things pretty much his own way, at least for a time. At this point it is not certain how far Reagan will go in trying to put into practice some of the things he talked about that so disturbed millions of people.

But this much is certain: in the first flush of victory the right-wingers have bared their teeth and thrown down the gauntlet; Reagan and his administration had better deliver for them, or else; and, they already have targeted more liberals and moderates of both parties who will be forced to walk the plank two years from now.

The challenge is clear.

To be sure, it is not a challenge to black America alone.

But higher percentages of us do stand to be crushed as the right-wing cracks its whip.

And we must be in the vanguard of the fight to put America back on the right road.

Consider some of the problem: the rightwingers are geared up and raring to go; liberal forces like Senators Birch Bayh, George McGovern Gaylord Nelson, Jacob Javits, John Culver and Frank Church were knocked out; there will be Senate chairmanship changes such as Strom Thurmond replacing Edward Kennedy, Judiciary, and Jesse Helms gaining more influence by replacing Herman Talmadge, Agriculture;

Reagan wants to turn welfare back to the states which already say they can't afford Medicaid costs; he intends to aid billions to the cost of defense and cut taxes, so he must plan to slash social programs that help poor people; he has a fuzzy plan for assisting cities; and, among other things, has indicated he will listen to rightwingers who support South Africa, more for aid private schools and? — —-- -busing amendment. wingers who support South Africa, more for aid private schools and anti-busing amendment.

Frankly, we think the real world

in which Ronald Reagan and his right-wing administration must function is so vastly different from what they seem to belive that long before two years have gone by they will stand before us a frustrated leadership unable to bring about the miracles they have promised — another prospect that troubles us.

That is why we must put our shoulders to the task at hand now.

As disappointed as blacks were with President Carter, whose overall record someday may look better than it does today, they gave him more than 83 percent of their votes in an effort to stop Reagan, someone they feared more.

The election problem was twofold: blacks did not turn out in as great numbers as we should have in many places; and the national desire for a change from the status quo especially the economic situation, was such that they as a group could not have stemmed the tide with what would have been an overall respectable vote.

But we were impressed with how black voters responded to the urgings of their leaders and fellow citizens to turn out and vote their interests.

We were encouraged enough to believe that two years from now we will be as ready to square off in the elections that year as will be the rightwing element.

By then we should have registered millions of new voters. We will know what senators and congressmen deserve our support and which don't — and we will vote our interests, and that of the country, all over the nation.

Where necessary we must urge good liberal candidates to seek office.

As we said earlier, this fight to get America back on the right track cannot be ours alone.

And it will not be. Senator George McGovern already has announced that he will form a National Coalition for Common Sense. Labor in the fight. Religious groups will join. Many others will help.

Our remaining friends in public office must know that their fates are not being left entirely to the rightwingers who seek to dictate a turning back of the clock.

They must not be left quaking in their boots as the National Conservative Political Action Committee's John Nolan boasts he would be if he were a liberal running in 1982.

The challenge now is to cut our losses and keep demanding, and fighting for, leadership that dreams of and works to improve the quality of life for all.

The Pittsburgh Press

Pittsburgh, Pa., November 7, 1980

As the size of Ronald Reagan's landslide sinks in, conservatives are starting to chortle that the old New Deal coalition of labor, blacks, Catholics, city dwellers and southerners is finished.

They rejoice prematurely.

The coalition that elected so many Democratic presidents is resilient. It was shattered in the 1972 McGovern debacle but re-formed to elect Jimmy Carter four years later. It will snap back again if Mr. Reagan, like Mr. Carter, fails to curb inflation and overweening government.

★ ★ ★

What may be ended by Mr. Reagan's sweep is the liberal mind-set that enacts a costly federal program for every problem, even when the problems don't exist. This penchant should be chilled by the people's response to Mr. Reagan's goal of "getting government off your backs."

In any case, so many prominent House and Senate liberals fell in Tuesday's massacre that the survivors will lack the numbers and foolhardiness to propose a law — and tax dollars — to cure every supposed ailment.

Mr. Reagan's ability to govern and push his policies rose markedly when the GOP, confounding the experts, took control of the Senate for the first time in 26 years. This will give him an unanticipated power base on Capitol Hill.

In addition, the GOP's gain of 33 seats

in the House hands the president-elect an "ideological majority" — Republicans plus like-minded conservative Democrats — in that chamber.

Thus the chances are good for Mr. Reagan's policy of personal income-tax cuts, spurs to business investment, boosted defense spending and, eventually, a balanced budget.

★ ★ ★

It may be unkind to mention dangers to Mr. Reagan's future even as he savors his smashing victory, but they cannot be safely ignored.

In any sane world he will have to negotiate a new nuclear-arms-limitation treaty with Russia. But Sens. Bayh, Church, Culver, Durkin, Javits, Magnuson, McGovern and Nelson — all backers of arms control — have been ousted from the Senate.

Their GOP successors are conservative and suspicious of the SALT process. Thus Mr Reagan could face a treaty rebuff as serious as the defeat of the League of Nations that destroyed Woodrow Wilson's presidency.

Another peril is that he could cut taxes but be unable to restrain spending. If that happens, the federal deficit will swell, inflation will take off again and interest rates will climb.

Mr. Reagan should need no reminder that just such a series of mishaps drove President Carter from office.

The Dispatch

Columbus, Ohio, November 5, 1980

RONALD REAGAN not only took the White House away from President Carter in Tuesday's election, he undoubtedly has changed the face of the United States government.

Even though polls were still open in the western states, Carter conceded defeat and offered cooperation in the transition prior to Reagan's inauguration. With that the president-elect declared that "I don't believe the American people are frightened of what lies ahead; together we're going to do what has to be done."

Reagan's victory was the greatest from a philosophical sense in the nation's recent history. That the victory swept out of the U.S. Senate several liberal stalwarts is evidence the people want a conservative fiscal policy and a reversal of the decline on both the domestic and foreign scenes.

The former California governor's victory in the presidential race will have a tremendous impact upon the composition of the new Congress.

The next U.S. Senate will see a GOP edge as seven liberal Democrats were among those falling by the wayside. But Ohio's effective

senior senator, John Glenn, won a second term handily.

As for the U.S. House, the Democrats saw their 117-seat margin shrink to about 50, foretelling a significant realignment of key committees.

The Ohio GOP's 13-10 control of the state delegation to the U.S. House will remain unchanged although there will be some new faces.

Notably, Samuel Devine, who has represented the Columbus area 12th District for 22 years, was defeated by Democrat Robert Shamansky, a Columbus attorney. The other Columbus area congressman, Chalmers Wylie of the 15th District, easily won his eighth term on Capitol Hill.

In carrying Ohio by a margin of about 450,000 votes over President Carter, Reagan received a verification of his image of America.

He sees the nation for what it is — energetic, promising and skilled.

And the voters saw Reagan for what he is — intelligent and steeped in common sense — attributes that should help in leading America back to what it ought to be.

HOSTAGE CRISIS:

Americans Return Home
After 444 Days in Captivity

The 52 Americans held in Iran for 14 months were released by Iran Jan. 20 after several days of tense negotiations and last-minute delays. After a week of medical care and relaxation at the U.S. Air Force Base in Wiesbaden, West Germany, they returned to the U.S. Jan. 27 to a tumultuous welcome from millions of Americans.

The tempo of negotiations for their release had quickened at the beginning of January. Iran had originally demanded $24 billion for releasing the captives, and the U.S. responded in early January with an offer to deposit more than $5 billion in frozen Iranian assets in the central bank of Algeria, which was acting as a go-between in the U.S.-Iranian negotiations. The final agreement, signed Jan. 19 by U.S. Deputy Secretary of State Warren Christopher in Algiers and Iranian Executive State Minister Behzad Nabavi in Teheran, called for the U.S. to deposit $8 billion in Iranian assets in the Bank of England. After the hostages' release, however, $5.2 billion of the money would be returned to the U.S. to pay off U.S. bank loans to Iran. The other major aspects of the agreement were: a lifting of U.S. trade sanctions, U.S. aid in returning assets of the late Shah Mohammed Riza Pahlevi to Iran and a U.S. pledge not to interfere in Iran's internal affairs.

There was some speculation that the incoming Reagan Administration would refuse to carry out parts of the deal. A State Department spokesman Jan. 21 said the administration "does not want to commit itself to follow through without having had a chance of going over the agreement." The next day, however, the Reagan Administration confirmed that it "fully intends to carry out the obligations" of the hostage accord.

THE WALL STREET JOURNAL.
New York, N.Y., January 21, 1981

The agreement the United States made with Iran for return of the hostages has the same moral standing as an agreement made with a kidnapper, that is to say none at all. This is not said in criticism of the Carter administration, which made the deal to save the hostages' lives. But now that the hostages are free, President Reagan should examine the agreement carefully and if its unfulfilled parts do not, on balance, benefit American interests, there should be no hesitation in renouncing it.

There will be arguments against such a course, no doubt. It will be said that no great nation, having made a commitment, should renege if it wants to be trusted in the future. It will be argued that such a move would cut the ground out from under those Iranian leaders who favored the deal and faced up to the wild men who would have held the hostages forever. It will be argued that we are only giving back to the Iranians what is lawfully theirs. It will be asked whether we would be able to do business with terrorists in the future if the need arose.

Those are all persuasive arguments, but they miss the core point:

This was not an agreement, it was extortion. And it is important for the world to know that extortionists are not entitled to the same legal and moral consideration as governments operating in accordance with international law.

There would be another implicit message: We are not worrying about how much future terrorists trust our word because future terrorists will not be dealt with in this manner. Having learned our lesson from this experience we will see to it that the next ones who try it are dealt with swiftly and with force. Whether they trust our word will be immaterial.

As to the Iranians who argued for negotiations, do we really feel we owe anything to anyone in Iran's power elite? They are all, after all, the creatures of the Ayatollah Khomeini. Anyone who was not is either now dead or in exile. Our initial mistake in Iran was in the idea that we could do business with such people.

There is finally the question of our giving back to the Iranians "their own property." If we are dealing here with legalisms, any Iranian assets that are free of liens might be considered their

property, but everything else falls into a different category. The U.S. negotiators took a very long leap when they agreed to submit to an international claims commission the claims of American nationals against Iranian assets held in the U.S. They were, in effect, pledging to take these cases out of U.S. courts, a pledge that has dubious constitutionality. As to the damages that can be claimed by the hostages themselves, the agreement seems to leave them with no recourse in the courts. As to delivering up any discoverable assets of the Shah's family, do we really want to finally capitulate to the Ayatollah's lust for vengeance against the Shah?

We do not want to treat the American negotiators harshly. They worked arduously for long hours under horrendous pressure and achieved their primary goal, getting the hostages released. But the other side, bargaining with human lives against money and contracts, had an unfair advantage. We should not hesitate to make it clear that an agreement negotiated under such conditions is worthless and equally clear that anyone who attempts the same thing in the future will not be treated so gently.

Roanoke Times & World-News
Roanoke, Va., January 23, 1981

The Wall Street Journal urges that the United States renounce the deal with Iran that brought home the 52 hostages. The agreement, it says, "has the same moral standing as an agreement made with a kidnaper, that is to say none at all." It meets every objection point by point with brilliant reasoning -- but it is the kind of reasoning that led Dr. Faustus to sell his soul to the devil.

In the unknown but certainly perilous future, there might be — there probably will be — other occasions in which the United States is negotiating with wicked people. Life and property might be at stake, war or peace might be at stake — and the credibility of future negotiators should not now be undercut by an impatient and emotional reaction to the work of nasty Iranians. To renege on the deal would not be in the American character; it would put us in the same classification as the Iranian malefactors and with them we do not wish to be classified.

To repeat the classic words of the late Winston Churchill, used in a wartime context which is not too dissimilar to the present one: "What kind of people do they think we are?"

It is possible, not probable but within easy imagination, that the American taxpayer himself will wind up paying part of the ransom. If American companies have lost their ability to collect honest debts in court, their only recourse would be to sue the government and, thus, themselves and other taxpayers. If such a burden there be, it must be endured. A fraction of it might be charged off to continuing education, in the reality that actions have consequences and that consequences cannot honorably be undone.

We understand exactly the fury and frustration of those who wish Americans to renege on the deal. We admire the intellectual brilliance *The Wall Street Journal* editorial page has put to the service of the cause. But the cause is a bad one. It arises from the same source of former President Carter's errors on the subject: impatience and emotionalism. That pool can contaminate ideas of the Right as well as Left, the conservatives as well as liberals. We were trapped by the Iranians because we did not do the things we ought to have done. If we renege on the deal that rescued the hostages, we will have done the things that we ought not to have done. Then, truly, there will be no health in us. President Reagan should choose the honorable course.

THE PLAIN DEALER
Cleveland, Ohio, January 23, 1981

A national sense of outrage at the barbaric treatment by Iran of members of the U.S. diplomatic mission must not be allowed to force America to act against its own best interests.

When so many Americans are quoted by reporters checking the national temper as saying "bomb them," including some ministers, or "keep the Iranian money," it is obvious that strong national emotions are at play calling for revenge. Yet the desire to inflict punishment, while understandable, should not drive reason out.

The need for a national catharsis, the purging of the emotional tensions built up over the long hostage crisis, appears served by a proposed congressional investigation and by President Reagan's policy of examining the basic agreement fully, and thoroughly reviewing the 10 executive orders signed by President Jimmy Carter on Monday. Some terms kept secret should be quickly made public.

However, the basic agreement should stand: the exchange of unencumbered Iranian assets for Americans held captive, repayment of most bank loans and international arbitration of most claims.

Yet some Carter executive orders have impacts that could well be reversed. One is the end to a trade embargo against Iran. Considering the illegal kidnaping of the diplomats, their brutal mistreatment and the ransom demanded for them, it is just too early for an American president to restore Iranian-American trade to business as usual. Some time must be allowed for cooling passions.

Another Carter order that should be examined closely is the one that would prevent the hostages from suing the Iranian government or Iranians for damages for their imprisonment and harsh treatment. It appears legal, and a hostage compensation commission will substitute for lawsuits. But it rubs the wrong way by appearing to eliminate a basic right of the victims of international brigandage to seek legal redress in the courts.

Courts are also expected to hear challenges to Carter's agreement to wipe out lawsuits and claims for business losses filed against Iranian assets that were not part of the $8 billion transferred for the release of the hostages. An estimated $4 billion additional is involved. Yet unless the Supreme Court rules otherwise, Reagan should not break the agreement calling for arbitration of claims in lieu of suits.

As much as America has come to dislike Iran, that country's strong, independent status is important to the welfare of the United States. That status keeps the Soviet Union from the warmwater port it has coveted for centuries, from the Persian Gulf oil fields on which America and the West depend, and from the flanks of independent, small nations.

America's current best interest lies in not further weakening an already weak Iranian government and driving it into a fatal bear hug. We do not have to trade with Iran, but we should not discourage our allies from doing so. And Iran should neither be bombed nor have its assets withheld.

One final point. When the United States gives its word, it should be kept. This is what this country is all about.

EVENING EXPRESS
Portland, Me., January 24, 1981

The United States must honor the agreement which was the instrument of release for the American captives in Iran.

Nothing must be permitted to influence the U.S. to do otherwise, not even the atrocities committed by the barbaric Iranians.

The Reagan administration has announced that the agreement will be honored. The announcement was contained in a prepared statement read by William Dyess, a State Department spokesman.

But further comments by Dyess and Vice President George Bush had the tone of fine-print footnotes that created a feeling of uneasiness.

Would reports of the foul treatment of the hostages affect the administration's study of the agreement? "It certainly won't make it any easier," said Dyess.

Former President Carter's report on his visit to the former captives in West Germany adds a "new dimension" to the administration's review of the agreements returning Iran's frozen assets, said the new vice president.

But no "new dimensions," no review can justify refusal by this country to meet the obligation to which it agreed. To do so would be to lend a measure of substance to some of the charges the Iranians have been hurling at the United States.

We must demonstrate the integrity which the Iranians lacked.

To default now would be a betrayal of the Algerian government which, at no little risk to its own relations in that part of the world, worked so diligently and effectively in our behalf.

The United States made a deal. Unless it is shown that there is something illegal about it, the country must stick to it.

The Washington Post
Washington, D.C., January 23, 1981

A ROUND of appeals has been made to President Reagan to renounce the deal Jimmy Carter's government made to get the hostages released. The objectors do have something of a point. It has been a dirtying experience to have to deal with the kidnappers and torturers in Tehran as though they were gentlemen in the international club. There does not seem to be a penny of "ransom," as conventionally defined, in the agreement, but undeniably it is distasteful to deal in money, even Iran's own money, to retrieve people illegally captured. It is quite true, moreover, that the United States can accept no moral obligation to kidnappers: if the country chose to default on the agreement, it would not have to defend itself on that score.

We feel, nonetheless, that the event is more complicated than that. If the United States has no moral obligation to kidnappers, it certainly has a moral obligation to their victims, including, in this context, to the victims of acts of terrorism to come. The hostages back from Tehran would not be hurt by renunciation of the agreement that brought them home, though American financial claimants might be. But future hostages could well be hurt by renunciation, which could chill the willingness of would-be compromisers and middlemen to bet on the American word in the next crisis. For that matter, a great many people in a great many situations depend on the American word. It is not a mere Boy Scout thing. A great power cannot trifle with it unless the burden lifted, or the benefit expected, is very great.

In this instance, the administration has been taking into account an essential political dimension in its cautious initial moves to honor "the obligations of the United States." To renounce the deal would be to treat Algeria shabbily for its considerable pains and to pitch into further disarray a region in which virtually every country except perhaps Iran hopes the United States will move back into a steadying role. Are these really acceptable costs?

Meanwhile, the specific terms of the deal are surely worth looking at. The country has the hostages. And of $12 billion in Iranian assets seized, the United States currently still holds $9 billion: $5 billion disbursed or held in escrow to pay off American banks and $4 billion-plus that won't be unblocked until satisfactory procedures are established to settle the claims of American companies.

It is often forgotten that, before the hostage crisis, American firms were having big trouble getting their money from the Iranian revolutionary regime. It was, for instance, threatening to default on "shah loans." The new agreement pays out the American banks at 100 cents on the dollar; that's already done. The companies are assured an international claims procedure underwritten by a "miraculous pitcher" fund in which the Iranians must keep at least $.5 billion at all times.

The drafters of the financial terms point out that Iran's is not the first revolution in which American businessmen have encountered turbulence. To cite one typical case, only when relations were normalized in 1978 was a claims agreement made with China; claimants got 42 cents on the dollar. In Cuba, meanwhile, Americans have claimed $1.5 billion for two decades and got nothing. We reserve a final judgment. One thing we are waiting to see, however, is whether the companies' mood to litigate will be affected by their own closer study of the terms. It would also be interesting to get their judgment on the official assertion that they are better off now than they were before the hostages were seized.

ASSASSINATION ATTEMPT:

Americans React with Shock, Horror to News of Reagan's Shooting

Six shots from a would-be assassin's handgun March 30 plunged the U.S. yet again into the nightmare of an attack on the President. John Warnock Hinckley, a 25-year-old drifter from Colorado, fired at Ronald Reagan as the President left the Washington Hilton Hotel after addressing a gathering of construction union officials. The President, believed at first to have escaped injury, suffered a bullet wound in the chest and underwent emergency surgery at George Washington University Hospital. Three other men were seriously injured: White House press secretary James Brady, Secret Service agent Timothy McCarthy and D.C. police officer Thomas Delahanty.

In the aftermath of the attack, stunned Americans wondered why Hinckley was able to come so close to the President without being questioned and why he was able to obtain a handgun despite a history of mental instability. Additional questions surrounded the security agencies' failure to take note of Hinckley long before. He had been arrested in Nashville, Tenn. for possession of concealed weapons on Oct. 9, 1980, the very day that former President Jimmy Carter was in the city. A search of Hinckley's Washington hotel room turned up letters revealing an infatuation with Jodie Foster, an actress who had appeared in the movie *Taxi Driver*, in which the assassination of a prominent political figure was plotted. Hinckley reportedly had written to Foster that he was planning to kill Reagan out of love for her.

The son of an oil-company executive, Hinckley had grown up in affluence but had failed to complete his studies or maintain a job. He had drifted around the country, at one time becoming a member of the National Socialist Party of America, known as America's chief Nazi party. His family, described as conservative and religious, said they were "grieved and heartbroken by this tragedy."

The Boston Globe

Boston, Mass., March 31, 1981

The sound of assassin's bullets, which in the past two decades reverberated so sickeningly from Dallas, Memphis, Los Angeles, Laurel, Md., San Francisco and Sacramento, has now echoed in the streets of the capital.

In what has become a distressingly familiar habit, sudden tableaus of anxiety formed in homes and offices yesterday as Americans clustered at the radio or television to find the latest details of the gunfire.

Four American Presidents – Lincoln, Garfield, McKinley and Kennedy – were killed by assassins. Theodore Roosevelt, Franklin Roosevelt, Harry Truman and Gerald Ford all survived assassination attempts. The prayers and hopes of millions of Americans are with Ronald Reagan as he recovers from his wounds.

The vulnerability of this massive continental society to any crazed and determined person with a gun was brought into dramatically high relief in those frightening moments outside a Washington hotel. Paradoxically, the assassination attempt also demonstrated the strength of this nation.

Visibly and swiftly, the government showed that it continued to function. As the President entered the hospital, his Administration was already working to reassure America and the world of that fact. Last week's big Washington news, the quarrel between Vice President Bush and Secretary of State Haig, seemed embarrassingly trivial.

Off the Senate floor, Sen. Russell Long of Louisiana, whose father was assassinated in the 1930s, and Sen. Edward Kennedy of Massachusetts, who lost two brothers to assassins in the 1960s, stared at a television set.

As did his brother, Robert, who spoke to a crowd of blacks in Indianapolis minutes after the assassination of Martin Luther King Jr. in 1968, Sen. Kennedy spoke instinctively and eloquently to a gallery crowded with tourists and schoolchildren. "My family has been touched by violence," he said. "Year after year, you read about it. My brothers John and Robert Kennedy, Martin Luther King, Medgar Evers, Al Lowenstein, Vernon Jordan, President Ford and now the attempt on President Reagan. I think all of us understand that all these good individuals had a common purpose – to make this a better country."

"Violence and hatred have no place in our society," Kennedy added. "Nonetheless, we see it continue in our society and in our country. I think all of us who care about our country . . . bear an important responsibility in whatever way we possibly can to rid this society of the kind of violence and hatred we have seen."

HOUSTON CHRONICLE

Houston, Texas, April 1, 1981

Emotional reactions to the shooting of President Reagan continue to flood across the nation. The feelings are honest ones, reflecting the deep concern of people for the man and for the nation he heads.

Houstonians and people around the world have expressed in prayers the hope for full recovery by President Reagan and the others wounded Monday. In uncounted messsages they have extended their support to Mrs. Reagan and the families of the others injured.

One of the great virtues of this country is that the president of the United States is accepted as the representative of all of us, whether we differ with him or not. That acceptance is what makes an act of violence against the president an act against one and all. The very fact he is so recognized makes him an even more tempting target for the deranged.

Once the shock of the Monday assassination attempt passed, and there came the resolve that this must never happen again, even at the cost of greater restrictions on public access to the president, one emotion continues to rise to the surface — anger. Anger that any individual would dare attempt to assassinate a president.

That such attempts have been made in the past, and have succeeded, doesn't lessen the force of that anger — it reinforces it, for the nation has come to know all too well the trauma of such an act.

The anger must, of course, be a controlled emotion, expressed more in the calmer terms of indignation and a determination to create a better society, but anger should not be discarded as unworthy. The alternative is passive acceptance of the shooting of a president of the United States as an inevitable event. It is not. It is an aberration. It is an abnormality. It is unacceptable. Violence is not to be taken for granted, whether it is directed against a president or against the weakest member of society.

If there is a choice between acceptance and anger, then let us be angry. By all that our nation stands for, violence is not and must not ever become an accepted part of our lives.

THE SAGINAW NEWS
Saginaw, Mich., April 3, 1981

We are finding out more about John W. Hinckley Jr. than we want to know, and more than he deserves — which is nothing.

Assassins seek fame, attention, a place in history they could achieve no other way. It is galling to grant any of this to the suspect. Knowing that it is impossible and unwise, we still wish that an example could be set of giving him no notice, much less the research into high-school careers and publishing of childhood photo albums.

That might help deter other would-be killers. But it is impossible because the public demands to know just who is accused of this awful deed, and why it was done.

It is unwise because, as we are learning, the suspect was apparently obsessed with matters that have nothing to do with enmity toward either the president as a person, or his policies. Mr. Reagan was attacked because, simply, he is the president.

From what we know so far, this man was no part of normal America. His motivation came from within himself, not from any quarrel with society.

For our own sakes, we need to recognize that what happened this week does not mean America is sick. It does mean that there are sick people in America. That there are so many of them is deeply troubling. But it would be grossly unfair to ourselves, and to our recovery from these events, to declare them the rule rather than the tragic exceptions they are.

Rockford Register Star
Rockford, Ill., March 31, 1981

First came the shock of disbelief — the hope that it couldn't be true, that it must not be true.

But it was all too horribly true. Once again the nation had come terribly close to yet another presidential assassination.

Then a stunned nation turned to prayers for the wounded Ronald Reagan — and to fears of what would come next, of what this nation has become.

Once again we are a nation being tested.

As the doctors worked over our wounded president, the machinery of our democracy struggled to deal with yet another mindless tragedy. Vice President George Bush rushed back to Washington from a speaking engagement in Texas. Secretary of State Alexander Haig went on national television with assurances that order was restored, that the government was functioning, that America would deal well with this latest crisis.

And the nation wrestled with its conscience. What is it about America that breeds this senseless violence? What is it about our way of life that exposes our national leaders to such mindless threats? What is it that leads any man to open fire from just a few feet away at the man chosen by Americans to lead them? How long can we as a nation continue to allow such violence to occur?

Beyond that was the bigger question: Is our system of democracy, our belief in freedom of the individual, badly flawed if such aberrations continue, if terror can continue to stalk the land?

Thus is the nation tested today.

As we pray for the speedy recovery of Ronald Reagan, we must pass the test of finding ways for our government to continue on the course he has charted. As we ponder the horror of yet another presidential assassination attempt, we must find ways to deal with terror while still preserving our two centuries of democracy. As we dwell on the tragedy of the present, and of those of the past, we must find methods to end such tragedies while preserving our American way of life.

It is the test of this nation to find solutions while retaining the freedoms held so dear by Ronald Reagan and by Jack Kennedy, Bobby Kennedy, Martin Luther King, Abraham Lincoln and so many, many others who have fallen victim to the terrorists in our midst.

The Charlotte Observer
Charlotte, N.C., March 31, 1981

The sound of gunfire, which has echoed again and again like a nightmare drumbeat through our memories of the past two decades, was heard again Monday. From the route of a Dallas parade, a Memphis motel balcony, a Los Angeles hotel corridor and the faraway battlefields of a bewildering war, violence continues to be a traumatic motif in the history of this generation of Americans.

And each time we ask who's to blame. Even when we clearly are confronted with the act of a deranged individual, we find ourselves wondering if there is this impulse to violence somewhere deep within our national character, some anachronistic distortion of the American spirit left over from our frontier past.

The idea that killing is, under some circumstances, an appropriate means to an end continues to be widely accepted. The idea that every American who is not obviously dangerous to society has a right to bear arms — even a gun small enough to be easily concealed — continues to be widely accepted. There may be no connection between those facts and the tragedies and near-tragedies of these 20 years, yet we find ourselves coming back to them each time the gunfire rings out again, and asking ourselves what sort of people we are.

Two things, at least, should be clear. Congress ought to establish a strict national policy of handgun control. And as much as the idea of an isolated president goes against the American grain, we need to worry again about the extent to which people have opportunities to get within pistol range of him.

The Philadelphia Inquirer
Philadelphia, Pa., March 31, 1981

The awful fascination tyrannized the mind, the consciousness. The events unfolded, live and in endlessly repetitive retrospect. The videotape was played over and over, slowed down, ran backwards. One's breath came in short, shallow pain. Suddenly it was more acute, in a spasm of physical empathy, as the news came through that President Reagan *had* been wounded, contrary to the very earliest reports. Dominating it all, the overriding feeling, as history unfolded tyrannically, was the ghastly immediacy of wishing, praying against reality. *Don't let it be true! Don't let it be happening.*

Not again.

What is it, what can it be, that drives America to this violence, this brutality? What grotesque sickness is lurking in the nation's vitals, latent for years, then breaking out in its full virulence in Dallas in 1963, then again and again, with the deaths of two Kennedys, Martin Luther King, others, and attempts on others: The targets strong men, the violence done by weak, thwarted, sinisterly inscrutable men and women?

What has happened to this most decent, most humanely established and dedicated of nations that to kill or try to kill its leaders has come to be part of the American way of life?

In Washington, as reporters and officials and the curious clustered outside the White House and George Washington Hospital, rain began to fall, as if the heavens were weeping on and for the seat of the government of the United States.

As well they might. As well they should. Sympathy, though, seems not enough, not good enough. Not for James S. Brady, that decent, careful man of 40, wounded in the brain. Not for Secret Service agent Timothy J. McCarthy, or District of Columbia police officer Thomas K. Delahanty wounded on protective duty in full light of day in the nation's capital, where safety should be — but is not — a basic assumption. Not, certainly, for Ronald Reagan, who with characteristic self-confidence and cheer joked with bystanders and physicians even as he was being moved toward surgery.

Overriding the sympathy, the rage, the senses of disgust and frustration is the clear imperative that the business of government, and of the nation, must and will go on. Again, as in each of the ghastly series of such acts of violence, it became vital to the structure, the law, the very civilization of the nation, that the response be methodical, punctilious in its legal orthodoxy. And every indication late yesterday in Washington and elsewhere was that just that was happening, and apparently had from the moment after the shots had been fired.

Government must go on, and will. The law, in its tragic incapacity to change what is past, must go forward, and will. The nation must examine, and re-examine, its conscience and its capacity to bear pain and the failure of its capacity to assure even to its leaders the most fundamental right of civilization, which is to continue to live unmolested.

Short minutes before the shots were fired outside the Washington Hilton yesterday afternoon, President Reagan told a gathering of American labor leaders that "It's time we place trust in ourselves .... Our destiny is not our fate, it is our choice .... Together, we'll make America great again."

That optimism, that faith, had a bitter taste soon after for all Americans, the bitterness deepening, wrenching at the stomach and the spirit, in the hours afterward. Without such confidence and good will, however, there can be nothing else to draw upon but despair and resignation. And that cannot be accepted.

LABOR:
Air Traffic Controllers Strike in Defiance of Federal Law

Most of the nation's 17,000 air traffic controllers walked off their jobs Aug. 3, causing delays and confusion in domestic and foreign flights. The Professional Air Traffic Controllers Organization called its 15,000 members out after rejecting the government's final offer on a new contract. PATCO had demanded a four-day, 32-hour work-week, a $10,000 across-the-board raise for all controllers and retirement after 20 years at 75% of pay, all of which would total $575 million. The Federal Aviation Administration had raised its final offer to $50 million in total compensation from an initial $40 million. An average controller's salary was $33,000 a year for a five-day, 40-hour week, and retirement benefits generally were paid after 25 years at 50% of average highest salary.

Washington's reaction to the strike was swift and reflected almost two years of advance planning. PATCO was fined more than $1 million, and its leaders were jailed briefly. President Ronald Reagan warned the controllers that they were violating their oath not to strike and would be fired if they did not return. Dismissal notices were sent out beginning Aug. 5. To keep air traffic moving, the government brought in military air traffic controllers to help the 2,000 non-union controllers, supervisors and 2,000 PATCO members who did not strike. Airports were chaotic for the first few days, but afterward the FAA reported that the system was operating at 75% of capacity. PATCO President Robert Poli asserted that the system was unsafe, but the FAA and most airline pilots disputed his claim.

THE ATLANTA CONSTITUTION
Atlanta, Ga., August 4, 1981

The Reagan administration is to be commended for its hard-nosed attitude toward striking air controllers. The Justice Department has obtained court orders against the striking Professional Air Traffic Controllers, demanding that the strike end. President Reagan says he will fire strikers who are not back on the job within 48 hours.

Fortunately, some PATCO members in Atlanta had the good sense to recognize that the strike is illegal, and they showed up for work. So the strike, at least in Atlanta, did not have the paralyzing effect it was designed to have.

In the past, strikes by public employees have been settled with little or no retribution against the strikers — although they were clearly in violation of the law. That should not happen in the case of the controllers' strike. The administration must take a hard line, and test in the Supreme Court, if need be, the law that prohibits controllers from striking.

PATCO is consciously attempting to create chaos in this country's transportation system. It is attempting to wound the nation by disrupting commerce and reducing tourist travel. It is attempting to extort a settlement from the government by bringing harm and misery to its citizens. And in doing so, PATCO also has plainly shown that it holds itself above the law.

If PATCO wishes to gain support and sympathy for its wage demands, it has chosen the worst path to that support.

And we reiterate our belief that the Reagan administration should not yield to the arrogance and scofflaw attitude of the striking controllers.

THE LINCOLN STAR
Lincoln, Neb., August 4, 1981

President Reagan's response to the air traffic controller's strike couldn't have been any tougher.

He has told them if they don't go back to work within 48 hours they'll be fired. The government has moved to impound their strike fund and decertify their union as a bargaining agent. Military air controllers have been moved in — scabs, if you will — to help that minority of civilian controllers who stayed on the job. The administration announced that union leaders and other members of the Professional Air Traffic Controllers Organization who are involved in the strike will be subject to criminal and civil prosecution.

About the only thing Reagan hasn't done is to hire goons with baseball bats to break up picket lines.

Still, as hard as the administration has come down on PATCO members, and as much as the American labor movement leadership might resent such a show of force, we'd guess Reagan has the support of an overwhelming majority of Americans on the issue.

Some 800,000 of us fly every day and the strike is affecting all passengers to some degree. It is disrupting business in a variety of ways and causing additional delays in the delivery of first class mail. It is an aggravating, inconvenient, penalizing, costly work shutdown. There might be a bit more public sympathy toward the strikers — considering the importance of their work and the stress involved with it — if the public did not perceive the controllers as already being well paid (at an average of $33,000 per year) and as asking for a far too costly package.

But there are drawbacks to lowering the boom with such a devastating swing. Reagan has left himself little or no room to maneuver if union members decide to tough it out. And he has let his anti-government bias show with the obvious signal that he feels public employees are members of an underclass of workers; that their problems are not as real as those suffered by workers in the private sector; that they are not deserving of the remedies open to others. That may result in short-term political gain that will be reflected in the next public opinion polls. But it could hurt him over the long run with an increasingly active, vocal political constituency: those who work for government at all levels.

Oregon
Journal
Portland, Ore., August 7, 1981

Air traffic control ought to fall into that category of public employment that should be barred legally from striking because it is a vital public service.

The current situation, however, indicates just how difficult it is to enforce such a law, for the air traffic controllers are striking in spite of the legal prohibition.

What is suggested, perhaps, is that an alternative means of resolving a labor dispute is needed when strikes are outlawed.

In Oregon, such public employees as police and firefighters are statutorily prevented from striking because of the effect on public safety.

They are, however, covered by binding arbitration. If they were stalemated with their governmental managers an outside, professional arbitrator would settle the dispute. Thus there is a means to resolve the issue even though a strike is not allowed.

Federal law contains no such alternative, however. But perhaps it should. Congress should give thought to binding arbitration for the categories of federal employees who should be barred from striking.

Even though there is no legal requirement for binding arbitration, the Reagan administration and the controllers' union might seek the services of an arbitrator to try to resolve the impasse.

However, President Reagan, in his ultimatum to the controllers and his follow-through in firing them, may have gone too far to allow the flexibility for such action.

The president is on the spot, trying to enforce a law being blatantly defied. But he may have taken such a hard line that there is no room to maneuver. If so, the nation may be in trouble in the sky for some time to come.

Chicago Tribune

Chicago, Ill., August 7, 1981

The striking air traffic controllers, individually and collectively, had better begin rethinking their position — and quickly. They have begun a job action that at this point they must know will fail. The President of the United States has put his prestige on the line, and he is not likely to make contract concessions. He has begun to fire and prosecute strikers. This will continue.

The controllers made a mistake in refusing the earlier government contract offer. They misjudged not only President Reagan's mettle but also the objective economic and political condi-

tions and the public's reaction. The President, whose popularity will rise or fall based on how the economy fares, could hardly have given in to a huge pay demand from one group of federal employes. If he had given in, this would have had a damaging effect on negotiations with public and private sector employes throughout the country.

The controllers, perhaps carried away by their own efforts to make people aware of the stresses of their job, thought the public would support them in a strike. The public has not, and this is because for the time being at least the need for austerity has become widely accepted.

The general appreciation the controllers had created, before the strike, of the importance and difficulty of their work would have helped them in the long term. It could still help them if the strike were ended.

And there is every reason to think that if the controllers were to begin reporting for work —

better yet, if the union called off the strike officially and agreed to live with the contract earlier agreed on — the Federal Aviation Administration might well recommend to President Reagan not to terminate their jobs.

In that case, President Reagan would probably be generous enough to accept the recommendation. He is a strong, uncompromising man, but he is not vindictive. He must carry his point, which is an important one; but once he does, he can afford to be gracious about it.

If the controllers let the abortive strike drag on, they will lose everything. They will lose whatever public sensitivity to their job's pressures they have managed to create. And, worse, they will lose their jobs. Though unions are not accustomed to accepting defeat, the controllers should put aside their emotions and accept reality. The question is no longer what they may gain but how much they are going to lose.

the Charleston Gazette

Charleston, W.Va., August 7, 1981

SURELY an air traffic controllers strike that inconveniences travels, disrupts the conduct of business and threatens mail deliveries will prompt many Americans to pause and reflect upon the concept of labor unions whose members are employees of the people. The conspicuous question, of course, is this: What is the value of the "no-strike" assurances invariably produced by advocates of public employee unions to soothe a doubting public?

We have seen in the case of "sick-outs" and the like that "no-strike" pledges in ordinary public employee contracts can be circumvented with impunity. As the air traffic controllers have shown, even strict law prohibiting strikes by government employees against the public safety can be ignored. Whether it can be ignored with impunity depends upon the stiffness of President Reagan's backbone.

Each striking air traffic controller gave his solemn oath that he would not participate in a strike against the government of the United States or any agency thereof. The strikers have done more than break the law. They have reneged on a promise to the people. We are in complete accord with President Reagan, who declared that those who did not report for work within 48 hours would forfeit their jobs and be fired.

We know of no other way to deal with the situation. We hope the president's strong language renders impossible any governmental shilly-shallying. If the president doesn't weaken in his resolve, a long overdue precedent may in the future strengthen public officials at all levels of government. Although the right to strike is cherished in America, it is a right that exists only in the case of private employment. It is a right that must be forfeited as a condition of public employment because, as the president said:

"Government cannot close down the assembly line. It has to provide without interruption the protective services which are the government's reason for being."

We hope the people of the United States can be made sufficiently aware of the distinction between public and private employment. It is a distinction public employee union leaders and their legislative supporters tend to fuzz.

Putting law and principle aside for a moment, let us look at the circumstances of air traffic controllers. Seven months ago they were offered an increase in pay that is twice the amount other government employees could expect. Members of the union, whose work is difficult and nerve-wracking, are well-paid. Everybody knows that government fringes and pensions are the envy of the privately employed. The union wants 17 times what was offered seven months ago.

But we will not comment on what would be a proper pay settlement. Our concern is with the illegal strike. It should be put down — crushed, if you will — by governmental authority.

St. Petersburg Times

St. Petersburg, Fla., August 6, 1981

In most labor disputes involving public employees, the government's objective is to create a climate of mutual understanding and free-flowing communication between the two sides for the purpose of restoring public service as quickly as possible.

In the bitter, illegal strike of the air traffic controllers against the Federal Aviation Administration (FAA), the government's goal seems to be to break the union and to intimidate and punish the strikers.

NEVER IN our memory has the federal government come down so harshly and with such force against any such group. President Reagan destroyed any possibility of a negotiated settlement by issuing a threatening, give-up-or-be-fired ultimatum. The government tried to seize the union's strike fund. When that turned out to be illegal, government lawyers found a judge to freeze the fund. Justice Department lawyers persuaded judges to impose enormous fines against the union and its leaders. They got injunctions ordering strikers back to work in 57 cities. They obtained 38 criminal indictments and they prepared 20 civil contempt citations. Five union leaders were jailed.

The controllers should not be striking because it is illegal. But as a free society, this nation still has not resolved how to treat public employees who have sincere grievances. Some states have tried to resolve the issue with compulsory arbitration, which is not the answer. Other states, including Florida, have established a process of mediation and conciliation that often is more successful.

Unfortunately, no such ray of hope exists for the air controllers. The FAA has a long history of incompetence and unresponsiveness in dealing with its employees and those it regulates, such as the airline pilots. After years of unsatisfactory complaining, many of the controllers have come to believe that their only choice is between striking and working under conditions so stress-

ful that they lead inevitably to illness and personal disaster. We don't know whether that perception is accurate or not, but it is an attitude with which the government must deal if it wants air controllers who are well adjusted and satisfied with their jobs.

IN SUCH conflicts with workers who are wanted back on the job, wise managers seek to find a middle ground where communication and compromise can occur. This is a principle of conduct with applications in all human affairs, foreign relations as well as labor disputes. With his threatening ultimatum, the President destroyed all hope for an honorable compromise. If such a threat were necessary, then it should have come from FAA Administrator J. Lynn Helms. The President might have been needed at a later time to take the steps, without any loss of face, that could have led to a settlement.

The forgotten issue is the safety of Americans traveling on airplanes. Supervisors have been able to maintain much of the airlines' schedules, but how long can they keep up the pace? If the government sticks by its firing of all the strikers, who is going to control the airplanes while new workers are trained? What will be the economic effects of many months or years of crippled air service?

FEW OF THESE questions seem to have been considered either by the strikers or the administration. Many passengers have answered them so far this week by staying away from the airport.

What the country needs is to find a way to put aside the bitterness and bluster of the past in order to find a way to resume reasonable negotiations. Unfortunately, both sides have pushed the dispute far beyond the point at which that still seems possible. Instead, there may be a long period of turmoil and recrimination that won't benefit anyone, especially people who must travel by air.

U.S.-SOVIET RELATIONS:
Soviet President Brezhnev Dies; Former KGB Chief Andropov Succeeds

Long-time Soviet leader Leonid I. Brezhnev died Nov. 10 of a heart attack. Although Brezhnev, 75, had appeared in ill health for many years, reports of his condition were not confirmed until the announcement of his death, delayed until Nov. 11. An official medical bulletin stated that heart failure was due to arteriosclerosis of the aorta, and revealed that Brezhnev had suffered several previous heart attacks. Western observers, who had long speculated on the succession, were surprised by the speed with which the Soviet leadership named Yuri V. Andropov to replace Brezhnev as general secretary of the Communist Party's Central Committee, the most powerful position in the Soviet hierarchy. Andropov, 68, had been a member of the Central Committee's Secretariat and was a former head of the state security police (KGB). He was unanimously elected Nov. 12 during an emergency session of the full CP Central Committee, according to the official Soviet news agency, Tass.

President Reagan sent a letter to the Soviet leadership Nov. 11, expressing regret for Brezhnev's death. Writing that Brezhnev was "one of the world's most important figures for nearly two decades," Reagan continued: "I look forward to conducting relations with the new leadership in the Soviet Union with the aim of expanding areas where our two nations can cooperate to mutual advantage." That evening, during a televised news conference at the White House, Reagan echoed the sentiments of his letter, and then went on to say that "we will continue to pursue every avenue for progress" in the reduction of nuclear forces. But, he said, "it takes two to tango," adding that it was up to the Soviets to demonstrate "that they want to tango also." In response to a question whether, in the wake of Brezhnev's death, he was planning to take a "first step" toward easing tensions with the Soviet Union, Reagan replied: "Well, there are some people that've said I took the first step with lifting the grain embargo. Have we gotten anything for it?" Reagan decided not to attend the funeral in Moscow, instead appointing Vice President George Bush to head the U.S. delegation.

THE INDIANAPOLIS STAR
Indianapolis, Ind., November 12, 1982

The death of Leonid Brezhnev ends another chapter in the long history of Soviet tyranny. Another now begins, its outlines a mixture of predictability and mystery.

Even professional Kremlin watchers can only speculate on what will happen in the months to come. Consensus, however, is that there will be a fairly prolonged and quiet interregnum out front while the power play for succession takes place behind the scenes.

Brezhnev's death has been expected for many months. Public appearances this year have often been characterized by a death mask pallor, a halting gait and the slurred speech that betrays heavy medication.

Symptomatic of the elitist nature of Soviet chronicles is the fact that the official announcement of the death was made 29 hours after the event. Moreover, the announcement, when it did come, was addressed, first, "to the party" and then "to the people."

Brezhnev's obvious ill health gave ample time to the governing Council of Ministers and the Politburo to prepare for almost any political or military eventuality. The clamps were screwed even tighter around any volatile area of the communist world. In Poland, no doubt, "troublemakers" have been locked up or are under surveillance. The Red Army is on alert.

To expect any dramatic, lightning-like turn of events is to ignore the iron rigidity of communism. Most likely, it will be business as usual until another party chieftain emerges at the top.

The Kremlin guard, however masterful at manipulating world opinion, is not now concerned with reaction in the West. Therefore, urgings from the detente lobby that the Reagan administration seize the opportunity for conciliatory overtures are naive and unrealistically optimistic.

The administration attitude now appears to be one of wait and see. And indeed that is all the West — and the millions of people under the Red yoke — can do. That and pray that somehow this moment will eventually produce a kinder twist in the world's fate.

THE BLADE
Toledo, Ohio, November 21, 1982

We are realists. We will stay that way. We are strong. We will stay that way. We're constructive, and we are ready to solve problems and will continue to be ready to do so, ready to respond.
— Secretary of State Shultz

THERE are, to be sure, certain assumptions in those statements that may be subject to argument or interpretation. But on balance they represent a reasonable approach to relations with the Soviet Union, which at the moment are very uncertain. Despite all the speculation as to how the Kremlin will act under party secretary Yuri Andropov, no one outside the Politburo has any great insight into the matter.

Some American observers believe that President Reagan should have made it a point to pay his respects personally to the late Soviet President Leonid Brezhnev at his funeral in Moscow. While this might have had some limited effect as a symbolic gesture, we are not persuaded that it would have been either useful or appropriate.

This country was adequately represented by Vice President Bush, summoned from an African diplomatic tour, by Secretary of State Shultz, and by Ambassador Arthur Hartman. Joseph Stalin did not pay a personal visit to Washington on the death of President Franklin Roosevelt — it was, of course, wartime — nor did Nikita Khrushchev come to this country after the assassination of President John Kennedy. Furthermore, it is doubtful that any great insights would be gained in the ponderous pomp and stolid ceremony of a state funeral in the Russian capital.

Insofar as U.S. policy toward the Soviet Union is concerned, with the advent of the Andropov government, it was summed up by Mr. Shultz about as well as possible. If the change in leadership within the Soviet Union means an opportunity for more meaningful dialogue between the superpowers, so much the better. But there will have to be some signals and concrete action from Moscow indicating that this is possible. In that respect, Secretary of State Shultz's words take on added meaning.

The Seattle Times
Seattle, Wash., November 14, 1982

IN STALIN'S day, Soviet propaganda assiduously cultivated the myth that Stalin was Lenin's closest associate. In fact, the young Stalin was just one of a number of early day Bolsheviks around the Founding Father — one not fully trusted by Lenin.

Now the myth of Stalin as Lenin's intimate confidant is being revived in a new form. In a speech nominating Yuri Andropov to succeed Leonid Brezhnev as general secretary of the Soviet Communist Party, Konstantin Chernenko described Andropov as Brezhnev's closest associate.

Actually, others, including Chernenko, were closer to the departed chief.

In his acceptance speech, Andropov offered this chilling thought: "We know well that the imperialists will never meet one's pleas for peace. It can only be defended by relying on the invincible might of the Soviet armed forces."

That word "never" is bothersome. Does he mean there is no hope for peace in the world?

Perhaps Andropov was merely engaging in overstated propaganda — like the two myths about who was whose "closest associate."

AKRON BEACON JOURNAL
Akron, Ohio, November 15, 1982

FOR A politician whose views have often seemed rigid, to put it mildly, Ronald Reagan continues to display amazing and justifiable adaptability from time to time in the White House.

His comments in the wake of Soviet president Leonid Brezhnev's death are the instant example.

Every American president has every reason to be firm with the Russians, but Mr. Reagan in his pre-presidential days was often bellicose about them.

Fortunately, in commenting on the Soviet leader's demise, the President clearly understood the need for restraint and calm language. Both in his initial reaction and in his comments at his Thursday night news conference, he struck the right tone of conciliation without weakness.

The Kremlin is a place of mystery and political intrigue. A major shift of power there may be more unsettling than in a free society such as ours.

In any event, there may be times for strong rhetoric about the goals and actions of the Soviet leadership. Right now is not one of those times, and it was reassuring to see that as President, Mr. Reagan understood that.

SYRACUSE
HERALD-JOURNAL
Syracuse, N.Y., November 12, 1982

Soviet President Leonid I. Brezhnev is dead. Where does the U.S.S.R. go from here?

That's the question Kremlin watchers will be debating from now until a clear leader emerges from the pack of those who want to be the "Head Red."

Soviet leadership transitions are always an uneasy time, there and abroad. Since the Russian revolution in 1917, only four men — Lenin, Stalin, Khrushchev and Brezhnev — have been able to consolidate political power and grab the top spot.

Lenin, the revolutionary, died before he could set the nation on the course he envisioned. Stalin's maniacal purges of his own people would have have been even more frightening internationally if he had had control of "the bomb." Khrushchev's mostly hollow outbursts of rhetoric and threats kept relations between the U.S. and U.S.S.R. frigid until Brezhnev's detente brought a period of thaw.

While talking peace, however, it was Brezhnev who directed a Soviet arms build up that brought it to near parity with the U.S. And when things began getting sticky in Czechoslovakia, Afghanistan and Poland, Brezhnev demonstrated how heavy-handed the Russian bear could still be.

Keeping its satellite states in line proved to have a higher priority than retaining good relations with the U.S. and things again turned cold.

We always hope for a moderate rather than a hardliner, someone who is always threatening to push the button and start World War III. Because of the Soviets' unique method of politics, whoever eventually surfaces assuredly be a tough infighter, or he never would have made it to the top.

Former KGB chief Yuri Andropov has been named chief of the Communist Party and would appear to be in charge at the moment. Breshnev's protege Konstantin Chernenko is expected to be named Soviet president later this month. Of course, there also may be someone who has been waiting for Breshnev's death to make his move.

The speculation and nervous tension now going on in this country must occur nearly every four years in the Soviet Union when the U.S. presidential elections roll around.

Twenty years ago, there was John Kennedy, who stood eyeball to eyeball with the Soviets and made them dismantle their missiles from Cuba. His successor, Lyndon Johnson, showed his determination to halt Communist expansionism by escalating the Vietnam conflict into a full-scale war effort.

Richard Nixon probably caused the Russians the greatest concern with his visits to Red China but he also helped estalish detente with the Soviets, a policy followed by his successor Gerald Ford.

Jimmy Carter started with detente but abandoned the policy when the Soviets' hobnail boots began crushing human rights movements in the Soviet Bloc.

Ronald Reagan's anti-Soviet administration actually may force the Soviet power brokers to pick an equally tough anti-American leader who would match Reagan's hardline stance.

No matter who becomes Soviet chief, however, Reagan can be assured that Soviet wooing of the Chinese will continue, as will the Russians' plans for the natural gas pipeline to Western Europe. The former is an important security matter for the Soviets; the latter is essential to its economy.

A new Soviet president can mean a new beginning for U.S.-U.S.S.R. relations, but only if the Reagan administration shows more flexibility than it has during the last two years of Brezhnev's tenure.

We know President Reagan can match Soviet hardline strategy with the toughest of former U.S. presidents. The question is: Can Reagan also show an ability to compromise in areas that might be to the U.S.'s and world's betterment in decades to come?

Reagan's first comments on Brezhnev's death had a conciliatory ring to them, but he is still talking about peace that can only be built upon a strong military foundation.

His decision not to attend Brezhnev's funeral is a signal that he is not ready to make a profound gesture of conciliation to the Soviets.

The Soviets have had only four leaders in 65 years. The new Soviet leader may well lead his nation through the end of this century. Reagan will be in office no more than six more years. The relationship he builds with the new Soviet chief may well determine Soviet-U.S. for the next two decades.

THE ARIZONA REPUBLIC
Phoenix, Ariz., November 14, 1982

WHY no one should ever say anything but good of the dead, at least until he's snugly in his grave, has always mystified us.

It's as old as the Romans. One of the few memorable Latin phrases is, *"De mortuis, nil nisi bonum."*

Of course, there's hardly anyone a determined minister can't find something good to say about at the funeral.

The political boss who robbed his city blind may have been a loving son, and the mobster who sold cocaine to kids may have never missed a Memorial Day parade.

Nobody is all bad.

This refusal to call a spade a spade is sickening. And never has there been anything as sickening as the unctuous statements that poured from world capitals after the death of Soviet leader Leonid Brezhnev.

Former Secretary of State Henry Kissinger described him as a man who wanted peace.

Pieter Dankert, president of the European Common Market's parliament, called him "a person devoted to peace."

The gush flowed ankle deep.

Let's set the record straight.

Brezhnev devoted his entire life to oppressing his people. The Gulag Archipelago is a monument to his brutality.

One of his first major acts after ascending to Nikita Khrushchev's throne was to send the Warsaw Pact armies into Czechoslovakia to suppress the flowering of democracy there.

Later, he poured weapons into North Vietnam to help in the conquest of the South.

He used Cuban surrogates to establish pro-Soviet governments in Angola, Ethiopia and South Yemen.

He ordered Poland's communist dictatorship to declare martial law.

He built the greatest peacetime war machine ever seen, and his last known words were a promise to his generals to give them more guns, tanks and planes.

He was about as peaceloving as a tiger on a rampage.

However, it's true that he was good to his mother.

SOVIET-WORLD RELATIONS:

South Korean Passenger Plane Shot Down after Violating Soviet Airspace

A South Korean commercial airliner en route from New York to Seoul was shot down Sept. 1 after overflying strategically sensitive Soviet territory. All 240 passengers and 29 crew members were believed killed when the plane, a Boeing 747, disappeared in the Sea of Japan after being struck by a heat-seeking missile launched by a Soviet jet fighter. According to Korean Air Lines, the dead passengers included 81 South Koreans, 61 Americans, 28 Japanese, 16 Filipinos, 10 Canadians, six Thais, four Australians and single passengers from India, Malaysia, Sweden and Vietnam. The 29 crew members were all South Korean. Among the U.S. passengers was Rep. Larry P. McDonald (D, Ga.), chairman of the extreme right-wing John Birch Society.

Accounts of the downing of the plane that began to emerge Sept. 1 were sketchy and marked by rhetoric that intensified steadily over the next few days. The Soviet Union Sept. 1 claimed that a plane flying without navigational lights had violated Soviet airspace and resisted efforts by Soviet planes to guide it. A statement carried by the official press agency, Tass, said ''the intruder plane did not react to the signals and warnings from the Soviet fighters and continued its flight in the direction of the Sea of Japan.'' U.S. Secretary of State George Shultz the same day charged that the U.S.S.R. had downed the South Korean plane, knowing that it was an unarmed civilian airliner. Shultz offered an unusual glimpse into U.S. intelligence gathering operations when he disclosed that the U.S. routinely monitored Soviet military transmissions. A replay of electronically recorded communications by a Soviet fighter pilot had indicated that he had sighted the South Korean plane, fired on it and reported it destroyed, Shultz revealed. Shultz acknowledged that Flight 007 had been flying over Soviet territory but did not explain why the jetliner had strayed so far off course. President Reagan Sept. 1 condemned the jet's destruction as a ''horrifying act of violence'' and demanded an explanation from the U.S.S.R.

The U.S. Sept. 4 disclosed that a U.S. reconaissance plane had been in the vicinity of the Korean Air Lines jet when it passed over the Kamchatka Peninsula. The admission followed the suggestion by a Soviet general that the South Korean plane had been mistaken for a U.S. RC-135. An RC-135 had in fact been flying a route that intersected that of the Korean Air Lines plane, the U.S. revealed, but a White House statement maintained that the closest the two planes ever came was about 75 nautical miles. U.S. officials noted that the shapes of the planes were considerably different, and that although they could not be distinguished on radar screens, the Soviet pilot, according to the transcripts, had made visual contact with the passenger plane.

President Reagan, in a nationally televised speech Sept. 5, denounced the Soviet Union for what he described as the ''Korean Air Line massacre.'' He avoided taking any major retaliatory initiatives, however, announcing only minor punitive measures that were widely viewed as symbolic and unlikely to have any appreciable effect on U.S.-Soviet relations. A majority of the countries in the North Atlantic Treaty Organization reportedly agreed at a meeting in Brussels Sept. 9 to impose a two-week ban on civilian flights to and from the Soviet Union. President Reagan Sept. 8 directed that the two U.S. offices of the Soviet airline Aeroflot be closed, and that the three Aeroflot officials be expelled from the U.S.

The Soviet Union was forced Sept. 12 to use its veto power to block a resolution stating that the United Nations Security Council ''deeply deplores the destruction of the Korean airliner and the tragic loss of civilian life therein.'' The vote was nine to two, with four abstentions. Poland joined the U.S.S.R. in voting against the resolution. The four countries that abstained were China, Nicaragua, Zimbabwe and Guyana.

THE INDIANAPOLIS STAR

Indianapolis, Ind., September 2, 1983

If the world needed proof of the brutal nature of the Soviet regime, it has it now in the senseless barbaric gunning down of a commercial Korean jetliner. The aircraft accidentally and innocently strayed into Soviet air space and the price paid was the lives of 265 human beings.

The tragedy was not precipitated by some trigger-happy military crew acting in haste and without consultation with superiors. The Korean aircraft was tracked on Soviet radar for more than two hours and the MiG fighters which intercepted it — as many as eight, according to reports — were in constant contact with their ground control.

Communications monitored by the Japanese report that there was visual contact with the Korean jet and that a MiG pilot confirmed the firing of a missile and the destruction of his ''target.''

There are no mitigating circumstances and no basis for plausible explanations. Diplomatic apologies and negotiated settlements are not appropriate. Among civilized people the incident is, pure and simple, the murder of 265 helpless people.

One of the terrible ironies is the death of Rep. Lawrence P. McDonald, D-Ga., national chairman of the John Birch Society, an organization frequently denounced as paranoiac about communism. McDonald, then, has become a victim of paranoia come true.

The real delusion, however, is that the Soviet Union is just another member of the family of nations. Rather, this incident confirms the contempt the Soviets have not only for international law but for the humaneness that marks a civilized society.

Rockford Register Star

Rockford, Ill., September 2, 1983

Inconceivable . . . appalling . . . outrageous . . . revolting . . . barbaric . . . completely inexcusable.

There simply are no words to adequately describe the shooting down of a peaceful passenger plane and the 269 persons aboard.

Soviet actions as spelled out in detailed reports from Washington and from Japan fully deserve the condemnation of the entire world.

Was there provocation? Probably in that the Boeing 747 apparently had wandered into Soviet air space. But how provocative can a jumbo airliner be? And under what twisted logic would such a "provocation" justify firing a deadly missile at an airliner?

Is there a possibility that this was the act of some irresponsible fighter pilot with an itchy trigger finger? Of course that possibility exists. But radio transmissions monitored in Japan clearly indicate Soviet fighter pilots in close communications with their ground command during the entire 2½ hours they trailed the jumbo jet.

And even if this tragedy was triggered, literally, by one irresponsible individual, what does that say about the nation which gives such a person a trigger to pull?

Washington and Tokyo are fully justified in the anger they've expressed officially to the Soviets and in their demands for explanation.

But we can't imagine an acceptable explanation for such a grave violation of international laws and such an humanitarian act.

No, the Soviets stand accused today before all mankind for a terribly violation against humanity.

ARGUS-LEADER

Sioux Falls, S.D., September 3, 1983

There are probably few things that the United States can do to gain any immediate satisfaction from the Soviet Union for shooting down a Korean Air Lines jumbo jet over or near Sakhalin Island, with the loss of 269 lives, including 51 Americans.

But what the United States already has accomplished — in telling the world how the Soviets tracked the flight for 2½ hours and directed its fighter planes to shoot down the .747 — may already have done a great deal to dissuade the Russians from shooting down another airliner.

The Soviets cannot be excused from shooting down the South Korean plane because of their paranoia about their defense installations in the Kamchatka Peninsula, the Kurile Islands and Sakhalin, an area near which the world's airliners fly between Alaska, Japan, South Korea and other Asiatic destinations.

It also has been said that the Soviets care very little for public opinion.

Nevertheless, President Yuri Andropov and his colleagues in the Kremlin will have to recognize the anger and sorrow that nearly every nation has displayed over this needless, brutal loss of civilian lives. The Soviet government should be persuaded to seek a humane, not barbaric ending to future incidents of this kind.

We can't imagine any scenario in which the United States would shoot down a Soviet airliner, or any other country's passenger jet which strayed off course. We also doubt that the Soviet Union would attack an American airliner.

The Soviets, however, have displayed no such concern for planes of South Korea, a country with which the Kremlin does not have diplomatic relations.

In 1978, Soviet planes fired on a South Korean airliner carrying 110 people which strayed into Russian air space north of Moscow on a polar flight from Paris to Seoul. The Korean pilot crash landed on a frozen lake; two passengers were killed and 13 injured.

Maj. Gen. George Keegan, former chief of U.S. air force intelligence, in a New York Times article said the South Koreans have been careless in flying too close to Soviet airspace and that they invited what happened Wednesday.

Another factor is that Soviet military forces involved in the incident no doubt reacted to the circumstances by strict adherence to regulations that call for challenging intruders. Possibly, the Korean pilots didn't obey visual signals from the Soviet planes to land or acknowledge warning shots. We doubt that the decision to shoot down the airliner was made in Moscow. We think local commanders were responsible.

Commercial American airlines have had no similar navigation or other problems in flying Far East routes. In any event, the tragedy should impel the Koreans to avoid repeating any mistakes they might have made.

President Ronald Reagan, Secretary of State George Shultz and other American leaders have expressed revulsion and anger at the Soviets' attack and their reluctance to admit what happened. Reagan has used very strong language against the Soviets — a step that should bring a response and full explanation from the Kremlin.

This country must continue talking to the Soviet Union, despite the loss of Rep. Larry McDonald, D-Ga., and other victims of the incident.

But such talks must be conducted in a realistic context. The United States will have to be as wary of trusting the Soviets as they are suspicious of any challenge — even by a South Korean airliner — to the sanctity of their territory.

Meantime, the United States and other countries aligned with the West should keep the pressure on the Soviets to explain, if they can, why they had to blast Korean Air Lines flight 7 from the skies.

U.S. willingness to use intelligence and other information to document the attack may deter the Soviet leadership from responding the same way sometime in the future when a foreign airliner, for whatever reason, violates airspace of the U.S.S.R.

Minneapolis Star and Tribune

Minneapolis, Minn., September 3, 1983

Simply "come clean," said the British foreign secretary to the Soviet ambassador yesterday in London. It was good advice. Better than anything else, coming clean might interrupt the torrent of contempt set flowing this week by the willful Soviet order to shoot down an off-course South Korean civilian plane.

For Moscow to admit a major misjudgment, and to punish those responsible, would soften the denunciations it will face next week when top diplomats of the West meet with Soviet-bloc nations to sign a document on security and cooperation. Compassion and compensation for the families of the dead would counter suspicions that a ruthless shooting was intended to demonstrate ruthless policies as well.

Any high-level humanitarian sign would help limit the Soviet Union's loss of popular respect. Restitution to the government of South Korea and formal regret for the deaths of citizens from other nations would lessen the chill that now threatens such key discussions as the arms talks in Geneva. And a straightforward Soviet account of how the attack developed might even turn up some trace of extenuating circumstance. It at least would allow discussion of proposals to prevent such tragedies from recurring.

But despite their obvious benefits for Soviet self-interest, such responses are unlikely. Coming clean is rarely in any government's repertory, and perhaps most rarely in the Soviet Union's. So instead of suffering diplomatic embarrassment and trying to get it behind them, Soviet leaders are making the damage worse. Their spokesmen make no mention of shooting to destroy the unarmed plane. They call its straying into Soviet air space a "preplanned act" of using civilian cover for "special intelligence aims." And all they see in the West's appalled reaction is a "hysterical anti-Soviet campaign."

The danger from this tragedy is not only to the Soviet Union. It is dangerous also for the foreign-policy aims of the United States and its allies. Indignation and dismay are right responses to a needless brutal act. But repeated recrimination and heated rhetoric cannot do much to shame the Soviet Union into different behavior. Perhaps nothing can. Thus symbolic pinpricks like ending flights to Moscow and grand boomerang gestures like another grain embargo do not hold much promise either. Such gestures cannot substitute for pursuit of wider U.S. foreign-policy goals: secure coexistence with a hostile superpower and reliable agreements on arms control no matter how repellent Soviet values and actions may be.

President Reagan and other Western leaders strike the right note by condemning the airplane atrocity yet not losing sight of aims that outweigh even so outrageous an incident. The West should continue on that cool-headed course, for no other is available to serve Western interests. If the Soviet Union unexpectedly comes clean, so much the better. But if Soviet leaders compound their own folly by shouting about spies on a common commercial flight, there's no way or need to stop them. The strongest stance for America and its friends is to state the facts, clearly and bluntly, and not shout back.

Rocky Mountain News

Denver, Colo., September 3, 1983

AMERICANS have justifiably reacted with fury over the Soviet Union's shooting down of a Korean airliner and many would like to see the United States take the strongest of retaliatory measures.

Obviously, the murderous act requires a strong official response from this country. But it would not be in the interest of the United States or of the world to overreact.

It is elemental that the attack be condemned in the sharpest terms and that a demand be made of the Soviet Union for a full explanation of the details of the episode and of what prompted it to kill 269 innocent passengers and crew of an unarmed commercial aircraft.

The United States also should take the lead in marshalling world opinion against the savagery of the Soviet regime.

Past that, though, officials face a delicate task in deciding how far to go.

In earlier times such an aggression would have been considered an act of war. But it goes without saying that a response that could escalate events into a shooting war is out of the question.

There have been demands in some quarters that the grain treaty just signed with the Soviet Union be revoked and that all trade with the Soviet Union be stopped. U.S. officials would have to weigh where the

consequences of such actions would fall heaviest — on us or them. In any event, responses of this nature would fail unless they were supported by other nations of the free world. So if the U.S. does decide to act, it ought to round up support first.

If the Soviet leadership has any sense, it will acknowledge that it made a terrible mistake and apologize. So far it has done nothing but lie and try to put the blame on others.

If there is any good that can come out of such a tragedy it is the opening of the eyes of everyone in the world as to exactly what kind of leaders they are dealing with in the Soviet Union.

The Idaho STATESMAN

Boise, Idaho, September 2, 1983

The question preying upon millions of minds today is how a Soviet fighter plane came to shoot down an unarmed Korean jetliner.

The Soviets' few statements — that the airliner failed to identify itself and that Soviet fighters attempted to escort it to an airfield — are not likely to assuage anyone's outrage. The attack, which apparently took the lives of all 269 people aboard the plane, defies rationality. There can be no justification.

Still, the Soviets must explain.

All that is known points to a deliberate decision by someone in the Soviet military to destroy a plane that, under the circumstances, could hardly have been taken for anything other than what it was.

The Soviets had tracked the Korean Air Lines Boeing 747 for 2½ hours. According to Secretary of State George Shultz, at least eight Soviet planes reacted to the KAL flight at one time or another. The Soviet pilot who fired the missile apparently had the 747 in sight when he fired. He was continually in contact with superiors on the ground and told them it was a 747.

Did the Soviets believe the plane, which they say violated Soviet airspace, presented some threat? If so, why? One would think that the innocent nature of such a plane would be evident even at night.

Did the Soviets try to persuade the Korean Air Lines pilot to alter his route, either by radio or through signals? Was there a warning shot fired?

What happened?

Such questions, which have been directed to the Soviets by our own State Department, are not raised out of mere curiosity. They lie at the heart of a matter of vital concern to everyone on Earth.

Peace today is maintained through an armed truce between the Soviets and the West, each side fearing and respecting the power of the other, each side depending upon the other's willingness and ability to act rationally.

On Thursday, the Soviets broke that truce with an act that, by all available accounts, makes no sense. None of us can rest easy until that act is explained and assurances are made that such a thing can never happen again. Much more explanation — plus an apology from President Yuri Andropov — must be forthcoming from the Soviets.

The Providence Journal

Providence, R.I., September 2, 1983

The loss of 265 lives aboard a South Korean jetliner has left the world shaken — more shaken, indeed, than most air tragedies do. Neither bad weather nor mechanical trouble seems to have been involved. Instead, according to U.S. accounts (derived from sensitive intelligence-gathering devices), the Boeing 747 jumbo jet — unarmed, on a routine civilian flight — was blasted out of the sky by a missile fired from a Soviet fighter near Soviet-owned Sakhalin Island north of Japan.

Such an attack is a barbaric outrage, as an incensed Washington was insisting yesterday. Shooting down an unarmed civilian aircraft can never be justified, regardless of whether the plane is offending a government by violating its air space. There are many ways to bring an intruding plane under control short of shooting it down. Did the Soviets try any such steps? The record is unclear. Regardless, shooting the plane down cannot be seen as anything other than a wanton, criminal act. Those aboard the downed Korean plane appear to have been murdered, as surely as if they had been lined up against a wall and shot.

It seems agreed that the Korean plane, Flight 007 en route from New York to Seoul by way of an Anchorage refueling stop, went off course and strayed into Soviet airspace — not once but twice. It first flew over the Kamchatka Peninsula and over the Sea of Okhotsk, and then over Sakhalin Island. Both U.S. and Soviet officials say the flight was tracked for two and a half hours. Tass, the Soviet press agency, said yesterday that the plane carried no navigation lights and failed to respond to radioed queries. Soviet air-defense fighters, added Tass, "tried to give it assistance in in directing it to the nearest

airfield." The Soviet account made no mention of the plane's having been shot down.

Full details of this grim and mysterious event may never be learned. So far as is known, the plane's crew sent no radio message to indicate that Soviet aircraft were nearby. All the crew and passengers are presumed lost, and the Soviets are unlikely to level with the rest of the world if one of their pilots did indeed shoot down the Korean jet. But the detailed U.S. account, unless it can be effectively refuted, depicts an example of callous behavior that even by Soviet standards has to be considered cold-blooded and brutal.

Technical and navigational questions abound. Was the pilot off course? If so, did he know it? And, if so, why is there no evidence of radio contact with some ground station, somewhere? If the Soviets indeed tried to establish radio contact, as they claim, what kept the Korean pilot from replying?

None of these questions, however, can alter the fact of an appalling international tragedy, one heavy with political overtones. The loss of the Korean plane underscores, in all-too-vivid fashion, the shaky state of East-West relations and the constant perils of a world dominated by heavily armed superpowers. If the Soviets shot down the jetliner, it was an act utterly impossible of justification or explanation, one providing all too grim a reminder of the Soviets' habit of behaving in world affairs according to their own rules. One hopes Soviet officials make decisions about their nuclear missiles with more care and thought than was evident in the episode of the Korean jetliner.

"THE SOVIET UNION APOLOGIZED TO THE WORLD TODAY AND ACCEPTED FULL RESPONSIBILITY FOR WHAT IT CALLED 'THIS DEPLORABLE LOSS OF INNOCENT LIFE' IN THE KOREAN AIRLINER INCIDENT. IN RELATED EVENTS, HELL FROZE OVER..."

Chicago Tribune

Chicago, Ill., September 3, 1983

The **Reagan** administration is considering what it can do to respond to the deadly Soviet attack on a Korean commercial jetliner. The President will undoubtedly be getting suggestions to cancel the grain deal with the Soviet Union or cut off arms control talks. Some of this advice will be coming from aides who favored these measures even before the Korean jet incident.

The first thing to consider is that the attack merely confirms what the West ought already to know about the Soviet Union—that it is a cruel and fearful regime that does not adhere to standards of decent conduct the free world holds dear. Any romantic ideas about the possibilities of fundamental change in the Soviet system in the forseeable future ought to have been dashed by the brutality of this attack, if they had somehow managed to survive Afghanistan and Warsaw.

But to respond to this incident by canceling the grain deal or cutting off arms talks would be wrong. The United States deals with the Soviet Union in trade matters because the U.S. has a national interest in doing so. The grain deal was a business arrangement not a marriage. And the negotiations toward limitations on nuclear weapons are necessary simply because the Soviet Union is a dangerous adversary, not because the Soviet Union is a trustworthy member of the community of Western values.

A better response to the attack on the Korean jet is to put together an international agreement to ban the Soviet Union from the commercial airline fraternity. No landing rights in the West. No overflight rights. Treat the Soviet airline as an outlaw until the Soviet Union makes some concession about its responsibility for the incident and some guarantee that such a thing will not happen again.

This approach would damage the Soviet Union without damaging Western interests. It would be a gesture of Western solidarity against the Soviet's most barbarous enforcement of its sovereignty. And it would be a measure that the West as a whole could hold to.

The Dispatch

Columbus, Ohio, September 9, 1983

There is precious little that decent nations can do to penalize the Kremlin for the murder of 269 civilians aboard a Korean Air Lines jet without victimizing their own people in the process. The ability of the world community to punish the Soviet Union must be limited to condemning the Kremlin at every available forum and to letting the Soviets strangle themselves in their own web of lies and drown themselves in the slimy "justifications" oozing from Moscow.

The episode does, however, provide a textbook lesson of how the trapped rats in the Kremlin react when all the world can see the horror of their deeds. This is not an obscure incident, such as the use of "yellow rain" in the hinterlands of Southeast Asia, or the massacre of civilians in the back hills of Afghanistan, or the subversion of freedom in Central America. It's all up front: on tapes of fighter pilot conversations as they move in for the kill, on video terminals as the tapes are translated for the U.N. Security Council, in the photos and family portraits of the victims, in the glimpses of bereaved relatives and friends and in the horrible realization of the fear that must have filled the final moments of life of all the passengers — most especially the little children. Unlike the bits and pieces of information that needed to be pieced together from Asia and Afghanistan, the evidence of Soviet villainy in the Korean Air Lines attack overwhelms the senses.

The urge to want to punish the Soviets is understandable but the need to control and channel anger must be paramount. Recent history demonstrates that embargoes and sanctions have little effect on the Kremlin. World opinion also fails to move the Soviet leaders. Indeed, one of the casualities of the jumbo jet attack is our own expectation that the Soviets would conform to generally accepted standards of behavior. They do not, and this requires that all nations that wish to remain free must arm themselves with the ability to counter Soviet adventurism. It requires that NATO nations deploy missiles in Western Europe to counter already deployed Soviet missiles in Eastern Europe unless the West can be absolutely certain that the Kremlin is removing and disassembling its missiles. It requires that any agreement entered into with the Soviet Union be verifiable.

And it requires that all the world remember the fate of Korean Air Lines Flight 007 and the behavior of the Soviet leaders in the days that followed the attack. The callousness, cowardice and duplicity evidenced in this episode must not be allowed to fade from our minds. And the shocking lesson learned must not fail to guide our future dealings with the gang at the Kremlin.

LEBANON:

Over 200 U.S. Marines Killed in Suicide Terrorist Attack

A building filled with sleeping U.S. troops was blown up Oct. 23 when a TNT-laden truck crashed into the Marine compound at the Beirut airport. The attack occurred shortly after dawn. Almost simultaneously, a second truck bomb blew up at a French paratroop barracks two miles away. Both buildings were reduced to rubble, and the extent of the death toll only gradually emerged over the following days. By Oct. 26, the number of Americans declared dead stood at 219, with another 75 wounded and 20 to 30 still missing. The French the same day listed 47 soldiers as dead, with another 15 wounded and 11 still missing. All had been members of the multinational peacekeeping force in Lebanon. The Marine death toll far exceeded that incurred in any single action of the Vietnam War. Many of the Marines' personnel records were destroyed in the explosion and ensuing fire, making it impossible to give an early accounting of the dead and missing, and producing days of agonizing uncertainty for many of the servicemen's families.

President Reagan expressed ''outrage'' over the ''vicious, cowardly and ruthless'' attack. ''I think we should all recognize that these deeds make so evident the bestial nature of those who would assume power if they could have their way and drive us out of the area,'' Reagan continued. ''We must be more determined than ever that they cannot take over that vital and strategic area of the earth, or for that matter, any other part of the earth.'' The question of responsibility for the twin attacks remained unanswered following the blasts, with speculation focusing primarily on fundamentalist Shiite groups with links to Iran and Syria. A caller to the Beirut office of Agence France-Presse Oct. 23 attributed both bombings to the Free Islamic Revolutionary Movement, a previously unknown group. Defense Secretary Caspar Weinberger said that circumstantial evidence ''points in the direction of Iran,'' and Secretary of State George Shultz cited Syria and the Soviet Union as ''bitter opponents'' of the multinational peacekeeping force. Reagan, while reaffirming the U.S. determination to remain in Lebanon and ruling out any widening of the war, stated that ''this despicable act will not go unpunished.''

Chicago Tribune
Chicago, Ill., October 25, 1983

Americans are hearing demands, anguished and sincere, that our Marines be withdrawn before still more of them die in the incomprehensible brutality of Lebanon. And they are hearing other demands, also sincere and understandable, for revenge against the fanatics who decimated the ranks of the Lebanon peacekeeping force.

But before considering either, it is important to remember the mission and the duty of the United States and its allies in Lebanon. It is the honorable mission of bringing peace to a vital part of the world, and the men in the shattered Battalion Landing Team headquarters died honorably in pursuit of it. To withdraw them with their mission still incomplete would encourage terrorism and dishonor the fallen soldiers and the proud tradition of the Corps. Marines do not, will not, flee from a mission—this country must not ask that of them.

Nor should Americans give in to retributive rage. Nobody, not the U.S. forces and not even the Lebanese themselves, can easily sort out the complex of religious and ethnic and familial hostilities to determine what particular faction, what particular mix of faith and ideology, is directly responsible for the Beirut atrocities. To attempt blindly to mete out punishment would violate one of the true lessons of Vietnam. The United States entered Vietnam with the mission of bringing a measure of stability while an indigenous government grew. But somewhere along the line in Vietnam that mission gradually gave way to one of attack and retribution. Our soldiers adopted the language and tactics of search-and-destroy, carpet bombing, body counts and free-fire zones. The result was confusion, demoralization and failure.

In the heart of the rubble of the Marine headquarters and the French barracks are scattered the earthly remains of two men whose fanatic devotion to a cause led them to undertake an attack that they knew would end with their certain deaths. They acted in concert with others as fanatical as they. Such fanaticism grew out of, and thrives upon, a bloody and seemingly endless cycle of atrocity and retribution. To add to that cycle now would increase the danger to members of the peacekeeping force without furthering the cause of peace. It would change the U.S. mission. It would be futile. It would fail.

The first task now is the purely military one of assessing the causes of the bombings. The terrorists were able to breach perimeter security and deliver their deadly loads of explosives. Those security gaps must be closed. But at the same time there ought to be no confusion on this point: the nature of the violence in Lebanon is such that complete security is not possible. Fixed forces acting in support of government troops will always be vulnerable to the sniper bullets, rocket grenades and random terrorism of guerrillas, but that vulnerability can be minimized.

The second task is the political and diplomatic one of getting the contending forces to the negotiating table. Before the bombings there had been some progress in that direction, and it was made possible largely by the presence of the peacekeeping force. The best way to isolate and defeat the fringe fanatics responsible for the bombing is to bring the general Lebanese community—which has suffered violence as a daily fact of life for more than a decade—into a peaceful accommodation.

The Marines and their French, Italian and British comrades are serving a noble cause of peace in Lebanon. For the sake of those who died, and those who continue to face great danger, that cause must neither be abandoned out of fear nor forgotten out of vengeful rage.

THE DENVER POST
Denver, Colo., October 24, 1983

BY THE TIME the wounded have finished dying, perhaps 200 U.S. Marines will have been killed in the craven attack on a Beirut hotel where they were sleeping Sunday night.

A group calling itself the Islamic Revolutionary Movement claimed ''credit'' for that attack and another in which at least 25 French soldiers died. The tactics were the essence of simplicity and cowardice: Pickup trucks loaded with hundreds of pounds of explosives were smashed into the buildings that served as temporary barracks for the peacekeeping troops.

President Reagan called it a ''despicable act.'' French Defense Minister Charles Hernu called the attacks ''odious and cowardly.'' Words are inadeqate to describe the cold inhumanity of such terrorists, who destroy without conscience and escape into anonymity and rootlessness. And fury will not bring back the dead.

We could say we told you so. The Post asserted in an editorial only six days ago that there is no longer a purpose to the American presence, and the murder of U.S. Marines, in Lebanon. We warned that it is impossible to avoid ensnarement in a perilous trap; that civil wars such as the one in Lebanon spawn irrational hatreds that can suck even the best-intentioned into their malignancy.

That was when only a handful had died. Now that many times that number have fallen, there will be those who insist that we have had a purpose thrust upon us — to avenge those deaths, and to ensure that no more will die.

That begs the issue. To insist that more risk their lives in an accelerated conflict without any clear goal in mind is belligerence only for the sake of belligerence. The national policy that has sent these American youths to their deaths in a faraway and foreign place has not been articulated, either by the president, or by Congress, who collaborated in extending the U.S. presence in Lebanon for 18 more months.

Perhaps it is fortunate that this travesty occurred somewhat outside the recognized structures of competing factions in Lebanon. Like the savagely similar attack against the U.S. embassy in Beirut last April, in which 49 diplomats died, this atrocity was blamed on pro-Iranian fanatics, though the two groups may not be identical.

This lack of government, this lack of credence or respectability, is perhaps fortunate. It means we don't know against whom to retaliate. It forces us to be wise instead of reflexive. We have little choice but to mourn, and not to pander to these sadists by giving them anything to gloat over.

And as the rubble is cleared, the dead buried and the wounded healed, we need to set forth clearly what our goals are in this terrible and ancient battle. We need to know what our troops are expected to accomplish that justifies such a bloody toll.

The Des Moines Register
Des Moines, Iowa, October 27, 1983

There can be no excuse for the incompetence that made more than 200 American Marines sitting ducks for a lone, suicidal assassin, but Marine Commandant Gen. Paul Kelley offered one, anyway — and succeeded only in proving how gross was the incompetence.

"I think one has to realize," Kelley said of the man who drove a truckload of explosives into the Marine command post, "that if you have a determined individual who is willing to risk his life . . . the chances are he is going to get through and do that."

If so, what possible excuse do the Marine officers have for concentrating their men in so vulnerable a position?

There was every reason to believe such an attack could occur; every reason to know there existed a "determined individual willing to risk his life" in that territory teeming with fanatics.

The assassin followed a course of attack almost identical to that of another assassin who destroyed the U.S. Embassy in Beirut just six months earlier, killing 49 — an attack from which Marine officers apparently learned nothing.

Two guard bunkers may not have been manned at the time of the attack, the Marines acknowledge; after all, it was Sunday morning. Military officers have known since at least 1941 that enemies do not always respect the American tradition of sleeping in on Sunday mornings.

If they are ever allowed out of the stockade, the officers responsible for allowing brave members of a proud corps to be sacrificed to stupidity should be busted to buck privates and remain at that rank until they learn some elementary lessons in defense.

THE INDIANAPOLIS NEWS
Indianapolis, Ind., October 24, 1983

"This night methinks is but the daylight sick." — Shakespeare

The days in Lebanon have been sick with fear and frustration for the American Marines as they jolted in their jeeps around the perimeter of the Beirut Airport. They have been called "keepers of the peace." But there is no peace.

The tough Marines made jokes of their jobs, as strong men in danger always do, wondering aloud who would be the unlucky one to catch the next sniper bullet. Several of them had already been hit at random by the mindless terrorists.

The evil shades of these acts of terror pale alongside the bloody suicide bombing that has killed at least 183 and wounded 80 Marines — most of them while they slept Sunday morning.

A pickup truck, loaded with explosives, ran at least three security check points to ram into the lobby of the four-story building in which the Marines were billeted. A group identified as the Islamic Revolution takes "credit" for the suicide bombing. In a chaotic nation where terror has a thousand names, however, why search for a special title?

What is known about this recurring and unspeakable terror is that it has originated mostly in the southern suburbs of Beirut, where predominantly Shiite Moslems are dug in.

This enclave of terror inexplicably surrounds the Marine encampment. Lebanese militiamen have not been able, or willing, to penetrate these Moslem neighborhoods. The area patrolled by the American Marines runs along the edge of the airport and is largely open terrain, exposed boldly to the densely populated neighborhood around it.

President Reagan, moved and angered by the tragedy, brought up a hindsight subject: Moving the Marines to a more defendable position.

The question is why was such a move not made much earlier? Marines have written letters home describing their position as that of "sitting ducks."

Their position itself was a military blunder of serious dimensions.

The second blunder was the poor security at the building where the Marines were sleeping. It is unthinkable that a pickup truck could run the security gauntlet and penetrate to the lobby of their quarters.

The President is rightly angered over the wanton terrorism, but he should also be angry with the military leaders who thought this was a daylight war.

After this, will the Marines resume their peacekeeper role? Yes, says the President, and the other national leaders agree — so far. The French have suffered new casualties, too.

But the President has some explaining to do. He must defend his convictions and policies more openly, describing precisely the prospects of Syria and the Soviet Union assuming control of all of Lebanon if the U.S. should pull out.

In the light of the Beirut massacre, the military role of the multinational forces will need to be revised. It is evident that President Gemayel's Lebanonese Army cannot be supported with the U.S. simply in the role of a "moral force" that now and then lobs shells at the terrorists.

Americans will be forced to assume major responsibility for routing the terrorists, and erasing the pockets of resistance. If they do this, they will be fighting in the villages and mountains of Lebanon.

One alternative to such an invasion is to pull out the Marines and maintain a military presence — and limited force — using only the Navy and Air Force. There is a possibility that such a plan would work as well as the current plan —and without such risk of life.

The third alternative is to withdraw, lock, stock and barrel, and let the "religious" factions do what they do best — kill each other day and night.

The President and his advisers — and the American people — face the making of a distasteful and dangerous choice.

THE BISMARCK TRIBUNE
Bismarck, N.D., October 25, 1983

The attacks against our Marines and French soldiers in Beirut were shocking, certainly.

And yet, given the situtation in Lebanon, only the most naive of us did not recognize that such a slaughter was possible.

And, today, only the most naive of us do not recognize that further acts of violence are possible against our soldiers and other "peacekeeping" forces in Lebanon.

The people with guns and explosives, after all, do not abide by the Marquess of Queensberry rules. The combatants in the Middle East are playing for keeps, and they'll do anything to win.

And now, perhaps the time has come to sit down and reappraise the U.S. mission in Lebanon and the alternatives for accomplishing that mission.

Our mission is to promote peace and stability and to prevent a Syrian (Soviet) takeover of the country.

Those are noble objectives, to be sure, but it is becoming increasingly evident that our presence is not doing the job. Our Marines — and the other "peacekeeping" forces — are in fact becoming the targets of forces that do not want us there, and it is hard to see how the we can prevent further U.S. casualities.

That being the case, perhaps a different tact might be more successful.

For one thing, perhaps we should step up our aid to the Lebanese government of Amin Gemayal. If, as we believe, the interests of the Gemayal government are the same as our interests, then Germayal should be given whatever is necessary — including moral and other support from the United Nations — to become quickly and firmly entrenched as the country's leader.

Furthermore, perhaps it's time to call on our friends, the Israelis, to move up from the south and resume a more active military role in Lebanon. There is a supreme irony in the fact that since the Israeli withdrawal, western nations, their hands tied by the "peacekeeping" part of their mission, have been bloodied nearly as badly as the Israelis were when they were in active combat.

Finally, it seems that the real enemy in the region — the Soviet Union — is getting off scot-free, and perhaps it is time for the nations of the West to firmly establish in everybody's mind the link between the Soviets and the unrest in the Middle East.

The Seattle Times
Seattle, Wash., October 24, 1983

IT IS not mere hindsight in the wake of the hideous weekend tragedy in Lebanon to say the Marines never should have been sent there.

When President Reagan voiced his anger against "those who sponsor these outrages," he unwittingly identified the problem. Who are "those"? The Middle East, as everyone minimally familiar with the region knows, is full of "crazies." Political fanaticism is mixed with religious fanaticism of unbounded dimensions. Any one of more than a score of extremist groups or sects could have been responsible for the greatest Marine loss of life since Vietnam and for the similar kamikaze-style attack on French paratroops.

A United Nations force made up of troops from small nations, such as Ireland and Norway, has been serving for years in southern Lebanon without serious incident. It is representatives of the big powers that draw the attention of the "crazies."

Although sending the Marines into the Lebanese caldron was a mistake, it would also be a mistake to withdraw them in the immediate aftermath of the weekend disaster. Such a move would be exactly what the perpetrators of the mass atrocities — the mysterious "those" — are hoping for.

Henry Kissinger's call for a coordinated effort to strengthen the Beirut government makes sense. The U.S. and its allies must either develop a clear purpose and strategy in the Middle East — with better safeguards for the peacekeeping troops — or eventually be replaced by a small-nation U.N. force such as should have been given the mission in the first place.

U.S.-WORLD RELATIONS:
U.S., Caribbean States Invade Grenada; World Reaction Negative

It was the first large-scale United States military intervention in the Western hemisphere since the invasion of the Dominican Republic in 1965. Nearly 2,000 U.S. Marines and Army Rangers began to land on the island of Grenada at about 5:30 a.m. eastern daylight time on Oct. 25, encountering more resistance than expected from Cuban construction workers at the Point Salines airport. The invasion was announced by President Reagan at a news conference just after 9 a.m. The President said the U.S. had received an "urgent, formal request from the Organization of Eastern Caribbean States" to "assist in a joint effort to restore order and democracy" in Grenada. (An internal power struggle among the members of the ruling New Jewel Movement had led to the death of Prime Minister Maurice Bishop, and the overthrow of his government, the week before.) Saying that "a brutal group of leftist thugs" had "violently seized power," Reagan maintained that the combined military action of the U.S. troops and contingents from Antigua, Barbados, Dominica, Jamaica, St. Lucia and St. Vincent was "forced on us by events that have no precedent in the eastern Caribbean and no place in any civilized society." (The 300 members of the Caribbean task force landed after both airports on the island had been secured by U.S. troops, and were reportedly to be used for security purposes.) Reagan said the U.S. objectives were to protect U.S. citizens, facilitate the evacuation of anyone wishing to leave and "to help in the restoration of democratic institutions in Grenada." The U.S. opened Pearls Airport Oct. 26, which had been closed since the coup, and began evacuating U.S. citizens. There had been approximately 1,100 U.S. citizens on Grenada, more than half of whom were associated with St. George's University School of Medicine, located east of the Port Salines airport. On the same day, some 800 U.S. paratroopers from the 82nd Airborne Division were airlifted into Grenada because there continued to be resistance from local militias and the Cubans who had been building the airport. Secretary of Defense Caspar Weinberger said at a news conference Oct. 26 that 600 Cubans had been captured, 20 of whom were wounded, and that caches of Soviet-made arms had also been found. (President Fidel Castro had stated that morning that there were 700 Cubans in Grenada, mostly construction workers. He claimed that 40 were military advisers.) The Reagan Administration had charged that the airport was constructed for use as a staging point for Soviet and Cuban aircraft, while Grenada, Cuba and the project's backers maintained that it was intended to facilitate tourism.

World leaders reacted negatively to the invasion, as did many Democrats in the U.S. Congress. Questions were raised about the legality of the attack with regard to international law, and members of Congress complained that they had not been consulted in advance. The issue of the applicability of the War Powers Resolution was also raised. British Prime Minister Margaret Thatcher told Parliament Oct. 25 that she had expressed "very considerable doubts" to President Reagan after learning of the planned invasion, and had advised him to reconsider.

The Union Leader
Manchester, N.H., October 31, 1983

The estimated 1,000 Cubans still holding out on the island of Grenada may be said to be facing a hopeless situation—militarily, that is.

But it may well be that Havana feels it has three powerful allies on its side that make continued resistance feasible, even desirable: time, the U.S. Congress and the liberal news media.

The longer it takes to pacify the island and initiate the first steps toward democratic government, thereby enabling U.S. forces to be withdrawn, the greater the opportunity for left-wing congressional opportunists, aided and abetted by Big Media, politically to exploit the issue and undermine U.S. policy there.

Where public reaction is concerned, it makes sense for the administration to crush resistance on the island as quickly as possible, before today's cheers become tomorrow's jeers.

The Detroit News
Detroit, Mich., October 23, 1983

These are shocking words, at least at first glance. Invading other countries isn't something the United States is supposed to do any longer. The world has become a more civilized place, you see. Besides, a show of force might make somebody mad at us — the Soviets or the Cubans, for instance.

But it's also possible to make a strong case that the time has come to stop wringing our hands and act decisively. Where the situation seems clear cut, we should prevent further Communist penetration of this hemisphere and help our neighbors who are the victims of oppression. And Grenada may be a good place to begin.

The tiny Caribbean island, located 90 miles north of Trinidad is the latest Latin American domino to topple to the Communists. Details are somewhat sketchy at this point, but we do know that Prime Minister Maurice Bishop was executed last week by forces loyal to former Deputy Prime Minister, Bernard Coard.

The hard-line Marxist had denounced Bishop because he was slow to convert the former British colony into a Communist state. Never mind that during his four-year rule, he had censored the press, canceled elections, stifled opposition parties, and jailed numerous "political detainees." Too, the Soviet Union and Cuba have established a strong presence in Grenada and he was building a new airport where Soviet and Cuban warplanes could land. But when Bishop was of no further use to the Communists, they had him shot.

Now the island is held hostage by Marxist thugs who have not only declared a 24-hour curfew, but told their troops to shoot to kill on sight.

It should not be beyond the wit and power of the United States to clean up this nightmare in which 110,000 Grenadians find themselves. Lyndon Johnson achieved the same thing in the Dominican Republic in the mid-1960s when that small country looked ready to slide into the abyss. We haven't heard any complaints from the Dominicans about American "imperialism."

There are, of course, complications. About 500 American medical students currently are in Grenada and they should be removed first. Lives might be lost if there is anyone foolish enough to resist a determined military move. But the State Department has been doing its best to negotiate a better deal for Grenada for four years, and a Soviet-style coup is what we got for the effort.

The use of force is, and should be, an absolute last resort. But if the United States is never willing to use the force it has, there is no point in having it. Oppressed peoples in Grenada and other areas of the world where the United States has vital interests will not thank us for keeping our moral skirts clean at the price of their freedom. In the case of Grenada, force should now be considered.

WORCESTER TELEGRAM.

Worcester, Mass., October 26, 1983

The decision to move troops from the United States and Caribbean countries into Grenada is another reminder that we live in a dangerous, unpredictable, violent world.

Although the Maurice Bishop regime on Grenada was no friend of ours, the militarist junta that murdered him and his aides is far worse. Even Cuba was outraged by the crime. Last week the Castro government called for "exemplary punishment" of those guilty and said it was reassessing its relations with Grenada.

Faced with dangerous situations like those in Lebanon and the Caribbean, the president of the United States can either act or talk. In cases where talk seems futile, President Reagan has decided to act. As always, the critics are ready to pounce. He saw a danger to American lives in Grenada. Some saw no danger. He saw the threat of a Soviet takeover on the island, which has a 10,000-foot reinforced airport runway. Others profess to see no risk.

We are inclined to back the president until events prove him wrong. We think the developments in Lebanon show an urgent need for a policy reappraisal. In Grenada, we see what he sees — a brutal takeover by a Marxist militarist faction that would be a Moscow puppet. That would surely mean further difficulties for Central America, now undergoing an agony of revolution and counter-revolution. It might imperil the sea lanes in the Eastern Caribbean, where so many oil tankers travel.

The president says that our intervention will last only long enough to re-establish order, protect American lives and provide the Grenadian people with a free choice for their political future. Those goals are shared by the member islands of the Organization of Eastern Caribbean States, which has endorsed and shared in the intervention.

This administration has repeatedly asserted that it would not allow another Soviet puppet outpost to be established in the Caribbean. The move into Grenada emphasizes the point so that no one can miss it.

It would be nice if the world were amenable to reason and negotiations, but such is not the case. It is a threatening world, full of risks and surprises. For the moment, President Reagan deserves the benefit of the doubt in his decision to intervene in Grenada.

BUFFALO EVENING NEWS

Buffalo, N.Y., October 26, 1983

The initial reaction to the joint U.S.-Caribbean military operation in Grenada must be one of confusion and concern at seeing American forces going into action in still another part of the world.

With U.S. ground or naval forces deployed in other world trouble spots in Lebanon, the Persian Gulf and Central America, many Americans will join some congressmen in wondering where such deployments will end.

To the extent that this action was necessary to prevent American civilians on Grenada from being hurt or taken hostage — and that is the primary reason cited by President Reagan and Secretary of State Shultz — it can certainly be justified. The U.S. government has a duty to do what it can to protect American citizens facing danger in foreign lands.

But there is contradictory information about the immediacy of the threat to the some 1,000 Americans on the island following the bloody military coup that replaced one leftist regime there with another. Furthermore, Mr. Reagan said the move was also made to comply with a request from the Organization of Eastern Caribbean States for "a joint effort to restore order and democracy on the island of Grenada." That is a worthy objective but one that suggests an effort to play a world policeman's role at a cost in American servicemen's lives.

That the Grenada invasion was a multilateral action involving six Caribbean nations as well as the United States should help to counter criticism of "gunboat diplomacy." But international legal questions will nonetheless be raised because the United States is a signatory to the Organization of American States charter barring intervention in the affairs of other states.

Obviously, America has a right to be worried about the spread of pro-Soviet Marxist regimes in this hemisphere, but whether present circumstances warranted the drastic step of military action is a question that remains to be resolved.

There is one point on which everyone can agree: the U.S. forces should be brought home as soon as possible and there should be no thought of any extended Lebanon-type commitment by American forces. That is the course the administration correctly indicates it will pursue, leaving to the other Caribbean states any longer-term stay on the island.

With American troops now engaged on two continents, there is reason for concern that U.S. resources are being spread too thin. Mr. Reagan should define the American role in these tinderbox areas of the world more closely to assure the American people that we are not drifting into a growing new dependency on military force.

The Times-Picayune
The States-Item

New Orleans, La., October 26, 1983

Enough was finally enough in Grenada for the United States and its neighbors in the Caribbean. In a swift move of preventive self-defense, troops from the United States, Barbados, Jamaica, Dominica, St. Lucia and St. Vincent invaded that unhappy island, in President Reagan's words, "to protect innocent lives, including up to 1,000 Americans ... to forestall further chaos, and third, to assist in the restoration of conditions of law and order and of governmental institutions to the island of Grenada, where a brutal group of leftist thugs violently seized power."

This was the first show of such force since President Johnson sent troops to the Dominican Republic in 1965 in a brief, successful effort to avert a Castro-style takeover. In Grenada, which has had only one election and has been ineptly ruled since its independence in 1974, a new, violent group has taken over by killing the prime minister and three Cabinet ministers and ordering a 24-hour curfew. President Reagan is right in describing Grenada as in "a very perilous and dangerous situation, with no government, with no constitution and no order other than a curfew and shoot on sight."

The new leader, Gen. Hudson Austin, is a far-leftist admirer of Cuba and the Soviet Union, and seems to add to that the personality of the brutal strongman-thief of the Batista-Somoza-Trujillo type. In pre-Castroist times, such a development in a small Latin country was of less concern to its neighbors, since traditional dictators were generally content with running their own countries.

Today, however, Castroist Cuba and Sandinista Nicaragua have set a pattern of exporting subversion that changes the rules for a rogue nation's neighbors. Thus the members of the Organization of Eastern Caribbean States and the United States got together to eliminate the threat.

Shocked comparisons to the Soviet invasion of Afghanistan and insistence on the inviolability of the principle of national self-determination are inappropriate to this situation. The last two of the three governments Grenada has had since 1974 were installed by coups, and there has been no demonstration that those governments represented the will of the Grenadian people. The point of the present invasion is to give the people the opportunity to choose their own government, not, as in Afghanistan, to impose by force a government of the invader's choosing.

Grave times call for grave undertakings, but a decisive move like the Grenada operation can solve rather than create problems by proving to adventurers — Nicaragua comes instantly to mind — that they must consider carefully the consequences of their actions.

POLITICS:
Mondale Chooses Ferraro as Running Mate

Walter Mondale, expected to become the Democratic presidential nominee, named Rep. Geraldine A. Ferraro (N.Y.) July 12 as his running mate. Should she receive confirmation by the Democratic National Convention, Ferraro will become the first woman in United States history to be a vice presidential candidate of a major party. Ferraro, 48, a former teacher and assistant prosecutor from Queens in New York City, is serving her third term in Congress. She is the mother of three children, a Roman Catholic and the daughter of an Italian immigrant. Her voting record has been liberal, traditionally Democratic, and she became the protege immediately upon her entry into Congress of House Speaker Tip O'Neill (D, Mass.). She became secretary of the Democratic Caucus in the House and is currently serving the Democrats nationally as chair of the party's platform committee. In announcing his decision at the state capitol in St. Paul, Minn., Mondale described Ferraro's record as "really the story of a classic American dream." "History speaks to us today," he said, and the message was "that America is for everyone who works hard and contributes to our blessed country."

Mondale had interviewed seven prospective candidates for the vice presidential spot, including two other women—Mayor Dianne Feinstein of San Francisco and Gov. Martha Layne Collins of Kentucky. Others interviewed for the post included Philadelphia Mayor W. Wilson Goode and San Antonio Mayor Henry Cisneros. The well-publicized search drew criticism from other prominent Democrats, some of whom levelled the familiar charge that Mondale was merely attempting to please special interest groups through his consideration of certain candidates. Jesse Jackson, also a candidate for the Democratic presidential nomination, assailed Mondale for failing to consider him as a running mate, and expressed doubt that Mondale was seriously considering a black to share the ticket. Sen. Gary Hart (Colo.), another challenger, described the search as "a little like pandering." Both contenders later softened their comments. Mondale had come under considerable pressure to pick a woman for the ticket. At the annual conference of the National Organization for Women June 29–July 1, the organization warned that there might be an attempt made to nominate a woman from the floor of the convention in the event that Mondale chose a man as his running mate.

The Orlando Sentinel
Orlando, Fla., July 13, 1984

Good for Walter Mondale. Liberal or conservative, male or female, all Americans can be proud that a woman will be on a major party's national ticket. Finally.

Mr. Mondale's choice of New York Rep. Geraldine Ferraro as his running mate shatters a barrier in American politics that's two centuries old. The decision will rattle sexist obstacles throughout American society.

The choice is historic even if in many ways it is also traditional. As usual with vice presidential choices, the soon-to-be nominee looked first for someone who could help him win the White House and to credentials second. But trailing President Reagan by 19 percent in the Gallup Poll, Mr. Mondale needs plenty of help.

Politically, Ms. Ferraro is bound to put some fire into a drab campaign and energize a cadre of campaign volunteers in the process. For sure it is the first blip from the routine.

For voters, and that's what counts, Thursday's surprise has started them measuring Ms. Ferraro against the office of vice president and its occupant, George Bush. It's good to see so much attention on the vice presidency. Experience says that many vice presidents really do move up. If Mr. Mondale wins this year, or if Mr. Bush succeeds his boss sooner or later, he would be the fifth vice president of the last 10 to become president.

So let both vice presidential candidates face the same intense scrutiny that Ms. Ferraro, as the first woman nominee, is sure to receive. Republicans already are ribbing her with Vice President Bush's resume of blue-ribbon appointments. Like Ronald Reagan in '80, she has little international experience. Yet she has climbed fast and impressed colleagues since entering Congress in 1979. This year she has been effective in heading the Democratic convention's platform committee.

A series of Ferraro-Bush debates would help fill in the blanks about her. Her performance in debate and on the stump also will answer whether Mr. Mondale made the right political choice. But this week, with Democratic delegates about to convene, the Ferraro choice looks good. Unlike her uncharismatic running mate, she brings excitement to the ticket.

This contrast for the vice presidency still is no pass key to the White House for Walter Mondale. The race is between President Reagan and his challenger. On that score, Mr. Mondale wobbled through the primaries in too traditional a stance to inspire a lot of confidence among voters or hope among followers.

Perhaps his boldness with his ticket forecasts a Thursday-night acceptance speech that puts new backbone in his program. That would be the best ticket back to the White House.

Arkansas Gazette.
Little Rock, Ark., July 13, 1984

Did someone say that Walter Mondale plays the game of politics so predictably that he bores his national audience? Whoever said it should meet Walter Mondale, the presidential nominee-apparent who has just decided that a woman shall become a nominee for vice president for the first time in the history of the Republic.

Mr. Mondale's selection of Geraldine Ferraro, a three-term member of Congress from a district in Queens, New York, to join him on the ballot was anything but predictable although Mrs. Ferraro had been one in the succession of officeholders Mondale interviewed at his home in Minnesota. It was, in fact, a bold move, one that could help or harm the ticket in the fall campaign. There are pluses and minuses, clearly, and fairly soon we shall know if the country is ready for a woman as a nominee for vice-president of the United States. Unquestionably the selection of Mrs. Ferraro will offend male chauvinists everywhere, and there are more of them than many of us imagine, but if the presence of a woman on the ticket turns on enough women voters then President Reagan and the Republican Party will be in trouble. Women are not, in fact, a "minority" in this country, as the census takers well know.

Mrs. Ferraro is a bright, attractive, 48-year-old mother of three who was hardly known to the general public before Mr. Mondale began his interviews but she will become widely known now, in the four months that lie ahead. Her credentials in office are not as good as those of a leading U. S. senator like Dale Bumpers, or of a powerful state executive like Governor Mario Cuomo of New York, but they are acceptable. In her six years of service in the U. S. House of Representatives, she has won considerable recognition for her work, her acumen, her party loyalty. She won one of the coveted positions on the House Budget Committee and recently served as chairman of the national party's platform committee. If she turns in a good performance in the general election campaign, she may prove to be an asset to the ticket and enhance the chances for rescuing the country from the Reagan administration.

In picking Mrs. Ferraro for his running mate, Mr. Mondale effectively quashed all the cynical criticism of the process he used in selection. The pilgrimage of potential nominees to Minnesota had been described by Rev. Jesse Jackson as a "P.R. parade" and Senator Gary Hart even suggested that Mr. Mondale was engaged in "pandering" to the so-called minorities. Now Mondale's good faith has been upheld in a dramatic way, despite the earlier criticisms of the second and third place candidates for the presidential nomination. No doubt the talk show impresarios will say that Geraldine Ferraro made an honest man of Walter Mondale.

Whatever the political arguments for and against choosing a woman, and specifically for and against the choice of Mrs. Ferraro, the decision has been made, the gamble taken. The role of Mrs. Ferraro in the race will add interest and extraordinary precedent to the November campaign. The ticket is complete, ready for ratification in San Francisco next week.

Certainly the Democratic cause will be well served now if the losers, Hart and Jackson, make no more than a ceremonial contest for the nomination. Further acrimony will serve no cause except that of the Republicans.

The Morning Union
Springfield, Mass., July 13, 1984

Suddenly Walter Mondale, the ho-hum Democratic challenger, the "old ideas" candidate liked by many but exciting to none, has become interesting.

His selection of U.S. Rep. Geraldine Ferraro as his running mate was a daring move, made at the risk of criticism that he knuckled under to pressure from the National Organization of Women.

By selecting the first woman ever to share a major party ticket, Mondale showed that he was capable of breaking new ground, even as he covered his political bases by naming a vice presidential candidate of Ms. Ferraro's caliber.

Ms. Ferraro, D-N.Y., would have been a good choice regardless of her sex. The daughter of Italian immigrants, she is a product of the blue-collar working class that she represents today in her Queens district.

The mother of three children and former schoolteacher has been there, as they say. She reached Congress the hard way, studying nights for a law degree and practicing from home for 13 years before becoming an assistant district attorney specializing in cases of child abuse, rape, domestic violence and crimes against the elderly.

□ □ □

Ms. Ferraro won her congressional seat to replace retiring veteran James Delaney, a conservative Democrat, in 1978. More liberal than Delaney, she was appointed secretary to the House Democratic caucus and to a seat on the Public Works and Transportation Committee. Last year, she was named to the House Budget Committee.

She's considered to be a tough, pragmatic politician — just the kind Mondale needs to balance the ticket. She's also a Roman Catholic, a forbidding factor in presidential politics until John F. Kennedy surmounted it in 1960.

Mondale took his time and his share of criticism in the selection process. For all of that, he announced his choice early, even before the Democratic convention in San Francisco. Another first for the Minnesotan.

Thus Mondale has gained a new image along with a running mate. He dared to be different, and — despite the fear among many Democrats that a woman on the ticket will be a liability — his new display of political nerve could turn out to be an asset.

The boredom is over. Voters of both parties are likely to pay attention now.

TULSA WORLD
Tulsa, Okla., July 13, 1984

WALTER Mondale has indeed made history by selecting a woman, Rep. Geraldine Ferraro of New York, as his running mate on the Democratic ticket. But the question is whether that choice will help the Democrats' chances for victory in November.

That is not a slap at Rep. Ferraro. It is a question of practical politics.

Ferraro, a third term congresswoman, seems as qualified as many other vice presidential candidates. Her resume pales a bit in comparison to Republican George Bush, perhaps, but she has Washington experience and has proved her capacity for hard political work.

As an Italian-American, a Catholic and a New Yorker, she adds diversity to the Democratic ticket. What political effect her gender will have is unclear. An ABC-Washington Post poll conducted last week indicated that a woman on the ticket could be a wash. Fifteen percent of registered Democrats said a woman vice president would make them more likely to vote for Mondale, but another 15 percent said such a choice would make them less likely to vote for Mondale.

The biggest drawback to Ferraro's selection is the manner in which it was made. Ethnicity, religion and geography have always played a role in selection of a vice presidential candi-

date. Now sex is added to the list. But since these factors are purely political and have no relation to a person's qualification for office, the wise presidential candidate does not emphasize them as decisvie considerations.

But Mondale made no effort at subtlety. He pandered publicly to race, nationality, regional bias and sex, treating them as the major factors in his selection process. As one wag put it, Mondale's home began to resemble Ellis Island — a port of entry for all minorities.

The strident voices of the National Organization for Women also take some of the shine off Rep. Ferraro's selection. NOW leaders said that if Mondale did not select a woman for vice president, they would nominate a candidate of their own at the convention.

Was Ferraro's selection made to appease NOW and head off a divisive floor fight? That will be the impression among many.

It should not have worked out this way. Ms. Ferraro brings legitimate strengths to the Democratic ticket. But Mondale's handling of the selection coupled with NOW's threats suggests, unfairly perhaps, that she was not picked for her qualifications but as a sop for feminist redhots.

The first woman to run for national office deserved better.

The Seattle Times
Seattle, Wash., July 13, 1984

WHILE New York's Geraldine Ferraro is regarded by her congressional colleagues as an energetic and highly skilled politician with authentic liberal credentials, she does not command respect for depth of knowledge on issues, especially foreign affairs.

Were it not for her gender, in fact, and for her image as an ardent feminist, it's fair to say she would not have been Walter Mondale's choice to share the Democratic presidential ticket this year. But Mondale made that choice yesterday, thereby — assuming their nomination at the San Francisco convention next week — assuring Ferraro of a secure niche in history and setting the stage for a dramatic break with the past in American presidential politics.

In becoming the first female to occupy a place on a major-party presidential ticket, Ferraro dislodges an illogical and inequitable barrier to women like the one that, until 1960, kept Catholics of either sex from seeking the nation's highest office.

Geraldine Ferraro

From a Democratic Party standpoint, she could give the Mondale campaign — dullsville since its beginnings last February — a decided lift. Her role as a prospective vice president will afford Democrats a fresh chance to exploit the gender gap that distances many American women from the Reagan administration. And her sprightly personal manner will lend some pizzazz to the wooden demeanor that has characterized the Mondale campaign so far.

Weighing a broader question, Ferraro's place on the ticket will create in November a useful opportunity to measure the maturity of the U.S. electorate — to test the extent to which American voters today are ready to overcome past prejudices and weigh candidates without regard to their sex. As a "first," Ferraro thus assumes a heavy burden because she will be subjected to far closer media scrutiny than any male vice-presidential candidate ever has received in either party.

On balance, the pluses surrounding Mondale's choice appear to outweigh the negatives. That is why the announcement is playing to generally favorable notices across the country, although the TV people — already worried about holding viewers for next week's convention — would have preferred that Mondale not extinguish one of the few elements of suspense remaining in this year's nominating process.

TERRORISM:

Palestinians Seize Cruise Ship; U.S. Intercepts Egyptian Jet

Four Palestinian terrorists hijacked an Italian cruise ship with more than 400 passengers and crew off Egypt Oct. 7 and demanded that Israel free 50 Palestinian prisoners. The heavily armed gunmen took over the *Achille Lauro*, a 23,629-ton luxury liner that normally held more than 1,000 people, and said that unless their demands were met they would start killing their hostages, beginning with the Americans and British. The terrorists also warned that they would blow up the ship if a rescue mission was attempted. Most of the ship's passengers had just disembarked for a land tour at Alexandria, leaving approximately 80 passengers—of Austrian, West German, French, British, Italian and American nationality—and 320 mostly Italian crew members aboard. Israeli, Italian, Egyptian and American officials repeatedly said that they would not make any concessions to the terrorists.

After being commandeered, the ship sailed to Tartus, Syria and then to Cyprus. Authorities in both countries refused to grant the ship port rights, and it was forced to return to Egypt. It was apparently off of Tartus Oct. 8 that the hijackers shot and killed Leon Klinghoffer, a disabled, 69-year-old New York City resident, and dumped his body overboard with his wheelchair. The action came after the hijackers, who had demanded to talk to negotiators, said: "We cannot wait any longer. We will start killing." Throughout the day Oct. 8, there were reports that one or possibly two Americans had been slain. The ship sailed back to Port Said Oct. 9, where the hijackers surrendered after negotiations with two PLO officials—Hani el-Hassan, an Arafat adviser, and Mohammad Abul Abbas, leader of the pro-Arafat faction of the Palestine Liberation Front (PLF)—and the ambassadors of Italy and West Germany. The hijackers had been given a pledge of safe conduct out of the country; the negotiators claimed they were not aware of Klinghoffer's death when this arrangement was made.

After the U.S. ambassador to Egypt, Nicholas Veliotes, boarded the *Achille Lauro* Oct. 9 and learned of Klinghoffer's slaying, he radioed the information to the American embassy in Cairo. He then said: "Call the [Egyptian] foreign minister, tell him what we've learned, tell him the circumstances, tell him that in view of this and the fact that we, and presumably they, didn't have those facts, we insist that they prosecute those sons of bitches." Italian Premier Bettino Craxi Oct. 9 learned of the death of Klinghoffer shortly before he was to announce what he thought was the peaceful resolution of the crisis. He then went ahead with a news conference in which he confirmed the U.S. passenger's slaying, calling the death "a terrible loss." Craxi also thanked the governments of Egypt, Syria and Cyprus, and particularly the PLO, for their help in ending the crisis.

On Oct. 10, an Egyptian Boeing 737 took off carrying the four hijackers, the two Palestinian negotiators, and armed Egyptian security men. On the order of President Reagan, F-14 Tomcat fighters were scrambled from the aircraft carrier U.S.S. *Saratoga*, which was sailing in the Aegean Sea. The fighters, accompanied by E2-C electronic surveillance planes, intercepted the Egyptian jet in international airspace in the vicinity of the island of Crete. The fighters then directed the Egyptian pilot to accompany them to a joint Italian-North Atlantic Treaty Organization base in Sicily, where the plane was surrounded by U.S. and Italian troops upon landing. White House spokesman Larry Speakes, in announcing the action, said that the Italian authorities agreed to take the hijackers into custody several hours after the plane landed. Speakes praised Italy for its role in the capture of the hijackers, as well as Tunisia, which had refused the Egyptian plane permission to land at Tunis. He also praised Egypt for its role in ending the hijacking and saving hostages' lives, but said the U.S. and Egypt differed strongly on the fate of the hijackers.

Italy Oct. 12 released Abbas, one of the two Palestinian negotiators who had been aboard the intercepted plane with the terrorists. The PLO splinter organization headed by Abbas two days later admitted responsiblity for the hijacking, but indicated that its original intention had been a suicide attack on the Israeli port of Ashdod. The U.S., which sought to prosecute Abbas for masterminding the hijacking, sharply protested Italy's action in freeing him. Abbas' whereabouts were currently unknown, although he had left Rome on a Yugoslav airliner bound for Belgrade. Yugoslavia was reported to have refused a U.S. request for his extradition.

Arkansas Gazette.
Little Rock, AR, October 12, 1985

Two days of terror for hundreds of passengers aboard an Italian cruise liner in the Mediterranean have ended after the death of an elderly, partially paralyzed New York man, and the four Palestinian hijackers are in the hands of Italian officials who vow to prosecute them. The fast-moving events surrounding the terrorist episode remain shrouded in the fog of claims and counterclaims by officials of several governments, suggesting that there may never be many clear answers.

The particular American interest in the terrorist incident is basically two-fold. The four armed members of the Palestinian splinter group essentially botched their original mission and in frustration, or incompetence or whatever they singled out the relative handful of Americans among the 500 or so hostages for abusive treatment, including the murder of the New York man. Secondly, American warplanes intercepted over the Mediterranean an Egyptian plane carrying the four captured hijackers and forced it to land in Sicily, where the four were taken into custody by Italian authorities.

The United States would like to take an even greater interest, but it is unlikely that Italy will extradite the four for trial in the United States. The crimes did occur on an Italian vessel in international waters, and, besides, Italy probably does not want to damage its generally open relations with the Palestine Liberation Organization, whose precise role in the incident is largely a matter of speculation in the absence of hard evidence.

No one should be naive enough to accept without question much of what has been said or left unsaid on all official sides about this act of terrorism and its aftermath. One of the many hard lessons of long-standing strife in the Middle East is that things often are not as they seem.

But as things appear right now, this, in capsule, probably is what happened. The four young terrorists boarded the Achille Lauro with the intention of debarking at the Israeli port of Ashdod, for mischief aimed at obtaining the release of about 50 Palestinians held by the Israelis or to retaliate in some way for the Israeli raid on PLO headquarters in Tunisia the previous week. They were discovered, panicked, and seized the vessel, and in a fit of rage killed the American. They agreed to surrender in exchange for safe passage out of nearby Egypt. The Egyptian plane carrying them toward Tunisia, which refused landing rights, was diverted by American F-14s to the NATO base in Sicily, marking the first direct military action the United States has taken toward stopping, or punishing, international terrorism directed against its citizens or interests.

It was, as they say, a "clean" operation by American forces in the area, requiring no bloodshed, but it easily could have been messy if the Egyptian pilot had refused to land where directed.

Certainly it would be a mistake to assume that this is the end of terrorist actions, that a show of American intelligence and military capability in diverting a plane will cause terrorists of any description to shy away from plying their cowardly trade. More likely, the entire episode from the hijacking of the vessel to the arrest of the four Palestinians in Sicily, will turn out to be simply one more turn in the cycle of violence and response in this troubled region.

St. Paul Pioneer Press & Dispatch
St. Paul, MN, October 12, 1985

Go ahead and cheer. The capture of the Achille Lauro pirates was neat, clean and satisfying. Tomorrow's complications can wait until tomorrow. Right now, congratulations are in order: to President Ronald Reagan, to the U.S. Navy and its aviators, to Italian Prime Minister Bettino Craxi and officials of other nations who helped (openly or otherwise) settle the hijacking and sack up the hijackers.

Is cheering unseemly because murder was done? Somewhat. Leon Klinghoffer, American citizen and Jew, 69 and crippled, had the only life he possessed blown away. Now he is recorded as the only casualty of the hijacking. Even the reports of his death became part of the intrigue. (Who knew of the murder and when?) Yet, the fact remains that many other unoffending humans could have met Mr. Klinghoffer's fate had things been handled much differently by those who dealt with the terrorists aboard the Achille Lauro.

The successful hijacking of the hijackers makes it easy to forgive whatever following of internal agendas was going on in Egypt, Italy and Tunisia. At least it *should* make it easy. Egypt is a deliverer, not a villain. Italy wants to share credit with the Palestine Liberation Organization for ending the hijacking.

The main point is the hijacking was ended and the pirates captured without greater loss of life. Personal points scored by Mr. Craxi, the PLO's Yasser Arafat, Egyptian President Hosni Mubarak and even Mr. Reagan are beside that point. It is not unreasonable to believe that the four men worked closely together, each for his own reasons, and regardless of post-deliverance statements.

Now the Italians have the Achille Lauro terrorists: four young Palestinians. The men appear not to have a friend in the world, but who would be surprised to find their release the object of the next outrage in this terror-ridden era? Italy knows about terrorist blackmail, but demanded as a right its obligation to try these four. That is courageous. The United States wants the pirates, too. Both nations may have to show nerve again; so, too, might their more reticent partners. They all did well once.

LAS VEGAS REVIEW-JOURNAL
Las Vegas, NV, October 11, 1985

Events were still unfolding rapidly last night, with the closing scenes of the hijacking of that Italian cruise ship still being acted out.

It was high drama as American warplanes reportedly intercepted an Egyptian aircraft carrying the four Palestinian gunmen who had grabbed control of the ship, terrorized the passengers and murdered an elderly American.

The Egyptian plane, escorted by U.S. fighters, was forced to land in Sicily where it was surrounded by U.S. military forces.

The Eygptian 737 aircraft was intercepted as it headed toward Tunisia from Cairo. When the craft touched down, American Navy Seals threw a ring of firepower around it.

It was too early to gauge the outcome of this operation, but indications are that Americans may have cause to stand up and cheer. For too long, the U.S. seemed a paper tiger — full of tough talk but unwilling to act.

The pirating of the Italian ship Achille Lauro was a vile act of terrorism.

One American — 69-year-old Leon Klinghoffer — paid the ultimate price. He died at the hands of the four Palestinian sea pirates who grabbed control of the cruise ship. Klinghoffer, who was partially paralyzed and confined to a wheelchair, was murdered, his body dumped into the Mediterranean. It was an obscene act, on a par with the cold-blooded execution of an American Navy man by Shiite terrorists during the takeover of a TWA jetliner earlier this year.

These murders alone are cause for outrage. But the American passengers who survived also were taunted, tramatized, threatened and subjected to gross indignities. Reports indicate American passengers aboard the Achille Lauro were forced to sit in the sun on the open deck with barrels of flammable liquid nearby. They were threatened with death by fire.

The terrorists apparently thought they had cut a deal with Egypt, and probably figured they were headed for safety in the terrorist havens of the Middle East. As of midday Thursday, it looked like the United States would again be humiliated by the Mideast's Terror Inc.

But the murderers of Leon Klinghoffer were in for a big surprise. They must have experienced something of that sinking feeling when those U.S. jets swooped in.

This decisive action by the United States is welcome indeed. Perhaps the era of U.S. paralysis in the face of brutal terror is coming to a deserved end.

The News Journal
Wilmington, DE, October 12, 1985

THE SOUND YOU hear is cheering.

Month after month, year after year the nameless, faceless purveyors of terror and misery commit atrocity and then escape untouched. Not this time.

With skill and precision, U.S. Navy F-14 Tomcat jet fighters intercepted the Egyptian plane taking four Palestinian thugs to safety. They forced the plane down in Sicily and turned the terrorists over to Italian authorities for prosecution.

Deep anger and unquenchable frustration have haunted the United States and other nations for years as the opportunities to strike back at terrorism vanished as quickly as the men and women who demonstrate bravery by holding guns at the heads of innocents. Not this time.

We must accept as a matter of good faith the decision by the Egyptian government to grant freedom to the four men who held 500 people hostage on the Achille Lauro. They did not know, they say, that murder had been done.

But murder was done. Leon Klinghoffer was killed — killed because he was an American.

President Reagan is to be commended for his swift and certain decision to demonstrate to terrorists that, when it is possible, the United States will do whatever is necessary to bring them to civilized justice.

Before his election in 1980, the president was rather harsh in his criticism of former President Jimmy Carter for his failure to strike a blow against terrorism. Yet, for five long years President Reagan has been forced, as his predecessor was, to endure humiliation from rag-tag rebels whose pursuit of liberation seemed to need regular injections of American blood to survive.

The capture of the four terrorists will not give Leon Klinghoffer back his life. Nor will it end terrorism. But their capture may give some comfort to Mr. Klinghoffer's family. And it surely eases the years of frustration felt by millions of people in the civilized world.

Portland Press Herald
Portland, ME, October 12, 1985

It looked like the same old story: Hijackers capturing innocent hostages, grabbing world headlines, making demands, committing murder, then ending the siege after receiving assurances of safe passage.

For once the story didn't end the usual way—in total frustration.

With the surprise interception by U.S. Navy jets of an Egyptian airliner bearing the hijackers of an Italian cruise ship to freedom, this time the tables were turned on terrorists. This time, it was one for our side.

Senate Majority Leader Robert Dole echoed the sentiments of most Americans when he said, "It's something we've needed for a long time."

Terrorists have been kicking us around for a long time now and getting away with it. Hostage-taking holds civilized societies in check. Direct action poses too great a threat to the innocent captives.

It's what allows terrorists to hold entire governments hostage to their deadly dramas, more often than not escaping punishment for their acts. So it's only natural that the national psyche should get a big lift out of a bold, successful response to a terrorist act like this one.

Let Egypt splutter at the use of military aircraft to stop their commercial airliner. Let critics complain that the U.S. action may escalate retaliatory acts. Let others point out that terrorism is not going to be wiped out by one dramatic instance of counterattack.

Just for now, just this once, we have a right to feel good about the way this particular story ended.

SPACE PROGRAM:

Space Shuttle Explodes; All Crew Members Are Killed

The space shuttle Challenger exploded shortly after launching Jan. 28. All seven crew members died in the explosion. A stunned nation mourned the lost astronauts and pondered the future of its winged craft space program. The National Aeronautics and Space Administration immediately grounded its remaining fleet of three shuttle orbiters. The disaster, the worst in the American space program, occurred only 74 seconds after takeoff at 11:38 a.m. from Cape Canaveral, Fla.

The craft was flying 1,977 miles per hour, 10 miles up and eight miles down range. These were the statistics being relayed by Stephen A. Nesbitt of Mission Control in Houston when an orange ball of fire appeared at the base of Challenger's external fuel tank. The tank held at liftoff a half-million gallons of liquid hydrogen and oxygen for powering the spacecraft's three main engines during ascent. Another show of fire flickered around the tank. Then, a few seconds after the first flame appeared, an intense fireball burst out amidship and the craft was instantly engulfed in a giant cloud of fire and smoke. The solid-fuel rocket boosters veered off, trailing white plumes of smoke that began to coil erratically downward. Debris rained into the ocean for an hour after the explosion, making the site of the fallout, about 18 miles offshore, unsafe to search. The long fallout also testified to the force of the explosion. By nightfall, no evidence had been found that the crew had survived.

The shuttle crew members lost were Francis R. Scobee, mission commander; Navy Comdr. Michael J. Smith, the pilot; Dr. Judith A. Resnick, an electrical engineer and mission specialist; Air Force Lt. Col. Ellison S. Onizuka; Gregory B. Jarvis, a Hughes Aircraft Co. engineer; and Christa McAuliffe, a Concord, N.H. high-school teacher selected by NASA to be the first "citizen observer" to ride the space shuttle. President Reagan addressed the nation from the Oval Office that afternoon, calling the crew members "pioneers" and "heroes."

U.S. space shuttles had flown 24 times without major mishap since the first flight of the orbiter Columbia in April 1981. The tragic flight was the first of 15 missions scheduled for 1986, the most ambitious year yet in the program. NASA suspended the shuttle program and named an interim review panel to collect and identify flight data from the mission, pending appointment of a formal investigating board.

The Washington Post

Washington, DC, January 29, 1986

"OH, THE humanity!" Those words, spoken by a weeping radio announcer as he witnessed the explosion and fire that consumed the dirigible Hindenburg nearly 50 years ago, must have come to the minds of some people yesterday as they watched the terrible short flight of the space shuttle Challenger. For a few moments that announcer in New Jersey in 1937 was doing his best as a journalist, describing a disaster that was to prove a turning point in the history of aviation. But suddenly he was overcome by the sight of fellow human beings dying.

The radio and television journalists who brought the first word of yesterday's loss were similarly affected. For a few moments they were, like the rest of us, shaken and horrified by what they had seen, by what was the last thing they or any of the rest of us had expected to see: the deaths of seven people we thought were beginning another routine voyage into space.

So routine, in fact, had these shuttle takeoffs and landings become that many of us didn't bother to turn on the television anymore. All had gone so well so many times that we tended to forget what a combustible combination of fuel and rocket engines is needed to lift a 100-ton craft into orbit—to move it in 10 minutes from Florida to a place high over the Indian Ocean. Remember the cartoons and columns making fun of a U.S. senator's shuttle trip—and printed *before* the flight? They were the work of people certain that nothing could go wrong.

Now we have seen how far wrong things can go. This disaster will undoubtedly have its impact on decisions to be made about the future of American space exploration. But that debate is for another day. There can be no questioning the spirit of the people who have gone aloft in this country's 55 space trips. We were reminded yesterday of the courage it takes to board these outlandish craft and head off beyond the atmosphere, and of the quality of the people who devote their lives to getting a chance to do so.

It was painful to see the reruns of the explosion, and even more painful to see once again the seven crew members and passengers boarding the ship, a cheerful, varied and interesting lot looking forward to a great adventure. The disaster that befell them occurred, horrifyingly, before the eyes of their loved ones and of schoolchildren across the country who were watching this launch as part of an educational project. It was awful to see, but if such things are to be done they should be done in the open. We need to know the people involved and to see their humanity—good people such as Christa McAuliffe, Gregory Jarvis, Michael Smith, Francis R. Scobee, Ellison Onizuka, Ronald McNair and Judith Resnik.

ARGUS-LEADER

Siouxi Falls, SD, January 29, 1986

The shocking spectacle was witnessed Tuesday by millions of television viewers.

A minute after liftoff, space shuttle Challenger exploded into a fireball, killing seven crew members and shattering some of America's hopes for space exploration.

Editorial

Among the victims was New Hampshire schoolteacher Christa McAuliffe, the first citizen passenger to ride a shuttle. Her death adds to the devastating setback suffered by the National Aeronautics and Space Administration.

Tuesday's unsuccessful flight followed 24 successful space shuttle missions, but it understandably raises questions about the future of the U.S. space program.

President Reagan canceled his State of the Union speech Tuesday and supplied the right answers during his alternative speech to the nation.

Reagan appropriately called Tuesday a day for mourning and remembering. But he also pledged to continue America's space program. U.S. journeys into space will not end, he said.

Victims of the flight should be mourned. And the nation's scientists must determine what went wrong and how to prevent it from happening again. But our journeys into space should not end.

The journey did not end 19 years ago, when three astronauts died in a launching pad fire while preparing for an Apollo flight. Our future and that of our children demands that we remain strong and committed in our hopes for the future.

As Reagan said, sometimes painful things happen along the way.

"The future doesn't belong to the fainthearted," Reagan said. "It belongs to the brave."

McAuliffe, the 37-year-old teacher selected from 11,146 teacher applicants to be the first to fly in NASA's citizen-in-space program, was to have beamed two lessons for live broadcast over the Public Broadcasting System into classrooms across the nation.

Instead, she and the other crew members — Francis R. Scobee, Michael J. Smith, Judith Resnik, Ronald E. McNair, Ellison S. Onizuka and Gregory B. Jarvis — taught us a lesson in purpose and dedication.

That lesson should not be wasted.

TULSA WORLD
Tulsa, OK, January 29, 1986

TRAGEDY came to Cape Canaveral Tuesday in a fiery explosion 10 miles above the Atlantic. Seven brave and talented Americans — the full crew of the space shuttle Challenger — died in the first in-flight fatal accident in nearly 25 years of American manned space exploration.

The free world, which had begun to take space flight for granted, was reminded with a shock that this is still a dangerous challenge and the men and women who venture beyond the space frontier are indeed made of the right stuff.

The best known Challenger crew member was Christa McAuliffe, 37-year-old New Hampshire teacher, the first private citizen in space. Her role in the space shuttle program was symbolic of America's commitment to the expansion of scientific knowledge and its dependence on a good public school system.

So the nation mourns the loss of an outstanding teacher and six other exceptional Americans — commander Francis R. Scobee, pilot Michael J. Smith, Judith Resnik, Ronald E. McNair, Ellison S. Onizuka and Gregory B. Jarvis.

They join a special pantheon of heroes — those who risk death in uncharted and dangerous places to expand human knowledge.

The tragedy will no doubt cripple the U.S. space program for a time. But after the inquiries and perhaps some finger-pointing, the quest will continue. The brave crew of space shuttle Challenger would demand nothing less.

CHARLESTON EVENING POST
Charleston, SC, January 31, 1986

Just as television brought the stark realities of the Vietnam war into the living rooms of America, so did its horrifying pictures of the explosion of the shuttle Challenger bring home to Americans the grave risks involved in space exploration.

That televised tragedy sharpened the national awareness is ironic, in that TV is the medium which has shaped the impressions most people have of U.S. space efforts. The astronauts and all the other people who work for the National Aeronautics and Space Administration have been so successful in achieving program objectives — no matter how distant — that they have made space travel look easy. Such deception (if that's the word) is the hallmark of the true professional, yet it inadvertently has led television watchers to take far too much for granted.

They sit before their TV sets and watch the drama of blast-off, see the spacecraft's graceful arc into the heavens and listen to the crisp radio messages between Mission Control and the mission commander. A week later they catch the Evening News on TV and watch the space shuttle return to earth on schedule and so precisely on the money that they equate it with a Grayhound bus pulling into the depot from Columbia.

As the televised pictures of the loss of Challenger and its gallant crew proved so graphically, that's not how it is at all in the space program. Real risks remain after 25 years. Some will remain so long as man reaches out toward the new frontier. The astronauts and the NASA scientists and administrators realize that. They've known it all along. They have talked about the probability of disaster, of something going wrong, but none has ever talked about putting the space program on hold because of risks.

No one connected with the program is talking that way now, nor should they be. The shuttle program should be postponed until NASA can determine what went wrong with Challenger, and what safeguards should be employed to avert death-dealing malfunctions in the future. When such determinations are made, and corrective actions taken space travel will be a little safer — thanks to seven brave men and women. Exploring space, like pioneering anywhere, can never be without risk, though. Television viewers should remind themselves of that fact of life as they watch spacecraft lift off in the future.

The Houston Post
Houston, TX, January 29, 1986

The Tuesday disaster which destroyed the space shuttle orbiter Challenger a little more than a minute into its ninth mission is a setback to the program and a tragedy for our nation and our community. Yet the astronauts who died knew and accepted the risks inherent in pushing man's capabilities beyond what they were before.

This disaster took the lives of seven of the select group chosen to fly in space, people among the best our civilization can muster. Those people were astronauts and the woman named to be our first private citizen in space. Most of them were our friends and fellow Houstonians.

It also cost us a billion-dollar orbiter — one-fourth of our fleet of manned spacecraft — and a $100 million satellite aboard it. The satellite, like a sister spacecraft already in orbit, would have increased our ability to communicate with other satellites and manned vehicles in orbit and enabled prompt transmission of great amounts of data as well as voice communication.

What has happened is bad enough, but it creates a potential for additional harm. If we allow it to weaken our resolve to continue to advance our knowledge and capabilities to function in space, that explosive fireball could reverberate negatively through the future of the space program, to its detriment — and to our own.

There have been more than 20 successful shuttle flights. Great care was taken in their preparation and launch, as well as during the flights themselves. The same great care was taken before Tuesday's launch. But great care is not always enough. Sometimes our best efforts are not sufficient — sometimes people err and sometimes equipment fails. Those errors and failures are costly in the demanding and perilous realm of space flight.

But it would be a poor monument to those who died were we to lose our determination to proceed with the work to which they had dedicated a great part of their lives. We must go forward in the full awareness of the hazards we encounter when we push back the unknown and the undoable. But we must, above all, go forward.

Edmonton Journal
Edmonton, Alta., January 31, 1986

The explosion of the space shuttle Challenger was a tragedy. But the fact that seven astronauts have died does not mean that robots should replace humans on future missions.

Men and women will remain in the forefront of space exploration as long as space continues to fascinate us. No machine can match the sensitivity and curiosity of a man or woman bent on probing the mysteries of nature. To deny humans access to space is to deny ourselves a chance at enlightment, at boundary-breaking and at life itself.

This attitude was embraced by the seven astronauts who died aboard the Challenger. Collectively, they represented humankind's commitment to a better future for all. Alert, intelligent and eager, they were willing to risk their lives for the pursuit of knowledge.

Unmanned space travel does offer some advantages. It's safer, less-costly and makes longer voyages into deep space possible. The satellite Voyager 2, which sent impressive and otherwise unobtainable pictures of Uranus and its moons to scientists on earth, is an incredible accomplishment.

A legitimate concern has been raised that the investigation into the shuttle disaster might siphon funds earmarked for unmanned space probes. Such action would be as ill-advised as the discontinuation of manned space flights. Each branch of space study has its purpose; one must not be recklessly sacrificed for the short-term gain of the other.

History teaches us that civilization pays a price for progress. Centuries ago, people perished in shipwrecks as man attempted to circumnavigate the globe and settle new continents. Our forbears weighed the risk of death against the promise of a better life and they pressed on.

The exploration of space offers the same risks and rewards. Our fascination with the unknown will not be denied.

Richmond Times-Dispatch
Richmond, VA, January 29, 1986

Social studies teacher Sharon Christa McAuliffe, one of the seven astronauts who perished yesterday in the explosion of the shuttle Challenger, had said that she hoped to "humanize the technology of the space age" for her students in Concord, N.H., and others involved in a Classroom Earth project across the nation. The catastrophe that befell Mission 51-L may have accomplished that purpose in a way yet another dazzlingly successful flight never could have. For it shocked Americans into a realization that no matter how sophisticated their space technology becomes, there will always be a significant element of human risk.

Mrs. McAuliffe had thought of herself — unpretentiously, for one who had won a first-in-space competition among 11,000 teachers — as an ordinary person who might convey some sense of the wonder and possibilities of space travel. "Like a woman on the Conestoga wagons pioneering the West," she said, "I too would be able to bring back my thoughts in my journal to make that a part of our history."

Well, many of those early pioneers who ventured beyond the boundaries of safe and secure turf never reached their destinations either. They fell victim to hostile elements of one kind or another. But without their willingness to blaze the trail, their many sacrifices, the limits of knowledge and opportunity would have remained narrowly constricted. Those who would help Mrs. McAuliffe's students (including those she never knew) cope with their grief would do well to place her, properly, in the framework of a long line of courageous pioneers. As President Reagan told the American people so eloquently: "The future doesn't belong to the fainthearted; it belongs to the brave."

Many Americans felt a special attachment to Mrs. McAuliffe and her family because of the media focus on Mr. Reagan's appropriate decision that a teacher should have the honor of being the first private citizen to ride the shuttle. But the other astronauts on the ill-fated mission were special people, too, and their families equally deserve the nation's profoundest sympathy in their personal loss.

One of those on board, Dr. Judith Resnick, an electrical engineer who in 1984 became only the second woman to go into space, was the sister of Dr. Charles Resnick, a Henrico County resident and professor at the Medical College of Virginia. The Resnick family, including the astronaut's young nephew and niece, were at the launch yesterday as were Mrs. McAuliffe's husband, two children and parents, and relatives of some of the other astronauts. Americans surely share in their sorrow.

The other astronauts were Cmdr. Francis R. Scobee, who had logged more than 6,500 hours in 45 types of aircraft; pilot Michael J. Smith, an astronaut since 1980 who was on his first mission; Ronald E. McNair, one of the first black astronauts; Ellison S. Onizuka, who had been the first Japanese-American in space; and Gregory B. Jarvis, a Hughes Aircraft payload specialist who had been waiting years for the chance to go on a mission.

The Challenger Seven now belong to the pantheon of American pioneers, explorers and heroes — and to history. They have written a page in the journal of space exploration as surely as if Christa McAuliffe had been able to return to pen it personally.

The Dispatch
Columbus, OH, January 29, 1986

The dream is a nightmare. The innocence is gone. The nation was stunned as the space shuttle *Challenger* was destroyed yesterday. The seven brave people who died in the tragedy will forever be remembered as pioneers who sought to walk among the stars to make life better here on Earth.

As we all are too painfully aware, the crew included Christa McAuliffe, the New Hampshire schoolteacher who sought to "humanize" space — to help make it real to thousands of youngsters who anticipated the launch and flight with the childish glee of a great adventure.

The other crew members included three trained pilots, an expert on lasers, an engineer and the second American woman (Ohioan Judith Resnik) to fly into space.

But none of their training, none of their skill could prevent the sudden explosion, the roaring flames, the sickening twisting of rockets roaring out of control, leaving behind the shuttle debris as it rained upon the Atlantic Ocean.

This split second in American space history stands in bleak contrast to the many hours of exuberant triumph the nation and the world have known as humanity reached out to the stars. Just this week, the world was treated to the breathtaking photographs as Voyager 2 — now two billion miles from Earth — sailed past Uranus, revealing eternity-old secrets in a conquest of the unknown. We were there among the Greek deities and our confidence knew no bounds.

That confidence has now been staggered, and our efforts must focus on finding out what went wrong. There is no place for dreams in the days ahead; no time to hope. We can pray, as we will, for the dead, and for all the rest of us who must live on in the sadness of this day.

THE SUN
Baltimore, MD, January 29, 1986

The selection of Christa McAuliffe as the first private-citizen space shuttle passenger was intended to be a lesson for the world on the human dimension of space exploration. President Reagan and National Aeronautics and Space Administration officials hoped Ms. McAuliffe, a Concord, N.H., schoolteacher, could help restore prestige to her profession as she helped to reduce the scale of complex space technology to proportions ordinary people could appreciate.

The fiery death of Ms. McAuliffe and her six Challenger crewmates, before the horrified gaze of TV viewers around the world, chillingly underscored another lesson on the courage of those working on the frontiers of the human environment. The sky beyond the Earth's atmosphere is a harsh, unforgiving place, open to human beings only through the use of huge, complicated machines. As was shown Jan. 27, 1967, by the agonizing deaths of the Apollo 1 astronauts and again by yesterday's devastating explosion of Challenger, the very power required to get into space poses great danger to the men and women who use it to reach for the stars.

Apollo's astronauts were working with equipment being invented as they tried it out, using techniques they developed to handle problems never before imagined. Their destination was the Moon. Many people doubted they would get there at all, much less return safely.

But Apollo pushed on, for the boundaries of human imagination are thrown into relief by the dimensions of a man. In 1968, astronauts flew around the Moon; a year later, they landed on it.

The Apollo program fulfilled a dream, but only shuttle craft can bring space into the realm of the practical. The industrialization of space, the development of orbital factories and laboratories to make products impossible to produce on the ground, can proceed only with reliable, large-payload vehicles to ferry equipment, supplies and technicians back and forth. The Hopkins and Hubble space telescopes, the largest optical instruments destined for space orbit, will have to ride shuttles on their assigned missions. Once again, the human factor will be required to operate and maintain them. This is something to ponder as the nation begins a showdown debate on manned versus unmanned space projects.

Ms. McAuliffe's name, and those of Lt. Col. Francis R. Scobee, Cmdr. Michael Smith, Ronald E. McNair, Lt. Col. Ellison S. Onizuka, Judy Resnik and Gregory Jarvis, must be placed beside all those pioneers who have died to extend the borders of human understanding. As Mr. Reagan said, these seven "were daring and brave, and they had that special grace, that special spirit that says, 'Give me a challenge, and I'll meet it with joy.'" As the saddened American people continue the quest for knowledge, all must remember that.

THE CHRISTIAN SCIENCE MONITOR
Boston, MA, January 29, 1986

IT is perhaps of the schoolchildren, millions in America alone, waiting expectantly for the Challenger space mission this week, that the tragic explosion after liftoff most makes one think. New Hampshire teacher Christa McAuliffe was among the passengers. She was to teach two lessons from space, which were to be viewed in hundreds of schools via the Public Broadcasting Service, during the six-day mission. The loss of Mrs. McAuliffe and the members of the Columbia crew makes us all reach for words of compassion and comfort.

Spaceflight needs to be viewed in the broadest of frameworks — as more than a personal adventure. It is an aspect of the human race's efforts to comprehend and master its universe.

From ocean voyages and the discovery of continents on Earth a few centuries ago, to the first steps by man on the moon's surface in 1969, to the hurtling of the Voyager II spacecraft past the planet Uranus's moons at the outer reaches of our solar system just this week, human familiarity with this magnificent universe has been accelerating. It is in the context of this larger adventure that this week's tragic event should be viewed.

Pioneers endure risks.

Columbus and other navigators lost whole crews. The first Apollo flight team, astronauts Grissom, White, and Chaffee, perished in a simulated launch in 1967. The disabled Apollo 13 had to be swung in a special arc around the moon in 1970 to be returned safely. A special honor is reserved for those who undertake such adventures.

On balance, the manned space program has been relatively free of serious mishap. There have been failures of equipment to function. In the current Challenger shuttle series, delays were frequent, often caused by misreadings of the weather. Disputes have arisen over the mix of military and commercial missions for the Challenger craft. The space program's top administrator has come under a legal cloud for private transactions. An air of impatience about the space program, and competition for federal funding for space exploration at a time of budget constraint, have been evident. But all this must be set against reasonable expectations for an experimental program that to this point has had remarkable success.

"I am a teacher first," Mrs. McAuliffe said of her role in the space mission.

Surely all are heartened and instructed by this sense of purpose which embraced her and her fellow space voyagers.

Chicago Tribune
Chicago, IL, January 30, 1986

In the first aftershock of the explosion of the space shuttle Challenger came the question: What will this mean to the children? How should it be explained? The President spoke to them directly in his painful national address. "It's all part of the process of exploration and discovery," he said. "It's all part of taking a chance and expanding man's horizons."

And the best that can come of this is a recognition of the real weight of those words, the way they should speak to all of us, including the President himself, reawakening the true spirit of the endeavor, its depth and seriousness.

The instinct to embrace the children at a moment like this is very powerful. They are innocent of the tragic sense that prepares people to contend with the horror. To them, space flight is pure adventure, a form of romance, in which death has no part.

Unusually large numbers of youngsters were watching the doomed launch Tuesday because there was a teacher along. This was to be a learning experience. They could identify with Christa McAuliffe because she was an extension of their own narrow world. Later in the mission, she was to teach a televised class period from space. But a little more than a minute after liftoff, the lesson became mortal.

Searing as it was for the children, for the adults it should have been more. Watching the awful image of the blast ought to have brought home a vivid, painful recognition that somewhere along the line we had begun to trivialize the exploration of space. The long, hard and dangerous work of reaching beyond our grasp had become so ordinary that network television had even stopped broadcasting it live.

Locked in its own political struggle—to get funding, to retain civilian control—the National Aeronautics and Space Administration had begun to try to stimulate the public imagination by public relations tricks. This was why a senator and a congressman and finally a teacher went aboard the shuttle. When the attention of the media strayed, in response to a flagging interest by the public, the program lost its political edge.

Mrs. McAuliffe's reasons for going were as fine and simple as the yearning to extend beyond the normal confines of experience and return to tell the tale. But the reasons she was invited were less perfectly noble, less important, more expedient. And if her death weighs specially on the mind, this must be why.

It would be a terrible mistake to let the sacrifice of seven lives destroy our confidence that exploration of space by human beings is worth the risk or the resources. Of course machines can do many things. But it is men and women who truly extend the human reach. No inanimate thing can have the intimate relation with wonderment that is the fundamental motive and animating spirit of all discovery.

But the shattering reality of force and fire 10 miles above the Earth, and in particular the death of Mrs. McAuliffe, should re-educate us all about the seriousness of what it means to investigate the heavens, and the stakes.

As adults, we had to explain to the children the meaning of what they saw Tuesday morning. But if we are to be adults ourselves, we must go on, chastened by the knowledge that we may have become jaded and indifferent, that we may have expected new thrills with every new mission, and that when the hard, slogging work of technological development and preparation for the next bold leap grew stale, the people in charge of the program tried to provide artificial substitutes.

From now on, the commitment should be as serious as the nature of the enterprise. It should be taken in the full knowledge that it is dangerous to the men and women who go aloft and that it may not provide immediate gratification to the appetite for novelty.

Reaffirming the more profound appetite—in President Reagan's words the yearning to explore and discover, to expand mankind's horizons—should be the consequence of the tragedy of Challenger.

We should no longer expect space crews to reflect any social or political purpose beyond the work of expanding knowledge. There need be no journalist, no mayor, no clergyman, no public representative. Anyone who reaches out into space belongs to the people and is the extension of the human species into the realm of the unknown. The astronauts are our hands, outstretched to the sky in a position that is at once vulnerable and humble and aspiring: the attitude of hope and fear, of awe.

WORCESTER TELEGRAM
Worcester, MA, January 29, 1986

The space shuttle had become routine. Since the first spectacular test mission in 1981, the sleek Challenger, Columbia and Discovery had gone up and beyond with what seemed to be humdrum efficiency. Fifty-two million miles without a major mishap. An amazing record and one we came to take for granted.

Then came Tuesday's terrible tragedy: An explosion about 10 miles above the Florida launch pad.

All seven aboard are lost, including the first private citizen in space, Christa McAuliffe of Concord, N.H., who went to high school in nearby Framingham.

Mrs. McAuliffe, 37, mother, vibrant teacher and caring citizen, was an example to her profession, her community and her pupils. She was high on learning, optimistic about people.

Over the last few weeks, her smiling, almost playful expression was much in the news and her spirit was obvious — and infectious.

America and much of the world weep for all of the lost crew members.

Now, NASA will sift through reams of computerized evidence and tapes. It will pore over what scraps of metal it can find as it relentlessly pursues the cause of this tragedy.

There is no worse setback than one that takes life. Our space program must now pause, take a hard look at its methods, procedures and goals, and then decide on the direction our manned-flight space program is to take.

Were Christa McAuliffe back in her New Hampshire classroom, she would tell her students that life goes on no matter what the setbacks. She would say unhesitatingly that there are new challenges to meet and new worlds to explore if ignorance is to be conquered.

That is the American spirit the brave little band aboard Challenger so clearly exemplified.

SOVIET UNION:

Crisis at Chernobyl Nuclear Plant Spreads Radiation, Fear

A serious accident at a nuclear-power plant in the Soviet Ukraine spewed clouds of radiation that eventually spread over other nations in Europe. The mishap, veiled in secrecy by Moscow, caused widespread fear and conjecture April 28-30. The accident involved the No. 4 reactor at the Chernobyl nuclear plant, located in the town of Pripyat, about 60 miles north of Kiev. Based on Western speculation and unconfirmed reports, there might have been thousands of Soviet casualties, mainly due to exposure to high levels of radiation in the accident area. Western experts also speculated that the accident might actually have occurred as early as April 24. Throughout the incident, Moscow had down-played the accident while denouncing the West for allegedly exaggerating the seriousness of the crisis. The Kremlin rebuffed most Western offers of assistance. The Soviet Union came under strong international condemnation for not initially revealing the accident and for withholding detailed information on the mishap. Western analysts noted that Moscow's secrecy conformed to a policy of not disclosing domestic mishaps. Evidence gathered outside the U.S.S.R suggested at least one other nuclear accident, with a high loss of life, had occurred in the country, at Kyshtym in the Ural Mountains in 1957.

The lack of detailed information prompted mounting speculation in the West. As early as April 28, some nuclear experts surmised that the stricken reactor had sustained at least a partial meltdown of its core. The supposition was prompted by the presence of isotopes and iodine in the Swedish fallout. A melting of the uranium fuel in a damaged reactor would cause the release of such isotopes. In turn, the speculation over a meltdown raised fears, particularly in Europe, of the possible cancers that could result from the radioactive fallout carried on the wind from Chernobyl.

THE SACRAMENTO BEE
Sacramento, CA, April 30, 1986

The official Soviet press is calling it a disaster, but as of this writing that's all we know. An unnamed Soviet diplomat in Sweden says the accident at the Chernobyl nuclear power plant in the Ukraine is the worst nuclear accident in history; an unnamed hospital worker in Kiev says 80 people died immediately and 2,000 more died on their way to the hospital; assorted anonymous reports put the number of evacuees in the tens of thousands. But it is so difficult to get this kind of information out of the Soviet Union that none of these reports is entirely reliable. In fact, the key reason for suspecting that something catastrophic has happened is the fact that Soviet officials have acknowledged any accident at all.

It's in this way that even the world's sympathy is kept out of the Soviet Union. Soviet officials have asked for Western advice about fighting graphite fire and for anti-radiation medicines. But that is such a breach of the usual insularity that it's got Western experts worrying about a possible meltdown or, worse yet, about a fire perhaps out of control at the Chernobyl site. The international cooperation — the Soviet acceptance of offers of international help and expressions of worldwide concern — that should have been routine is instead so rare as to be ominous, and so partial as to be dangerous.

Like some terrible allegory for the one world we live in, the Chernobyl plant provided electricity chiefly to Hungary and other Eastern European nations; U.S. contractors helped build the housing for the 40,000 people who lived at its outskirts; whatever tragedy that has happened there, it was first detected when radioactive gases reached Sweden; that cloud blew over Finland, Norway and Poland, as well as Kiev and Leningrad, and it's expected to migrate over the Arctic and past the west coasts of Canada and the United States within a few days. This didn't happen to an isolated foreign village. The world isn't like that anymore.

Not that there appears to be any significant danger to the rest of the world in this case. Although too little is known about Chernobyl, the experts say the radioactive gas that's migrating poses no human health hazard, and whatever other damage has happened seems to be contained in the Ukraine.

But the warning couldn't be more glaring. If the Soviet Union had allowed itself to learn from other countries' mistakes, it would not have waited so long to start designing containment buildings for its nuclear power plant reactors. (Apparently at least two of the four Chernobyl reactors had not even these elemental protective facilities.) If the Soviet Union hadn't kept its own counsel, Scandinavia wouldn't now be registering fallout.

The United States and the other Western nations have offered their aid. How could they not, when thousands of people may have been hurt or killed, when a radioactive fire may be burning out of control, when radioactive isotopes may be contaminating the water supply for Kiev, the Soviets' third largest city? But it remains to be seen if they will force their help beyond the immediate tragedy — if they'll put up an ongoing fight against the informational distance the Soviets like to keep. And it remains to be seen if the Soviets will accept it.

The Des Moines Register
Des Moines, IA, April 30, 1986

International agreements require that a nation warn its neighbors if a release of dangerous radiation threatens them. But the Soviet Union did not acknowledge the accident at its atomic-power plant near Kiev until hours after monitors in Scandinavian countries reported high readings.

Unless and until the Soviet Union gives a full accounting, the extent of the damage may never be known. The Soviet disinclination to level with the rest of the world, coupled with a cavalier disregard for the safety of Soviet citizens and others, helps make these nuclear plants dangerous far beyond Soviet borders.

Nuclear plants produce power from heat generated by an atomic reaction. The reaction must be carefully controlled. In America, federal regulations mandate overlapping safety systems to minimize the danger — but accidents still happen.

Two of the most notable occurred in 1975 at Browns Ferry, Ala., and in 1979 at Three Mile Island outside Harrisburg, Pa. Backup safety systems kept the accidents from becoming disasters. But most Soviet atomic reactors lack the containment vessels that are intended to prevent escape of radioactive material.

Early reports indicate the Kiev accident may not be life-threatening far downwind, but, because of radiation's long-term effects, it could be decades before any damage to humans is known.

With luck, the radioactive substances traveling farthest from the plant will be the least lethal, and the more dangerous substances will be deposited as solids near the plant itself. But there is cobalt in the iron water-pipes of Soviet reactors, says Dr. Robert Wilson of Harvard University. If that cobalt absorbed neutrons from the reactor in an accident and the cooling water containing it were to reach the atmosphere, cobalt 60 — a particularly deadly isotope — could be carried for thousands of miles.

The growing reliance on nuclear power by the Soviet Union and much of Europe shortens the odds against disaster and makes international cooperation increasingly important. The international community must message the Soviet Union that others do not share its indifference to the welfare of humanity.

THE PLAIN DEALER

Clevevland, OH, April 30, 1986

At the start, there were only vague and distant clues that the accident at a Soviet nuclear power plant was extreme. In Scandinavia, radiation levels began to rise. Then, after being challenged by Sweden for an explanation, the Soviets allowed a terse, four-sentence news story to be buried in Monday evening's 9-o'clock news. Ordinarily, the Soviet news apparatus would have stifled that information entirely. Now, the Soviets are calling the accident a "disaster." They asked for firefighting help and have warned against travel to the area. At least three cities have been evacuated. The best conclusion is that at least one of four reactors at the huge Chernobyl facility, near Kiev, underwent a catastrophic fuel meltdown.

The Soviet reluctance to report such events is appalling and reckless. No one is yet sure how severely other nations have been jeopardized. Even if the effects are trivial, the Soviet report was late, and might not have been issued at all were it not for Scandinavian monitoring. It's bad enough that the Soviets withhold such information from their own citizens. It's criminal when they withhold that information from other nations threatened by the consequences of Soviet mishaps.

The reaction of the Soviets to the frightening accident clearly has been inadequate. What is not clear, however, is how the political fallout will affect the American nuclear landscape. Despite the confidence of utilities and atomic-minded technocrats, America's nuclear industry is beset with problems. Some claim that Washington's regulatory framework for nuclear power plants is too lax. They will say—again—that meltdowns could happen here (as they nearly did at Three Mile Island and, on a smaller scale, at the Davis-Besse plant at Oak Harbor). Problems with financing, waste disposal, inefficient and confused regulations, oversupply, fall-offs in demand and widespread fears have brought the nuclear industry to a virtual standstill. There have been no new orders for plants since 1978; 110 plants have been canceled since 1973.

The Soviet calamity could further retard nuclear development, in the United States and elsewhere. It shows, with horrifying clarity, the desperate consequences of error. It is evidence that stringent regulatory restraints on nuclear power are essential. Soviet safety procedures are less strict than American controls, but that doesn't mean American controls are adequate, or that their enforcement is complete. Indeed, it might be that the Nuclear Regulatory Commission could be made more effective by being made more efficient. Industry spokesmen accuse the system of being "congealed."

Already, the Reagan administration has offered to assist the Soviets. Moscow's request for help from West Germany and Sweden suggests that it is unable to cope with the crisis alone.

The Chernobyl accident should prompt two additional responses. First: A rejection of claims that nuclear power is over-regulated in the United States. Disasters might be rare, but close calls are not. Second: An NRC review of the regulatory system with an eye to making it more efficient and more exacting. Without those steps, it will become increasingly difficult to accept the nuclear industry's grand optimism and casual assurances.

The Washington Post

Washington, DC, April 30, 1986

THE CATASTROPHE at the Chernobyl nuclear reactor will heighten all of the doubts and questions about this unforgiving technology. Since it is a valuable source of power for which many countries will continue to have great need, the Soviet Union—and other governments as well—owe the world a response that is candid and substantial, acknowledging the dimensions of this accident and offering people some reason to think that it will not be repeated.

The United States and other Western countries have offered any assistance that could prove helpful in this dire emergency. This is urgent and the right thing to do. All required help must be made available to limit the illness and death and the spread of radiation. The emergency, like the airborne poison, knows no national boundaries. But much more than cleanup is going to be required from both East and West. The meltdown at Chernobyl demonstrates a need for clearer and more useful international standards for notification and for safety enforcement in the world's growing nuclear power industry.

The Soviets owed their neighbors downwind a prompt warning of the disaster. Instead, characteristically, they said nothing until the Swedes, 800 miles away, began picking up the evidence of it. That is unacceptable. Even now the Soviets refuse to provide an accurate description of the accident. If it's true that the graphite pile is on fire, it may be out of control for some considerable time.

International safety standards would be difficult to achieve, but perhaps not totally impossible. The structure already exists. The International Atomic Energy Agency, based in Vienna, has devoted most of its limited resources over the years to restraining the spread of nuclear weapons. Since the United States and the Soviet Union have similar interests here, their relations in the IAEA have been less bad than elsewhere. Last summer, for the first time, the Soviets allowed an IAEA inspection team to go through one of their nuclear power plants. One of the inspectors was an American. The IAEA has been giving increasing attention to safety over the past decade, and it provides a forum for drafting nuclear safety conventions. Similarly, its nonproliferation inspections offer the precedent for at least limited safety enforcement.

Safety standards run into obvious resistance wherever civilian power facilities touch a country's weapons production. The two are highly intermingled in the Soviet Union. The Chernobyl reactor is a type that the Soviets have used to produce both power for industry and plutonium for weapons. Comprehensive inspections are hardly a realistic goal. But something short of that might prove possible. Presumably even the Soviets now realize that they have much to gain from higher standards of performance.

No doubt this disaster will strengthen the campaigns against nuclear power in many countries. But not in the Soviet Union, where the need for electricity is severe and the most available alternate source, oil, can be sold for hard currency in the West. The Soviet Union now has the world's third largest nuclear generating system—after the United States and France—and it will continue to build. The cloud of radioactive debris that the wind carried across the Soviet border is the best kind of reason for the West to try to work with the Soviets on reactor safety and management. Progress will be slow, but any progress at all is worth achieving. The incentives are, demonstrably, imperative.

WORCESTER TELEGRAM.

Worcester, MA, April 30, 1986

While it might be some time before the full extent of the Soviet atomic power plant accident is known, it serves as a sobering reminder of the dangers inherent in our nuclear age.

The severity of the mishap, which spread discernible radioactive material over Scandinavia, is not known; there aren't any reliable estimates of possible casualties. The Soviets usually restrict information in such cases, particularly when the news is bad, but the phrasing of reports from Eastern Europe indicates that the problem is extremely serious.

The accident occurred at the giant Chernobyl nuclear power plant, about 80 miles north of the Ukrainian capital of Kiev, in a populated area. Soviet authorities admitted that something had transpired only after Sweden, Finland and Denmark reported abnormally high radioactivity levels in their skies. The announcement marked the first time Moscow has acknowledged a nuclear accident within its borders, even though in the late 1950s a major disaster at a remote plutonium processing plant in the Central Soviet Union reportedly killed or injured thousands.

U.S. experts suggest that an accident is more likely to occur in a Soviet nuclear power plant than at plants in the United States. The Chernobyl facility is said to have an outdated graphite-moderated reactor, with fewer safety measures than shared by modern American plants. Indeed, in the Three Mile Island incident in 1979, the worst in U.S. history, only a small amount of radiation was released. Evidently, Chernobyl did not have a radiation containment structure, considered crucial to safety.

Inevitably, the Soviet accident will be used to fuel the fire kept alive by opponents of nuclear power plants in this country. In Massachusetts, Gov. Michael Dukakis recently declared that the not yet on line Seabrook nuclear plant on the New Hampshire coast should be closed during the summer until shelters are built to house beach crowds in case of disaster. Protests at Seabrook and other sites may result in the aftermath of what is now being described as a nuclear fire in the Soviet Union.

If the accident near Kiev has caused injuries and loss of life, America will offer compassion. And if the Soviet government needs technical assistance from the West, that, too, would be forthcoming. While ideologies and power politics divide East and West, when it comes to coping with nuclear calamities, all of the splits are forgotten. Nuclear devastation is the common foe.

The Globe and Mail

Toronto, Ont., April 30, 1986

It has been a nuclear world for four decades, but keeping the beast in its cage — for weapons or wattage — remains an uncertain business. The characteristic Soviet attempt to contain much of the detail of what happened at its Chernobyl power plant near Kiev makes it difficult for the moment to assess the dimensions of the mishap, but it was certainly no trifle.

If, well over 1,000 kilometres away in Sweden, radiation levels high enough to arouse suspicion of a *local* problem were detected, the levels in the vicinity of Kiev must have been awesome. Any accident that would induce Soviet authorities to look to the West for assistance is one of some consequence. Soviet news sources have guardedly conceded two deaths, evacuation of the area around the plant and structural damage to the building housing the reactor.

It is well understood by both the defenders and opponents of nuclear power stations that, once out of control, they can turn extremely nasty. We have had some experience of this in the past few decades, fortunately encountering nothing that claimed large numbers of lives. The most frightening U.S. experience occurred in 1979 when one of the Three Mile Island reactors near Harrisburg, Penn., lost its coolant, causing the reactor fuel to overheat. Although the escape of radioactivity was small and no one died, much of the U.S. ardor for nuclear power cooled in the heat of the mishap.

A substantial melting of the reactor core, possibly the worst consequence of a reactor mishap, is thought to have occurred at the Chernobyl plant — the evidence resting on the presence of cobalt, radioactive iodine and cesium in the gases drifting over Scandinavia. There has been speculation that a graphite fire — difficult to control — broke out in the reactor.

A good deal of national pride seems to be built into the design of Soviet reactors. The trait can be found elsewhere, but in this case it leads to irony: the praise heaped on the Chernobyl unit in the February issue of Soviet Life magazine. An eight-page article in the U.S. edition described the plant as a model of safety. "The huge reactor is housed in a concrete silo, and it has environmental protection systems," said the article. "Even if the incredible should happen, the automatic control and safety systems would shut down the reactor in a matter of minutes." Vitali Sklydarov, the Ukraine's minister of power and electrification, added that there was no danger in having towns next to the plant, and said that "the odds of a meltdown are one in 10,000 years. The plants have safe and reliable controls that are protected from any breakdown with three safety lines."

Concrete silo, environmental protection, automatic control, safe and reliable. The assurances add up, but the core melts down. Battle will doubtless be joined again on whether we should be generating electrical power by this means; an uneasy public will be pulled this way and that, reminded at every turn of the awful example of the Soviet reactor.

It should be remembered that, while there is no perfect design — nuclear power being in its infancy — some are better than others. In the aftermath of the most recent disaster, Western experts noted that at least two of the four Chernobyl reactors had no radiation containment buildings — a feature credited with greatly reducing the ill effects of the Three Mile Island mishap.

In time we may learn what went wrong in the Chernobyl plant. Meanwhile, we will watch closely what may be the first major effort to cope with civil nuclear disaster.

The Kansas City Times

Kansas City, MO, April 30, 1986

The peaceful use of nuclear power has been dealt a stunning blow. The disaster at the Chernobyl station in the Soviet Union illustrates the tremendous danger posed by man's meddling with the atom. At this point, however, it certainly does not mean the plug should be pulled on nuclear plants worldwide.

Simply put, the immediate cry to abandon such facilities is unrealistic. They supply 15 percent of the electrical power in this country, almost 20 percent in Great Britain and almost two-thirds of the electricity in France. The figure is around 10 percent in the Soviet Union. Closing nuclear complexes is not the proper initial response to the Chernobyl accident.

Two other reactions are much more logical.

The first step is to find out exactly what went wrong in the Ukraine so similar accidents can be avoided. This may be difficult, given the secrecy of the Soviets. But the worst nuclear disaster in history has occurred, with casualties yet and perhaps never to be known, poisoning an undetermined number with dangerous radiation. Scientists should focus all their attention on how the accident happened and what short- and long-term effects it will have.

Nuclear plants can be run safely, as the operation of dozens of facilities over the last decade indicates. But improvements can and must be made following the nightmare at Chernobyl.

The second proper response to the tragedy is an important one, and it applies to the 100 or so plants in the United States.

Operators here must redouble their efforts to ensure that their facilities are running safely — and prove it to the public. This is not as simple as it sounds. Previous investigations, often prompted by opponents of nuclear power, have pointed out that problems have plagued plants throughout the country. Wolf Creek in Kansas and Callaway County in Missouri had their share during construction.

The United States has a strong point in its favor on this matter. The accident at Three Mile Island seven years ago prompted billions of dollars in modifications at plants already operating or under construction. This is where critics of nuclear power have had their strongest influence. It has been a highly positive one, despite protests by some utilities. Certainly, at times like these the improvements appear to have been a wise investment indeed.

Inevitably, more questions will surface in the days ahead. Can such a disaster happen here? Perhaps, probably in a different shape or form. Still, experts already have pointed out there are many key differences between the Chernobyl plant and those built in this country, including the two nearby facilities.

Should we move away from nuclear power? Such a path looks more appealing today than last week. True, alternate forms of energy are fraught with problems, both in economic terms — for solar — and in environmental terms — for coal.

But the latest tragedy should give the world pause before it pursues further development of nuclear power. For now, let's make sure that what we have is working as correctly and safely as possible.

●

The Soviet penchant for secrecy has deep roots in old Russia. It has always been a closed society, fearful of the outside, burying the most harmless information on the inside, suspicious and mistrustful.

That routine news is withheld from Soviet citizens is expected. Fear of embarrassment, fear of discontent, the pathetic worry that the people might suspect imperfection in the system — all come together in a conspiracy of vast and deliberate ignorance.

The tragedy of Chernobyl cannot be hidden. Yet surely the new openness of Mikhail Gorbachev ought to be reflected in consideration of neighbors whose skies will be clouded by radioactive drift. Nothing was known of the catastrophe until monitors in Scandinavia picked up the fallout.

When German warplanes were splitting the air on June 22, 1941, Radio Moscow continued as usual for hours, prattling on about the achievements of the workers. The Tashkent earthquake of 1966 was a non-event. A forest fire and famine in the Vladimir area in 1972 were unreported. Pages of the encyclopedia are excised. And on and on.

It is old stuff. In 1518 the monk Maxim the Greek visited Moscow to revise liturgy. He was not allowed to leave; he died in a monastary 38 years later. He was told: "We are in fear: thou, a man of learning, comest to us and hast seen here of our best and worst, and when thou goest hence *thou wilt tell of everything*."

THE TAMPA TRIBUNE
Tampa, FL, April 30, 1986

History's worst civilian nuclear disaster has occurred in the Soviet Union but — at least thus far — poses a serious threat only to that nation.

Moscow is secretive about what occurred at the four-reactor plant at Chernobyl, 60 miles north of Kiev in the Ukraine. The Kremlin said nothing of the accident, which apparently occurred Saturday, until queried by Scandinavian nations after increased airborne radiation was detected Monday, first in Sweden, then in Finland, Norway, and Denmark. The levels found are above allowable emissions in those countries, but not dangerous. Since Monday, however, winds have shifted back toward the Soviet Union. If the Soviets were lying when they said late yesterday the nuclear situation has been "stabilized," another wind shift could have more serious results.

The first Soviet announcement was terse, but a Moscow request to Sweden and West Germany yesterday for advice on controlling graphite fires in reactors led nuclear scientists to assume that an inexplicable "massive loss of coolant" within the reactor brought on core meltdown, igniting the thick layer of graphite the Soviets use to control radiation. U.S. experts say the graphite could have "smoldered like charcoal" for a long time before the fire became apparent. Such a fire is worse than meltdown because it creates much more radioactive fallout, and is so difficult to extinguish (water would immediately turn to radioactive steam) it may just have to burn itself out.

The accident is far worse than that at the Three Mile Island plant in Pennsylvania in 1979. Scientists liken it to what occurred at an experimental reactor at Windscale, England, in 1957, when graphite rods caught fire and burned for five days. Although there were no human fatalities, fallout from Windscale caused radioactive contamination of nearby dairy grazing lands, and tons of milk were dumped as a result.

A second Soviet announcement admitted that two people were killed and more than 30,000 had been evacuated from the area. Unconfirmed reports by telephone or travelers from Kiev yesterday said, however, the death toll exceeded 2,000, and that the bodies were being buried in a nearby nuclear waste dump rather than in cemeteries.

Scientists minimize the chances of a similar accident in the West. Western power plants use water rather than graphite to absorb neutrons thrown off by the fission reaction, so the fallout hazard is much less. In addition, Soviet water coolant pipes are basically iron, with some cobalt. Absorption of neutrons converts that element into the dangerous and long-lived cobalt 60 isotope which, when released into the atmosphere, may drift for thousands of miles.

The major difference marking the Chernobyl disaster is that the plant's reactors have no containment shelters, the standard concrete and steel shell-like structures so visible on Western reactors. The Soviets adopted the shells less than a decade ago, and by then the Chernobyl reactors were already operating or nearing completion. Zhores Medvedev, the exiled Soviet scientist, says other safety elements in USSR nuclear power plants fall far short of Western requirements.

Whatever the immediate casualties, Jens Scheer, a West German who is the foremost authority on the Soviet nuclear program, said the accident could result in 10,000 deaths from lung cancer in a 300-mile radius of the plant in the next 10 years. Medvedev noted that the plant's proximity to the Dnieper River could endanger the water supply of Kiev, a city of 2.4 million people. Other scientists foresaw extensive environmental damage which could gravely reduce the wheat crop in the Ukraine for years to come.

Charlie Porter, head of the Environmental Protection Agency's radiation monitoring, said it was doubtful that fallout in the United States would be dangerous, although adding there is no way yet to be sure. Current wind patterns indicate most radiation increases will be in the American Northwest, although a major storm could move some effects into the upper Midwest.

The catastrophe at Chernobyl is no reason to abandon nuclear power generation in the West. It does, however, argue for rigid safety standards in design, construction and operation (one rumor in Kiev is that a worker at Chernobyl fell asleep and did not see warnings of trouble in the instruments he was assigned to monitor).

It also suggests that the leaders of the world's nuclear powers reassess their faltering efforts toward control and reduction of nuclear weapons. If the Soviet death toll is indeed 2,000, it is catastrophic. It is, however, only one-fiftieth of that exacted by the first atom bomb dropped on Hiroshima, and that bomb had one-fiftieth the power of the warhead most commonly carried in multiple-warhead intercontinental missiles.

That does *not* suggest that President Reagan madly rush to unilateral nuclear disarmament, as Mikhail Gorbachev surely will not. All we are saying is that the existence of thousands of weapons capable of taking a toll *2,500 times* that at Chernobyl is a reality worth thinking about.

The Washington Times
Washington, DC, April 30, 1986

Though the Soviets are holding their tongues, nuclear experts believe that the accident at the Chernobyl power station is the worst of the Atomic Age. The core of a nuclear reactor there appears to have melted down, venting a plume of poisonous gases that has irradiated everything in the vicinity and cast a radioactive pall over Scandinavia as well. The full story may remain unknown for months or longer, but the implications are clear now.

In matters nuclear, as in so many other matters, the Soviets are not to be trusted. Central to their self-esteem is the pretense that calamities do not occur inside the U.S.S.R. Unless foreigners are aboard, airplane crashes go unreported. Natural disasters are rarely discussed. Nuclear accidents are the price other countries pay for careless management. Had the wind blown east instead of into Scandinavia, Moscow would have hidden this disaster, too.

As it is, the information is skimpy enough. "An accident has occurred," Moscow TV reported tersely three days after the meltdown. "Aid is being given to those affected." Privately the Kremlin has appealed to Sweden and West Germany for advice on extinguishing a "nuclear fire," or burning graphite — far more serious than a core meltdown alone.

Western experts long have warned that Moscow's disregard of safety precautions — reinforced concrete shells, for example — imperiled Soviet nuclear plants. Putting nuclear power plants under military control several years ago did nothing to correct the problem and may have increased the danger. The Chernobyl blowup, then, should come as no surprise.

Thus far only Russia and Scandinavia have been dusted, but shifting winds may spread the debris to Poland, Czechoslovakia, East Germany, and Hungary as well. Even the northwestern U.S. may feel the effects. Inside the Soviet Union, hundreds, even thousands, of persons may have died already, and slow radiation poisoning could kill thousands more. Kiev, home to 2.3 million, is barely 60 miles from the Chernobyl plant.

Moscow should receive whatever help we can give, and the Reagan administration was right to offer its assistance. But as events at Chernobyl demonstrate anew, what this secretive and suspicious regime continues not to deserve is our trust.

NARCOTICS:

President, First Lady Urge Antidrug 'Crusade'

President Reagan and his wife, Nancy, Sept. 14 broadcast a television and radio appeal for a "national crusade" against drug abuse. It was the first time Reagan and his wife have delivered a joint television address during Reagan's presidency. Narcotics abuse has inspired a recent surge in national concern. The talk came a day before Reagan unveiled a legislative package of anti-drug proposals. President Reagan said the government would "continue to act aggressively" against the narcotics problem, but that "nothing would be more effective than for Americans simply to quit using illegal drugs." He called for "a massive change in national attitudes" toward drugs. Mrs. Reagan said: "There's no moral middle ground. Indifference is not an option. We want you to help create an outspoken intolerance for drug use." Adding a personal appeal to young people, she declared: "Say 'yes' to life. And when it comes to drugs and alcohol, just say 'no.'" "Just say 'no'" is the slogan of the antidrug publicity campaign Mrs. Reagan launched after coming to the White House. The drive is aimed at preventing future drug abuse by appealing to children aged seven to 14. By one count, the drive had spurred the establishment of 10,000 clubs, in which at least 200,000 children have pledged not to use drugs. However, government spending for antidrug education and other prevention programs has fallen by 5% under the Reagan Administration, the New York Times reported Sept. 14. Time magazine reported in its Sept. 15 issue that the Department of Education spent so little on the matter that there was no record of the funds.

Reagan Sept. 15 signed an executive order requiring that federal employees who hold "sensitive" posts be tested for use of illegal drugs. The same day, he unveiled his package of proposed legislation for fighting the narcotics problem. The Reagan antidrug package was one of several to be prepared after a recent increase in public anger and concern over narcotics. The House of Representatives had passed a sweeping and far more expensive antinarcotics bill a few days before Reagan presented his package. (See pp. 1038-1047.) Administration officials said they did not know how many people would be tested under the President's new executive order. The order instructed all heads of executive agencies to set up testing programs under guidelines to be issued by the Department of Health and Human Services.

The Chattanooga Times
Chattanooga, TN, September 19, 1986

By making a televised appeal for a nationwide crusade against illegal drugs, President and Mrs. Reagan lent the force and prestige of their respective positions to a serious social problem and provided educational leadership as well. To the extent that the appeal energizes efforts around the country to combat a problem that victimizes young and old alike, the Reagans' joint speech will be especially valuable.

The president outlined several goals, including schools and workplaces that are free of drugs, expanded efforts in the research and treatment of drug abuse and tougher punishment for those who deal in drugs. Another prime goal was the effort to make the public more aware of the consequences of illegal drug use. That will probably be easier to accomplish, given the response by Congress and the White House to the drug problem, not to mention the numerous reports by the press.

Predictably, some complained that the Reagans' White House speech was political. That's true to an extent, but the same can be said of the congressional measures being pushed by Republicans and Democrats. But although the use of politics to promote a matter of public concern is not entirely wrong in and of itself, there is always the danger that political excess can subvert dispassionate consideration of the issue. For example, in the announcement Tuesday of his candidacy for the Republican presidential nomination, former Delaware Gov. Pierre S. du Pont called for mandatory drug testing of all teen-agers, a dumb idea if there ever was one.

Mr. Reagan didn't go that far after his television speech, but he did sign an executive order requiring mandatory drug tests for all federal employees in sensitive positions. Members of the military and other security agencies are already subject to such tests. It's anybody's guess, however, how many government employees will actually be tested, since the president's order leaves that decision to the heads of government agencies.

The inherent ambiguity of the president's order suggests it is vulnerable to constitutional challenge, and indeed some lower court decisions have already held that mandatory tests for public employees are unconstitutional. The reason is simple: Such tests force individuals, whether or not they are suspected of drug abuse, to prove their innocence.

We are seeing the application of that kind of thinking here in Chattanooga. Responding to a letter from the firemen's union requesting a suspension of mandatory, across-the-board drug testing for firefighters without guidelines, Fire and Police Commissioner Tom Kennedy said the tests were begun because of "problems" of drug use. But instead of testing only those suspected of drug use, the requirement was imposed on all.

It won't be easy to make a dent in the drug abuse problem, but it can be done without sacrificing our civil liberties. The proposed increase in spending for antidrug efforts would strengthen law enforcement and reinvigorate drug education and treatment programs which the administration reduced in 1981. More promising than increased spending and new programs, however, is the president's assertion that "we seek a massive change in national attitudes (to) separate the drugs from the customer." Whether that is accomplished by education, peer pressure ("Just say no") or law enforcement, the hope is that it can be done without succumbing to counterproductive measures.

The Evening Telegram
St. John's, Nfld.
September 17, 1986

When the President of the United States and the Prime Minister of Canada say drug use is an epidemic and call for a crusade against drug use, then it is obvious North American society has a drug problem.

President Ronald Reagan and his wife Nancy appeared on national television in the U.S. Sunday to appeal to Americans to fight drug abuse.

Monday morning, the president signed an order making drug tests mandatory for federal employees; last week, the House of Representatives ordered the U.S. military to intercept drugs at the nation's borders and called for the death penalty for drug dealers.

Sunday, Prime Minister Brian Mulroney promised "important" legislation to deal with drug abuse in Canada.

Drug abuse is a serious problem in North America.

There has been scandal after scandal in professional sports over drug abuse.

Two federal crown corporations screen job applicants for drug use. Other Canadian companies have drug and alcohol treatment programs for employees.

An estimated 25 per cent of U.S. firms have mandatory drug-testing programs; more companies are considering such programs.

Tougher laws, drug testing programs, use of the military to stop smuggling and the death penalty for dealers do not address the problem of why people use drugs.

What is it about North American society that encourages, or persuades, people to use illegal drugs?

·The answer to that question is as important as the legal efforts to curb illegal drug use.

Until it is answered, there will always be a problem with use of illegal drugs.

The News and Observer
Raleigh, NC, September 17, 1986

Fanned by the winds of an election year, the drug abuse issue has caught fire. What ought to have been a constant, careful effort to limit this damaging and deplorable indulgence has now flared into semi-hysteria, typified by President Reagan's directive that many federal workers undergo drug testing and by the call in the House of Representatives for military action to catch drug smugglers.

The president would have justification for a systematic drug testing program for those workers whose activities directly affect the lives and safety of others. The public has an obvious stake in ensuring that air traffic controllers, for example, are stone-cold sober. But the president casts his testing dragnet far too wide, entangling up to 1 million of the 2.8 million federal civil servants.

Besides law enforcement officers and health-care workers, Reagan says those to be tested will include presidential appointees, anyone handling classified information, anyone whose job relates to national security and anyone in a "sensitive" position. His order seems to cover the gamut from the director of central intelligence to the lowliest Pentagon secretary. Meanwhile, he also directs agency heads to establish voluntary testing programs for other employees and stipulates testing for new hires.

The president acts as though drug abuse were known to be a significant problem among federal employees, even those at the highest levels. While federal workers certainly are not immune from the pressures and temptations that affect other Americans, it is insulting and absurd for Reagan to imply that cracking down on them constitutes real progress in stamping out illegal drugs. In his zeal to project a get-tough image, he sacrifices the rights of employees for whom he, as chief executive, is responsible.

Requiring someone to take a drug test is equivalent to searching their body. Testing therefore ought normally be conducted under the spirit of the Fourth Amendment, which allows a search only when there is probable cause to believe that it will yield evidence of a crime.

It is reasonable to require an employee to undergo testing when suspected drug abuse threatens job performance. But except in cases where public safety is an overriding concern, it is repugnant to force employees to submit to tests when no such suspicion exists. Even "voluntary" testing puts employees in an untenable position. They experience pressure to submit or risk retaliation from their employer.

Reagan proposes $900 million in federal spending to round out his anti-drug plan. Half of the money would be spent to curb smuggling and the rest divided among various education and treatment programs. The House, trying to outclass the president in its drug-war fervor, would spend twice as much while scrapping the long-standing rule against military involvement in law enforcement.

The president tells Congress he'll pay for his proposals by cutting other programs, which will create difficulties elsewhere in the budget. The House wants to put pressure on Reagan to raise taxes, which he resists. Neither side talks about alcohol abuse, certainly as big a problem as illegal drugs.

What's most likely to survive the campaign frenzy is the drug-testing program — relatively inexpensive to the taxpayers, but costly in terms of the rights of people who work for the federal government.

Lexington Herald-Leader
Lexington, KY, September 17, 1986

President Reagan's anti-drug proposals are a vast improvement over the cynical mishmash that the House of Representatives pushed out last week. The president's suggestions are more reasoned, more feasible and less hysterical. Still, they leave much to be desired as a blueprint for a successful effort to curb drug abuse.

The part of his proposal that is likely to attract the most attention — mandatory drug tests for more than 1 million government workers — will generate plenty of controversy but make at best a symbolic bow in the direction of the problem.

His proposal to spend another $500 million on stopping drugs at the border sounds better than it is. We have already spent hundreds of millions in an effort to stop the cocaine import trade in Florida, with the result that more of it is coming in than ever.

Where the president's program is markedly better than the House's is his proposal that could make for more money for drug education and treatment. But even so, the president's proposal stops short of the sort of effort that is needed.

Many drug experts are trying to figure out why all this sudden uproar. National figures suggest that drug abuse is leveling off. Use of some drugs is declining. Fewer people are smoking or drinking strong alcoholic beverages.

Why is this happening? Education efforts have led people to conclude that such behavior is sensible. That's another element in the argument for more education, more treatment and less hysteria.

The Forum
Fargo, ND, September 16, 1986

President and Mrs. Reagan brought the war on drugs to the people via national television Sunday night. On Monday the president announced a series of proposals that will cost $3 billion.

He has cautioned that "As much financing as we commit, however, we would be fooling ourselves if we thought that massive new amounts of money alone will provide the solution."

The most effective method of combatting drugs is still education and good example. This may sound too goody-goody to some, but we believe that the U.S. Department of Education has the best idea.

It has issued a handbook on how to drive the drug problem out of the nation's schools. One million copies are being distributed to every public and private school and every school superintendent in the country.

The 78-page booklet, "Schools Without Drugs" is aimed at educators, parents and students, laying out facts about drugs and providing a detailed explanation of educators' rights to search students for drugs and suspend or expel offenders.

The booklet describes physical and mental signs of drug use: blood shot eyes, possession of large amounts of money and a downward turn in student grades.

Listed is a 12-point plan for ridding schools of drugs. It recommends clear rules and strong enforcement, and it involves the police in education and enforcement.

The plan advises schools to conduct anonymous surveys and consult with the police to identify the extent of the drug problem. It states that the community should be advised frankly of the results.

While the plan involves second chances and treatment, it recommends expelling some offenders, especially pushers.

While the worst of the nation's problems may not be in schools, it is so very vital that young people are given the right start in their attitude toward drugs.

Young people must learn that "no" can be the best word in their vocabulary. That's a cliche, but only because it's so true.

There is no doubt that the deaths of athletes Len Bias and Don Rogers from using cocaine have had a lot to do with the new awareness of the dangers of drugs.

Public figures, especially athletes, influence the behavior of young people. Public service announcements in the media by athletes and entertainers against drugs are important.

The best influence on behavior, however, should be that of parents. Parents who not only do not use drugs, but who talk to their offspring about life's problems — of which drugs are only one — have an inside track on getting kids to say "no" when they should.

Surgeon General Wants AIDS Classes

U.S. Surgeon General C. Everett Koop issued a report October 22, 1986 calling for education of school children "at the lowest grade possible" about sex and the fatal disease AIDS. The unusually explicit 36-page report, available to the public in booklet form, was the federal government's first major statement on how to contain the spread of AIDS. The White House had requested the paper, and Koop himself was the author. He discussed the report at a Washington, D.C. news conference.

Koop said sex education, including material on AIDS, should begin in elementary school. He added that the AIDS epidemic could foster agreement among "diverse groups of parents and educators with opposing views on inclusion of sex education in the curricula." Programs targeting blacks, Hispanics and other groups that showed high rates of infection would be useful, he said. The Reagan administration had been criticized for not providing enough AIDS education funds, but Koop said there was now enough money.

Parents and teachers would have to deal frankly with the subject of AIDS, the Koop report said. "Many people, especially your youth, are not receiving information that is vital to their future health and well-being because of our resistance in dealing with the subjects of sex, sexual practices and homosexuality," the surgeon general wrote. "This silence must end. We can no longer sidestep frank, open discussions about sexual practices—homosexual and heterosexual." Homosexual contact accounted for most AIDS cases, but transmission by heterosexual contact was expected to grow, Koop told reporters. His report emphasized that the disease was "not spread by common everyday contact," such as shaking hands, social kissing or sneezing. Sexual relations and the sharing of intravenous drug needles and syringes accounted for most AIDS cases, Koop said. Koop said "protective behavior" was called for so long as there was any question at all as to the health of the sex partner. "The best protection against infection right now—barring abstinence—is use of a condom," he said. "A condom should be used during sexual relations, from start to finish, with anyone whom you know or suspect is infected." The Koop report urged individuals with high-risk sexual pasts to check for infection by taking blood tests.

But the surgeon general dismissed calls for compulsory testing and said quarantine of AIDS victims would be medically pointless. "It's time to...recognize that we are fighting a disease—not people," he said at his news conference.

A White House advisory commission on AIDS held its first full-scale meeting September 9-10, 1987 in Washington, D.C. Perhaps the most impassioned testimony by a federal official came from Surgeon General Koop. Citing reports that more doctors and other health workers were refusing to treat AIDS patients, Koop Sept. 10 warned that "the ethical foundations of health care itself" were threatened by a "fearful and irrational minority." He suggested that health workers would have little to worry about if they carefully followed "the sensible and rather elementary guidelines" issued by the federal Centers for Disease Control, which prescribed the use of gloves and other protective measures to avoid contamination.

The Washington Post

Washington, DC, October 24, 1986

IT ISN'T OFTEN that Planned Parenthood and the Reagan administration see eye to eye, but a national crisis has brought them together on at least one subject: AIDS. A report issued earlier this week by Surgeon General C. Everett Koop drew praise from the family-planning group specifically because it urges sex education in schools at the earliest possible grade. But that recommendation is not the only noteworthy item in Dr. Koop's frank and sensible report.

Wednesday's statement was prepared at the request of President Reagan and is styled "a report to the American people on AIDS." No reader could come away complacent about the statistics presented on the spread and deadliness of the disease, but the report contains more than facts. It exhorts Americans to put aside prejudices they may have against homosexuals and intravenous drug users, to help the victims of this epidemic and to stop talking nonsense about quarantines, universal blood tests and tattoos for those who test positive. Perhaps most gratifying to those who view the surgeon general as a conservative, he approaches this sensitive subject without making value judgments, only medical ones. "It is time," he says, "to put self-defeating attitudes aside and recognize that we are fighting a disease—not people."

On the issue of sex education, Dr. Koop is forthright. "There is now no doubt that we need sex education in schools and that it include information on sexual practices that may put our children at risk for AIDS." This risk applies primarily to homosexuals and intravenous drug users, and the report contains specific instructions on how people in these categories can reduce their exposure. But, as the most recent data on the spread of AIDS confirm, it is not limited to these groups, and the disease is spreading, through sexual contact, to the general population. Abstinence and the maintenance of mutually faithful monogamous relationships, whether homosexual or heterosexual, are the only sure means of avoiding sexually transmitted AIDS. But the report acknowledges that not everyone will accept such restrictions. It goes on to describe the steps that can be taken to reduce the risk.

Dr. Koop's statement sets a standard for other government officials—federal, state and local—in dealing with AIDS and its victims. Without a hint of mean-spiritedness or hesitation, he says three things. We must help and not condemn those who suffer. We must take precautions against the spread of AIDS. We must educate our children about the dangers of this disease. That's good advice, and it should be heeded.

The Augusta Chronicle

Augusta, GA
October 29, 1986

Surgeon General C. Everett Koop, in his long-awaited report on AIDS, has drawn both praise and criticism for calling for sex education in the schools to combat the spread of the fatal disease.

We understand where the critics are coming from. In the past the nation has had some unhappy experiences with sex education — which was used in many cases as a radical forum to promote a "value free" society based on "situation ethics." Under the aegis of being taught about sex, kids were encouraged to engage in it.

Koop makes it clear this is not the kind of sex education he has in mind. He thinks kids should be taught, beginning at an early age, that sex can be fatal to your health. He recommends total abstinence for teenagers.

The surgeon general's report also says the only safe sex is "mutually faithful monogamous relationships" and urges the use of condoms if there is any doubt. That's certainly good advice for adults, particularly since statistics indicate AIDS is beginning to break out of the homosexual and drug communities into the heterosexual community.

Our only quarrel with the report is that it would start sex education in elementary school, which is a little too young. Few 8-year-olds are prepared intellectually or psychologically to deal with the subtle human complexities involved in sex and AIDS.

But the thrust of Koop's report — that leaving our children ignorant about sex will endanger their lives — is right on target. Parents have been terribly remiss in educating their children about sex. The job often falls to schools by default.

What is needed now is for concerned citizens across the nation to work with their local school districts in helping to establish responsible sex education courses that will both teach our kids what they need to know and reflect contemporary local standards.

The curricula shouldn't become radicalized again if Koop's advice is taken — and local School Boards keep a sharp eye on how the courses are taught.

BUFFALO EVENING NEWS
Buffalo, NY, October 23, 1986

SURGEON GENERAL C. Everett Koop, in his long-awaited report on AIDS, lays great stress on education, which is, indeed, one of the few means so far at our disposal in fighting the dread disease.

The disease, formally known as acquired immunity deficiency syndrome, was discovered only a few years ago, and it has been spreading at a rapid rate. So far, 26,566 Americans have been diagnosed as having AIDS, and 14,977 of them have died. There is no cure and no known survivor.

Koop's reasoned report should put the disease in proper perspective as a serious national health problem but one that is no cause for panic. He dispels some of the mystery about the disease, stressing that it "is not spread by casual, non-sexual contact" and that new infections can be prevented through precautionary measures.

Since AIDS is spread mostly by intimate sexual contact, especially homosexual contact, it is vital that information about the disease be disseminated so that proper precautions can be taken. While heterosexual transmission of the disease is still low in this country, it is rising rapidly in other countries, and Koop warned that "freewheeling, casual sex" is "a dangerous game."

Unfortunately, this much-needed information is not getting through to those who need it, particularly many young people. Koop said there was a reticence about dealing with subjects like sex, sexual practices and homosexuality.

"This silence must end," he said. "We can no longer afford to sidestep frank, open discussions about sexual practices — homosexual and heterosexual." Education regarding AIDS, Koop said, should start at an early age, with both parents and schools taking a role.

Sex education in the schools has always been a controversial subject, and the forthright stand taken by Koop is especially noteworthy because of his conservative background. Koop once described the gay rights movement as "anti-family."

Now, however, in the effort to control AIDS, he said that "there is now no doubt that we need sex education in schools and that it include information on heterosexual and homosexual relationships."

Koop noted that when AIDS was first discovered among homosexuals, some people felt that people from certain groups "deserved" their illness. "Let us put those feelings behind us," Koop said in the report. "We are fighting a disease, not people." He opposed compulsory testing, quarantines or the tattooing of infected persons — all ideas that have been proposed as a means of controlling AIDS.

While the number of people known to be infected is at present comparatively small, they may be just the tip of the iceberg. Hundreds of thousands of people could be carriers of AIDS without knowing it.

With the outlook for a preventive vaccine fairly remote at present, the fight against this insidious disease must be carried on with the weapons we have — education concerning the spread of the disease and how to prevent infection.

The Miami Herald
Miami, FL, November 7, 1986

FIRST THE Reagan Administration's conservative and often-moralistic Surgeon General fired a blast at hysterical and punitive treatment of AIDS victims. Now a special committee from the National Academy of Sciences and the Institute of Medicine has followed with a chilling report that warns of potential "catastrophe" as AIDS seeps into the general population. The academic committee suggests a $2-billion-a-year national campaign of research, education, and treatment to curb the burgeoning epidemic.

Surgeon General Everett Koop issued a report urging education at an early age and dismissing quarantines as useless as well as cruel. He suggests teaching children about anal intercourse and other homosexual and heterosexual practices so they can "grow up knowing the behavior to avoid to protect themselves."

The science groups' report projects that AIDS cases among heterosexuals will increase by 1991 to about 7,000 from the current 1,100. Pediatric cases from *in utero* infection will increase to more than 3,000.

Its rapid spread makes clear that AIDS can strike any sexually active person, even a monogamous person whose sex partner has had even *one* other, infected partner. Clearly, AIDS has the potential to become a modern-day Black Plague.

The Surgeon General and the nation's most respected biomedical experts properly are seeking a balanced approach to AIDS and its victims, an approach grounded in knowledge, compassion, and realism. They deserve the careful attention of every governmental and private agency that is grappling with the ever-increasing threat.

★ ★ ★

South Florida not only is a focal point of AIDS cases, it's also a leading center of AIDS research. Yet such is the fear of AIDS that those trying to help its victims — and potential victims — find theirs at best a frustrating endeavor.

Consider the American Society of Interior Designers' South Florida chapter. The group has enlisted Diahann Carroll and Peter Allen to appear at a Nov. 16 black-tie dinner capping "A Designers Weekend" Nov. 14-16. Profits, if any, will go to the University of Miami's AIDS Research Fund, the Health Crisis Network, and Center One.

Ticket sales are going slowly, says co-chairman Judi Male. She attributes the poor response to people's reluctance to recognize that AIDS — like heart disease, cancer, or other afflictions — can affect *them* too. The evidence cited above attests to that.

South Floridians who wish to support AIDS research couldn't find a better avenue than "A Designers Weekend." For ticket and other information, please call 576-2739.

The Chattanooga Times
Chattanooga, TN, October 29, 1986

With the number of confirmed cases spiraling upward, the dread disease AIDS, or acquired immune deficiency syndrome, is considered an epidemic in this country; the disease is spreading in other countries as well. That makes Surgeon General C. Everett Koop's report on AIDS last week valuable. At a time when so many treat AIDS as a taboo subject, Dr. Koop has addressed the matter with remarkable candor.

So far as is known, AIDS is inevitably fatal, so the only way to combat it now, Dr. Koop said, is by prevention. Despite some slight hints of a breakthrough, scientists have been unable to come up with a cure or a long-term treatment that arrests the fatal deterioration of the body's immune system.

Although the principal victims of AIDS are homosexuals, the disease is now occurring increasingly among heterosexuals as well. Dr. Koop said the AIDS epidemic had already killed nearly 15,000 Americans and that 12 times that number could die by 1991 unless preventive measures are taken. Simple precautions taken by partners during sexual intercourse would drastically reduce, if not eliminate, the incidence of the disease's transmission from one person to another. Granted, that would help neither the relatively small number of hemophiliacs stricken by AIDS through the transfusions of contaminated blood nor users of illegal drugs who contract the disease with unsterile needles. But the number of AIDS cases would drop dramatically if precautions reduced the sexual transmission of the disease.

Dr. Koop's candid recommendations are a breath of fresh air in the public discussion of this matter. He is putting the health of our people, particularly young men and women, above the fears of those who think that instruction in sexual hygiene will encourage sexual activity. He wrote in his report: "Many people, especially our youth, are not receiving information that is vital to their future health and well-being because of our reticence in dealing with the subjects of sex, sexual practices and homosexuality. We can no longer afford to sidestep frank, open discussions about sexual practices — homosexual and heterosexual. Education about AIDS should start at an early age so that children can grow up knowing the behaviors to avoid to protect themselves from exposure to the AIDS virus." (Dr. Koop's report is available from the U.S. Public Health Service by writing to AIDS, P.O. Box 1452, Washington, D.C. 20044.)

Sexual promiscuity, the hopes of some to the contrary notwithstanding, will not disappear if we simply refuse to provide adequate sex education. And the evidence is clear that AIDS no longer infects only those who some say "deserve" it — the homosexuals. The subject is too important in terms of public health to ignore the dangers. Dr. Koop's report is an outstanding public service. The question now is whether its recommendations will be followed.

U.S. FOREIGN POLICY:

U.S. Profits From Iran Arms Deal Found Sent to Nicaraguan Contras

President Reagan Nov. 25 said he had not been informed about an aspect of his Iranian policy and as a consequence had accepted the resignation of national security adviser Vice Adm. John Poindexter and fired a key aide, Lt. Col. Oliver North. This was followed by the disclosure that $10 million to $30 million in profits from the Israeli-brokered sale of American arms to Iran had been secretly diverted to help the contra rebels fighting the Nicaraguan government. The revelation of the Nicaraguan connection, following a week of unprecedented public bickering among top administration officials over who was to blame, left Reagan facing the most serious crisis of his presidency.

Both Republican and Democratic leaders on Capitol Hill expressed shock at the news and promised full-scale and wide-ranging congressional investigations. They noted that a number of laws might have been broken by the diversion of funds at a time when United States aid to the contras had been banned by Congress. Some lawmakers described Reagan's foreign policy as being in "total disarray." They viewed the claim that a major covert operation had been run out of the White House without the President's knowledge as having raised damaging questions about his competence and credibility.

Reagan made a brief statement to reporters. He said that the previous week he had directed Attorney General Edwin Meese 3rd to review the Iranian arms-supply policy, which had been aimed chiefly at establishing links with Teheran and winning the freedom of U.S. hostages in Lebanon. He said a preliminary report of Meese's findings had "led me to conclude that I was not fully informed on the nature of one of the activities undertaken in connection with this initiative." He said, "This action raises some serious questions of propriety." Reagan said he would "appoint a special review board to conduct a comprehensive review of the National Security Council (NSC) staff in the conduct of foreign and national security policy. The NSC, which was created as a policy coordinating and advisory body, had run the Iran arms operation—skirting Congress and the State and Defense Departments in the process. Reagan said further actions would wait until after he received the reports from the Justice Department and the special review board. "I am deeply troubled that the implementation of a policy aimed at resolving a truly tragic situation in the Middle East has resulted in such a controversy," Reagan continued. "As I've stated previously, I believe our policy goals toward Iran were well founded." But in one respect, the policy's implementation "was seriously flawed," he said.

According to Meese, a preliminary investigation by the Justice Department had established the following outline of what happened: Between January and September of 1986 the Central Intelligence Agency (CIA), under NSC direction, sent $12 million in Defense Department weapons stocks to Israel, which had agreed to broker the covert U.S.-Iranian contacts. "Representatives of Israel," not necessarily in the Israeli government, sold the arms to Iran with a premium of $10 million to $30 million added on top of their cost. The Israelis gave $12 million, plus transport costs, of the Iranian payment to the CIA, which in turn reimbursed the Pentagon. Either the Israelis or the Iranian representatives, acting with the knowledge of North, then transferred the extra funds to Swiss bank accounts controlled by "the forces in Central America which are opposing the Sandinista government there." Meese said that none of the other members of the NSC—including CIA Director William Casey, Secretary of State George Shultz and Defense Secretary Caspar Weinberger—had known about the Nicaraguan aspect. Meese said President Reagan knew nothing until the day before.

Some U.S. officials Nov. 25 noted that the disclosure of the skimming off of Iranian arms profits for the contras could partly explain how the rebels had been able to finance their resupply operation over the previous two years, when U.S. aid had been cut off. It was suggested that, at least since early 1986, the Iranian funds had paid for a large part of the resupply effort, which involved hundreds of covert drops over Nicaragua. The rebels, along with Lt. Col. Oliver North and other Administration officials, had maintained that the money needed to keep the aid flowing came from anonymous private doners in the U.S. and abroad. Meanwhile, Adolfo Calero, political leader of the largest contra force, Nov. 25 in Miami denied that his group had received any of the Iranian money. He said the rebels "have no access" to any Swiss bank accounts of the type described by Meese.

The Washington Post

Washington, DC, November 26, 1986

PERHAPS AN accident will save us, Louis XVI was supposed to have said as the French monarchy crashed around him. A kindred thought might have occurred to the Reagan administration as it disclosed the tale of the Israelis diverting part of Iran's arms payments to the Nicaraguan contras. Here at last was an opportunity to show command, to come clean, to feed the lions and still to preserve the defense of the administration's embattled policies respecting terrorism and Iran—although the disputed content of these policies appears to have been set aside for the duration. President Reagan did all of this yesterday, with the sturdy help of Attorney General Edwin Meese.

It begs belief that a mere lieutenant colonel on the National Security Council staff, even an ultimate gung-ho Marine such as the now-fired Oliver North, could have been, as Mr. Meese said, the sole person in the know. It invites further incredulity and dismay that his superior, the now-reassigned national security adviser, John Poindexter, could have known "generally" of the North operation and failed to look further into it or to inform his chief. Presumably the inquiry being pressed by the Justice Department—far from the only inquiry now under way—will shed more light on this bizarre affair.

In the meantime, it is good that President Reagan has finally, belatedly, seen fit to name a commission to look into the "role and procedures" of the NSC staff. It would serve the president poorly to appoint people of less than "wise man" stature. The commission will be under pressure to expand its study into and beyond the whole string of NSC operations with which elements of the Reagan administration have sought to plug the widening gap between presidential ambition and public acceptability over the past year. For it is evident that once again the secrecy option has encouraged the pursuit of policies that were not always accepted and were sometimes explicitly opposed by Congress, that were not always supported by or even disclosed to the full ranks of the administration and that trifled with the law.

The administration's sudden stumble upon the diversion scandal compelled the president to consider personnel changes he earlier had resisted. Col. North is gone; he became something of a notorious legend without ever becoming a known public man. Adm. Poindexter leaves with the reputation of having been too ready to offer the president salutes and shortcuts.

President Reagan was a man under pressure yesterday. The pressure is going to stay on. As his handoff of the podium to his attorney general showed, he is a president who puts immense reliance on subordinates. He needs strong Cabinet officers, especially a strong secretary of state; he is lucky to have one already. Incidentally, Mr. Meese, though he didn't seem happy with Secretary Shultz's acknowledged difference with administration policy on arms transfers to Iran, did "verify"—his word—the secretary's account of the fragmentary nature of his knowledge of events. The president also needs a strong national security adviser, one who understands the proper role of that ambiguous and difficult office, avoids the traps of secret power and helps Mr. Reagan recover from the damage he has sustained in the past few weeks.

The Oregonian
Portland, OR, November 26, 1986

Some time ago, President Reagan charged that there was a secret terrorist connection linking such distant countries as Iran and Nicaragua. The reaction at the time was skeptical, but the link has now been found: It was operating out of the basement of the White House.

National Security Adviser John Poindexter and his free-lance agent Lt. Col. Oliver North should have been removed last week, just because of the disastrous effect of their secret course of selling arms to Iran. Tuesday's revelations that the money from the sale went into a secret Swiss bank account for the Contras only shows how far out of control the foreign relations of the United States have gone.

Last week, the situation appeared appalling. This week, it got worse.

The president says, and there seems no reason to disbelieve him, that he did not know where the money had gone. It is hard to say whether this is better or worse than if he had. His ignorance may provide an alibi to some violations of law, but it suggests that his laxity of control is worse than his bitterest enemies had ever charged.

"Follow the money," was the moral of the last major presidential scandal, and in this case it did not need much following. It took the Justice Department at most three days to uncover the creative Contra financing, and the key figure was not exactly well-hidden: North worked directly for Poindexter, who worked directly for Reagan.

The president may claim to be shocked by North's activities, but hardly surprised. This administration repeatedly has declared itself to be above the law in foreign policy activities, especially regarding Nicaragua.

When Congress refused to provide aid for the Contras, the Reaga administration winkingly encouraged private American citizens to go to war. When the CIA decided to mine Nicaragua's harbors — an internationally recognized act of war — the agency ignored even its legal responsibility to notify Congress. When Nicaragua sued in the World Court, the United States declared itself outside the court's jurisdiction.

To Oliver North, the leap from this attitude to a course of embezzling against communism could not have seemed great. To the administration, and the Senate, and the American people, the lesson is underlined again: A foreign policy conducted under the table will go lower than ever expected.

THE COMMERCIAL APPEAL
Memphis, TN, November 26, 1986

PRESIDENT Reagan's arms-for-Iran crisis has taken a drastic turn for the worse with the disclosure that money from the sale was secretly — and probably illegally — used to support the anti-Sandinista guerrillas in Nicaragua.

In an uncomfortable announcement, Reagan admitted he did not know his National Security Council was running money to the contras, adding to the impression that he has lost touch with foreign-policy details.

The deepening scandal caused Reagan to accept the resignation of his national security adviser, Vice Adm. John Poindexter, and to dismiss Poindexter's key aide, Lt. Col. Oliver North, who handled the transfer of funds.

According to Atty. Gen. Edwin Meese, who investigated the matter for Reagan, Israel sold American weapons to Iran and deposited the proceeds in a contra account in a Swiss bank. Meese said no one higher than Poindexter and North knew about the maneuver, which, if correct, would be a bizarre way to conduct policy.

What makes the action perhaps criminal is that it took place after Congress passed and Reagan signed a law barring all but a bit of humanitarian aid to the anti-Marxist Nicaraguans. To slip them between $10 million and $30 million, which undoubtedly they used for arms, would violate both the spirit and letter of the law.

The bombshell comes at a dreadful time for the President. He is still reeling from criticism of the arms-for-hostages deal, which he is almost alone in defending. Now he faces a Watergate-style scandal involving White House wrongdoing.

Congressional Democrats have pledged a series of investigations, which they will try to keep running until the 1988 elections. The prospect is for serious damage to Reagan and his party.

Like all presidents in trouble, Reagan will appoint a commission — this time a board to review the work of the National Security Council. No review is needed; the NSC should act as it was meant to — giving the President all the options, not running covert operations like a mini-CIA without congressional oversight.

Instead of a review board, Reagan should appoint an experienced, respected figure to head 'the NSC — Brent Scowcroft, for example. Then the public would know that the council's advisory role was in good hands while the White House coped with the political crisis it brought on itself.

The Birmingham News
Birmingham, AL, November 27, 1986

The stunning revelation that profits from clandestine U.S. arms sales to Iran had been diverted to the anti-government Contras in Nicaragua left President Reagan with little choice but to fire the man responsible and to accept the resignation of that aide's supervisor, who knew something of the deal.

So Lt. Col. Oliver North, a can-do Marine officer on the National Security Council staff who had helped plan such successful operations as the Grenada liberation and the hijacking of the *Achille Lauro* hijackers, is out the door. With him goes Vice Adm. John Poindexter, who asked to be relieved of his assignment as assistant to the president for national security affairs.

And outside the White House, the critics are yelling for more bloodletting. They want Mr. Reagan's scalp, or at least Donald Regan's.

But what exactly has happened here? It appears that an overzealous operative in the administration has taken some of Mr. Reagan's laudable policy goals — opening new communication with Iran and providing support for the freedom fighters in Nicaragua — and mixed them together in an ingenious way that is certainly against the expressed will of Congress and most probably against the law.

Worst of all, North apparently did not tell his boss, Poindexter, exactly what he was doing. And Poindexter did not tell the president anything.

Many questions remain about the operation that Attorney General Edwin Meese described Tuesday. He says arms worth about $12 million were provided to Israel, which sold them to "representatives of Iran." Money to cover the full cost of the arms was given to the United States, while some $10 million to $30 million in profits were deposited in Swiss bank accounts for the Nicaraguan rebels.

Why did the Iranians pay so much more than the arms were worth? How much did the Israelis know about where the money was going? How much of the money is now in Contra hands, and how has it been spent?

But the most important question is why was a lieutenant colonel on the National Security Council staff making foreign policy? And why didn't the president know more about what was going on?

Mr. Reagan has always been more interested in the broad direction of foreign policy than in the details of its implementation. In most cases, this approach has worked well for him. While some leaders have been unable to see the forest for the trees, Mr. Reagan has been able to look over the whole landscape and map a strong and direct course to his foreign policy goals.

He trusted his aides to follow that course, and to steer around the political and legal pitfalls along the way. That trust was betrayed. The implementation of Mr. Reagan's policy was, in his own words, "seriously flawed."

Now Mr. Reagan has said he will name a special commission to examine the role of the National Security Council staff and the Justice Department will continue to investigate the money angle.

We hope these two probes will answer all the remaining questions about the Iran arms deal so that Mr. Reagan can put this foreign policy fiasco behind him and move on to more important matters of state.

IRAN-CONTRA ARMS SCANDAL:

Tower Commission Blames Reagan, Aides for 'Chaos' in Scandal

President Reagan, confused and unaware, allowed himself to be misled by dishonest staff members who organized the trade of arms to Iran for hostages held in Lebanon and pursued a secret war against the Nicarguan government, a special commission appointed to review the National Security Council (NSC) concluded Feb. 26. (See 1986, pp. 1268-1287, 1334-1345; 1987, pp. 16-21, 110-121.) The 300-page document quoted dozens of secret communications among senior national security officials, showing how U.S. policy evolved into "chaos" as "amateurish" staff members failed to subject their complex dealings with Iran, Israel, the contra rebels in Nicaragua and various arms dealers to a comprehensive policy review. The report charged that Reagan had failed to "insist upon accountability and performance review," allowing the NSC process to collapse.

While carefully wording its criticisms of Reagan's "personal management style," the report bluntly assailed numerous other top officials:

■ White House chief of staff Donald Regan "must bear responsibility for the chaos," the report said, charging that "more than almost any chief of staff of recent memory, he asserted personal control over the White House staff and sought to extend this control to the national security adviser."

■ Former national security adviser Robert McFarlane failed to fully inform cabinet members about the progress of the Iran initiative. His successor, Vice. Adm. John Poindexter, "actively misled" cabinet members.

■ Secretary of State George Shultz and Defense Secretary Caspar Weinberger, while opposing the initiative, "actively distanced themselves from the march of events."

■ The former director of the Central Intelligence Agency (CIA), William Casey, was blamed for allowing the CIA to lose control of the operation to the NSC and for failing to tell Reagan or Congress about it.

The commission had been appointed to study the workings of the NSC and to make recommendations on ways to change the NSC process so that disasters like the Iran-contra operation would not recur. But the members of the panel went beyond its mandate, concluding that "the NSC process did not fail; it simply was largely ignored." The panel recommended no major changes in the law authorizing the NSC but examined the Iran-contra affair in great detail as a "case study" of how the process was ignored.

The commission, formally, the President's Special Review Board, had been appointed by Reagan in November 1986, following the Administration's announcement that it had discovered that funds from the arms sales had been diverted to the contras. The panel's members were John Tower, a former Republican senator from Texas who chaired the Senate Armed Services Committee; Brent Scowcroft, a retired Air Force general who had served as national security adviser under President Gerald Ford; and Edmund Muskie, a former Democratic senator from Maine who had briefly been secretary of state under President Jimmy Carter.

The three members of the panel held a press conference to announce the release of the report. They were introduced to the press and a national television audience by Reagan, who had promised to "carefully study" the report and respond to it in a televised address in the coming week. At the press conference, the commission members were cautious in their criticisms and insistent that, despite their differing political views, they had not disagreed over the substance of their report. "The President did make mistakes," Tower asserted. He added that "every president has made some mistakes from time to time, some of far greater consequence than the ones President Reagan has made." Tower said that Reagan had not been involved in an effort to cover-up the scandal. "We don't use the term cover-up," he said. But Tower asserted that "there was a deliberate effort to mislead" by those who prepared a chronology for Reagan in in November 1986. In its account of the arms shipments, the report confirmed that the deal originated with two motives: President Reagan's emotional commitment to the release of the hostages held in Lebanon and a "latent and unresolved" geopolitical interest in better U.S. ties to Iran to prevent the Soviet Union from gaining a foothold in that strategically important nation. After the arms shipments began, however, they quickly evolved into a strict arms-for-hostages trade, the commission reported.

THE SACRAMENTO BEE
Sacramento, CA, February 27, 1987

The words the Tower Commission used were all of a kind. The president's supervision of the National Security Council was too casual; the NSC, which is the president's creature, will not work unless the president makes it work; the president did not *wittingly* mislead the American people and the Congress; the inference is that he believed the lies prepared for him to read on television to the American people. The commission talked about the fact that the president's advisers have a responsibility to keep him informed, even if it requires lights to flash and bells to ring — in other words, even if his aides have to take him firmly by the lapels and shake him.

Yet finally, there is no one but the president who's to blame, not in some abstract institutional sense, but within the most common-sense meaning of the term. The manipulators and deceivers were his people, carrying out the policy of a man who still seems to regard a major reversal regarding the selling of arms to terrorists as no more memorable than what he had for dinner on some August evening two years ago. The commission correctly recommends no major institutional changes in the NSC system; the NSC is the president's creature and should be responsive to him. But that, of course, means he must manage it, must be concerned, energetic and curious enough to keep it under control and to understand what he and it are doing. Is this president, particularly in his present state, able to manage that?

There is a surreal quality in the fact that the commission's scathing report — a report full of horrendous details about the deceptions of the NSC staff and the incuriosity and neglect of the president — was presented at the White House with the president's praise and blessing, as if this concerned some distant event, a mine disaster perhaps, or the technicalities of nuclear policy. The form and mutual compliments of the presentation suggest that here is a government pulling together to deal with its problems.

But the substance suggests something very different. The plain conclusions of the Tower report, the disclosures surrounding it, the president's revealing remarks concerning his inability to recall his decision authorizing the arms sale, his own uncertain state of health, the politically weakened — if not paralyzed — state of his administration and, most of all, the near-impossibility that at this late stage and age in the president's career he will be able to change the mind-set of a lifetime, make it highly unlikely that things can change very much. When the president appeared with the commission Thursday morning, he seemed shaken and distracted.

White House Chief of Staff Donald Regan will probably go — by now his dismissal has come to be generally regarded as a minimum condition for any restoration of confidence in the president — but that's hardly enough. The president will go on television early next week with his promised response. When he does the nation may get an indication of how much more he is able to deliver. At this point, the burden seems overwhelming.

The Washington Post

Washington, DC, February 27, 1987

FROM JOHN TOWER, Edmund Muskie and Brent Scowcroft comes an incisive and painstaking report that becomes the new base line for both an understanding of the Iran-contra affair and for addressing the astonishing lapses and derelictions in policy making that created this mess in the first place. It is devastating.

The report adds to the store of what was known about unorthodox funding, from various sources, including profits from the Iran arms sales, for the Nicaraguan contras. Its centerpiece, however, is the rich and freshly detailed picture it draws of what one of the rogues, Lt. Col. Oliver North, called at one point "the damndest operation I have ever seen."

The report is principally a catalogue of the human failings that no policy process, however deftly organized, run or even reformed, could altogether screen out. Adm. John Poindexter, at one time national security adviser, seems out of his depth, devious, furtive, negligently focused on narrow operational goals, forever concerned that the list of those in the know be shortened, that this one or that one be walled out. His aide, Col. North, inventing fantasies, bullying his way around, is absolutely off the wall, with an unfortunate talent for mesmerizing his superiors. Read Robert McFarlane's statement to him that "if the world only knew how many times you have kept a semblance of integrity and gumption to U.S. policy, they would make you Secretary of State." (That Col. North was not made secretary of state is one of the few blessings one can think of in reading this report.) On his own account, Mr.

McFarlane is at best confusing and at times disingenuous. George Shultz and Caspar Weinberger, though more right in tactical judgment where the national security cowboys were wrong, unaccountably failed to raise their strong dissents to the consistent hollers that alone might have awakened the president. Meanwhile, Donald Regan, chief of staff, was carrying on a monumental dereliction of duty to the president he ostensibly served.

President Reagan is reaping a measure of praise for opening himself to the Tower Commission's critique. The commission was inclined to believe, furthermore, that he was telling the truth. But it is chilling to see a president so utterly given to sentiment over the hostages, so incurious and uncritical about the events that were unfolding around him and so vulnerable to the weaknesses of character and lapses of judgment of the people in whom he had put his trust. His was an administration in the back seat of a car rolling down a hill with no one at the wheel.

The commission has some intelligent things to say about the possibilities and the limits of tinkering with the policy-making mechanism. As experienced Washington hands, however, the commission's members realize that no process can save a president from himself. This is where it places the principal responsibility for this affair. Mr. Reagan introduced the commission at the White House yesterday and, appearing somewhat shaken, at once left the stage. When he returns to it, next week, he will be under brutal pressure to show he has learned from this ordeal and has the strength to pass beyond it.

Minneapolis Star and Tribune

Minneapolis, MN, February 27, 1987

The explosion you heard Wednesday was the Tower Commission delivering its report on National Security Council mismanagement of the Iran-contras affair. Everyone knew the impact would be greater than imagined at the commission's inception last fall, but the shock was stunning nonetheless. The commission pictures top White House advisers as inept or worse. It does not spare the secretaries of state and defense, who opposed the arms-for-hostage dealings but failed to exert their full influence. Nor does it spare the man at the top. President Reagan therefore will have much to account for when he addresses the nation on television next week.

But Reagan will do so without the same burden Richard Nixon carried as the dimensions of the Watergate scandal became known. This is more a case of presidential ineffectiveness than of venality. Public support for Reagan remains substantial despite public disapproval of much of what his administration has done. Concern for Reagan, even sympathy, are more evident than the antipathy so often exhibited toward Nixon.

In the commission's report the damning comment that sums up its critique of the president is this: He "did not seem to be aware of the way in which the (Iran arms sales) operation was implemented and the full consequences of U.S. participation." Commission chairman John Tower, a conservative Republican and a Reagan ally, offered his own

summing up in yesterday's press conference. The president was poorly advised, Tower said, and poorly served, and he should have monitored what his advisers were doing.

Those low-key comments were apt. So were several by the other panelists, former Secretary of State Edmund Muskie and former National Security Adviser Brent Scowcroft. But the report itself best conveys the flavor of a tangentially involved president nodding vague approval to advisers operating in duplicitous, unprofessional and perhaps illegal ways. For example:

". . . even if the president in some sense consented to or approved the transactions, a serious question of law remains . . . . The consent did not meet the conditions of the Arms Export Control Act" and "was never reduced to writing. It appears to have been conveyed to only one person. The president himself has no memory of it . . . the requirement for congressional notification was ignored."

Tower and his colleagues have produced a report that deals harshly and, it appears, fairly with the Reagan administration's national-security apparatus. The president's response yesterday was a promise to make the necessary reforms. We hope he realizes, finally, how grave were the mistakes he mentioned so casually in his State of the Union speech. The first test of recognition will come next week when he speaks to the nation.

The Hutchinson News

Hutchinson, KS
February 27, 1987

Moses did the job with 10 short commandments.

The Tower Commission decided it needed to write a book.

The Tower Commission was President Reagan's official investigator of the Iranian scandal. In its huge report Thursday, the commission gave the president the benefit of the doubt. It viewed him as merely ignorant and incompetent. It viewed his chief aides as liars and thieves of public property.

The Tower Commission's findings are consistent. Ronald Reagan is out of touch with reality, with his administration, and with the guiding principles of this nation as shown by his reliance on people like Regan, North, Poindexter, Casey, Watt, Burford, Deaver and Meese.

He has surrounded himself with incompetents whom he describes as heroes, in a frighteningly unreal world in which the rewriting of history and truth is embraced as readily as the writing of fiction and illusion.

And he still does not see it.

"I think it's possible to forget," he quipped on the eve of the report's release.

"Everybody that can remember what they were doing on Aug. 8, 1985, raise your hands," he said, trying idiotically to excuse his purported ignorance of approving one of the more calamitous decisions in the history of American foreign policy.

He had promised never to trade with terrorists. Yet he not only secretly agreed to trade with terrorists, he sent them arms even as they tortured to death a leading American foreign agent. Before the nation last fall, he went on national television to argue how small the shipments of arms to the thugs were, even as his aides were working feverishly to doctor the official records.

A greater authority will judge compliance with two of those Ten Commandments.

But a nation must instantly repudiate the lies, thefts, stupidity and incompetence of an administration that has wrecked foreign policy, created havoc in the nation's domestic heartland and holds a finger on the button that could unleash 30,000 nuclear warheads.

CENTRAL AMERICA:

Central America Nations Sign Regional Peace Plan

The presidents of five Central American nations Aug. 7 in Guatemala City signed a preliminary peace agreement that called for cease-fires in conflicts in the region. The pact also called for democratic reforms (a provision aimed primarily at Nicaragua), dialogue between governments and unarmed opposition groups, and political amnesty. The agreement encompassed the main points of a proposal put forward in February by Costa Rican President Oscar Arias Sanchez.

The Guatemala City proposal differed in a number of ways from one advanced by United States President Reagan three days earlier. The major difference was that the Guatemalan plan called for measures including cease-fires and democratization to take place simultaneously within ninety days. The Reagan plan set a 60-day deadline for a cease-fire and for the completion of talks in Nicaragua on establishing a framework for free elections. It also called for the withdrawal of Soviet-bloc and other foreign advisers from Nicaragua within 60 days. The hastily presented Reagan plan reportedly did much to draw the Central American presidents together. El Salvador's communications minisiter, Adolfo Rey Prendes, commented Aug. 7 that the Reagan proposal had caused "indisputable worry" that it would push aside the Arias plan and give Nicaragua a pretext for withdrawing from the peace process. Commenting on the Guatemala City agreement, President Reagan Aug. 8 was cautious in his support. He said he welcomed the commitment to peace and democracy but added that there was a long way to go before the plan was successful. Reagan said his administration's acceptance depended on U.S. interests and those of the "Nicaraguan resistance."

The Central American plan, if carried out, would end the fighting in El Salvador, Nicaragua and Guatemala and bring democratic reform in Nicaragua. The pact was signed by Presidents Arias, Vinicio Cerezo Arevalo of Guatemala, Daniel Ortega Saavedra of Nicaragua, Jose Napolean Duarte of El Salvador, and Jose Azcona Hoyo of Honduras. It was unveiled by Arias at the end of a two-day summit. Diplomatic wrangling among the five nations had almost scuttled the Arias plan. The Guatemala City summit originally had been scheduled for June 25-26 but was postponed June 12 at the request of President Duarte. Nicaragua charged that the U.S. was behind the postponement, as Duarte's request came too soon after a trip to El Salvador by Philip Habib, the U.S. special envoy to Central America. Habib also visited Costa Rica, El Salvador and Guatemala.

President Reagan June 17 had met with Arias in Washington, D.C. and expressed reservations about the peace plan, specifically its perceived leniancy toward Nicaragua. Reagan told Arias that the military effort by the contras was the only way to put pressure on the Sandinistas. Arias June 18 criticized U.S. aid to the contras for giving the Sandinista government an excuse to implement repressive policies. He said his peace plan was imcompatible with continued aid.

The Aug. 7 agreement, titled "Procedure for the Establishment of a Strong and Lasting Peace in Central America," outlined two stages; national reconciliation and international verification and follow-up.

The recommended procedures included:

■ Dialogue between governments in the region and all "unarmed internal political groups" or those who had accepted amnesty, as the first step toward national reconciliation. Countries where divisions had arisen would decree an amnesty and "irregular forces" would release their prisoners. Compliance with this and other procedures would be verified by a National Reconciliation Commission in each country.

■ Cease-fires in countries where irregular forces were operating.

■ Promotion of "an authentic, democratic, pluralist and participatory process" in each country, with respect for human rights and social justice.

■ "Free, pluralist and honest" municipal, legislative and presidential elections held in accordance with the constitutions of each country and monitored by international observers. Elections for a Central American parliament would be held simultaneously in the five nations in the first half of 1988.

■ "Urgent attentions" to the problem of resettling refugees and persons displaced by conflicts in the region.

The Washington Post

Washington, DC, August 7, 1987

THE REAGAN administration's latest reach for peace in Central America takes place under the dark cloud cast by the Iran-contra hearings. It has enraged some of the president's pro-contra constituents. More menacing to its prospects of acceptance by Congress, Democratic skeptics insist it is merely a gimmick to tranquilize doubters and buy the next slice of contra aid. But we think it would be extraordinarily shortsighted to let debate over the move degenerate into an examination of suspected motives. Far better to stipulate these, to recognize that a moment of potential transition may have arrived and to look hard for ways to make the most of it.

Oliver North notwithstanding, President Reagan's public command of the Nicaraguan issue has slipped badly. He is within sight of his administration's terminal stages with no firm prospect at all of achieving what may be his most cherished foreign goal—undoing the Sandinistas. He could yet decide to pass the problem and the blame to his successors and political adversaries. The far better alternative, however, and the one we hope is guiding the president now, is to do what he can to move the struggle within Nicaragua back within political lines. To do that, the White House appears to be inviting some erstwhile critics in Congress to join Mr. Reagan in the launching of a diplomatic initiative. The president is also taking the further political risk of putting contra-aid renewal on the back burner; he cannot know whether it will be possible to crank the program up again in the fall.

Daniel Ortega, too, has his problems. Americans may debate the question of the contras, but the Sandinistas know their weight and sting and cannot dismiss the possibility of their remaining in the field. At the same time, Nicaragua's neighbors and fellow Latins, divided among themselves and from the United States on many things, agree that a turn toward pluralism in Managua is the key to the region's stability and security. These are the two large considerations inclining the Sandinistas to explore what the new American posture means. They are even warier than Americans, since what is to Americans at most a problem in regional foreign policy is to the Sandinistas a matter of the whole future of their revolution. Nonetheless, the Managua regime was quick to respond to the American initiative with an offer to resume the direct dialogue the two sides broke off in 1985. The offer is not new, and like every other tactical choice, it carries its own traps. But at this stage, a clear channel for authoritative exchange has an obvious value. The administration was too hasty in setting a condition—a prior cease-fire—for it.

A cease-fire, mutual suspension of foreign military support, a political opening sufficient to civilianize Nicaragua's search for its future, the participation of Nicaragua's fellow Latins: these are the basic elements of all "plans" for this embattled country, including the Arias plan, which this one resembles in its emphasis on political change. But what is new about the latest American move is that it seems less a plan than a solicitation for a double process. On one level, the more realistic elements within the Reagan administration are trying to draw the president toward an endgame that will let him achieve some respectable part of his goal of preventing consolidation of a "second Cuba." On another level, the United States seeks to draw a suspicious and repressive Nicaraguan regime from a military struggle to a political one.

There will be time enough later for any recriminations, for those given to them—and for another whack at the aid issue, if that turns out to be necessary. Right now it is time for Americans, Nicaraguans and, not least, other Central Americans and Latins to see if peace and some measure of pluralism can still be saved.

The Clarion-Ledger
JACKSON
DAILY NEWS
Jackson, MS, August 11, 1987

Peace in Nicaragua appears to be gaining new impetus from the recent initiatives disclosed by President Reagan and by the presidents of five Central American nations. Indeed, the two plans are very similar and the latter has already received the backing of President Reagan and House Speaker Jim Wright. However, this resort to diplomacy is very fragile and faces many obstacles.

Reagan has indicated a willingness to compromise on the Contra-Sandinista conflict in Nicaragua, but whether the Contras and the Sandinistas will come around on the issue is gravely in doubt. Nicaragua President Daniel Ortega labeled Reagan's proposal last week a "publicity stunt" if the United States refuses to negotiate directly. To which Secretary of State George Shultz said, "no way."

The Central American plan, based on a proposal by President Oscar Arias of Costa Rica, seems to be the main instrument in the new peace efforts. It calls for a cease-fire in 3 ½ months in Nicaragua's civil war and the leftist insurgency in El Salvador. The deadline seems more realistic than Reagan's proposed 60 days for negotiating a cease-fire and a timetable for making democratic reforms in Nicaragua.

The Arias plan also calls for reconciliation between the governments and opposition groups in El Salvador and Nicaragua, steps to assure democracy in each of the five nations which are a party to the plan and an end to outside aid to irregular forces. A tall order, indeed.

Meanwhile, a September deadline nears in Congress on another $100 million plus in military aid to the Contras.

Mistrusting motives of the principals on the issue tends to doom the peace effort no matter its merits. But those in Congress and the administration who hold different views must recognize the narrowing of choices. As put by one observer, the United States can pay, shoot or negotiate. The latter by all means must come first.

The Houston Post
Houston, TX, August 7, 1987

The new Central American peace plan the Reagan administration and House Speaker Jim Wright, D-Texas, have fielded is a gamble. But it is also a welcome first step in building a bipartisan U.S. policy toward the troubled region and Nicaragua's Soviet-backed regime.

If the Sandinista government wants to settle its civil war with the U.S.-backed Contra rebels, it can agree to 1) a cease-fire, 2) major democratic reforms, and 3) a halt to Soviet-bloc military aid. All this would have to be negotiated by Sept. 30. In return, we will suspend arms to the Contras. We also want regional talks on removing foreign military personnel and balancing armed forces. And we will consider lifting our embargo against Nicaragua and renewing aid.

The peace plan's chances of success are slim. Even so, Secretary of State George Shultz was right Thursday in rejecting Nicaraguan President Daniel Ortega's call for direct talks on it. Managua's Marxist leaders want us to bear the onus for their problems. But since the 1979 revolution that overthrew the Somoza dictatorship, they have suppressed political opposition, the church and the press. And with Soviet and Cuban help, they have built a powerful military machine.

Another obstacle to the plan is in the U.S. Congress. Liberal Democrats, who have criticized Reagan for using military force rather than negotiating, now charge that this is a ploy to win more Contra aid when current funds run out Sept. 30. That would be a risky gimmick, however, which could backfire in a total aid cutoff.

Conservative Republicans complain that the Contras are being "hung out to dry." But rebel leaders have cautiously supported the initiative, though they want a voice in the negotiations.

Despite the cool reception the plan received from Central American presidents meeting in Guatemala Thursday, it has merit. It rightly stresses regional solutions to Central America's problems. And unlike some other peace proposals the presidents have before them, it doesn't shortchange our security interests.

LAS VEGAS
REVIEW-JOURNAL
Las Vegas, NV, August 7, 1987

In foreign policy the pursuit of peace is quite obviously laudable. Equally important and equally laudable in the teleology of American foreign policy is the pursuit of liberty.

Simply stated, American foreign policy should not involve the blind pursuit of "peace" at any price. It is America's destiny to advance the cause of liberty in the world.

It would be foolish to deny that the United States has a spotless record in this regard. During the 1950s, at the height of the red scare and in the throes of McCarthyism, the United States saw fit to support just about any tin horn dictator who embraced anti-communism. That approach didn't win us many friends in the underdeveloped world.

This is not to say that opposing communism is not a worthy cause or a valid undertaking. It is. Communism, this scientific form of dictatorship, is the most efficient system of oppression ever devised by mankind. The United States must oppose communism and its spread, and other forms of tyranny. But, in so doing, this country must also be prepared to foster, in the place of tyrannies, systems of government under which people can live free.

The U.S. complaint with Nicaragua is not that nation's socialism. Nicaragua's economic system is not the concern. No, the concern is the evolving dictatorship that has stripped Nicaraguan citizens of the freedom of speech, the freedom of association, the freedom to assemble, the freedom of the press, the right to judicial due process, the freedom from political persecution.

If Nicaragua wants a socialist economy, fine. If it wants to be truly non-aligned, fine. What the United States should not tolerate is a full-blown dictatorship, a base for Soviet adventures in the Western Hemisphere.

The Sandinistas came to power with promises of free elections, a pluralistic political system and basic human freedoms. The Sandinistas have not kept their word. They spurned economic aid from the United States and began importing Soviet and Cuban advisers and sophisticated East Bloc weapons, all the while converting Nicaragua into a totalitarian state.

A liberation army, the Contras, arose to oppose the regime. The Contras, whose numbers include peasants and young people, former Sandinistas and some members of the old Somoza National Guard, are backed — intermittently — by the United States.

The Contra war does not sit well with many Democrats in Congress, as well as some of the leaders of other Central American nations. They would prefer a negotiated rather than an armed solution to the Nicaragua problem.

Now the Reagan administration and the Democratic leadership in Congress have, in a surprising move, agreed to offer the Sandinistas a deal: The United States will drop funding for the Contras if the Sandinistas agree to restore civil liberties to the Nicaraguan people, renounce Soviet and East Bloc military aid, call a cease fire and set a timetable for elections.

It is a peace plan that could work. It is true that no communist government has ever been negotiated out of existence, but there's a first time for everything, and this might be it.

The only other alternatives for Nicaragua are protracted guerrilla war with the Contras or protracted misery for the Nicaraguan people under the boot of a totalitarian state.

The Reagan administration and Congress should pursue this peace plan with the utmost urgency. If it works, the Nicaraguan people could enjoy both peace and liberty.

WALL STREET:

World Stock Prices Collapse

In panicked selling, the Dow Jones industrial average fell an astounding 508.32 points on Monday, Oct. 19. After rebounding in the next two days, United States stock prices turned downward again. World stock markets followed a similar pattern, with the London exchange experiencing record declines October 19 and 20. The Tokyo market suffered a record 14.9% loss Oct. 20. In the U.S., the Federal Reserve loosened credit and banks lowered their prime lending rates in response to the crash and fears of recession. The crash sparked a bipartisan determination to reduce the U.S. budget deficit. President Ronald Reagan Oct. 22 told a news conference that he was willing to meet with congressional Democrats and implied that he might consider tax increases. Computerized program trading of stocks was widely blamed for amplifying market volatility. Such trades were temporarily curtailed by the stock exchanges. Some corporate mergers were called off because of the sudden stock market volatility. A few smaller Wall Street firms were in deep trouble, while larger firms planned to trim growth. Major companies took the suddenly lower stock prices as an opportunity to buy back some of their shares. The U.S. government was running a stopgap appropriation as the budget process remained deadlocked. The international plunge in stock prices adversely affected privatization plans of the British and French governments.

The 508.32-point collapse was by far the largest in Wall Street history. The two previous record drops—95.46 and 108.36 points—had been recorded the previous week, when the Dow fell 261.43 points in three days. The Dow's rebounds of 102.27 points Oct. 20 and 186.84 Oct. 21 also set records as the biggest one-day increases. While the Dow had posted a number of absolute record declines in recent years, none had approached the 12.9% one-day percentage decline in the 1929 crash that foreshadowed the Great Depression. But the decline on Oct. 19, which came to be dubbed Black Monday, was 22.6%—the largest decline since prior to World War I.

Securities and Exchange Commission (SEC) Chairman David Ruder Oct. 20 frightened some traders by suggesting early in the day that he might call for a "very temporary" suspension of trading. The SEC later took the unusual step of announcing that it was "not discussing the nation's securities market." Princeton University economist Stanford Grossman said that suspending trading would be "a sure way to cause a panic."

Reagan administration officials met throughout the day Oct. 19 but concluded that there was nothing they could do immediately to stem the panic. President Reagan issued an official statement that said, "everyone is a little puzzled" because "nothing is wrong with the economy." Some observers lambasted administration comments about the sound economy because of their similarity to President Herbert Hoover's statement after the 1929 market crash that the economy remained "on a sound and prosperous basis."

In the U.S., the stock collapse spurred fears that a long-anticipated recession would come sooner and be more devastating than expected. Even as President Reagan Oct. 20 was insisting that the economy was fundamentally sound, the Federal Reserve Board was acting to reduce interest rates in order to increase liquidity for troubled financial institutions and to ease fears that higher rates would lead to recession. Democrats sought to take the initiative by assailing the President for budget deficits, and the President in turn blamed them, but agreed to consider almost any Democratic proposal to cut the deficit, even one that would raise taxes.

U.S. Treasury Secretary James Baker 3rd, on a scheduled trip to Western Europe, met in Bonn Oct. 19-20 with West German officials and then rushed back to the U.S. Baker's public criticism of West German economic policies, as well as his thinly veiled threat to allow a further decline in the value of the dollar, had widely been viewed as a factor in the previous week's stock market declines.

In the U.S. business world, some smaller Wall Street firms lost most of their money, and rumors swirled that the biggest firms were insolvent. Several mergers were called off because of the sudden volatility, but some corporate raiders took advantage of lower stock prices to increase their stakes in potential takeover targets. Several major companies announced they would buy back their own shares. These buybacks figured heavily in the market's comeback Oct. 20.

The Star-Ledger

Newark, NJ, October 28, 1987

One of the ground rules set for the "budget summit" was a moratorium on critical comments which could deflect from the thus far elusive goal of reducing the federal deficit. If it is observed by White House and congressional conferees, it would remove the bipartisan sniping that has frustrated efforts to bring the deficit to a manageable level.

The budget talks are a response to the stock market crash which sent two distinctly different messages to the Reagan administration and Congress. Both were directly related to the same issue—taxes. In what was obviously an overreaction, Treasury Secretary James Baker blamed Democratic legislators who were working on a tax hike measure for helping to fuel the stock-selling stampede.

Democratic congressmen viewed the Wall Street debacle in a much different perspective, a financial crisis that clearly underscored an urgent need to responsibly address recurring budget deficits that have rolled up the largest federal debt in the nation's history.

The accelerated buildup of the enormous debt in the last several years was a joint venture, an uneasy collaboration on spending and revenue policies that involved the White House and Congress. The huge debt problem had its regrettable genesis in the tax cuts proposed by the Reagan administration and approved by the legislative branch.

The tax reductions served as a stimulus for a soft economy. But they also had the debilitating effect of reducing the revenue potential—revenues that would have cushioned the record spending that the President insisted was needed to beef up the military. While Democratic congressmen resisted some White House demands for cuts in domestic programs, they went along—sometimes grudgingly—with sharp increases in defense appropriations.

The reckoning for these unsound fiscal and monetary policies was not long in surfacing in stubborn annual deficits and recurring budgetary confrontations between the legislative and executive branches, which finally forced the passage of the Gramm-Rudman mandatory budget-cutting law.

But it has become apparent that spending cutbacks—$23 billion in budget deficit reductions are being discussed—were not enough, that they would have to be supplemented with additional revenues in order to effectively reduce the deficit. Until he began wavering after the market collapse, the President had been adamant against anything resembling a tax hike, but indicated he would go along with hikes in user fees.

There's a critical drawback to the Reagan proposal—it won't generate enough revenues to significantly alleviate the deficit. Opposing a tax rise makes for good politics, but it's not realistic monetary policy. The Wall Street crisis should be sufficiently compelling for the White House to do some serious reassessing of its revenue positions in light of the drastically changed conditions generated in part by institutionalized, oversized federal deficits.

THE KANSAS CITY STAR
Kansas City, MO, October 20, 1987

The West German fear of inflation is understandable in light of the monetary disaster of the 1920s, yet for the last few months the Germans have seemed intent on fighting the last financial war. In its refusal to expand the West German economy, the Bundesbank is threatening the system of managed exchange rates, and contributing to the chaos in the financial markets.

Tension between Bonn and Washington has grown as the Germans have repeatedly tightened monetary policy, in violation of the spirit of the February Louvre agreement. In that gathering, Germany and Japan agreed to increase consumer demand, play a greater role in spurring world growth, and help ease trade imbalances.

Japanese growth is increasing, but the Germans have been tightening their money supply. Four times since last July the Bundesbank has raised a key interest rate—despite a sluggish economy, a hefty trade surplus, an inflation rate of only 1 percent and an unemployment rate of 9 percent.

Monday the West Germans added more money to the banking system, but some analysts doubted the move will head off another short-term interest rate increase. The addition of liquidity was apparently in response to a weekend report that the United States planned to let the dollar fall below the Louvre trading range. Although Treasury Secretary James Baker reiterated warnings that the U.S. may favor a lower dollar, he denied reports that a lower target price had been adopted.

Higher interest rates by our major trading partners puts upward pressure on U.S. rates, threatening the economic expansion. A West German lending-rate boost Oct. 6, for example, sent the Dow Jones Industrial Average reeling by nearly 92 points.

Despite Baker's denial, the threat of a plummeting dollar no doubt played a role in Monday's wild ride on Wall Street.

The tiff between Washington and Bonn threatens not only the fragile system of managed exchange rates and the relative stability they offer, but also undermines the trend toward greater economic coordination among the major industrial countries. On Monday, West Germany reaffirmed its commitment to the Louvre agreement. The statement would be more convincing if the Bundesbank were managing a thriving economy, rather than a stagnant one. But if there was ever a need for greater cooperation among the major industrial powers it is now.

THE COMMERCIAL APPEAL
Memphis, TN, October 20/21, 1987

Monday's massive selloff of stocks on Wall Street has created panic selling throughout world financial markets. At its close, the Dow-Jones average — one of the most closely-followed indices — had dropped 508 points.

Only last Friday, the Dow-Jones set a one-day record by tumbling 108 points. Compared to Monday's furious action, that seemed mild.

Comparisons between 1987 and 1929 are inescapable. And, indeed, the five-year bull market that added trillions of dollars to stock values showed many of the symptoms that preceded the 1929 crash. Both came at a time when the market never really reflected the sluggish growth in the economy. And both came from investors who kept pouring money into stocks regardless of the performance of individual companies.

But there's one important difference between 1929 and 1987: Now there is no clear sign of an economic downturn. In 1929, signs of a recession were already apparent. The Dow-Jones began a spectacular rise in the '20s from the 75 mark to 381.17 on Sept. 3, 1929. And on Oct. 28, the Dow fell 38.33 points to 260.64 — a loss of 12.8 percent of the market. The next day, it fell another 30.57 points, or 11.73 percent of the market.

Compare that to the staggering losses suffered last week and this. Friday's 108-point drop was 4.6 percent of the market — and Monday's was another 22 percent.

Other world markets were similarly battered. The Canadian market had its worst recorded day. The London Stock Exchange lost 10.8 percent of its value. Exchanges in Tokyo, Hong Kong, and other financial capitals were similarly shaken.

It may take months before the full impact of Wall Street's panic selloff can be assessed. Will the market hit bottom and stage a spectacular resurgence? Or will it drift aimlessly? It's anyone's guess — and certainly the Wall Street "experts" are as mystified as anyone else.

THE BILLINGS GAZETTE
Billings, MT, October 20, 1987

Nichibei represents the melding of the of the Japanese characters representing the sun country (Japan) and the rice country (America).

The *nichibei* economy is the symbolic melding of the financial affairs of both countries into an unstable interdependency.

And that has frightening implications for this country.

A recent article in the economics section of Business Week magazine suggests that this nation's economy is a boat made of rice paper, and unless something is done the bottom could be torn out by the early 1990s.

Norman Jonas writes that there are a number of reasons for the peril:

● Japan runs huge trade surpluses. This, in conjunction with the Japanese people's propensity for saving, gives that country vast amounts of capital for investment, particularly in America.

● The United States is running huge trade deficits. Additionally, the national deficit is the largest in history. We have proved through the 1980s that we do not have the will — from president through freshman congressman to the man on the street — to bring spending into balance with revenue.

● When American companies were given tax breaks under Reagan's trickle-down economic theory, the companies chose quick profits over building for the future. We desperately needed investment in plants, equipment, research and education. Instead, the companies played take-over games that resulted in an inflated stock market. As a result some of our industries have been crippled and can no longer compete in the world market.

● The United States is spending 6.5 percent of its gross national product on national defense. Japan sits under the American arms umbrella and spends only about 1 percent of its GNP on defense. That allows Japan to prosper while we live in a false economy built on the whims of the Japanese investors.

● Basically, the Japanese "lend" money to America which allows us to continue our profligate deficit spending and, in turn, have tapped key American technology and some of the nation's vast natural resources. The Japanese are taking a firmer grip on America's purse strings and future.

● And the American stockmarket shuddered and plummeted more than 500 points Monday, creating panic around the world. If Japan should decide that the American economy is too shaky to warrant the huge investments of the past, the impact would be devastating.

Meanwhile, the sentiment for protectionist trade policies is growing, and that could be deadly. We need to join efforts with Japan in order to resolve our growing dependency on each other.

And first order of the day is bringing the national budget closer to balance. Unfortunately, we don't seem to have the leadership in Washington or the resolve on the streets to get that done.

Edmonton Journal

Edmonton, Alta., October 21, 1987

Though comparisons are tempting this week's chaotic stock markets do not herald a repeat of the Great Depression which began 58 years ago.

The world economy is more integrated now than it was then; the corrective steps necessary for sustained economic growth are well known.

If anything, the stock market slide brings share values closer to reality eliminating the paper-profit speculation that had driven prices to record highs.

More fundamental, it forces politicians to make the economic decisions necessary to avoid a global recession.

The Bank of Canada has already moved to lower interest rates. The rate on treasury bills has been cut and the bank rate could fall half a point when it is set Thursday.

Lowering the cost of borrowing money should restore some stability to the panicky market and allow for a sober reassessment of the value of companies.

Similar action must be taken by the U.S. The unnecessarily high cost of borrowing money, caused largely by an American national debt of seemingly insatiable appetite, drains western industrial economies.

To satisfy Washington's spending investors the world over have been chasing the high rate of return offered to those who underwrite the U.S. debt.

This investment would spur the economy were it to increase wealth and productivity. Unfortunately, a large part of the U.S. deficit goes to finance military spending which is unproductive and does nothing to increase wealth.

Yet the spinoff of this huge investment is an aura of prosperity — and it is this illusion which has faded with the stock-market correction.

While there is considerable strength inherent in the consumer-led economies of the U.S. and most western industrial nations, it has been skewed by America's penchant for running up debt.

At the same time, the U.S. dollar has been overvalued. This in turn has led to a prodigious American trade deficit which inspires protectionism at home.

Worry about the debt; the trade deficit, and fears of inflation's driving interest rates even higher, triggered a panic in the stock markets — augmented by computers programmed to automatically sell off stocks at certain levels.

America's first step is to devalue the U.S. dollar to make its exports more competitive. The best way to do so is to reduce the U.S. budget deficit — particularly military spending, thereby reducing interest rates.

As a corollary, the western world's most successful export economies — West Germany and Japan — should be willing to increase their share of imports. If comparative advantage is allowed to reign in a climate of fair and liberalized trade, economic prosperity will follow.

Japan's announced willingness to boost imports, combined with a lower U.S. dollar, should help restore confidence.

Another imperative is to rewrite the debts of Latin American and other developing nations which are large markets for western goods and services.

Profligacy has saddled Latin America with huge debts — and huge interest charges.

If long-term debt could be deferred, the wealth which debtor nations create would be applied to trade, leading to prosperity which would benefit all — and ultimately assuring the repayment of the principal on those past debts.

Yet the immediate cure for stock-market jitters is calm action by governments to restore confidence.

The Bank of Canada's move is only a beginning. Without a fundamental revision of western economic and trade policy, this week's shock could be a foretaste of worse to come.

THE DAILY HERALD

Biloxi, MS, October 21, 1987

You may not own a single stock, bond or other investment but Monday's stock market crash will almost certainly touch your life in some way. It's ramifications will rumble through the economy for some time.

Financial experts do not yet agree on what it all means. The Dow Jones Industrial Average plunged 508.32 points to 1738.42. The 22.6 percent drop almost doubled the 12.8 percent fall that triggered the Great Depression 58 years ago.

Will that economic misery be repeated? It is highly unlikely. Major bulwarks are built into the economic system to prevent a recurrence of the Depression. Chief among these are the laws, regulations and insurance for the banking system, which was vulnerable to widespread failures after 1929, and limits on the amounts investors may borrow to buy stocks.

More caution in spending is expected of individuals and of corporations. How much more depends on whether the market rebounds to recoup some of the loss.

Taking the blame are the huge budget deficit, a stubborn trade deficit and the weak dollar.

Yet, the national unemployment rate remains below 6 percent. The Gross National Product has been plodding along with a slow increase, with a 2.25 percent growth predicted this year and 2.75 percent for 1988. Those forecasts may no longer be valid after the drop wiped out $503 billion worth of stock value.

Congressmen could help if they quit dilly-dallying with the budget deficit, now in excess of $2 trillion. The Gramm-Rudman-Hollings anti-deficit act will activate automatic cuts, unless Congress trims $23 billion from the debt by Nov. 20. Democrats want a tax hike of about $12 billion to stall the Gramm-Rudman-Hollings activation, but President Reagan is adamantly opposed to a tax hike and has the veto power. The scenario indicates another stalemate when action is needed.

Congress has habitually ignored warnings of the dangers of a continually increasing budget deficit, a continuing trade deficit and a weakened dollar. Will its members ignore Monday's stock market disaster also?

DESERET NEWS

Salt Lake City, UT, October 25, 1987

Instantly after the stock-market earthquake, nearly everyone knew what had to be done. The federal deficits must be reduced. America has been living too long on borrowed money.

A lot of people have been saying that for a long time, and also saying that there is no realistic way to end the deficits without a tax increase. Taxes should have been increased two or three years ago, and the present crisis might not have happened. Now, however, a tax increase must be approached very cautiously.

For once, President Reagan is right about taxes — more or less. Any tax increase included in a deficit-reduction agreement shouldn't be of the kind that will greatly slow the economy.

It must be assumed that the stock-market dive foreshadows a recession, and a tax increase during a recession could make the slowdown worse. A general tax increase probably should be avoided, yet deficit-reduction is imperative. What to do?

One choice might be an oil-import tax. That wouldn't raise enough to end the deficits, but it would make a big dent. In addition, it would boost the depressed U.S. oil patch, would encourage renewed energy conservation and would lessen a growing and dangerous dependence on foreign oil.

It's not an entirely happy choice because an increase in energy prices would have some slowing effect on the economy, but that would have to be weighed against the greater peril of not reducing the deficits.

On the spending side, an across-the-board freeze on spending levels of the kind favored for years by Iowa Senator Charles Grassley could make a big impact while avoiding a fight over what to cut and what not to cut.

The Record

Hackensack, NJ, October 21, 1987

Monday's collapse on Wall Street was an overwhelming vote of no confidence in President Reagan, Treasury Secretary James A. Baker III, and the absurd doctrine of supply-side economics. For months, Reagan administration officials have been assuring investors that the economy was fundamentally healthy. And the markets tended to believe them, despite indications that the prosperity was actually built on an ever-expanding mountain of debt.

Earlier this year, however, disbelief set in. As debt grew, interest rates — the return investors demand for financing all the debt — began inching upwards. The stock market soon took fright. From its high of 2722.42 on Aug. 25, the Dow-Jones average skidded to 2482 by Oct. 9, a 9 percent fall. Last week it fell another 9.5 percent.

At various points, Secretary Baker attempted to halt the slide, but succeeded only in making things worse. Last weekend, in chastising West Germany for raising its own interest rates, he indicated that the dollar might have to fall a few more points against the West German mark. But a cheaper dollar would bring about inflation — it would take more dollars to buy the same amount of goods — and a lower return for foreign investors. This was just what the stock market, already nervous, did not want to hear. On Monday, Wall Street panicked.

If Mr. Baker thinks that a cheaper dollar and a war of nerves with West Germany are the cure for the economy's ills, it's no wonder that investors no longer trust his pronouncements. The Reagan administration's policy of low taxes, big spending, and unrestrained borrowing initially drove the markets into a frenzy of delight — but now, because they have gone much too far, are driving them to a frenzy of despair. The markets want something very different: sound fiscal policies, something approaching a balanced budget, and an end to the irresponsi-ble supply-side dogma that tax cuts will return the country to economic health.

Unfortunately, Washington is in no position to give them those things. The time to raise taxes was two or three years ago, when the economy was still relatively strong. The economy would have slowed, but the federal budget deficit would have narrowed and long-term confidence would have been strengthened. Now, however, it is probably too late. Raising taxes in today's nerve-wracked climate could prove to be a repeat of Herbert Hoover's suicidal balanced-budget policies of the early Thirties. With higher taxes eating up money that could otherwise be used for consumer spending and investment, the economy would contract. The contraction would almost certainly tip the country over into recession or even depression.

But failing to deal with the deficit could be even worse. And if the economy is flooded with more money — as the Federal Reserve began doing yesterday in an effort to lower interest rates and calm the markets — the danger of inflation is seriously heightened.

Thus, Mr. Baker is damned if he does and damned if he doesn't. Six years of headlong borrowing and wild spending have left him and the president with few long-term options. To the economy's long-term woes — deep budget and trade deficits, a weakening dollar — has been added a psychological problem: Monday's crash is likely to make consumers and investors far more reluctant than before to spend money. Despite yesterday's mini-recovery on Wall Street, the long-term prospects are for a sharp economic contraction — with painful results, particularly for the New York-New Jersey regional economy, with its heavy dependence on the financial markets.

"It's morning in America," President Reagan declared in 1984. Thanks to Monday's crash, it's now the morning after.

THE DAILY OKLAHOMAN
Oklahoma City, OK
October 27, 1987

MANY economists predict at least a mild recession early next year, and that may be the best news President Reagan will get this week.

Without checking the record, one could probably figure the "experts" are wrong about as often as they are right. They have been forecasting the failure of Reagan's economic policies almost since he took office in 1981. But the economy continues to roll along in robust health.

The latest government statistics show the annual growth rate of the real gross national product increased to 3.8 percent in the third quarter from 2.5 percent in the second quarter. Yet the consumer price index last month edged up only 0.2 percent, indicating that inflation was held in check.

The reports reflect economic conditions before the Oct. 19 stock market crash, of course. Some analysts tie the plunge to the nation's budget and trade deficits, which they blame on Reaganomics. These numbers have been bad for some time, so why would they trigger such a massive sell-off now? Indeed, the budget deficit has been shrinking. The experts should look elsewhere for a scapegoat.

Newsday

Long Island, NY, October 29, 1987

Wall Street sent Washington a message Monday: The Dow Jones industrial average plunged 156 points — a fall second only to the 508-point tumble on Black Monday last week. The latest dive was a vote of no confidence in the nation's political leadership or its ability to deal with persistent federal budget deficits.

The same day, President Ronald Reagan convened a long-overdue summit meeting with congressional leaders on the budget. The message that the political leaders must send back to Wall Street is clear, and it goes like this:

"We're serious about addressing the deficit — not just this week, not just to calm the churning markets, but because we recognize it *must* be done." Mere words won't do; what's necessary now is action — painful, cost-cutting, revenue-raising action.

The first requirement is to cut the current fiscal year's projected deficit by $25 billion to $30 billion. Anything less won't convince anybody that Washington is serious, since the Gramm-Rudman Act will force $23 billion in cuts even if Reagan and Congress do nothing further.

Second, the negotiators must agree on a program that leads directly to further deficit reductions in later years — either a plan that commits Washington to specific spending cuts in 1989, as Sen. Bob Dole (R-Kan.) suggests, or one with a mechanism that produces reductions in the future.

Congress already has put together plans to avoid the procrustean Gramm-Rudman cuts by splitting the $23 billion evenly between spending reductions and new revenues. That's a good formula, which avoids severe stress on any part of the budget.

The White House, in contrast, talks of a budget freeze for 1988 — in part because it would better protect defense spending. That won't do. Freezes ignore changing needs, and that's not only bad policy but also politically unsustainable for very long. What's needed is a long-term approach.

There's not time to scrutinize federal spending with the utmost care, but Congress can surely find cuts of $15 billion or so; that's less than 2 percent of total projected federal spending. And if the legislators and the White House will commit themselves to begin rethinking federal spending programs, so much the better.

On the revenue side, the House and the Senate have employed similar tactics: closing a few loopholes here and limiting deductions there. But both, perversely, have also come up with several billion dollars in new tax breaks for favored constituents.

Aside from those new breaks, which should be summarily scrapped, much in both plans is sound. But the new revenues they propose wouldn't expand next year or the year after, when the deficit will still be a problem.

Here's a good alternative:

• Freeze 1987 tax rates for three years. Next year the rates for higher income taxpayers are slated to drop, reducing tax revenue and shifting the tax burden to people of more modest means. Keeping the existing tax structure would bring in about $8.6 billion in 1988, according to the Congressional Budget Office.

• Then impose a 1 or 2 percent surtax on all personal and corporate tax returns. That would raise $5 billion to $10 billion.

A surtax has several advantages: It spreads the burden across all taxpayers in rough proportion to their ability to pay. It's highly visible, clearly a temporary measure and no excuse for avoiding more fundamental budget questions. And it can be adjusted to meet shifting fiscal policy needs. If other deficit-slashing measures fall short, it could be increased; if the economy stumbles and needs a boost from a tax cut, it could be reduced.

Most important, it would show that Washington is ready to deal with the deficit in a systematic way — not just cobble up some stopgap this year and hope for the return of fair weather later on.

POLITICS:

Bush-Quayle Ticket Wins U.S. Presidential Election

Vice President George Herbert Walker Bush (R) was elected Nov. 8 to be the 41st president of the U.S., defeating Massachusetts Gov. Michael S. Dukakis (D). Bush won a 54%-46% victory in the popular vote and an overwhelming 426-112 victory in the electoral vote. Bush's running mate, Sen. J. Danforth (Dan) Quayle (R, Ind.), became the vice president-elect. Sen. Lloyd M. Bentsen Jr. (D, Texas) had been the Democratic vice presidential nominee.

Bush would add the presidency to his long resume in public service, which included a variety of high-level appointments but only one previous elective office besides the vice presidency, the House of Representatives in 1966. Bush became the first sitting vice president to win the presidency since Martin Van Buren in 1836.

But Democrats more than held their own in other offices, preserving the overall political balance between a Republican White House and a Democratic Congress. That situation led many commentators to call the election an endorsement of the status quo. Democrats gained one seat overall in the Senate for a new majority of 55-45. They added a probable three seats to their majority in the House and posted a net gain of one governorship. As in 1986, ticket splitting was pronounced. In Texas, roughly 400,000 voters voted for different parties for president and Senate.

Bush and Quayle won a 54% to 46% victory in the popular vote over Dukakis and Bentsen. In unofficial returns with 99% of the nation's precincts reporting, Bush had 47,946,422 votes to 41,016,429 for Dukakis. Bush carried 40 states to Dukakis's 10, including all of the southern tier of the country, coast to coast. Bush ended up with a massive victory in the electoral college, claiming 426 electoral votes to 112 for Dukakis, with 270 needed to win.

Dukakis carried only a scattering of states in the East, Midwest and West. He won Massachusetts, Rhode Island, New York, West Virginia, Iowa, Wisconsin, Minnesota, Oregon, Washington, Hawaii and the District of Columbia. He fell just short in two other large states that were crucial to his final, fallback victory strategy, Pennsylvania and Illinois.

Of the eight states with 20 or more electoral votes, Bush lost only one, New York, which went for Dukakis by 52%-48%. The other largest states, with Bush's winning percentages, were: California (52%), Texas (56%), Pennsylvania (51%), Illinois (51%), Ohio (55%), Florida (61%), and Michigan (54%). Bush swept the deep South and the mountain West with vote totals at the 60% level or better. A number of other states were close enough, however, that a swing of fewer than 600,000 votes in nine states could have barely tipped the electoral vote to Dukakis.

Bush on election night made a gesture at healing the wounds opened in what was widely viewed as a negative campaign. (See pp. 1206-1213.) In his victory speech at his headquarters in Houston, Bush said, "A campaign is a disagreement, and disagreements divide. But an election is a decision and decisions clear the way for harmony and peace. I mean to be a president of all the people, and I want to work for the hopes and interests not only of my supporters but of the governor's and of those who didn't vote at all.

"To those who supported me, I will try to be worthy of your trust, and to those who did not, I will try to earn it, and my hand is out to you, and I want to be your president, too," Bush said.

Dukakis, in his concession 20 minutes earlier, had said he would continue to fight for "families all across America" in working with the new administration. Dukakis had gone from a 14%-17% lead in the preference polls in June to a 14%-17% deficit in late October, meaning he had turned away nearly one potential supporter in six during the campaign. Dukakis campaign manager John Sasso, told one interviewer on election night, "Clearly there are things you would do over if you had the opportunity to." The mistake the Dukakis forces were most often faulted for was not responding directly to the charges of the Bush camp until it was too late.

Dukakis's showing of 10 states and 112 electoral votes was actually the best by a Democratic presidential candidate since Jimmy Carter's victory in 1976. The outcome was that close only because of an energetic closing push by Dukakis in key targeted states.

The Chattanooga Times

Chattanooga, TN, November 9, 1988

Riding the key themes of peace and prosperity, George Bush registered a substantial victory Tuesday in his quest for the presidency. His defeat of Massachusetts Gov. Michael Dukakis reflected not only the smooth functioning of a highly professional campaign, but an ability to use themes that struck responsive chords among millions of voters.

If nothing else, the Bush victory illustrated once again the Democrats' tendency to underestimate their opponent in a national campaign. Even though Mr. Dukakis himself expected his lead over the vice president to slip after the GOP convention, the slippage turned into a power dive as the Bush forces began to define and dominate the agenda for the campaign. Not until the last couple of weeks of the campaign did Mr. Dukakis begin hitting themes to which the audiences could respond favorably.

The Bush triumph, however, is more than a victory of strategy and tactics, although they were essential. Mr. Bush was able to point to economic conditions of the late 1970s, contrast them with the relative low interest, inflation and unemployment rates of today and suggest that economic disaster would result from a Dukakis administration. It was a shrewd appeal to voters' justified fears for their economic well-being, although neither Mr. Bush nor Mr. Dukakis adequately addressed the two major threats to the nation's — and Americans' — economies: the budget and trade deficits.

In his successful drive to the presidency, Mr. Bush promised to continue the Reagan administration's domestic and foreign policies, so that in one sense the election became a referendum on the Reagan presidency. But Mr. Bush, the former congressman, CIA director, ambassador, party head and vice president, also stressed his government experience, which he said would serve the nation well, particularly in its relations with the Soviet Union.

Every new president gives a new definition to the nation's highest office, and Mr. Bush will be no exception. To that extent, then, Americans must hope that Mr. Bush will grow in his new responsibilities. He will first have to unify the nation. That will not be an easy task in light of the negativism — indeed, the downright nastiness — that characterized much of his campaign, more so than the Dukakis effort. In short, Mr. Bush will have to move quickly to exemplify the type of leadership Americans have a right to expect from their president.

Mr. Bush's success as a national leader will depend in large part on his ability to fashion a workable relationship with Congress, both houses of which will remain solidly Democratic. Mr. Reagan won several victories during his eight years, chiefly because he won substantial mandates in the 1980 and 1984 elections. It's an open question, however, whether Mr. Bush will emerge with the type of mandate he will need to get his legislative program through Congress.

The next four years are guaranteed to bring enormous challenges to Mr. Bush and his national constituency. He has demonstrated a capacity for leadership by virtue of his successful campaign. Now he must show himself capable of the even greater task of leading the nation.

Richmond Times-Dispatch

Richmond, VA, November 11, 1988

The most bizarre feature of this election season was not Mike Dukakis' ride in a tank or George Bush's paeans to a "kinder, gentler" nation before socking it to his opponent again. It was the bulging ballot in California, which had citizens of the Golden State voting on 29 statewide propositions plus a number of local issues in many areas.

In San Francisco, for example, there were 25 purely local propositions. Thus, voters in the city by the bay were asked to wade through 54 ballot questions in addition to voting for candidates in the presidential, congressional, legislative and local races. Will voters have to start packing a snack before they enter the polling place?

Political analyst Neal R. Peirce has observed correctly that this is an "experiment in direct democracy" that "appears to be running amok." Originally, initiative and referendum techniques were seen as a citizens' counterweight to the influence of vested interests. Howard Jarvis became something of a folk hero 10 years ago with the success of his tax-capping Proposition 13 in California. Perversely, though, the ballot initiative has become a tool of the special interests,

which can manipulate public opinion to get their causes on the ballot. Californians were confronted with five propositions dealing with automobile insurance alone, for example, with contradictory proposals pushed by the industry, trial lawyers and the Ralph Nader organization.

In a republic, citizens ideally elect representatives to make the basic governmental decisions and then hold them accountable for their actions. The system is not perfect, but it beats the chaos of direct democracy by a long shot. Now and again, someone introduces a bill in the Virginia General Assembly calling for the initiative and referendum. One look at the electoral chaos in California should be sufficient to convince Virginia lawmakers to keeping saying no to such legislation. They should represent their constituents as best they can, make the tough calls when they have to, and protect the ballot from the monied manipulators. Referenda on such major policy departures as the lottery and pari-mutuel are justified on occasion, but representative government depends on representatives having the fortitude to make decisions for the people.

The Washington Post

Washington, DC, November 14, 1988

"**MANDATE**" is one of those words that have come to suggest more than they mean. It has also taken on a kind of high-minded bronze glow. Newly elected officials must and invariably do profess that they have a mandate from the people to do whatever they have it in mind to do anyhow, and they always manage to convey the idea that their mandate has the force of a court order. Right now the argument is being waged over whether President-Elect Bush has a mandate or can now create a mandate if he neglected to get one in the first place.

Many of the Democrats lamenting the absence of a mandate and—get this—comparing the situation unfavorably with the glory days when Ronald Reagan supposedly came to town *with* a mandate, neglect to mention, or perhaps merely to recall, that they 1) hated the contents of Mr. Reagan's mandate and 2) found any number of inventive ways to argue from the electoral arithmetic that President Reagan didn't have a mandate at all to perpetrate the most controversial things he had in mind. They also seem always to imply that a mandate is exclusively for creating new programs, not, as in the Reagan case, for eliminating a lot of them.

Well what about Mr. Bush? Do we know why he was elected? That is, does he have a mandate not to raise taxes or merely not to be Michael Dukakis or what? Can you ever know which part of an elected official's campaign spiel was being validated by the voters? Generally, we believe these mandates are no more than certain broad areas of assent, certain go-ahead signals the electorate has given. Dwight Eisenhower had a mandate to end the war in Korea, Richard Nixon to end the war in Vietnam and to restore order to the nation's turbulent, demonstration-ridden politics (which he didn't quite do). Jimmy Carter, who beat the transitional Gerald Ford, had a mandate not to be Richard Nixon and to make us forget the Watergate horror. Ronald Reagan had a mandate

to toughen up the nation's foreign policy and defense (and balance its budget and not raise taxes).

In this broad sense, we suppose Mr. Bush's mandate is to continue with the basic policies of the Reagan years in an incremental, undramatic manner. Surely it is not to promulgate a bunch of high-octane, high-cost domestic programs (especially when the filling station no longer accepts the federal credit card), and it is not to kill off those programs that have survived the ax of the Reagan years either. His mandate must mainly be to improve and slightly rejigger those that already exist, unless he is finally willing to raise the revenues required for more. In foreign policy and defense, he is surely charged with consolidating the gains of the past eight years. He is going to have to make some choices on defense expenditures, whether he likes doing it or not.

The truth of the matter is that the whole argument over the nature of Mr. Bush's mandate is in a sense merely incidental to a much larger and more immediate issue: How, on the basis of his campaign rhetoric and whatever the voters consider his mandate to be, a newly installed President Bush will handle the challenge of creeping Gramm-Rudman deadlines, burgeoning federal government costs and a Democratic Congress not exactly bursting with enthusiasm to help him out of the fiscal and financial pressures that are intensifying. His mandate in this poorly focused election may not have been to fix the budget deficit, but until he does, he can do little else. (See below.) Given all this, we expect Mr. Bush's plans cannot be grandiose; his claims and demands will not be dramatic. He will reveal himself as a man whose hope is to make the so-called Reagan revolution work, to somewhat extend its social sympathies and to vindicate the past eight years in the next four. He will also be doing a lot of bailing out. If you will pardon the expression, in this context we think the Bush presidency is more likely to be about competence than ideology.

The Honolulu Advertiser

Honolulu, HI, November 9, 1988

Vice President George Bush's margin — in the popular vote and especially in the Electoral College — is undeniably impressive. He is to be congratulated.

Some will call it a landslide, but others still termed it a mudslide, and that remains part of his problem as president-elect.

In any event, the American people have voted for "peace and prosperity," for a continuation of Reaganism even without Ronald Reagan and for the patriotic, socially conservative "mainstream" values Bush espoused so well.

Now one question is whether this big Bush victory is a mandate and, if so, for what. His campaign was long on negatives and short on new ideas or meaningful promises, except for his "read my lips" pledge not to raise taxes. Considering that the federal deficit, with its immediate and future repercussions, is the most pressing domestic problem, that's going to be difficult.

So the honeymoon may be short for George Bush, who had better hope he has Reagan's famous luck if not his charisma.

While choosing a Cabinet and other advisers, Bush must restore relations with Democratic leaders after a negative, condescending campaign. That's especially so with the Democratic Congress, and some felt his speech on winning last night was at least a start.

Once again Americans have opted for "divided government" as a check on the "imperial presidency" and on any tendency toward rash or extreme actions by either party. Lately we seem content with the high-profile, symbolically potent position of the presidency, with its heavy responsibility for defense and foreign relations, to be in Republican hands.

But like Reagan, Bush's "coattails" are short. When it comes to running the country on domestic matters, Americans pick Democratic majorities in Congress, as well as most state governorships and legislatures.

The nation is in for four more years of this sometimes quarrelsome, often frustrating, but in the long run comfortably cautious form of governance.

TERRORISM:

Bomb Blamed in Pan Am Crash

A Pan Am jetliner flying from London to New York City broke apart and crashed into the village of Lockerbie in southwest Scotland Dec. 21. All 243 passengers and 15 crew members on board were killed in the crash. As of Dec. 24, at least 11 residents of Lockerbie were also reported dead, or missing and believed dead.

Although investigators were not immediately able to determine the cause of the crash, speculation centered on either a structural failure or sabotage in the form of an on-board bomb.

An anonymous caller claiming to represent the Guardians of the Islamic Revolution, a pro-Iranian group, Dec. 22 telephoned news agencies in London and claimed responsibility. However, Iran officially denied any connection with the crash.

Investigators who examined the plane's cockpit and flight data recordings said Dec. 23 that the cockpit voice recording showed nothing unusual, except for a faint, unidentified noise just before the recording cut off. The data recording had also ended abruptly at the same time, they said. That fact suggested that a massive failure had instantly severed the plane's electrical systems.

The plane, a Boeing 747, had been cruising at an altitude of 31,000 feet when it disappeared from radar screens. No distress call was received. Wreckage from the crash was scattered over an area of least 10 miles wide.

The airliner, Pan Am's Flight 103, had left London's Heathrow Airport and was headed for New York's Kennedy International Airport when the disaster occurred. An earlier leg of the flight had originated in Frankfurt, West Germany on a different aircraft, a Boeing 727.

The Federal Aviation Administration reported Dec. 22 that the U.S. government had alerted embassies in Europe of a possible attack after a bomb threat was received Dec. 5. A caller had told the U.S. embassy in Finland that a Pan Am plane flying from Frankfurt to the U.S. would be the target of a bombing attempt within the next two weeks.

Finnish authorities Dec. 22 said that they had been monitoring the caller's activities and they doubted that there was a connection between the telephone threat and the crash. However, news of the warning prompted widespread complaints that the public had not been informed of the possible risk. U.S. President Ronald Reagan responded to the criticism Dec. 23. "If you stop to think about it," he said, "such a public statement, with nothing but a telephone call to go on, would literally have closed down all the air traffic in the world."

British investigators confirmed Dec. 28 that the crash of Pan Am flight 103 in Lockerbie, Scotland on Dec. 21 had been caused by a powerful explosive device. The British Department of Transport's Air Accidents Investigation, which was heading the inquiry, reported that "conclusive evidence of a detonating high explosive" had been found in part of a metal luggage holder from the wreckage.

The department also said that residue recovered from the debris indicated that a plastic explosive had been the type of explosive used to blow up the plane. Some experts speculated that the material might have been Sentek, a plastic explosive manufactured in Czechoslovakia that was popular with terrorist groups.

President-elect George Bush responded Dec. 29 by saying that the U.S. should "seek hard and punish firmly, decisively those who did this, if you could ever find them." But Bush refused to discuss whether he would consider military action against the bombers, if the bomb was found to have been planted by a terrorist group. "The most imprudent thing a responsible official can do is discuss what kind of action would be taken or would not be taken," he said. "That would be imprudent and I wouldn't do that."

St. Petersburg Times

St. Petersburg, FL,
December 23, 1988

News that a Pan American jumbo jet had crashed in Scotland did not come as a total surprise to everyone. Not to the terrorists who probably sabotaged it. Not to the anonymous caller who earlier this month had warned a U.S. embassy of just such a plot. And not to the numerous American officials who knew of the threat but had not told the public.

There are good reasons, of course, for civil aviation authorities not to divulge every bomb threat they receive. Experience teaches that such publicity only encourages more threats.

But there must have been something different about the call that was received Dec. 5 at the U.S. embassy at Helsinki. The State Department acknowledges that it warned that a bomb would be carried "unwittingly" aboard a Pan American flight from Frankfurt. CBS News, quoting anonymous sources, said the caller even specified that a Finnish woman would be involved and that the Abu Nidal terrorist organization would be responsible. The State Department took the threat seriously enough that it not only notified the airline industry but posted warnings to employees at all American embassies.

If the threat was taken seriously enough to warn diplomats who might fly that route, why was it not taken seriously enough to warn the public? Why did the Federal Aviation Administration expressly forbid Pan American from notifying the public? Was this yet another instance of the FAA looking out for the financial security of the airline industry instead of the safety of its passengers?

The families of those who died in the airplane and on the ground are entitled to unambiguous explanations. A congressional investigation would appear to be the most appropriate context. Among the other questions that should be answered to a moral certainty: What additional security precautions were taken in response to the threat?

Officials were insisting Thursday that it remains to be proved that the aircraft was sabotaged or that the Dec. 5 warning was related. Legally, that's correct. But the coincidences speak loudly for themselves.

Protecting aircraft from all sabotage is a daunting task. How to be certain? The first thing is to empty the plane and search every seat, compartment and crevice. Then search the passengers and their luggage, person by person and bag by bag. Then call in the bomb-sniffing dogs and search again. To do that with every flight would mean inconvenience and delays that the public would find unacceptable. For the reasons noted, airline officials would not want to say how often they have been doing it. However often, it now seems that it was not often enough.

THE ARIZONA REPUBLIC
Phoenix, AZ, December 23, 1988

ALTHOUGH the evidence is preliminary and speculative, indications point to an on-board explosion as the probable cause of the mid-flight destruction of Pan Am Flight 103.

There is, of course, no want of potential perpetrators of such an atrocity — a radical faction of the Palestine Liberation Organization wanting to embarrass the newly moderate Yasser Arafat, a renegade Shiite group seeking revenge for the downing of an Iranian airliner by the *USS Vincennes*, the Irish Republican Army, which has a tradition of Christmastime barbarism. The list is long.

A previously uncelebrated Iranian group — the Guardians of the Islamic Revolution — has taken credit for the attack, and the U.S. State Department has confirmed that it had warnings of a December attack on Pan Am. But such threats are common, and terrorist groups, hoping to enhance their reputations, habitually claim responsibility for such disasters.

The aircraft's mid-air disintegration, however, seems more consistent with an explosion than with some undetected structural failure. If the Anglo-American investigation turns up evidence that Pan Am 747 was blown out of the sky by a suitcase full of plastique, the incident will demonstrate a disquieting truth about terrorism: no matter how good the security, a few trained and determined terrorists occasionally will slip through.

The Pan Am flight, which departed Heathrow for New York, originated in Frankfurt. The flight entailed a change of planes and the transfer of baggage in Great Britain. Both Britain and West Germany have had more than their share of experience with terrorism, and security arrangements at Frankfurt and Heathrow are among the best in the world.

It is impossible, however, to render open societies invulnerable to terrorist attack. Good intelligence can sniff out many terrorist operations before they begin, and beefed-up security can make terrorism more difficult. The most efficient way to attack terrorism, however, is through tactics the West, with rare exceptions, has been unwilling to employ.

The modern international terrorist cannot operate effectively without the sanctuary and support of sympathetic governments. Because they had lacked the logistical base enjoyed by the PLO's Abu Nidal faction in Syria or the Hezbollah group in Iran and Lebanon, such European terrorist cells as the Baader-Meinhof Gang and the Red Brigades have been all but wiped out.

With the exception of President Reagan's bombing of Libya — which effectively subdued Col. Moammar Khadafy's deadly friends — Western powers have permitted the terrorists to rest easy in their sanctuaries while planning new atrocities. Until these terrorists are run to ground, the West can only lick its wounds, comfort the afflicted and mourn the needless loss of life.

THE ☀ SUN
Baltimore, MD, December 23, 1988

The spectacular fall of a Pan Am jumbo jet onto a sleepy village in Scotland has intruded the ugly fear of terrorism where Christmas joy should have been for thousands of American and European families. Flight 103 mysteriously disappeared from British radar screens about the same time people on the ground in Scotland saw bright flashes in the sky, pointing to an explosion. Only a catastrophic event could shut off power to the Boeing 747's radar transponder, experts say, and a mid-air collision has been ruled out. Investigators are still not sure, but reports of a caller announcing the imminent placing of a bomb aboard a Pan Am flight from Frankfurt two weeks ago have turned all eyes toward the terrorist threat.

Speculation has centered on whether U.S. authorities should have warned the public as well the airline when the threat occurred. In hindsight, it sounds like a fair demand, but prudence demands a more sober look. Such threats are, after all, not uncommon. Telling the public to avoid Pan Am flights from Frankfurt could just as well have played into a terrorist's hands. The sort of people who secret bombs onto private airliners and kill hundreds of civilians are not above using panic as a weapon, or even targeting another airline after scaring people toward its flights. Allowing anonymous callers to speak so directly to the public may thus put too much power into the hands of those least likely to act in a responsible manner.

Investigators are still probing the charred remains of the downed airliner and its passengers in the bloodied village of Lockerbie, Scotland, and have not ruled out the possibility that an accident caused the crash after all. And if terrorism is finally determined to be the cause, that will strengthen, not weaken, the requirement for a calm examination of what can be done to lessen its hazards.

Civilized men and women do not inflict bloody tragedy on innocent people whose activities bear little relation to their grievances. Security can be tightened at air terminals in efforts to trap those who are willing to create such carnage, and police agencies can try to identify the groups behind them. But millions of people take to the skies every day in the United States alone, and thousands more fly trans-ocean routes regularly. Security can never be air-tight, nor can criminal minds be prevented from inventing ever more devious schemes to get around it.

For now, all that can be done is to recover the bodies and offer condolences to the families, American, Scottish and British, of the hundreds killed in the air and those lost on the ground. Their holidays have been ruined horribly, scarred with memories that will return year after year, and no condolences can change that. Such a tragedy dims the spirit of the nation when it should be shining its brightest but this, too, shall pass. Decency must prevail in the end.

The Hutchinson News
Hutchinson, KS, December 23, 1988

Lockerbie, Scotland, was the site of the battle, but as Wednesday's Pan Am tragedy shows so clearly, most of the world is the war zone.

Whether the terrorists were Iranian fanatics or Palestinian fanatics, the result is tragedy reaching into the homes of virtually everyone in the civilized world.

In cities such as Buhler, where links to one of the victims is direct, the tragedy is compounded, for the community will grieve for neighbors it knows as well as for good people unknown.

The murders and the murderers are so despicable that most any rational person would be willing to step forward and throw the switch to execute the criminals involved. And that may be the only way that the war by the terrorists may be won.

First, however, the war against the terrorists must be started. And that will require far more than blind retaliation or United Nations resolutions of outrage.

An international commitment must be made to fight terrorism, whether it comes from the Palestinians, the Iranians, or the Irish Republican Army. That commitment obviously has not been made previously, and until it is made, the war against terrorism will succeed no more than the war against drugs has succeeded.

International intelligence gathering is essential, and must come with the support of decent governments who commit the resources needed and the supervision required to conduct civilized agencies.

The breeding grounds of international terrorism must be examined and corrected. Merely slaughtering today's heinous terrorists, if that were possible, would not win the war if the world continues to breed heinous terrorists with the same diseases.

Innocent bystanders are always killed in wars.

In the current war of international terrorists, however, there are no innocent bystanders.

We're all in the trenches, sharing today with one local family and the families of 280 others grief over the latest casualties.

ENVIRONMENT & POLLUTION:

Largest U.S. Oil Spill
Fouls Alaska Marine Habitat

The largest oil spill in U.S. history began at 12:04 a.m. Alaskan time (5:04 a.m. Eastern Standard Time) March 24 when the *Exxon Valdez*, loaded with 1,260,000 barrels of crude oil, ran aground on a reef in the Gulf of Alaska, 25 miles from Valdez, the southern terminal of the Alyeska pipeline.

The reef, Bligh Reef, was clearly marked on charts, and the 987-foot tanker was off course, with the third mate, and not the captain, at the helm. The whereabouts of the captain, Joseph Hazelwood, at the time of the accident was not immediately explained. The third mate, Gregory Cousins, was not certified to pilot the tanker in those waters, Prince William Sound, a channeled crossing studded with icebergs.

A Coast Guard investigator found "probable cause" to have the blood of the captain, the third mate and the helmsman tested for alcohol, it was announced March 25. The results, announced March 30, were that the captain had unacceptably high levels of alcohol in his blood even nine hours after the accident.

Efforts to contain the spill lagged from the start. "The initial response was inadequate and didn't match the planned, outlined response measures to be taken in a spill," Dennis Kelso, commissioner of the Alaska Department of Environmental Conservation, said March 25. "As of 24 hours into the spill, we stil haven't seen adequate containment."

Frank Iarossi, president of Exxon Shipping Co., which owned the *Exxon Valdez*, said March 25 that Exxon accepted full responsibility for the spill.

Estimates of the spill put it at 240,000 barrels. Another million barrels or so remained on the *Exxon Valdez* and was being siphoned off into a companion ship. But in the first two days, when calm seas prevailed, little was done to contain the spill, which quickly mounted to a 12-square-mile mass inside a 100-square-mile area containing smaller slicks.

Winds of 70 miles an hour hit the area March 27. Containment booms were ripped apart, and attempts to use a chemical cleaning agent on the oil were abandoned. The *Exxon Valdez* itself shifted 12 degrees overnight, causing fears of a breakup and loss of the rest of the oil into the sound.

President Bush March 28 dispatched a delegation of federal officials to the scene of the spill to survey the damage. "There is a sense that nobody is in charge there," a senior White House official remarked at the time. The slick, by then, had grown into a 40-mile-long patch, split into numerous fingers reaching out for the estuaries that harbored a multitude of marine life. The spill soiled islands and threatened the sound's $100 million-a-year fishing industry.

At the White House March 28, President Bush, announcing his team for an on-site inspection, was asked if the spill changed his position in support of exploratory oil drilling in the Alaska National Wildlife Refuge. Ten environmental groups, at a joint news conference the same day, urged the president to order an independent study on the possibility of developing the refuge without harm to the wildlife there.

Bush said he saw "no connection" on that point. They've been shipping oil out of there for a long, long time and never had anything of this magnitude or this concern," he said. "So the big thing is to correct it."

When the White House team reported back March 30, Bush called the oil spill "a major tragedy." But the administration decided against taking over the cleanup. Although it got off to a slow start, officials said, the cleanup was now proceeding well and a federal takeover would be "counterproductive."

Exxon official Iarossi was asked March 27 if the oil companies had been deceptive in their prior assurances of cleanup plans. When the pipeline and oil-port project was being debated, oil company officials had given assurances that action to contain a major spill would be underway within five hours of an accident, but it was two or three days after the *Exxon Valdez* ran aground before Exxon's part of the effort took shape. Iarossi said nobody had anticipated a spill of the magnitude that occurred.

Alaska state officials announced March 29 that they were beginning a criminal investigation of the accident.

Arkansas Gazette

Little Rock, AR, March 29, 1989

Big Oil's Big Spill in Alaska has happened, as many concerned about the environment had dreaded would be the case even before now. Exxon's shipping people are busy trying to clean up the 100-square-mile slick after a slow start, and no doubt its public relations people are scrambling full speed ahead to control the political damage.

Even though the odds have favored a major environmental disaster since the opening of the North Slope fields, there is no reason this particular accident should have happened. So far, the investigation is concentrating on crew error as a possible cause, but the National Transportation Safety Board should not ignore the possibility that some blame could rest with those much higher in the petroleum giant, even those with policy responsibilities.

The 987-foot tanker, the Exxon Valdez, left the shipping lanes last Friday to avoid ice but ran aground on a charted reef in Prince William Sound after leaving the port of Valdez with 1.2 million barrels of oil from the North Slope. About 240,000 barrels of the crude were released into the sound. Grave threat is posed to wildlife and fish. Even if the spill is quickly contained the damaging effects will be felt for many years.

Monetary damages will be in the tens of millions of dollars, and unfortunately these costs will be widely shared. Already gasoline consumers throughout the rest of the country have seen prices rise simply because sellers jump in anticipation, or on the fiction, of an oil shortage. It is true that 20 percent of domestic production is from the North Slope, but shipments through Valdez have been resumed after only three or four days.

Big Oil has been getting a relatively smooth ride on environmental issues in recent years, but it — or Exxon — will have a lot of explaining to do after this incident. Congress simply must take a closer look at the proposal to allow exploration in the Arctic National Wildlife Refuge on a coastal plain east of the North Slope oil fields. President Bush already has given his approval — if the drilling can be done within environmental guidelines.

Sen. Max Baucus of Montana, chairman of the Senate environmental protection subcommittee, has raised a welcome and proper flag of caution:

"Unfortunately the oil spill . . . is the latest and most tragic evidence of the gap that exists between past industry assurances and actual industry performance in preventing environmental damage."

A heavy burden of proof showing there will be no environmental damage rests on the shoulders of Big Oil before the nation dare allow intrusions in the Arctic National Wildlife Refuge.

The Houston Post
Houston, TX, March 29, 1989

EXXON CORP. CERTAINLY HAS its hands full trying to contain a giant oil spill in Prince William Sound, appease environmentalists, and answer questions about what happened.

The big question facing the oil company is how this 10.1-million-gallon, 100-square-mile spill occurred. Who is to blame for this horror that has fouled beaches on four uninhabited islands, and is threatening sensitive salmon-spawning areas as well as the region's abundant herring, marine mammals and seabirds? An even bigger question is how any similar spill can be prevented in the future.

What happened? According to Exxon officials, Exxon Valdez Capt. Joseph Hazelwood was not on the bridge when the vessel left shipping lanes to avoid ice and ran aground. The third mate, who did not have certification to pilot the ship at night in those waters, was in charge. Right now, authorities are investigating reports that Hazelwood had drinking problems. "We look at all areas in an investigation and that's an area of concern," National Transportation Safety Board spokesman Bill Woody said of reports that Hazelwood has had a a history of drunken driving convictions.

Hazelwood probably will be required to testify at hearings that begin April 4, but investigators said the results of drug and alcohol tests on crew members may be made public in two or three days.

The harbor was finally reopened yesterday and a fleet of tankers anchored offshore moved in to pick up oil for the first time since the biggest spill in U.S. history closed the port at the southern end of the Alaskan pipeline on Friday.

President Bush said the federal government would consider taking over the cleanup after top officials travel to Alaska "to take a hard look at where this disaster stands." That might be a good idea. Exxon needs all the help it can get cleaning up this mess. And the federal government should look into some possible regulations that might help prevent this type of disaster from occurring again.

Toronto, Ont., March 31, 1989

This reality dwarfs fiction. The Alaskan oil spill drooling its killer path down the West Coast reads like a script that would be rejected if someone tried to sell it to Hollywood.

But it's real enough, an environmental nightmare that is also an indictment of an oil giant.

As the story oozes out, Exxon's negligence and incompetence staggers the mind even as it brutalizes an ocean.

It's incomprehensible given the concern for the environment on the lips of the whole world.

Mega corporations were supposed to have been whipped into ship shape by heightened public concern about our vulnerable environment.

But Exxon has acted like a throwback to an era when big companies used all the world as a garbage dump.

How better to measure Exxon's callous irresponsibility than to consider its massive tanker was captained by a man who hasn't been able to drive a car because of a drinking problem.

And he was asleep while a ship the length of three football fields was being guided through dangerous waters by an unqualified third mate.

Exxon took charge of the cleanup after the largest spill in American history and has botched that too.

There are larger questions. The U.S. government was warned spills were inevitable when it approved the dangerous tanker route. So why was it not ready to initiate an instant massive cleanup?

Alaska has launched a criminal investigation. From here, it looks like they won't want for targets. They have a shooting gallery full. We want them to blaze away.

After all, words and warnings haven't managed to climb the Olympian heights of Exxon management. The huge bills for beach cleanups and fishermen's claims may stop Exxon from falling asleep again.

But President George Bush should also be on notice.

He should be oiling his environmental protection agencies to assure it never happens again. Because no matter how much is spent now, another beautiful nook in the world has been ruined by carelessness and concern for the almighty bottom line.

Times-Colonist
Victoria, B.C. , March 28, 1989

While there was a healthy dollop of politicking in Premier Vander Zalm's well-publicized weekend plane trip to Alaska to see the largest oil spill in U.S. history, it's good that he went and it would be even better if he proves sincere in his claim that after seeing this disaster for himself, "now I'm wary about oil tankers."

That fresh concern prompted Vander Zalm to ask deputy environment minister Richard Dalon to review oil shipments along the coast and to take a new look at allowing oil drilling off the B.C. coast.

Andrew Thompson, former head of the West Coast Oil Ports inquiry, dismissed Vander Zalm's apparent conversion as "grandstanding," noting that oil tankers come under federal jurisdiction. NDP opposition leader Mike Harcourt called the premier's trip useless.

The criticism is ironic. Just three months ago, when oil from a Washington coast spill was beginning to foul Vancouver Island beaches, environmental groups and opposition critics roasted B.C. Environment Minister Bruce Strachan for not hurrying off to check the damage for himself, and roundly condemned him for trying to justify his inaction on grounds that B.C. had no jurisdiction in the matter.

Jurisdiction or not, B.C. and Washington state have since formed a joint Task Force on Oil Spills, and representatives from the group (Dalon, who is task force chairman, and Fred Olson of the Washington state department of ecology) were with Vander Zalm on his inspection trip, as was Provincial Emergency Program director Murray Stewart.

The fact that Vander Zalm also convinced Alaska to join the task force (Dalon stayed behind to work out the details) made the trip worthwhile. But while his boss was making some good moves, Strachan was once again noticeable by his absence. For that matter, federal Environment Minister Lucien Bouchard hadn't been heard from by Monday, nor was there any sign that any of our federal officials made it to Alaska.

It's unfortunate that these key men in environmental protection couldn't drop whatever else they were doing to take a first-hand look at the tragedy off Valdez and see to it that their technical experts learn all they can from this painful lesson. While some research has been done into how oil behaves when it's dumped into the ocean, the oil spill at Grays Harbor, Wash., just three months ago was a potent reminder that much needs to be learned.

As for U.S. Coast Guard assurances that the Valdez spill won't likely spread to Canadian waters, it's worth recalling a week after the Grays Harbor spill, 150 kilometres south of Victoria, officials declared the oil had dissipated and virtually stopped washing ashore, with hardly a trace left on the beaches. Within two days, it became apparent that the oil was drifting north and fouling Washington state and Vancouver Island beaches.

The oil spill task force was a good idea; lifting the moratorium on offshore oil exploration was not. And Vander Zalm should make note of one of Harcourt's better suggestions — promotion of an international team approach to coping with oil disasters.

The oil tanker companies can pay the bills.

Chinese Troops Crush Pro-democracy Protests

Tens of thousands of Chinese army troops, supported by tanks and armored personnel carriers, swept into downtown Beijing June 3-4 to crush a student-led pro-democracy movement that had begun in mid-April. (See pp. 560-569.)

The bloody military crackdown, which came two weeks after the government had imposed martial law in Beijing, provoked a wave of antigovernment sentiment in the capital and numerous other Chinese cities, and was harshly condemned by nations around the world.

Although casualty figures were difficult to verify, the Western press estimated that at least several hundred and possibly as many as 5,000 people were killed in the nighttime assault and its aftermath, and that as many as 10,000 others were injured. The casualties included both protesters and soldiers, as well as civilian bystanders caught up in the disorder. Official Chinese accounts of the incident, presented variously by military and government spokesmen, were contradictory. The official statements listed death tolls ranging from zero to 300, with most of the casualties reported to be soldiers.

In the days immediately following the crackdown, there were persistent reports in the Western press that rival Chinese army units were facing off against one another, sparking fears that the country was headed toward civil war. The uncertainty surrounding the loyalty of the military appeared to indicate that the ongoing leadership struggle at the top of the Communist Party – reportedly involving China's paramount leader, Deng Ziaoping, Premier Li Peng, President Yang Shangkun and the party's general secretary, Zhao Ziyang – had yet to be resolved.

Contributing to the sense of uncertainty in China was the fact that none of the nation's top leaders had appeared in public for at least a week, leaving outside observers in the dark as to who was running the country. Rumors were widely circulated among Chinese in the capital that Deng was in the hospital near death from cancer or had already died. Other reports asserted that Premier Li Peng had been shot by one of his guards in an attempted assasination. Western press and diplomatic sources said the rumors were impossible to confirm or discount.

Shortly after midnight June 3, somewhere between 2,000 and 10,000 unarmed soldiers began a march down a central thoroughfare in the capital, headed toward Tiananmen Square. The move appeared to be an attempt to clear the vast 100-acre square of protesters without using force. The soldiers advanced to within several hundred yards of the square but then found their path blocked by tens of thousands of jeering students and workers.

The confrontation with the unarmed troops seemed to revive the pro-democracy movement. Hundreds of thousands of people in the capital poured into the streets during the morning of June 3 to show their support for the protesters. The wild celebration by citizens was short-lived, however, as new clashes broke out at midday between demonstrators and soldiers and police.

According to Western press accounts, which were sketchy and sometimes contradictory, the all-out military assault against the protesters began about midnight June 4. Dozens of tanks and armored personnel carriers and thousands of combat troops armed with automatic rifles and machine guns moved toward the central square from several points around the city. Civilians once again moved to block the army units from reaching the square but, unlike previous occasions, the troops did not back down. The confrontations, most of which took place within a 10-block radius of the square, quickly turned bloody as soldiers first fired warning shots into the air above the demonstrators' heads and then began firing directly into the crowd.

At 7:40 a.m., the government announced that "the rebellion has been suppressed and the soldiers are now in charge" of the square.

Chicago Tribune

Chicago, IL, June 5, 1989

To comprehend the slaughter conducted in Beijing's Tienanmen Square over the weekend, the place to begin is not in the news accounts, the thoughts of Chairman Mao or even Chinese history. The best explanation came in the nightmare vision of George Orwell's "1984": "If you want a picture of the future, imagine a boot stamping on a human face—forever."

That was the picture the world saw of Chinese communism, and a horrific picture it was: Troops firing AK-47s indiscriminately into crowds. Students lying in their tents, crushed beneath the treads of army tanks. A girl who has just heard that her brother has been killed, running toward a line of soldiers, who riddle her with bullets even after she has fallen to the ground. Many hundreds, perhaps thousands, died; many hundreds more lay wounded.

Amid the atrocities, there were inspiring acts of courage, defiance and compassion: Unarmed students seizing an abandoned tank and adorning its turrets with flags reading "Democracy" and "Freedom." A crowd facing the soldiers, chanting, "Fascists! Fascists!" Doctors, their mouths red with blood, frantically giving artificial respiration to victims.

In all the tense anticipation of how the occupation of Teinanmen Square might end, no one imagined how savage it would be. The Chinese movement for democracy had been so gentle, so reasoned, so just, that it hardly seemed possible it could be crushed.

The people cut down by the army were armed with nothing more than fire bombs and rocks, taken up only after the assault had begun; most of them weren't armed at all. The danger they presented was not of disorder and violence. It was of awakening the imaginations of their fellow Chinese.

In that the protesters triumphed. From a spontaneous march following the death of a favorite party leader in April, the demonstrations swelled with each day into one the most authentic mass movements in Chinese history.

But flames can be snuffed, and this one may have been. The last hope of the movement was that when they were ordered to attack the protesters, the soldiers of the People's Army would refuse. But they obeyed. As long as the party and the army are united against the people, the people can be suppressed.

In responding to what has happened, the United States needs to act strongly but not recklessly. No one in China should have any doubt that our government and people are on the side of the movement for democracy. One way Washington can dramatize its feelings is to stop selling arms to the regime.

But broad economic sanctions probably would be a mistake. What brought China out of the dark ages of Mao Zedong's rule was its opening to the West. Thousands of Chinese have gone abroad as students; millions have been exposed to foreign news and foreign thinking; countless numbers have been captivated by the democracy and liberty they have heard about. The key to fostering democracy is keeping China open to commerce in goods and ideas.

By turning so violently against its own people, the regime has forfeited any pretense that it rules by popular consent. It has given vivid proof that China needs a radical change in its government. Eventually, it will have to pay for its crime.

At midnight Saturday, a 28-year-old man who supported the students, bleeding from a stomach wound, looked up at a foreign reporter and gasped, "Look at me and think." The world and the Chinese people have looked, and they cannot help but think.

St. Paul Pioneer Press & Dispatch

St. Paul, MN, June 13, 1989

The cosmic storm building between the United States and China over dissident Fang Lizhi promises to thunder through the human rights community with massive force. The United States must refuse to hand over Dr. Fang to the witchhunters in Beijing or risk all moral credibility.

The Chinese government on Sunday ordered the arrests of Dr. Fang, an astrophysicist, and his wife, Li Shuxian, for what authorities said were counterrevolutionary activities — that is, supporting the democracy movement. The two prominent dissidents sought refuge in the U.S. Embassy in Beijing after the unthinkable massacre happened June 4 in Tiananmen Square.

The United States has been riding a fine line well in relations with China since senior leader Deng Xiaoping and his elderly cohorts abrogated the rule of law so carefully built up over the last decade. It is wise to try to salvage what is possible for when the bloody purges and hatemongering give way to renewed reason at some imponderable time in the future.

Dr. Fang's plight, however, is real and it is happening now. The Bush administration must continue to protect him. There are no foreseeable circumstances in this tangled tale that would warrant turning the dissident over to the vengeful Chinese authorities.

In some ways the Fang case is a simplistic symbol of chaos the Chinese old guard has unleashed on its people. But it is a valid symbol, one that the world is watching.

None knows better than the prominent astrophysicist that, to borrow the Chinese idiom, there is great havoc under heaven.

Edmonton Journal

Edmonton, Alta., June 5, 1989

The Beijing Spring is over, but China's long march to democracy is not.

The weekend massacre in Tiananmen Square will in no way advance the position of China's government, or of the old guard who now appear to control it.

Indeed, it is difficult to imagine that the slaughter will do anything other than enrage and inspire the millions of Chinese who took the streets during the month of protests for democracy.

By killing the people whose trust it claims to exercise, China's government has lost its legitimacy.

It no longer has a moral or ethical basis on which to govern, it may rule only by the brute force of arms — provided it can continue to find soldiers willing to slaughter unarmed civilians.

There can be no justification, no mitigation, for the bloodshed in Tiananmen Square. The democracy movement in the square was singular for its nonviolence. In the face of past attempts by soldiers to enforce martial law, thousands of people used their bodies to block the military advance. Even then, there had been no attempt to escalate the confrontation into bloodshed.

The violence began only when an old man on his sickbed decided that enough was enough. Deng Xiaoping, supreme leader of China, suffering from cancer, reverted to the habit of a lifetime in ordering the armed assault that cleared the square — at a cost of several hundred lives.

The images of people crushed by the tanks, shot by random machine-gun fire, stand in stark contrast to the pacifism of the protesters during the month the square was occupied. Only days ago, soldiers of the People's Liberation Army joined the demonstrators, singing along with them, accepting flowers and flashing peace signs.

The soldiers who carried out Deng's order were from outside the Beijing military command. But their act has wrought a fundamental change in revolutionary China. Since 1949, the military has enjoyed a special status because its title reflected its role — the People's Liberation Army.

Now the army of liberation becomes an army of oppression, the army of the people is turned against the people. How many soldiers will accept the new situation? Only a fortnight ago, 100 senior military commanders in the Beijing region denounced martial law. How can Deng and his supporters hope to maintain the loyalty of the entire army? And without it, how can they hope to maintain control over a country of a billion people?

The propaganda line after the massacre was that the army moved in to restore order and had the support of the students and of the population at large. But in an age of mass media, this facade soon will unravel.

Having gone this far, Deng and his supporters will have no choice but to maintain an authoritarian course. They clearly have rejected any negotiations or popular reform. But the hardliners are in a hopeless position. They may maintain power for a few months or perhaps at best a few years. By ordering in the army, they have signed the death warrant of the *ancien regime*. In this, at least, the people of Tiananmen Square did not die in vain.

Calgary Herald

Calgary, Alta., June 6, 1989

Chinese students began occupying Tiananmen Square in April with but one demand — a public dialogue with China's Communist leadership to discuss political reform.

China's old guard blurted out their unequivocal answer Sunday and punctuated it with machine-gun fire in the dark.

Savagely, senselessly, China's hardliners chose to shoot blindly rather than talk with their own people. With estimates of the dead varying from several hundred to several thousand, it was a textbook display of reactionary repression.

Thomas Jefferson wrote in 1787, "The tree of liberty must be refreshed from time to time with the blood of patriots and tyrants. It is its natural manure."

China's tree of liberty was last weekend freshened only with the blood of patriots. The tyrants shed nothing. Not even crocodile tears.

The brutal arrogance of Chinese troops bears a chilling resemblance to the conduct of Soviet troops who rolled into Budapest to squelch a popular movement in 1956.

The difference, however, is that the Chinese massacre cannot be summed up neatly as a clash between capitalist and communist ideology.

Quite simply, this bloodbath was sanctioned because China's old guard leaders felt threatened. Like tin-pot dictators the world over, Deng Xiaoping chose the military solution.

No matter how reasonable, pacifist or patriotic the students actually were, they were perceived to be a threat. Deng would not deign to acknowledge one single demand. Like the emperors and warlords before him, he chose brute force over dialogue.

But should the 84-year-old live long enough, he is certain to discover that his solution is really no solution at all.

The outrage of the international community is nothing compared to the bitter seed he has planted among his own people. Feelings of wrath and betrayal are sure to dog Deng and his successors. One 36-year-old Communist party official put it this way, "We don't want to overthrow the government, but we never thought the government could be so inhumane."

Chinese yearning for a freer society and less corruption by their Communist leaders will be able to point to the Soviet model.

Mikhail Gorbachev has recognized that the Soviet Union could not achieve economic reforms without political reforms, too. Deng, who has been successful in opening up China's vast market to trade and investment, must come to the same realization.

His administration is not fighting "the dregs of society" but intelligent, articulate young people with a hankering for free thoughts and free speech.

The Chinese army has trashed the student uprising and wrecked their papier mache goddess of liberty. But like Jefferson's tree, the blood spilled has not slaked the Chinese people's thirst for reform.

Arkansas Gazette

Little Rock, AR, June 6, 1989

The bloody military assault in Beijing must be deplored and condemned among all civilized peoples, as it already has been by most of Chinese society. A government so shaky that it turns guns and tanks on its own people surely cannot sustain legitimacy.

Even from the government's point of view the decision to order loyal troops against unarmed, peacefully demonstrating students in Tiananmen Square makes no sense. What support the government still had after weeks of demonstrations for democracy and freedom within the system already in place surely has greatly dissipated.

If the hard-line faction can continue to rule at all, it will be only by the force of arms, bringing more bloody confrontation and tragedy on a truly heroic scale. The calls for reform issue from the nation's young people, its future. They cannot be denied for long, although in the short term their prospects for reshaping the political, economic and social order of their homeland are bleak. More bloodshed lurks grimly in the wings.

What can the United States and other nations do? Unfortunately, not nearly as much as their emotional response to brutal slaughter tugs at them to do. In time, sharper and more dramatic steps might be in order, but for now it is hard to find fault with President Bush's initial moves. For the time being there will be no break in diplomatic relations, on the sound reasoning that in a popular struggle for freedom and democracy a continuing American presence might be helpful to those whose cause we champion.

Events could shift dramatically. China's military is known for its factions; earlier contingents sent to Tiananmen Square were reluctant to move against the students and older sympathizers.

★　★　★

In one small step, Bush yesterday suspended all military sales to China and visits to the United States by Chinese military leaders. Chinese students in the United States who wish to extend their stay here will be looked upon favorably by American officials.

These and other measures may be sufficient for the moment, but if the violence escalates and persists, American interests would be the same as those who represent China's democratic future. If the Soviet Union is as committed to sweeping, peaceful change within its own country as it seems to be, it too would be obligated to align itself with China's future.

In the meantime, America's heart must go out to those who thirst so much for democracy that they, like their fallen comrades, may have to pay a dear price in its solemn pursuit.

The Register-Guard

Eugene, OR, June 6, 1989

Deng Xiaoping blew it. He turned the last chapter of his own career from a triumph into a travesty. And he imposed on the nation he leads an appalling, utterly pointless tragedy.

The students in Tiananmen Square were a military threat to no one. They had no guns or knives. Their weapons were words and ideas — often confused, always idealistic, ideas — but still only that. The students did not deserve to be shot by soldiers and crushed by tanks as their punishment for refusing to leave a public square.

This enormously sad moment for China spoils what had been a time of hope. Deng had turned the country around economically, pushing marketplace pragmatism and abandoning many of the controls that had stifled progress in the factories and the fields. This part of the drive toward modernism had worked well, even though imperfectly.

But many had commented earlier that the old warrior/politician did not have *political* modernism in his repertoire. He could no more give up authoritarianism than stop smoking. That analysis received shocking confirmation over the weekend.

It's true, of course, that the students had attracted massive support throughout the country. That undoubtedly frightened the leaders, chiefly men who have been in charge since China's Communist revolution. Although the specific thoughts of "the people" in support of the student demonstrations were in some ways vague and unformed, there was no doubt about a strong, shared criticism of those in power.

At the same time, it was absurd for the government to try to excuse sending in armed troops on the ground that protest leaders were counterrevolutionaries plotting to overthrow the government. Some of the official government statements issued after the shooting resembled the statements Southern sheriffs and politicians used to make about "communists" and "outside agitators" secretly controlling the civil rights movement.

What will happen now? There is bound to be a national wave of revulsion against the government for the massacre of civilians. That could manifest itself in a variety of ways; widespread strikes are likely. In any case, the reaction of the people will not make governing the nation easy.

Even an authoritarian government must have a minimum level of acceptance among the governed. So ultimately, this experience will discredit China's present generation of leaders and hasten the installation of successors who can claim at least some distance from the Tiananmen Square decision-making.

In the meantime, the old men still in power face hostility at home and condemnation abroad. Against that background, the inevitable jockeying among them will add to the national instability that their misguided resort to violence has produced.

THE SAGINAW NEWS

Saginaw, MI, June 5, 1989

The people of China re-learned a hard lesson. Raw power does grow out of the barrel of a gun.

The leaders of China may yet learn another — that of an idea whose time has come.

Over the weekend, the tanks of desperation, not the times of democracy, prevailed.

"Don't shoot the people," pleaded the crowds in Tiananmen Square. The soldiers shot the people. The army listened instead to a ruling elite that failed to understand that the streets were full not of chaos, but of hope.

In a massive betrayal of the masses themselves, China's government crushed China's people. In a contradiction of the party tenets the protesters espoused — some died singing the "Internationale," the Communist hymn — the clear will of students, farmers, workers, even bureaucrats, disappeared into a storm of gas and bullets.

Few thought it would end this way. The demonstrators were peaceful, even patriotic. Armed only with the desire for a better future, they asked for nothing more than the chance to achieve it.

But something snapped in Premier Li Peng, himself the victim of atrocities during the days of Red Guard terror. And as the crowds heeded a warning that "We can't let any more blood flow," armor toppled the figure called the "goddess of democracy," modeled on the Statue of Liberty.

Statues can be brought down; not so easily can a national spirit be quelled. If the brutality augurs a new period of suppression, then a mighty nation of a billion people must wait a little longer to assert its might. These seven weeks showed, however, from every corner of China, a new mood that can be put down, but not kept down.

It was Mao who said, "To be attacked by the enemy is not a bad thing, but a good thing." At least the real enemy of the people of China has identified itself, and must stare down the barrel of a power that cannot, sooner or later, be denied.

The London Free Press

London, Ont., June 5, 1989

June 1, 1989, should long live as a day of infamy in Chinese history — the day when soldiers in Beijing's Tiananmen square opened fire with tanks, machine guns and rifles on thousands of relatively unarmed civilians calling for freedom and democracy.

The world has not seen any act of political repression quite so ferocious since Soviet tanks moved through the streets of Budapest in 1956, gunning down hundreds of Hungarian freedom fighters. In the case of China, though, it's a horrible case of fratricide: Chinese soldiers killing Chinese citizens at the command of their own Chinese authorities.

Appropriately enough, External Affairs Minister Joe Clark quickly called in the Chinese ambassador on Sunday to express the outrage of Canadians and call upon the Chinese government to stop "the aggressive and senseless killing by its armed forces." Similar statements have come from U.S. President George Bush and the leaders of all the other genuine multi-party democracies. Perhaps, the tough old men commanding the troops in Beijing will pay little heed, but it's enough that the brave students who occupied Tiananmen square will hear and be encouraged.

In addition, Immigration Minister Barbara McDougall should make plain that Chinese students attending school in Canada are welcome to stay in this country so long as the current turmoil persists. Here is a clear and compelling case for a major exemption from the generally valid rule that refugee claimants must apply from outside the country.

Correspondingly, the Bush administration should also offer sanctuary to the thousands of Chinese students studying in the U.S. and immediately cut off military aid to the Beijing regime. There is no reason to fear that vigorous measures to denounce the atrocities in Beijing will force the Chinese government back into a closer embrace with the Soviet Union. Regardless of ideology, any Chinese leader will want to keep his distance from Moscow in order to protect China's independent national interests.

What will happen next in China? No one can know for sure, but it's evident that government officials have to be concerned that they have lost almost all respect among the Chinese people.

Mao Tse-tung, the first ruler of Communist China, was notorious for insisting that power came out of the barrel of a gun, but he also inspired a great many gun-toting people with a fanatical belief in Communist idealism. That faith is now dead; it remains to be seen how long his successors can cling to power by brute force alone.

Las Vegas Review-Journal

Las Vegas, NV, June 6, 1989

The geriatric leaders of the "People's" Republic of China have reared up to smite the Chinese people, and all hopes for a peaceful transition to a more democratic form of government have been brutally crushed.

Although the hopes for a peaceful transition have vanished, it is still possible that democratic-minded forces will prevail — but only after a violent upheaval that depends on elements of the army taking the side of pro-democracy protesters. Indeed, reports out of China Monday suggested internecine fighting within the army, perhaps presaging full-blown civil war or a sustained rebellion against the communist leadership. Alas, Chinese democracy is not destined to be born without a mighty struggle.

As we watch the unfolding of what promises to be one of the major historical events of the 20th century, it is essential that the United States be on the right side of that history.

The butchery in Tiananmen Square deserves America's forceful condemnation. We support the call by Nevada Sens. Harry Reid, Richard Bryan and a bipartisan collection of others in Congress to condemn the brutality and — at the very least — cut off weapons sales to the Chinese government. The United States does have a major strategic stake in maintaining good relations with China; but to avert our faces at the bloodbath in Beijing would be unconscionable.

China represents a fascinating case study in what happens when a communist nation begins to abandon the Marxist economic model. Communist rulers always have justified repression of basic human rights by arguing that other "rights" — i.e. Marxist economic "rights" — take precedence over the bourgeois rights of free speech, free assembly, etc., enjoyed in the Western democracies.

When a communist state essentially admits Marxist economic theory has failed, and when it begins to dismantle the economic superstructure of Marxism — as China has during the 1980s — it loses any "justification" for dictatorship. In essence, when a communist state abandons communist economic theory, it becomes nothing but an old-line dictatorship, no different from any other run-of-the-mill tyranny. Socialist theories are chucked into the slop bucket and all that remains to sustain the dictatorship is naked power.

Mao said: "Every communist must grasp the truth: Political power grows out of the barrel of a gun." And so the students in Tiananmen Square have learned.

EASTERN EUROPE:

East Germany Opens Borders, Including Berlin Wall

East Germany Nov. 9 announced relaxation of restrictions on the travel and immigration of its citizens to the West. The action virtually opened the country's borders, including the Berlin Wall. (See pp. 1280-1285)

The announcement climaxed a week of monumental developments. During the period Nov. 2-8, East German leader Egon Krenz visited Moscow and Warsaw, more than half a million people staged a pro-democracy protest in East Berlin, as many as 50,000 East Germans fled to West Germany through Czechoslovakia, the East German government resigned, the Politburo of the ruling Socialist Unity (Communist) Party was purged, a reformist was named premier and the regime suggested a willingness to hold free elections.

Krenz, the successor to ousted hard-line leader Erich Honecker, exhibited surprising flexibility as he struggled with rising demands for change.

The West – trying to adapt to the dizzying pace of liberalization in the U.S.S.R., Poland and Hungary – was caught off guard by the developments in East Germany, once the embodiment of uncompromising orthodox communism. (See 1986, pp. 902-907)

The East German government Nov. 9 lifted the restrictions that had curbed legal travel and immigration to the West. East Germans no longer required special permission from the state for private journeys or emigration. Exit visas were to be issued "immediately" to those who wanted them.

"Permanent emigration is allowed across all border crossing points between East Germany and West Germany and West Berlin," the announcement said.

Some Western observers believed the East Berlin regime hoped to stem the flight to West Germany by using reverse psychology: If people knew they were free to leave, perhaps they would decide to stay.

Within hours of the announcement, thousands of jubilant East Germans and West Germans met at the Berlin Wall for an impromptu celebration that lasted into Nov. 10.

Near the historic Brandenburg Gate, hundreds of youths from both countries danced atop the wall without interference from East Germany's border guards. Many curious East Berliners crossed through the wall's checkpoints simply by showing their identity cards to the sentries.

"The long-awaited day has arrived," said West Berlin Mayor Walter Momper Nov. 9. "The Berlin Wall no longer divides Berliners."

The wall had been the symbol of East-West divisions since its construction in 1961. Some people used hammers and chisels to chip pieces from the barrier, an action carried around the world in television coverage.

West German Chancellor Helmut Kohl, visiting Poland Nov. 9 welcomed the East German move: "It is hard to estimate what consequences this step will have. Our interest must be that our compatriots stay in their homeland."

U.S. President George Bush Nov. 9 hailed the development as a "dramatic happening for East Germany and, of course, for freedom." But he cautioned that it was too early to think in terms of German reunification.

Tens of thousands of East Germans poured into West Berlin Nov. 10 on foot and by car and special shuttle buses. They were greeted by thousands of West Berliners, who offered the visitors flowers, champagne and candy at the crossing points. The sounds of ringing church bells, honking car horns and singing filled the air. A holiday atmosphere prevailed on both sides of the wall. In West Berlin, long-separated friends and relatives were reunited in tearful scenes.

The vast majority of East Germans returned to their country. West German authorities estimated that 40,000 entered West Berlin Nov. 9-10, and that 1,500 had elected to stay on the western side.

The Phoenix Gazette
Phoenix, AZ, November 10, 1989

They danced in the streets of West Berlin Thursday night, as 28 years of infamous history melted away under the pressure of a subjugated population that no longer would submit to its masters.

In the end, the East German rulers discovered that the only way to keep their people in was to allow them to leave. More than 200,000 East Germans have left since January — more than 50,000 in the past week — in a population drain that threatens the country's basic industries.

"We know this need of citizens to travel or leave the country," said Guenter Schabowski, a member of the Politburo who made the dramatic announcement Thursday that unleashed 28 years of emotions. The East German government acted not out of generosity of spirit but because events forced it to take a desperate gamble; they've tried everything else, why not try a little freedom?

While the euphoria of the moment will shortly fade to the reality that East Germany has many serious problems that will not evaporate, give the Germans their celebration. They have certainly earned it, enduring for four decades in a divided nation occupied by the victors of World War II.

If any instant analysis is accurate, it most certainly is that the Postwar Era ended Thursday night as the Iron Curtain was shredded. Now we move into a new era, in which German reunification is a serious proposition rather than a useful propaganda slogan. This is uncharted territory.

Another analysis is that the crumbling of the communist bloc is continuing at a dizzying pace, driven by inescapable economic realities. East Germany erected a wall 28 years ago not to keep Westerners out of its people's paradise, but to hold its people in when the economic and political freedoms of West Germany proved so much more compelling than the drab deprivation of East Germany's failed communist state.

Readers often complain that the news is so unpleasant. They ask, "Isn't there any good news?" It is hard to imagine better news than the erosion of communism throughout Eastern Europe before our very eyes, and the recognition by tyrannical regimes that basic human freedoms must be acknowledged. Today there is good news, and it is on the front pages in big, black type.

Good news? This is more than that; it is an epochal change that will be in history books for future generations to study. And East Germans will tell their grandchildren of that magical night when the gates opened and they danced in the streets of Berlin, free once again after so long.

The Evening Gazette

Worcester, MA, November 12, 1989

Events in East Germany have been unfolding with such astonishing speed that we've found it impossible to comment on them in a timely fashion. Barely has one victory for freedom been won before the next made it old news.

But if history attaches a date on which the cold war finally ended, it is apt to be Nov. 10, 1989. That was the day when the Berlin Wall that oppression built was rendered obsolete by the forces of freedom.

What few people thought possible in their lifetime seemed so simple in the end: Scores of happy Germans from the East walked or drove across checkpoints to the West to enjoy the sights and sounds of the Kurfuersterdam, one of Europe's most elegant shopping avenues.

Some crossed over from the West for a look. As bewildered East German border guards looked on, others celebrated along the hated wall.

Not since Oct. 23, 1956, when a meeting of Hungarian students grew to a massive uprising within hours, has any popular movement been so swift and overwhelming. But unlike 1956, this time there was no rancor, no threats, no shots fired — only the people's uncontrollable desire to be free.

Nothing can overshadow the joy of that day. Yet the continuing disintegration of East Germany will pose a formidable challenge to the government in Bonn, to the Soviet Union, to the United States and its European allies. The disappearance of a communist buffer state between East and West will reshape the face of Europe and international politics.

But dealing with this challenge should be a happy task compared with enduring what the past offered. For Germans, Hungarians, Poles and others, nothing matters right now but the demise of the "wall of shame" and the promise of a brighter future.

The "leading rule of the Communist Party" in a large part of Europe is being replaced by a giant victory party shared by millions of people who are celebrating a dream come true.

The Hutchinson News

Hutchinson, KS, November 9, 1989

As the Iron Curtain continues to erode brick by brick, will a new, modern wall replace the fading one?

The ease with which East Germans are flooding into West Germany should not have surprised the Bonn government, which only now is realizing the economic and social burden that is coming with the tide.

At the confluence of the acceptance of East Germans and the West German resolve to provide them sanctuary is a growing intolerance reflected by the strain in the system and the fear that is beginning to rise among West Germans that these East German refugees may eventually become competitors.

Already about 175,000 people have made the trek from east to west in search of a less restrictive life under a more flexible and less rigid government.

West Germany, with 8 percent unemployment and a housing problem of its own, cannot for long tolerate the continuing migration of new refugees. This is the pragmatic and unfortunate truth to an adventure that has inspired hope among democratic nations throughout the world.

Chancellor Helmut Kohl's West German government should have anticipated the flood of refugees.

The Iron Curtain has split Germany since 1962 and has offered one half of that former unified population a repressive regime with little hope for change — until now.

If the flow continues — and there is no reason to doubt it won't — West Germans may embrace the extremes of nationalism and begin to place a new wall in the way of Germans seeking a new life in the West.

West Germans require much patience. Patience that East Germany will eventually reform sooner and not later. And that West Germany can withstand the economic and social burdens that come with being a sanctuary, as the United States has been, until reforms make life in the east more tolerable.

The resignation Tuesday of the entire 44-man East German Cabinet, bowing to pressure for reforms from East German citizens, ought to ease the concerns of worried West Germans.

But despite the swift changes taking place, it would be unfortunate if the growing tide of refugees causes West Germany to adopt restrictive policies regulating immigration, transforming itself — bit by bit — into a shape resembling the closed and oppressive regime its new refugees so recently escaped.

The Phoenix Gazette

Phoenix, AZ, November 10, 1989

They danced in the streets of West Berlin Thursday night, as 28 years of infamous history melted away under the pressure of a subjugated population that no longer would submit to its masters.

In the end, the East German rulers discovered that the only way to keep their people in was to allow them to leave. More than 200,000 East Germans have left since January — more than 50,000 in the past week — in a population drain that threatens the country's basic industries.

"We know this need of citizens to travel or leave the country," said Guenter Schabowski, a member of the Politburo who made the dramatic announcement Thursday that unleashed 28 years of emotions. The East German government acted not out of generosity of spirit but because events forced it to take a desperate gamble; they've tried everything else, why not try a little freedom?

While the euphoria of the moment will shortly fade to the reality that East Germany has many serious problems that will not evaporate, give the Germans their celebration. They have certainly earned it, enduring for four decades in a divided nation occupied by the victors of World War II.

If any instant analysis is accurate, it most certainly is that the Postwar Era ended Thursday night as the Iron Curtain was shredded. Now we move into a new era, in which German reunification is a serious proposition rather than a useful propaganda slogan. This is uncharted territory.

Another analysis is that the crumbling of the communist bloc is continuing at a dizzying pace, driven by inescapable economic realities. East Germany erected a wall 28 years ago not to keep Westerners out of its people's paradise, but to hold its people in when the economic and political freedoms of West Germany proved so much more compelling than the drab deprivation of East Germany's failed communist state.

Readers often complain that the news is so unpleasant. They ask, "Isn't there any good news?" It is hard to imagine better news than the erosion of communism throughout Eastern Europe before our very eyes, and the recognition by tyrannical regimes that basic human freedoms must be acknowledged. Today there is good news, and it is on the front pages in big, black type.

Good news? This is more than that; it is an epochal change that will be in history books for future generations to study. And East Germans will tell their grandchildren of that magical night when the gates opened and they danced in the streets of Berlin, free once again after so long.

The Globe and Mail

Toronto, Ont., November 11, 1989

Life in East Germany changed more this week than it had during the previous 40 years. The government quit, half the Communist Party leadership was fired, the borders were opened and free elections were promised. It is anybody's guess what will happen over the weekend.

As the Germans dance on the ruins of the Berlin Wall, the rest of us are left to pace the corridors of memory, wondering what kind of world is about to be born. The sound of celebrations at the Brandenburg Gate echoes throughout the nations of the East and the West, reawakening old fears.

Precisely 50 years after the world was last dragged into total war, the German question has re-emerged in yet another form. After the brutal simplicities of the Cold War era, the world has again become rich with complication and unforeseeable danger.

In the United States, many intellectuals and ideologues want to declare victory and celebrate as the collapse of communism quickens throughout Eastern Europe. "Democracy has won the political battle, the market has won the economic battle, the Cold War is finished," historian Arthur Schlesinger, a key adviser to John F. Kennedy, assured an American television audience this week.

But President George Bush has pointedly refused to crack open the champagne. "We are handling [the events in Eastern Europe] in a way where we're not trying to give anybody a hard time," he said late Thursday night.

The liberal revolution in Central Europe has tremendous implications for the Western allies. But political, economic and social developments in Poland, Hungary and now East Germany have far outrun the process of demilitarization.

Though these countries appear to be hurtling headlong toward some form of democracy, they are still bristling with tactical nuclear weapons and are host to huge numbers of Soviet and Warsaw Pact troops. The generals of the North Atlantic Treaty Organization must be asking themselves whether they have become obsolete or more vital than ever.

From Moscow, Mikhail Gorbachev congratulated the East Germans for their reform efforts and suggested that the Soviet Union could live with a non-Communist government. But Mr. Gorbachev was also careful to let the West know that he considers the reunification of the Germanys unthinkable until NATO and the Warsaw Pact are dissolved.

His caution is understandable. But the Germans may not be prepared to put their political evolution on hold for the next decade while the Warsaw Pact and NATO work out terms for dismantling the war machines built up during the past four decades.

What Mr. Gorbachev probably wants above all else right now is a breathing space during which he can seek to moderate the pace of change within the Eastern Bloc. Inside the Soviet Union, he faces potential opposition from reactionary Russians who may not be satisfied to sit idly by as their empire disintegrates. At the very least, he must preserve the illusion that he is still leading the revolutionary attempt to renew and restore socialism.

If the very conservative forces in the Red Army decide that the situation in East Germany (or any of the domestic republics) is getting out of control, Mr. Gorbachev will come under intense pressure to slow the pace of change.

When Mr. Gorbachev and Mr. Bush meet in Malta next month, they will be faced with the challenge of producing methods for coping with the creative instability of this new age. These deliberations will require courage and vision as well as the caution both have already shown.

The greater the pace of change, the greater the need for trust, lest change defeat itself by inviting disillusionment, reaction and even repression.

TULSA WORLD

Tulsa, OK, November 11, 1989

WINSTON Churchill described the Communist prison of Soviet-dominated Eastern Europe in his famous speech at Fulton, Mo. "An iron curtain has descended on the continent."

For 28 years the Berlin Wall was the concrete embodiment of the Iron Curtain. Thursday the wall, the symbol, came tumbling down, figuratively if not yet literally.

Communist authorities suddenly opened East German borders to free travel, in an effort to slow the stream of people into the West in recent weeks and to quell spontaneous demonstrations that have spread to several East German cities.

The opening touched off a euphoric celebration. Germans from East and West danced atop the wall. Others chipped off concrete souvenirs. Some embraced relatives they hadn't seen for years. Some simply drove from the East to visit the famed shopping area, the Kurfuerstendamm, in the West.

"The Wall is Gone! Berlin is Again Berlin," headlined one German newspaper. Said one young East German: "It was so simple to come over. The feeling is just indescribable."

It is difficult for most Americans to comprehend the significance of the event. The majority of Americans — those born after the end of World War II — have witnessed in recent months the greatest political upheaval to occur during their lifetime, first in China and then in East Germany and other countries in communist Europe.

The lifting of the Iron Curtain equals anything to date. Dare we hope for the actual demolition of the Wall? A re-unified Germany? Who knows?

FORT WORTH STAR-TELEGRAM

Fort Worth, TX, November 11, 1989

The opening of the Berlin Wall provides one of the bittersweet moments in history, a moment that evokes brooding reflections on the past and kindles hope for the future.

Out of the past comes a grainy picture of that gray day in 1961 when the workers came with the concrete, bricks and barbed wire that physically divided Berlin into two cities, separating families and friends, while onlookers watched in stunned disbelief.

Out of old headlines and TV footage come stories of daring escapes over, under and around the wall and of failed escape attempts that ended in tragedy.

During the 28 years of the wall's existence, almost 200 people were killed trying to flee East Germany through it.

Echoes of challenges hurled at the wall reverberate in the memories of two generations. A young U.S. president addresses a crowd of West Berliners near the monument to oppression and stirs them by shouting, "Ich bin ein Berliner."

Years later, an older U.S. president speaks to an audience in Berlin and pleads, "Mr. Gorbachev, tear down that wall."

Gorbachev took Ronald Reagan at his word. Although it was Egon Krenz, the new East German leader of less than three weeks, who opened the country's borders, Gorbachev unleashed the forces that led to that dramatic breakthrough.

One would have to be a hopeless pessimist not to see this remarkable event as a harbinger of bright promise for East and West Germany and a pivotal point in East-West relations. It is an occasion for rejoicing at the snowballing momentum gained by the forces pushing for more freedom in Eastern Europe.

It is not, however, a time for gloating, as some have chosen to do about the triumph of democracy and market-driven economic systems over Marxist systems. Much still remains to be done, and such bombast could be counterproductive.

Clearly, the United States and the Western democracies must respond creatively to rapid-fire changes that are transforming Eastern Europe and East Germany in particular. East Germany will need economic assistance from the West in order to provide the opportunities to keep its best and brightest people from leaving.

Opening its borders was the only recourse East Germany had to stop the population hemorrhage through Hungary and Czechoslovakia. Since they know they can now leave anytime they choose, East Germans will be more inclined to stay and wait to see if the government is serious about meaningful economic reforms and political democratization. That is best for the West and particularly West Germany, which would be extremely hard-pressed to take in very many more East Germans.

The prospect of a freer, more prosperous East Germany, of course, raises the issue of German reunification, which no one really wants to tackle at this time. Indeed, there is no reason to complicate matters now by grappling with that vexing question.

Although the concrete, mortar and bricks still stand, for all intents and purposes the Berlin wall is down. It is a moment for bittersweet reflection on what it stood for and dedication to keeping it down.

THE SACRAMENTO BEE

Sacramento, CA, November 11, 1989

The Berlin Wall still stands, but it has been breached, perhaps irrevocably. Once the hated symbol of Communist repression and barbarism, the Wall has now become a monument to the inability of bricks, mortar and barbed wire to hold in check the passion for freedom. Upon that Wall, where desperate East Germans once died, machine gunned in their flight to the West, hundreds of their countrymen now dance, exhilarating in their new freedom to travel. An amazed world dances with them.

Recognizing that it could not stem the tide of East Germans flooding around the Wall through Czechoslovakia, the East German regime, its authority crumbling, has thrown open the Wall itself. It plainly hopes its dramatic gesture will convince East Germans intent on fleeing that real reform is in the offing. "This means that the Berlin Wall has no more meaning," an East German official said Thursday.

But if the Wall has no more meaning, neither will the regime that remains in the East. For the crisis in East Germany to end, the state must re-establish its legitimacy through reform — free speech, free elections and a freer economy. In a speech published Thursday, Egon Krenz, the East German party leader, himself called for such changes. The East German Communists have room to do all that — Moscow has announced that East Germany can choose its own political path, provided it remains in the Warsaw Pact. Whether Krenz will carry through on his vague promises of reform is the open question.

Both Moscow and Washington must hope that he will. The crisis in East Germany, with its exodus of the best and brightest, is unsettling for all of Europe, and there appears no way to reassemble the old order by force or repression. An orderly transition in the pluralist direction Poland and Hungary are already traveling is the only humane resolution of the East German crisis.

As much as such a transition would satisfy the West's desire for freedom in the Eastern bloc, it will create new perils and uncertainties. Forty years of armed confrontation between freedom and communism in Central Europe, as trying and dangerous as it has been at times, nevertheless has yielded stability and peace in Europe. A free East Germany, followed by pressures for German reunification, would drastically transform the strategic equation, calling into question the policies and routines of two generations of leaders, East and West.

Washington, Moscow and their allies need urgently to be considering what new diplomatic order will follow the collapse of the old. When the familiar rules disappear, the diplomatic game becomes more dangerous. The collapse of the Berlin Wall is a time for cheering, but also for caution, thought, mutual understanding and movement toward a European structure that preserves peace even as it welcomes freedom.

The Charlotte Observer

Charlotte, NC, November 10, 1989

The Berlin Wall went up in 1961 to stop the flight of East Germany's brightest and most skilled. Now its gates apparently are being opened for the same reason: to try to dam the new flood of East Germans to the West.

The wall is still in place. But hundreds of East Germans were seen passing through its gates and other border crossings Thursday night even without the visas that are supposed to be required, though freely granted, under the new policy. If the policy is implemented as promised, the most infamous part of the Iron Curtain will have lost its utility as a prison wall.

For the East German regime, it is a bold and risky move. Even with the borders still hedged about with fortifications and regulations, more than 200,000 East Germans have left this year by a variety of legal and illegal means. Since restrictions on leaving through Czechoslovakia were lifted last week, more than 50,000 have taken that route out. Now the leadership is gambling that opening the borders will reduce the fervor to leave and calm the massive demonstrations that brought hundreds of thousands of East Germans into the streets.

The year's events have shaken the communist government, swept much of its key leadership from power and virtually shattered its foundations.

Gone is Erich Honecker, who supervised the building of the wall and has defended it fiercely ever since. In his place since mid-October has been Egon Krenz. Though long known as an eagerly conforming disciple of Marxist rigidity, he has now seen his country move further toward freedom in a period of weeks than most dreamed of moving in years.

In West Berlin, the TV cameras showed dancing in the streets, even on top of the wall itself. In Washington — and surely in other capitals — the joy was more muted. Though Soviet leader Mikhail Gorbachev has long since demonstrated his tolerance and encouragement for reform in Poland, Hungary and his own country, the history of revolutions makes even their fans nervous. Nobody wants chaos that could bring out the troops — whether East German or Soviet — or persuade Moscow's hardliners that the Gorbachev policies threaten not just communist power but Soviet security.

The task for us in the West is to encourage the East German leadership to stand by its new promises of free travel and free elections, while working to ensure that this revolution is both peaceful and lasting. It is a wonderful moment, but still a terribly fragile and risky one.

The Washington Post

Washington, DC, November 10, 1989

EAST GERMANS no longer have to climb out the back window to leave home. In the latest amazing decision in this amazing week, their government has said they can use the front door. They no longer have to make the detour through Czechoslovakia but now can walk directly into West Germany through the border checkpoints. That goes a long way toward meeting one of the demonstrators' demands, but it doesn't quite get there. It's not yet an open border.

East German travelers, whether going west only for a visit or for good, will still need visas issued by the police. They will still have to pass through heavily guarded gates that they know could be shut again at any moment without warning. It's only by doing as the Hungarians did last May and by beginning to tear down the fences and walls that the East German government can hope to make its people believe this week's changes are irreversible.

The Berlin Wall is one of the ugliest monuments in the world, the only structure in Europe that is actually improved by the graffiti scrawled across it. The wall is the great symbol of the division of Europe into two parts, one in which great personal freedom prevails and one in which it does not. A group of prominent East German Communists published a letter yesterday urging the demolition of the wall.

And why not? The wall was built 28 years ago to cut off the heavy flow of East Germans escaping through Berlin, the last unguarded exit between eastern and western Europe. But if the government is prepared to tolerate an outflow on the current scale—because it fears that the alternative might be a violent explosion—then the wall has no purpose except to threaten a clamp-down in the future. Since it is the threat of a future clamp-down that is inciting those tens of thousands of East Germans to flee, East Germany would manifestly be better off without the wall. The one thing that the East German government could do most quickly to win a degree of respect is to bulldoze it.

To stabilize their shaken country and to persuade their alienated people to remain, East Germany's rulers are going to have to provide three things: freedom of movement, elections and a rising standard of living. Freedom of movement can be established immediately if the regime is courageous. Elections will take a little longer. But if and when they are in sight, West Germany is prepared to offer economic aid on a scale that promises rapid economic growth.

East Germany has changed unbelievably in a few weeks, to the enormous benefit of its people. Even greater changes are now possible. Perhaps if Germany and the world are fortunate the next great advance will be at the Berlin Wall.

CENTRAL AMERICA:

Panama's Noriega Surrenders to U.S.

Ousted Panamanian dictator Gen. Manuel Antonio Noriega Jan. 3 surrendered to U.S. officials, 10 days after he had taken refuge in the Vatican's diplomatic mission in Panama City. (See 1989, pp. 1474-1495)

Following his surrender, Noriega was taken to a U.S. military base in Panama City, where he was formally arrested by agents from the U.S. Drug Enforcement Administration on outstanding indictments charging that he had aided drug trafficking. (See 1988, pp. 134-141)

He was then flown to Homestead Air Force Base in southern Florida and was arraigned in federal district court in Miami Jan. 4. Appearing in court in full military uniform, he refused to enter a plea because, his lawyer Frank A. Rubino said, he was a "political prisoner" who was immune to prosecution. U.S. District Judge William M. Hoeveler then entered a plea of not guilty on Noriega's behalf.

President George Bush had announced Noriega's surrender in a nationally televised address Jan. 3. "This evening, Gen. Noriega turned himself in to U.S. authorities in Panama with the full knowledge of the Panamanian government," Bush said. "The return of Gen. Noriega marks a significant milestone in Operation Just Cause" – the administration's code-name for the U.S. invasion of Panama.

Bush thanked the Vatican and the papal nuncio in Panama for their "even-handed statesmanlike assistance," and he said, "The United States is committted to providing Gen. Noriega fair trial."

Bush also said that an economic team under the direction of Deputy Secretary of State Lawrence S. Eagleburger had just returned from Panama on a fact-finding mission intended as a first step in the reconstruction of Panama's damaged economy. (See pp. 10-13)

Noriega reportedly turned himself in to U.S. authorities following several days of subtle tactics on the part of papal officials, who sought to pressure Noriega into leaving the nunciature of his own accord.

Although papal officials had initially insisted that they would not turn Noriega over to the U.S., they reportedly changed their minds after Panama's bishops sent a letter to Pope Paul II denouncing Noriega's long-standing violations of human rights. According to Panamanian Archbishop Marcos McGrath Jan. 4, the letter prompted the Vatican to announce Dec. 30 that Noriega "was not considered to be in diplomatic or political asylum but a person in refuge against whom there were criminal charges."

U.S. administration officials Jan. 4 claimed that Noriega had surrendered after being told by papal nuncio Msgr. Jose Sebastian Laboa on Jan. 3 that his refuge would expire at noon the next day. Laboa Jan. 5 denied the report, however, and insisted, "The only pressures here were those of circumstance. I told him up to the last minute, 'You can stay here.' We will never throw you out.'"

Laboa admitted that he had used psychological pressure on Noriega. "From the very start I had a plan" to "create a psychological environment" that would convince Noriega to leave, Laboa said. He noted that he had told Noriega, "The best thing was to hand himself over to the Americans" because Panamanians were more hostile to him and because if he made a deal quickly he could avoid the severe punishment that would follow a protracted stalemate.

Archbishop McGrath Jan. 3 suggested that Noriega might also have been influenced by a demonstration held earlier that day, in which some 10,000 to 20,000 Panamanians had rallied near the nunciature shouting "Justice" and "Assassin" and demanding that Noriega be handed over to the U.S.

In the end, Noriega left after demanding several minor conditions that were accepted by U.S. officials: that he be allowed to telephone family and friends in Panama before leaving the country, that he wear his military uniform and surrender to a similar-ranking U.S. general and that the press be kept away from the event.

Following the announcement of Noriega's surrender Jan. 3, crowds took to the streets in Panama City to cheer his downfall.

Arkansas Gazette

Little Rock, AR, January 5, 1990

Assured he would not be prosecuted under a law carrying the death penalty, Gen. Manuel Antonio Noriega has surrendered to the United States military forces and been arrested by the Drug Enforcement Administration. He was arraigned on lesser drug-dealing charges yesterday in Florida.

Now that he is in the hands of American authorities, Noriega deserves all that he may get from the American system of justice, starting with a fair trial. He is not a desirable character, by any definition available in Panama or anywhere else, and ran Panama like a despicable thug. But being a dictator in a sovereign country is not a violation of American law. By invading Panama in order to capture the strongman, the United States may well have violated international law. And now our courts will decide if Noriega has violated United States drug laws.

And so it goes. President Bush felt it was worth the price of invasion — 26 American dead and more than 300 wounded — to get his man. The other stated reasons, in our view, were more window dressing than anything else, or at least subordinate to Noriega's arrest.

In any event, the focus now shifts to the courtroom, and short of an astonishing decision by Noriega to plead guilty, the whole sordid episode involving this tinhorn dictator is far short of being over.

It is general knowledge that Noriega once worked for the CIA and that he had contact with George Bush, perhaps when Bush was Director of Central Intelligence and perhaps when he was vice president. There are interesting tales to be told on the witness stand. And Noriega's lawyers will almost certainly demand access to classified or sensitive (embarrassing) documents for use in his defense. The possible legal complications are obvious, especially in light of administration refusal to release classified documents in some of the Iran-Contra cases in federal court.

With Noriega in the United States, American troops dispatched on Dec. 20 should be sent back home as quickly as possible, and efforts should be made on a civilian level to help Panama recover from effects of the invasion. And the pertinent question lingers: Was the invasion, regardless of the stated objectives, worth the price?

THE KANSAS CITY STAR

Kansas City, MO, January 5, 1990

The U.S. victory in Panama appears complete. American officials listed four goals for the intervention there, and the surrender of Gen. Manuel Noriega allows them to check off the final item.

President Bush tried a lot of other options in dealing with Noriega before finally resorting to military force. There were costs to the intervention, including the deaths of American soldiers and Panamanian civilians. Yet the cost of allowing the status quo to continue had become unacceptably high, both for the U.S. and for the people of Panama.

The sight of Panamanians cheering in the streets and hugging American soldiers at the news that Noriega was gone is a gratifying one. It does much to offset the public grousing of other nations in the region and elsewhere.

Noriega's arrival in the U.S., however, should be the cause for some trepidation. This was the administration's goal. Now that it has been achieved, the U.S. will have to live with the consequences.

A Noriega trial could be a messy affair. The questions about whether the U.S. can legally try a foreign leader—and they are questions worth pondering—are only the beginning.

President Bush and other American officials have had to abruptly shift gears. Having denounced Noriega as a despicable, drug-dealing tyrant, they must now declare that the newly apprehended suspect—presumed innocent until proven guilty, of course—can receive a fair trial. Meanwhile, some U.S. lawmakers continue to refer to Noriega as "the international snake," "on his way to the pokey," and so forth.

Sen. Nancy Landon Kassebaum of Kansas spoke for many Americans in saying that she hoped "we won't be tied up in our own legal knots." But there isn't much chance that we won't.

One of Noriega's attorneys, Steven Kollin, has already begun complaining about "this unparalleled pretrial publicity." It's hard to argue that he's exaggerating on this point.

Kollin has also promised to request "certain sensitive documents" from the U.S. government. As we have learned from the Iran-contra affair, this can be a fruitful defensive tactic. It certainly promises to be so in Noriega's case, given his reported ties with the Central Intelligence Agency and the Pentagon.

Finally, there is disconcerting talk about weaknesses in the legal case against Noriega. What if he is found innocent? Wouldn't that be embarrassing and—more important—damaging to U.S. credibility in many places besides Panama?

These sorts of concerns can be traced to the confusion of law enforcement and the conduct of foreign policy. They are distinct spheres, with different rules and different objectives. The idea of trying Noriega in an American court may carry a certain amount of emotional satisfaction, but in terms of this country's larger objectives it might not turn out to be a very smart move.

The Washington Post

Washington, DC, January 5, 1990

IT WAS a deft piece of diplomacy that the pope's ambassador carried off in bringing Gen. Manuel Noriega to his decision to abandon sanctuary and deliver himself to American justice. His choice solved a difficult Vatican problem, which was to be faithful to church traditions of sanctuary without protecting criminal conduct. It solved an even greater Panamanian problem, which was to offload a figure whose presence could have capsized the project of rebuilding. In taking Gen. Noriega, the United States did a major service for a grateful Panama, one it perhaps owed for having created the National Guard and seated the general in the first place. But it took a major burden upon itself.

The Reagan administration indicted the general on drug-trafficking charges two years ago, more, it seems, to press the war on drugs than to bargain him out of power. The Bush administration brought its own passion to the case for both purposes. The president went after Gen. Noriega with an almost personal fury and ended up elevating his capture and prosecution to a status as an objective of the invasion.

But from the start, the United States has been in the dubious position of reaching across national borders to apply American priorities and law to a foreign national—and not just any national: a head of government. It takes only a little reflection to comprehend the great license the United States has demanded for itself in using its armed forces to pursue a foreign criminal suspect, the concern this may generate elsewhere and the example this sets for other countries that may have American citizens in their sights.

President Bush counts the landing of Gen. Noriega as a success and vindication of the intervention. He would do better to emphasize purposes that are more legitimate, universal and defensible. In this instance, it is plenty that, after other remedies had been tried in vain, he used American power effectively and with relatively few casualties to protect American citizens, the Panama Canal and the canal treaties. Further, the intervention ousted a corrupt dictatorship and gave Panamanians back a government of their own choosing.

This leaves the United States with a large role in helping repair damage done by the embargo, the fighting and the looting—the human toll, of course, is beyond repair—and in stepping aside expeditiously as Panamanians take up the work of moving from the forms of democracy to the substance.

Washington, DC, January 5, 1990

THE REAGAN administration denied that the indictments of Gen. Manuel Noriega in 1988 were political acts. The Justice Department said the action had been taken only in the normal course of events and because for the first time prosecutors had a solid case against the general. That is what the department must now prove. But in the process it has shifted the standard for judging Gen. Noriega from the expansive political one that has previously prevailed to the narrower, harder tests that must be met in court. It remains to be seen to whose advantage that shift works out.

The president has rightly said that Gen. Noriega must have a "fair trial." Of course he must, not least because it was partly in the name of such bulwarks as fair trials and the rest of due process—like honoring election results—that the troops were sent in to oust him. But it would be a huge embarrassment if he were acquitted, since the troops were also sent in on grounds that he was complicit in the drug trade, as the indictment alleges, and a thug.

His lawyers have already indicated some of the likely lines of his defense. They will say that he cannot have an impartial trial, that no jury can be found that has not been bent by the weight of pretrial publicity, the advance conviction of their client on page one and on TV by every national authority figure from the president down. The Oliver North case suggests that this won't wash, and we don't think it should—but it's there. The indictments—there are two, both charging the general with taking large amounts of money for allowing his country to be used as a way station and money laundry in the drug trade—also rest on the testimony of rather unsavory characters. The defense lawyers will try to impeach them on the stand, but that is a fact of life in many drug cases.

Potentially more difficult than either of these is the familiar problem of classified material. The lawyers have indicated they will seek to introduce large amounts of it in open court, presumably to show that the general was often acting, if not on the instructions or with the approval of various U.S. agencies and operatives, then at least with their knowledge and without their interference or censure. The devil made or surely let him do it, they will say. The theory is partly that this will be a mitigating factor in the eyes of a jury, even more that it will be too embarrassing for the government to let appear—that the government will be forced to drop its case on national security grounds rather than give him materials that the court may say he is entitled to in his defense.

Iran-contra charges against a former CIA station chief were just thrown out by a district judge on these grounds; the CIA and Justice Department wouldn't produce the required materials. In the Noriega case there will be enormous pressure on the agencies to be more forthcoming. That at least is a good side effect of putting him on trial.

Chicago Tribune

Chicago, IL, January 5, 1990

When the U.S. invasion came, Gen. Manuel Antonio Noriega, the erstwhile Panamanian strongman whose rallying cry during his two-year standoff with Ronald Reagan and George Bush was *"¡Ni un paso atrás!"* ("Not one step back!"), did a lot of running away from his determined pursuers.

But in the end, he put on his white dress uniform and took a big step forward—out of the shelter of the Vatican embassy in Panama City and into the waiting arms of the American military.

Turning himself in to be flown to Florida to face trial on charges he helped the Colombian drug cartels was certainly not something he relished. But the alternatives were scarce and potentially more unpleasant.

Noriega, who was arraigned on Thursday in federal court in Miami, made the best deal he could before he left the Papal Nuncio's residence, where he had been given refuge Christmas Eve.

He was allowed to surrender in uniform to an American general and have his family notified, he was permitted to make some phone calls and, most important, he got assurances of a fair trial on charges that do not carry the death penalty.

People have called Manuel Noriega a lot of things, a dictator, a thug, a greedy crook to name a few. But nobody ever accused him of outright stupidity. Only Cuba, which the Vatican felt was unsuitable, had offered to take him if the U.S. and Panama could be persuaded to let him go into exile.

Meanwhile, the new Panamanian attorney general was talking about murder charges. And the new president was telling the Vatican the justice system is in such sorry shape his government couldn't guarantee due process for the deposed dictator. All this, while mobs outside were howling for his scalp.

On the other hand, President Bush, understandably delighted to have the troublesome Noriega in custody at last, reaffirmed that the U.S. is committed to giving him a fair trial. For good reason, Noriega believed that. He will be entitled to all the safeguards of the American justice system. And nowhere on Earth could he get a better guarantee of fairness.

Noriega, it is widely accepted, is an all-around bad guy. But when he goes to trial in the U.S., he will be as innocent until proven guilty as any person who ever went to court. In fact, Americans—as they often do—are likely to get frustrated by proceedings that could last months, even years. It's certainly possible he may never go to trial, or may be acquitted.

Already, concerns are being expressed that his alleged former CIA connections will cause the government to deny the defense evidence it says is vital, paving the way for a dismissal of charges. Or that the court may decide evidence seized during the invasion is tainted—obtained without search warrants.

Whatever the outcome, George Bush has made his point that the United States is "serious in its determination that those charged with promoting the distribution of drugs cannot escape the scrutiny of justice." That is, as he said, a good "clear signal" to send to the world's drug dealers. And bringing in Noriega is an unqualified victory in the President's ongoing battle to de-wimp his image.

The Vatican also came off well in what could have been an intolerably messy process. Never having granted Noriega political asylum, but only refuge in an asserted desire to end hostilities, it managed to arrange his voluntary departure from the embassy without capitulating to U.S. demands he be handed over.

That was a neat trick, but the quiet dignity with which the Papal Nuncio and others handled the matter left the Vatican with its historic credibility as a provider of refuge well intact. All in all, it was nicely put together by the diplomats on all sides. Let's hope it speeds the day when U.S. forces can depart and let the Panamanians run their country again.

FORT WORTH STAR-TELEGRAM

Fort Worth, TX, January 5, 1990

We got him. The trick now is to keep him and see that justice is done.

The surrender of Gen. Manuel Antonio Noriega closes one chapter of the U.S.-Panama saga and opens another, which, for sheer melodrama, may be every bit as suspenseful.

When Noriega was brought to the United States after two weeks in the Vatican Embassy in Panama, it signaled the beginning of the end of the armed incursion into that country by U.S. troops. The next installment might not be so easy on any of the participants.

Both sides in the new drama, which the vast majority of Americans understandably view as a classic matchup of good vs. evil, could be excused for worrying about the uncertainty of the American justice system.

The United States obviously believes that it has a solid drug-trafficking case against the deposed dictator, but so many shadowy issues exist at its outer edges that no one can be certain that all the evidence will be heard. Noriega's known connections with the CIA and the Drug Enforcement Administration, for example, could cause the prosecution some serious headaches.

His attorney's expressed doubts concerning the possibility of a fair trial in light of the publicity surrounding the case are reason for legitimate concern. Many of this government's ringing anti-Noriega statements during the last few months were justified and undoubtedly struck a responsive chord with the American public, but they are apt to work in the Panamanian's favor within the unemotional confines of a judge's chambers.

Despite some cautiously worded denials by U.S. officials, the possibility still exists that some type of deal has already been struck between Noriega and the U.S. government. Noriega is a cunning animal, and he did not remain in power for six years by being stupid or naive. His options may have been limited, but it is a cinch that he weighed them all carefully before agreeing to throw himself on the mercy of an American court.

If this were an ideal world, justice would be swift and uncompromising. The charges against Noriega are of sufficient severity that, assuming conviction, he should spend the rest of his life behind bars. In the real world, unfortunately, justice does not always prevail. We can only hope that, in this instance, it will.

AKRON BEACON JOURNAL

Akron, OH, January 9, 1990

Q. SO WE GOT Noriega and we're going to try him in Miami. It looks like it's going to be a legal circus, doesn't it?

A. Perhaps. His attorneys, as is the case with all vigorous lawyers for defendants in criminal cases, are raising every issue they can think of.

Q. How can the United States justify abducting the head of a foreign country to this country for trial? Can that be legal?

A. The Bush administration says legal procedures were followed, noting that Noriega turned himself over to U.S. authorities.

Q. Yes, but won't the way we got him jeopardize the chance that he'll ever come to trial?

A. Perhaps, but that's why we have a judicial system, to sort out and decide all such claims. This case is before a federal court, which is better equipped than most state courts to answer and determine whether any legal objections are valid or not.

Q. The president, the administration, the media and many others have branded Noriega a thug, a crook and a drug kingpin so many times, how can he possibly get a fair trial? Can't he get off on that basis?

A. Not necessarily. There are many other cases in which notorious people have been successfully tried and convicted despite lots of pretrial publicity. It's up to the judge, step-by-step, to ensure that the defendant gets a fair trial, and judges have numerous ways of doing that.

Q. Won't the Noriega trial bring out a lot of embarrassing material about our government's earlier involvement with him, including connections with George Bush before he was president?

A. That could happen. However, that's no reason not to prosecute him. And the president himself has said he's not bothered by any evidence that might come out.

Q. Isn't there a risk that Noriega could be found not guilty by a jury or get off on some technicality? How would the United States look then?

A. There's always that risk in any trial. The administration says it is confident of its case. The United States might look as though it had failed, but Noriega would still be out of power in Panama. In the meantime, both he and those prosecuting him for drug-dealing activities will get the case heard under the American system of justice.

Q. What happens to him if he does get off?

A. That's unknown at this point. By then, there could be other charges pending against him, either in this country or in Panama. Obviously, Noriega thought he could get a fairer trial here than he could in Panama, where they know him better than the United States does.

St. Louis Review

St. Louis, MO, January 12, 1990

The Accademia, the school for Vatican diplomats, is one of the oldest institutions of its kind. For some years now, the Accademia has been under the direction of an American, Archbishop Justin Rigali, formerly a priest of the Los Angeles Archdiocese. During the past month, the skill and resourcefulness of Vatican diplomacy has been put to the test in Panama and has proved its mettle.

In the centuries in which the pope was also the ruler of the papal states, the burden of serving as a temporal ruler was often a hindrance to the spiritual role of the pope. In negotiating the Lateran Treaty of 1929, the genius of Pope Pius XI brought about recognition of Vatican City as an independent political entity, while limiting the territory of the papal domain to a scant 108 acres. This enables the pope and his representatives to serve society with no suggestion of political or territorial gain.

In Panama, the role of the papal nuncio was clearly humanitarian. In admitting Manuel Noriega to the nunciature, Archbishop Jose Sebastian Laboa helped to bring the fighting to an end, saving lives and property. In his precise and correct relations with Panama, the United States and the world community, Archbishop Laboa maintained the inviolability of accredited embassies without offense to any of the parties.

Ultimately, it was the skill of the papal nuncio that helped Noriega to decide that surrender to the Americans was the best option available. In the entire incident, we have seen Vatican diplomacy at its very best in the service of peace and justice.

For those who complain that this is an instance of the Church interfering in world politics, we see it rather as the Church serving as an honest broker in the cause of peace. The Church can never be so other-worldly that it has nothing to contribute in time of crisis. If anything, the fact that the Vatican representative is, above all, a priest, enabled him to approach the situation with a greater perception of its many facets.

DIARIO LAS AMERICAS

Miami, FL, January 5, 1990

There is no doubt whatsoever that the overthrow and capture of the former chief of the Panamanian Armed Forces, dictator Manuel Antonio Noriega, is surrounded by exceptional characteristics in the history of the American continent. Of course, the type of dictatorship endured by the Panamanian people was also one of exceptional characteristics. A different outcome was practically impossible because of the conduct of the Noriega dictatorship.

On the night of Wednesday, January 3rd, first from the White House and later from the Panama Canal Zone, the news was oficially divulged that the diplomatic asylum of former dictator Noriega in the Apostolic Nunciature in Panama had ended, and that it had been agreed that he would surrender to the American authorities to be taken to Miami where he is under indictment for drug trafficking, according to formal accusations made years ago.

Logically, that news, which was issued in a statement by President Bush from the press conference room of the White House, went around the world where it was received with great interest. From now on, everything regarding former dictator Noriega has nothing to do with the armed struggle for his necessary overthrow and the persecution in the Panamanian capital to capture him. From now on, the fundamental revolves around this judicial process that, undoubtedly, will have sensational characteristics.

It is fitting to emphasize this, because in many countries of the world, perhaps in many of the Western Hemisphere, it might be thought that the insistence of the President of the U.S. in behalf of Panamanian democracy scourged by the military dictatorthip, and against Noriega, might imply a bias in the Judiciary or something similar. And this does not happen at all in the United States of America. If any mistake might be made in this trial it could be for any reason, but not because the courts try to please the President of the Republic.

It is very difficult to predict how long the trial will last and the aspects that it will cover, as well as the surprises that might spring from it.

The Birmingham News

Birmingham, AL, January 4, 1990

When President Bush sent 14,000 troops to Panama, his intent was to end Manuel Noriega's despotic rule and to remove the threat to the Panama Canal posed by the cocaine-dealing buddy of Fidel Castro and Daniel Ortega.

With Noriega's surrender Wednesday night to U.S. authorities, that mission has been accomplished. If convicted on all charges he faces in this nation, Noriega could be sentenced to 145 years in prison and fined $1.1 million.

We hope he gets the maximum and is forever denied an opportunity to re-establish the grip he held on Panama.

Noriega was apparently tipped hours before U.S. troops arrived to oust him Dec. 20. He went into hiding as our soldiers were helping the legitimately elected government of President Guillermo Endara replace Noriega cronies.

Christmas Eve, like an unwanted present, Noriega turned up in the Vatican embassy appealing to the church for sanctuary. Though hardly a political refugee, Noriega was allowed temporary asylum while the Vatican considered the U.S. request that he be handed over for trial in Florida.

Finally, Wednesday night, perhaps fearing what the 20,000 Panamanians protesting outside the embassy would do to him, Noriega turned himself in to U.S. authorities and was quickly flown to Miami to face arraignment in a federal court.

Now that Noriega has been captured the U.S. must concentrate on its remaining responsibilities to Panama. We must help President Endara maintain order and restore economic stability to a nation that has been devastated by sanctions imposed by the U.S. to topple the Noriega government.

In restoring order to Panama we will be ensuring the safety of the canal and the thousands of American citizens who live in the Canal Zone.

Noriega's trial will be complicated because of his former ties to the CIA, but we hope justice will prevail and he is put behind bars for a long time.

With U.S. assistance, President Endara should be able to successfully restore Panama to prosperity and democracy. And that will keep any wishing to emulate Noriega from similarly forcing their will on Panama.

SAVINGS & LOAN CRISIS:

Brady Sets Sharply Higher Bailout Tab

The Bush administration May 23 said for the first time that it had greatly underestimated the cost of the savings-and-loan-industry bailout and that new funds were necessary for the program to proceed. (See pp. 350-353)

Testifying before the Senate Banking Committee, Treasury Secretary Nicholas F. Brady estimated that the cost of insuring deposits at insolvent thrifts from 1989 through 1992 would be between $17 billion and $57 billion more than the $73 billion the administration had originally requested in its 1989 thrift bailout law.

According to the most optimistic scenario, direct bailout costs would be about $90 billion, Brady said. That would account for bailouts from 1989 through 1992, and for the cost of replenishing the fund that would pay for bailouts after 1992.

But Brady said that if real-estate prices continued to sag and thrifts continued to fail at a greater pace than the administration had initially anticipated, the cost could balloon to over $130 billion. Neither estimate took into account interest payments on the funds borrowed to finance the bailout or additional costs of thrift rescues in 1988.

Brady said that with those costs added, the bailout over the next 10 years could cost nearly $300 billion, almost double the $166 billion the administration had originally estimated.

The worst-case scenario provided for the possibility that 1,037 thrifts with $350 billion in assets – about 40% of the industry – might eventually have to be seized by the government. The Resolution Trust Corp. (RTC), which sold insolvent thrifts, had already taken control of 423 thrifts. The Office of Thrift Supervision, which oversaw the savings and loan industry, May 23 projected that 299 more thrifts would definitely fail, with 315 additional thrifts likely to be declared insolvent if real-estate prices did not recover.

Brady said the new estimates meant that Congress would have to allocate more funds to the bailout program. The money could be appreciated either as a fixed sum or as an unlimited allocation that would pay whatever costs became apparent, he said. But he cautioned that a fixed sum would likely be inadequate, since the bailout figures could easily be revised upward again.

The Washington Post
Washington, DC, May 23, 1990

WHILE President Bush doubtless had many reasons to seek a budget compromise with Congress, the most compelling one is the soaring cost of the S&L cleanup. His proposed budget last January made very little provision for the S&Ls—one of its many evasions and, as it turns out, the most dangerous. His budget also overestimated revenues and underestimated interest costs, but some of those errors were visible last winter. The surprise this spring has been the acceleration of the federal regulators' drive to end the bankrupt S&Ls' losses by closing them down.

Last summer Congress gave the administration $50 billion to cover the deposit insurance losses as it shut or sold off these S&Ls. It had spent $9 billion by April. Then William Seidman, chairman of the Federal Deposit Insurance Corp., who is running this operation, announced that it was going into high gear with a gigantic plan that would put 141 of the bankrupts out of business by the end of June. That is estimated to cost another $19 billion of the insurance money. But there will still be hundreds of S&Ls, failed or failing, to deal with. The implication is that by the end of the fiscal year in September, the administration will have gone through most of the deposit insurance money that Congress provided, with the job still far from finished.

But covering the insurance losses is only part of the cost to the government. It also needs money—working capital—to acquire the failed S&Ls' assets, mostly foreclosed real estate, and hold them until it can sell them off. Presumably this money will eventually come back to the taxpayers. But in the meantime it is counted in the budget as spending.

Largely because of the S&Ls, it now appears that the budget deficit this year will be some $60 billion higher than the president's estimate last January of $124 billion. The S&L outlays are extremely hard to forecast, but any realistic calculation of next year's deficit would have to run at least twice as high as the limit of $64 billion set by the budget law.

It would be possible to hold down these costs by slowing the resolution of the failed S&Ls and allowing some of them to continue longer in business. But they are losing money heavily, and to let them go on would merely run up the ultimate costs to the taxpayer. The administration is right to push the cleanup as fast as it can. If the consequence is to force the White House to come to terms at last with the arithmetic of the budget and the need for more taxes, that will be further reason for applause.

The New York Times
New York, NY, May 29, 1990

No less an authority than the Federal Reserve chairman, Alan Greenspan, says the eventual cost of the savings and loan bailout could exceed a half-trillion dollars. *A half-trillion.* And Treasury Secretary Nicholas Brady admits that taxpayers will bear most of that burden.

It is scandalous, all agree, but unlike any earlier scandal. By any measure, it is the largest by far. Forget the relatively puny bailouts of Chrysler, Lockheed and New York City. (Even the Marshall Plan, which bailed out Western Europe 40 years ago, cost a mere $65 billion in today's dollars.)

A greater outrage is that most of the perpetrators will escape. For that, the responsible parties are members of Congress who legislated the thrifts' license to splurge and steal, Reagan Administration officials who ignored the storm warnings and hundreds of incompetent and corrupt S & L owners and managers who dallied with their depositors' trust.

A few politicians have paid, and more may pay as inquiries proceed. Former Representative Fernand St Germain of Rhode Island, co-author of the law that turned the S & L's loose, was defeated for re-election. Speaker Jim Wright's downfall was due partly to his badgering of Federal regulators. Five senators' reputations, if not their seats, are at risk because they intervened with regulators on behalf of a big campaign donor, Charles Keating, and his now-bankrupt Lincoln Savings and Loan.

Some industry high-fliers have paid, too. Close to 50 thrift officials, developers, accountants and others have been convicted, and F.B.I. Director William Sessions says his agents have found fraud "pervasive" industrywide. But even if Government prosecutors were more vigorous, most of the funds are gone.

So who really pays? Mostly the taxpayer; to a lesser extent the surviving thrifts, which now pay higher fees for Federal deposit insurance.

Estimates of the damage vary widely because the experts still don't agree on how to measure it. Secretary Brady says the cost might reach $130 billion; the General Accounting Office says $325 billion, and Mr. Greenspan says a half-trillion.

Why the huge differences? Mr. Brady doesn't count most of the huge interest payments for 30 or 40 years on the billions he must borrow to finance the bailout; and no one knows what the interest rates will be. He also omits billions laid out for failed thrifts before last year, when the bailout package was enacted.

Another unknown is what the Government will recoup from selling the immensely varied assets of the thrifts it takes over — real estate, junk bonds, amusement parks. Finally, there is no way to know just how many thrifts will be taken over.

One thing is clear. In 1987, when the Reagan Administration first acknowledged a problem — the deposit insurance fund was running low — it asked Congress for $15 billion. The savings and loan industry, wanting desperately to avoid scrutiny, insisted that $5 billion would be enough. Congress finally voted $11 billion.

Those figures show how easily a lax Administration, an irresponsible Congress and a recklessly deregulated industry played with other people's money. That's why the taxpayer will now pay. Perhaps a half-trillion.

The Houston Post

Houston, TX, May 29, 1990

THE BUSH ADMINISTRATION has decided to come clean about the cost of the savings and loan fiasco. Treasury Secretary Nicholas Brady told Congress last week that the bill to clean up the mess could reach $90 billion to $130 billion — not the $73 billion estimated last year.

Brady warned the Senate Banking Committee that the government may eventually have to close or sell more than 1,000 ailing thrifts, about 40 percent of the industry. That is twice the number the administration originally thought regulators might have to take over.

Even before these sharply raised projections, the savings and loan scandal was called the biggest financial debacle in U.S. history. It grew out of a combination of lax federal regulation, wheeler-dealer lending practices, and the collapse of oil and real estate prices — all of which hit Texas especially hard.

Until last week, the administration had insisted that the $73 billion Congress appropriated last year would be sufficient to cover depositors' federally insured losses in insolvent S&Ls

and meet other expenses. Brady cited a soft real estate market and higher interest rates as the chief contributors to the rise in costs.

The current budget negotiations between the administration and Congress were largely responsible for smoking out the grim truth about the extent of the increase. Negotiators must decide how to provide the new funding needed while meeting the deficit target set by the Gramm-Rudman budget-balancing law.

The new higher estimates do not include the cost of disposing of 200 bankrupt thrifts before the bailout law was enacted, creating the Resolution Trust Corp., which deals with insolvent S&Ls. Nor do they include interest on money the government is borrowing to finance liquidation of these institutions. The General Accounting Office, Congress' research arm, says this could boost the thrift rescue cost to as much as $500 billion over the next 30 years.

Brady told Congress that interest isn't included in accounting for government programs. Why not? It must be paid — in this case by at least two generations of taxpayers.

MILWAUKEE SENTINEL

Milwaukee, WI, May 25, 1990

It isn't as if nobody expected it. But when Treasury Secretary Nicholas Brady said it, it became official.

The US savings and loan industry — or racket — is in worse shape than ever outside of Wisconsin and getting worse. Before running its course, the biggest government bailout in history may cost the American taxpayer $300 billion in principal and interest to finance the rescue.

That's $2,000 for every citizen, according to many estimates.

There can be no solace taken in the fact that the administration is finally issuing a realistic assessment of the depth of the crisis. It could still grow to $500 billion — or twice that — before being brought under control.

President Bush tells the American public the crisis causes him "great concern." But S&Ls are still failing at a frightening rate.

And guess what?

No one has gone to jail. Politicians of the highest standing who trafficked with major figures in the scandal have not been brought to account.

People ought to care, but they don't. For the average American couch potato, the bailout is not a priority item. It is a distraction, at best. They're insured, so who cares?

Give me my "Twin Peaks" and stop bugging me!

The industry, as the title of a recent Milwaukee Sentinel series pointed out, has been "Anything but Thrifty."

"Mismanagement, fraud and government neglect will burden taxpayers well into the next century as the country struggles to correct the disastrous mistakes that threaten to destroy the savings and loan industry," the series said.

Inflation, depressed home values, unemployment, a tightening of commercial credit and more expensive, and harder to obtain, mortgages — all these are the consequences of the crisis. And future generations will pay for it.

Some blame the deregulation of the industry in the '80s and the subsequent spree of questionable investments and schemes that executives devised to make money and attract customers.

It was a wild scene. What was supposed to create opportunity for savers degenerated into greedy owners and shady dealings. Meantime, profitable thrifts, like those in Wisconsin, are shouldering much of the burden for the huge bailout.

It's unfair. But that's what is happening — and at a price that is unimaginable, but real.

For that price, someone should pay. The most galling thing about the savings and loan disaster is that no one has paid — except the innocent and truly thrifty.

St. Paul Pioneer Press & Dispatch

St. Paul, MN, May 29, 1990

Long after others in the bailing brigade saw the need for bigger buckets, the Bush administration raised its estimate of how much the government will have to borrow because of the savings and loan disaster.

Prosecutions could even serve to raise public confidence in government.

When Treasury Secretary Nicholas Brady last week raised the official figures on borrowing from $50 billion to between $90 billion and $130 billion, he put something on the table that should prove useful to budget negotiators. The new numbers were followed by President Bush's rhetorical confidence that Congress and the administration can pick a number and manage S&L cost decisions based on mutual accord.

Maybe. And that certainly would be welcome. But if the politicians pick that number and treat it like a victory, like a solution, the folks footing the bill should think about using Election Day as an opportunity for feedback.

That, however, requires the voter to do some thinking. The problem with that is not dimwitted voters. It's the numbers and nuances that are numbing. Who can comprehend $500 billion, which the Government Accounting Office, Congress' research arm, says is liable to be the bottom line in the S&L bailout? And, with so many players in the cast of the culpable, how can the political process assign blame? And after some kind of search for justice, how can the country hope to cure the pernicious economic anemia caused by paying for the terminal illnesses of S&Ls?

A reasonable place is the most visible one: prosecuting the amazing backlog of S&L fraud cases overflowing FBI file cabinets. Anyone listening to the grumblings on buses and in elevators carrying Americans to honest work knows there is a thirst for justice — if not blood.

Crooks and quick-buck hustlers are not the only cause of the S&L mess. But pressure to prosecute on behalf of the American people is reasonable. It could even serve to raise public confidence in government.

Testimony earlier this month revealed that the FBI has 21,000 unaddressed S&L referrals about possible fraud. Of those, more than 200 involve in excess of $1 million. Not all of these would go on to prosecution, but they deserve timely investigation. Why aren't these unaddressed cases being moved forward? The FBI and U.S. attorneys received half the additional staff they sought last year to handle S&L cases. Too expensive to hire them? Congress authorized an additional $75 million to pursue prosecutions, but the Bush administration allocated only $50 million of that.

No wonder the folks on the buses and in the elevators are cynical.

MIDDLE EAST:

Iraqi Forces Invade, Occupy Kuwait

Iraqi troops and tanks stormed across the border into Kuwait in the early morning hours of Aug. 2 and quickly seized effective control of the oil-rich desert sheikdom at the head of the Persian Gulf. Although the invasion had been preceded by two weeks of Iraqi military threats, most of the world was caught by surprise by Iraqi President Saddam Hussein's sudden act of aggression.

Initial reports indicated that at least 200 Kuwaitis had been killed or wounded in the lightning assault before most armed resistance was crushed by the massive invasion force. The ruling emir, Sheik Jabir al-Ahmad, fled to Saudi Arabia.

Iraq claimed that its troops had been invited in to restore order by an "interim free government" of Kuwaiti revolutionaries who had overthrown the Sabah dynasty, which had ruled the emirate for two and a half centuries. But independent accounts agreed that the Iraqi invaders had ousted the Sabah government with the intention of installing a pro-Iraqi regime.

In seizing control of Kuwait and its oil fields, Hussein apparently sought to turn Iraq virtually overnight into a regional superpower with economic clout to match its military might. Together, Iraq and Kuwait possessed proven oil reserves of some 195 billion barrels. That was 20% of the world supply, more than 25% of the Organization of Petroleum Exporting Countries's (OPEC) total and second only to Saudi Arabia's 255 billion barrels. World oil prices shot up in response to the crisis in the gulf, and financial markets were plunged into turmoil.

The U.S. strongly condemned the Iraqi invasion. President Bush Aug. 2 ordered economic sanctions against Baghdad and quickly froze both Iraq's and Kuwait's assets in the U.S. Although he declined to rule out the possible use of force. American military options were widely seen as being limited, due to both Iraq's armed strength and the lack of U.S. military bases in the region.

Britain and France also moved to freeze Kuwait's extensive foreign assets to prevent Iraq from getting control of them. The United Nations Security Council swiftly and unanimously condemned the attack, and the Soviet Union said it was suspending arms deliveries to Baghdad, until now its ally.

In contrast to the near-universal condemnation of the invasion in most of the international community, the reaction in the Arab world was muted. Iraq's attack represented the first time in modern history that one Arab had invaded another, but most Arab country governments initially had little to say beyond urging a diplomatic solution and opposing foreign intervention. The conservative Persian Gulf monarchies, including Saudi Arabia, were widely seen to be leery of antagonizing Iraq after it had shown its willingness to use force.

Earlier, talks on oil and border disputes between Iraq and Kuwait in the Saudi city of Jidda had been broken off Aug. 1 after only one two-hour session. The collapse of the talks raised tensions and sparked a rise in oil prices.

The regional crisis had begun July 17, when Hussein accused Kuwait and the United Arab Emirates of plotting with the U.S. to keep oil prices low by flouting their OPEC export quotas. Low oil prices had stunted Iraqi revenues and hurt Hussein's efforts to rebuild an economy weighed down by debts and wrecked by Iraq's 1980-88 war with Iran. (See 1988, pp. 848-859)

The Star-Ledger

Newark, NJ, August 3, 1990

In many parts of the world, totalitarian regimes have been replaced by democratic governments. But that does not mean that the specter of repression and war has disappeared. The area that poses the greatest threat to peace remains the Mideast.

President Saddam Hussein of Iraq has emerged as the latest in a series of dictators to enhance their power by menacing their neighbors. The difference now is that President Hussein has gone from threats to overt aggression, dispatching troops into neighboring Kuwait and overrunning that oil-rich nation.

The motives for this unprovoked attack are classic ones in the tragedy of warfare—power and greed. The claim by President Hussein that he was responding to entreaties for assistance by Kuwaiti dissidents can be dismissed as pure piffle.

What really motivates the Iraqi dictator is a desire to expand his influence and his territory at the expense of his neighbors. Simultaneously, he increases his wealth by taking over the enormous petroleum reserves of Kuwait.

President Bush was quick to denounce the "naked aggression" of Iraq and to take such steps as are available to the United States. This includes freezing the considerable assets of Iraq that are on deposit in the U.S. and banning the delivery of Iraqi oil and other imports. An American military option does not now appear likely or desirable.

The menacing actions of President Hussein had sometimes been overshadowed by the more spectacular antics of the ruler of one of Iraq's neighbors, the late Ayatollah Khomeini of Iran. But President Hussein could well prove to have a more dangerous potential for disturbing the peace.

The true nature of President Hussein's view of politics and warfare became evident during the Iraq-Iran war, when Iraqi forces used poison gas to slaughter Iranian civilians. Such attacks continued, despite the warnings of an international panel on chemical warfare.

There are other alarming aspects of Iraq's military posture. During the Iraq-Iran war, when Saudi Arabia, an ally of Iraq, didn't supply aid in quantities sufficient for President Hussein, Iraq conducted a bombing raid against its own ally. There are other reports that Iraq is in possession of a nuclear arsenal and is prepared to use it.

The latest incident involving Kuwait is a further example of Iraqi militarism. Both Iraq and Kuwait are members of OPEC, the international oil cartel. President Hussein objected to Kuwait selling oil cheaply. He has now taken irresponsible steps that have sent oil prices rocketing.

The nations of the world should realize now the dangers of Iraqi militarism and prepare to take appropriate action. Iraq should be on notice that this type of conduct will not be tolerated and that sanctions, an economic boycott and perhaps other measures as well will be taken if this aggressive and irresponsible action is not reversed.

The Philadelphia Inquirer / TONY AUTH

Calgary Herald

Calgary, Alta., August 3, 1990

When Iraq was at war with fundamentalist Iran, the West was too willing to overlook Iraq's dismal human rights record and its growing hostility toward its other neighbors.

But with its latest display of naked aggression, it is clear the international community must work together to check Iraqi President Saddam Hussein.

He may be able to bully tiny Kuwait into submission, but sooner or later, even a strongman must be made to pay a price.

Last week, the entire Mideast thought the so-called Butcher of Baghdad was bluffing. Now that he has brazenly overrun tiny Kuwait, Hussein has proven himself a danger even to his Arab brethren.

By way of justification, Hussein claims Iraq has been robbed of the money it needs to restore its economy, ravaged by the 1980-88 Gulf War with Iran.

Iraq is laden with $80-billion worth of debt. It claims Kuwait profiteered from that war and that it is further crimping an Iraqi recovery by dumping more than its OPEC quota of oil on to the market, thereby keeping the price of oil down.

Hussein threatened to attack Kuwait if the tiny emirate did not forgive him the estimated $15 billion in war debts he owes to it, cut back its oil production and promise to pay reparations to Iraq for oil the Iraqis claimed the Kuwaitis stole from Iraq during the war.

But Kuwait promised last week to stop dumping and agreed to raise the cartel minimum price $3 to $21 per barrel. .

Not content to police OPEC and bully it into a higher target price for cartel oil, Hussein has resorted to brute force the like of which the world has not seen for some time.

Given that Hussein has used poison gas against Iraq's Kurdish minority, has brutally suppressed all internal dissent and has threatened to lob chemical weapons at Israel, the world should have known what Hussein is really made of.

Now that the ugly truth has been confirmed, a concerted international effort must be made to isolate and sanction Iraq.

THE DAILY OKLAHOMAN

Oklahoma City, OK, August 3, 1990

IRAQ'S lightning-quick invasion of Kuwait provokes a number of observations about the new era of international relations.

In the not-too-distant past, the Soviet Union might have staunchly defended Iraqi President Saddam Hussein's use of troops to overrun the tiny kingdom after talks broke down in a dispute over an oil-rich border area. Instead, Moscow called on Baghdad to immediately withdraw its forces.

Indeed, virtually the entire community of nations joined the United States in condemning the power play, which from all indications was motivated by a desire to keep oil prices at a high level. Notable exceptions were China and some, but not all, Arab countries.

Such unity of opinion directed against the Arab world's strongest and most militant military power is encouraging, because it is this type of Third World conflict that the United States must be prepared to deal with after all the superpower treaties are signed.

The invasion confirms anew energy industry warnings that the United States is becoming too dependent on foreign oil and could become' vulnerable to another Arab oil embargo. Half of America's oil now comes from overseas, much of it from the Persian Gulf region.

Iraq's aggressive action also bears out warnings from Israel that Saddam poses a genuine threat to stability in the Middle East. Iraq is heavily armed from its eight-year war with Iran, which ended in 1988. Saddam has a vast arsenal of conventional and chemical weapons.

Perhaps it is not too much to hope that the invasion of Kuwait might serve as a wakeup call to Americans who might have been lulled by premature declarations of peace sounded by members of Congress who want to slash the U.S. defense budget.

As long as there are terrorist nations like Iraq in the world, hostilities are inevitable. It is essential that the United States maintain sufficient military strength to protect our interests throughout the world and help preserve the peace for all nations.

PERSIAN GULF CRISIS:

U.S.-Led Coalition Attacks Iraq After U.N. Deadline Passes

An international force led by the U.S. Jan. 16 launched air and missile attacks on Iraq and Iraqi-occupied Kuwait. The attack was launched less than 17 hours after the expiration of a United Nations Security Council deadline for Iraq to withdraw from Kuwait, which it had invaded on Aug. 2, 1990. [See *Editorials On File* 1991, pp. 870-883, 1364-1371; 1991, pp. 2-11. See also *Facts On File World News Digest* 1991, pp. 25A1-30D3; for previous developments see *Facts On File* 1990, pp. 565A1, 581A1; 1991, pp. 9A1]

The first official word of the attack came just after 7:00 p.m. in Washington, D.C. when President Bush's spokesman, Marlin M. Fitzwater, announced that "the liberation of Kuwait has begun" under the codename Operation Desert Storm. The U.S. Congress Jan. 12 had voted Bush the authority to use "all means necessary" to drive Iraq from Kuwait. [See *Editorials On File* 1991, pp. 12-23. See also *Facts On File World News Digest* 1991, p. 32A1]

The first U.S. planes launched against Iraq left their bases at about 4:50 p.m. eastern standard time Jan. 16 and began to hit their targets around 7:00 p.m. (Those times corresponded with 12:50 a.m. Jan. 17 Baghdad time for the launch and 3:00 a.m. Jan. 17 for the strike. Unless otherwise noted, *Editorials On File* and *Facts On File* use U.S. Eastern Standard Time.)

The international forces aligned against Iraqi President Saddam Hussein began the attack with air and missile strikes launched from bases in Saudi Arabia and from ships in the region. The massive strikes made extensive use of U.S. high-technology weaponry.

U.S. officials Jan. 17 indicated that the air offensive was going well, but they stressed that the war was in its earliest stages and cautioned against over-optimism. Rules restricting press reporting and the lack of independently confirmed information from inside Iraq made it impossible to assess the overall result of the early allied assault. [See *Editorials On File* 1991, pp. 24-27. See also *Facts On File World News Digest* 1991, p. 14E3]

Iraq Jan. 17 responded by firing eight long-range Scud missiles into Israel. But Iraq did not deliver the chemical weapons attack that had been threatened in the past. Israel, which was not a member of the international military coalition against Iraq, reported only slight casualties and did not immediately retaliate against Iraq. [See *Editorials On File* 1991, pp. 84-91. See also *Facts On File World News Digest* 1991, p. 28F2]

At a briefing on the morning of Jan. 17, U.S. officials said one American plane had been lost and its pilot, later identified as 33-year-old Navy Lt. Cmdr. Michael S. Speicher, killed. In addition, two British planes and one Kuwaiti craft were reported downed. In its first military statement Jan. 17, Iraq reported 23 civilians dead and 66 wounded.

There were 28 nations with troops, planes or ships in the allied military coalition. U.S. army and marine units made up about 70% of all ground combat forces. Air forces from the U.S., Great Britain, Kuwait, France and Italy participated in attacks during the first two days of hostilities. [See *Facts On File World News Digest* 1991, p. 26A3]

Since Iraq had invaded Kuwait, the U.N. Security Council had passed 12 resolutions calling for Iraq to withdraw and imposing economic sanctions. The last of the resolutions, Resolution 678, passed Nov. 29, 1990, had authorized the use of "all necessary means" to drive Iraq from Kuwait if it failed to withdraw by Jan. 15, 1991. [See *Facts On File World News Digest* 1990, p. 888D1]

The last major diplomatic effort to avoid war had ended in failure Jan. 13, when U.N. Secretary General Javier Perez de Cuellar left Baghdad without making any progress in meetings with Saddam Hussein. That mission came four days after the failure of talks in Geneva, Switzerland between U.S. Secretary of State James A. Baker 3rd and Iraqi Foreign Minister Tariq Aziz.

Chicago Tribune

Chicago, Illinois, January 17, 1991

Now the battle has been joined. It thunders over lands as ancient as war.

If fortune is kind, the violence will end quickly and decisively and with mercy to civilians and soldiers on both sides. It will end with the United States and the United Nations victorious and the principle of international decency triumphant. Iv will end with the vindication, as President Bush said Wednesday night, of the rule of law and the unconditional defeat of the primitive rule of the jungle.

And yet the means of achieving these ends are terrible. War itself is the jungle. It may be necessary, as it was for the United States and its allies, but war is always a dark and terrifying place in which the worst seems to become best.

Violence that horrifies can deliver us from violence. Ruthless concentration of will and fire can be a form of kindness, proving to the enemy the futility of further struggle. And, most central of all, war makes an essential virtue of the willingness to spill blood.

War touches the most extreme elements of the human spirit. It draws upon sources of sacrifice and courage and strength of character unimaginable in other settings. But, too, it hearkens up impulses human beings did not shed as they evolved the more humane disciplines of civilization.

Thanks to TV, the United States was able to witness in real time the relentless hammering of Baghdad and its environs. The attack was in one sense a profound relief. The waiting had become excruciating, like the vigil at a prison before an execution. War had become inevitable, and time had become almost unbearable.

And yet there were human beings under the bombs, and many of them surely died horrible deaths. It was exhilarating to witness the success of the U.S. and UN air strikes, and yet what lingers is less the excitement than a pall of regret at what Iraq's tyrant has brought down upon his people.

●●●

The battle was joined when the bombs fell on Baghdad in the dead of night, but those bombs did not trigger the Persian Gulf War. It has been going on since Aug. 2, when Saddam Hussein's legions swept into Kuwait.

Yet ever since it became apparent that a gulf conflict was a real possibility, some Americans seem to have been as eager as the Iraqis to forget about Kuwait.

It wasn't the most attractive nation in the world. It was an oligarchy; women were repressed; human rights and civil liberties on the Western model were not always perfectly observed. But Kuwait was hardly alone in those failings. And it was a member of the United Nations, its existence recognized by all, including Iraq.

Nevertheless, Saddam Hussein last August ordered his armies to invade and occupy it. They did so—ruthlessly, committing horrifying atrocities in the process. Then Saddam annexed it to Iraq. Kuwait had been, as they say in police states, "disappeared." And the war began.

All of the diplomacy since then has been an act of forbearance on the part of the United States and other members of the UN who responded to the appeal for help put out by Kuwait's unlovely, but legitimate, government. And the diplomatic activity continued even after the UN deadline had expired, with nation after nation—including this one—appealling to Saddam Hussein to bring his armies home.

He spurned every attempt.

The attack Wednesday night was not really the start of the war. It was a counterattack.

St. Paul Pioneer Press & Dispatch
St. Paul, Minnesota, January 17, 1991

Even with the 5½ months of warning, the enormity of the news hit with breathtaking force. The United States is at war. The *danse macabre* moves across the Persian Gulf and pushes the world over a new brink.

> **Hope for an early end to this grim task.**

President Bush followed the expected but horrifying news with a suitable and historic address to the people of the United States. But realities carried live on television from the Mideast made his message symbolic rather than full of information.

War came as we feared and anticipated: from the skies in the dead of a dark desert night. Into Kuwait. Into Iraq. Fire and death with the mission to liberate Kuwait, taken by raw aggression last Aug. 2 to further Iraqi President Saddam Hussein's vision of empire.

Like no other war, this one, because of the miracles of technology, will come into America's homes with immediacy and impact that may astonish. But the information age also affords opportunities for those of us who wait and worry far away from Operation Desert Storm. There is a way to evaluate and stay in spirit with Americans and allies pressing the campaign in Iraq.

Watch and hope. Keep the troops and their families in your heart. Hope for an early end to this grim task, with minimum casualties. Hope for containment of hostilities. Hope. Watch. And stand now together as Americans walking toward destiny under the command of a president elected to the most awesome and lonely job in this broken and bleeding world.

The Des Moines Register
Des Moines, Iowa, January 17, 1991

Though war had been anticipated for days, nothing could diminish the sense of dread that accompanied word that "flashes of light" were being seen in Baghdad shortly before 6 p.m. Wednesday. Well before the White House announced that "the liberation of Kuwait has begun," Americans had heard the stunning reports from CNN news crews that air strikes were under way.

Joint Chiefs of Staff Chairman Colin Powell days ago told American troops in the gulf that, "When we launch it, we will launch it violently, we will launch it in a way that will make it decisive so we can get it over as quickly as possible and there's no question who won."

Late Wednesday it was far from over, but there was little question air forces were following through with what Powell had forecast. The initial strikes were described as "massive" and successful.

It was a masterful, well-organized attack, leading to hope that civilian deaths would be minimized. Using elements of surprise and operating with precision, the air forces involved in Operation Desert Storm returned from their missions safely. There could be hope, as well, that the fighting would not be prolonged.

President Bush, in a speech aimed at reassuring Americans that all diplomatic means to settle the Kuwaiti issue had been exhausted, emphasized his view that sanctions would not be sufficient to end Saddam Hussein's occupation of Kuwait. "The world could wait no longer," he said.

He has been less than convincing on that point. Sanctions could have been continued for much longer. There have been signs that they were beginning to have an impact in isolating Saddam; there has been no indication that the 28-nation coalition aligned against the Iraqi dictator was breaking down.

Nor is there much indication that the president has considered what will happen after the current conflict is resolved. He said Wednesday night that American troops would be brought home as soon as possible. But there is no assurance that the current fight will result in a more peaceful Middle East, that world oil supplies will be any more secure, that American forces won't be needed in the region for months if not years.

As for the "New World Order" proclaimed by Bush, with B-52s and F-16s and Stealth fighters remaining the chosen method of resolving conflict, it seems far away indeed.

There will be future debate of those issues. For now, the primary thoughts of Americans will be with their sons and daughters in the gulf, and with the hope that Saddam quickly can be made to recognize the inevitable and back down.

Bush made it clear, in his speech two hours after the attack began, that American forces would be given "the best possible support" to achieve their mission. Now that the attack is under way, they should have nothing less.

ARGUS-LEADER
Sioux Falls, South Dakota, January 17, 1991

Like many Americans, we are not convinced that liberating Kuwait — President Bush's stated objective — is worth the risk of American lives. But we share the belief that Wednesday's military strike was necessary to stop Iraq's ruthless leader, Saddam Hussein.

Iraq's August takeover of Kuwait, a tiny, oil-rich nation governed by a ruling family, was Saddam's greatest mistake. But this battle is not about wealth or natural resources; it is about stopping a man whose demented vision threatens the well-being of the world.

The debate over whether to take on Saddam became moot surprisingly soon Wednesday, when U.S.-led forces led heavy aerial bombardments of military targets in Iraq. Attention shifts now to how long the fighting will last.

Overnight air attacks took a massive toll on Iraq's military potential. But don't look for this to be a two-day skirmish.

Iraq, although not a superpower, has one of the largest military forces in the world, and it is battle-hardened from an eight-year war with Iran.

Saddam has never left any doubt that he would strike back, and his record supports his threatening rhetoric. This is a man who used chemical weapons against Kurdish rebels in his own country. He has suggested that he would attack Israel in an attempt to unite the Arab world against the United States. And he has threatened to strike back with random acts of terrorism throughout the world.

Wednesday's bombardment may have been devastating to Iraq's military, but don't count it out yet.

The United States and its allies must maintain their willingness to strike hard and fast, rather than allow fighting to drag out.

Bush promised again Wednesday night that this would not be another Vietnam. But this isn't a foray into Grenada or Panama, either.

Fortunately, the United States is not acting alone. It has been joined by other world powers, including Great Britain and France.

An argument could be made that the United Nations forces should have stepped up military enforcement of economic sanctions before they started dropping bombs. But that debate is moot. Now that the fighting has started, the issue is one of resolve.

Bush justified the bombing raid effectively in a nationally televised speech by saying it had become apparent that economic sanctions would not convince Saddam to withdraw from Kuwait. Bush also noted that Saddam had met every peace overture with contempt. The world could wait no longer, he said.

"We will not fail," Bush promised.

He and other administration officials were reassuring in unreassuring conditions.

More than 1 million troops are massed on opposite sides — 425,000 of them Americans — in what Saddam says will be the mother of all wars.

U.S. troops deployed five months ago were part of a defensive operation called Desert Shield, a code-name that has given way to an offensive operation called Desert Storm.

This is not an easy war to justify. The United States was not attacked. But it was threatened.

A new world order is due and, as Bush says, may be coming. But it may not come without considerable pain. The United States must be willing to endure.

THE CHRISTIAN SCIENCE MONITOR
Boston, Massachusetts, January 18, 1991

NOW that allied planes have started to bomb Iraqi troops and defense installations, the time for prayer has not ended. No, prayers for peace – in which so many people around the world have joined earnestly in recent days – are needed more urgently than ever.

Those prayers should not be for victory in a strictly military sense. Mere triumph of arms will be ephemeral if it is not accompanied by a heightened world commitment to justice, compassion, and international understanding and cooperation, and to the amelioration of those conditions that produce war: hatred, poverty, ignorance, fear, mad ambition.

We hope for a quick cessation of hostilities. In particular, we hope that the present air phase of the Gulf war will, with minimal loss of life, prove decisive, making unnecessary the clash of huge land armies.

But we also support the success of the forces allied in support of the United Nations. Their goal of enforcing UN resolutions and reversing the Iraqi invasion of Kuwait is just.

Sadly, warfare takes on a dynamic of its own. The destructive force of modern weapons and the speed and maneuverability of modern forces have slashed the margin of error and the time in which to make military decisions.

As the United States and allies unleash massive firepower against Iraq, the need to use force effectively and to protect allied troops may not permit the fine military calibrations one would prefer. Civilians in Iraq and Kuwait may suffer grievously. To the greatest extent consistent with the safe accomplishment of their mission, American commanders must not use force wantonly.

Planning for political and security arrangements in the Middle East after the war must move into high gear. Among the great postwar imponderables are the extent of demoralization and political collapse within Iraq and the reaction of Arab masses to Iraq's defeat. So planning for many different possible outcomes is needed.

America's leaders must also resolve to make this war a catalyst for the resolution of the Israeli-Palestinian dispute. The US correctly resisted formal "linkage" in its dealings with Saddam Hussein. But in fact, linkage exists and will remain.

The US will have a moral and political obligation to moderate Arabs resolutely to broker a just solution. The defeat of Israel's most dangerous enemy in the region should ease its security concerns. Conditions could be ripe for a settlement, but it will require firm US involvement.

The Atlanta Journal AND THE ATLANTA CONSTITUTION
Atlanta, Georgia, January 17, 1991

It has begun, the war we barely could make out on the horizon 5½ months ago, the war that kept looming larger in front of us.

Let us be clear, however, where responsibility for the collision with Iraq lies, first and foremost. It is Saddam Hussein who put himself and his people in their current precarious position, and it is he who rejected every single opportunity for extrication. Taking into account the man's cruelty and his cunning, but most of all his egomaniacal ambitions, it is no wartime bluster to say that we fight for a just cause against evil personified.

Americans may still debate, in retrospect, the wisdom of employing force over economic sanctions, which President Bush said Wednesday night he had concluded could not do the job of forcing Iraq out of Kuwait. But the fact is, there never was any conflict over the objective of the two policies: to remove the Iraqi aggressors from Kuwait.

Now that we are engaged in war, with all its confusion and raw emotions, we must try to stay focused on that goal. Naturally, we must take advantage of our tremendous edge in firepower so as to minimize the losses on our side. Still, we must not allow ourselves to be swept up in a fury over punishing blows from Iraq, if any come, to expand our mission — say, to destroy Iraq as a capable participant in the region's postwar affairs.

That way lies additional allied casualties and more postwar grief when the remains of Iraq could become easy pickings for the likes of Syria or Iran. It is very possible that a defeat in Kuwait would spell the end of Saddam, and even if it doesn't, he and his army will be reduced to a manageable size.

If a new world order is to emerge from the ashes of the Persian Gulf war, as Mr. Bush hoped again last night, the world needs to do much more than merely sign on to non-aggression resolutions in the United Nations. It has to back its moral stance with effective and visible support in the killing fields. And America, too, has to change some old habits.

By accepting America's role as leader of the charge against Saddam, the world implicitly acknowledged the sole remaining superpower's dominant influence. But by not being willing to shed its blood or share more equitably the financial cost of deterring global larceny, the world risks passing up on the opportunity to create a post-Cold War order in which multilateral institutions such as the United Nations could function more effectively as an arbiter of international disputes.

For America, the question now is whether a nation that's long used to being a "Lone Ranger" in policing the world in its own interests can adapt to the new role of a sheriff leading the posse to enforce the law of nations. The gulf war doesn't augur well for this. Washington was so consumed by the Saddam threat, it reverted to its old habits of making questionable alliances (with Syria, for one), twisting arms and rejecting suggestions that did not fall within its own defined parameters on how the crisis ought to be resolved.

But such refinements are for another day, with war behind us. For now, the successful rescue of Kuwait, with as little loss of life as possible, and the self-restraint to limit our mission to just and wise war aims are the sad business at hand. America has entered this war without anger but with purpose. We must fight it that way, too.

WALT HANDELSMAN ©1991 THE TIMES-PICAYUNE

The Philadelphia Inquirer
Philadelphia, Pennsylvania, January 17, 1991

Even as war in the Persian Gulf drew near, most of the world prayed that Saddam Hussein would withdraw from Kuwait. And when the United Nations' deadline came and went, many people still felt that President Bush should hold his fire. But last evening came the news: U.S.-led forces had gone on the attack in America's first major war since Vietnam. Suddenly, the debate over whether to fight or wait was history, and concern for brave souls on the firing line was foremost.

The start of war does not — indeed, it cannot — extinguish our conviction that President Bush switched too soon from embargo to war. Like millions of Americans (but apparently not a majority), we believed that the time for war had still not arrived — not before the embargo had clearly failed, not before diplomacy had been given yet another chance.

But President Bush chose otherwise, concluding, as he told the nation last night, that "only force will make him leave." And he did so after Congress had passionately debated all the options and given him the clear authority to do so. Not even his critics will be able to say that he exceeded his constitutional authority.

At this grave moment, all Americans can be united in respect for the service, the bravery and the potential sacrifice of the hundreds of thousands of men and women in harm's way. This is also a time to reach out to their relatives and friends.

Now, too, without rancor or partisanship, Americans can join in hoping that this war will end soon, that the United Nations will achieve its objective of liberating Kuwait and that the human toll — on all sides — will be less than feared. Finally, this is a time to pray that nations will build a just and lasting peace on the ashes of this war.

AKRON BEACON JOURNAL
Akron, Ohio, January 17, 1991

OPERATION Desert Storm began as so many observers expected, with a massive air strike against Iraq in the early morning hours. American F-15 fighters led the assault, triggering the antiaircraft fire that flashed in the dark skies over Baghdad. "The battle has been joined," as President Bush told the nation.

For many, the moment they first learned of the attack, around seven in the evening, will be etched forever in their memories. Those with family and friends serving in the Persian Gulf, however, are likely to remember first not where they stood, but where their sons and daughters and husbands and wives are stationed in this new theater of war.

There should be no illusions about the risks. Perhaps this battle will be won swiftly. But Saddam Hussein has shown that he's capable of shocking brutality even for wartime. He's used chemical weapons on his countrymen, as well as his foes.

Our thoughts should be with those who've taken up this fight for us and others around the world. Their sacrifice is as great as citizens can give to their country.

When the president named specific soldiers deployed in the gulf — "Hollywood, Walter, J.P. and Jackie" — it was a poignant reminder of the precious lives this country has put at stake. War is uncertain. In a flash, a fight in the Middle East can widen; it's only the distance from here to Cincinnati between Tel Aviv and the Iraqi border.

And yet, the unprecedented coalition of nations lined up against Saddam testifies to the worthiness of this fight.

It's a fight the allied nations didn't want. Saddam wanted it. Without provocation, he invaded Kuwait.

And for more than five months, he's delayed, hoping to preserve the fruits of his aggression. He's shunned countless opportunities to reach a negotiated settlement, including those most recently presented by Arab countries, the French and the United Nations. Even hints of an international conference to deal with the Palestinian issue, which he has cynically trumpeted, have been turned aside.

This week, as the Jan. 15 deadline loomed, Javier Perez de Cuellar, the UN secretary general, ruefully noted that Saddam seemed more interested in serving him tea and cookies than talking about peace.

The economic sanctions imposed by the United Nations against Iraq have been impressive, but, as the president noted, it had become increasingly clear that they alone wouldn't force Saddam from Kuwait. The allied position became far more credible when it included the willingness to use force, and once threatened, force had to be used when the deadline passed.

Vital American interests are at stake in the gulf. Neither the United States, nor its allies, can afford to have Saddam Hussein control almost half of the world's oil reserves, and the influence that would give him over the world's economy.

His thirst for an empire and his pursuit of nuclear weapons promise instability in one of the world's most critical and volatile regions. If he hadn't been confronted now, it's likely the fight would have come later. And allied soldiers would have faced an even more powerful enemy.

Along with everyone else, we hope the air strikes will convince Saddam to get out of Kuwait. It's up to him. He can come to his senses or trigger a land war. The fight shouldn't stop until Kuwait is freed from the hands of this brutal aggressor.

Rockford Register Star
Rockford, Illinois, January 17, 1991

■ **Hostilities commence:** Let's pray for a brief war in the Persian Gulf and an honorable vigil at home.

The advent of war in the Persian Gulf brings with it the hopes and prayers of countless people around the world that the conflict will be mercifully brief with a minimum of casualties. The hope also is that the war will decisively vanquish Saddam Hussein and thereby deter such aggression as Iraq has displayed in violently annexing Kuwait.

With those of all our compatriots, our hearts go out to those American men and women serving their country in the theater of war and to their hopeful families and friends here at home. For these brave young people, prayers are on our lips, lights are in our windows, and yellow ribbons adorn all our old oak trees. We await the safe and victorious return of our men and women in uniform.

While hostilities now render moot questions of whether a strategy of continued economic sanctions against Iraq would have been preferable, other questions concerning American and allied objectives remain valid. Among these is whether the ultimate goals include the liquidation of Saddam and the destruction of his country.

These issues are especially important considering the awesome firepower available to allied forces, including nuclear weaponry on American naval vessels in the Middle East.

As much as anybody else, we want to see no effort spared to give full support to American troops. Still, our hope is that the need can be met with a minimum of violence against innocent civilians. Our foes, as President Bush has noted, are Saddam's government and military, not the Iraqi people.

Another important consideration here on the home front is that war fever not blind us to the rights and civilities mandated by our Constitution. Under our First Amendment, the issues raised by this war remain open to peaceful debate. Nobody has the right to stifle legitimate dissent. But by the same token, no dissenter has a right to resort to violent or otherwise unlawful means of protest.

It is important, too, to remember that Americans of Arabic descent — or of any other race or ethnic origin — are still Americans. Their loyalties should not be unduly questioned. Neither should those of the millions of Americans who embrace the Islamic faith. This war is not against Arabs or Moslems. It is against the aggression of Saddam Hussein.

Let us hope that the war ends soon — and, for the liberators of Kuwait, victoriously. Let us also hope and pray that this episode serves mainly to deter any future military conflicts anywhere in the world, for war in the final analysis is evil.

U.S. SUPREME COURT:

Thomas Narrowly Confirmed as 106th Supreme Court Justice

After one of the most bitter and divisive confirmation battles in the 202-year history of the Supreme Court, the Senate Oct. 15 confirmed Judge Clarence Thomas as the court's 106th associate justice. The 52–48 vote came after three days of televised Senate Judiciary Committee hearings Oct. 11–14 on charges of sexual harassment made against Thomas by a former aide, Anita F. Hill. [See *Editorials On File* 1991, pp. 1148-1173. See also *Facts On File World News Digest* 1991, p. 769A1. For previous developments see *Facts On File* 1991, p. 756E1]

The vote was the closest for a Supreme Court justice in the 20th century. Thomas, who would replace retired Justice Thurgood Marshall, would be the second black to sit on the high court.

After the hearings, the Senate had one full day of debate Oct. 15 before the vote on Thomas's confirmation was held. The Bush administration tried to retain behind Thomas the coalition of Republicans and Southern Democrats who had supported the nominee before Hill's charges arose.

Three Democrats who had openly supported Thomas in September—Joseph Lieberman of Connecticut and Richard H. Bryan and Harry Reid, both of Nevada—switched their votes and opposed his confirmation Oct. 15. They were joined by three other Democrats who had hinted their early support for Thomas. Those were Bob Graham of Florida, Daniel Patrick Moynihan of New York and Robert C. Byrd of West Virginia.

Byrd Oct. 15 took the Senate floor in an impassioned speech on the importance of protecting the judicial process from any cloud of doubt over Thomas's fitness for the Supreme Court. He criticized his fellow Democrats for being intimidated by Thomas's charges of racism and said, "I think it was blatant intimidation and, I'm sorry to say, it worked. I sat there thinking, Who's going to ask him some tough questions? Are they afraid of him?"

He added, "I believe Anita Hill. I did not see on that face the knotted brow of satanic revenge."

Other senators, however, said Thomas deserved the benefit of the doubt. Sen. Alan J. Dixon (D, Ill.) cited criminal court precedent when he explained his decision to back Thomas. He said, "The accused gets the benefit of the doubt."

Sen. Nancy Landon Kassebaum (Kan.), the only woman Republican in the Senate, voted for Thomas, but she chastised the Judiciary Committee for subjecting Hill to an "intellectual witch hunt." She said Thomas would "live under a cloud of suspicion he can never fully escape."

The two Republicans who voted against Thomas, Sens. Bob Packwood of Oregon and James M. Jeffords of Vermont, both said they had made their decision before the hearings on Hill's charges.

Senate Majority leader Sen. George Mitchell (D, Maine) Oct. 15 announced that he would order an investigation of the leaks to the news media of Hill's affidavit to the committee and possibly of copies of the FBI report on her charges. [See *Facts On File* 1991, p. 757C2]

The six Republican senators on the Judiciary Committee, led by Strom Thurmond of South Carolina, had called for an FBI investigation to determine who was responsible for the leak. Throughout the hearings, Republicans charged that Democratic senators' staff members had given confidential committee documents to the media to force hearings on Hill's charges.

The Senate Oct. 16 began a reappraisal of the Supreme Court confirmation process after public criticism swelled in the wake of Thomas's confirmation.

Sens. Sam Nunn (D, Ga.) and Paul Simon (D, Ill.) made proposals for alterations to the process. Both proposals called for more Senate involvement in selecting candidates for confirmation.

President Bush Oct. 16 said all sides agreed that "the present process is simply not fair." He said he was working on suggestions for improvements.

The Times-Picayune
New Orleans, Louisiana, October 16, 1991

Now that the vote is over, Clarence Thomas and Anita Hill can begin to rebuild their lives and reputations.

They have plenty of time to do it. Both young, both secure in the support of their family and friends, they have years to mold their careers, to make their marks.

But the biggest mark already has been left on us.

The most savage confirmation hearing in memory has left a nation of men and women wrestling with their consciences and their memories. It has caused us to remember and to wonder about what we've done and what has been done to us. It has shaped the debate over sexual harassment in the workplace for years to come.

No one knows what form that debate will take. Some columnists have written, in all apparent seriousness, that the Thomas hearings have created a climate in which men and women will be too fearful to make social contact with the opposite sex. They won't be able to flirt, they will never get together, with drastic consequences for the propagation of the human race.

Others worry that Judge Thomas' confirmation hearings send a clear signal to women that it will do no good to complain about the way men treat them on the job. If someone as professional and well spoken as Anita Hill was not believed, what are the chances of an ordinary woman being believed?

They worry that the Thomas hearings — and the outcome of those hearings — only reinforce the code of silence with which women have long met unwelcome sexual attention from men.

We subscribe to a third, more optimistic theory. It holds that what has happened in the Senate hearing room over the past week has for the first time forced the nation to attend to a very real problem that has never been dealt with openly before.

People who never thought about sexual harassment before are thinking about it. People who never talked about it before are talking and arguing and sometimes even communicating.

U.S. Senators were confronted with their own embarrassing lack of understanding and foresight, and sometimes, their own embarrassing pasts.

As a nation, we have had an education in the sometimes difficult relations between men and women in the workplace. Our consciousness, whether we like it or not, has been raised.

There are many questions left to be answered, many disagreements to overcome.

But at least we're talking.

The Providence Journal
Providence, Rhode Island, October 16, 1991

It will be interesting to see how the Senate contends with this remarkable nominee — and tragic if his journey from Pinpoint, Ga., is disrupted by politics in Washington, D.C.

So said these newspapers last July, when President Bush nominated Clarence Thomas to the Supreme Court. Now that Judge Thomas is Justice Thomas, we may possess some semblance of an answer.

We suspect this morning, as we have guessed in the past, that Clarence Thomas will prove worthy of this distinction. In the short run, the Supreme Court will benefit from the presence of an independent-minded black jurist. In the long run, his skeptical nature and inquisitive mind will mix principle with experience, and grant the Court some wisdom. It is true that Clarence Thomas is by no means *the* most qualified person to sit on the Court — who is? — but it is also true that, at age 43, he brings to the nation's highest tribunal an inspiring personal background, a record of accomplishment, an inquisitive intellect, and the courage of his convictions. These are valuable assets.

Justice Thomas will be neither the most saintly, nor the least worthy, human being to sit on the Supreme Court. Americans will argue about the events of this past weekend, but if nothing else is certain, it is palpably true that Justice Thomas is human. There are worse emotions than anger, and bitter experience may teach some useful lessons. You never can tell what the Court might do to justices: Hugo Black was once a member of the Ku Klux Klan, William O. Douglas was a legendary lecher, Earl Warren presided over the internment of Japanese-Americans during the Second World War.

Clarence Thomas has survived this ordeal, will prosper and grow.

Our concern is not so much with Clarence Thomas, but with the process by which the Senate tortures judicial nominees. Ever since the public assassination of Robert Bork's character in 1987, the landscape has been altered. The constitutional duty to advise and consent seems to have evolved into a partisan mandate to subvert and destroy. What is the purpose of these protracted sessions? And why should special interest groups wield decisive influence?

The answer, of course, is divided government. As long as the executive branch is the province of one party, and the legislative branch is the property of another, conflict is inevitable. There are two solutions only. The first, of course, is for the party that controls the executive branch to gain control of the Senate — or vice versa. The second, and more plausible, course of action is for people to make their views known to Congress. If Americans are appalled by the 107 days of Clarence Thomas's ordeal, they should let their representatives know exactly why.

THE BLADE
Toledo, Ohio, October 23, 1991

AMERICANS are rightly accused of being unaware of the history and culture of other nations, but it works the other way too. Many Europeans, for example, never did seem to understand the issues involved in the stormy confirmation hearings for Supreme Court nominee Clarence Thomas.

In general, sophisticated Europeans were inclined to put the hearings down to the puritannical morality of Americans that crops up from time to time, noting that they would not let their views of a politician's personal life affect their judgment of his record as a public servant. This is not true, of course. British leaders are sometimes toppled, at least in part because of sex scandals.

In the aftermath of the hearings over allegations of sexual harassment against Judge Thomas some commentators say the issue really became a matter of race rather than gender. Race still is a major issue and a determinant of viewpoints on many issues. It is, as the late Swedish sociologists Gunnar and Alvah Myrdal pointed out in their monumental work on the subject of race relations in this country, "The American Dilemma."

We have some company in this respect, however. Europeans, too, are increasingly disturbed by Third World immigrants in their midst, many of whom are are people of color. European countries do a better job of controlling illegal immigrants, but it is becoming increasingly difficult for Europeans to ignore the efforts of people from Africa, Asia, and even eastern parts of their own continent to better their lives by moving to a western European country. The United States does not always do well as a melting pot, but it has decades of experience in assimilating peoples of different races, creeds, and nationalities.

Undoubtedly, the sexual harassment charges had a good deal to do with the enormous television audience that ignored some rather dull baseball playoffs to check out the scene of Clarence Thomas and Anita Hill. They were also fascinated and repelled by their contacts with those denizens of the Cave of the Winds, the U.S. Senate.

Puritanism was not the central issue of the Thomas confirmation hearings. Race was an issue — or became one — and sexual harassment was an issue. The hearings exposed some flaws in our society, but they exist in most other societies, too, and they seldom get attention. Sexism is a fundamental aspect of most Asian societies, for example.

The hearings — virtually a national town meeting of the air — contained embarrassing moments for some Americans, and especially some self-important politicians. But they were not, as European critics have suggested, an embarrassment for America as a whole.

Portland Press Herald
Portland, Maine, October 17, 1991

More than any U.S. Supreme Court justice before him, perhaps, Clarence Thomas will begin work on the court bearing a very heavy burden.

First will be the charges of sexual harassment brought against him, unproved but exceedingly troublesome to many, nonetheless, because of the apparent credibility of his accuser.

Many people, particularly women – particularly victimized women, whose number is legion – will think of Thomas first as a suspected abuser, then as a Supreme Court justice. Several of the early cases with which he is expected to deal concern questions of sexual harassment and pornography, which will bring added pain to the new justice.

In a sense, Thomas' traumatic confirmation hearing will never end.

He also will carry the burden of being "expected," in some quarters, to be the conservative justice his mostly Republican supporters visualize him to be. Supporters and opponents alike see his as almost an automatic vote on the court to overturn the Roe vs. Wade abortion decision, for example.

In fact, Thomas will go his own way on the court, just as he has gone his own way in life, whether or not that disappoints those who support him so vociferously now. Growing up in poverty, as Thomas did, enduring the taunts and the discrimination of his more privileged school peers, seeing firsthand the suffering of so many – all this cannot help but have shaped the new justice's values and his life's philosophy.

No one should assume this man is going to carry water for anyone.

Be that as it may, Thomas also will bear the burden of being a role model to black Americans when so many disagree with many of his public statements to date. Again, how he performs on the court will be the greater test of how he is regarded by black Americans and other minorities in time.

Ultimately, it will be the American people who render the final judgment on Thomas. A young man, he may serve for three decades or more, and it's how he will be regarded at the end of that time, rather than at the beginning of it, that will be his true measure.

For now, he should have Americans' prayers as he takes up the burdens and challenges of his high office.

EUROPE:

Soviet Union Disbands; Gorbachev Resigns

The Soviet Union officially disbanded Dec. 25, replaced by a Commonwealth of Independent States made up of 11 of the 12 former Soviet constituent republics. The demise of the U.S.S.R. came shortly after Soviet President Mikhail S. Gorbachev announced his immediate resignation in a nationally televised address. [See *Editorials On File* 1991, pp. 1396-1413. See also *Facts On File World News Digest* 1991, p. 969A1. For previous developments see *Facts On File* 1991, p. 945A1, A2. For data on the republics, see *Facts On File* 1991, p. 641A2]

The Soviet Union, formed in 1922, was dissolved with little ceremony 33 minutes after Gorbachev's resignation, when the giant red Soviet flag atop the Kremlin was replaced by the white, red and blue flag of prerevolution Russia.

The U.S. and other countries, while expressing regret at Gorbachev's decision, nonetheless quickly moved to recognize the new realities: The U.S.S.R. no longer existed, and Russian President Boris N. Yeltsin had pushed aside Gorbachev to assume de facto leadership of the region.

Events of Dec. 19 and Dec. 21 made Gorbachev a head of state in name only, leaving him no recourse but to step down.

On Dec. 19, President Yeltsin issued decrees directing the Russian government to seize the Kremlin and to take over or replace the functions of the entire Soviet central government with the exceptions of the ministries of defense and atomic energy.

For example, Gosbank—the Soviet central bank—was taken over by the Russian state bank. The U.S.S.R.'s embassies and consulates became Russian diplomatic facilities. And the Soviet and Russian interior ministries, plus the domestic-intelligence wing of the KGB (Soviet state security agency), were merged into a new Russian ministry.

Gorbachev denounced the decrees as illegal, but he could no nothing to block them.

The unofficial end of the Soviet Union came on Dec. 21, when all of the republics except Georgia, which was embroiled in a civil war, signed agreements to create the commonwealth. The pact was signed at a meeting of the republics' presidents in Alma-Ata, the capital of the Central Asian republic of Kazakhstan. The former Soviet Baltic republics (Estonia, Latvia and Lithuania) were not party to the agreements. [For texts of the Commonwealth agreements, see box *Facts On File* 1991, p. 972A1]

President Gorbachev stepped down in a brief, bitter speech to the country Dec. 25. In power six years and 10 months, he was the last Soviet leader. [See *Facts On File* 1985, p. 177A1. For a text of Gorbachev's resignation speech, see *Facts On File* 1991, p. 970A1]

Before going on the air, Gorbachev telephoned U.S. President Bush and was reported to have thanked the American leader for his support.

In his address, Gorbachev reminded the people of his personal triumphs. But, he added, "The policy prevailed of dismembering this country and disuniting the state, with which I cannot agree."

Gorbachev had done more than any other figure to end the Cold War and curb the arms race. He had put the Soviet Union on the road to democracy, freed political prisoners, opened Jewish emigration, pulled Soviet troops out of Afghanistan, and attempted to reform the Soviet Union's archaic system of central economic planning. He had introduced the concepts of *perestroika* (restructuring), *glasnost* (openness), "new thinking" (pragmatism) and "democratization." [For a listing of key events of the Gorbachev years, see *Facts On File* 1991, p. 971A1]

Analysts noted that Gorbachev—still a committed Marxist—could not have foreseen that his reforms ultimately would lead to the fall of communism in Eastern Europe and in the Soviet Union. They also noted the contradictions during his reign. For example, while pushing for democracy, he himself never ran in a popular election. While advocating market reforms, he had resisted the introduction of true capitalism. While supporting more autonomy for the Soviet republics, he had opposed the independence movements that gained impetus as a result of his own policies.

ST. LOUIS POST-DISPATCH
St. Louis, Missouri, December 27, 1991

"He didn't know how to make sausage, but he did know how to give freedom. And if someone believes that the former is more important than the latter, he is likely never to have either." So the newspaper *Komsomolskaya Pravda* aptly appraised the precious gift that Mikhail Gorbachev gave to his fellow citizens. And it was precisely because he offered freedom, not sausage, that Mr. Gorbachev, the former president of a former superpower, resigned.

Mr. Gorbachev originally wanted to do both. When he came to power in 1985, he was fully aware that the Soviet Union was saddled with a moribund economy and a corrupt political system. He introduced glasnost, openness or the freedom to speak and remember, as a way to stimulate perestroika, or economic restructuring. Without freedom, believed Mr. Gorbachev, the Soviets wouldn't have sausage.

To realize how radical this view was, consider the geriatric Chinese leaders who believe that economic reform could be achieved without political freedom, indeed that economic reform would substitute for freedom. That view culminated in Tiananmen Square, not the euphoric Red Square in August.

Once freedom is introduced, the consequences are unpredictable. Certainly Mr. Gorbachev didn't know that his reforms would end in the death of the Soviet Union. For a long time, Mr. Gorbachev thought the system could be reformed. Without that vision of socialism with a human face animating his moves, he may never have been so bold — or so successful. As writer Victor Yerofeyev put it, "He had just enough intelligence to change everything but not enough to see that everything would be destroyed."

Mr. Gorbachev accomplished his historical task of setting his country on the way to freedom. Under his stewardship, the hegemony of the Communist Party was shattered, and a rudimentary system of multiple parties and representative institutions was born. The monolithic press shattered into a media of many voices and inclinations. Ideas blossomed.

Mr. Gorbachev presided over the remarkably peaceful collapse of the Soviet external and internal empire. It was not his job to build the successor state or states. Freedom and democracy also mean that the people have a voice in building their future. As much as Mr. Gorbachev wanted the Soviet Union to continue, the people didn't — so the once mighty nation collapsed and the Commonwealth of Independent States arose in its wake.

The commonwealth is likely to be but a transitional arrangement. At the moment, it exists primarily as a mechanism for transfering the responsibilities of the Soviet state to Russia primarily and the other republics. While the world's attention was focused on Soviet nuclear weapons, there remain major questions about the future of the former Soviet army, navy and air force that will take time to resolve.

If the commonwealth respects current borders, keeps them open and relies on a common currency and military, it may actually be the nucleus of a new union. Other forces, such as nationalism and the violence in Georgia, are just as likely to doom the commonwealth. It would be foolhardy to say what the commonwealth will look like a year from now.

But one thing is crystal clear. With Mr. Gorbachev gone, the next generation of leaders, most especially Russian President Boris Yeltsin, must now grapple with the dialectic of sausage and freedom. Will they succeed as well in their historic mission as Mr. Gorbachev did with his?

The Seattle Times

Seattle, Washington, December 27, 1991

FOR all the political momentum Mikhail Gorbachev inspired, he left no clear picture of where he intended the Union of Soviet Socialist Republics to go.

Both are now history. His resignation Wednesday came moments before the red flag with its hammer and sickle were lowered from atop the Kremlin.

Gorbachev came to power in 1985 with a keen grasp of what ailed his country, but historians will record that he was reluctant to follow his own prescriptions for radical therapy.

His youthfulness was invigorating after three doddering predecessors, and more important, his age gave Gorbachev emotional distance from Soviet history in World War II.

Gorbachev operated with a measure of detachment and skepticism about the military's drain on the economy. As early as May 1986, he told a Central Committee conference, "We are encircled not by invincible armies but by superior economies."

His grip on the real enemy of the Communist state allowed him to extricate the Soviet Union from its own Vietnam-like quagmire in Afghanistan, negotiate for arms controls, and push for an end to Cold War relations with Western powers.

British Prime Minister Margaret Thatcher declared he was a man with whom she and others could do business. They were comfortable with one another in the ether levels of superpower politics. What happened on his own turf was his problem.

If Gorbachev was a visionary on the international scene, his insight was less acute at home.

After decades of totalitarian rule, the political freedom of glasnost was a tonic. Perestroika's tinkering with the economy inflicted hardships that were never understood as movement toward an identifiable goal.

Gorbachev was haunted by his own ambivalence. He artfully finessed conservative elements who resisted all change, but could not bring himself to follow through on substantive reform.

In their book, "Gorbachev, Heretic in the Kremlin," Dusko Doder and Louise Branson, Moscow bureau chiefs for the The New York Times and The Sunday Times of London, remind readers he banned all business deals that might damage the central planning system.

In his desire to preserve the Soviet state, Gorbachev cemented bonds with the most reactionary elements of the security forces, the Communist Party, and regional military commands. As the end drew near, they tried to dump him.

Gorbachev dispatched elite military units to Baltic republics to crush uprisings. He refused to cede power to the nationalist movements that found a voice in his Russian rival, Boris Yeltsin.

In the fall of 1990, Gorbachev reversed his own democratic rhetoric to push hard for direct presidential control. On Dec. 20, 1990, his foreign minister, Eduard Shevardnadze, resigned with a warning, "Dictatorship is coming."

Twelve months and five days after – in the midst of growing economic hardship and failure to check independence movements – Gorbachev surrendered his powerless title.

His epitaph may be something on the order of "No Follow Through." Gorbachev did not have the power and vision to change the nation. He was not ruthless enough to hold it together.

Gorbachev is admired, even beloved, abroad. At home, people are contemplating his place in history as they stand in bread lines.

CHICAGO Sun-Times

Chicago, Illinois, December 27, 1991

And while we're wishing them all well, we also wish we could count on more than Boris Yeltsin's word for it that there is no need to fear a nuclear attack from the former Soviet Union.

The Russian president says the leaders of the three other republics with strategic weapons, Ukraine, Byelorussia and Kazakhstan, have agreed to grant him control of the entire existing nuclear arsenal and that "we will do all we can to prevent this nuclear button" from ever being used.

His peers in those republics seem less definitive on this, though, and the president of Kazakhstan has let it be known that he has not approved withdrawal of any nuclear weapons from his turf.

Can we get a warranty on Yeltsin's assurances?

San Francisco Chronicle

San Francisco, California, December 25, 1991

IT IS SOBERING to realize that Mikhail Gorbachev, whose resignation as president of the Soviet Union is expected to be announced today, has actually been at the helm for a mere six and a half years. That so much fundamental change could occur in such relatively little time, and with such little bloodshed, defies our traditional notions about the plodding pace of political change.

He was an intrepid helmsman at a time of whirlpools

"Time is nature's way of making sure everything doesn't happen all at once," somebody once said. But Gorbachev interfered with such natural laws. Emerging from the gloom and stagnation of the Brezhnev era, he perceived that if change did not occur on a massive and urgent scale, time would run out for the atrophied power of Soviet communism and the union itself.

In 1985, Gorbachev understood that he could either be the last dictator of a fading empire, resisting change into his own Brezhnevian dotage; or he could open the floodgates, via glasnost and perestroika, and — given enough skill and courage — become the first leader of a renewed and dynamic superpower.

To his eternal credit — and what should be the gratitude of the world — Gorbachev chose the latter, believing he could master the mighty forces he set loose. The fact that it did not work out that way — that the changes eventually swallowed up the transformer — reflects not so much on Gorbachev's lack of vision or skill as on the transcending power of political liberation itself.

When Gorbachev gave the Soviet people the freedom to speak their minds, he also gave them, for the first time, a reason to use their minds — and their hearts. With today's perfect, 20-20 hindsight, it is clear that from that point on no single helmsman could remain secure at the heart of the whirlpool.

In the end, by gracefully relinquishing the official reins of his once formidable power, he adds yet another first to his remarkable tally of achievements: the freeing of his empire's Eastern European satellites, the ending of the East-West Cold War and the resulting nuclear de-escalation, the initiation of the economic and political transformation of the Soviet Union, and the introduction of political pluralism in the world's largest nation.

AND SO THE END has come for Gorbachev, and for the Soviet Union itself, while the powers he unleashed still run rampant, transforming not only the former union but the entire geopolitical world.

While the final verdict must be reserved to the historians, no one who has lived through the last six and a half tumultuous years needs a text book to know that the world has been enriched by a great man.

THE DAILY OKLAHOMAN

Oklahoma City, Oklahoma,
December 31, 1991

INSTABILITY in the former Soviet Union may produce the most dangerous scenario since President John F. Kennedy and Nikita Khrushchev faced off during the Cuban missile crisis 30 years ago.

While a nuclear attack on the United States seems remote, the specter of nuclear weapons falling into the hands of smaller, extremist nations is terrifying.

Russian leader Boris Yeltsin has attempted to convince the world the vast nuclear stockpile is under tight control, but events make it clear he is not totally in control of the arsenal.

Although Yeltsin may have the codes needed to fire missiles, the warheads are physically located in other former republics from where they could be sold and delivered to other nations. Of particular concern is the proximity of at least one of the former republics to Iran.

The so-called "Muslim Bomb" has been the dream of several nations, including Iran, Iraq, Pakistan and Libya. We can be certain leaders of all the countries are seeking ways to exploit the situation to their advantage.

The instability increases the chances for enriched materials used to make nuclear weapons to find an outlet to other countries. Also, the nuclear scientists who developed the Soviet arsenal can command high prices if they should defect to other nations.

The world will not be able to breathe easily until the 27,000 nuclear weapons in the former Soviet Union are brought under tight controls.

In the hands of terrorists even one nuclear bomb could be disastrous. While the United States can detect and track missiles fired at our shores, it is defenseless against a nuclear device placed in a ship bound for New York harbor.

The Atlanta Journal
THE ATLANTA CONSTITUTION
Atlanta, Georgia, December 27, 1991

Mikhail Gorbachev still possesses the vigor of an ex-farmhand, a hard-edged intelligence, untapped reserves of self-confidence and a flair for the dramatic public gesture. It seems risky to write the political obituary of such a hardy corpse, but Mr. Gorbachev finally ran afoul of so many constituencies it is difficult to imagine a second political life for him.

Mikhail Gorbachev

The privileged holders of Communist Party cards consider him a traitor to his class in what was supposed to be a classless society. Many idled military officers deplore the low estate to which they and the former superpower that they served have plummeted. Liberal reformers who once considered him a soulmate have written him off as vacillating or manipulative, more interested in his own survival than in systemic renewal. And the bulk of his countrymen hold him accountable because the once all-powerful system no longer provides for their basic needs.

Still, to hear average Muscovites on the street Wednesday ruminating upon his resignation, one could get the impression his rehabilitation had just begun, if grudgingly. For all the mounting inconveniences and deprivation they have endured during Mr. Gorbachev's six years in power, some thoughtful Russians are willing to concede their sacrifices have been worthwhile because, at long last, they no longer are living a lie.

Indeed, glasnost — openness — has surely worked better than perestroika, Mr. Gorbachev's sputtering attempt at economic reform. If glasnost's champion, Mr. Gorbachev, fudged now and then, at least he made it possible for truths to be unearthed, disseminated and discussed openly in a society that has been kept in the dark for centuries.

On the larger world stage, Mr. Gorbachev probably had as much effect on 20th century history as Winston Churchill, another defender of empire who lived to see its liquidation. However, Mr. Gorbachev made his mark less by what he did than what he didn't do.

He could have stepped up the war in Afghanistan, but he didn't. He could have conducted Cold War business as usual, the insurgencies and the terrorism and the arms race, but he didn't. He could have intervened when Soviet clients in Eastern Europe began toppling left and right, but he didn't — not even when Germany reunited as a full partner in the European Community and (gulp!) NATO.

As a result of his actions and his failures to act, intended or not, the Soviet Union is no more, its Communist Party is defunct and the country's once-vaunted military is in disarray. One nation dominated from the center has been transformed into a dozen republics.

When Mr. Gorbachev took power in 1985, he had the savvy to realize what his predecessors did not: that his country was in steep decline. His biggest mistake was to think a structural overhaul would do when a complete replacement was called for. His own dithering compounded his problems; he conceded as much in his farewell speech.

With it all, power has been transferred and an empire disassembled on Mr. Gorbachev's watch with mercifully little blood being shed, a remarkable feat in Russian history. The general tone that he set while in office and the grace with which he relinquished it contributed greatly to the smooth transition and may be his most valuable legacy to his people.

St. Petersburg Times
St. Petersburg, Florida, December 26, 1991

Mikhail Gorbachev's resignation, long a foregone conclusion, came at a time when most of the West was preoccupied with celebrating Christmas. But his formal departure deserves to be noted as the end of a remarkable political and personal drama.

The achievements of the eighth and last leader of the now-officially-defunct Union of Soviet Socialist Republics are unparalleled in the 20th century. Gorbachev transformed his country's totalitarian Communist system, removed the Iron Curtain from Eastern Europe, inspired arms-control agreements and set the stage for political accords in a number of regional trouble spots. His failures, however, were equally spectacular. Too often, he found himself reacting to rather than out front of the momentous events he unleashed.

History's final judgment of Gorbachev will depend to a great extent on what eventually emerges from the ferment he set in motion. As he departs, there is anything but certainty that Boris Yeltsin's shaky confederation of former Soviet republics can solve mounting economic, political and social crises. Especially troubling is the question of whether some 27,000 nuclear weapons are in secure hands.

Gorbachev himself seemed all but convinced Wednesday that Yeltsin's experiment would fail. "Today is a dangerous time," he warned after his resignation speech.

In a nationally televised address, President George Bush warmly praised the courage of a former enemy who helped free the world from the grip of a Cold War arms race. One way we can repay that courage is to heed Gorbachev's caveats, and help to finish the work he started.

The Phoenix Gazette
Phoenix, Arizona, December 28, 1991

Who would have imagined that Lenin's body would outlast Soviet communism?

The Soviet Union is ashes, but the embalmed remains of Vladimir Lenin endure. Few people visit the Soviet Union without viewing the wax-like figure in the glass box on Red Square. The faithful regularly stand in line several hours to pay their respects. But the faithful are less numerous than they used to be and their numbers are likely to keep shrinking.

If the patriarch of communism is removed, it won't be the first time that a body has been taken from the mausoleum. Josef Stalin shared the structure for eight years, until Nikita Khrushchev's revelations caused him to be evicted.

According to his will, Lenin wanted to rest beside his mother and sister in Volkovo Cemetery in St. Petersburg — the city that used to be called Leningrad.

The union has been buried. It's only fitting that Lenin be extended the same courtesy.

The Virginian-Pilot
Norfolk, Virginia, December 27, 1991

It's official: The Soviet Union — a Russian empire fashioned and maintained by force — is no more. The Commonwealth of Independent States, its successor, is in business.

Perhaps the commonwealth will flourish. Perhaps future historians will say Russian Federation President Boris Yeltsin, who leads the biggest, richest and most populous of the 11 states composing the commonwealth, fostered prosperity.

But perhaps not. Ex-Soviet President Mikhail Gorbachev, who abandoned his office Wednesday, is hailed by President Bush and other national leaders for destroying the totalitarian Soviet regime, freeing Eastern Europe and ending the Cold War. But he is reviled at home for wrecking the economy. Will Mr. Yeltsin and the leaders of the other states trigger a speedy economic renaissance?

Not likely. Mr. Yeltsin will push economic development. But if the commonwealth doesn't improve living standards, Mr. Yeltsin will also be unpopular.

Supplanting a 70-year-old command economy with one based on private enterprise, private property, free markets and convertible currency is a lengthy chore. Prolonged economic pain for the common-wealth is the prospect. Continuing hardship — shortages of jobs, food, shelter — could sharpen ethnic rivalries; ignite trade wars, civil wars and cross-border wars; and revive dictatorship. With its expertise, private investment, trade and assorted aid, the West may hold the key that staves off anarchy and tyranny.

The top Western concerns are the nuclear missiles that remain scattered about four commonwealth states. But Mr. Yeltsin alone controls the button, and the commonwealth promises to honor all arms-control agreements. That's reassuring.

Is a return to the Stalinist days of brutal repression on a continental scale in the cards? Not likely either, although elements of the military, the KGB security police and the deposed Soviet bureaucracy may grab for power, especially if discontent flares into upheaval. But because Mr. Gorbachev opened the Soviet Union to the world, outside ties are obstacles to aspiring despots. Among other things, the West would exact economic and diplomatic penalties from counterrevolutionaries.

Mr. Gorbachev confronted complex, perilous challenges. He bested many, but many remain. Hope that his successors succeed where he failed.

UNITED STATES AFFAIRS:

Riots Erupt in Los Angeles after Video Beating Verdict

A California Superior Court jury in suburban Simi Valley April 29 acquitted four white Los Angeles police officers on all but one charge stemming from a March 1991 beating of black motorist Rodney G. King. The beating, videotaped by a resident of a nearby apartment complex, was broadcast around the world and provoked outrage at police brutality nationwide. In the hours after the verdict was announced, looting and violence broke out across the predominantly black and Hispanic South-Central section of Los Angeles despite appeals for calm from city officials and black leaders. As the sun set, the attacks grew increasingly more violent, and more than 100 arson fires engulfed much of the area. About a dozen people were reported killed by day's end. [See *Editorials On File* 1991, pp. 778-783, 420-423, 352-357. See also *Facts On File World News Digest* 1992, p. 304D1. For previous developments see *Facts On File* 1991, p. 575F1]

Los Angeles Mayor Tom Bradley (D) April 29 declared a local state of emergency, and California Gov. Pete Wilson (R) ordered the National Guard to report for duty, to assist local police trying to control the growing anarchy. The riots were said to be the worst since the August 1965 Watts riots in Los Angeles in which 34 people were killed over six days. [See *Facts On File* 1965, p. 293E2]

The 81-second videotape of the beating, the prosecution's key piece of evidence, showed police officers repeatedly kicking King and hitting him more than 50 times with their batons as he lay on the ground. Nonetheless, the jury acquitted Sgt. Stacey Koon and officers Timothy E. Wind and Theodore J. Briseno of all charges against them, including assault with a deadly weapon, excessive use of force by a police officer, filing a false report and acting as an accessory after the fact. The fourth defendant, Officer Laurence M. Powell, who was seen delivering most of the blows, was acquitted on charges of assault with a deadly weapon and filing a false police report.

The jury, after deliberating for 32 hours over seven days, deadlocked on a single count accusing Powell of assault under color of police authority. Judge Stanley M. Weisberg said he would hold a hearing May 15 to determine if Powell would be retried on the charge.

Koon, Powell and Briseno had been suspended without pay since the incident. Wind, a rookie at the time of the beating, had been fired.

Remaining anonymous, as they had during the trial, several jurors spoke with national news organizations April 29 explaining how the jury had reached its verdicts. One woman told KNBC-TV in Los Angeles that she had voted for acquittal because King had resisted arrest and was "in full control" of the situation both before and during the beating.

The six-man, six-woman jury that acquitted the police officers had no black members. It was made up of 10 whites, one Asian and one Hispanic. Simi Valley, where the trial was held, was located 45 miles (70 km) northwest of Los Angeles in Ventura County. It was a predominantly white bedroom community where many police officers and firefighters lived.

(In July 1991, the California Second District Court of Appeal had granted a change of venue to avoid having the judicial process tainted by pretrial publicity. Judge Weisberg chose the new venue in November 1991, after the first judge in the case, Judge Bernard Kamins, was removed by the appeals court in August.)

In a televised address, Mayor Bradley, who was black, appealed for calm and expressed outrage at the verdict, saying, "Today the system failed us." He added, "The jury's verdict will never blind us to what we saw on that videotape. The men who beat Rodney King do not deserve to wear the uniform of the L.A.P.D."

Los Angeles Police Chief Daryl F. Gates said, "I don't think anyone has come out of this a winner. I'm hopeful that we can all move on."

THE BUFFALO NEWS
Buffalo, New York, May 1, 1992

LIKE RELIGION, democracy sometimes is a test of faith, demanding that practitioners accept the unexplainable even when there is no evidence for doing so.

So it is with the appalling Rodney King verdict that asks a nation not to believe its eyes, and yet still to believe that "the system" works.

It is a staggering miscarriage of justice that asks African-Americans in particular — but anyone who might come in contact with police — to believe that the law protects them from unjustified abuse, when this verdict clearly says it does not.

Perhaps the only way to look at it is like lightning — one hopes it can't strike twice, that no other jury could rationalize so fatuous a decision.

But that is meager consolation for the millions of Americans for whom the verdict hit like a blunt kick — or nightstick blow — in the stomach. The notion that what the country saw on tape is deemed appropriate police conduct takes all the wind out of a populace that thought it had long passed the point where unbridled state violence against minorities could be condoned.

Jurors talking anonymously said incredibly that King — writhing on the ground after being shocked with a stun gun and clubbed 56 times — "controlled the situation." He did that, according to this twisted logic, by running from police and initially resisting arrest.

What that says is that once anyone tussles with police, all bets are off. The concept of using the minimum force necessary goes out the window. Police are free to cite imagined fears — like saying King was high on PCP when he wasn't — as justification for continuing a savage beating far beyond what is necessary to make an arrest. Giving police such license should frighten anyone.

And then there is the subtly disturbing admission that King's failure to testify had an impact — even though it was not supposed to under the law. Some will second-guess prosecutors, but there was no reason to put King on the stand. The damning tape spoke for itself; and King, after all, was not on trial. At least, he was not supposed to be.

But juror comments make it clear he was. And the message implicit in that is that a disheveled-looking African-American who's been drinking has somehow relinquished the right not to be abused. Los Angeles police certainly thought so; their racist comments among themselves after the incident made that clear.

This jury — which included no blacks and was convened in mostly white Ventura County after the trial was moved from Los Angeles — apparently thought so, too.

The U.S. Justice Department is reviewing the case to determine whether to prosecute under federal civil rights laws. The three of the four defendants still in the department also face internal hearings, and one could be retried on a single charge. Civil suits also will follow.

But none of that can make up for this jury's betrayal of justice. Restoring the faith will not be easy.

The Hartford Courant
Hartford, Connecticut, May 1, 1992

The surprising verdict was "not only an insult to the black race, but an insult to the human race." So said an African-American minister Wednesday after a jury acquitted four white Los Angeles police officers in the beating of a black suspect, Rodney G. King.

He was right. The system failed. If ever the term "miscarriage of justice" truly applied, it is to this case.

Americans don't always agree with jury verdicts, but they usually accept them. In our system, it is presumed, correctly, that juries have more information, that they've fully heard both sides of the argument and that they've been carefully instructed in the law by the judge. Because of all that, we give juries the benefit of the doubt. They know what we don't know.

But not in the Rodney King case. It makes no difference that he was a convicted felon or that he drunkenly led the police on a high-speed chase or that the officers said they were afraid of him. It makes no difference that the jury heard all the evidence.

Thanks to a video tape fortuitously made by a neighbor, millions of Americans saw the accused officers mercilessly beat Mr. King with batons and kick him while he was on the ground. They used excessive force by any measure, and that's against the law. But the jury allowed what the law forbids.

Millions of Americans read the accounts of smug, racist communications between the offending officers and headquarters — the "gorillas in the mist" comments, the laughter, the casual references to the frequency of beatings by police.

The public was able to put the video image and the officers' words together to form a complete picture of racially motivated brutality.

Yet the jury seemed to ignore the obvious. Its verdict demonstrates how blindly trusting many Americans are of the police, no matter how badly some officers might betray that trust. The verdict demonstrated, too, that when a venue is changed — as this one was from the city to a bedroom community — to give the defendants a fair trial, the result can be that the victim is denied a fair trial. There were no blacks on this jury; it was white except for an Asian and a Hispanic.

Sadly, the acquittals spawned violence and bloodshed in Los Angeles. Criminals took advantage of righteous anger to loot stores, burn buildings and beat and shoot innocent people, black and white. But the black community suffered the most from the out-of-control violent reaction to an injustice. As much as the verdict hurt, as great the despair, the violence must stop. It serves no good purpose and only begets more hate and unhappiness.

The Rodney King nightmare is an awful stain on America. Robert S. Strauss, U.S. ambassador to Moscow, said on the Larry King show Wednesday night that all he could tell Russians is that democracy allows for such results as the acquittal verdict. Yes, it would be fair for them to conclude that democracy allows for injustice and racism.

Some good has come out of the King beating. L.A. Police Chief Daryl F. Gates, who created a climate of brutality and intolerance in his department, is leaving. He will be replaced by a black chief, Willie L. Williams, who has to rebuild the force. Amidst the anger, there should be hope. What happens next could be important to every city, from Los Angeles to Hartford.

But that does not mean efforts should cease to bring Mr. King's tormenters to justice. The U.S. Justice Department is investigating whether to bring charges of civil-rights violations against the officers. The Bush administration should have the courage to act.

THE SUN
Baltimore, Maryland, May 1, 1992

The brutal beating of Rodney King last spring was sufficient to unseat the entrenched Los Angeles police chief, Daryl Gates. But it was not sufficient to convict the four police officers who beat Mr. King. Something is wrong. It is not enough to say the verdict was wrong, as almost anyone who saw the videotape of the beating would conclude. But was the jury wrong, or does blame lie with the legal machinations and judicial decisions which gave birth to the jury?

Lesson after lesson in the past 25 years teaches that the perception that justice has been thwarted by racism is the single most volatile element in civil riots. Police brutality also fuels unrest in minority communities. The fact that the videotaped beating of Mr. King by four white police officers did not touch off rioting when it was broadcast again and again last year underscores the cry of anguish that exploded Wednesday night in South Los Angeles. White and black Angelenos alike initially expected a fair trial for the policemen, judged by a cross-section selected from their communities. Instead, the trial was moved from the central city area where the incident occurred — and the trial should have taken place — to a distant suburb populated by a narrow segment of the population. A downtown jury could have freed the policemen without a perception that justice had been cheated. A jury without a single African American could not.

Most police departments and judicial systems have come a long way since the epidemic of urban unrest of the '60s and '70s. But clearly not all the lessons have been learned in Los Angeles and perhaps elsewhere. Justice must not only be served; it must be perceived to be served. And not just by the majority of a community — by all of it, particularly the minorities who are most alienated from the social fabric of our communities. That means not only community relations programs, sensitivity training and more nonwhite police commanders. It also means everyday police work that is firm, fair and professional — that does nothing to foment civil disorder but also knows how to deal with it if it occurs. It means a judiciary that is not so remote it exacerbates social tensions.

The courts of California have spoken in the King case. They have ill-served the cause of justice. Now it is up to the protector of civil rights of last resort, the federal government, to see that justice is both served and seen to be served.

THE SPOKESMAN-REVIEW
Spokane, Washington, April 30, 1992

Rodney King was no choir boy, that's for sure.

He was a drunk parolee with a second-degree robbery conviction on March 3, 1991, when he led Los Angeles police officers on a high-speed auto chase that ended in an L.A. suburb. He climbed from his car in a manner that some of the 15 lawmen on hand deemed menacing.

Most Americans have seen the videotape of what happened next — something the law-enforcement officer in charge described as "a managed and controlled use of force."

It involved kicking, clubbing and a 50,000-volt stun gun. It lasted nearly a minute and a half and resulted in King's suffering 11 skull fractures, a crushed cheekbone, a broken ankle, internal injuries, a burn and brain damage.

Managed? Controlled? Absurd.

Yet a Los Angeles Superior Court jury apparently bought it. After nearly three months of trial and seven days of deliberation, they acquitted the four officers of all charges except for one excessive-force count against one officer and they deadlocked on that.

Justice was not done. Justice, like Rodney King, was brutalized.

What prompted the jury to reach its stunning conclusion? Were they saying a black man is fair game for a herd of baton-wielding white police officers? Were they expressing their frustration with crime and sending a message that parolees lose their constitutional protections?

Let's hope it was merely a case of 12 sincere people, faced with a tough job, innocently reached a horribly wrong decision.

Unfortunately, the verdict has seared the sensitivities of those who already believe bigotry contaminates the justice system.

After all, even Los Angeles Police Chief Daryl Gates — who once observed that blacks are more susceptible to choke holds than "normal people" and who resigned over the King incident — had said the beating "brought shame and dishonor upon the police profession."

During the trial, hospital nurses who treated King described police officers as taunting and mocking him. A California highway patrolwoman who first stopped King testified that she had him subdued before Los Angeles police took over. The officers' own comments, recorded over police radio afterward, reflected a cavalier, gloating attitude. Even one of the defendants, Officer Theodore Briseno, said he thought the beating was wrong.

This isn't an indictment against our system of justice which works more often than not. But sometimes it errs, as it did in this case.

For a brighter, and thankfully more typical, discussion of the character of law-enforcement professionals, keep reading . . .

The Arizona Republic
Phoenix, Arizona, May 2, 1992

Through the smoke and fiery rhetoric, several truths may be discerned from this week's mayhem in south-central Los Angeles, where more than a score are dead and hundreds injured.

One truth has to do with the agents of violence, who are commonly misidentified. Another has to do with how those who have sworn to keep the peace, not to wring their hands and issue platitudes, need to respond to chaos, even chaos of overwhelming magnitude. The two truths are not unrelated.

Since the Watts riots of 1965 and the widespread violence touched off by the murder three years later of Dr. Martin Luther King Jr., America seems to have learned little about either the origins of urban violence or how to contain it. Despite voluminous reports from the McCone and Kerner Commissions, the initial response of Los Angeles officials this week remains the standard. As millions of TV viewers looked on aghast, the L.A. police watched from the sidelines while swarms of hoodlums ransacked stores and lugged sofas and cases of whiskey to waiting automobiles.

The police did not intervene, it is clear, because they had no orders to do so. Indeed, they seem to have been ordered to avoid the least "provocation," for fear that the rioters might be antagonized. So here were the police, who a year earlier had yanked a motorist from his car and beaten him senseless, effectively paralyzed in the face of a general breakdown of law and order.

Why? Part of the reason may have to do with the common mistake of confusing legitimate protest and lawlessness. Americans of all races were outraged by the jury's verdict in the Rodney King case — a verdict rendered in stubborn defiance of the visible facts. But the overwhelming majority did not pillage or riot. Those who did are in no way representative of the black community in Los Angeles or any other city. These are not people who are "disenchanted with the system." They are people who prey on the system. They constitute a criminal underclass, and it is as criminals that they should be treated.

That this is not the general perception is the fault largely of those who shape public opinion, including some public officials. Speaking on the Cable News Network yesterday, former California Gov. Jerry Brown, who aspires to be president of the United States, expressed passionate dismay at the torching and looting of his state's largest city. Yet he harbored no apparent animus toward the rioters and looters. His irritation was reserved for what he called "an institutionalized injustice across America." This is a widespread and — what is worse — paralysis-inducing analysis.

Is there injustice in America? Of course. Was the King verdict an instance of it? So it seems. But to observe that society is imperfect or that some Americans, conspicuously African-Americans, have been the victims of injustice in no way explains the disorders in Los Angeles. The riots, as we say, are the work of a lawless minority. Most African-Americans are as appalled as everyone else. To suggest otherwise, to lump them together with the rioting riffraff — this itself constitutes a gross injustice.

Such stereotyping distorts reality and spreads confusion in a situation demanding clear heads. What Los Angeles requires now most of all is an end to lawlessness, and muddled moralizing is unlikely to bring it about.

The Providence Journal
Providence, Rhode Island, May 1, 1992

The horrific death and destruction that have followed the astounding acquittals of four Los Angeles police officers in the Rodney King case have obscured an important fact: That a jury, and not the media or its audience, is called upon to render such judgments, and must be as free as possible from mass hysteria and political pressure if it is to perform this difficult duty responsibly.

And whatever our views of the King case, a civilized society depends upon our accepting court decisions — no matter the nature of the charges — without violence.

Of course, with the tape of Mr. King's beating available for all to see, the acquittals were sure to arouse rage. Worsening that anger was the unfortunate fact that no black citizens were on the jury. And who knows what the public perception would have been if Mr. King had himself taken the stand?

Certainly the images of one man being struck repeatedly by four heavily armed officers were sickening, as were the scenes of innocent people being beaten, some to death, after the verdict. That Mr. King is black and the officers are white has inevitably spawned racial hatreds, and led to charges that the jurors are racist. (Though we note that the rioting and looting included many young whites as well as blacks, which suggests that this controversy may have provided some people with an opportunity to have a macabre, and lucrative, good time.)

But until evidence can be shown to the contrary, we must accept — if not approve — the verdicts. While most of the public has only seen the infamous videotape, the jury was required not only to study the tape, over and over, frame by frame, but also the history of the eight-mile car chase of Mr. King, police training and procedure, the perceptions of the officers and many other factors in interminable detail.

There is no proof of jurors' racism — at least not yet. But it might cool tempers to note that the bias issue is far from legally settled. A federal civil rights probe of the officers' actions is likely, one of the officers may be retried on one count, and there will be suits and internal Police Department actions galore that may continue for years.

Meanwhile, all citizens should peacefully accept the verdict, lest one more bulwark against violence — our court system — be fatally undermined, to the particular peril of society's weakest members.

MILWAUKEE SENTINEL
Milwaukee, Wisconsin, May 5, 1992

Just as shocking as the acquittal of the four Los Angeles police officers charged in the Rodney G. King beating last week was the obvious lack of official preparedness for its violent aftermath.

Even President Bush was surprised by the verdict. In retrospect, the groundwork for the riots was laid by the furor over the videotaped recording of the beating that had apparently left the entire nation convinced that the officers would be convicted.

Los Angeles Police Chief Daryl Gates, a lame duck who shared the blame for the incident and is scheduled to leave his post in June, was attending a political fund-raiser when the violence began.

This had to contribute to the slow response to the rioting by police. And officers on the front lines of the fray complained of not receiving any direction.

Meantime, although California Gov. Pete Wilson called out the National Guard promptly, the guardsmen reportedly remained in staging areas for hours because of lack of ammunition.

This is unthinkable in an era when violence, particularly the kind inspired by racial strife, is fairly commonplace. Certainly, the memory of the Watts riots should have left Los Angeles and all of California on guard.

With the physical damage done, however, it now remains for the political damage to be sorted out.

Wilson has taken a good first step by asking Peter Ueberroth, who managed the 1984 Olympics in Los Angeles, to assume the Olympian task of restoring the minority community's economic base, which suffered most from the trashing and burning of minority-owned or -operated businesses.

Appropriately, Ueberroth has insisted on a commitment of cooperation from the various ethnic groups involved.

Meantime, Bush has committed himself to tackling the long-range problem of law and order, while his expected opponent for the presidency, Arkansas Gov. Bill Clinton, has proclaimed the Los Angeles riots "a fire bell in the night."

If this means that the issue of urban decay — involving the root causes of crime and discontent such as unemployment, housing, poverty and infrastructure — will receive more than a passing concern as the primary election campaign winds down, something good may yet spring from this disaster.

Meantime, Bush must use the high profile to which the issue has been raised to push Congress toward acting on urban problems now. That fire bell is not only tolling for the president, but for the lawmakers, too.

The LeaderPost
Regina, Saskatchewan, May 2, 1992

French President Mitterrand yesterday said the Los Angeles rioting stemmed from George Bush's conservative social policies. That is utter rot, coming from a country that has recently seen — and will see more — anti-immigrant riots.

Others say glibly that the L.A. riots are the product of incomprehensible acquittals of policemen following the shocking videotape of police beating a black man. The acquittals were almost coincidental: looting, burning and mayhem would likely have followed

convictions. The social underclasses have been primed for anarchy and it mattered not which match was used.

The 1967 Detroit riot began with a routine police raid on a "blind pig" illegal bar. The pillaging and 43 deaths that followed had nothing to do with the ostensible cause.

Other '60s and later riots in Baltimore, Washington, Chicago, Liberty City and Watts similarly were not directly related to injustice but to the pattern of joblessness, deprivation and despair. The difference this time is that fury and anarchy are not

confined to blighted areas, but have skipped to other major centres, including affluent ones.

U.S. federal troops were joining national guardsmen to restore order in L.A. Disorder, however, is just a sleeping dog, whether in France, the U.S., Nagorno Karabakh or Canada: every so often it awakes.

A truly major societal restructuring is needed throughout the world to provide its peoples with a sense of worth, of hope, and of peace.

TULSA WORLD
Tulsa, Oklahoma, May 5, 1992

THE LOS Angeles riots have produced the predictable flood of good ideas and good intentions aimed at the black underclass. Suggestions range from federally funded car pools to special college aid for prospective black police officers. There are the familiar calls for tax-favored enterprise zones to boost jobs in poor areas, more federal job programs, public housing and the rest.

Some of these are useful. Others are worth trying.

But what is missing from this message is this: Any great change that comes about in the ghetto and the black underclass must have impetus and leadership from within. It cannot be done altogether from the outside.

There are limits to what white, middle class society can or will do. There are certainly limits to what government programs can accomplish.

It is foolish and cruel to say that if poor blacks want help they will have to help themselves, and let it go at

that. There is much that must be done by the larger society. Better education is one example.

But it is also cruel and foolish to leave the impression with troubled people, black or white, that their deliverance is dependent on the rest of society.

Blacks are particularly handicapped by a history of slavery and segregation. But these handicaps can be overcome. Every year, thousands of black families work their way out of the mean streets into the middle class.

The rhetoric from politicians, sociologists and others following the Los Angeles tragedy is supposed to sound encouraging. We are ready to help; white America can do better to atone for past wrongs.

But much of it is, on second hearing, disheartening. It assumes that poor black people can't be expected to help themselves. That they are not responsible. It is a benign but terribly crippling kind of racial bias.

St. Louis Review
St. Louis, Missouri, May 8, 1992

"We condemn the beating, the judicial process that gave rise to the verdict and the violence that has ensued." This key phrase in the statement on the Rodney King case issued by the Human Rights Commission of the Archdiocese of St. Louis also sums up our reaction to recent events in Los Angeles. If it is an ill wind that blows no good, this wind became a gale force. As we sit — still somewhat stunned by the jury's verdict, the people's outrage and the resultant looting and rioting — we become aware that this is what happens when a nation pays no heed to the festering wounds of its people.

Over the past decades this nation has experienced serious strains on the fabric of racial concord but nothing indicating that we were about to reap the whirlwind of last week in Los Angeles and other cities across the country. Fifty-five people are reported killed with 2,000 injured. Some estimate that up to

10,000 businesses were ruined, resulting in the loss of 25,000 jobs. Truly all in that area have been affected, but all of us who profess to be Americans and religious feel this pain.

What occurred in Los Angeles was not all that different from racial and ethnic conflicts raging in what was Yugoslavia or Beirut or Belfast for that matter. Outbursts of violence, killing, looting and burning are but outward evidences of the smoldering embers of prejudice and fear that can continue for hundreds of years unless serious long-range efforts are put forth to break this infernal cycle. We like to think that our nation attended to these problems in the late '60s and early '70s, forgetting that new generations presented with new problems continue to cry out for improved opportunities for communication, nonviolent conflict resolution and access to power in democratic institutions.

We can cast about for various groups to blame for the outcome of the Rodney King beating trial and the consequent outcry and riots. Our search should not be limited to California or even Washington. Just about every large city and its suburbs have similar embers of prejudice waiting to be fanned into a fire storm of social unrest. Our search should not be limited to blacks and whites. In our newly enlarged mosaic of racial and ethnic populations we must include Hispanics, Asians and Native Americans. It is not just the Democrats or Republicans who have implemented faulty programs of social planning. There is plenty of room to blame independent voters and those who never vote. We must also include churches, schools and charitable agencies who have eluded the mantle of responsibility in failing to bring people together for worship, education and communication. It is time to set our faces to the wind. We must all face the future together or muddle once again into chaos.

U.S. PRESIDENTIAL CAMPAIGN:

Clinton Wins U.S. Presidency by Large Electoral Margin

Arkansas Gov. Bill Clinton (D) Nov. 3 was elected the 42nd president of the U.S., ending 12 consecutive years of Republican control of the White House. Clinton, born in 1946, would become the first member of the post–World War II generation to lead the nation. [See *Editorials On File* 1988, pp. 1258-1271. See also *Facts On File World News Digest* 1992, p. 825A1. For previous developments see *Facts On File* 1992, p. 811F3]

Clinton won 32 states from all regions of the country. According to unofficial results, Clinton captured 43,728,275 votes, or 43% of the national total, President Bush won 38,167,416 votes, or 38%, and independent candidate Ross Perot won 19,237,247 votes, or 19%. Clinton won 370 electoral votes, to 168 for Bush.

Clinton's inauguration was set for Jan. 20, 1993. His running mate, Sen. Al Gore (D, Tenn.), 44, would be inaugurated as vice president, replacing Bush's running mate, incumbent Vice President Dan Quayle.

Clinton's looming success became apparent early in the evening of election day when he was declared the winner in Georgia, where the GOP had hoped to win, and New Hampshire and Vermont, both traditionally Republican states. And when the closely contested industrial "swing states"—New Jersey, Pennsylvania, Ohio, Michigan and Illinois—were called for Clinton, his victory was clear.

California, New York and the industrial Midwest, where the most electoral votes were concentrated, formed the core of Clinton's victory. The governor also won all six New England states and several states from the formerly solid GOP regions of the South and West. Clinton won four of the 11 states of the old Confederacy, including his and Gore's respective home states of Arkansas and Tennessee.

Clinton won nine states that no Democrat had won since 1964: New Hampshire, Vermont, California, Montana, Colorado, New Mexico, Illinois, New Jersey and Nevada. Clinton was the first Democrat ever to win the presidency without carrying Texas.

Bush's loss was marked by the disintegration of the Republican coalition put together by Ronald Reagan: independents, Southerners, Roman Catholics, working-class Democrats and suburban voters.

Clinton was only the second Democrat after Jimmy Carter in 1976 to win the White House since President Lyndon B. Johnson's landslide in 1964.

President Bush conceded the race at 11:00 p.m. Eastern standard time before a gathering of supporters in Houston.

"The people have spoken, and we respect the majesty of the democratic system," Bush told the crestfallen crowd. Of Clinton, he said, "I wish him well in the White House. And I want the country to know that our entire administration will work closely with his team to insure the smooth transition of power. There is important work to be done, and America must always come first. . . . I ask that we stand behind our new president."

Perot conceded at a celebratory gathering of his supporters in Dallas, where a band played and he danced on stage with his wife and daughters. He offered warm congratulations to Clinton, led the crowd in three cheers of "hip, hip, hooray" for Bush and offered several not-so-subtle indications that he might run again, such as holding up a bumper sticker reading, "Perot '96."

The president-elect gave his victory speech at about 12:30 a.m. Eastern time Nov. 4 to jubilant supporters gathered in front of the Old State House in Little Rock, Ark. He and Gore, who also spoke, appeared before the crowd with their families.

Clinton said, "I accept tonight the responsibility that you have given me to be the leader of this, the greatest country in human history. I accept it with a full heart and a joyous spirit. But I ask you to be Americans again, too. To be interested not just in getting, but in giving; not just in placing blame but now in assuming responsibility. . . . We need a new spirit of community, a sense that we're all in this together."

The Washington Times

Washington, D.C., November 5, 1992

The Democrats ran a superb campaign, the Republicans suffered from an incumbent candidate whose actions and inaction inflicted severe damage on himself, the people spoke, and congratulations are in order for President-elect Bill Clinton and his running mate, Al Gore.

Mr. Clinton's tenacity borders on Terminatorhood. He absorbed blow after seemingly devastating blow but reconstituted himself quickly and completely. He looked unshakeably confident throughout. Perhaps when he made the decision to seek his party's nomination more than a year ago, when George Bush's approval ratings were still high and his re-election appeared to be a cinch, Mr. Clinton was merely positioning himself for a second run in 1996. But he quickly seized on the president's mounting weakness, and he never let go.

To be sure, he eventually got some substantial help from a press corps most of which, despite its insistence on its impartiality, clearly wanted him to win. The decisions about what was and what was not an issue, what was and what was not a story, reflected that desire. There are, however, two things that people who would like to blame the media for Mr. Clinton's success should note. In the first place, during the primary campaign, Mr. Clinton by no means got a free pass from the press. In fact, his way of responding to charges that surfaced in the media during the primary might offer some lessons to Republicans who find themselves enmeshed in scandals, real or manufactured. In the second place, if the inclinations of the elite media actually determined electoral outcomes, the results of elections in 1980, 1984 and 1988 would have been possible. The media do not dictate the outcome of presidential elections. Voters do, based on their assessment of the candidate and his message.

And what was that assessment? Well, it will take time to study the exit polls. But a few preliminary observations:

Mr. Bush's attacks on Mr. Clinton's character and candor took a toll. Few were the voters who said that the quality they most admired in Mr. Clinton was his honesty. On the other hand, Mr. Bush was himself badly damaged by the betrayal of his tax pledge. And the attacks on him for neither knowing nor caring much about domestic matters — a portrait of a callous ignoramus — were barbed enough to sting badly. In the end, neither man was much liked.

On to the message, then. Mr. Bush was naturally vulnerable to attacks on his credibility, and the Democrats did not hesitate to exploit that vulnerability. One of the most effective scenes from the Clinton campaign was the candidate's appearance at the Astrodome in Houston, scene of "Read my lips." It mattered little, it seems, what Mr. Bush had to offer. Many voters never even got to that question. They were willing to take their leave on credibility alone.

Whatever Mr. Clinton's credibility problems, they were no worse. As for the substance of his message, here, too, many voters found little to worry them. Clearly, Mr. Clinton was going to *do something*; to the extent that inaction itself was a problem, he offered a solution. And he was careful to distinguish himself from past nominees of his party. He was no old-style Democrat. He seemed to accept the notion that "tax-and-spend" and "liberal" were fair labels to apply to other Democrats, but he insisted that they did not apply to him. And he even offered a sort of tax pledge of his own, saying that while those who profited most from the tax cuts of the Reagan years — those earning $200,000 a year or more — would have to pay more, he would not raise taxes on the middle class to pay for his programs.

In all of this, Mr. Clinton may think he allowed himself wiggle room. But voters heard his description of a moderate — almost conservative — Democrat. And that is what they are expecting.

If Mr. Clinton is actually something else, he is in for serious trouble with the public. And if he is as moderate as he says, he is in for serious trouble with the more liberal Democrats who rule Capitol Hill. Politics will be fascinating during the Clinton administration.

Richmond Times-Dispatch
Richmond, Virginia, November 4, 1992

And then there was one.

Two years ago, Bill Clinton promised Arkansas voters that if they re-elected him their governor he would serve a full four-year term. On January 20, 1993, he will take the oath of office of the President of the United States.

Last night ended the easy part. Soon the hard stuff of governing will begin. Although a President leads a nation and not merely a party, he cannot be everything to everyone. Leadership means making some people mad. Perhaps Clinton's most daunting challenge will come from his own party. When a Democrat sweeps into

Clinton

Washington, the flotsam also washes ashore. The Left undid Jimmy Carter. The new administration will draw from a pool that never reconciled itself to the progress of the Reagan years. For 12 years the party of "change" resisted *change*.

Give Clinton credit. While other Democrats — including his running-mate — looked at last year's polls and beat a path for the tall grass, Clinton ran anyway. He kept his eyes on the prize. It belongs to him.

During the campaign, Clinton promised much. He recited the word "change" as though it were a morning and evening prayer. Yet for all his talk of a newness, Clinton himself is cut from old political cloth. Politics is his only career. His journey to Pennsylvania Avenue began, apparently, in the womb. Clinton moved from Hope to Oxford and back to Little Rock and immediately began running for office. He is the first baby-boomer (and yuppie) elected President.

George Bush is the last of a line. Never again will America have a President who fought in World War II. Bush belongs to a culture and a class populists love to hate, but he and many like him in both parties — *e.g.,* Dean Acheson, John Foster Dulles — contributed immeasurably to the defeat of Nazism and Communism, the totalitarian twins.

Why did Bush lose? "What we have here," said the warden in "Cool Hand Luke," "is a failure to communicate." With the exception of the tense weeks leading to Desert Storm, Bush failed to articulate a rationale for his presidency. The parts of his administration's policies were superior to the sum. But Bush never presented them as a coherent whole. Yes, he lacked the vision thing. And at some point, garbled syntax reflects garbled thought. Although exit polls last night suggested taxes did not rank among the electorate's primary concerns, Bush's 1990 tax capitulation likely sealed his fate. From then on, how could he speak of trust? Bush squandered the Reagan legacy. Therein lay his despair.

Ross Perot's vote confounded the experts — including, ahem, your servants. It did not collapse. His voters went to the polls and told both parties to stick it in their kazoos. What might Perot have achieved if not for the midsummer comedy of his withdrawal? His vote should not comfort Clinton. Although Perotnistas expressed their disgust with the Bush *status quo*, they similarly scorned the Clinton alternative. Would they have rallied to Jack Kemp?

Virginia is blessed. Once again it declined to join the gadarene rush. Yet Bush's diminished percentage in the only Southern state Carter did not take in 1976 only reinforced the measure of his national decline. In the state's more notable House races, Democrat Leslie Byrne claimed the 11th; Republican Bob Goodlatte won a landslide in the 6th; incumbent Republican Herb Bateman brushed aside a dubious challenger; and Democrat Bobby Scott scored an impressive and historic win in the 3rd (Scott should rise to the top of the Democrats' freshman class). Incumbents Tom Bliley (a Republican) and Norman Sisisky (a Democrat) won deserved re-election in the 7th and 4th Districts respectively.

Last night's most distressing news came from the exit polls, which said voters did not rate "trust" among their presidential concerns. If so, then perhaps it is because each of the three major candidates had trust questions of his own — Clinton (Gennifer and the draft), Bush (taxes and Iran/Contra), Perot (general kookiness). Trust is a synonym for character. And as Alexander Hamilton and the Founders knew, character outranks all other qualifications for the presidency. Starting today, Clinton's task is to transcend himself.

Although the U.S. invests too much capital in politics in general and the presidency in general, to wish a President other than well is to wish the nation harm. In January, the Democrats will control all the levers of national elected power. The Republicans and Perot's people will become the loyal opposition. For the next four years may they play the role more responsibly than their colleagues across the aisle played it during the past 12.

Calgary Herald
Calgary, Alberta, November 5, 1992

Celebratory parties and campaign rhetoric aside, president-elect Bill Clinton faces a daunting challenge from the day he moves into the White House.

His country's problems are no secret. The U.S. is mired in a frightening recession. Hundreds of thousands of jobs have been lost. Money for education and job training is in short supply. Major cities have become battle zones. The rural hinterland is in decay. The war on drugs has been a fiasco. Quality of life has become a precious commodity, available to only the very rich.

Clearly no one man can resolve all these issues. But Clinton has made the most dangerous of all election promises: he has vowed to restore the American dream.

Not only may that be impossible — from an economic standpoint — but were it possible, which dream would it be? The dream visualized by Black Americans? The mental picture painted by Hispanic Americans? The dream all but forgotten by poor Americans? The dream of self-sufficient, self-reliant, isolationist Americans?

Unlike George Bush, whose Republican mandate paved a clear way for both internal and external policies, Clinton faces the unenviable task of responding to the hodge-podge of demanding special interest groups that call the Democratic Party home.

Not only will the new president have to decipher and address their cacophony of needs, but he will have to do so with a sense of urgency that will appease a country hungry for better times.

Like constituencies around the world, the American electorate wants change now. They want jobs now. They want better, more accessible health care. They want to hold the line on immigration. They want a return to traditional values — whatever those may be. And they want everything now.

Internationally, Clinton will find himself forced to play a variety of roles. Peacemaker. Bully. Friend. Confidante. Statesman. Strategist. And of course, Great Father.

Is he up to the assignment?

Will he be able to massage a satisfactory conclusion to the long-running, acrimonious GATT discussions? Will he be able to appease Democrats who want the North American Free Trade Agreement torn up, or at least dramatically overhauled, without endangering the economic future of a continent? Will he be able to appease increasingly militant protectionists who believe the U.S. economy will never return to its halcyon days unless imports are curbed?

Many of these objectives are contradictory. Unlike his predecessor, Clinton will not have the luxury of muddling along a path designed to appease everyone. Americans do not want the status quo maintained. They want change. Clinton has promised to repaint the American landscape with a new brush. The audience awaits his first strokes.

Not only must they be brilliant, but his choice of colors must be universally appealing. There is little room for experimentation. Nothing short of a virtuoso performance will do.

THE CONGRESS AND I WILL MOVE TOGETHER!

GUN LOBBY
BIG LABOR
AGRICULTURE
INSURANCE
TOBACCO
TEACHERS UNION
TRIAL LAWYERS
HIGHWAY ETC.
AMERICAN MEDICAL ASSN
OIL

AUTH

11·17·92 THE PHILADELPHIA INQUIRER. UNIVERSAL PRESS SYNDICATE.

StarPhoenix

Saskatoon, Saskatchewan, November 5, 1992

In rejecting George Bush, strongly supporting independent Ross Perot and granting a massive presidential victory to Bill Clinton, Americans sent their political leaders a clear message.

In essence, voters said it was time to cast aside old-style politics in favor of a government responsive to their needs of jobs and economic growth. In that sentiment, Americans were no different from the Japanese, Britons or the French, who have recently made it clear they expect more from politicians than mere platitudes.

In Canada, federal party leaders are dreaming if they believe they will escape unscathed in the next election. Prime Minister Brian Mulroney has already vowed to lead his Conservatives into the 1993 election, the Liberals appear complacent with the rarely-heard-from Jean Chretien and the New Democrats are plodding along with Audrey McLaughlin.

President-elect Clinton, the first 'baby-boomer'' poised to take over his nation's top post, represents a changing of the guard in U.S. politics. Even Perot's appeal was as an outsider, a person who carried no baggage of decades in politics.

Compare that to the options facing Canadians in 1993. The three major party leaders have already been discredited by the electorate, as evidenced by the referendum debacle.

McLaughlin was being misguidedly optimistic Tuesday by expressing hope that the American taste for new political blood will extend to Canada. Little does she realize that she, too, is seen by voters as one of the old gang. Mulroney and Chretien, with their tonnes of political baggage, fare no better.

It's time for Canada's major political parties to take stock of their leadership. Waiting until after the next election will be too late.

THE INDIANAPOLIS NEWS
Indianapolis, Indiana, November 4, 1992

Come January, America will have a new president.

Yesterday, Americans made Arkansas Gov. William Jefferson Clinton the 42nd president of the United States. Clinton won 355 electoral votes to President George Bush's 183.

That sounds like a more resounding victory than it was. In the popular vote, Bush ran much closer to Clinton. He picked up 38 percent of the votes cast yesterday. Clinton grabbed 43 percent. Ross Perot snared the other 19 percent.

Thus, Clinton's electoral landslide disguises the fact that he will enter the White House as a minority president. And that will greatly influence the shape and direction of a Clinton administration.

Unlike Ronald Reagan — the last challenger to oust an incumbent from the Rose Garden — Bill Clinton will not enter the White House with a mandate. Fewer than half the Americans who cast their ballots yesterday gave their support to the Arkansas governor.

That means that Clinton will not have the mass of Americans behind him if he tries to radically redesign or realign this country or its government. Clinton will have to compromise, will have to search for common ground between Democrats and Republicans. He will have to find ways to bring Americans together.

That is a challenge that will tax the president-elect's touted political skills because he inherits the leadership of a divided and uncertain country.

This division and uncertainty — creations of the end of Cold War and the beginning of a period of worldwide economic realignment and readjustment — were largely responsible for Clinton's victory and Bush's defeat.

In some ways, President Bush was a victim of the Republican Party's successes during the 1980s. It was under a Reagan-Bush administration that the United States adopted a policy of increasing the pressure on the economy of the Soviet Union by stepping up military spending.

It was that policy that helped end the Cold War and made it possible for the United States and the world to step away from the shadow of nuclear destruction.

Ironically, it was the disappearance of that threat — during George Bush's presidency — that made the election of President Bush less imperative. Absent the danger of sudden annihilation, the president's great strengths in foreign policy seemed less essential.

And made it possible for a governor from a small state like Arkansas to become president.

Bill Clinton and his running mate, Sen. Al Gore, already have said, in interviews with The News, that their first priority as president and vice president will be to reinvigorate the American economy. As their specific plans to accomplish that goal become known, we will analyze and, no doubt, occasionally criticize them.

But that is still in the future.

For now, it is enough simply to congratulate Bill Clinton and Al Gore and wish them well as they adopt the awesome responsibilities that come with serving as president and vice president of the United States.

Lincoln Journal

Lincoln, Nebraska, November 4, 1992

"If he runs the country as well as he ran this campaign, the country will be all right."

— Vice President Dan Quayle

A country that is "all right" instead of frayed by resentments, fragmented by personal worries and worried about the future is a universal hope today.

THE ARIZONA REPUBLIC
Phoenix, Arizona, November 4, 1992

THIS morning President-elect Bill Clinton awakened with the judgment of the American people behind him. With his scrambled eggs and orange juice also should come the realization that, despite all the up-beat rhetoric of the campaign, the course he sets for America probably will be the most crucial since the dark days of the Great Depression.

By their nature U.S. presidential campaigns are insular affairs. Americans invariably turn inward, for the business of picking a president requires them to put national interests first. True to form, the campaign of 1992, as was clear from the outset, was not going to be about America's role as the remaining superpower or about winning a lightning war in the Middle East or about extending the conservative revolution that began when Ronald Reagan deposed Jimmy Carter 12 years earlier. Rather, it was going to be about the economy, which was mired in a shallow but nonetheless relentless recession.

Yet in focusing on the economy, the three major candidates succumbed, in varying degrees, to the misperception that recession was a peculiarly American problem requiring essentially American solutions. Only George Bush seemed to grasp, and then only tangentially, that the recession, while having national features, was global in nature — a perspective sometimes used to mask his own stewardship.

As America slowly emerges from its election-year cocoon, the harsh reality will appear vastly different.

Last week Japanese Prime Minister Kiichi Miyazawa conceded that his country was facing a prolonged and severe downturn — was, if not in the midst of recession, then poised at the outskirts. Figures from Japanese lenders and industries confirmed this forlorn view. From March to September non-performing loans at leading Japanese banks rose an astounding 54 percent — an increase in bad debt that, Japanese bankers say, will take years to correct. Meanwhile, consumer-electronics giant JVC and Japan Air Lines, among other sufferers, reported sharp declines in semi-annual profits.

Germany, the European half of the postwar miracle (defeated nations transformed into conquering economic powers), continues to struggle through costly reunification, and Chancellor Helmut Kohl hints at a tax increase in 1995 — a hint that, in the interim, could wreck business and consumer confidence. France struggles with rising unemployment, now up to 10.3 percent. Britain, its currency battered and its newly re-elected Conservative government dangerously unsettled over the closure of coal pits, lumbers along aimlessly in what already is its worst economic downturn since the Great Depression.

And this is not half of it. Lacking a General Agreement on Tariffs and Trade, the United States and the European Community glower at each other and ponder the prospect of a trade war. The former Soviet Union, still in tatters, is little closer to a market economy than it was under communism. Drought and starvation continue to ravage large parts of southern Africa. Latin America remains buried under horrendous, decade-old debt.

None of this is to suggest that domestic issues will require no attention from the White House for the next four years. Certainly they will. But as the candidates were glad-handing their way toward November, even more indicators offered hints that recovery was not going to arrive with a quick fix, but as a result of long-term effort. The takeover of General Motors by outside directors assured that GM, the world's largest corporation, would step up layoffs. Other corporations, most notably American Express last week, also have announced plans to reduce the work force, meaning that many more Americans will begin the year with pink slips, not pay raises.

Meanwhile, the military-industrial complex, the massive accretion of half a century of Cold War, cries out to be reduced to sensible peacetime proportions, but dismantling will not be easily achieved. Such mammoth public works projects as high-speed rail hold out the promise of new jobs, but years will be required before the first nickel reaches the pockets of American workers. The rising deficit, a problem hammered mercilessly by independent candidate Ross Perot, must be slowed and eventually eliminated. Likewise, the national debt, now at $4 trillion, must be scaled back if we are to avert the inevitable alternative — hyperinflation on a Brazilian scale, with accompanying political chaos.

All is not glum, to be sure. America still possesses the largest consumer market in the world, and our system of government, which Lord Macaulay derided as all sail and no anchor, remains seaworthy well into a third century. Yet if the United States is to rescue the unemployed, the underemployed and those who see their industries shutting down, the time for introspection is past. If we are to retain our leadership in the world, our president must assemble a program of recovery that not only takes care of the needs at home, but revs up the sputtering global economy as well.

This will be no easy task, and every attempt will be resisted, even by our friends. But we must persevere or see the world, and us with it, slip ever deeper into despair, its remarkable progress toward peace, global stability, political freedom and material well-being painfully arrested.

That is the challenge, Mr. President-elect, and for the next four years it will be disproportionately yours.

"Making it all right" is now the challenge before President-elect Bill Clinton, as much the least disliked option before the American electorate Tuesday as the people's wildly enthusiastic choice.

The youthful, all-Dixie team of Arkansan Clinton, 46, and Tennessean Al Gore, 44, should bring to the immense task an energy — and a vision — lacking in the White House for too long.

The electoral landscape modified by American voters Tuesday, mostly at the top, opens on a great opportunity.

No longer a legislature of one political persuasion and an executive of the other. Therefore, no more excuses for gridlock. No more partisan one-upmanship. If the nation's cry can be collapsed into a single shout beamed at Washington, it would be Ross Perot's command: Fix it!

So count this newspaper as one intending to hold the Clinton administration and the Democratic majorities in the House and Senate responsible, and accountable, for moving quickly on problems of jobs, health care and deficit reduction.

Flares of legislative activism will not be enough, either. Measurable results toward clear goals are a must in the next four years. Otherwise Clinton will join the lengthening list of one-term presidents.

(He might also be reminded that not since Franklin Roosevelt, in a time of different peril, has an elected Democrat served out at least two terms in the Oval Office.)

The governmental energy Clinton promised throughout the campaign, his bent toward a more overt private-public partnership to juice the economy, should be examined without prejudice.

What the 42nd president-to-be has not sufficiently stressed — but now must — are the national sacrifices inherent in changing the status quo. And not just temporary adjustments in direction, but some leading to permanent changes in lifestyle; even value systems. We have done it before.

The United States cannot survive an extension of the borrow-and-spend policies of the last dozen years, where the obscene size of annual interest on the growing national debt actually exceeds the yearly national deficit. We cannot be a global superpower, with a hollowed-out internal economy, any more than can Russia.

We cannot truly be a healthy body, either, suffering bouts of persistent racial and religiously-themed trench warfare.

America ever has been a dynamic nation, not a static society. It responds to troubles and grievances. Filling the mind and heart with confidence is mostly our shared history. Americans come with an admixture of idealism, pragmatism and optimism.

Politician William Jefferson Clinton must know those just happen to be the trademarks of our most successful leaders, too.

AFRICA:

First U.S. Forces Arrive in Somali Capital

About 1,800 U.S. Marines Dec. 9 arrived in the Somali capital of Mogadishu as the vanguard of "Operation Restore Hope," an American-led mission under the auspices of the United Nations to bring aid to the famine-stricken East African country. Sporadic gunfire was heard throughout the day, but there was no armed resistance to the American arrival, and no casualties were reported. [See *Editorials On File* 1992, pp. 1420-1425. See also *Facts On File World News Digest* 1992, p. 925A1. For previous developments see *Facts On File* 1992, p. 905A1]

The troops secured the city's port from looters. Although warehouses there were stocked with thousands of tons of donated grain, almost none of it had been distributed since early November because of tensions between rival warlords.

The troops also began repair work on Mogadishu's international airport so that it could accommodate round-the-clock relief flights. The U.N. World Food Program landed a C-130 Hercules supply jet on the runway Dec. 9, the first supply jet to land there in six months.

From positions off the coast in the Indian Ocean, U.S. boats, helicopters and hovercraft ferried ashore soldiers, vehicles and building materials. (Somalia's infrastructure was devastated from warfare and neglect. According to U.S. officials, anything the soldiers needed—such as food, fuel or electricity—they would have to bring or create themselves.)

The Americans disembarked from pre-positioned ships that had been stationed off the coast for several days. The U.S. Navy had deployed four large ships in the area from its base at the Indian Ocean island of Diego Garcia: *Tripoli,* an amphibious assault ship carrying 23 helicopters; *Rushmore,* a dock landing vessel; *Juneau,* a transport dock ship; and *Lummus,* a massive supply ship. Expected to arrive soon was a battle group from the Persian Gulf consisting of the aircraft carrier *Ranger,* the cruiser *Valley Forge* and the destroyer *Kinkaid.*

When in full swing, the U.S. operation would involve 16,000 Marines from the First Marine Expeditionary Force based at Camp Pendleton, Calif. and 10,000 soldiers from the Army's light infantry 10th Mountain Division at Fort Drum, N.Y. Troops from the Air Force would also take part. The operation was under the command of Lt. Gen. Robert B. Johnson of the Marine Corps.

The Pentagon envisioned a four-phase operation. In the first phase, Marines would take control of the port and airport in Mogadishu and then travel west to secure the airstrip in the city of Baidoa in the country's interior. In the second, Army soldiers would occupy other towns, including Belet Uen. The third phase would involve moving into the southern coastal city of Kismayu. Relief operations would be transferred to a U.N. peace-keeping force in the fourth phase.

In a televised speech, U.S. President Bush Dec. 4 formally issued orders for the Somalia intervention.

The two main warlords in Mogadishu, the Somali capital, Dec. 11 signed a peace accord that took effect immediately. The agreement was brokered by the U.S.'s special envoy to Somalia, Robert Oakley.

The warlord rivals, Gen. Mohammed Farah Aidid and Ali Mahdi Mohammed, embraced as they met each other face to face for the first time in over a year. The signing took place at a guest house owned by an American firm, Consolidated Oil Co. The house was serving as the unofficial U.S. embassy in Somalia.

The leaders agreed to have their militiamen withdraw their weapons from Mogadishu within 48 hours. They pledged to remove checkpoints from the "green line" that divided their territories and also promised to halt propaganda about each other.

Rockford Register Star

Rockford, Illinois, December 10, 1992

In Somalia, restoring hope will be the easy part. The trick will be in sustaining it.

The deployment of 28,000 U.S. troops to protect food shipments to starving Somalis is a humanitarian mission of the highest order. "Somebody dialed 911 and we came," Col. Greg Newbold said of Operation Restore Hope, which began Tuesday night with the landing of 1,800 Marines at the main port of Mogadishu.

But the mission will be neither quick nor easy if the United States is to provide more than passing relief to the crisis. It will be one thing to feed people and force a temporary cease-fire in the country's civil war; it will be yet another to prevent more famines and encourage hostile clans to make peace.

Food might be delivered to all the starving in two to three months, the time frame given by Defense Secretary Dick Cheney. Colin Powell, chairman of the Joint Chiefs of Staff, was even more optimistic, predicting an end to the crisis within a month. But instead of asking how soon the plight of the hungry will be addressed, we should be wondering how long that relief will last.

> **Somalia will need more than a military solution.**

There are estimates that even a relatively short relief operation will cost the United States upwards of $300 million. As expensive as that is, it would be cheaper — and certainly less tragic — if Americans would stick around and search for a permanent solution, rather than wait for the next catastrophe. The United States, which eagerly provided arms to Somalia when it was a Cold War pawn, must now decide the best way to disarm the country — either by incentive or by force.

To create peaceful zones for food shipments is not enough. It isn't only hunger that has killed 300,000 people and may kill another quarter of a million before the year is out. It is also the clans and their ever-present weapons.

Rapid population growth has forced Somali farmers to reuse fallow land, reducing the soil's ability to retain moisture and creating desert-like conditions. Famines are the natural result. They can be averted, however, through extensive agricultural help and teaching. This assistance could be offered under the auspices of the United Nations.

Such common-sense solutions belie the growing notion that Somalia is a quagmire for the United States and the international community. But if we care only about restoring hope and not about shepherding recovery, about troop deployment instead of sustained commitment, we should not be surprised when our services are needed again.

THE ASHEVILLE CITIZEN

Asheville, North Carolina, December 12, 1992

The starving people of Somalia have become a beneficiary of the conclusion of the Cold War.

The current military mission to stabilize Somalia so that the victims of the famine can be fed could never have taken place in the tense atmosphere of American-Soviet rivalry.

The last great famine in the horn of Africa points out the difference. When drought ravaged Ethiopia in 1984-85, millions died because a coordinated world response was not possible. Part of the reason was that Ethiopia was a client state of the old Soviet Union, and neighboring Somalia was a client state of the United States. Neither party would have permitted a military force to take a humanitarian action because of paranoia over political gamesmanship.

There was more concern over protecting access to Middle East oil than aiding starving men, women and children.

Somalia may become an example of what can be accomplished in a world where the needs of human beings finally are put above those of politics.

TULSA WORLD

Tulsa, Oklahoma, December 5, 1992

THE UNITED Nations military relief mission to Somalia is not Desert Storm. But it does have this in common with the UN intervention against Iraq in Kuwait two years ago: It shows that the civilized world has advanced to the point that it can take limited action against international outlaws.

The emphasis is on "limited." President Bush has emphasized the strict limits on what U.S. and UN forces will be expected to do in Somalia. Their mission, slightly oversimplified, will be to ride shotgun on relief supplies to starving civilians. These supplies have been repeatedly stopped or stolen by armed bands. Although some shooting is likely, this is a much more restrained effort than Operation Desert Storm.

The important thing about the mission is the message it sends to international outlaws everywhere. There are limits to the world's tolerance of brigandage and oppression against innocent civilians.

There are limits to the power of a world police force of any kind. Politics, terrain and geography dictate that outside intervention will work for some victims of oppression but not for others. Somalia is lucky in that it is largely a desert country. It is easier to carry out military movements in a desert than in mountains or cities.

Still, Sen. David Boren is absolutely right in his proposal to formalize this new world intolerance of oppression. He wants a permanent international force to handle problems such as those facing the starving people of Somalia.

It's time.

Tulsa, Oklahoma, December 8, 1992

RELIEF columns got through the bandit-infested Somalian countryside during the weekend to areas that have been without food for weeks. This good news was reported even before the new international military force arrived on the scene. It is a good omen.

The United Nations decision to use military force to relieve some famished areas of Somalia may or may not have influenced the conduct of thugs who have been hijacking relief vehicles and stealing supplies. But if the decision alone has not made an impression, everyone involved in the operation is pretty sure that the actual presence of troops — including U.S. marines — will have a pacifying effect.

Polls show that a great majority of Americans support this combined military and humanitarian venture. A few pessimists disagree. They ask: Are we setting a precedent to intervene in every troubled place on the globe?

The answer, of course, is no. The United States and other U.N. members are intervening because help is desperately needed, and it can be given with limited risk.

Americans cannot intervene everywhere. But where we can help without great danger or loss of life, it is the right thing to do.

MILWAUKEE SENTINEL

Milwaukee, Wisconsin, December 7, 1992

The anniversary of America's most terrible military defeat dawned today with U.S. troops preparing to go off to a war of another kind in Somalia.

This time, the GIs are participating in an exercise which is something of an invasion and an act of mercy.

How history will remember those participating in Operation Restore Hope cannot be predicted. We would hope that no battle will result from this exercise, but that cannot be certain.

Without question, those who participate in the mission will be worthy of commendation.

Certainly, loved ones back home can be proud of all who participate in this expedition and rest assured that they deserve to be held in the highest esteem.

We salute those who died at Pearl Harbor 51 years ago and their comrades who went on to win the greatest military victory in the nation's history.

And we salute those who are on their way to Somalia. As President Bush appropriately put it, "the humanitarian mission they undertake is in the finest traditions of the service."

RAPID CITY JOURNAL

Rapid City, South Dakota, December 2, 1992

The shadow of Vietnam has long cast itself on U.S. foreign policy decisions. And it should. America needs to forever keep in mind the lessons learned from its experience in Vietnam.

President Bush showed he understood those lessons by our nation's clearly defined role in the Persian Gulf war, and again in his offer last week to send 30,000 U.S. troops to Somalia. The United Nations Security Council is debating whether to accept the plan that would limit U.S. involvement to protecting aid shipments and relief workers and to bringing about a cease-fire, after which the U.S. force would be replaced by U.N. peacekeepers.

The Journal's view

A stronger military presence is needed in Somalia to prevent millions of people from starving to death. Relief workers estimate that 200,000 metric tons of food intended to feed hungry Somalians has been stolen by warring factions of bandits. Another 12,000 metric tons of food sits in warehouses, not being delivered because of fear it will be stolen.

Meanwhile, according to estimates of relief workers, 300,000 people have died from the effects of drought and warfare, and another 2 million lives are at risk. The deployment of U.S. troops in Somalia could make the difference for those 2 million people.

But as Bush seems to understand, the role of U.S. troops in Somalia must be clearly defined. They should be there only as a relief measure, not as an open-ended attempt to establish social and political order. That should be the U.N.'s responsibility, and there must be assurances that the U.N., with the backing of other countries, will make a commitment and begin working toward that end.

Under the plan, U.S. lives would be at risk. That is a risk that our nation should accept in order to save the lives of many innocent Somalians.

LAW ENFORCEMENT:

Scores Die as Besieged Texas Cult Compound Burns Down

The compound of a religious cult near Waco, Texas burned to the ground April 19 in what the Federal Bureau of Investigation described as a mass suicide. The heavily armed cult, the Branch Davidians, had been in a stand-off with law-enforcement officials for 51 days. [See *Editorials On File* 1993, pp. 444-445, 272-277. See also *Facts On File World News Digest* 1993, p. 282E1. For previous developments see *Facts On File* 1993, p. 240A1–G3]

The blaze occurred hours after federal agents in armored vehicles had begun battering the compound's walls and pumping tear gas into the structure. In the wake of the fire, critics questioned the appropriateness of the federal agents' actions.

Nine cultists escaped the fire at the compound, which was located 10 miles (16 km) northeast of Waco. Among the survivors was a woman who had run out of the compound and then attempted to run back in, according to the FBI. An FBI agent had grabbed the woman and, as she struggled, dragged her to safety.

The FBI had calculated that 86 cult members, including leader and self-proclaimed messiah David Koresh, had perished in the flames, it was reported April 21. Seventeen children were believed to have died in the inferno. Thirty-six bodies were found in the charred ruins of the compound April 21.

Bob Ricks, a senior FBI agent, April 19 said that negotiators had telephoned the compound early that day and warned Schneider, Koresh's aide, of their plans to begin pumping tear gas into the compound. Ricks said the negotiators had asked that the cult members surrender peacefully. In response, Ricks said, Schneider had angrily slammed down the phone and thrown it out the compound door.

Shortly after that conversation, at about 6:00 a.m. local time April 19, the FBI proceeded with their plan, using armored vehicles that knocked holes in the compound's walls and then shot the tear gas inside. The FBI said that the vehicles were met with a barrage of gunfire from the cult members as they approached the compound. The bureau said it had not returned any fire.

At a mid-morning news conference before the blaze, Ricks April 19 had described the tear-gas attack as "the next logical step in a series to bring this episode to an end." He said the goal of the assault was to make the cultists' "environment as uncomfortable as possible."

Shortly after 1:00 p.m., flames appeared in a window of the compound some distance away from the armored vehicles. The rapidly spreading fire, fueled by winds of up to 30 miles per hour (50 kmph), consumed the compound in less than half an hour. Ricks said that the Davidians had used lantern fuel to ignite the blaze. During the blaze there was a powerful explosion, possibly of the cult's stockpiled weapons or ammunition, which filled the air with a dark cloud of smoke.

There were no firetrucks on the scene, and by the time they arrived from Waco and adjacent towns, the fire was out of control. "We cannot roll fire trucks to a scene where people could shoot them," Ricks explained. However, he conceded that officials had not expected a fire.

Attorney General Janet Reno, speaking at a press conference April 19, publicly took responsibility for the decision to shoot tear gas into the compound. "I made the decision," Reno said. "I'm accountable. The buck stops with me."

Reno had briefed President Clinton the day before the attack, according to White House officials. Clinton later April 19 issued a brief statement emphasizing that the plan had been "recommended" by federal law-enforcement agencies. "I told the attorney general to do what she thought was right, and I stand by that decision," the statement said.

In a news conference April 20, Clinton said that he bore "full responsibility" for the outcome of the operation. The news conference was seen as an attempt to counter suggestions that the White House had had Reno take the blame for the incident in order to protect the president.

THE ARIZONA REPUBLIC
Phoenix, Arizona, April 20, 1993

THE ill-fated federal raid on a religious cult's compound near Waco, Texas, that began tragically with questionable tactics, ended horrifically some 51 days later with even more questions being asked.

What is known is that more than 80 people, including as many as 25 children, died yesterday when flames destroyed the Branch Davidian compound. According to federal authorities, the blaze, deliberately set by cult members, rapidly raced through the compound's wooden buildings, consuming everything in its path.

Fewer than 10 of the nearly 100 cult members thought to be alive inside the compound survived. One of them, a woman "in flames," as the FBI put it, seen outside the compound was dragged to safety by an agent as she tried to re-enter the inferno. Whether the fires were started is part of a mass suicide effort ordered by cult leader David Koresh or meant for some other purpose is unknown.

The beginning of the deadly end to the siege started early Monday, after federal officials, including Attorney General Janet Reno, decided over the weekend to take aggressive action to end the standoff, which began on Feb. 28 with a bungled raid by Bureau of Alcohol Tobacco and Firearms agents. When the smoke clear that day, four agents had been killed and 16 wounded. Cult leaders said six of their members had been killed.

The initial raid supposedly was ordered because the Davidians were thought to be stockpiling illegal weapons, including machine guns, yet it was clear from the outset that the ATF agents were unprepared for the ensuing battle. Federal officials say the cultists were tipped off in advance of the raid.

Saying that they feared a mass suicide or that the cultists were preparing for another deadly confrontation, the FBI, after issuing warnings, began ripping holes in the walls of the compound with armored vehicles and spraying a non-toxic chemical agent to force out the cultists. "We believed this thing had to be brought to a logical conclusion," said an FBI spokesman.

Instead of exiting, however, cult members fired at the agents. About six hours after the FBI began battering the buildings, the fires began. Within an hour the blaze had consumed the compound.

The debate over the government's decision to provoke an end to the siege likely will rage on for months. Mr. Koresh, a self-styled prophet, had named the compound Ranch Apocalypse. In the end, he was proven right.

LEXINGTON HERALD-LEADER
Lexington, Kentucky, April 21, 1993

If you're looking for originality, look elsewhere. Our questions about the Waco disaster are the same as everybody's.

What was the hurry?

Why didn't authorities just wait out David Koresh and his followers?

Was the decision to invade the Branch Davidian compound motivated by fears for the safety of the innocent children inside? Or was it motivated by nothing more than a lack of patience and pressure to stop wasting money on the siege?

How could the authorities, including Attorney General Janet Reno, have so badly misread the situation? How could they have ignored the clear signs that Koresh would react violently?

How could this whole affair have been so badly handled from the beginning by a series of federal agencies and officials?

There are no answers yet, but there must be. That's why the pending congressional hearings and the internal investigations in the Justice and Treasury departments are so important.

These inquiries will serve a larger purpose than simply establishing responsibility. They also will give the public some badly needed information.

Perhaps new information will emerge that will explain the decision of Reno and other Justice Department authorities to act so boldly after more than two months of restraint. Perhaps some extenuating circumstances will emerge. Or perhaps it may simply become clear that Reno's decision was nothing but a carefully calculated risk that had to be taken.

Perhaps.

But whatever the investigations reveal, the questions must be answered. It's too late to save the people who died in the Branch Davidian compound, but it's not too late to discover why and how this affair came to such a tragic end and to learn from that knowledge.

The Union Leader
Manchester, New Hampshire, April 21, 1993

The post-mortems have already begun in earnest on what caused the 51-day stand-off between federal authorities and David Koresh and his followers to conclude Monday in a fiery Götterdämmerung at the David Davidians' encampment outside Waco, Texas.

(Despite the claims of Koresh, this self-proclaimed earthly "Jesus," this was not the twilight of the gods that he apparently envisioned. It was a barbaric murder of the innocents.)

But before the second-guessing and finger pointing reaches the frenetic stage, as it invariably does, before the media "experts" start blaming, say, Ronald Reagan or the Second Amendment to the Constitution, more emphasis — much more — should be placed on the indescribable human tragedy of 86 human beings, reportedly including 24 children, having their lives snuffed out because of the megalomania of one con man, an armed and dangerous thug and child molester masquerading as a religious leader.

Especially should our thoughts turn to the children — tragic, innocent victims of events they could not control — who were deprived of the opportunity to mature and experience the joys of life on this earth and the gratification that derives from overcoming its travails.

It is they especially who were cheated out of life by this pathological liar David Koresh, this fraud whose every action mocked what a Christian is supposed to be and served as such a convenient propaganda tool for pagans in the news media and academe who seek to demonize all of Christianity.

The adults who perished in Monday's conflagration at "Ranch Apocalypse" at least had the opportunity to determine the course of their lives. They made the decisions that led to their own deaths and, tragically, to the deaths of these innocent children as well.

To be sure, there is a need for public debate and investigation of "what went wrong," of whether the authorities conducted themselves in a professional manner, of whether this day of death and destruction was at all preventable. When human lives are lost in any nation that considers itself civilized, there must be a period of evaluation and introspection.

But, first, let us not forget to weep for these children —assuming, of course, that the daily slaughter of other tiny innocents has not rendered us too callous to do so.

Portland Press Herald
Portland, Maine, April 21, 1993

The cult compound that became a funeral pyre for more than 80 souls on Monday should be remembered as something more. It should be a charred landmark on the Justice Department's path to revising its procedures for dealing with such volatile situations. The 51-day standoff was handled badly from the start. The questions began when agents from the Bureau of Alcohol, Tobacco and Firearms blundered into a firefight that left four agents dead and an unknown number slain inside the compound.

Things got worse when the FBI took over. The FBI knew it was dealing with an unstable personality, yet it persisted in stepping up the pressure, to the point of starting to knock the compound down in the final assault. Common sense should have told anyone that such a provocation could send David Koresh, the Branch Davidian leader, over the edge, since he had dwelled on the "apocalypse" scene from the start.

It was not a surprise that the conflagration followed. In a sense, it would have been a surprise if it had not.

Pending the findings of two congressional investigations, Attorney General Janet Reno should order a full-scale revamping of training procedures for agents facing crisis situations. Far greater emphasis has to be placed on the art of conflict resolution, whereby conflict is managed rather than "eliminated," often through third-party mediation. Potential mediators not only were available in the Waco standoff, but two already were at work through the Branch Davidians' lawyer. The pair, religion experts specializing in apocalyptic groups, had suggested to Koresh he write out his interpretation of the book of Revelation. He was doing that when the FBI assault began.

Americans with no special training at all are asking what would have been wrong with simply waiting the Davidians out. The compound could have been cordoned off, and a watch maintained indefinitely by the Texas Rangers. The costly, heavy federal presence wasn't needed. In time, many more of the cult members and their children likely would have come out, just as a steady stream had done since Feb. 28. By the time Koresh had finished his "interpretation," he might have wanted the whole ordeal to end peacefully.

Now, we'll never know – and an estimated 86 more people lay dead that better procedures might have saved.

SOUTH AFRICA:

Mandela and ANC Claim Election Victory

African National Congress President Nelson Mandela May 2 claimed a landslide victory for the ANC in South Africa's first all-race elections, which had been held April 26–29. After early results were released May 2, Mandela proclaimed that black South Africans who had been disenfranchised for decades under the apartheid system of racial separation were "free at last." [See *Editorials On File* 1994, pp. 496-505. See also *Facts On File World News Digest* 1994, p. 313A1. For previous developmetns see *Facts On File* 1994, p. 270B3]

Mandela, who had spent 27 years in South African prisons before being released in 1990, was expected to be inaugurated as president of a "national unity" government May 10.

In a historic moment that effectively dissolved the last remnants of apartheid, the ANC leader April 27 had cast the first ballot of his lifetime, joining an estimated 22.7 million eligible voters who participated in the four days of polling. Most of those voters, like Mandela, were getting their first chance to help decide the shape of their nation's government. The elections marked the end of a decades-long struggle led by black organizations, including the ANC, that had sought liberation from three centuries of white-minority rule. The National Party formally had implemented apartheid after coming to power in 1948. [For a chronology of South Africa's recent history, see *Facts On File* 1994, p. 317A1]

The days leading up to the voting had been marred by bombings, allegedly orchestrated by white rightists, that left more than 20 people dead and dozens more injured. However, voters, undeterred by the violence, began standing on line at some polling stations at 4:00 a.m., with many waiting as long as 12 hours to cast their first ballots ever. While violence subsided during the elections, instances of alleged voting irregularities and of logistical problems plagued the polling process. But political leaders, international observers and analysts generally agreed that the elections overall were free and fair.

A new South African national flag was raised at 12:01 a.m. April 26, replacing a flag that had been introduced in 1928. With the new flag, the country's new constitution and bill of rights took effect. The black homelands that had served as a symbol of apartheid for decades were dissolved, and nine new all-race provinces came into being. [See map, *Facts On File* 1994, p. 314A1; 1993, p. 873A1; 1982 p. 234E1]

The nine provinces created under the new constitution were Northern Transvaal; Eastern Transvaal; Pretoria, Witwatersrand, Vereeniging (PWV); North West; Orange Free State; KwaZulu/Natal; Eastern Cape; Northern Cape; and Western Cape. [For a map of preelection South Africa, see *Facts On File* 1982, p. 179C1]

As the new flag—a geometric pattern of red, white, blue, green, gold and black—was raised in Johannesburg, residents sang the country's new anthems— "Nkosi Sikelele iAfrika" ("God Bless Africa"), the antiapartheid anthem, and "Die Stem" ("The Call"), the traditional Afrikaner anthem.

Mandela, 75, May 2 declared victory over President F. W. de Klerk, 58, at the ANC's election headquarters in Johannesburg. Less than half the votes had been counted, but the ANC was polling more than 62% of

Mandela acknowledged the cooperation that de Klerk had offered in launching initiatives to dismantle apartheid. He congratulated de Klerk for "the many days, weeks and months and the four years that we have worked together, quarreled [and] addressed sensitive problems." To his supporters, Mandela said, "I stand here before you filled with a deep pride and joy. Pride in the ordinary, humble people of this country—you have shown such a calm, patient determination to reclaim this country as your own. And joy that we can loudly proclaim from the rooftops: free at last!"

The Charlotte Observer
Charlotte, North Carolina, May 1, 1994

Sometimes the rush of world events obscures the almost incredible nature of what's happening. A few days before the South African election, the major concern was whether there would be widespread bloodshed. Once the election began, the major concern was whether there would be enough ballots to accommodate the people of all races who stood in long lines at the polls to participate in the rebirth of a nation. In some areas, voter turnout exceeded 90%.

The rebirth of South Africa is equal to the other political miracle of the end of this century, the fall of communism, in everything but scale. The main characters in the story, F.W. de Klerk and Nelson Mandela, are heroes of mythic stature — the former prisoner and his former jailer, old adversaries joined in a momentous enterprise, the creation of a new nation.

Mr. Mandela has devoted his life to the struggle for black citizenship in his native land. Prime Minister De Klerk had devoted his life to the maintenance of white power. Imprisoned for 27 years, Mr. Mandela never wavered. In time the prime minister saw that the shift in power from the white minority to the black majority was inevitable, and willingly gave up his own and his party's power in hopes of making the transition a peaceful one.

The violence that marred the period leading up to the election no doubt will continue to some degree for some time. The cause of the violence is clear. Extremist groups that had power don't want to give it up.

The result has never been in doubt: a huge majority for the African National Congress, followed by the election of Nelson Mandela as South Africa's first black president.

What will happen next is less certain. Mr. Mandela will face a difficult challenge. Apartheid is dead, but its legacy lives on. Some 30-40% of South Africans cannot read. Many of the blacks expected to fill government offices have little experience at such work. Indeed, the success of the black-dominated government will depend in large degree on the cooperation of whites, who have better education and better professional training. If the election is followed by political and racial unrest, that could lead to an exodus of talent that would make the task of nation-building even more difficult.

Still, there is reason to hope in South Africa. Look at what has occurred already. A month ago, Zulu leaders were vowing to boycott the election, and woe to Zulus who didn't follow their lead. Last week, after a compromise, Zulus were flocking peacefully to the polls. Five years ago the ANC was outlawed as a terrorist organization. Its leaders were in exile or in jail. Now Nelson Mandela will lead a government that includes F.W. de Klerk, who first imprisoned him and then set him free.

The greatest of miracles are those that open people's eyes and change their hearts. In South Africa, such miracles are occurring every day.

TULSA WORLD
Tulsa, Oklahoma, April 30, 1994

SOUTH Africa's history-making elections, the first in which people of all races are permitted to participate, evoke two strong, conflicting feelings.

First, it is impossible not to be moved by stories and pictures of black South Africans streaming to — in some cases, overrunning — the polls to cast their first-ever votes in a nation that until now was ruled by a white minority.

Despite ill-prepared polling places, despite the car bombs and shootings by terrorists whose aim was to disrupt the democratic process, voters by the millions went to the polls, beginning with the elderly and disabled on Tuesday and contining Wednesday and Thursday with the general voting population. So heavy was the crush that government officials vowed to keep some rural polling places open after Thursday's deadline to accommodate those who wished to vote.

Such wholehearted participation in the face of huge obstacles should be the envy of every democratic country.

Second, it is easy to believe that the turmoil, unrest and violence that has marked the election is a forerunner of what is in store for South Africa as it continues to struggle with the transition from minority rule to democracy. Longstanding conflicts among factions that have much to lose or gain as the new government is established — activist white racists, a minority of the former minority ruling class; the African National Congress; and some tribes such as the Zulus — won't be easily resolved.

Unhappily, the prognosis is for continued unrest and bloodshed. Those who cherish democracy can only hope that after the initial wave of euphoria passes, South Africans can sustain their enthusiasm for democracy, and make it work in South Africa.

The Globe and Mail
Toronto, Ontario, May 4, 1994

MAY 2, 1994, was a miraculous day in South Africa, and the two men most responsible for the miracle, F. W. de Klerk and Nelson Mandela, welcomed it with fitting grace. President de Klerk, conceding victory to Mr. Mandela's African National Congress in last week's election, offered "friendship and co-operation" to his successor and "enthusiastically" pledged his support "in the spirit of national reconciliation." Mr. Mandela, who is to be inaugurated next Tuesday in Pretoria, congratulated Mr. de Klerk and other party leaders, promising to co-operate closely with them in the coming government of national unity. "I hold out a hand of friendship to the leaders of all parties and their members," he said at Monday night's victory celebration.

However appropriate to the moment, the spirit of amity is not likely to last. Amid the conciliatory words were clear signals of the battles that lie ahead as the national unity government grapples with the enormous problems facing the new South Africa. The central battle will be over the economy.

Mr. de Klerk's National Party stands squarely for free enterprise. Only with such a system, said Mr. de Klerk on Monday, "can we ensure that we will generate the wealth which we need to address the pressing social needs of large sections of our population. We must ensure that social services are affordable, caring and effective." Mr. Mandela obviously wants a strong economy too. But he also wants to employ the resources of government to improve the social conditions of the non-white majority. With that aim, the ANC has promised to spend $11-billion (U.S.) to provide houses, jobs, education and medical services.

On Monday, he made it quite clear that he does not consider that program negotiable. "If there are attempts on the part of anybody to undermine that program, there will be serious tensions in the government of national unity," he said, ". . . and nobody will be entitled to participate in that government of national unity to oppose that plan."

These are troubling words for the future leader of a cabinet that, under the interim constitution drawn up last year with the ANC's full participation, is supposed to operate by consensus. Although no one could disagree with the goals of the ANC reconstruction plan, there is plenty of room for argument over its cost and, even more important, the means of financing it. If Mr. Mandela intends to increase taxes — and he will have to if he wants to reach his ambitious goals — how big will the increases be? What effect will they have on the already battered South African economy and, by extension, its currency, the rand?

The fear of the National Party, of course, is that Mr. Mandela will attempt to squeeze the money out of white South Africans — just as whites squeezed cheap labour out of blacks to finance their relatively prosperous way of life. That might be just, but is it smart? Would whites then begin fleeing South Africa as they did when black majority rule came to neighbouring Zimbabwe? Would Mr. Mandela in effect kill the goose that lays the golden egg?

More than federalism, more than tribalism, more even than crime and violence, this is the prosaic question that will dominate the government of national unity. No matter how determined he is to bring in his reconstruction program, Mr. Mandela must allow other parties to have a voice in determining the answer.

The Star-Ledger
Newark, New Jersey, May 5, 1994

For more than a century, the history of the South African state has been that of a majority ruled by a minority.

In the 19th century, South Africa was part of the British empire and government policies were decided in London, not Johannesburg. When the Boer government replaced the British, it substituted one form of anti-democratic regime for another. The apartheid laws it passed, which not only denied blacks the right to vote but imposed a cruel form of racial segregation, were a retrogression in terms of fairness and justice.

Now, at last, democracy and simple justice, unfettered by racial considerations, will get a chance to rule this long-troubled land. Next week, the first South African parliament to be selected through free elections without racial barriers to voting will meet to elect Nelson Mandela president. Later, the 75-year-old Mr. Mandela will be inaugurated as president, capping a dream that seemed impossible indeed when the apartheid government imprisoned him more than three decades ago for committing the unpardonable sin of seeking free elections.

For years, South Africa has been regularly rocked by racially inspired violence, and when white militants staged several pre-election bombings, it seemed likely that the election days would see the same violence. Surprisingly, this did not happen. Once the tide of free elections began to roll, violence disappeared.

That the long struggle for racial justice in South Africa should be resolved through free elections is something even the most rabid opponents of apartheid did not foresee until comparatively recently. That violence was averted is an example of how much the good will and earnest intentions of two men can matter.

When F.W. de Klerk became president of South Africa, he appeared to be just one more Boer head of state who would make apartheid the cornerstone of his presidency. Instead, he moved in the opposite direction, dismantling step by step the nation's segregation statutes. Even more surprisingly, he released Mr. Mandela from prison.

Once released after 27 years in captivity, Mr. Mandela might have proved to be a man consumed by hatred, one who would seek revenge for the wrongs done to him and his people. Instead, he has been an advocate of harmony and moderation. He has pledged to make his government representative of all the people of South Africa, not just of his ruling African National Congress, which won an overwhelming election victory.

And so South Africa, in the words of Mr. Mandela and of the old hymn once quoted by Dr. Martin Luther King Jr., is "free at last!" One can only hope that the era of good feeling and racial harmony that now widely prevails will continue as the nation moves into its new era.

The Evening Gazette

Worcester, Massachusetts, May 4, 1994

The spectacle of long-sought freedom unfolding this week in South Africa is occasion for renewed, worldwide dedication to the cause of democracy rooted in human rights and free enterprise.

Those who predicted that dire events would accompany free elections in this traditional bastion of apartheid were drowned out by the ecstatic celebrations of the nation's 30 million blacks who are, indeed, "free at last."

The graciousness with which President F.W. de Klerk conceded defeat and the dignity with which Nelson Mandela proclaimed victory set the proper tone for difficult business that lies ahead.

Wisely, Mandela has put a five-year timeline on the first phase of promised reforms: construction of a million houses, a public works employment program and free, compulsory education for all.

To accomplish these ambitious goals, Mandela will need de Klerk, who, as one of two vice presidents, will be his key link to the civil service responsible for carrying out the reforms.

While Mandela's African National Congress party polled well over 60 percent of the vote, de Klerk's National Party was, as expected, a solid second. Significantly, the Freedom Front, which favors a white separatist homeland, garnered less than 5 percent of the total vote.

Clearly, moderation and reconciliation carried the day.

The way ahead will not be easy, but a great divide has been crossed. Mandela summed up the mood in his moving statement Monday night: "Let our celebrations be in keeping with the mood set in the elections, peaceful, respectful and disciplined, showing we are a people ready to assume the responsibilities of government."

It is a joyous moment for South Africa and for the world.

THE TAMPA TRIBUNE

Tampa, Florida, May 7, 1994

After the deserved celebrations of South Africa's new democracy comes the hard work of crafting a new constitution.

Nelson Mandela's African National Congress won a landslide victory, and while counting is incomplete, the ANC is expected to come very close to the two-thirds majority needed to write the constitution as it pleases. The ANC generously promised to include all parties in the historic process, and even if it does gain the two-thirds majority, compromise would be a wise move.

A constitution born of hard-argued give and take will be best designed to serve all South Africans.

The democracy South Africa has given itself is a remarkable achievement, and is largely due to the charismatic leadership of two gifted politicians, Mandela and outgoing President F.W. de Klerk. Whether their accomplishment will fulfill its potential will depend not on what they say today but what fundamentals of freedom they set in constitutional concrete.

The experience of the United States proves that a constitution properly written and intelligently amended can lead future generations peacefully through crises not imagined by the authors of the document.

As Americans have shown the world, the freedom to vote is no guarantee for everyone of either equality or justice. Even where the majority believes in national unity and fairness, an independent judiciary is required to enforce laws fairly and defend fundamental human rights.

The South African electorate presents a unique combination of challenges. Some people there are calling for kings and others for communism. Some want a strong central government and others want power so fragmented as to allow states to set up independent fascist governments.

In the recent elections, Mandela and de Klerk were masters of restrained campaigning: Both appealed to voters' hopes more than their fears, and in so doing kept sparks away from explosive emotions. They seem to understand Mark Twain's ironic observation: "In our country we have those three unspeakably precious things: freedom of speech, freedom of conscience, and the prudence never to practice either."

Now is the time to celebrate South Africa's victory of democracy, and to realize that for the victory to stay won, the game must be replayed with prudence time after time.

WISCONSIN ⚜ STATE JOURNAL

Madison, Wisconsin, May 5, 1994

Writing this week in the Wall Street Journal, Leon Louw of the Free Market Foundation of South Africa offered this sobering analysis of the all-race elections that buried the corpse of apartheid and elevated the once-imprisoned Nelson Mandela into that nation's presidency.

"South Africa must avoid simply shifting from one form of centralized state authoritarianism to another. The absence of apartheid does not mean the presence of liberty. . . . The United States now must call for a truly free and democratic South Africa, one committed to the protection of the widest range of civil and human rights and political and economic freedoms."

Although there is no small amount of irony in white South Africans suddenly becoming nervous about losing their civil rights, Louw is correct in warning that South Africa's first-ever free elections cannot guarantee a working democracy. Indeed, some of the hard-left elements of the African National Congress can be expected to press for "reforms" that will be viewed by many South Africans — black and white — as Marxist-style redistribution, regulation and retaliation.

So far, however, there is no evidence that Mandela and the ANC plan to turn their 63 percent mandate into an excuse to shut everyone else out of the government. In fact, the exact opposite seemed true in Mandela's post-victory remarks and in the comments of F.W. de Klerk, the current president and the last of South Africa's apartheid-era rulers.

Mandela, forever gracious, forever the wise "Madiba," an affectionate term for old man, immediately extended his hand to parties that had run against the ANC. He hinted that even those that had not won 5 percent of the national vote — the threshold required for a Cabinet seat — would be given positions. "An ANC government will serve all the people of South Africa, not just ANC members," he vowed.

According to election rules, the party with the second largest number of votes is entitled to a deputy presidency. That means de Klerk, with 23 percent of the vote, will remain in a position of authority in the new South African government. The only question is how far Mandela and the ANC will go to accommodate the Inkatha Zulu Party of Mangosuthu Buthelezi.

Privileged South Africans — meaning, for the most part, white South Africans — cannot hope for life to remain the same. South Africa is dogged by huge disparities in employment, income, education and housing, to name a few of apartheid's legacies. For decades, whites hoarded much of the country's wealth. Now they'll have to use some of it to create jobs, new housing and better schools for blacks.

That's as it should be. What should not come to be is a "new" South Africa where one form of oppression is traded for another. Only if all South Africans, white, black or colored, can live as equals will the nation move forward economically. Mandela and de Klerk already understand that; let's hope others follow their lead.

LAS VEGAS REVIEW-JOURNAL
Las Vegas, Nevada, May 6, 1994

A new nation bursts upon the scene — the new South Africa, which has just completed, in more or less peaceful fashion, its first all-race election.

As expected, Nelson Mandela and his African National Congress pulled down a landslide majority of the vote.

One must admire Mandela's steely determination, his steadfast leadership and forebearance in the long struggle for racial parity in a nation where a white minority lorded it over a black majority for 342 years. Much of the credit for South Africa's transition to real democracy also belongs to outgoing President F. W. de Klerk, who pushed for the rapid dismantling of the hated apartheid system.

The new South Africa faces vexing problems, including the complex task of trying to give black and mixed-race citizens their due. Mandela promises sweeping land reform and the establishment of a national commission charged with sorting out the ownership of both urban and farm lands to which both blacks and whites lay claim. This will be an arduous, and perhaps bloody process.

Mandela's stated commitment to civil rights and democracy will be sorely tested as the months pass. He says he hopes to forge a consensus which takes in the views of the entire political spectrum which, in South Africa, runs from separatist white rightists and Zulu nationalists to the hard-line communists in Mandela's own governing party. It's difficult to see what form of "consensus" could be forged out of such divergent forces. One hopes the ANC's communist underpinnings do not serve to sway the government toward authoritarian or totalitarian rule. We hope the election was not a prelude to the replacement of white tyranny with black tyranny.

THE CHRISTIAN SCIENCE MONITOR
Boston, Massachusetts, May 2, 1994

BY any reckoning, South Africa has added its name to the list of late 20th-century improbables. The joy and awe apparent in the voices of black South Africans as they voted for the first time should serve as a reminder to jaded Western electorates of the preciousness of their franchise.

That the reins of power so far have shifted relatively peacefully from the morally repugnant and deeply entrenched apartheid system to black-majority rule is cause for gratitude. Yet if statesmanship was needed to bring the country this far, it will be all the more important during the next five years, as South Africa develops a more permanent government structure.

At this writing, the elections have propelled the African National Congress, led by Nelson Mandela, into its anticipated leadership position. Outgoing President Frederik de Klerk is almost assured a role as one of two deputy presidents in the five-year government of reconciliation. And even Chief Mangosuthu Buthelezi, who heads the Inkatha Freedom Party and who kept the country on edge until the final week of the campaign by threatening to boycott the elections, appears to have earned a cabinet seat.

What remains to be determined is the ANC's margin of victory. If it captures 67 percent of the seats in the national parliament, it will be able to write the country's new constitution virtually unchecked. The burden to resist a winner-takes-all mentality from setting in could fall on Mr. Mandela's personal persuasiveness, which is said to be considerable. With less than 67 percent, accommodation with other parties will become a political necessity. That need is indicated by the strong showing in provincial legislative races by the National Party in Western Cape Province and by Inkatha in Natal Province. Inkatha in particular has held out for a more federal system that grants greater authority to the provinces than would the ANC, which wants a strong central government.

EDITORIALS

To his credit, Mandela is setting the right tone for the transition. In news interviews during recent days, he has offered an amnesty to law enforcement officials who killed or tortured blacks for political reasons during the apartheid. Only people who committed such crimes recently would be prosecuted. He indicated that the government would continue to help underwrite the cost of schooling for ethnic minorities, while still trying to narrow a 2-to-1 funding gap that favors whites. And he said he favors holding taxes down to attract foreign investment.

That investment will be critical to South Africa's future. In that regard, the 43 remaining state and local governments in the United States that still have anti-apartheid sanctions on their books should remove them. It is insufficient to say that legislative calendars are clogged; they were opened speedily enough when sanctions ●were enacted.

Calgary Herald
Calgary, Alberta, May 3, 1994

Not content with authoring one of the most remarkable stories in the history of democracy, Nelson Mandela continues to break new political ground.

With his African National Congress party in the process of recording a resounding victory in South Africa's first democratic elections, Mandela has opted to extend the olive branch of inclusion to virtually all of the political factions that have surfaced — including those responsible for his own 27-year imprisonment.

Even before the ballots had been counted, Mandela promised that, if elected to the presidency, his government would allow every party a voice in parliament, rely heavily on the mostly white business sector for economic guidance, forgive past crimes and in general, conduct itself in a non-sectarian, democratic fashion.

His promises stand in direct contrast to the destructive politics and genocidal policies that have ruined Somalia, Rwanda and other non-African states like Bosnia — and while they have yet to prove entirely workable, reflect the exceptional farsighted character of Mandela.

With the eyes of the world still trained on South Africa, it is obvious Mandela is determined to show that under his leadership, his country can overcome the huge challenge that democracy has brought.

Even the politics of inclusion, which Mandela appears committed to pursuing, is not without danger.

By offering to create a government in which members of opposition parties are invited to sit as cabinet members, Mandela may be saddling South Africa with a system that creates a host of new, potentially explosive, dynamics.

As well, the new government will have to quickly exhibit the will to address and begin to defuse the myriad of racial, economic and social tensions that have marked South Africa's oppressive, violent history.

Most important, all of Mandela's legendary patience and vision will be needed if he is to steer his country through the gamut of expectations, needs, disappointments, hopes, heartaches, and opportunities that are sure to present themselves on an almost daily basis.

The new government — and Mandela's vision — will face many formidable challenges. But few will be as imposing as the task of writing a new constitution.

Because South Africa's constitution will have to reflect not only present realities, but past and future considerations, it will come into existence only after extensive give and take from the country's vast array of special-interest groups.

If Mandela can facilitate the successful creation of a new constitution within a reasonable time period, there will be no limits — economically, politically and socially — to what the new South Africa can accomplish.

If, on the other hand, Mandela's policies of inclusion and reconciliation are not pervasive enough to produce a fair and acceptable constitution, this week's celebrations of the democratic spirit may prove premature.

GREAT BRITAIN & NORTHERN IRELAND:

IRA Declares Cease-Fire in 25-Year Conflict

The outlawed Provisional Irish Republican Army Aug. 31 announced a cease-fire in its 25-year-old armed struggle to end British rule in the U.K. province of Northern Ireland, also known as Ulster. The sectarian conflict, which pitted the IRA's Roman Catholic fighters against British troops and Protestant paramilitary forces, had killed more than 3,000 people since 1969, most of them civilians. [See *Editorials On File* 1993, pp. 1458-1465. See also *Facts On File World News Digest* 1994, p. 613A1. For previous developments see *Facts On File* 1994, p. 416A1]

The IRA declared the truce in a brief, four-paragraph statement issued on the morning of Aug. 31. It began: "Recognizing the potential of the current situation and in order to enhance the democratic peace process and underline our definitive commitment to its success, the leadership of Oglaigh na h-Eirann [the IRA's Gaelic name] have decided that as of midnight Wednesday, Aug. 31, there will be a complete cessation of military operations. All our units have been instructed accordingly." The statement said it was now time to rely on political solutions to the conflict in Northern Ireland.

The statement did not declare the truce to be permanent and did not say whether its continuance would depend on any specific actions by the U.K. government. Nor did it say whether the IRA would surrender its huge weapons supplies.

For several days before the announcement, there had been a flurry of news reports in the British and U.S. press indicating that an IRA truce was imminent. The declaration followed months of mostly secret talks between the U.K., Ireland, Ulster's Catholic leaders, Sinn Fein (the IRA's legal political wing) and the IRA itself. In November 1993, Britain had acknowledged its secret contacts with the IRA, and the following month British Prime Minister John Major and Irish Prime Minister Albert Reynolds issued a joint peace plan for Ulster, the so-called Downing Street Declaration. [See *Facts On File* 1993, pp. 938C1, 889A1]

The omission of the word "permanent" from the IRA cease-fire announcement was controversial because the requirement of a permanent cease-fire had been set out in the Downing Street Declaration. Britain continued to maintain that it would not enter into formal talks with Sinn Fein until it unequivocally renounced violence and until three months after the start of a permanent cease-fire by the IRA.

(Previously, the IRA's longest unilateral truce had been in 1975, when a cease-fire was nominally in force for much of the year, although it was punctuated by violence. The IRA had also called three-day Christmas truces annually since 1990, and most recently had called a brief halt to hostilities in April. [See *Facts On File* 1994, p. 263A3; 1975, pp. 952D1, 865D3])

The IRA announcement did not specifically mention the group's long-standing goal of uniting the six counties of Ulster with the Irish Republic, but it reiterated "our commitment to our republican objectives."

In the days leading up to the cease-fire declaration, British officials had insisted that they had made no concessions to the IRA, and Major and Reynolds reiterated that point Aug. 31. Major maintained that there would be no change in the status of Northern Ireland without the consent of the majority of its citizens. He said, "Northern Ireland is part of the United Kingdom for so long as people in Northern Ireland wish to remain part of the U.K. They will do so with the support of this government and, I hope, future governments."

(Protestants—most of whom were believed to favor continued union with the U.K.—still held the demographic edge in Northern Ireland, accounting for about 57% of Ulster's 1.6 million population, as compared with the Catholic minority's 43%. The Irish Republic, on the other hand, was an overwhelmingly Catholic country.)

The "troubles"—as the conflict was known in Northern Ireland—began in the 1960s as a civil-rights struggle by Catholics, who had long suffered political and economic discrimination at the hands of Ulster's Protestant majority.

The Washington Post

Washington, D.C., September 8, 1994

IT WAS startling but cheering to see pictures this week of Irish Prime Minister Albert Reynolds smiling and shaking hands with Gerry Adams, the leader of Sinn Fein. The two have been antagonists for years as political leaders in the Irish Republic sought to stem IRA violence and build peace in Northern Ireland in cooperation with the British. With the cease-fire, a new hope has arisen. While it may be jarring to hear the head of the IRA's political arm expressing sorrow for all the deaths that have occurred in the last 25 years and reaching out to his "Protestant brothers in the north," those are at least the right words for this early stage in reconciliation.

Across the water in London, however, another meeting about the future of Ulster did not go well. The Rev. Ian Paisley, the most intransigent of the Protestant leaders in the province and the one most likely to find the most hostile and defiant words for any occasion, confronted British Prime Minister John Major. At the private meeting, he charged Mr. Major with having made a secret deal to sell out the loyalists who are the majority in the province. When Mr. Paisley refused to accept the prime minister's personal assurance that this was not the case, the meeting was ended abruptly. The prime minister was undoubtedly provoked and exasperated by Mr. Paisley's characteristic belligerence, but it is a shame nevertheless that prospects for reconciliation on this front were not advanced. Peacemakers have learned not to expect cooperation from Mr. Paisley himself, but surely now that the fighting has ended—for the time being, at least—their most important task is to reassure Mr. Paisley's followers and other Protestants that they have not been betrayed.

At every stage of the long process toward peace, it has been made clear that the future of Northern Ireland will be determined only by the people of the province itself. Political leaders in London and Dublin have provided that assurance repeatedly. Moreover, even though demographics will probably give Ulster Catholics a majority within 35 or 40 years, there is no reason to assume that all Catholics will favor union with the Irish Republic. There are real economic and other advantages to maintaining the link with Britain instead.

Ian Paisley has a constituency, and many men and women look to him for leadership. It would be wonderful if the opportunity created by the cease-fire allowed him to be reassuring, cooperative and even hopeful about his country's future. But whether or not he chooses to move forward with others, the Protestants of the north must be convinced that they have more to gain than lose in this new situation. Peace is only the first prize. Foreign investment, economic stability and the respect of the international community will surely follow, and these benefits will flow to citizens on both sides of the old barriers.

ALBUQUERQUE JOURNAL

Albuquerque, New Mexico, September 2, 1994

The Irish Republican Army's declaration of a cease-fire holds the best promise yet, that after 25 years, the political and sectarian violence in Northern Ireland could end.

The IRA has promised to stop attacks on Protestants and British troops in Northern Ireland. Britain, however, has ruled out peace talks until it is assured the violence has stopped for good.

The cease-fire announcement carries forward the process started late last year with a bilateral declaration of principles for peace. In that document, London and Dublin stipulated that the IRA's political arm, Sinn Fein, could join other parties in determining Northern Ireland's future only after three violence-free months of a cease-fire had transpired.

Nationalism, grudges and religious bigotry nursed through generations won't end with a simple declaration by the IRA. But there is hope on all sides that the cease-fire will hold, even though there have been other truces — 10 in all — since the current cycle of violence began in 1969.

The division that characterizes Northern Ireland began in the 17th century when Protestant Scottish and English farmers displaced native Irish Catholics from their prime land. In 1641 Irish rebels killed the farmers or ran them out of their homes. In the 18th century there was openly sectarian fighting between the Protestant Peep O'Day Boys and the Defenders on the Catholic side.

Those old antagonisms won't die easily, yet the IRA's announcement of a "complete cessation of military operations" could set the stage for joint talks on the future of Northern Ireland. But the age-old conflict remains. The Protestant majority wants to retain its ties to Britain. The Catholic minority regards itself as Irish.

The peace process might be helped if 18,000 British troops, most of whom are deployed in Catholic areas against the IRA, are withdrawn, which seems unlikely.

More than 3,100 people have been killed in Northern Ireland in political and sectarian violence during the last 25 years. About half of the victims were killed by the IRA, while loyalists, security forces and splinter republican groups are blamed for the remaining deaths. The two main Protestant groups — the Ulster Volunteer Force and the larger Ulster Defense Association — have been blamed for killing 30 people this year, nearly twice the 17 deaths claimed by the IRA.

John Hume, a Catholic political leader, identifies the primary challenge as reaching "agreement among our divided people." James Molyneaux, leader of the Ulster Unionist Party, the largest Protestant party in Northern Ireland, cautiously welcomed the announcement. "I hope the authors of the statement mean what they say — that it is a permanent, total, complete cessation of terrorism."

In the days and weeks to come, extremists on the Protestant side may try to draw the IRA back into the conflict by targeting Catholics. The IRA will be judged by its responses and actions rather than by its words.

Gerry Adams, president of Sinn Fein, the IRA's political party ally, observed that "This struggle is not over. This struggle is into a new phase."

President Clinton declared that the IRA's announcement "can mark the beginning of a new era that holds the promise of peace for all the people of Northern Ireland."

Optimistic words. The promise of a lasting peace will be fulfilled only when Northern Ireland's nationalism, ancient grudges and religious bigotry are tempered greatly or permanently laid to rest.

Winnipeg Free Press

Winnipeg, Manitoba, September 2, 1994

Ireland took another step toward peace and unification yesterday when the Irish Republican Army announced that it was abandoning violence in order to join the search for a political settlement in Ulster.

After the miraculously rapid progress toward peace and democracy that this year has brought in the Middle East and South Africa, renunciation of violence by the

IRA may seem like small potatoes, but it is still an outstanding success for the policy of British Prime Minister John Major and Irish Prime Minister Albert Reynolds.

The two prime ministers last December announced that they could both accept annexation of Northern Ireland to the Irish Republic, though never against the wishes of a majority of the inhabitants. This was a dramatic reversal of policy for both countries. The republic had always claimed the whole island, whether the people of the North liked it or not. Previous British governments had no thought of detaching Northern Ireland from the United Kingdom.

The December joint declaration left the Irish nationalist movement and the Ulster unionists in isolation and in danger of irrelevance. Once the governments had decided to discuss terms and procedures for reunification, those who refused to consider reunification became mere irritants. Once it was admitted that the people of Ulster cannot be compelled to join the republic against their will, then those who seek unification through coercion were wasting their time.

The Ulster unionists still have the majority of Northern Ireland's people with them, for the Protestant 60 per cent of the six northern counties do not wish to join the republic. But once the shooting and the bombing stop and the British Army presence is reduced, a new generation of Ulster leaders may emerge who are willing to consider some connection with the republic — for tourist promotion, perhaps, or joint cattle-breeding projects.

Plenty of Ulster Protestants will cling proudly to their ancient hatreds and fears, but Northern Ireland is made up mainly of reasonable people who, in time, will be able to look calmly at the idea of joining the republic by gradual stages. Some will find it an appealing idea. Some who cannot stomach it will cross the sea to England. Eventually, a majority for union will be found and a referendum will carry.

Those few who have lived by murder, robbery, extortion and kidnapping these last 25 years will not easily shake the habit. We will know that the leopard's spots have changed when the IRA starts turning in the recalcitrant ones who cannot bring themselves to put away the guns.

The Star-Ledger

Newark, New Jersey, September 2, 1994

After 25 years of senseless killing, the IRA declaration of a cease-fire this week could mark a hopeful turn in Northern Ireland. True, the truce promises only a moratorium, but it does offer a reprieve from political violence that has taken several thousand lives and sets the stage for negotiations directed at the long-elusive goal of a peaceful future for divided Ireland.

The IRA truce is an outgrowth of a peace campaign launched last year by Britain and Ireland, which pledged that there could be no change in the status of Northern Ireland without the approval of a majority of its people.

Sinn Fein, the IRA's political arm, was invited to join in negotiations if the IRA permanently ended its armed resistance. Irish Prime Minister Albert Reynolds said the IRA has met that condition and "there could be no turning back." But British Prime Minister John Major warily underscored a "need to be clear that this is indeed intended to be a permanent renunciation of violence, that is to say, for good."

The parties are in the opening phase of an extremely difficult process. They must try to produce an equitable plan, one that will require concessions by both sides — setting up a system of government in Northern Ireland acceptable to Protestant Unionists and Catholic Nationalists.

The IRA cease-fire came about through a constructive collaboration between Sinn Fein President Gerry Adams and John Hume, the leader of the main Catholic-based party, which wants Ireland united peacefully. They engaged in secret talks last year to explore the possibility of Sinn Fein pursuing its goals without the IRA. Their talks persuaded the British and Irish governments to offer Sinn Fein a place in renewed negotiations but only if the IRA agreed to stop the killings permanently.

Getting all the Catholic Nationalists talking on the same wavelength was a trying process. But it will be far more difficult to get militant Protestants to sit down with Sinn Fein. While the Catholic faction has been able to bend and accept change, the Protestants have continued to resist change and have been unwilling or unable to offer a positive program.

"There's no de Klerk figure emerging on the Protestant Union side," said Tim Hogan, author of a history of the IRA, referring to the former president of South Africa, F.W. de Klerk, who helped end apartheid. There has been some flexibility, but a formidable faction of Protestant militants has remained intractable in its opposition to a united Ireland.

The IRA cease-fire is not likely to decrease the intransigent Protestant resistance to political and economic changes in Northern Ireland. But it may lay the groundwork for an end to the political violence. With or without unification, there is no justification and no future for the use of violence in Northern Ireland.

The Record

Hackensack, New Jersey, September 1, 1994

THE "complete" cease-fire declared by the Irish Republican Army this week could be the long-awaited first step toward peace in Northern Ireland.

The cease-fire is expected to allow Sinn Fein, the political arm of the IRA, to take part in negotiations on the future of the British province. More than 3,000 Catholics and Protestants have died in 25 years of violence in war-torn Northern Ireland.

John Hume, Northern Ireland's top Catholic politician, said this week: "We have a historic opportunity to resolve our problems, if we take it . . . The first step, the major step, is to create a totally peaceful atmosphere."

Now it's up to all the parties to the negotiations, including the British government, the Irish government, and the IRA, to begin their work in earnest. Britain has offered to talk with leaders of Sinn Fein within three months of a permanent cease-fire.

The Clinton administration deserves some credit for encouraging the truce. Last winter, the White House granted a visa to Sinn Fein leader Gerry Adams, and this week to Joseph Cahill of the IRA, to come to the United States to talk to supporters about the cease-fire.

In recent months the world has seen several great breakthroughs that would have seemed almost impossible a few years ago. Substantive peace talks in the Middle East, the fall of apartheid and the rise of democracy in South Africa, and now the IRA laying down its arms.

The Salt Lake Tribune

Salt Lake City, Utah, September 1, 1994

In this decade of stunning peacemaking, the date of August 31, 1994 — the day that the Irish Republican Army declared a "complete cessation of military operations" on its part — may take a prominent place on the list of '90s breakthroughs.

Granted, real peace in Northern Ireland can only be achieved if the other perpetrators of violence in Ulster over the last quarter-century — the Unionist terrorists who oppose absorption into a unified Ireland — lay down their arms as well. They have increased their bloody activities since peace overtures were launched last year, and it is questionable that IRA guns could remain silent in the wake of stepped-up Unionist attacks.

The concern over Protestant violence, though, simply amplifies how the landscape has changed in Northern Ireland: It is the minority Catholics, whose sense of economic and political desperation instigated "the troubles" 25 years ago, who are now the agents for peace, while the Protestant majority senses a desperation of its own, born of the fear of eventual British desertion.

That transformation can be traced through the footsteps of John Hume, the leader of Northern Ireland's moderate Catholics, who greatly outnumber the IRA radicals. He began meeting last year with Gerry Adams, the leader of Sinn Fein (the IRA's political front), and the two of them devised a peace proposal last fall — a forerunner to the December proposal by Irish and British government leaders.

The framers of the latter agreement, known as the Downing Street Declaration, were prime ministers John Major of England and Albert Reynolds of Ireland, and they deserve credit for influencing the IRA's cease-fire, even if it took eight months. The declaration offered Sinn Fein a seat at negotiations over Northern Ireland's future, as long as the IRA permanently renounced violence, as it seems to have done Wednesday.

While Mr. Adams delayed his response for months, all the while trying to enhance his public image with gambits like his American trip last February, it seemed he was building political capital at the expense of Messrs. Major and Reynolds. But the longer he refused to embrace the peace proposal, the more time began to turn against him. And when the IRA rejected the peace plan last month, it earned public condemnation from all corners.

The IRA had simply become so marginalized that it ultimately had little choice but to lay down its arms. Not only does it command little support in Northern Ireland and almost none in the Irish Republic, its goal of Irish unification has also lost much of its appeal with Irish Catholics, both north and south. After taking some 2,000 lives over the last 25 years, through cowardly bombings and random shootings, the IRA thugs were left with little reason to keep fighting.

Still, its official announcement Wednesday, inevitable as it may have been, marks an historic moment. If the Unionist terrorists can follow the lead of the IRA terrorists, then the prospects for peace in Northern Ireland — built on the Downing Street Declaration principle of self-determination by the people of Ulster — may be real indeed. After 25 years of violence, Irish eyes would truly be smiling.

The Miami Herald

Miami, Florida, September 9, 1994

When the Irish Republican Army declared its "complete cessation" of violence last week, the reaction in London — which has seen too much IRA bloodshed — was naturally wary. In Washington and Dublin, though, it seemed to border on euphoria.

That became especially clear when Vice President Al Gore met Irish Prime Minister Albert Reynolds in Shannon, Ireland, the other day. The two men fairly gushed with enthusiasm for the prospects of peace in Northern Ireland, leaving British Prime Minister John Major to play the role of wet blanket.

President Clinton and Mr. Gore deservedly take a certain pride in the event: Irish sources say that the two men played a helpful role in nudging the IRA toward a gesture of peace. And the administration reportedly envisions a $200 million aid package for the province if the peace proves lasting. All of that puts the United States in the right role — as facilitator and encourager — behind Irish and British peacemakers.

But the causes of Northern Ireland's problems aren't mainly economic; they're political. They're unlikely to respond much to goodwill from Washington or any other foreign capital. Nor will they be solved by a few words from the IRA, no matter how unprecedented and hopeful those words may seem after 25 years of organized cruelty. In all those respects, Mr. Major's reaction has been more on the money.

Political killings in Northern Ireland

BUT CAN IT LAST?
Northern Ireland's 'Troubles' can't end without a lasting IRA cease-fire. But that's only the beginning.

---

are merely the external flourish of a grotesque and thriving underworld. In parts of Belfast, your religion determines where you can safely park your car, even what taxis you ride. Painted curbstones designate streets either Catholic or Protestant. Hundreds of jobs depend on the protection rackets. Whole industries subsist on replacing shattered windows and cleaning up after bombings. In this landscape, one vague declaration by one band of toughs is barely a start.

Mr. Reynolds, a key broker in bringing the IRA nearer to the peace table, has good reason to put the best face on the so-far "complete" cease-fire. But his enthusiasm is a strategic necessity; it shouldn't be mistaken for a mirror of reality. It is aimed at reinforcing the IRA's pacifist faction while nudging a still-wary Britain. It is not a neutral assessment of the evidence.

If the IRA's "complete" cease-fire also proves permanent — and resists whatever outrages the unionist opposition has in hand — then hard talks, a gradual peace, and a slow healing *may* follow. U.S. economic aid might then help a little, if that stage ever is reached.

But that, like all the historic events of the past two weeks, would be just one small, indispensable step in a 100-mile journey. The real work of peace will occur only in small increments on the streets of Belfast and Derry and all the grief-weary Northern Irish communities where memories will not simply fade like so many traces of blood.

Rockford Register Star

Rockford, Illinois, September 6, 1994

The road to peace is invariably filled with obstacles, and perhaps nowhere is that more apparent than in Northern Ireland.

Last week's announcement of a "complete cessation" of attacks by the Irish Republican Army has raised hopes for an end to sectarian violence that has killed more than 3,100 people and wounded another 30,000 in the past quarter-century. Talks that could eventually lead to a united Ireland are planned.

But the announcement has also raised concerns from some in the Protestant majority in Northern Ireland that they will be forgotten in the creation of a united Ireland, which would have a Catholic majority. Violence attributed to militant groups followed the cease-fire announcement

---

Lack of trust is big roadblock to peace in Northern Ireland.

---

by a matter of hours, and other incidents are likely to follow. Many Protestants don't want to cut Ulster's ties to Britain.

The biggest roadblock to peace may be the lack of trust shown by all sides of the complicated equation: The British government has had trouble deciding if the IRA's language indicated a permanent cease-fire; Protestant groups suspect that secret deals were made among the British government, Irish government and the IRA to ensure the halt in attacks; and the IRA's political wing, Sinn Fein, says the British are hung up on semantics.

The cease-fire announcement by the IRA — permanent or not — was the biggest single step toward peace in that troubled area since the latest skirmish in an old war broke out 25 years ago. It will take further bold steps to overcome generations of hatred and mistrust.

The road to peace is and will continue to be a dangerous one. But in this case, there's no other way to reach the destination of a lasting peace.

The Orlando Sentinel

Orlando, Florida, September 22, 1994

Twice in the past year, peace has reared its head cautiously in Northern Ireland. That has raised expectations that the conundrum, once termed "insoluble Ireland," might be resolved.

It's about time. People in Northern Ireland have suffered enough through centuries of strife, particularly the incessant conflict and the deaths of thousands in the past few decades.

The earlier event concerned a gesture by a British prime minister in conjunction with the Irish government to kindle discussions — although it was more comprehensive than efforts in the past.

This week's declaration of a cease-fire by the Irish Republican Army, however, is potentially even more significant in that it may usher in an environment that makes productive talks possible.

Indeed, renouncing violence was a condition set forth by London for moving forward on the British offer.

Skeptics, of course, abound, eager to predict the early demise of the commitment.

This cease-fire — which took effect Thursday — is different, though, in that it appears free of conditions and is open-ended.

Of course, the tragedies may not be over.

When British Prime Minister John Major pushed his peace plan last December, the concern was that the IRA or its Protestant extremist equivalents could shun the gesture and thwart progress.

Now that the IRA seems to have come around, the Protestants remain potentially disruptive. That must be prevented.

Mindless bloodletting has produced nothing but misery in Northern Ireland. Without a pause for serious negotiations, there can never be an enduring solution. A majority seems to realize that, and most sides to the conflict suggest that they're prepared to move in a similar direction.

In sum, it's still too early for rejoicing, for declaring the conflict over and for praising this as a historic moment.

There is, however, a historic *opportunity* that bears approaching with a balance of realism and hope. It is that potential that all participants in the Northern Ireland situation must seize with vigor, lest the page not turn to a new chapter of peace.

MIDDLE EAST:

Jordan, Israel Sign Draft Pact For Full Diplomatic Ties

Israel and the Hashemite Kingdom of Jordan Oct. 17 initialed a draft peace treaty that set the stage for fully normalized relations between the two erstwhile enemies. The formal treaty signing, conditionally set for late October after approval of the pact by the respective national legislatures, would mark the second such treaty between Israel and an Arab nation, being preceded only by the Israeli–Egyptian accord finalized in 1979. [See *Editorials On File* 1994, pp. 834-847. See also *Facts On File World News Digest* 1994, p. 767B3. For previous developments see *Facts On File* 1994, p. 725E2; 1979, p. 221A1]

The draft accord was hammered out during a night of negotiations in which Jordanian and Israeli negotiators, meeting in the Jordanian capital, Amman, resolved long-standing differences over disputed territory, water rights and security issues. The agreement capped a series of intensive negotiations between the two sides that had followed the signing in July of the so-called Washington Declaration. The declaration had formally ended the 46-year-long state of war between Israel and Jordan. [See *Facts On File* 1994, p. 525A1]

The decision by Jordan's King Hussein to take the final step toward full ties with Israel represented a clear rupture in the already weakened ranks of Arab unity, and drew heated responses from Syria's President Hafez al-Assad and Palestine Liberation Organization (PLO) Chairman Yasir Arafat. Syria, the PLO, Jordan and Lebanon earlier had seemingly agreed that neither would sign a full treaty with Israel until each of the other parties had negotiated terms for peace with the Jewish state. [See *Facts On File* 1993, pp. 704A1, 645D2]

Israeli Prime Minister Yitzhak Rabin immediately returned to Israel and the same day secured his cabinet's unanimous approval for the draft accord. The cabinet of the Jordanian premier, Abdel Salem al-Majali, unanimously adopted the draft Oct. 18. That left Israeli and Jordanian negotiators with the task of determining the final wording of the peace treaty, including annexes to the pact, at which point it would be submitted for parliamentary approval in both countries.

Rabin, who had been accompanied to Amman by Israeli Foreign Minister Shimon Peres, and Majali had signed the draft document for their two countries.

Rabin Oct. 17 hailed the agreement, saying, "No one [particular side] lost, no one won, we all won."

U.S. President Clinton, in characterizing the draft as "an extraordinary achievement," said he would attend the formal signing, set for the border area at Eilat, Israel and Aqaba, Jordan.

Neither Israel nor Jordan immediately released details of the accord, but the principal terms of the 25-clause agreement emerged from local sources Oct. 17–18.

In addition to the regular diplomatic relations, upgraded commercial ties and eased travel and tourism arrangements that the accord would sanction between the two countries, Israel agreed—in a complicated deal—to return to Jordan some 120 square miles (310 sq km) of territory along their southern border seized by the Israelis in the 1948–49 Arab–Israeli war. However, since some of the land had long been farmed by Israeli settlers, Jordan agreed to lease about 12 square miles back to the Israeli government.

Israel was to divert yearly to Jordan about 13 billion gallons (50 billion liters) of water, which represented a fraction of Jordan's original claim on disputed water resources. The two nations reportedly agreed to further develop the amount of water available to each by constructing dams on the Jordan River, which demarcated much of their border, and the Yarmuk River, which flowed eastward into Jordan from the Sea of Galilee.

On the issue of security, Jordan agreed not to form alliances with other nations against Israel and to prevent third parties from using Jordanian territory to stage anti-Israeli attacks.

An Israeli–Jordanian peace treaty would acknowledge the sovereignty of both nations within their internationally accepted borders.

THE BLADE
Toledo, Ohio, October 20, 1994

WHILE a world still attempts to assimilate the notion of a Nobel Peace Prize given to any prominent political figure in the Middle East — given the region's long history of violence — one wonders what sort of Nobel prize might be given to Jordan's King Hussein, given the remarkable step toward peace he helped achieve this week.

Certainly he would deserve a prize for endurance and longevity in office — he has ruled since 1953. Or for that matter a share in the peace prize. Jordan and Israel's freshly signed peace treaty will open diplomatic and commercial relations and ease travel between the two countries. Jordan is the first Arab nation to sign a peace treaty with Israel since Egypt did so in 1979.

The two nations have had variable relations in the past 46 years, sometimes at war, but in recent years carried on what appeared to be almost normal relations. Arguably, it is a more important development than the much-hailed accord between Israel and the Palestine Liberation Organization.

Both nations have much to gain. For Jordan it is the tangible gain of a precious resource — 13 billion gallons of water a year — which will be diverted to a largely arid land. For Israel it is a further step toward cementing permanent relations with its Arab neighbors — in the long run Israel's only certain guarantee of national security.

The Blade once described King Hussein as "an enigma inside a cynic wrapped in the persona of a survivor/statesman." King Hussein was on the wrong side in the Gulf war, and for a time was given the diplomatic cold shoulder by Washington. But that is over. The two sides negotiated, with the United States providing its good offices. Announcement of the end to the state of war took place last July in the so-called Washington Declaration. That was the first time the Israeli and Jordanian leaders had met in public.

"No one lost, no one won, we all won," Israel Prime Minister Yitzhak Rabin commented.

"Between us, hopefully it's a fresh beginning, a fresh start," King Hussein said at the ceremony in the Royal Guest Palace where the peace ceremonies took place.

Many issues remain to be settled, but the biggest one apparently was the division of water resources. The troubled waters having been bridged by this historic agreement, perhaps this is really the most hopeful step yet toward peace in the Middle East.

THE DAILY OKLAHOMAN
Oklahoma City, Oklahoma, October 20, 1994

PEACE accords signed between Israel and Jordan this week comprise important building blocks to a comprehensive Middle East settlement, but the tedious process is still a long way from completion.

Israel has now reached peace agreements with three important players in the regional tender box — Egypt, Jordan and the Palestine Liberation Organization.

Yet to be completed are peace arrangements between Syria and Israel. Syrian Foreign Minister Farouk al-Sharaa had it right when he said, "We hope the Israeli government will realize the fact that without achieving peace with Syria and Lebanon, there will be no peace in the region."

Because Lebanon remains a surrogate of Syria, talks with Syria are crucial to an overall settlement. Syria alone has the power to stifle Iranian mischief via Lebanon and curtail PLO extremists who regularly carry on guerrilla operations against the Jewish state.

There remains a long road to travel toward peace in the Middle East, but the journey seems much shorter than it did just a year ago.

THE TENNESSEAN
Nashville, Tennessee, October 18, 1994

SADDAM Hussein offered the United Nations a bargain too good to be true.

He'll recognize Kuwait's sovereignty if the United Nations will lift the embargo. That deserves consideration at some point, but not while he's threatening.

In the meantime, the United States and its allies need to find a way to keep him at bay. The Clinton administration has proposed a promising course of action. The plan would force Hussein to keep his 20,000 Republican Guard forces out of the south, with assurances that they would not be deployed again in that area. Regular Iraqi army forces in the area that have been used to deal with the Shiite rebellion would be allowed to remain.

The plan makes sense. It would keep Iraq away from Kuwait, but allow Iraqis to continue fending off a possible attack by Iran that could only complicate the region's problems.

Defense Secretary William Perry argued for drawing a line deeper in the sand at the 32nd parallel, where an accompanying no-fly zone begins. But administration officials feared that a demilitarized zone would only encourage Hussein to test allied resolve with forays on the ground, similar to those he has occasionally made in the air. And it would leave the region vulnerable to Iran, still a threat to an already volatile area.

The thornier question of finishing the job begun in the Gulf War and taking Hussein out permanently has thus far been avoided. While it's a popular solution at home, the possible consequences are so grave that allies are right to restrain that impulse until more consideration is given.

A more immediate threat is the commitment of allies to addressing the Iraq

Talk of lifting embargo is premature

situation. France has offered its share of troops and weapons, but officials ridiculously postured that the crisis was manufactured by the United States out of domestic political needs. The idea is ludicrous. The United States has plenty to do in Haiti without an eruption in the Persian Gulf again. Besides, the world ignored the massing of Iraqi troops on the Kuwaiti border the last time and Kuwait was overrun. A more likely explanation is that Hussein wanted to embarrass President Clinton during an election year.

France as well as Russia both had lucrative business interests in Baghdad before the Gulf War. Russia is currently working on a joint oil production agreement with the Iraqis. Together with China, the Russians and French have lobbied for the lifting of the embargo against Iraq which the Security Council has thus far wisely rejected.

Right now, Hussein doesn't deserve a reward for his behavior. Iraq clearly threatened upheaval in Kuwait again and the allies were right to respond with a show of force. A united force broke Hussein's forces before in the Gulf War. Now, they should remain united to further defeat him.

At some point in the future, lifting the embargo must be discussed. But for the immediate future, the allied task should be to turn Iraqi troops away from the Kuwaiti borders and find a way to keep them there. The sooner that's accomplished, the sooner everyone can go home. ■

THE KANSAS CITY STAR
Kansas City, Missouri, October 19, 1994

The draft peace treaty between Israel and Jordan is a welcome indication that peace efforts, despite the resistance of murderous fanatics, continue to move forward.

The benefits of the peace treaty for the predominantly Palestinian country of Jordan appear to be enormous. Jordan, which suffers from a worsening shortage of water, will receive significant amounts of water from Israel as part of the peace agreement. Closer ties with Israel may well lead to further assistance for Jordan in developing adequate sources of water.

Additional water is critical to Jordan's economic future. In addition, a solid peace treaty with Israel can give Jordanians better transportation systems, more economies of scale, more tourists, all sorts of technical assistance and expertise, access to some top-flight educational institutions, more exposure to a working democracy and a free press, greater security against the likes of Syria and Iraq, a voice in the debate over the future of Jerusalem . . . the list goes on and on.

Jordan is even getting back some territory that it lost to Israel back in the 1940s — and lease payments for some of the land as well.

There are economic benefits for Israel, too. But the chief attraction of the treaty for the Jewish state is that it represents another step toward a future in which the country may not have to focus so much of its energy on security issues.

Jordan is no great military power. But it shares a long border with Israel and its borders are uncomfortably close to the heavily populated areas in the middle of Israel. Jordanian-held territory once pinched the midsection of Israel to a width of only a few miles.

If all the final hitches can be worked out in the coming days, Jordan will become the second Arab state to sign a full-fledged treaty with Israel. The two countries, together with Egypt, have the potential to form a core of international stability and cooperation in the heart of the Middle East.

The killing of an Israeli soldier last week gave a horrifying reminder of the evil forces which still confront those who seek to make peace.

Attention now shifts to Syria. The brutal regime in Damascus must decide whether it will take advantage of Israeli's peace overtures and move forward with its neighbors, or continue along the same bloody path to nowhere that it has been following for decades.

THE [●] SUN
Baltimore, Maryland, October 29, 1994

And so it has come to pass that the American president is to make peace next week at the River Jordan between the Israelites, who hold sway over the lands on the West Bank, and the Hashemite monarch who rules the East Bank.

Yet the Palestinians who constitute the majority of those living on each side of the storied waterway remain restive, eager for full statehood, even muttering rebellion against the leader who has dared to abandon his revolutionary ways and cooperate with the Jewish state he fought so long.

Indeed it is the extremists in the Hamas organization who remain the biggest threat to the peace goals of Israel's Prime Minister Yitzhak Rabin, Jordan's King Hussein and the head of the Palestinian Authority in Gaza and Jericho, Yasser Arafat. If these unlikely allies, enemies for so long, can pacify the bulk of the Palestinian people, the dream of an overarching Middle East peace may at last be realized. Even the Syrians, long the most adamant of the anti-Israel coalition, seem prepared to join the process as their relations with the United States continue to improve. They, in turn, can bring Lebanon along.

Events appear to be tumbling over themselves in interlocking crescendo. In the past turbulent week, Hamas has kidnapped and killed an Israeli soldier, Nachshon Waxman, sent its followers into the streets of Gaza to protest Mr. Arafat's roundup of 160 extremists and has even warned the Palestinian Liberation Organization not to replace the Israeli government as Hamas' oppressor.

The question then becomes, can Mr. Arafat control militants resisting his peace efforts? It is a question that must resonate with King Hussein, whose regime was at war with the Palestinians in its midst a quarter-century ago, and with Mr. Rabin, whose peace policies were rocked by the kidnapping and the subsequent failed attempt to free poor Corporal Waxman from his captors.

Yet all the top leaders in this drama are wily if they are anything. Mr. Rabin's initialing of a draft peace agreement settling serious land and water issues with Jordan is as popular in Israel as his pact with the PLO is not. It could offset a national trauma over the soldier's death. Mr. Arafat may yet use the incident as a pretext for attempting to disarm his adversaries in Hamas, this on the assumption that the extremists in the Palestinian cause are isolated as never before. And King Hussein may see this as his moment to assert independence of the Syrians by becoming the second Arab state, after Egypt, to make peace with Israel.

In these events, the U.S. is active in Israeli-Arab negotiations and stands guardian over oil states of the Persian Gulf, protecting them from Iraq and Iran and thereby nudging Saudi Arabia into a modus vivendi with Israel. The symbol of President Clinton extending his arms over the Rabin-Arafat handshake on the White House lawn may soon be augmented by his embrace of the Israeli-Jordanian pact at the river Jews and Arabs most revere.

The Oregonian
Portland, Oregon, October 19, 1994

In another remarkable week for U.S. foreign policy, the United States has seen Israeli-Jordanian peace come to fruition and has reached an agreement of its own with North Korea aimed at scaling back Pyongyang's nuclear program.

The Israeli-Jordanian agreement, still to be signed, will end 46 years of hostility between the two countries.

It marks the first time since Egypt in 1979 that Israel has managed to make peace with any Arab neighbor state. That fact alone should put more pressure on Syria — Israel's most bellicose neighbor — to shorten its timetable for negotiations with Israel.

The North Korean agreement, reached in Geneva but still to be approved in Washington and Pyongyang, would all but end North Korea's capacity to make nuclear weapons. "All but" is the key phrase here. The agreement will require close monitoring for a decade to see that its terms are carried out. Even so, this welcome development would assure continuing, closer contacts between North Korea and the outside world and thus greatly lessen the danger of nuclear proliferation.

North Korea apparently has agreed to phase out its plutonium-producing nuclear installations, including one operating graphite reactor, two others under construction, and a spent-fuel reprocessing plant.

It would throw its past plutonium production open to inspection by the International Atomic Energy Agency, stop expanding its nuclear plants and agree to stop producing plutonium from an estimated 8,000 spent fuel rods. It also would resume talks with South Korea, suspended when North Korean leader Kim Il Sung died.

In exchange the United States pledged that the West would help North Korea build two modern light-water reactors, which produce far less plutonium than the older graphite variety. It also would provide coal and oil until the reactors are finished at a cost of about $4 billion.

The hitch in all this — the reason that close monitoring is a must — is that North Korea would store its plutonium-rich spent fuel rods until the new reactors are completed. Only then would it turn the rods over to another country. Only then would it be required to fully dismantle its weapons-related installations.

That's far from perfect, but it's a hopeful start. Continuing negotiations and contacts are essential to making it work and to ending the threat of nuclear madness in Asia.

Pittsburgh Post-Gazette
Pittsburgh, Pennsylvania, October 20, 1994

It seems that no victory for peace in the Middle East is very old before it is blotted by an act of violence. On Monday the leaders of Israel and Jordan initialed a historic peace agreement. Yesterday, rejoicing in Israel over reconciliation with an important neighbor and erstwhile enemy gave way to tears over a terrorist bombing of a bus in Tel Aviv, in which 22 people were killed.

Like previous outrages, this attack by Islamic extremists is meant to derail negotiations between Israelis and Palestinians. Israel and the PLO — whose leader, Yasser Arafat, promptly denounced the attack — mustn't allow that to happen. Important as the Israeli-Jordanian agreement is, the more complex Israeli-Palestinian relationship remains crucial to a durable peace.

The so-called "Jordan option," in which Israel would turn over most if not all of the West Bank to Jordan, which administered the area before the 1967 Six-Day War, is a diplomatic dead letter. (However, Israel has recognized a Jordanian role in the Muslim holy places of Jerusalem.) In deciding to open talks with the PLO, Israel recognized that Palestinian nationalism, a negligible force in 1967, is now something to be reckoned with.

The question is how that nationalism will be expressed, and at what cost to Israel. For all his fumbling and procrastination, Mr. Arafat is a serious partner for peace. The Islamic militants of Hamas, on the other hand, have yet to be reconciled to Israeli-Palestinian coexistence.

The terror attack in Tel Aviv, for which followers of Hamas have claimed responsibility, is thus aimed at both the PLO and at Israel. Israel already has moved to block Palestinians from the West Bank and Gaza from entering Israel, a move that will alienate Palestinians, and there will be pressure on Mr. Rabin to postpone talks with the PLO.

Mr. Arafat reacted to yesterday's act of terror by saying that "pushing forward with the peace process and implementing the rest of the agreement is the only way to respond to the enemies of peace."

He is right, with this qualification: The peace process must include more cooperation between Israel and the PLO to contain violence by Palestinians opposed to peace. Specifically, Mr. Arafat must heed Israeli complaints that Palestinian authorities aren't doing more to curb Hamas terrorists. Otherwise the terrorists may get their way.

THE ARIZONA REPUBLIC
Phoenix, Arizona, October 20, 1994

IF one had just awakened from a yearlong sleep and caught the headlines the other day from Israel, the probable reaction would be along the lines of, "So, what else is new?"

An Israeli soldier had been kidnapped by Palestinian terrorists, and a rescue attempt by Israeli commandos on the hostage-takers' lair had ended tragically. The kidnapped soldier, one commando and three of the terrorists were killed in the shootout.

So what else is new?

Well, what's new is that just hours before the botched raid, it was announced that Israeli Prime Minister Yitzhak Rabin and Foreign Minister Shimon Peres would share the 1994 Nobel Peace Prize with the Palestine Liberation Organization's Yasser Arafat. The PLO-directed police force in Gaza worked with Israeli security forces to try and track down the terrorists.

Moreover, a few more hours after the tragic shootout, Israel and Jordan announced that they had agreed to a draft peace treaty to be signed as early as next week. The pact would end 46 years of a state of war between the two countries and make Jordan the second Arab nation, behind Egypt, to make peace with Israel.

When Rabin and Arafat got the peace process started last year with their now-famous handshake in Washington, everyone predicted that there would be ups and downs along the way. The events of the past few days, running the gamut, from sorrow to euphoria, are indicative of the roller coaster of emotions and passions involved.

If a measure of encouragement can be gleaned from the latest act of Palestinian-Israeli violence, it is that the PLO police force, called on to take sides in the hunt for the kidnappers, actually aided the Israeli effort by rounding up suspected Hamas radicals and by providing some intelligence to the security forces.

To provide effective government in the territories, the PLO will have to demonstrate it can rule by law, fairly, predictably and effectively. One way the quality of enforcement will be judged is how it deals with such radical movements as Hamas, the Islamic group that makes no bones about its intentions to disrupt the peace process.

In the short run, it would be naive to think that even with greater PLO-Israeli cooperation on security matters, politically inspired violence will be wiped out. Extremists on both sides — the Hebron massacre earlier this year being a case in point — can be counted on to try and torpedo the peace process. The danger is that moderates on either side will overreact to the violence, which, thankfully, they did not do in the latest episode.

The longer-term prospects for Israeli-Palestinian coexistence no doubt will depend on how well Arafat and the PLO leadership can open up legitimate avenues of political expression for the more radical elements in the territories and provide much-needed social and economic services. An arrangement with Syria, still in the talking stages, that would cut off support in the region for anti-Israel terrorism, would help as well.

While violence in the region is certainly not new, polls show that the degree of condemnation for it on both sides has grown appreciably during the past year. Hopefully, it's a trend that more and more Israelis and Palestinians can learn to live with.

Portland Press Herald
Portland, Maine, October 18, 1994

The waters of the Jordan River spring from the slopes of Mount Hermon and flow south beneath the occupied Golan Heights to the Sea of Galilee. There the river widens a bit until it reaches the Dead Sea, which has no outlet. The Jordan, which for most of its length separates Israel and the occupied West Bank from the country of the same name, now flows more peacefully than it has in nearly half a century.

That's because a 46-year state of war between Israel and Jordan is ending.

Monday, in an agreement as epochal as the U.S.-brokered Camp David Accord that brought peace between Israel and Egypt in 1979, Israeli and Jordanian diplomats initialed a peace accord in Amman, Jordan's capital. It made Jordan only the second Arab nation to agree to a formal peace treaty with Israel since the latter nation's founding as a Jewish homeland in 1948.

The draft treaty is expected to be signed on Oct. 27 on the border between the two nations in a ceremony to which President Clinton has been invited. Clinton oversaw negotiations last summer in Washington that resulted in a non-belligerency pact being signed July 25.

The strength of the movement toward peace in this long-troubled area receives further testimony as negotiations between Israeli and Palestinian representatives are set to resume today. They were halted last week because tensions in Israel were running extremely high over the kidnapping and killing of a young Israeli soldier by terrorists.

On a third front, negotiations remain stalled between Israel and another Arab neighbor, Syria.

Israel still controls a good-sized piece of Syrian territory on the Golan Heights – including Mount Hermon. It captured the Golan in 1967 to forestall a Syrian invasion, and kept it because the hills provide a commanding perch over northern Israel. So the Israelis rightfully want strong guarantees – and perhaps an international peacekeeping force – to keep the Golan from ever being used by an aggressor again.

Movement toward that end may now come more quickly, as Syria finds itself increasingly isolated from the rest of Israel's neighbors.

In the meantime, and with increasing speed, history is being written on the banks of the River Jordan – in ink instead of blood. That's the only lasting way.

THE BUFFALO NEWS
Buffalo, New York, October 20, 1994

ISRAEL AND JORDAN ended 46 years of an uneasy form of co-existence last July with an agreement to renounce their belligerency. Now, the news is even better. Their initialed new treaty, set for formal signatures next week, brightens chances for prosperity and peaceful relations.

It will open the route to regular diplomatic contact, more convenient travel and expanded commercial ties.

Central to this tentative agreement initialed by Jordan's King Hussein and Israel's Prime Minister Yitzhak Rabin would appear to be advances in two sensitive policy areas: territory and water.

Reportedly, Israel will divert 13.2 billion gallons of water a year to parched Jordan. That is about 10 percent of what it now consumes. The two nations will cooperate in constructing dams to make fuller use of this vital but dangerously scarce resource.

Israel has reportedly returned all the land demanded by Jordan but will lease a portion of it for agricultural uses.

All of this goes to prove that if overriding conditions change, the two nations can with a little creative attention work out solutions to even very deep-seated religious and ethnic problems. It's enough to spawn fragile hope for settlements in such cockpits of conflict as Northern Ireland and — dare we mention it? — Bosnia.

The agreement's timing demonstrates to diehard extremists that violence — such as the abduction of the Israeli soldier last week — won't derail diplomacy.

If sticky territorial issues can be resolved with Jordan, those involving the Golan Heights, captured by Israel in 1967 from Syria, ought to yield to resolution as well. Optimists could even suspect that if King Hussein has come around, Syria's President Hafez al-Assad may not be too far behind.

U.S. POLITICS:

Republicans Win Control of U.S. House and Senate

The Republican Party swept to a landmark victory in U.S. general elections Nov. 8, wresting majorities from the Democratic Party in the House and Senate. In the wake of the voting, the GOP would control both houses of Congress for the first time in 40 years when the 104th Congress convened in January 1995. [See *Facts On File World News Digest* 1994, p. 825A1. For previous developments see *Facts On File* 1994, pp. 811D3, 795B1; 1954, p. 362D2]

Public dissatisfaction with the administration of President Clinton and fears about crime and the economy were translated into voter rejection of Democratic leadership in Congress and at the state level. With several races still undecided as of Nov. 10, defeated Democratic incumbents included 33 House members—among them Speaker Thomas S. Foley (Wash.) and former House Ways and Means Committee Chairman Dan Rostenkowski (Ill.)—as well as four governors and two senators. No Republican incumbent lost a congressional or gubernatorial race.

The GOP's successes marked the end of an era in the House, where the Democrats had held majorities for all but four years since 1932 and had held unbroken control since 1954. Republicans made a net gain of at least 50 House seats, assuring themselves of a majority. [See *Facts On File* 1994, p. 828D2]

The new results completed a pattern of turnover in the House; in the 104th Congress, at least 240 House seats would be held by people who had first been elected to the chamber in or after 1990.

Republicans won eight previously Democratic Senate seats and enlisted a defecting Democratic senator, Richard C. Shelby of Alabama, giving them a 53–46 majority in the upper chamber. One Senate race, between incumbent Dianne Feinstein (D, Calif.) and Rep. Michael Huffington (R, Calif.), remained undecided as of Nov. 10. The GOP had held a Senate majority for only six of the previous 40 years, between 1981 and 1987. [See *Facts On File* 1994, p. 832E2]

The parties of sitting presidents historically suffered losses in midterm elections. But the Democrats' combined losses in the House and Senate were the worst since 1958, when the GOP under President Dwight D. Eisenhower lost 48 House seats and 13 Senate seats. The setbacks to the Democrats in the House were the worst in that chamber since 1948, when Republicans lost 75 seats and a majority. [See *Facts On File* 1958, p. 355E2; 1948, p. 356M]

Analysts generally agreed that the 104th Congress would be ideologically polarized to a greater degree than the current one, since in many cases moderate lawmakers of both parties were replaced or defeated by staunch GOP conservatives. That result raised the specter of continued legislative "gridlock" between liberal Democrats and conservative Republicans, as well as of impasses between a GOP-dominated Congress and a Democratic White House.

The elections also left Republicans holding a majority of the nation's governorships for the first time since 1970, with Republicans gaining at least 11 statehouses to control a total of 30. The capture of formerly Democratic seats in New York, Texas and Pennsylvania left the GOP in charge in seven of the nation's eight most populous states. The GOP also made big gains in state legislatures. [See *Facts On File* 1994, pp. 838G3, 835B3; 1970, p. 806E3]

Increasing disapproval of Congress and government had been a factor in congressional elections in 1990 and 1992. But the 1994 election made it apparent that the Republican Party had been successful in capitalizing on that sentiment by representing its candidates—including incumbents—as agents of change.

Many campaign issues that were pivotal in GOP victories were summarized in the "Contract with America," a document signed by more than 300 Republican House candidates in September. The contract committed the party to enacting a range of reforms that appealed explicitly to antigoverment sentiment; among them were sweeping tax cuts, a balanced-budget amendment, sharp cuts in welfare spending and term limits for legislators. [See *Facts On File* 1994, p. 703B3; for the text of the contract, see p. 827A1]

The Des Moines Register

Des Moines, Iowa, November 10, 1994

Tuesday marked a major turning point in our nation's political history. After four decades on the outside looking in, Republicans have taken control of the Congress they have so loved to hate for so long. The party faces an opportunity denied it through two long generations in which it could frequently win the presidency but never rule the body that passed the laws and spent the money.

The long wait is over, the outs are in, the future is open.

Elections '94

National

The party that winced at what it saw as an erosion of American values can now offer up its remedies, not merely as an ideological wish list but with the votes to put meat on the bones.

Tuesday's vote proved that the troops are with them. Analysts will write volumes interpreting the biggest landslide since Johnson-vs.-Goldwater '64, theorizing and agonizing in search of explanations for the apparent anomaly of a huge political shake-up at a time when the nation is at peace, the harvests bountiful and the economy perking.

But whether the prime mover was the lure of the Republican call or disgust with the Democratic social-activist agenda, there is no mistaking what the electorate bought.

Republicans promised a balanced budget plus a tax cut. They promised to reduce the size of government, and will now tell us how and where. The vote validates the appeal of their tough stance on crime and welfare, problems that have bled society of its resources and its sense of security for decades.

In short, the Republicans' longing for a chance to rectify years of what they viewed as Democratic mismanagement is over; the opportunity is at hand. Leaders such as Senator Bob Dole and Congressman Newt Gingrich who bristled at the "obstructionist" charges hurled by the majority Democrats can now, as leaders of a new majority, offer constructive alternatives to a receptive Congress.

Throughout a long and proud history, the articulators of Republicanism have championed individual responsibility, faith in the innate wisdom of the citizen, and the proven virtues of thrift, hard work and a neighborly mutual respect. They have extolled government as the servant of the people rather than their master; laws as a means to equalize opportunity, rather than to evenly distribute the rewards; democracy as a challenge to the eager and enthusiastic, not as a security blanket for the laconic and lazy.

All the party asked was a chance. Now it's there.

May they make the best of it.

WISCONSIN STATE JOURNAL

Madison, Wisconsin, November 11, 1994

Can the Republicans govern? That question is being repeated from Maine to California today as the GOP's Election Day tidal wave recedes to reveal a dramatically different political shoreline in Congress and most statehouses.

The short answer: They don't have a choice. They must learn or suffer the same fate as the Democrats they have displaced.

Republicans in the U.S. Senate and House of Representatives are practiced at the politics of serving in the minority, as well they should be after 40 years of virtually unbroken Democratic rule in both houses. They have precious little experience, however, in the politics of running day-to-day life in the U.S. Capitol.

With the exception of those GOP senators who served in the majority for six years in the early 1980s, none of the Republicans on Capitol Hill knows what it's like to serve on the majority side of the aisle. Can career bomb-throwers such as Newt Gingrich make the transition from not-so-loyal opposition to Speaker of the House? Will Bob Dole spend less time on criticizing the policies of President Clinton and more on steering the Republican agenda through the Senate?

There is reason to hope that Gingrich, Dole and a flock of GOP committee chairmen in both houses will rise to the task. Republican leaders realize that voters haven't kicked out the Democrats just so the GOP can have a bigger platform for nay-saying tactics. They want to see Republicans pass legislation such as the balanced budget amendment and line-item budget veto, and to do so in forms that will be acceptable to members of both parties.

Gingrich has already sworn off undertaking new political witchhunts against Clinton and even talked Wednesday of compromise. "There's no reason we can't sit down and try to have a serious discussion in the next few days about places where we do agree," the Georgia Republican said.

While many will doubt whether Gingrich and Co. are sincere bearers of olive branches, Wisconsin offers homegrown proof of what can happen when someone in the minority becomes a majoritarian.

Gov. Tommy Thompson, who won two-thirds of the vote Tuesday on his way to capturing his third term, served most of his legislative career in the minority. Democrats even called him "Dr. No." Is there any doubt that Thompson quickly learned how to govern — and during years in which both houses of the Wisconsin Legislature were controlled by Democrats?

A question no less worthy of contemplation is this: Will Democrats learn from their stinging defeat? This was not an election about throwing all incumbents out of office — it was about giving Democratic incumbents the heave-ho. Not a single Republican who sought re-election to the House or Senate lost on Tuesday. But scores of incumbent Democrats with familiar names — Tom Foley, Dan Rostenkowski, Jack Brooks, Neal Smith — fell by the Election Day wayside.

The Republicans want to recapture the White House in 1996, but they cannot do so by using the same tactics they employed while they were the minority party. Likewise, President Clinton cannot win a second term (or even be nominated for one) unless he and his party learn from their historic repudiation by the voters.

The Wichita
Eagle-Beacon

Wichita, Kansas, November 13, 1994

Kansas women have a long tradition of political successes. The state was one of the first to give women the right to vote and the first to see a city elect a female mayor. There have been three Kansas women who have served in the U.S. House of Representatives.

And due to the emergence of a Republican majority in Congress, Sen. Nancy Kassebaum will soon become the chairman of the Senate Labor Committee, the first woman to chair a major committee in the Senate in nearly 50 years. In addition, Rep. Jan Meyers will be the new House Small Business Committee chairman. And in her race for re-election to her 3rd District seat, she faced another woman, attorney and Democrat Judy Hancock, the first time ever that two women have run against each other in a Kansas congressional contest.

The lieutenant governor-elect, Sheila Frahm, will be the first woman to serve in that position in Kansas. The Graves-Frahm administration will take over from the first woman governor in the state, Joan Finney. Other first-time female state office holders in 1995 will be the new attorney general, Republican Carla Stovall, and the new insurance commissioner, Democrat Kathleen Sebelius. Democrat Sally Thompson will continue to be the state treasurer.

In Sedgwick County, for the first time there will be two women on the County Commission. Melody McCray-Miller will become the first African-American woman elected to the commission. Incumbent Betsy Gwin was re-elected on Nov. 8. The only woman running for a contested local judgeship, Democrat Rebecca Pilshaw, was elected, too. Although the Legislature is still dominated by men, more than 20 women won election to the House, some of them over incumbents. And in District 74, Republican Ellen Samuelson pulled off an extraordinary write-in campaign win.

Throughout Kansas — from the early days of Argonia Mayor Susan Salter to Wichita Mayor Elma Broadfoot today — women have been a growing and important part of the state's political leadership. And election 1994 has proven to be another exceptional year for women leaders.

THE LINCOLN STAR

Lincoln, Nebraska, November 11, 1994

This week's election results can be explained only in multiples. No single explanation will suffice.

There was a real shift to the right philosophically. This week we also heard the voice of incoherent anger, an expression of anxiety about the economic future, and a personal repudiation of the president.

It was a repudiation of Clinton, sort of. Some seething Americans are venting their spleen (with encouragement from the Rushes and beyond) on anyone with the slightest liberal stripe.

But many less-strident voters are simply not emotionally drawn to this president.

It is the character thing. Some men view him as being a wimp (married to a strong, intelligent woman, able to tear up at other's pain). Some women have no respect for his womanizing.

It would be too great a leap to assume that a majority of Americans now favor a very limited role for federal government.

This is a tilt to the right. But many Americans want the "right" right. They don't want a movie sequel — "Look Mom, They Shrunk the Government." They do want to see government operate with more efficiency and not expand.

Many Americans in the middle understand that government tinkering is sometimes meddlesome, inefficient and not worth the taxes. But they also believe that government can be part of the solution.

The vote also was an expression of anger. There was personal anger based on fear about an uncertain future in an economy that is pinching the middle class and not producing enough new mid-pay jobs.

And there was general anger at a frustrating two-party political system that produces clever sound bites but little action at the federal level.

Republicans have reason to be elated. But they should not count what is not yet hatched.

The American public is fickle. Just look at what happened to former President Bush between the Gulf War and the election.

Many Americans are not wedded to any particular party. They can and will take their votes elsewhere if those they elect put partisan interests and personal power above solutions.

A Congress of all sound and fury is entertaining, but it is not what the electorate has ordered

The Detroit News

Detroit, Michigan, November 12, 1994

The Salt Lake Tribune

Salt Lake City, Utah, November 11, 1994

Newt Gingrich admits that his future role as speaker of the House will require of him less of the attack-dog approach that he employed as House minority whip. Too bad he couldn't start the new Republican era with that understanding.

The day after the election that swept the GOP to control of the House for the first time in 40 years, Mr. Gingrich demonstrated that his transition from rhetorical terrorist to cooperative statesman may take awhile: He called the Clintons counterculture McGovernicks. Apparently, that's an insult, but it's really an example of the Gingrich corner's false definition of American "values."

Counterculture is defined as "the culture and lifestyle of those people who reject the dominant values and behavior of society." George McGovern, the Democratic candidate for president in 1972, finds that word to be an odd definition of himself, so much so that he has written a response to Mr. Gingrich's comment.

Mr. McGovern, now 72, has actually lived a life that would be described by almost anybody as ideally reflective of American values: He grew up in the American heartland during the Depression, worked his way through school, served courageously in World War II and earned a Distinguished Flying Cross, enjoyed a successful career and has been married to the same woman for more than a half-century, having raised five children. That's "counterculture"?

Mr. Gingrich, on the other hand, accepted student deferments in the late '60s during the Vietnam War and is once-divorced — nothing out of the ordinary for members of his generation, but certainly nothing that gives him any standing to spit out Mr. McGovern's name as if he were the evil genius of anti-American values.

This, of course, is the problem with the "values" crowd: They have a hard time keeping their political ideas separate from the personal values that many of them would sooner impose on others than on themselves. Clearly, Mr. McGovern's life exemplifies anything but "counterculture" values, and Mr. Gingrich knows it.

Where Mr. Gingrich and Mr. McGovern differ is in their ideas about the role of government in American life. That's fine. Mr. Gingrich now has the opportunity to try out his ideas. What he does not have is the go-ahead to impose on anyone any set of personal "values" — certainly not if they're much different from those of the admirable lifestyle of George McGovern.

With the Republican tidal wave now washing through Congress, the question of term limits for members of Congress may soon be on the floor. Term limit legislation has been bottled up by the ruling Democrats. Newly ousted House Speaker Tom Foley even sued his own constituents in the state of Washington to block a state term limit provision.

Voters in seven states — Alaska, Colorado, Idaho, Maine, Massachusetts, Nebraska and Nevada — this week adopted measures imposing term limits on the people they send to Congress. This week's vote brings the total number of states adopting term limits on federal lawmakers to 22, including Michigan.

There can be no doubt that voters in each of the states have the right to limit the terms of their state legislators. But the U.S. Constitution places no term limits on federal lawmakers. The question is whether the voters of individual states can impose such limits. The issue will be tested in the U.S. Supreme Court, when a challenge to an Arkansas term limit measure will be heard.

In our view, voters of the several states should have that option, in keeping with the federal structure of government created by the Constitution. Deciding whether it is better for a state to have term-limited members or to have members who can run up seniority should be a trade-off that individual state voters can weigh. But if the high court sees the issue differently,

Congress has the authority to send the states a constitutional amendment for ratification. And it should.

It may well be argued that the huge change in American politics witnessed this week — with voters giving the GOP control of the Congress for the first time in 40 years — indicates that term limits aren't necessary. An awful lot of incumbents just had their terms limited the old-fashioned way.

Well, yes. But it did take 40 years. Why? Because of the power of incumbency. With the dissolution of the Soviet Union, no other major nation's legislative chamber was dominated for so long by one party as was the U.S. House of Representatives. And that majority used all of the power at its command to entrench itself in office.

With Republicans in control of the White House for 20 out of the last 25 years, the House still couldn't be budged — until now. The House was the personification of Lord Acton's famous dictum: "Power tends to corrupt and absolute power corrupts absolutely."

But Acton's dictum applies to Republicans as well as Democrats. A look at the new GOP House committee chairmen — one of whom was elected more than 30 years ago and many of whom were elected more than 20 years ago — makes a pretty good case for term limits.

The people of the states ought to have a right to be heard on the issue. And the new Congress, if it is serious about reform, should see that they do.

Detroit, Michigan, November 10, 1994

With a gain of at least 48 seats in the House and eight seats in the Senate, Republicans will control Congress for the first time in more than 40 years. They ran chiefly on a pledge to cut taxes and control the deficit through spending restraint. If they are to remain a governing party, they will have to deliver on that agenda.

The first thing Republicans should do is approve the pending General Agreement on Tariffs and Trade (GATT) legislation. GATT will be up for a vote in a lame duck session this month. It is essentially a worldwide tax cut. It would reduce tariffs and other trade barriers as well as protect patents and copyrights.

Contrary to critics, the trade agreement would not require more intrusive regulation. In fact, document language that encourages nations to adopt similar labor and environmental standards may prompt the United States to discard some of its more misguided environmental regulations.

Second, Republicans should push hard for major tax reform. President Clinton ran in 1992 promising a middle-class tax cut, but delivered a tax hike instead. There is talk now of an increased family deduction, but that is tinkering at the margins of the tax code.

The Republicans instead should go for something more radical — say, a flat income tax. The flat tax has been floating around in various guises for more than a decade. Most recently, U.S. Rep. Dick Armey, now touted as Republican majority leader in the House, has proposed a 17-percent flat tax.

The idea has a bipartisan pedigree. It was proposed with various permutations in the early 1980s by Democratic Sen. Bill Bradley of New Jersey, Democratic House Majority Leader Dick Gephardt of Missouri and California Democratic Rep. Leon Panetta, now Mr. Clinton's chief of staff.

Whatever its shape, it would have to be crafted in such a way as to avert a tax hike on low-income taxpayers, who now pay 15 percent, but that could be managed. Various studies have placed the "cost" in lost revenue of a flat tax at as much as $50 billion, but other studies have placed the cost of compliance with our current convoluted tax system at six billion man-hours, a deadweight loss to the economy of several hundred billion dollars per year.

A flat tax would still tax the rich more heavily than the less well-off — 10 percent of $10,000 is $1,000 but

10 percent of $100,000 is $10,000 — but we currently apply increasing rates of taxation to higher levels of income. The message: Economic success should be punished. In addition to its other virtues, a flat tax would signal that the government would reward rather than penalize economic effort — which would inevitably promote economic growth.

Polls suggest Americans don't want to go back to the economic policies of the 1980s, which liberals interpret to mean no tax cuts. What Americans are really worried about, we suspect, is the deficit. They want any tax cuts closely tied to a genuine reduction in spending. There are two ways a GOP Congress could structurally handle that.

First, it could adopt the "A to Z" bill, proposed by Reps Mike Andrews, D-Texas, and Bill Zeliff, R-New Hampshire. The bill would set aside several hours on the agenda of the House in which any member of the House could challenge any item in the budget, ask for a justification of the spending and then demand a "yes" or "no" vote on the item.

Such an open-air debate would automatically have a restraining effect on spending — which is why the old House barons worked so hard to bury the bill. The "A to Z" bill is a form of legislative line-item veto. But there is no reason the president should not be granted an executive line-item veto, which is now wielded by the governors of more than 40 states.

With both the executive and legislative branches granted the power — and thus the responsibility — of dealing with federal spending, both branches would run out of excuses for deficits.

Ultimately, moderation in taxes and encouragement of economic growth would have the most telling effect on deficits. The error of the 1980s was that the Democratic Congress insisted on using "deficit reduction" as a cover for tax increases that would sustain traditional spending patterns. Voters have now awakened to that game, and they obviously hope that a Republican Congress will act differently.

There is nothing in this agenda with which President Clinton could reasonably disagree. Indeed, he has specifically endorsed two of the ideas, and the flat-tax goal has the support of significant segments of his party. If he is truly looking for "cooperation" with the new Republican majority, here is his chance to prove it.

THE SACRAMENTO BEE
Sacramento, California, November 10, 1994

The historic Republican surge to gain control of Congress for the first time in four decades was more than a victory for change. It was an election about party in a country where parties aren't supposed to matter much anymore.

On Tuesday, party mattered a lot if you were a Democrat seeking office. It mattered in the Senate, where Democrats lost all the open races. It mattered in the House, where Democrats lost most open seats and failed to unseat a single Republican incumbent. It mattered in states such as New York and Texas, where prominent governors Mario Cuomo and Ann Richards went down to defeat, and it mattered in state legislatures around the country, where Democrats fell back to parity with Republicans for the first time since 1968.

Voters were not undiscriminating in registering their protest. Whatever their unhappiness with Democrats, they were not so heedless as to elect a demagogic liar such as Oliver North or a rich but empty suit such as Michael Huffington. They re-elected successful Democratic leaders such as Gov. Lawton Chiles and Sens. Joseph Lieberman, Bob Kerrey and Dianne Feinstein. But they were emphatic in whom they didn't like, including such entrenched Democratic leaders as Speaker Tom Foley and, by implication, a president who has not broadened his base beyond the minority that elected him.

Republicans are deservedly jubilant. But the election was also a victory for democracy. It proved for all the naysayers and term-limit gimmick-peddlers that political action contributions and the force of incumbency are no obstacle to change when voters are determined to clean house. And after the Democrats' 40-year stint in control of the House, some house cleaning was overdue.

As is true in many elections, the voters were more clear Tuesday about what they didn't want than what they do want. But the majority are plainly disturbed about crime levels that are too high; about a broken welfare system and the breakdown of social norms and families; about overintrusive and unbalanced regulation; about the stagnant incomes of many middle-class families; about special-interest influence and Washington's insiderism.

It will now be up to Republicans, in control of the dominant branch of government, to come up with a plausible program to address those concerns. To do that, they will need the cooperation of President Clinton, who campaigned in 1992 on a similar agenda, and, because the Republican majority is so narrow, of congressional Democrats.

But congressional Republicans will also need more realism of their own. The "Contract With America" that so many GOP House candidates signed was tailored for campaigning, not governing; it promised a reprise of the 1980s tax cuts and spending increases that does not pencil out and will probably not get by the Senate, let alone the White House.

The voters have given a congressional party accustomed to opposition the responsibility of delivering real answers to the country's problems, not two years of partisan sniping. Given how quickly voters have judged, and censured, Clinton's shortcomings, Tuesday's victors surely must understand that any lease on power in this impatient country is short-term and contingent on performance.

★   ★   ★

In California, as in the nation, there was no doubt about Tuesday's message, or about Gov. Pete Wilson's ability to exploit it – control immigration, control crime, revitalize the state's economic prospects and return to traditional social values – and turn it into a hefty electoral victory.

Whether the actual vote made the realization of those objectives any more likely is a tougher question. The passage of Proposition 187 will certainly send a message to Washington about enforcement of immigration controls that both the administration and the new Republican majorities in Congress are not likely to ignore. But the magnitude of its negative effects in the state will depend a great deal on how the governor and the courts now handle it. To his credit, Wilson, in his acceptance statement Tuesday night, tried to lower the decibels on the issue and to talk about unity, not division.

Similarly, the passage of the "three strikes" measure, Proposition 184, exacerbates the state's fiscal problems and reduces the Legislature's ability to deal with them. The governor Tuesday talked about education, but whether either the state's finances or the yet-undetermined leadership of the Assembly will permit any serious school reform is equally uncertain.

The great hope has to be that the Legislature's newly discovered ability to work together – shown in such things as passage of workers' compensation reforms – will grow and not wither in these new political circumstances.

If Tuesday's vote is understood as a call from voters for a less partisan, less divisive, more centrist Legislature, then a great deal will have been accomplished. But at this point that's more of a devout wish than a sure thing. Unfortunately, little in the vote made it any easier to govern or to get around the supermajority requirements that have hamstrung this state for a generation.

California voters made some fine distinctions: They did not allow themselves to be bamboozled by Huffington's $25 million-plus media assault or by a tobacco industry spending its millions to cloak itself as a promoter of reasonable smoking controls. If voters can make the same distinctions about what government now proceeds to do, progress may yet be made.

DESERET NEWS
Salt Lake City, Utah, November 10, 1994

Give President Clinton credit. Judging by his conciliatory words and subdued demeanor at his post-election news conference Wednesday afternoon, the beleaguered chief executive evidently got the stern message from the voters.

The question now is whether he is willing and able to match his professed conversion to bipartisanship with concrete deeds.

To express this reservation is not to detract from Clinton's performance at the news conference, which had its impressive moments.

It would have been easier for him to have remained cloistered in the Oval Office and licked his wounds in private. Or he could have become defensive and combative. Instead, he chose to put his chagrin on public display — and face some tough, pointed questions about his past record and new stab at conciliation.

For this stance, bravo! Congratulations, too, for demonstrating that he knows how to listen and draw the proper conclusions after the voters have spoken. Hence, his candid acknowledgment that the public is calling for less intrusive and costly but more efficient government — and his admission that he is not widely perceived as having delivered on this score.

So far, so good. But some reservations are still in order because Clinton sounded moderate and mainstream during the 1992 election, then jolted many of his supporters after he entered the White House with a series of liberal appointments and his efforts to force gays upon the reluctant military.

Besides, there are no painless solutions to many of the budgetary and other problems facing the nation. Moreover, the election did not and could not eliminate the basic philosophical and policy differences between the two major political parties. Some confrontation and conflict between the new Republican Congress and the Clinton White House is unavoidable.

Consequently, even though voters have told Washington with unmistakable clarity that business as usual won't do, a key question remains: Though this message may have penetrated the mind of the Clinton team, has it penetrated its heart? If not, the same message may have to be repeated even more forcefully two years from now.

OKLAHOMA CITY BOMBING:

Federal Building Bombed; Scores Killed in Terror Attack

A massive car bomb exploded outside a federal office building in Oklahoma City, the capital of Oklahoma, early April 19, ripping away the north face of the nine-story structure. The blast's death toll was expected to top 200, with 78 confirmed dead as of four days after the explosion. Of the fatalities, at least 13 were children who had been in the building's day-care center. More than 400 people were injured by the blast, and about 150 of the building's estimated 550 workers were missing and thought to be dead. [See *Facts On File World News Digest* 1995, p. 277A1]

Authorities April 20 said that there were two suspects in the bombings. Both were described as white males, weakening widespread speculation that the attack might have been the work of Middle Eastern terrorists. Officials said that the unidentified suspects' motive was unknown.

The bombing was the deadliest terrorist attack ever in the U.S. Many in Oklahoma City, whose population was 450,000, expressed shock that such an attack took place in the so-called heartland of the U.S., an area not associated with terrorism. Observers said that the incident illustrated how vulnerable the nation was to such attacks.

The bombing occurred shortly after 9:00 a.m. local time, when most employees at the building, the Alfred P. Murrah Federal Building, were beginning their work day. Law-enforcement officials cited in the *New York Times* April 20 said that there had been no bomb threats prior to the blast and no believable claims following the explosion.

The bomb, which officials concluded had been made with ammonium nitrate and fuel oil, was similar in type and intensity to that used in the 1993 attack on the World Trade Center in New York City. That bombing, undertaken by Moslem extremists, had killed six people and injured about 1,000. Authorities investigating the Oklahoma blast stressed April 20 that no link to the trade center bombing had been made. [See *Editorials On File* 1993, p. 258-271See also *Facts On File* 1994, p. 376B2]

Some officials noted that the bombing occurred on the second anniversary of a federal attack on the compound of the Branch Davidians religious cult near Waco, Texas in which at least 75 cultists had died. Cultists had blamed the Bureau of Alcohol, Tobacco and Firearms (ATF), an office of which was located in the Oklahoma City building, for the initial confrontation that led to the April 1993 raid. Investigators reportedly were looking into that link. [See *Editorials On File* 1993, pp. 450-459. See also *Facts On File* 1993, p. 282E1]

Other federal agencies housed in the building included the Social Security Administration, the Housing and Urban Development Department, the Veterans Affairs Department, the Secret Service and the Drug Enforcement Administration. Most workers were located on the hard-hit north side of the building. Explosive experts estimated that the bomb weighed 1,000 to 1,200 pounds (450 to 540 kg).

The car bomb, which had gone off near the curb outside the building's entrance, created a crater 20 feet (six meters) wide and eight feet deep. The explosion left a pile of debris about two stories high in front of the federal building and damaged other buildings dozens of blocks away from the blast site. The explosion also set ablaze cars located across the street from the building.

In the wake of the Oklahoma incident, numerous federal and local government buildings across the country were evacuated or shut down April 19–20 due to bomb threats, all of which turned out to be false. Security at many government buildings was bolstered.

President Clinton April 20 warned against jumping to conclusions amid speculation that the attack was the work of Middle Eastern terrorists. "We should not stereotype anybody," Clinton said. (Two large Arab-American groups, the Arab-American Anti-Discrimination Committee and the Arab-American Institute, had condemned the bombing.)

Oklahoma Gov. Frank A. Keating (R) April 19 said, "Obviously, no amateur did this. Whoever did this was an animal."

THE ARIZONA REPUBLIC
Phoenix, Arizona, April 21, 1995

THE terrorists did their job well: They made us afraid, which is the goal of terrorism.

And the horror of it.

Their savage images are etched in our collective consciousness:

A bombed-out day-care center.

Offices blown apart.

Mothers calling to children who will never answer.

Beyond the sadness and a sense of disbelief there is anger.

But the anger is not satisfying.

The president of the most powerful nation on Earth sounds strangely impotent when he says, "The United States will not tolerate, and I will not allow, the people of this country to be intimidated by evil cowards."

But we are intimidated.

The pictures from Oklahoma City are very intimidating.

Our experts tell us it can happen anywhere. And we heighten security at federal buildings. They tell us we've been lucky so far. And we watch what happened in a place where luck ran out.

Despite the World Trade Center bombing, we always saw terrorism as something that happened somewhere else. Far away. In other lands.

Now it is in our heartland. Our hearts.

From our sorrow and our anger, we could move to resignation. We could embrace the anesthetic of apathy. We could bow to the message of the terrorists that human lives have no value and human endeavors have no meaning because they can all be blasted into oblivion in a second.

If we do that, we have made the work of those who bombed the Alfred P. Murrah building in Oklahoma City more successful than they ever imagined.

From our sorrow and our anger, we could move to paranoia. We could decide that living in a free and open society isn't worth the risk. We could act like a society under siege. Adopt a fortress mentality. Barricade every public building against enemies foreign and domestic. Real and imagined.

If we do that, we hand the terrorists another victory.

From our sorrow and our anger, we could remember our humanity because that is what is under attack.

We could hold tighter to those who survived the bomb in Oklahoma City and to those who survive the vagaries of everyday life every day. Our co-workers. Our friends. Our families.

As we stiffen our national resolve to find and punish those who brought terror into our hearts, we could celebrate the bravery of those who have the guts not to give up. Those who continue to search for survivors because they will not concede that the missing are lost.

Those who will not give terrorism the victory it craves.

DAILY NEWS

New York City, New York, April 20, 1995

THOSE WERE SOME of the words President Clinton used to describe the horrific blast in Oklahoma City yesterday. Yet words ultimately fail to capture the depth of depravity needed to bomb an office building, killing dozens, many of them children. How could they? How could anyone?

The picture at right evokes chills of revulsion, especially for parents who fear for their children under normal circumstances. Daily, it's ever more clear that these are not normal times. America, even in its serene heartland, is no longer immune from the madness that has spread poison gas in Japan and detonated car bombs from the Mideast to Madrid.

America must respond. Clinton already has. By sending elite FBI agents and other law enforcement units to Oklahoma City, he moved to deliver on his pledge that, "justice will be swift, certain and severe."

"These people are killers," Clinton said, "and they must be treated like killers."

Officials also secured other public buildings around America — clearing at least three federal buildings after threats and heightening security in the Capitol itself. The threat may be, for the moment, faceless, nameless. But the nation's response must be clear: Safety, security, strength, resolve. Unity.

YET LONG AFTER the dead have been buried, the rubble cleared and the guilty punished, the questions will remain, starting with the most basic: Why? What human being deliberately causes such pain and suffering to so many? Do those responsible see the pictures of the bloodied, bandaged and body bags and feel good? Can there be satisfaction in murdering babies and terrorizing a nation?

These and many more questions were everywhere yesterday — in the faces of those searching through the Oklahoma wreckage. In the face of the dazed young woman, clutching a baby and a large black purse, being led to safety. In the shock-filled eyes of the blond-haired woman, sitting on a curb, blood streaming down her forehead. In the slumped shoulders of the police officer, who lay down his head in utter despair on the hood of a car.

THERE CAN BE no answers. At least none that make sense. That much was learned from the last time we went through this — a little over two years ago, when the World Trade Center rocked from a terrorist bomb. Six people died, 1,000 were injured. A city was frightened. And to what aim? It's abundantly clear that those who were convicted of carrying out the bombing achieved nothing more than murder — and their own imprisonment. Nothing but terror — for the sole sake of terror.

So it is now in Oklahoma City. Whoever lays claim to the carnage will have achieved nothing — save the wrath of all who believe in peace, in the right to safety, in the sanctity of each and every human life. When they are caught, there will be words, but there will be little understanding. For there can be no comprehension of the destruction wrought.

While there are no answers to the madness, many exist in the goodness. Those who rushed in to rescue, heal and give blood showed that humanity will, in the end, triumph over evil. As Clinton beseeched, all Americans can help. "Pray for the friends and family of the dead and wounded. Pray for the people of Oklahoma City. May God's grace be with them." Amen.

ALBUQUERQUE JOURNAL

Albuquerque, New Mexico, April 20, 1995

To terrorists, their victims are symbols of The Enemy. On Wednesday, dozens of "symbols" — some of them as young as one year of age — bled and died in the bombing of the federal building in Oklahoma City.

Any man, woman or child in America could have been the target of the cowards who apparently left a bomb in a car outside the building and then fled the scene. It just so happened that the Oklahoma federal building was deemed the appropriate "symbol" this time for whatever hatreds and grievances the terrorists harbor.

Compared to Europe and other parts of the world, America had been relatively unscarred by terrorist acts within our borders until the World Trade Center bombing in February 1993. Now, with the explosion that ripped out the entire side of the Oklahoma City federal building, terrorists have targeted the heartland of America — a city far from international centers of government and finance.

The viciousness of the act is shocking to people who can't fathom how a small child could be considered A Thing, A Symbol. The youngsters in the federal building day care center, ages 1 to 7 years of age, probably had enough physical strength among them to move a large couch a few inches. Those fragile lives, obliterated by explosives that can rip steel and concrete apart, are irreplaceable.

The horror in Oklahoma City can make average Americans feel vulnerable and even helpless. However, while it's impossible to guard against every terrorist act, it *is* possible to lessen the chance that some acts will be successful. America has reached the point where its citizens must adopt some of the ultra-vigilant practices of nations where such acts are more common — practices like screening people with metal detectors in even more buildings, reporting any seemingly abandoned suitcases or packages, not allowing strangers to park their cars near buildings.

But while actions are important in dealing with terrorism, so are attitudes. A danger in this is that America's professional cynics may sneer about the effectiveness of expressions of outrage over the bombing. What good, after all, does it do to say how horrible terrorism is? This is what good it does: It sends the message to the world, and reaffirms in our own nation, the belief that America will not allow itself to become easy prey for terrorists.

Every death at the hands of terrorists matters. And every expression of outrage matters — in New York City, in Oklahoma City and in Albuquerque. It's heartbreaking to witness the slaughter of Americans who committed the "crime" of going to work or sitting in a crib in a day care center. Expressions of grief are a natural reaction to an atrocity. And they help Americans remember that we share common feelings and beliefs, such as the basic understanding that children and other innocent victims are not to be used as symbols in fanatics' grievances.

In other words, Americans are in this together. We need each other if we are to successfully fight terrorism, in whatever form it may take. Widespread, deep anger over such acts can help prevent America from becoming a place where terrorists can gain a long-term foothold. Outrage spurs the kind of aggressive investigation and prosecution of terrorists that sends a message to the world: Terrorists have a slim chance of getting away with it in America. Just ask the World Trade Center defendants.

Perhaps the persons who left the car bomb outside the Oklahoma federal building see themselves in distorted, heroic terms — as fighters of The Enemy. But Americans see them as they really are — bloodthirsty, cowardly murderers who will be tracked down until they are brought to justice.

The Washington Times

Washington, D.C., April 20, 1995

The awful reality of terrorism on American soil erupted again yesterday as a bomb blasted a giant crater in a downtown Oklahoma City federal office building. Nine floors of the building collapsed and the entire front was torn away; office workers found themselves in free fall; glass and concrete fragments shot across city streets, injuring pedestrians. As of this writing, confirmed casualties had risen to 19 dead and some 200 wounded, but many remained trapped beneath the crumbled concrete. Chances are slim that they will be pulled out alive.

The act was made even more appalling by the fact that the building housed — along with offices of the FBI, the IRS, the Bureau of Alcohol, Tobacco and Firearms and the Secret Service, all potential targets — a federal day care center. In fact, most of those who died at the hands of the terrorists were infants and children, by the latest count 17. It is the worst act of terrorism ever committed on American soil, outranking in sheer destructiveness and carnage the 1993 New York Trade Center bombing (which killed six and injured 1,000) and it's enough to make you sick to contemplate what kind of human being would do this to innocent people going about their daily business.

No one, so far, has claimed responsibility for the bombing, and all we have is an FBI advisory that three suspects are being sought, two of them of Middle Eastern description, who were seen driving away from the area in a brown van at around 9 a.m. Whether there is any connection with the Waco conflagration, of which Wednesday was the second anniversary, remains to be determined. But this much at least can be said: The fight against terrorism may have entered a new phase, judging by the magnitude and ambitiousness of recent terrorist acts, starting with the World Trade Center bombing. After a downturn following collapse of the Soviet empire, terrorism is back with a vengeance.

In March, we saw the Tokyo subway chemical warfare attack (and on Wednesday, an apparent copy-cat gassing which left Tokyo railway passengers sickened, but not fatally harmed). The quantities of deadly chemicals stockpiled by the Aum Supreme Truth sect are reportedly enough to wipe out millions of people. We have seen Palestinian suicide bombers one after another hurl themselves against targets in Israel, killing 60 people since "peace" was signed.

We have also had the report from the U.N. weapons inspection team that Iraq has failed to account for huge amounts of materials for deadly chemical and biological agents. This may be a coincidence, but only last week, Saddam Hussein responded with virulently anti-American demonstrations to the U.N. Security Council's offer to let him sell $2 billion worth of oil, predicated on Iraq's commitment to use the proceeds to buy food and much-needed medical supplies. Nor are the Islamic fundamentalist groups sponsored by Iran, some of which base their U.S. operations in Oklahoma City, friends of this country at all. Add to all that, the chilling nuclear ambitions of countries like Iran, Iraq and Libya. While the Japanese attack seems almost certainly the act of a home-grown madman, state-sponsored terrorism bordering on warfare may be what we have to face today and in the future.

Is the United States prepared to counter this terrorist threat? No one can ever be prepared for the kind of horror inflicted on Oklahoma City on this peaceful Wednesday morning. Nor can any government of an open and free society ever wholly eliminate that risk. However, we can express our outrage and determination, and we can place states that sponsor terrorism on notice that we will be employing all our resources to find and punish the guilty parties, as well as those who back them.

Los Angeles Times

Los Angeles, California, April 20, 1995

Can one find any meaning in the blast that ripped away nearly half of the nine-story Alfred P. Murrah Federal Building in downtown Oklahoma City? What political cause, what religious zeal, what personal grievance could possibly have benefited from killing so many civilians, including children playing in a day-care center? The heart aches at the stupefying hate and ignorance of the callous and—as President Clinton aptly put it—"evil cowards" who planted this terrible bomb and ran.

From the smoking rubble presumably will come clues to the motive. There was speculation, given the similarities to the 1993 bombing of the World Trade Center in New York, that the crime was a terrorist attack by Islamic extremists. Others noted that the explosion came on the second anniversary of federal agents' deadly assault on the Branch Davidian religious sect in Waco, Tex., 275 miles away. The Oklahoma City building housed the offices of the FBI and the Bureau of Alcohol, Tobacco and Firearms that coordinated the Texas raid.

What can justify an attack on innocents?

Whatever the motive, this apparent spread of terrorism to the heartland, far from such centers of financial and political power as New York and Washington, is chilling. Who would have expected Oklahoma City, a quiet state capital of 450,000 where selling a mixed drink was illegal in most circumstances until the 1980s, would be the site of the worst terrorist attack ever on American soil? The bomb, thought to have weighed more than 1,000 pounds and to have been hidden in a vehicle parked in front of the federal building, was more powerful even than the one that killed six and injured hundreds at the World Trade Center.

Coming so soon after the deadly sarin nerve gas attack in the Tokyo subway and Wednesday's apparent release of phosgene gas in the Yokohama subway, the Oklahoma explosion serves to underscore the vulnerability of modern cities. Though Los Angeles lacks the urban density of a Tokyo or a New York, it is no less vulnerable to terrorist massacres.

All manner of lessons will be drawn from the Oklahoma City outrage. Perhaps the most absurd comes from the president of the National Treasury Employees Union, who saw a connection to the complaints of Congress members "who feed the ugly notion that federal employees are responsible for all this nation's ills."

Such embarrassments aside, until the perpetrators are convicted no far-reaching conclusions can be drawn. What is clear is that Americans, urban and rural alike, will have to get used to tougher security measures. (Some European countries have by now become accustomed to Draconian security at airports and to having no sidewalk trash cans in which bombs might be hidden.) Clearly, federal buildings at least will have to tighten security, especially those measures aimed at preventing car bombings. Authorities around the nation, including in Orange County, were properly cautious after Wednesday's bombing, temporarily evacuating some federal buildings after bomb threats were received.

For now, the bombers have gained what they almost certainly wanted—a measure of fear and confusion. But these feelings are temporary. Americans cherish their rights of movement and of access to government agencies—rights that ironically make it easier for terrorists who would destroy their freedoms. We will not be cowed.

THE LINCOLN STAR

Lincoln, Nebraska, April 21, 1995

The bombing of the federal building in Oklahoma City releases strong emotions.

We are frightened because of a renewed sense of vulnerability. We no longer feel safe in our own workplaces.

We are sick at heart over the loss of life, the senseless deaths of innocent people, the killing of babies.

We are outraged over the sheer senselessness of the act.

We are puzzled by the irrational hatred that could lead someone to kill innocent people.

Who would do something like this? How could someone hate a government or an institution so much that they would kill innocent people?

At the same time, we are heartened and moved by the strong and compassionate response to the disaster, by the sacrifice of those who are working to save lives.

As we move through this emotional wringer, Americans may want to lash out. We certainly will want to find those responsible for the killing and bring them to justice.

If it becomes clear that a Middle Eastern, Muslim terrorist group is responsible, there likely will be a backlash.

One easy response will be to take frustration and anger out on people who look like our stereotype of a Middle Easterner.

That is an easy and ugly way to vent our anger over this despicable bombing.

Any harassment of innocent people, who share only a physical similarity to our vision of a terrorist, is just as irrational as the killing of innocent individual Americans by those who hate America.

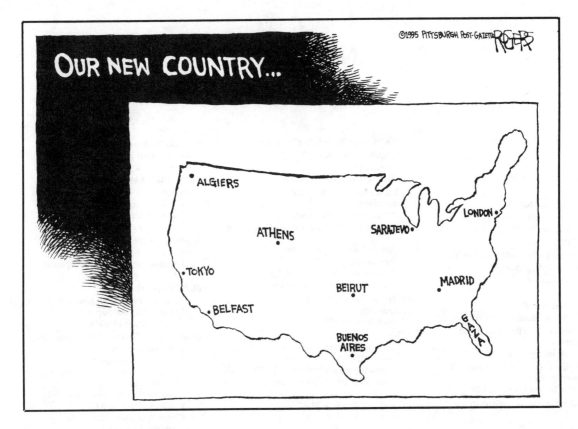

OUR NEW COUNTRY...

©1995 PITTSBURGH POST-GAZETTE ROGERS

ALGIERS
ATHENS
TOKYO
BELFAST
SARAJEVO
LONDON
BEIRUT
MADRID
BUENOS AIRES
GAZA

The San Diego Union-Tribune.

San Diego, California, April 20, 1995

A bomb exploding in the American heartland, Oklahoma City, far from the Middle East or Europe any other place associated with car bombs.

It is a shock. We gulp and hold our breath. Dozens so far are known to be dead and scores are missing in a building where 500 people worked, which contained a day care center.

Information is incomplete, yet it is obvious this was a deliberate attack. The building and people in it were targeted. It was a Beirut-style car bomb.

This was by far the worst terrorist act in U.S. history, worse than the 1993 explosion at the World Trade Center in New York City, which took six lives.

The perpetrators of that bombing are currently on trial in New York, a trial dwarfing in significance the O.J. Simpson trial, though you wouldn't know it. Is there a link between the New York trial and the Oklahoma City bombing?

It can't be ruled out.

But other clues lead in different directions. Oklahoma City's federal building houses the Bureau of Alcohol, Tobacco and Firearms, and the explosion came on the second anniversary of the ATF's raid on the compound of the Branch Davidian religious sect in Waco, Texas, about 275 miles south of Oklahoma City in which 71 people died.

If that is not a link, it is a startling coincidence.

Though far from the lands where great conflicts have been fought, America is not immune to terrorism. Our interests are worldwide, and even when terrorists cannot reach our shores, they reach our planes, our diplomats, our soldiers.

Twelve years ago we lost 241 Marines to a car bomb in Beirut, Marines who had gone there not as combatants but as peacekeepers.

The nature of terrorism, what makes it the scourge it is, one requiring a ceaseless effort to hunt down its sources and perpetrators, is that it is directed against civilians.

Terrorists do not distinguish between the armed and the unarmed, the hostile and the friendly, the guilty and the innocent. Terrorism can be as random as the poison gas in Tokyo's subway or as precise as the barracks bomb in Beirut. The aim is to frighten, to terrorize and to kill.

Terrorists, even the most experienced, rarely get away. They have motives and they leave trails. Oklahoma City's bombers will be caught.

"We will find the people who did this," said President Clinton yesterday. "When we do, justice will be swift, certain and severe."

There should be no doubt about that.

The Hutchinson News

Hutchinson, Kansas, April 20, 1995

The devastating bomb explosion in Oklahoma City's federal building brings the terrorism to our back yard.

America is under siege and we need to stop it. The World Trade Center and now Oklahoma City.

Even if this proves not to be members of the cultish Branch Davidians, out of Waco, Texas, Islamic fundamentalists, or whoever, it is a terrorist act.

President Clinton must address this situation immediately. He should give it top priority.

The investigation must be thorough and swift. When a conclusion is reached and suspects apprehended, punishment of same must be as harsh as possible.

Security measures at all federal buildings must be tightened. Ways of permanently making it tougher to bomb our buildings must be implemented.

Sadly, though, a realization also must creep into our collective psyches: America is no longer immune from terrorism at home.

It's here. What, if anything, can we do about it?

INDEX